perspectives

on health and

human rights

perspectives

on health and

human rights

edited by
Sofia Gruskin, Michael A. Grodin,
George J. Annas, Stephen P. Marks

Routledge
Taylor & Francis Group
NEW YORK AND LONDON

Published in 2005 by
Routledge
Taylor & Francis Group
270 Madison Avenue
New York, NY 10016

Published in Great Britain by
Routledge
Taylor & Francis Group
2 Park Square
Milton Park, Abingdon
Oxon OX14 4RN

Printed in the United States of America on acid-free paper
10 9 8 7 6 5 4 3 2 1

International Standard Book Number-10: 0-415-94806-1 (Hardcover) 0-415-94807-X (Softcover)
International Standard Book Number-13: 978-0-415-94806-7 (Hardcover) 978-0-415-94807-4 (Softcover)
Library of Congress Card Number 2004010575

Library of Congress Cataloging-in-Publication Data

Perspectives on health and human rights / edited by Sofia Gruskin [et al.].
    p. cm.
  Follow-up/companion volume to: Health and human rights. 1999.
  Includes bibliographical references and index.
  ISBN 0-415-94806-1 (hardback : alk. paper) -- ISBN 0-415-94807-X (pbk. : alk. paper)
  1. Public health--Moral and ethical aspects. 2. Human rights--Health aspects. I. Gruskin, Sofia.
II. Health and human rights.
  [DNLM: 1. Human Rights. 2. Public Health Administration. 3. Ethics, Medical. 4. Health Planning.
5. World Health. WA 530.1 P467 2004]

RA427.25.P47 2004
174.2--dc22
                                           2004010575

Taylor & Francis Group
is the Academic Division of T&F Informa plc.

**Visit the Taylor & Francis Web site at
http://www.taylorandfrancis.com**

**and the Routledge Web site at
http://www.routledge-ny.com**

We are at the threshold of a rebirth—a set of new perspectives—so clearly possible because (to paraphrase Newton) we stand on the shoulders of giants—in health and human rights—who have preceded us. Now we have the responsibility to move forward by recognizing that true interdependence and real interconnectedness requires that we—from health and from human rights—advance together: equal partners in the belief that the world can change.

Jonathan Mann
1947-1998

Contents

Acknowledgments

This book would not have been completed without the administrative support of Mark Hancock, Cliff Lubitz, and Carolyn D'Aquila. We would like to thank Albina du Boisrouvray and Dean Robert Meenan of the Boston University School of Public Health for their lasting support. Michael Bickerstaff and Julie Spadaro of Taylor and Francis were extremely helpful in guiding this book to fruition. Finally, we owe our sincere thanks to the many health and human rights students with whom we have had the privilege of teaching and learning over the past years.

Introduction

Approaches, Methods and Strategies in Health and Human Rights

Sofia Gruskin, Michael A. Grodin, George J. Annas, and Stephen P. Marks

Since the publication of *Health and Human Rights: A Reader* in 1999, attention to human rights in public health has shifted increasingly from the question, *Why* should we deal with human rights? to a new question: *How* should we deal with human rights? That human rights are regarded as fundamental to public health work is not surprising. In some ways, given the progressive nature of the public health tradition, what is a bit surprising is how long this recognition has taken. Those of us who work to bridge the fields of health and human rights represent a broad range of disciplines and use very different tools and strategies to do our work. We are not a monolithic entity, and we do not always agree on the best approaches for bringing health and human rights together. It is, however, fair to say that, while the nine parts of this volume bring together very different approaches, methods, and strategies for action, a common element is an abiding commitment to human rights and to improving the health of the world's populations. This common commitment is underscored in Part I, dealing with the conceptual underpinnings of the linkage of health and human rights.

Approaches to Emerging Issues in Health and Human Rights

This volume brings together previously published articles. These articles reflect a shared perspective that health is largely influenced by the environments in which people live and that we need to bring more attention to reducing the

xiii

gaps between those who enjoy higher standards of health and quality services and those who, for a mix of civil, political, economic, social or cultural reasons, are more vulnerable to ill-health and to inadequate access to health-related services. The entry points represented here focus on both the causes and the consequences of these inequalities. And each either implicitly or explicitly draws on human rights norms and standards, whether the focus is on the underlying determinants of health, the ways that health policies, programs and services are delivered, or the tools used to measure success or failure. Central to this concern for inequalities and determinants of health is the process of development and the challenges to achieving economic progress in ways that reduce these inequalities. Some examples of health-related thinking and analysis of human rights in development are provided in Part II.

For a variety of reasons, many of the actors with responsibilities in health, including governments, non-governmental organizations and intergovernmental agencies (such as those of the United Nations system), are bringing the language of human rights into their work. This is the case whether people are working in health advocacy, providing direct services, implementing programs or defining health policy. Yet, the ways in which they use this language and even the same legal documents in doing work related to health are very different. The same rights have been used in one way by advocates who are using them to support advocacy and civil society mobilization—for example, in pushing for the right to HIV treatment—and in other ways by the treaty-monitoring bodies and others who analyze and critique what a government is or is not doing in relation to health. Some bring pressure on behalf of those deprived of adequate health while others work to hold legally accountable those who have the obligation to ensure the availability, acceptability, accessibility and quality of health systems, including their outcomes among different population groups. Human rights have also been used by governments and NGOs as a framework for designing, implementing or monitoring their own policies and programs, sometimes also called a "rights-based approach." Legal accountability, including the role of non-state actors, is a key concern in considering the human rights aspects of emerging technologies, some of which are raised in Part III.

The pieces in this volume represent a wide variety of perspectives on human rights. Some authors use human rights in a highly legal sense, basing their arguments on international agreements rather than on the perspective of any particular country or cultural setting. Other authors are pushing to expand these definitions and working to build the legal and political structures that can support expanded definitions. Still others are more concerned with how the notion of human rights can inform their work whether or not these rights have per se been legally recognized. Attention to the similarities and differences in these approaches is critical to the effectiveness of the health and human rights movement. They represent different paradigms, and clarity is required as to where they connect, where they conflict and where they overlap. The inclusion of these very different approaches in this collection is a testament to our belief that the emerging field of health and human rights needs quality reflection and research from different perspectives, all of which can contribute to population health, even as their differences should be acknowledged and understood. Different approaches have their place at different times and in different situations, and the explicit acknowledgment of the differences in how human rights have been, and can be, relevant to public health work is imperative to our ability to strengthen our collective impact in the future.

The selections on sexual and reproductive health in Part IV illustrate this diversity of approaches. It is well known that risk-reduction strategies—such as behavioral change interventions and condom promotion in HIV prevention efforts—have been of limited effectiveness when they have failed to engage underlying individual and societal issues. For example, contraception, counseling, access to quality health services, education and information have all been understood to be central to improving women's reproductive and sexual health. Yet, individual women have to have the ability to control and make decisions about their lives, even just to access the services that are available. A woman's vulnerability to ill health is affected by a cluster of relevant human rights, each of which points the way towards a range of likely interventions both inside and outside the health sector. In addition to the rights to health and to information, nondiscrimination, and the rights to education, bodily integrity, personal security, privacy, and to equal rights in marriage and divorce are each relevant to an individual woman's ability to make and act upon the free and informed decisions she needs for her health. These rights are therefore necessary not only in and of themselves but also for government to fulfill its responsibility for ensuring reproductive and sexual health.

Violence is a public health issue of considerable magnitude, involving a wide range of phenomena from homicide and assaults within families to war and genocide. It is addressed through public health programming within criminal law, human rights law and humanitarian law. Issues concerning violence are priority concerns of health and human rights, such as the "war" on terrorism and its consequences, which are relevant not only for the populations of Afghanistan and Iraq but also for victims of terrorism and the consequences of policies of anti-terrorism across the globe. Part V provides the examples of capital punishment, maternal morality, humanitarian protection, and economic sanctions.

Methods and Strategies of Health and Human Rights

The relevance, strengths, but also limitations of quantitative methods for work in health and human rights are brought out in the selections in Part VI. Many of the problems in refining methods applicable to health and human rights stem from some of the underlying assumptions of each field. While an essential focus of public health is improving health outcomes, human rights, as defined in international human rights law, are fundamentally about what governments can do to us, cannot do to us, and should do for us.

Human rights are traditionally expressed essentially in terms of the obligations of agents of the state, including those who are working in health, whether within departments of health or in other sectors of government whose actions may influence health. As some of the pieces presented here make clear, the consensus that exists around human rights norms can make it possible to find common ground among diverse partners within and between government structures and between government actors and the people they work with outside in determining, for example, what factors to consider in assessing inequalities in health.

Governmental responsibility for health from a human rights perspective refers not only to government's duty not to violate human rights directly, but also to its responsibility to ensure the conditions that enable people to realize their rights as fully as possible. Every country in the world is party at least to one human rights treaty that includes health-related human rights and is therefore legally responsible and accountable under international law in some way for human rights as they relate to health. The United States government does not recognize the right to health as such, but 151 other countries (at the beginning of 2005), both resource-rich and resource-poor, are bound by the full range of obligations of the right to health. The sections in Part VII on the human right to health provide both a general analysis of the normative obligations of the right to health under international law, and illustrations of their application within national contexts.

For many in public health, work in health and human rights is driven by the recognition that the respect, protection and fulfillment of all human rights, be they civil, political, economic, social or cultural, is necessary primarily because they are critical to improving the health status of individuals and populations. These practitioners and advocates focus on the ways in which human rights can improve the design, implementation and evaluation of health policies, programs and practices. In short, this perspective suggests that studies that are done or interventions that are carried out should explicitly consider the civil, political, economic, social and cultural factors that surround them. Thus they should consciously take into account such factors as gender relations, religious beliefs, homophobia, and racism, that individually, and in combination, influence the extent to which individuals and communities are protected from discrimination, inequality, stigmatization and exclusion, as well as their ability to access services and to make and carry out free and informed decisions about their lives. This approach to the design, implementation and evaluation of health interventions focuses more completely on who falls ill, why, and what is done about it than on methods that do not explicitly consider the links between human rights and health. Part VIII, on mobilizing for health and human rights, contains examples of challenges and efforts to use human rights to design, implement and evaluate health interventions. It is complemented by a final section which describes additional resources for research and action.

Some Complex Challenges

As is apparent from the work presented here, consensus on the linkages between health and human rights has moved far enough to begin challenging traditional ways of working in public health and even in human rights. The experience of the past decade has provided rich examples of the value of bringing health and human rights together for advocacy and accountability purposes, as well as for the policy and program responses to health, although more hard evidence needs to be collected documenting the effectiveness of these approaches. Notwithstanding the notable successes of the past decade, many of which are described within this volume, a backlash has developed in high-level policymaking circles and amongst some public health officials against the integration of human rights into health work. Recent developments, supported by the current US administration, such as increasing federal funding for abstinence-until-marriage sex education programs, which prohibit accurate discussion about the health benefits of contraception, including condoms, in preventing unintended pregnancy, sexually transmitted infections (STIs), and HIV/AIDS, present serious challenges. At the 2001 United Nations General Assembly Special Session on HIV/AIDS, several governments, led by the United States, were reticent to endorse a human rights based approach to HIV/AIDS, preferring weaker language. At the United Nations General Assembly Special Session on Children in 2002, the rights of adolescents to access appropriate and scientifically accurate reproductive and sexual health information and services was seriously challenged by an alliance of states that included the United States, Sudan, Iran, and the Holy See. What is at stake is more than the domestic political agenda that drives US foreign policy in this area, or of religious dogma behind the positions of the Holy See, Sudan or Iran. The commitment to ensuring access to information and services goes to the heart of human rights-based approaches to health and reflects the consensus of health professionals in all regions of the world. Only sustained and enhanced attention to health and human rights by practitioners, advocates and academics will avoid the loss of hard-won advances in health policies and programs.

Attempts to question—and in some cases to deny completely—the existence of the right to health are a related problem. For example, the United States justified their opposition to the mandate of the United Nations Special Rapporteur on the Right to Health (appointed in 2002) because "the proposed mandate of a Special Rapporteur was part of an effort to promote legal entitlements in the health field and eventually in other areas. An assertion of legal entitlements could manifest itself in the form of lawsuits for health benefits that few, if any, governments could afford to pay."[1] This view poses a serious challenge that is more than a technical legal point; to treat health as a human right in the context of resource constraints requires a deliberate governmental policy to respect, protect, and fulfill the human right to health, and goes against economic arguments which doubt the value of a normative entitlement to health given scarce resources. People concerned with health and human rights will need to face this challenge by developing policy options that maximize health within available resources in ways that are consistent with legal obligations under the right to health.

Legitimate concern over potential large-scale health crises, such as sudden acute respiratory syndrome (SARS) and bioterrorism, have also brought back to the fore questions about the compatibility of public health and human rights approaches to health and well-being. Since the tragedy of September 11, 2001, some in public health have argued that in times of war and epidemics it is necessary to trade the protection of human rights for health security. This is almost always a false argument, since human rights and health security, far from being incompatible, almost always go hand in hand. The major human rights instruments were all developed in the post-World War II era and during the Cold War, and thus permitted some restrictions on liberty in wartime and other public emergencies, as well as for the protection of public health in a democratic society. Most public health concerns can be addressed without any infringements on human rights at all, but at times public health measures needed to curb the spread of disease do require restrictions on the rights of those already infected or at risk. However, as the SARS epidemic of 2003 demonstrated, even when there is heightened fear of widespread disease and death, voluntary measures, including voluntary home quarantines, are effective when the public is kept accurately informed and reasonable steps are taken by public health officials. Human rights are not only critical in the short-term response to terrorism and new epidemics, they are critical to our long-term survival as well. As Richard Horton, the editor of the *Lancet*, put it less than a month after 9/11:

> Principles of harm reduction are more realistic and practicable than false notions of a war on terrorism. Attacking hunger, disease, poverty, and social exclusion might do more good than air marshals, asylum restrictions, and identity cards. Global security will be achieved only by building stable and strong societies. Health is an undervalued measure of our global security.[2]

A continuing issue of concern to public health over the next few years will be the integration of the human rights principles of non-discrimination, equality, and participation into various domains of health. A health and human rights approach will focus on the information, education, health and other social services being provided, to whom they are being provided, in what ways they are being provided, and who and what is being left out and in what ways are they being left out. It will question and address how decisions are made about the types of studies and interventions undertaken and funded, as well as the ones that are not funded. Who is making these decisions, and according to what criteria? Have the affected communities been able to meaningfully participate in the decisions that will potentially affect their health? Explicit application of human rights norms and standards will not necessarily change the results, although it may, but a conscious focus on transparency in how these questions are answered is now understood to be useful in highlighting accountability as well as the processes by which these decisions are reached. And ultimately this work should prove useful in reducing the gaps between those who enjoy better health and better services and those who are more vulnerable to inadequate health services and structures.

Where Do We Go From Here?

Over the next few years, it will be important to document and analyze our efforts in these areas. We need to better organize the knowledge we are accumulating around the processes of linking health and human rights, testing new frameworks and comparing and validating the approaches that are currently used. The efforts of the United Nations Special Rapporteur on the Right to Health, the Committee on Economic, Social and Cultural Rights, and other actors engaged in working with the General Comment on the Right to Health, highlight the complementarity of these approaches, and we believe these efforts will provide useful signposts for those engaged in this work in the future.

As the previously-published articles collected here make clear, human rights provides a framework of analysis and a method of work that can be useful to public health, and public health provides tools and methods that can help to strengthen human rights work. Bringing human rights and public health work together is not about starting completely afresh or throwing out what works; it is rather about adding new tools to do our work better. Explicit attention will be needed over the next several years to better document the evidence how human rights are useful to public health work and the value of bringing public health concerns more prominently into human rights work. However, neither field can be expected to solve the problems of the other. The work of health and human rights is to bridge these two worlds, drawing on new resources and new actors. The next generation of practitioners working in health and human rights will need to be equally comfortable functioning in both worlds. Each field brings to the table not only a common concern for better health, but also its own disciplines, even as the boundaries between disciplines are increasingly blurred. The regrouping of communities—public health workers, clinicians, ethicists, epidemiologists, economists, human rights workers—has the potential to improve physical, mental and social well-being. For this work to be useful and to remain relevant, there has to be constant interaction between the conceptual work being done around the linkages between human rights and health and the realities being faced by those working directly on the front lines of practice. The readers of this volume will, in the last analysis and through their own efforts, determine whether this challenge is met in the future.

Notes

1. UN Press Release ECOSOC/6027, July 29, 2002.
2. Richard Horton, "Public Health: A Neglected Counterterrorist Measure," *Lancet* 2001; 358: 1112.

I

The Links Between Health and Human Rights

Health and human rights is a young but rapidly growing, and dynamic field. At this stage of its development, it is neither possible nor desirable to define it comprehensively or authoritatively. Nonetheless, the primarily descriptive material we brought together six years ago in *Health and Human Rights: A Reader* merits expansion. In that book we relied heavily on Jonathan Mann's three basic observations that led him to conclude health and human rights were natural allies in the quest to improve the human condition globally: human rights abuses can dramatically affect health, health can be dramatically worsened when human rights are ignored, and health and human rights can act synergistically with each other for global human betterment. These observations, Mann noted modestly, lead to a "hypothesis that promotion and protection of rights and health are inextricably linked [and that this] requires much creative exploration and rigorous evaluation."[1]

The linkages between health and human rights have been the subject of exploration from a variety of perspectives over the past five years. Amartya Sen, for example, has observed that "among the most important freedom we can have is freedom from avoidable ill-health and from escapable mortality" and concluded that health improvement requires improvements in participatory politics in which "the public must see itself not merely as a patient, but also as an agent of change."[2] Along these same lines, Paul Farmer has focused his work on equality and social justice, arguing that the world is suffering from plagues of inequalities as much as from plagues of infections.

In this part we present three chapters that address the conceptual foundations of the health and human rights field. Sofia Gruskin and Daniel Tarantola introduce us to the field of health and human rights by outlining its brief history, including the recognition, definition and application of the "right to health," exploring the reciprocal impact of health and human rights, and addressing some concrete ways in which health and human rights can be optimized in practice. This opening chapter, like the book it begins, urges movement from theory to action, including the systematic use of human rights analysis in health policy development; using human rights to inform health systems and practice; and developing a health and human rights research agenda to study and document the reciprocal impacts between health and human rights.

The other two chapters specifically address the international human rights movement that began after World War II, and was most fully articulated in the 1948 Universal Declaration of Human Rights, and its specific relationship to human health. In the first of these two, the immediate past Director-General of the World Health Organization, Gro Harlem Brundtland, sets forth her conviction that in order for WHO to meet its goals of providing the world's peoples with "the highest attainable standard of physical, mental and social well-being," more is required than new vaccines and other medical technologies: human rights must be taken seriously. George Annas would not disagree, and he broadens the health and human rights framework to suggest how it might affect not only the actions of governments, but also the actions of private corporations, public health officials, and physicians. He concludes that "by broadening our perspective, the language of human rights highlights basic needs, such as equality, education, nutrition, and sanitation and improvement in each of these areas can have a major role in improving health."

Notes

1. Jonathan M. Mann, Lawrence Gostin, Sofia Gruskin, Troyn Brennan, Zita Lazzarini, and Harvey Fineberg, "Health and Human Rights," in *Health and Human Rights: A Reader*, eds. Jonathan M. Mann, Sofia Gruskin, Michael A. Grodin, and George J. Annas (New York: Routledge, 1999).
2. Amartya Sen, "Health in Development," *Bulletin of the World Health Organization* (1999); 77: 619.

1
Health and Human Rights

Sofia Gruskin and Daniel Tarantola

Introduction

Since the creation of the United Nations over 50 years ago, international responsibility for health and for human rights has been increasingly acknowledged. Yet the actual links between health and human rights had not been recognized even a decade ago. Generally thought to be fundamentally antagonistic, these two worlds had evolved along parallel but distinctly separate tracks until a number of recent events helped to bring them together.

Conceptually one can point to the HIV/AIDS pandemic, to women's health issues, including violence, and to the blatant violations of human rights which occurred in such places as the Balkans and the Great Lakes region in Africa as having brought attention to the intrinsic connections that exist between health and human rights. Each of these issues helped to illustrate distinct, but linked, pieces of the health and human rights paradigm. While the relationship between health and human rights with respect to these and similar issues may always have made sense intuitively, the development of a 'health and human rights' language in the last few years has allowed for the connections between health and human rights to be explicitly named, and therefore for conceptual, analytical, policy, and programmatic work to begin to bridge these disparate disciplines and to move forward. In the last few years human rights have increasingly been at the centre of analysis and action in regard to health and development issues. The level of institutional and state political commitment to health and human rights has, in fact, never been higher. This is true within the work of the United Nations system but, even more importantly, can also be seen in the work of governments and non-governmental organizations at both the national and international level.

From HIV/AIDS and Human Rights to Health and Human Rights

The importance of the HIV/AIDS pandemic as a catalyst for beginning to define some of the structural connections between health and human rights cannot be overemphasized. The first time that human rights were explictly named in a public health strategy was only in the late 1980s, when the call for human rights and for compassion and solidarity with people living with HIV/AIDS was embodied in the first World Health Organization (WHO) global response to AIDS (WHO 1987). This approach was motivated by moral outrage but also, even more importantly, by the recognition that protecting the human rights of people living with HIV/AIDS was a necessary element of the worldwide public health response to the emerging epidemics. The implications of this call were far reaching. Framing this public health strategy in human rights terms—although initially focused on the rights of people living with HIV/AIDS rather than on the broad array of human rights influencing people's vulnerability to the epidemic—allowed it to become anchored in international law, thereby making governments and intergovernmental organizations publicly accountable for their actions towards people living with HIV/AIDS (Mann and Tarantola 1998). The groundbreaking contribution of this era lies in the recognition of the applicability of international law to HIV/AIDS issues and in the attention this approach then generated to the links between other health issues and human rights—and therefore to the ultimate responsibility and accountability of the state under international law for issues relating to health and well being (Mann et al. 1994).

International Conferences and the United Nations System

The series of international conferences held in the past decade under the auspices of the United Nations system have also been of critical importance in helping to clarify the links between health and human rights. While all of these conferences, ranging from the World Summit for Children held in 1990 to the World Conference against Racism held in 2001, are relevant to health and human rights concerns, the two most crucial in articulating the health and human rights link were the 1994 International Conference on Population and Development and the 1995 Fourth World Conference on Women. These conferences brought together policy-makers, activists, and representatives from local, national, and international agencies, as well as government representatives. The negotiated documents resulted in the first concrete links between health and human rights in international consensus documents and helped to focus attention to the dual obligations of governments regarding both health and human rights (see in particular Chapters IV to VII of the *Report of the International Conference on Population and Development*, and Chapter IV (C) 'Women and health' and Chapter IV (I) 'Human rights of women' of the Fourth World Conference on Women (ICPD 1994; FWCW 1995)). These documents were of use to governments and others in shaping policy and programmatic work which explicitly dealt with these links, as well as to activists and non-governmental organizations in framing their advocacy for government responsibility for health in the human rights language of responsibility and accountability.

In recent years there has been a substantial increase in attention and resources devoted to implementation of health and human rights within virtually all United Nations development agencies and programmes, due in large part to these international conference processes. All of the organizations and agencies of the United Nations have, albeit to varying degrees, begun to consider the relevance of human rights to their work in the health field (Alston 1997). The 1997 Programme for Reform put out by United Nations Secretary-General Kofi Annan, however, has been most crucial in moving the United Nations system's conceptual attention to human rights towards implementation and action within their own work. The Programme for Reform designates human rights as among the core activities of the United Nations system (UN 1997a; UNGA 1997). The document states that human rights are to be understood to cut across the four substantive fields of the United Nations' work: peace and security, economic and social affairs, development co-operation, and humanitarian affairs. Each of the agencies with responsibility for health currently has policy documents at various stages of elaboration which concern health and human rights, and technical staff responsible for the integration or implementation of human rights into at least some aspects of their work, a situation that would have been unimaginable even a few years ago.

1. The United Nations International Children's Emergency Fund (UNICEF) has restructured its policy and programmatic framework around the Convention on the Rights of the Child (UNICEF 2000).
2. The Joint United Nations Programme on HIV/AIDS (UNAIDS) recognizes human rights as a theme relevant to all aspects of its policy and programme work; see *UNAIDS Strategic Plan 1996 to 2000* (revised December 1995), pp. 5, 6, and 13 where the importance of contextual factors that increase vulnerability to HIV/AIDS is recognized, including existing discrimination against certain groups, and where human rights are cited as core values and guiding principles for the mission of UNAIDS.
3. A Memorandum of Understanding now exists between the United Nations Development Programme and the Office of the High Commissioner for Human Rights (UNDP 1999).
4. The United Nations Development Programme Human Development Report for the year 2000 has an explicit focus on human rights, and the WHO is currently preparing its first strategy on health and human rights (WHO 1999b).

Likewise, the bodies of the United Nations system with responsibility for human rights are also paying increasing attention to health-related concerns. This is most easily seen in the recent attention to HIV/AIDS and reproductive health by the human rights treaty monitoring bodies (UNHCHR 1996, 1997, 1998a, b). However, this commitment extends to the recent appointment of two health-related focal points in the Office of the High Commissioner for Human Rights: one responsible for integrating HIV/AIDS issues into the work of the human rights bodies and structures, and the other serving as a general liaison for all health and human rights issues.

State and Non-State Actors Entering the Arena of Health and Human Rights

Governments are also increasingly recognizing the relevance of human rights to their health and development work, and calling for technical assistance in the field of human rights. This is true in developing and industrialized countries alike. In Nepal, a comprehensive workshop was recently held on tuberculosis and human rights (WHO 1999b). An open debate in South Africa recently focused on the human rights implications of a proposed new regulation concerning AIDS reporting and AIDS-status disclosure to third persons (South Africa Government Gazette 1999). In Colombia, the Convention on the Elimination of All Forms of Discrimination Against Women is being used as a framework for mobilization around much of the work in family planning (Plata and Yanuzova 1993; Corporación Casa de la Mujer 1998). Within the United States, President Clinton issued an Executive Order in commemoration of Human Rights Day in 1998 that obliges the United States to respect and implement fully its obligations under the international human rights treaties to which it is a party and to 'promote respect for international human rights in our relationships with all other countries' (Clinton 1998). As a result, all United States federal agencies, including those with health-related responsibilities, have been directed to re-examine their policies and strategies from the perspective of international human rights standards.

Non-governmental organizations, such as Amnesty International and Human Rights Watch, are also increasingly considering the implications of the health and human rights connection for their own work. Non-governmental organizations that focus on health or development issues, many of which previously saw human rights as having little relevance to their work, are increasingly using not only the rhetoric of human rights but also its method of analysis to help shape their interventions. One prime example is the recent decision of the International Council of AIDS Service Organizations (ICASO) to name the promotion of human rights in the context of HIV/AIDS as one of its fundamental organizing principles (ICASO 1998). In addition, human rights nongovernmental organizations are expanding their formerly tight focus on civil and political rights to pay increasing attention to economic, social, and cultural rights, including the right to health. These developments are helping to shape new forms of advocacy and to put increased pressure on governments to take responsibility for the health of their populations. The current challenge is to ensure that the increased rhetorical attention to rights translates into policies, national legislation, and actions that will effectively impact on the underlying conditions necessary for health, as well as the ways in which health policies, programmes, and services are conceptualized and delivered.

Academics and researchers are also increasingly finding the links between health and human rights to be of critical importance in expanding their domains of work (Alfredsson and Tomasevski 1998; Toebes 1999). Academic centres with an explicit focus on the links between health and human rights are beginning to appear in a number of places, some with a focus on specific substantive issues, and others concerned with health and human rights more broadly (for example, the François-Xavier Bagnoud Center for Health and Human Rights at the Harvard School of Public Health, as well as the Macfarlane Burnett Centre for Medical Research in Australia, the Programme on Gender, Sexuality, Health and Human Rights at the Mailman School of Public Health at Columbia University. The Netherlands Institute of Human Rights, and the Department of Community Health at the University of Cape Town, South Africa). In the last several years, institutions around the globe have begun to offer courses in health and human rights, international conferences on health and human rights have been held in a number of locations, and professional health journals such as *The Lancet*, the *Journal of the American Medical Association*, and the *American Journal of Public Health* have devoted space to exploring health and human rights issues (Brenner 1996; Sonis et al. 1996; Leaning 1997; Fluss 1999). The first course on health and human rights was offered at the Harvard School of Public Health in 1992. Since then, courses on health and human rights have been increasingly offered in countries such as the United States, France, Sweden, Brazil, South Africa, and Zimbabwe. Efforts are currently under way to document existing courses on health and human rights.

Understanding the implications of linking health and human rights is of increasing importance to policy-makers, government officials, and activists— indeed, to anyone concerned with health issues, human rights issues, or the links between the two (Marks 1997). This chapter demonstrates the relationship between health and human rights, and provides a glimpse of some of the conceptual, analytical, and practical approaches to bringing health and human rights together that are currently being explored. It begins by explaining the basic concepts and procedures of human rights, with specific emphasis on their relation to health. It goes on to explore the framework of health as it relates to human rights promotion and protection. The next section considers the reciprocal relationships between health and human rights, with an emphasis on the human rights impact of public health policies and programmes and the impact of neglect or violation of human rights on health. Attention is then given to suggested methods for increasing the synergy between health and human rights, both as a method of analysis and as an approach to the design, implementation, and evaluation of health policies and programmes. This last section offers a method for considering the practical application of health and human rights concepts to policy and programmatic work.

What Are Human Rights?

While human rights thinking and practice has a long history, the importance of human rights for governmental action and accountability was first widely recognized only after the Second World War. Agreement between nation-states that all people are 'born free and equal in dignity and rights' was reached in 1945 when the promotion of human rights was identified as a principal purpose of the newly created United Nations (UN 1945). The United Nations Charter established general obligations that apply to all its member states, including respect for human rights and dignity. Then, in 1948, the Universal Declaration of Human Rights was adopted as a common standard of achievement for all peoples and all nations (UN 1948). The basic characteristics of human rights are that they are the rights of individuals, which inhere in individuals because they are human, that they apply to people everywhere in the world, and that they are principally concerned with the relationship between the individual and the state. In practical terms, international human rights law is about defining what governments can do to us, cannot do to us, and should do for us. For example, governments obviously should not do things like torture people, imprison them arbitrarily, or invade their privacy. Governments should ensure that all people in a society have shelter, food, medical care, and basic education.

The Universal Declaration of Human Rights can well be understood to be the cornerstone of the modern human rights movement. The preamble to the Universal Declaration of Human Rights proposes that human rights and dignity are self-evident, the 'highest aspiration of the common people', and the 'foundation of freedom, justice and peace'. 'Social progress and better standards of life' including the 'prevention of barbarous acts which have outraged the conscience of mankind', and, broadly speaking, individual and collective well being, are understood to depend upon the 'promotion of universal respect for and observance of human rights' (UN 1948). Although the Universal Declaration of Human Rights is not a legally binding document, nations have endowed it with a tremendous legitimacy through their actions, including invoking it legally and politically at the national and international levels. Portions of the Universal Declaration of Human Rights are cited in the majority of national constitutions drafted since it came into being, and governments often cite the Universal Declaration of Human Rights in their negotiations with other governments, as well as in their accusations against each other of violating human rights. A useful compilation can be found in Hannum (1998).

Under the auspices of the United Nations, more that 20 multilateral human rights treaties have been formulated since the adoption of the Universal Declaration of Human Rights. These treaties create legally binding obligations on the nations that have ratified them, thereby giving them the status and power of international law. Countries that become party to international human rights treaties accept certain procedures and responsibilities, including periodic submission of reports on their compliance with the substantive provisions of the texts to international monitoring bodies. The key international human rights treaties, the International Covenant on Economic, Social and Cultural Rights (ICESCR 1966) and the International Covenant on Civil and Political Rights (ICCPR 1966), further elaborate the content of the rights set out in the Universal Declaration of Human Rights and contain legally binding obligations for the governments that ratify them. As of January 2000, 142 countries had ratified the ICESCR and 144 had ratified the ICCPR. Together with the Universal Declaration of Human Rights and the United Nations Charter, these documents are often called the 'International Bill of Human Rights' (Humphrey 1976). Building upon these core documents, other international human rights treatles have focused on either specific populations (for example, the International Convention on the Elimination of All Forms of Racial Discrimination (ICERD 1965), the Convention on the Elimination of All Forms of Discrimination Against Women (CEDAW 1979), and the Convention on the Rights of the Child (CRC 1989)), or on specific issues (for example, the Convention against Torture and other Cruel, Inhuman or Degrading Treatment or Punishment (UN 1984a)).

There are also regional human rights treaties, which essentially concern the same sets of rights but are only open for signature by states in the relevant region, such as the African Charter on Human and Peoples' Rights (1982), the American Convention on Human Rights (1969), and the European Convention on the Protection of Human Rights (1950). Only the Asian region does not contain such a treaty. Additionally, there are numerous international declarations, resolutions, and recommendations which, although not strictly binding in a legal sense, express the political commitment of governments to promote and protect human rights and provide broadly recognized norms and standards relevant to the topic at hand (for example, the Declaration on the Elimination of All Forms of Intolerance and of Discrimination Based on Religion or Belief [UN 1981, 1993a]).

In the past decade, the series of international conferences held under the auspices of the United Nations have, to a great degree, helped give recognizable content to many of the rights contained in the various human rights treaties. Out of each of these conference processes has come a declaration and programme of action reflecting the consensus of the nations of the world. Though technically 'non-binding' commitments, these documents demonstrate that there is a consensus of the world community that international human rights treaty norms encompass the relationship between health and human rights, including reproductive rights, and that there are steps that ought to be taken at the local, national, and international levels to advance these concerns.

While these conference declarations and programmes of action represent nothing more than the political commitments of the governments present at their inception, the fact that they are then adopted at the next session of the United Nations General Assembly gives them a degree of formal standing. Although the declarations and programmes of action from the 1994 International Conference on Population and Development (ICPD 1994) and the 1995 Fourth World Conference on Women (FWCW 1995) have been of particular relevance, the 1993 World Conference on Human Rights (UN 1993c, 1998a) and the 1995 World Summit for Social Development (UN 1995b) have also helped explicate the relevance of the health and human rights framework to government action. Individually and collectively, these documents have been of critical importance in helping to elaborate provisions relevant to vulnerable groups, women's human rights, and broader concepts of health and human rights. Those commitments have helped to create new approaches for considering the extent of government accountability for health issues, as well as for determining the content of health issues using a rights framework. In so doing, these conference documents are helping to clarify the evolving meaning of the relationship between health and human rights and the steps needed for implementation (Gruskin 1998).

A Human Rights Perspective on Health

The rights that form the corpus of human rights law are found in the international human rights documents. While it is possible to identify different categories of rights, it is also critical to rights discourse and action to recognize that all rights are interdependent and interrelated, and that individuals rarely suffer neglect or violation of a particular right in isolation. For historical reasons, the rights described in the human rights documents have been divided into civil and political rights on the one hand and economic, social, and cultural rights on the other. Civil and political rights include the rights to liberty, to security of person, to freedom of movement, to vote, and not to be subjected to cruel, inhuman, or degrading treatment or punishment or to arbitrary arrest or detention. Economic, social, and cultural rights include the rights to the highest attainable standard of health, work, social security, adequate food, clothing and housing, and education, and the right to enjoy the benefits of scientific progress and its applications. Although the Universal Declaration of Human Rights contains both categories of rights, these rights were artificially split into two treaties due to Cold War politics, with the United States championing civil and political rights, and the former Soviet Union those rights considered to be more economic, social, and cultural in nature (Steiner and Alston 1996). Since the end of the Cold War, acknowledgement of the indivisibility and interdependence of rights has, once again, become commonplace (UN 1993c). The Convention on the Rights of the Child, the first human rights treaty to be opened for signature after the end of the Cold War, is the only one so far to include civil, political, and economic and social rights considerations not only within the same treaty but within the same right. (See, in particular Article 6, which in guaranteeing the right to life includes both the more civil and political provision which states that 'every child has the inherent right to life' and the more economic and social provision in which 'State Parties shall ensure to the maximum extent possible the survival and development of the child' (UNCRC 1989).)

Health and government responsibility for health is codified in these documents in several ways. The right to the highest attainable standard of health appears in one form or another in most of them. More importantly, nearly every article of every document can be understood to have clear implications for health (Mann et al. 1994). While the rights to information, education, housing and safe working conditions, and social security, for example, are particularly relevant to the health and human rights relationship, specific reference must be made to three rights: the right to non-discrimination, the right to the benefits of scientific progress, and the right to health.

Non-Discrimination

The principle of non-discrimination is key to human rights thinking and practice. Under international human rights law, all people should be treated equally and given equal opportunity. Within the international human rights framework, discrimination is a breach of a government's human rights obligations (Bilder 1992). Adverse discrimination occurs when a distinction is made against a person which results in their being treated unfairly or unjustly. In general, groups that are discriminated against tend to be those that do not share the characteristics of the dominant groups within a society. Thus, discrimination frequently reinforces social inequalities and denies equal opportunities. Common forms of discrimination include racism, gender-based discrimination, and homophobia. Each of the major human rights treaties specifically details the principle of non-discrimination with respect to race, colour, sex, language, religion, political or other opinion, national or social origin, property, birth, and, as it is called, 'other status'.

Governmental responsibility for this right includes ensuring equal protection under the law, as well as in relation to such issues as housing, employment, and medical care. The prohibition of discrimination does not mean that differences should not be acknowledged, only that different treatment must be based on objective and reasonable criteria. Although the international human rights documents do not explicitly prohibit discrimination on the basis of health status, the United Nations Commission on Human Rights has stated that 'all are equal before the law and entitled to equal protection of the law from all discrimination and from all incitement to discrimination relating to their state of health' (UN 1992a, 1993b; UNCHR 1994).

Right to Enjoy the Benefits of Scientific Progress

Closely allied to many of the issues relevant to health is the right to 'enjoy the benefits of scientific progress and its applications', recognized explicitly in the ICESCR. Article 15. This right includes governmental obligations for the steps necessary to conserve, develop, and diffuse science and scientific research, as well as freedom of scientific inquiry. The implications of this right for health issues have been explored recently with respect to access to drugs for the developing world, to name one important example (Lailemant et al. 1994; Reich 2000). In fact, this right is increasingly being cited by activist groups, non-governmental organizations, and others concerned by the large and growing disparities and inequities between wealthier and poorer populations regarding access to antiretroviral therapies and other forms of HIV/AIDS care. In addition, the relevance of this right to concerns about the development of vaccines that adequately respond to the specific needs of all populations, both in the North and the South, has recently been cited (Beloqui et al. 1998; Fluss and Little 1999). (See, for example, Statement from the Community AIDS Movement in Africa, presented at the Meeting on the International Partnership against HIV/ AIDS in Africa, New York, United Nations Headquarters, 6–7 December 1999.) While this right has long been recognized as relevant to governmental obligations under the ICESCR, its implications for health and health-related issues are only just beginning to be recognized.

The Right to Health

The human right to health should be understood, in the first instance, with reference to the description of health set forth in the preamble of the WHO Constitution and repeated in many subsequent documents (WHO 1946). Health is a 'state of complete physical, mental, and social well-being, and not merely the absence of disease or infirmity' (WHO 1946). This definition has important conceptual and practical implications, and it illustrates the indivisibility and interdependence of rights as they relate to health (Leary 1994; Tomasevski 1995a; Kirby 1999; Toebes 1999). Rights relating to discrimination, autonomy, information, education, and participation are an integral and indivisible part of the achievement of the highest attainable standard of health, just as the enjoyment of health is inseparable from that of other rights, whether categorized as civil and political, economic, social, or cultural. While the right to health has been set out in a number of international legal instruments, government obligations under this right are quite narrowly defined. As first elaborated in the ICESCR, the right is set forth only as 'the right to the highest attainable standard of physical and mental health', with obligations understood to encompass both the underlying preconditions necessary for health and the provision of medical care.

It is worth noting that the apparent tension between the broad definition of health proposed by the WHO, which includes the notion of social well being, and the more restrictive definition set out in the ICESCR reflects the very different purposes of these two documents. The WHO definition projects a vision of the ideal state of health as an eternal and universal goal to strive constantly towards, and has as its main purpose defining directions for the work of the Organization and its member states. The ICESCR definition differentiates two attributes of health—physical and mental well being—and is specifically concerned with assigning particular responsibilities to the governmental health sector; it assigns obligations relevant to social well being to the same governments under other articles of the treaty. The right to health as stated in the ICESCR (Box 1.1) is the principal framework for understanding governmental obligations under the right to health.

Governmental Obligations for Health Under International Human Rights Law

Governments are responsible not only for not directly violating rights, but also for ensuring the conditions which enable individuals to realize their rights as fully as possible. This is understood as an obligation to respect, protect, and fulfil rights, and governments are legally responsible for complying with this

---

Box 1.1 Article 12 of the United Nations International Covenant on Economic, Social and Cultural Rights (ICESCR)

1. The States Parties to the present Covenant recognize the right of everyone to the enjoyment of the highest attainable standard of physical and mental health.
2. The steps to be take by the States Parties to the present Covenant to achieve the full realization of this right shall include those necessary for:
   (a) the provision for the reduction of the stillbirth rate and of infant mortality and for the healthy development of the child
   (b) the improvement of all aspects of environmental and industrial hygiene
   (c) the prevention, treatment, and control of epidemic, endemic, occupational, and other diseases
   (d) the creation of conditions which would assure to all medical service and medical attention in the event of sickness.

---

range of obligations for every right in every human rights document they have ratified (Eide 1995a,b; Maastricht Guidelines on Violations of Economic, Social and Cultural Rights 1997).

Respecting, Protecting, and Fulfilling Human Rights

Governmental obligations towards ensuring the right to health are summarized below as an illustration of the range of issues relevant to respecting, protecting, and fulfilling human rights.

1. *Respecting* the right means that a state cannot violate the right directly. A government violates its responsibility to respect the right to health when it is immediately responsible for providing medical care to certain populations, such as prisoners or the military, and it arbitrarily decides to withhold that care.

2. *Protecting* the right means that a state has to prevent violations of rights by non-state actors and offer some sort of redress that people know about and can access if a violation occurs. This means that the state would be responsible for making it illegal to deny insurance or health care to people on the basis of a health condition, and that they would be responsible for ensuring safety nets and some system of redress that people know about and can access if a violation does occur.

3. *Fulfilling* the right means that a state has to take all appropriate measures—including but not limited to legislative, administrative, budgetary, and judicial—towards fulfillment of the right, including to promote the right in question. A state could be found to be in violation of the right to health if it failed to allocate sufficient resources incrementally to meet the public health needs of all of the communities within its borders.

In all countries, resource and other constraints can make it impossible for a government to fulfill all rights immediately and completely. The human rights machinery recognizes this and acknowledges that, in practical terms, a commitment to the right to health requires more than just passing a law. It will require financial resources, trained personnel, facilities, and, more than anything else, a sustainable infrastructure. Therefore, realization of rights is generally understood to be a matter of progressive realization of making steady progress towards a goal (ICESCR Article 2.1; Alston and Quinn 1987). The principle of 'progressive realization' is fundamental to the achievement of human rights. This is critical for resource-poor countries that are responsible for striving towards human rights goals to the maximum extent possible. It is also of relevance to wealthier countries in that they are responsible for respecting, protecting, and fulfilling human rights not only within their own borders, but through their engagement in international assistance and cooperation (UN 1984b).

Valid Limitations on Human Rights

In spite of the importance attached to human rights, there are situations where it is considered legitimate to restrict rights in order to achieve a broader public good. As described in the International Covenant on Civil and Political Rights, the public good can take precedence to 'secure due recognition and respect for the rights and freedoms of others; meet the just requirements of morality, public order, and the general welfare; and in times of emergency, when there are threats to the vital interests of the nation' (ICCPR Article 4). Public health is one such recognized public good. (The specific power of the state to restrict rights in the name of public health can be understood to be derived from Article 12 (c) of the ICESCR, which gives governments the right to take the steps they deem necessary for the 'prevention, treatment and control of epidemic, endemic, occupational and other diseases'.) Traditional public health measures have generally focused on curbing the spread of disease by imposing restrictions on the rights of those already infected or thought to be most vulnerable to becoming infected. In fact, coercion, compulsion, and restriction have historically been significant components of public health measures (Smith 1911; Schmidt 1995; Cohen 1998). Although the restrictions on rights that have occurred in the context of public health have generally had as their first concern protection of the public's health, it is also true that the measures taken have often been excessive. Interference with freedom of movement when instituting quarantine or isolation for a serious communicable disease—for example, Ebola fever, syphilis, typhoid, or untreated tuberculosis—is an example of a restriction on rights that may in certain circumstances be necessary for the public good and therefore could be considered legitimate under international human rights law. Conversely, arbitrary measures taken by public health authorities that fail to consider other valid alternatives may be found to be abusive of both human rights principles and public health 'best practice'. In recent times, measures taken around the world in response to HIV/AIDS provides some examples of this type of abuse (Cohen and Wiseberg 1990; UN 1992a, 1994; HRI 1998).

Certain rights are absolute, which means that restrictions may never be placed on them, even if justified as necessary for the public good. These include such rights as the right to be free from torture, slavery, or servitude, the right to a fair trial, and the right to freedom of thought. (See, for example, Article 4 of the ICCPR, which states that '[n]o derogation from articles 6, 7, 8 (paragraphs 1 and 2), 11, 15, 16, 18 may be made under this provision'.) Paradoxically, the right to life, which might at first glance appear to be inalienable, is not absolute; what is forbidden is the arbitrary deprivation of life. Interference with most rights can be legitimately justified as necessary under narrowly defined circumstances in many situations relevant to public health. (See, for example, Article 4 of the ICCPR, which states that '[I]n time of public emergency which threatens the life of the nation and the existence of which is officially proclaimed, the States Parties to the present Covenant may take measures derogating from their obligations under the present Covenant to the extent strictly required by the exigencies of the situation, provided that such measures are not inconsistent with their other obligations under international law and do not involve discrimination solely on the ground of race, colour, sex, language, religion or social origin'.)

Limitations on rights, however, are considered a serious issue under international human rights law, regardless of the apparent importance of the public good involved. When a government limits the exercise or enjoyment of a right, this action must be taken as a last resort and will only be considered legitimate if the following criteria are met (UNECOSOC 1985).

1. The restriction is provided for and carried out in accordance with the law;
2. The restriction is in the Interest of a legitimate objective of general interest;
3. The restriction is strictly necessary in a democratic society to achieve the objective;
4. There are no less intrusive and restrictive means available to reach the same goal; and
5. The restriction is not imposed arbitrarily, i.e., in an unreasonable or otherwise discriminatory manner.

This approach, often called the Siracusa Principles because they were conceptualized at a meeting in Siracusa. Italy, has long been recognized by those concerned with human rights monitoring and implementation as relevant to analysing a government's actions, and it has also recently begun to be considered a useful tool by those responsible within government for health-related policies and programmes (WHO/UNAIDS 1999). This framework, although still rudimentary, may be helpful in identifying public health actions that are abusive, whether intentionally or unintentionally.

Human Rights Monitoring Mechanisms Relevant to Health

The degree of governmental compliance with the obligations to respect, protect, and fulfill human rights are of direct relevance to the people affected, but they are also of interest to the international community. The accountability of governments for their legal commitments is monitored at the international level through the reporting process and, in many places, at the national level by governments themselves through the creation of commissions and ombudspersons, as well as by non-governmental organizations.

Reporting Under the Human Rights Treaties

As mentioned above, once a government has ratified a human rights treaty, it is obliged to report every several years to the specific body responsible for monitoring government action under that treaty. Governments are responsible for showing the ways that they are and are not in compliance with the treaty provisions, and must show constant improvement in their efforts to respect, protect, and fulfill the rights in question (UN 1996). Each of the treaty bodies meets several times a year to review a number of the government reports submitted. The process is very formal, with the government under review submitting a copy of its report approximately 2 months before the meeting. The report is officially presented at the meeting by a high-ranking government official, and the treaty body engages in formal dialogue with the country in question. Health-oriented United Nations Institutions, such as the WHO, UNAIDS, or UNICEF, are invited to provide the treaty bodies with information on the state of health and the performance of health systems in the country under review. Non-governmental organizations can also submit informal reports (often termed shadow reports) providing additional information, as well as stating their views on the situations and issues at stake. At the conclusion of the session, the treaty body prepares concluding comments and observations, which are made part of the substantive record. These comments address the extent to which the government in question is in compliance with its treaty provisions and provide concrete suggestions for actions to be taken by the country in order for it to be found in compliance at its next review. While this process can be extremely useful, there is, unfortunately, a tremendous backlog, largely because governments are often late with their reports, and none of the treaty bodies meets for a sufficient amount of time each year to cover all of the countries that are responsible for reporting to it.

All of the human rights treaty bodies have expressed a commitment to exploring the implications of health broadly defined, as well as the specific issues raised by both HIV/AIDS and reproductive health concerns, for governmental obligations under the treaties (UNDAW 1996; UNHCHR 1996; Boerefon and Toebes 1998; UNFPA 1998). While several of the treaties contain specific health-related provisions, the added impetus to pay attention to health in the context of monitoring work can largely be attributed to the interest generated from international conferences and the political commitments made there about governmental responsibility for ensuring the human rights of individuals in relation to health.

For each of the human rights treaties, general guidelines for reporting provide guidance to governments as to how to present the information about their compliance with their obligations to the treaty bodies (UN 1996). The information requested by the treaty bodies concerning health-related issues explains what governments are doing with respect to both the underlying preconditions for health and the ways in which health policies, programmes, and services are designed and implemented. From a health perspective, however, the actual information requested under current requirements has been largely insufficient to get at this range of issues. The general guidelines provided to governments for reporting on the right to health under the ICESCR are included in Box 1.2. They provide a concrete example of what the treaty body with primary responsibility for implementation of the right to health considers in determining if, and the degree to which, a government is in compliance with its obligations for the right to health.

The increasing links among the work of the treaty bodies, the United Nations specialized agencies, and non-governmental organizations are useful to the treaty monitoring process, but they are also beginning to contribute directly to the enhancement of the implementation of human rights at the country level by governments as well as other actors. The role of the technical and specialized agencies, funds, and programmes of the United Nations in the treaty monitoring process is growing, with respect to both provision of information and interactions with the treaty bodies and governments in question. This includes primarily UNICEF, UNAIDS, and the WHO but also, increasingly, the International Labour Organization (ILO), the United Nations Development Programme (UNDP), and the United Nations Population Fund (UNFPA). These agencies and programmes have increasingly been providing the treaty bodies with statistical information and other data collected as part of their routine work concerning the country in question to assist the treaty bodies in their review of government compliance. They have also been providing treaty bodies with guidelines and other examples of 'best practice' they have produced, which can assist the treaty bodies in their analysis of the information provided by the government and in the drafting of their concluding comments and observations. To date, however, the input of these agencies has been somewhat uncoordinated, even within the same institution, often resulting in heavy servicing of some treaty bodies in some specific ways while virtually ignoring others. As a result, a country may be heavily questioned by one treaty body as to a particular aspect of their compliance with their health-related obligations under one treaty, but not questioned at all by another treaty body responsible for monitoring similar health-related obligations. In addition, owing to lack of resources and the relative newness of their engagement with this process, the United Nations agencies, funds, and programmes do not provide even the treaty bodies they do work with equivalent information on all countries reporting at a particular time. Thus, while one country may be heavily questioned by a treaty body as a result of information provided by a particular agency, the next country immediately under review may not even be questioned superficially on comparable issues. UNICEF has been most involved in the treaty monitoring process. For example, it has expended considerable resources on helping governments to prepare their reports as well as increasingly framing technical assistance to countries according to the provisions of the Convention on the Rights of the Child (UNICEF 1998). This approach to the work of United Nations agencies and programmes at the country level has increasingly been considered of interest

Box 1.2 Guidelines for Reporting on Article 12 of the ICESCR (ECOSOC 1991; Alston 1991)

1. Please supply information on the physical and mental health of your population, both in the aggregate and with respect to different groups within your society. How has the health situation changed over time with regard to these groups? In case your government has recently submitted reports on the health situation in your country to the WHO you may wish to refer to the relevant parts of these reports rather than repeat the information here.

2. Please indicate whether your country has a national health policy. Please indicate whether a commitment to the WHO primary health care approach has been adopted as part of the health policy of your country. If so, what measures have been taken to implement primary health care?

3. Please indicate what percentage of your gross national product as well as of your national and/or regional budget(s) is spent on health. What percentage of those resources is allocated to primary health care? How does this compare with 5 years ago and 10 years ago?

4. Please provide, where available, indicators as defined by the WHO, relating to the following issues:

    (a) infant mortality rate (in addition to the national value, please provide the rate by sex, urban/rural division, and also, if possible, by socioeconomic or ethnic group and geographical area. Please include national definitions of urban/rural and other subdivisions)

    (b) population access to safe water (please disaggregate urban/rural)

    (c) population access to adequate excrete disposal facilities (please disaggregate urban/rural)

    (d) infants immunized against diphtheria, pertussis, tetanus, measles, poliomyelitis, and tuberculosis (please disaggregate urban/rural and by sex)

    (e) life expectancy (please disaggregate urban/rural, by socio-economic group, and by sex)

    (f) proportion of the population having access to trained personnel for the treatment of common diseases and injuries, with regular supply of 20 essential drugs, within 1 hour's walk or travel

    (g) proportion of pregnant women having access to trained personnel during pregnancy and proportion attended by such personnel for delivery. Please provide figures on the maternity mortality rate, both before and after childbirth

    (h) proportion of infants having access to trained personnel for care.

Box 1.2 (cont.)

(Please provide breakdowns by urban/rural and socio-economic groups for indicators (f) to (h).)

5. Can it be discerned from the breakdown of the indicators employed in paragraph 4, or by other means, that there are any groups in your country whose health situation is significantly worse than that of the majority of the population? Please define these groups as precisely as possible and give specifics. Which geographical areas in your country, if any, are worse off with regard to the health of their population?

   (a) During the reporting period, have there been any changes in national policies, laws, and practices negatively affecting the health situation of these groups or areas? If so, please describe these changes and their impact.

   (b) Please indicate what measures are considered necessary by your government to improve the physical and mental health situation of such vulnerable and disadvantaged groups in such worse off areas.

   (c) Please explain the policy measures your government has taken to the maximum of available resources, to realize such improvement. Indicate time related goals and benchmarks for measuring your achievement in this regard.

   (d) Please describe the effect of these measures on the health of the vulnerable and disadvantaged groups or worse-off areas under consideration and report on the successes, problems, and shortcomings of these measures.

   (e) Please describe the measures taken by your government in order to reduce the stillbirth rate and infant mortality and to provide for the healthy development of the child.

   (f) Please list the measures taken by your government to improve all aspects of environmental and industrial hygiene.

   (g) Please describe the measures taken by your government to prevent, treat, and control epidemic, endemic, and occupational and other diseases.

   (h) Please describe the measures taken by your government to assure to all medical service and medical attention in the event of sickness.

   (i) Please describe the effect of the measures, listed in subparagraphs (e) to (h) on the situation of the vulnerable and disadvantaged groups in your society and in any worse-off areas. Report on difficulties and failures as well as on positive results.

6. Please indicate the measures taken by your government to ensure that the rising costs of health care for the elderly do not lead to infringements on these persons' right to health.

Box 1.2 (cont.)

7. Please indicate what measures have been taken in your country to maximize community participation in the planning organization, operation, and control of primary health care.
8. Please indicate what measures have been taken in your country to provide education concerning prevailing health problems and the measures of preventing and controlling them.
9. Please indicate the role of international assistance in the full realization of the right enshrined in Article 12.

---

by the other technical agencies of the United Nations, especially UNAIDS and the WHO, and may help to frame some of their future work.

Non-governmental organizations have a critical role to play in monitoring government compliance with treaty provisions. Within countries, non-governmental organizations are increasingly using government obligations under the human rights treaties, as well as the concluding comments and observations of the treaty bodies, in their advocacy efforts. The input of non-governmental organizations is also crucial at the international level in that they are able to provide treaty monitoring bodies with additional outside information on the action (or inaction) of the government in question, which can then be used by the treaty body in its dialogue with that government. Although non-governmental organizations are sometimes present during the formal dialogue, this information is most often presented in shadow reports. There is no formal mechanism, however, for ensuring that this information reaches the treaty bodies, and, unfortunately, non-governmental organizations generally do not coordinate with each other on the information they provide. At times, the same information about a particular situation has been presented to a treaty body from numerous sources, while other potentially critical information of a more general nature is never provided. In addition, many local non-governmental organizations are unaware of or lack access to the treaty monitoring process, resulting in a number of problems. First, only the most publicized cases come to the attention of the monitoring body. Second, the lack of functioning non-governmental organizations in a majority of countries results in both a dearth of information from countries with some of the worst human rights records and a privileging of the information provided by well-established international human rights non-governmental organizations such as Amnesty International and Human Rights Watch, which have more contracts and closer relationships with the treaty body members than other organizations do. This last point is of particular concern in relation to health-related human rights issues, as these issues generally fall outside the purview of mainstream human rights organizations, and therefore little alternative information on health-related issues reaches

the relevant bodies (UNAIDS 1997). As a result, while the utility of the involvement of non-governmental organizations to this process is at this point undis-
puted, mechanisms for ensuring their involvement in a comprehensive way,
particularly with respect to health-related information, still remain to be worked
out.

General Recommendations and General Comments Concerning Health

In the past 5 years, there have been increasing efforts to draft authoritative
interpretations of the right to health in order to ensure state responsibility and
accountability with respect to health in a structured way. These authoritative
interpretations have taken the form of general comments or general recommendations, which are drafted and endorsed by the treaty monitoring body in
question and which form the basis of the treaty body's formal understanding
of the content of a particular right or issue. These general comments or general
recommendations then help to serve as a guide for governments concerning
the issues that they must consider in making their periodic reports under the
guidelines, for non-governmental organizations in their monitoring of governmental action and for the treaty bodies themselves in their dialogue and interaction with governments in the context of the monitoring process (UN 1996).
While these comments and recommendations are meant only to provide interpretation, their formulation does have real implications for whether or not a
government is judged to be in compliance with its treaty obligations. For example, the right to health as formulated in international treaties contains no
mention of primary health care. This is mainly because the concept of primary
health care had not yet been internationally recognized at the time that the
ICESCR was drafted. While the guidelines for reporting contain substantive
mention of primary health care, the relationship between a primary health
care approach and government obligations under the treaty are not detailed.
Thus, in the absence of a general comment or recommendation emphasizing a
primary health care approach, it is difficult to judge a country that pays little or
no attention to primary health care not to be in compliance with its health-
related obligations.

Until very recently, no general comments or recommendations had been
issued by any of the treaty bodies specifically related to health. In 1999, the
United Nations Committee on the Elimination of Discrimination Against
Women (CEDAW), which monitors governmental compliance under the
Women's Convention, issued a General Recommendation on Health (CEDAW
1999), and in 2000 the Committee on Economic, Social and Cultural Rights,
the body responsible for monitoring the ICESCR, issued a General Comment
on the Right to Health (ICESCR 2000). Nonetheless, a number of the general
comments and recommendations previously issued by the treaty bodies have
had clear health-related implications. These include the General Comments

on disability (UN 1994), housing (UN 1997b), and food (UN 1995a) issued by the UNCESCR, and the General Recommendations concerning HIV/AIDS (CEDAW 1990b), female circumcision (CEDAW 1990a), and violence against women (CEDAW 1989) issued by the CEDAW.

At the outset of the twenty-first century, the translation of the right to health into guidelines and other tools useful to national and international monitoring of governmental and intergovernmental obligations is still in its infancy. The ICESCR General Comment on the Right to the Highest Attainable Standard of Health, which was adopted in 2000 (ICESCR 2000), may help to provide some useful guidelines. In parallel, as described below, the WHO is developing a new set of tools and recommendations aimed at redirecting the attention given to monitoring global health indicators from disease-specific morbidity and mortality trends towards others that are more reflective of the degree to which health and human rights principles are respected, protected, and fulfilled (WHO 2000c). How and to what extent these instruments will be put to use and how effective they will be in advancing the health and human rights agenda has yet to be seen, but there are several factors that, even at this early stage, allow for guarded optimism. First, the treaty bodies and international organizations concerned with health are doing this work based on open dialogue and a degree of collaboration that greatly exceeds the level and quality of interagency collaboration traditionally observed within the United Nations machinery. This is exemplified by the sharing of goals and the collective technical co-operation that has prevailed in the current processes of defining obligations and monitoring methods and standards relevant to health and human rights in the process of operationalizing both the international treaties and the recommendations promulgated at the international conferences (UNDAW 1996; UNDP 1998b; WHO 2000b). Potentially, this work will help not only to monitor what governments are doing, but also to build their capacity to incorporate health and human rights principles into their policies and programmes.

In several countries, including Brazil, Thailand, and South Africa, human rights principles relevant to health have recently found their way into national legislation and new constitutions, thereby ensuring citizens the right to seek fulfilment of their right to care, for example, through national juridical means (Hannum 1998). As the methods and tools for monitoring and accountability of health-related issues mature, it is likely that cases of human rights violations related to health will increasingly be heard both within countries and at the regional and international level. A focus on monitoring and redress of violations of the right to health is but one means of ensuring action using the human rights documents. Equally important are the steps being taken to build national and international capacity to develop and reform public policy and laws in line with international human rights norms and standards as they apply to health (UNFPA 1998). This work requires institutional changes, as well as capacity building within both governmental systems and international organizations. The Director-General of the WHO has cited the need to integrate efforts towards this goal, noting: 'Even when governments are well-intentioned, they may have difficulty fulfilling their health and human rights obligations. Governments, the WHO and other intergovernmental agencies should strive to create the conditions favorable to health, even in situations where the base of public finance threatens to collapse' (Brundtland 1998).

The process of 'mainstreaming human rights', currently well underway in the United Nations system, is specifically aimed toward this goal (UN 1997a). Mainstreaming human rights is 'the process of assessing the human rights implications of any planned action, including legislation, policies or programmes, in all areas and at all levels. It is a strategy for making human rights an integral dimension of the design, implementation, monitoring and evaluation of policies and programmes in political, economic and social spheres' (UN 1997a). Two examples illustrate how this is done. In the 1990s, UNICEF adopted the Convention on the Rights of the Child (CRC), thereby ensuring that their policy and programmatic work would be guided by the principles and standards established by the CRC, as well as the Convention on the Elimination of All Forms of Discrimination Against Women. The 1996 Mission Statement says explicitly that pursuit of the rights of children and women is a fundamental purpose of the organization. These efforts have led to a restructuring of UNICEF and a rights-based approach to all programming efforts at all levels of its work (UNICEF 1998). In the WHO, a similar process began in 1999 with the aim of defining the goals of human rights mainstreaming for their national and international health work (WHO 1999c). A process was begun following the 1998 World Health Assembly Resolution that set out the need to 'promote and support the rights and principles, actions and responsibilities enunciated in the [World Health Declaration] through concerted action, full participation and partnership, calling on all peoples and institutions to share the vision of health for all in the twenty-first century, and to endeavor in common to realize it' (WHO 1998d). In 2000, work began towards a strategy document which would incorporate health and human rights into the policy and programme work of the WHO. Towards this aim, health and human rights are considered relevant to each of the WHO's four strategic directions (WHO 1999c):

- reducing excess mortality, morbidity, and disability, especially in poor and marginalized populations
- promoting healthy lifestyles and reducing risk factors to human health that arise from environmental, economic, social, and behavioural causes
- developing health systems that equitably improve health outcomes, respond to people's legitimate demands, and are financially fair

- developing an enabling policy and institutional environment in the health sector and promoting an effective health dimension to social, economic, environmental, and development policy.

These strategic directions are discussed more extensively below with specific reference to their health and human rights implications. To pursue these directions, the WHO is proposing to contribute to the building of skills and knowledge within the WHO and within countries; to perform an internal review of its policies and programmes to verify their conformity with health and human rights principles; to further its co-operation with the Office of the High Commissioner for Human Rights and the treaty monitoring bodies; to disseminate information; and to develop and refine human rights-sensitive monitoring and evaluation processes applicable nationally and internationally.

A Health Perspective on Human Rights

As stated above, over 50 years ago, the Constitution of the WHO projected a vision of health as a state of complete physical, mental, and social well being— a definition of health that is more relevant today than ever (WHO 1946). It recognized that the enjoyment of the highest attainable standard of health was one of the fundamental rights of every human being and that governments have a responsibility for the health of their peoples, which can be fulfilled only through the provision of adequate health and social measures. The 1978 Alma-Ata Declaration (WHO/UNICEF 1979) called on nations to ensure the availability of the essentials of primary health care, including:

- education concerning health problems and the methods for preventing and controlling them
- promotion of food supply and proper nutrition
- an adequate supply of safe water and basic sanitation
- maternal and child health care, including family planning
- immunization against major infectious diseases
- prevention and control of locally endemic diseases
- appropriate treatment of common disease and injuries
- provision of essential drugs.

In 1998, the World Health Assembly reaffirmed the commitment of nations to strive towards these goals in a World Health Declaration that stressed the 'will to promote health by addressing the basic determinants and prerequisites for health' and the urgent priority 'to pay the greatest attention to those most in need, burdened by ill health, receiving inadequate services for health or affected by poverty' (WHO 1998d). These ambitious objectives of health development must be examined from the perspective of the role of governments in ensuring equal and equitable access to medical care and health promotion while striving to create the underlying conditions necessary for health.

This section begins with a discussion of the traditional dichotomy between the roles and functions of medicine and those of public health, which will help begin to frame the content of governmental obligations towards individuals and populations for health under international human rights law. Health will then be placed in the broader context of human development in order to underscore the relevance of a broad array of governmental obligations, well beyond the health sector, that may impact on health. The four strategic directions to health development mentioned above will then be presented as an approach relevant to the development of both a health and human rights analysis and monitoring and accountability. Finally, a new grouping of these issues will be proposed as an entry point into their analysis from a human rights perspective, leading to a pathway for action.

Medicine, Public Health, and Human Rights

Health as it connects to human rights analysis and implementation concerns two related but different disciplines: medicine and public health. Historically the territorial boundaries of medicine and public health reflected not only professional interest and skill, but also the environments within which these skills were practised: homes, clinics, hospitals, and clinical laboratories on the one hand; institutes, public health laboratories, offices, and field projects on the other (Detels et al. 1997). Recently, the apparent differences between the two professions—the first primarily understood to focus on the health of individuals, the second on the health of populations—have profoundly impacted the ways in which the relationship between health and human rights has been understood by different actors. From a rights perspective, this ancient division resulted in the assumption that, of the two, medicine was more concerned with the health and rights of the individual (for example, in creating conditions enabling a particular individual to access care), while the primary focus of public health was the protection of collective interests, even at the cost of arbitrarily restricting individual rights (Mann 1997b). For example, coercion and restrictions of rights had been critical to traditional smallpox eradication efforts (Fenner et al. 1988). Yet as the human rights approach has made increasingly clear, this stark differentiation between medicine and public health is no longer fully relevant either to human rights or to health. Although they apply different methods of work, both medicine and public health seek to ensure every person's right to achieve the highest attainable standard of health, and both have a strong focus on the individual. Medicine is more concerned with analysing, diagnosing, and treating disease, as well as preventing ill health in individuals through such methods as immunization, appropriate diet, or prophylactic therapies. Public health seeks to address health and ill health by focusing on individual and collective determinants, be they behavioural, social, economic, or other contextual factors.

Three sets of factors have contributed to blurring traditional boundaries between medicine and public health. First, the transitions in health status through which many populations have been recently evolving have called for a closer understanding of the links between individual health, public health, and the environment (Shrader-Frechetter 1991; Gubler 1998). Current thinking about optimal strategies for disease control have evolved, as efforts to confront the most serious global health threats (including cancer, mental disorders, cardiovascular and other chronic diseases, reproductive and sexual health, infectious diseases, and violence) have increasingly emphasized the role of personal behaviour within a broad social context (Murray and Lopez 1996; WHO 1999a). The transition of the global disease burden from communicable to non-communicable diseases (which are heavily dependent on lifestyle), has evoked a medical need to care for patients in their own social contexts. There has been increasing understanding that behaviours and their social, economic, and cultural contexts are inextricably linked with the biology of health and disease, and are therefore relevant to individual care (Krieger and Sidney 1996).

Second, the tools and technologies of each field have been found to be of increasing utility to the other. For example, new technologies developed through biomedical research in such fields as immunology, molecular biology, and genetics are of increasing relevance to public health (Barry and Molyneux 1992; Andrews 1995; Aluwihare 1998). Scientific discoveries in molecular virology have provided tools that are as useful to individual diagnosis and care as they are to epidemiology, vaccine development, and public health programmes (Hunter 1999). Likewise, traditional public health tools, drawn from epidemiology, ecology, and social and behavioural sciences, have demonstrated their usefulness in deciphering powerful determinants of health and of disease outcomes, thus creating stronger bridges between biomedical care and public health interventions (Terragni 1993; Krieger and Zierler 1997).

Third, the human rights framework has shown that the state's human rights responsibilities to respect, protect, and fulfill rights relating to health include obligations concerning both medicine and public health. In the context of a health and human rights analysis, a challenge to the now artificial dichotomy between medicine and public health is not merely rhetorical or of analytical interest; it also brings into play the range of obligations of the state towards every individual. The health and human rights paradigm is relevant to clinical practice, community health, large-scale health programme development, implementation, and policy. The synergistic health and human rights perspective aims to guarantee that every individual can achieve the highest attainable standard of physical, mental, and social well being. Human rights are progressively being understood to offer an approach for considering the broader societal dimensions and contexts of the well being of individuals and populations, and therefore to be of utility to all those concerned with health.

Globalization and Health Development

The definition of health enshrined in the WHO Constitution was an important step in helping to move health thinking beyond a limited biomedical- and pathology-based perspective towards the more positive domain of well being, understood to include recognition of individuals and their need to realize aspirations, to satisfy needs, and to change or cope with their environments. The societal dimensions of this effort were emphasized in both the Alma-Ata Declaration (WHO 1979) and the Ottawa Charter for Health Promotion (1986). The Alma-Ata Declaration describes health as a social goal whose realization requires the action of many social and economic sectors in addition to the health sector. The Ottawa Charter proposes that the fundamental conditions and resources for health are peace, shelter, education, food, income, a stable ecosystem, sustainable resources, social justice, and equity.

When the WHO was created to improve health 50 years ago, there were hopes that antibiotics and the progress achieved in vaccines and biomedical technology would provide the tools sufficient to enable individuals worldwide to reach the highest attainable standard of physical, mental, and social well being (Tomasevski 1995b). However, decades later, as reflected in both the Alma-Ata Declaration and the Ottawa Charter, it is clear that, regardless of the effectiveness of technologies, the underlying civil, cultural, economic, political, and social conditions at both a global and local level have to be addressed as well. The major determinants of better health are increasingly understood to lie outside the health system and to include better education and information, as well as fulfilment of an array of rights which are relevant to, but not intrinsically connected with, the right to health (Carrin and Politi 1996). Thus health requires attention to the increasingly complex relationship of people to their environment and an understanding of respecting, protecting, and fulfilling human rights as a necessary prerequisite for the health of individuals and populations.

Globalization and the direct and indirect impacts of intensifying global flows of money, trade, information, culture, and people on health and related aspects of human development, have brought out a new set of human rights issues (Brundtland 2000). These issues need particular attention, as they have largely been ignored. The process of globalization has proceeded at a much faster pace than the development of policies aimed at maximizing its benefits to human development and preventing or mitigating its harmful effects.

Globalization, and the privatization of the means of production and services that inherently accompanies it, can contribute to the advancement of health through the sharing of information, technologies, and resources, as well as through the competition it generates to provide more effective, more widely available, and higher-quality services. Globalization can create new employment opportunities in some populations or sectors of the economy, but at times may do so to the detriment of others. It can also stimulate the spread of health hazards and disease as a result of intensified population mobility, or through the worldwide marketing of harmful substances, such as tobacco and alcohol. If poorly conceived and monitored, globalization can contribute to the widening of inequalities by increasing the autonomy and well being of some sectors of the population while producing negative consequences for others without access to safety nets to support the fulfilment of essential needs (Cooper Well et al. 1990; UN 1995c; WHO 1995; Al-Mazrou et al. 1997; Hallack 1999; Heggenhougen 1999; Brundtland 2000). In the wake of globalization and privatization, increasing attention must be paid to the role of non-state actors because they are now influencing the health and well being of people to an unprecedented extent, comparable even to the influence of governments (UNHCHR 2000). The role of the state is to ensure that all human beings are guaranteed their basic human rights, including the right to the highest attainable standard of health, whether this obligation is fulfilled directly through government-run services or through private intermediaries. Governmental roles and responsibilities are increasingly being delegated to non-state actors (for example, biomedical research institutions, international foundations, health insurance companies, care providers, health management organizations, and the pharmaceutical industry) whose accountability for what they do, do not do, or should do about people's health is poorly defined and inadequately monitored. There is a universal need to reinforce the commitment and capacity of governments to ensure that actions taken by the private sector and other actors in civil society relevant to health and other aspects of human development, both within and outside the boundaries of nation-states, are informed by and comply with human rights principles. Current structures are generally insufficient for non-governmental organizations or governments to monitor effectively and hold corporations operating on a national scale accountable. This problem is compounded when these companies are multinational (Hossain 1999; Orford 1999; UNHCHR 2000).

Attention to health reveals that multinationals are more than agents of economic change whose decisions are increasingly affecting the distribution of wealth, the fabric of society, and the creation of conditions favourable to advancing health; they are also increasingly the institutions called upon by political and social forces to create and operate alternative mechanisms to extend health and social services and to make available new and affordable vaccines and drugs (Kolodner 1994). Yet because they are multinational, they largely escape the realm of legal accountability within states, and, while they may choose to adopt ethical guidelines and codes of conduct, there is no international human rights law that directly applies to them or to their actions. The fora where world issues are debated have expanded from assemblies of governments—for example, under the United Nations umbrella—to gatherings and congresses such as the Davos forum that give a prominent role to these non-state actors, demonstrating that the state and non-state actors leading the world economy have become inseparable partners. From a health and human rights perspective, the desirable forms and extent of responsibility for multinational actors within the international legal system have yet to be defined in ways that help to shape international trade agreements effectively and to ensure their accountability. This is the next and most important challenge in the world of human rights, and it will have far-reaching health consequences.

Strategic Directions to Better Health

Human rights can help to provide an approach for redefining the ways in which governments and the international community as a whole are accountable for what is done and not done about the health of people (Mann et al. 1994). This requires an understanding of the content of the health issues most relevant to the health and well being of individuals and populations, as well as of those actions which ought to be taken at the national level to move towards health development.

As the approaches set out by the WHO are relevant to all its member states, this discussion will be framed around the strategic framework laid out by the WHO in its 1999 corporate strategy (WHO 1999b). From a strategic perspective, the issues relevant to health development can be understood to lie along four converging axes: (a) reducing excess mortality, morbidity, and disability; (b) promoting healthy lifestyles and reducing risk factors to human health that arise from environmental, economic, social, and behavioural causes; (c) developing health systems that equitably improve health outcomes, respond to people's legitimate demands, and are financially fair; (d) developing an enabling policy and institutional environment in the health sector while promoting an effective health dimension to social, economic, environmental, and development policy. Each of these approaches is briefly discussed below.

Reducing Excess Mortality, Morbidity, and Disability

Recent WHO information reveals that six preventable or curable diseases cause 90 per cent of infectious disease deaths worldwide, as well as half of all premature deaths, most of which occur in children and young adults living in developing countries (Murray and Lopez 1996; WHO 1999a). Reduction of excess mortality, morbidity, and disability calls for a combination of sound health interventions—some of a clinical nature, such as diagnosis and treatment of communicable and non-communicable diseases, and others building on large-scale programmes to inform, immunize, or apply population-based prophylactic therapies. From a health and human rights perspective, it is worth recognizing that the growing health disparity between countries of the North and the South creates compelling needs both for every country to develop effective disease prevention and control programmes targeted to their specific needs, and for global sharing of technology and resources in order to enable poorer countries to accelerate progress in health development. Therefore, priority must be given both locally and globally to poor and marginalized communities.

Promoting Healthy Lifestyles and Reducing Risk Factors to Human Health that Arise From Environmental, Economic, Social, and Behavioural Causes

Modern public health recognizes the influence of external factors on the ability of individuals to adopt healthy behaviours or to access care when ill health has set in. As stated above, health promotion is the process of enabling people to increase control over and improve their health. To do so, individuals or groups must be informed and able to identify and realize aspirations, satisfy needs, and change or cope with their environment. The concept of interventions aimed at reducing risk is familiar to those working on such health issues as HIV/AIDS and other sexually transmitted diseases, tobacco, and other types of substance use or occupational hazards (Mann et al. 1992; Mann and Tarantola 1996b,c; WHO 1998b). Risk reduction interventions can also bring attention to the inadequacy of public services to address such issues as reproductive health, access to safe blood transfusion, or access to clean water. Some authors have distinguished the notion of risk, defined as a statistical probability of suffering from ill health, from that of 'vulnerability', which impacts on risk via societal, programme-related, or individual factors (Mann and Tarantola 1996b,c; Tarantola 1998). Others have further extended this analysis by defining 'susceptibility' as the influence of external or individual factors on risk and 'vulnerability' as the degree to which individual, communities, or nations are able to cope effectively with the impacts of ill health (Barnett and Whiteside 1999). Still others have grouped these factors among the 'underlying preconditions for health', including policy, legal, and institutional environments, which have traditionally been dealt with as separate issues (Mann et al. 1994; Mann and Tarantola 1996a). All of these paradigms recognize the importance of integrating morbidity, mortality, and disability reduction programmes with interventions to mitigate or address the factors underlying the occurrence of these events. Reducing susceptibility or vulnerability requires understanding of who is affected and how and to what extent these people are exposed to and able to cope with the factors that impact on their health, and then designing interventions that can enable them to cope effectively. From a health and human rights perspective, this process is linked to the need to create conditions conducive to health through information, education, and the development or strengthening of health systems and social support programmes that promote healthy behaviours, impact on risk-taking behaviours, and increase individual and collective commitment and capacity to engage in these processes.

Developing Health Systems that Equitably Improve Health Outcomes, Respond to People's Legitimate Demands, and Are Financially Fair

In this context, 'health systems' can be understood as the set of public or private structures, services, actions, and people whose main aim is to promote health and prevent and treat disease. In order to progress towards these aims, health systems must be sufficiently accessible, efficient, and affordable, and of good quality (WHO 2000d). The WHO *World Health Report 2000* has proposed measures that reflect responsibility and create the grounds for accountability within health systems with regard to three dimensions of health: health outcomes, fairness, and responsiveness (WHO 2000d). The responsibilities of health systems in relation to health outcomes largely determines the type of services, interventions, and technologies they offer. If analysed on the basis of health outcomes, the accountability demanded of health systems must take into consideration the capacity of these systems to recognize and respond to health issues, as well as such factors as personal behaviours or unforseen social, economic, or environmental situations or events. From an accountability perspective, it is worth recognizing that some of these latter factors may impact on health outcomes but are beyond the responsibilities assigned to health systems. They must be taken into account in other ways—for example, in relation to governmental accountability for education, employment, freedom of movement or association, or in relation to other rights that impact on health.

Underlying this attention to the responsibility and accountability of health systems is the concept of equality, which implies that health systems are capable of defining and recognizing the characteristics and specific needs of populations within a nation who experience a disproportionate level of mortality, morbidity, and disability. This, in turn, requires that health data be collected and analysed with a degree of sensitivity and specificity sufficient to determine who is likely to require additional attention; what behaviours and practices have to be supported, induced, or changed; what service provisions have to be enhanced and in what ways; and what financial mechanisms are necessary to provide the safety nets necessary to ensure that those who need more actually receive more. Therefore, it follows that the information used to develop, monitor, and evaluate policies and programmes must accurately reflect characteristics that may be associated with discrimination and inequality, including sex, age, rural/urban location, and other relevant behavioural, social, and economic factors (Barton Smith 1998).

The WHO *World Health Report 2000* proposes that 'the way health care is financed is perfectly fair when the burden that health spending represents on the household, or its relative health financial contribution is identical for all households, independent of their income, their health status or their use of the health system' (WHO 2000d). Although the principle of fairness is not articulated as such in human rights treaties, it builds on an array of rights, such as non-discrimination, equality, and participation, that, together with obligations directly related to health, can be used to consider the responsibilities of governments for health systems. The financing of health systems must be considered from the perspective of competing human development priorities within a nation, as well as that of the intrinsic priorities within health systems themselves. No global benchmark can therefore be proposed to establish the minimum national spending for health systems, whether from public or private sources, and the debate must remain open as to the extent to which and the ways in which governments will invest in the health of their populations. Within health systems, the decisions concerning allocation of public funds for specific health initiatives can draw from epidemiological, economic, or political considerations and can use a variety of methods and processes, including cost-effectiveness analysis, as well as human rights considerations. The concept of financial fairness implies that these systems should enable all individuals to seek and receive services that are commensurate to their needs and economically affordable.

Finally, the concept of responsiveness imposes on health systems a requirement that they be sensitive to people's aspirations, needs, and demands with full respect for human rights, and that they offer support and services. The principles of non-discrimination, protection of confidentiality (privacy), and respect for people's dignity are central to both the design of health systems and to the attitude and practices of health providers. From a health and human rights perspective, each of the components considered necessary for health systems to improve health outcomes equitably raises additional issues to be considered from the perspective of governmental responsibility and accountability.

Developing an Enabling Policy and Institutional Environment in the Health Sector While Promoting an Effective Health Dimension to Social, Economic, Environmental, and Development Policy

If it is clear that policies and practices within health systems may impact positively or negatively on health, it is also clear that policies and practices concerned with the broad spectrum of human development may also impact significantly on health status and health-seeking behaviours (Cooper Well *et al.* 1990). A large-scale industrial project may, for example, create selective migratory movements that may result in accentuated health hazards, whether these are linked to inadequate working conditions, housing, or social or cultural uprooting (Shenker 1992; ILO 1996). The association between enhanced vulnerability to HIV/AIDS among migrant labourers and economically motivated mobility in Africa and Asia provides one example (UNAIDS/IOM 1998). Similarly, factors such as the amount of pollution that industries have generated, or the impact that the use of pesticides in agriculture has had on the health of some populations, imply that health impacts must be considered at all stages of human development programmes (McMichael 1993). From a health and human rights perspective, this requires attention to health impacts in the design of human development programmes; this would include preventing or counterbalancing their potential negative health effects, as well as ensuring that health indicators are built into the monitoring of human development initiatives (WHO 1992; Watson et al. 1998).

The four strategic elements of health as briefly described above provide a useful framework for analysing the interface between health and rights. Indeed, each of these elements involves governmental obligations that are relevant to policies and programmes directly impacting on health, as well as those more broadly concerned with human development.

Health Development and Human Rights

While the above categorization of strategic directions for health is useful because it reflects the approach being taken by the WHO and is guiding the current global health agenda, a perspective of governmental human rights obligations towards health development emerges more clearly if these strategies are divided into the following three domains.

1. The highest attainable standard of health. This is measured by morbidity, mortality, and disability, by positive health measures of growth and development in children, and by demographic variables, reproductive health, healthy lifestyles, behaviours, and practices in adults. The focus here is on health outcomes affecting individuals and populations.
2. Access to health systems which provide affordable and good-quality preventive, curative, and palliative care services and related social support. The focus here is on health systems.
3. A societal and physical environment conducive to health promotion and protection, including access to education, information, and other positive expressions of rights necessary for health as well as protection from violence, environmental and occupational hazards, harmful traditional practices, and other factors that may impact directly and negatively on health. The focus here is on the societal and environmental preconditions for health.

The development and application of governmental policies transcends all three of these domains of health development and is equally relevant to governmental responsibilities both to promote and protect health and to respect, protect, and fulfil human rights (Roemer and Roemer 1990; UNDP 1998a). A systematic analysis of the responsibilities of governments for health, considered with respect to their obligations under international human rights law, begins to lead us towards the practice of health and human rights.

Recognizing the Reciprocal Impact of Health and Human Rights

There are two approaches to analysing the relationship between health and human rights that help not only to illustrate their connection, but also to provide a framework for considering the implications of the health and human rights relationship for government responsibility and accountability (Mann et al. 1994). The first focuses consideration on the ways in which health policies, programmes, and practices can promote or violate rights in the ways they are designed or implemented. Health policies, programmes, and practices in and of themselves can promote and protect or, conversely, restrict and violate human rights, whether by design, neglect, or ignorance. The second approach examines how violations or lack of attention to human rights can have serious health consequences. The promotion, protection, restriction, or violation of human rights all can be seen to have direct and indirect impacts on health and well being. Looking at health through a human rights lens means recognizing not only the technical and operational aspects of health interventions but also the civil, political, economic, social, and cultural factors that surround them. These factors may include, for example, gender relations, religious beliefs, homophobia, or racism, which individually and in synergy influence the extent to which individuals are able to access services or to make and effect free and informed decisions about their lives—and, therefore, the extent of their vulnerability to ill health. Thus, health and human rights interact in numerous ways, both direct and indirect (Mann et al. 1994). Public health and human rights each recognize the ultimate responsibility of governments to create the enabling conditions necessary for people to make choices, cope with changing patterns of vulnerability, and keep themselves and their families healthy. Using human rights concepts, one can look at the extent to which governments are respecting, protecting, and fulfilling their obligations for all rights—civil political, economic, social, and cultural—and how these government actions influence both the patterns of mortality, morbidity, and disability within a population and what is done about them.

The Impact of Health Policies, Programmes, and Practices on Human Rights

A human rights framework can help to identify potential burdens on the lives of individuals and populations that are created by health policies, programmes, and practices. An obvious example, as was recognized in the International Conference on Population Development Programme of Action, is demographic goal-driven family planning programmes, which may by their very nature violate basic human rights (ICPD 1994). More subtle human rights issues may arise from health programmes that fail to provide services to certain populations or are not appropriately tailored to meet the needs of marginalized groups (Altman 1998; Beyrer 1998; Jackson 1998; Stevens 1998; Wodak 1998).

Responsibilities for public health are largely carried out through policies and programmes promulgated, implemented, and, at the very least, supported by the state. Therefore, a human rights approach to public health requires analysis of every stage of the design, implementation, and evaluation of health policies and programmes. This section teases out some of the issues that a human rights analysis can raise at various stages of policy and programme design and implementation. HIV/AIDS, sexual health, and reproductive health will serve as primary examples in this section because, in recent years, these issues have been especially important in illuminating the impact that health policies and programmes can have on human rights.

Human rights considerations arise at the initial formulation of health policies and programmes. Relevant issues would be raised, for example, if a state decides to approach a health issue in a particular way but refuses to disclose the scientific basis of its decisions or permit any debate on its merits, or if a government wilfully or neglectfully fails to consult with members of affected communities in reaching its decisions, or in any number of ways refuses to inform or involve the public in policy or programme development. Human rights issues may also interact with the development of health policies and programmes when prioritization of certain health issues is based less on actual need than on existing discrimination against certain population groups (Gilmore 1996). This can occur when, for example, minor health issues that predominantly impact the dominant group are systematically given higher priority in research, resource allocation, and policy and programme development than other more major health problems. Restrictive laws and policies that deliberately focus on certain population groups without sufficient data, epidemiological and otherwise, to support their approach may raise an additional host of human rights concerns. Two examples might be policies concerning the involuntary sterilization of women from certain population groups that are justified as necessary for their health and well being (Lombardo 1996; Comite Latinoamericano para la Defensa de los Derechos de la Mujer 1999), and sodomy statutes criminalizing same-sex sexual behaviour that are justified as necessary to prevent the spread of HIV/AIDS (UNHRC 1994).

Human rights also need to be considered when choosing which data are collected to determine the type and extent of health problems affecting a population, as this choice has a direct impact on the policies and programmes that are designed and implemented (Zierler et al. 2000). The choice of issues to be assessed and the way in which a population is defined in these assessments are of primary relevance (Braveman 1998). A state's failure to recognize or acknowledge health problems that particularly impact on a marginalized group, or to consider the impacts of particular health issues on all members of a population, may not only violate the right to non-discrimination, but may also lead to neglect of necessary services, which in turn may adversely affect the realization of other human rights (Cook 1994; Hendriks 1995; Miller et al. 1995). Examples of this would include the almost complete lack of attention and resources devoted to the early detection of cervical cancer by a number of governments, or state-controlled reproductive health programmes that exist for some population groups but exclude certain marginalized communities from their consideration and outreach (WHO 1994b). Likewise, the scarcity or absence of HIV-related services in a number of places can well be understood to have resulted in a disproportionate burden of health consequences that could have been prevented or alleviated through simple and affordable prevention messages and methods of early diagnosis and treatment.

Once a decision is made that a particular health problem will be dealt with, human rights issues can come into play in both the articulation and the implementation of the health policy or programme. An example is programmes that provide contraception to young boys but deny access to young girls, with the stated rationale that access might prompt girls to be sexually active (Radhakrishna et al. 1997; Youth Research 1997). From a human rights perspective, this distinction can be understood to be treating young girls unfairly and unjustly on the basis of their sex. The prohibition of discrimination in the human rights documents does not mean that differences should not be acknowledged, but rather that different treatment must be based on reasonable and objective criteria (Cook 1992; Coliver 1995). Therefore, applying different approaches to girls and boys in policy and programme development must be based on a valid recognition of gender-related differentials in risk and vulnerability with respect to the particular health issue and with an attempt to minimize the influence of prescribed gender roles and cultural norms in making this determination (Moody 1989; Holder 1992).

The severity of the devastating tuberculosis epidemic in developing countries, and in marginalized communities in affluent nations, draws attention to the relevance of a human rights analysis for the implementation of a health policy and programme (Raviglione et al. 1995; WHO 1999c). While the directly observed therapy strategy (DOTS) is widely recognized for its efficacy in controlling tuberculosis, the issues raised by the very different ways this strategy is administered in different countries, and to different population groups, demonstrates how discrimination may be relevant to the ways in which health programmes are implemented (WHO 2000a). Many health practitioners argue that the speed with which tuberculosis is spreading and the potential impact of individual non-compliance to treatment are likely to aggravate both the spread of the disease and the currently observed prevalence of multiple-drug resistance (WHO 1998c). The DOTS strategy aims to combat this by enrolling patients diagnosed with active tuberculosis in a programme where drugs are administered under the direct observation of a care provider, rather than self-administered by the patient (WHO 1994a). The strategy requires frequent visits by patients to the site where drugs are administered, which can potentially involve work absenteeism and in some cases out-of-pocket travel expenses. In small communities, the strategy may also lead to breaches of the right to privacy, as frequent visits to a treatment point may be associated with the stigma commonly attached to the disease. In cases of non-compliance to regular treatment administered in this way, measures up to and including mandatory hospital admission may be taken to motivate defaulting patients to comply. There is ample evidence to suggest, however, that in a number of places the level of coercion exercised by health practitioners in the decision to apply DOTS, as well as in the application of mandatory institutionalization, is directly associated with the levels of discrimination against particular population groups within the society in question (Farmer et al. 1991; Bayer et al. 1993; Schmidt 1995; Efferen 1997; Heymann and Sell 1999).

Attention must also be given to whether health and social services take into account logistic, financial, and sociocultural barriers to access and enjoyment, as a failure to do so can result in discrimination in practice, if not in law (Focht-New 1996). This includes attention to the factors that may impact on service utilization, such as hours of service and accessibility via public transportation. Issues are also raised by decisions concerning the location of prevention and treatment services for certain health issues. An extreme example relates to the location of sexually transmitted disease diagnosis, prevention, and care services, which may be integrated into the reproductive health services generally available to women or offered only in centres dedicated to sexually transmitted disease prevention and treatment. Evidence suggests that individuals, and women in particular, are less likely to take advantage of sexually transmitted disease services that operate under this latter designation for fear of stigma and discrimination within the community if they are seen at the facility (Weiss and Gupta 1993; d'Cruz-Grote 1996).

Laws and policies that may seem neutral but neglect to detail sufficiently the steps necessary for their implementation may raise additional human rights issues. Illustrative of such a situation are laws and policies that mandate the reporting of HIV infection but fail to spell out the actors responsible for doing so, or fail to take into account a lack of infrastructure to ensure that privacy can be respected and that mechanisms for redress exist if breaches of confidentiality occur (Gruskin and Tarantola 2000). Indeed, collecting personal information from individuals about their health status (for example, HIV infection, cancer, or genetic disorders), or behaviours (for example, sexual orientation or the use of alcohol or other substances) has the potential for misuse by the state, whether directly or because this information is intentionally or inadvertently made available to others. In recent times the most explicit examples of the impact of misuse or neglect of privacy protections are found in the context of HIV/AIDS. Misuse of personal information related to HIV status has led to restrictions on the right to marry and found a family, the right to work and education, as well as, in extreme cases, limitations on freedom of movement, arbitrary detention, or exile, and even cruel, inhuman, and degrading treatment. The release of information concerning a person's HIV status to others has, in many places, led to loss of employment and housing, as well as harassment and verbal and physical attacks (Cohen and Wiseberg 1990; Gruskin et al. 1996; UNDP 1998b).

Decisions on how data are collected have a direct influence on the policies and programmes that are put into place. For example, differentials determined by sex or gender roles in relation to HIV/sexually transmitted disease infection are generally not systematically considered in the collection and analysis of HIV/sexually transmitted disease epidemiological data, nor are they sufficiently studied or built into the design of prevention and care programmes. In countries where an HIV/AIDS epidemic has matured, some 15- to 16-year-old girls attending antenatal clinics for their first pregnancy are already infected with HIV, and no information is available as to the cause of this infection (that is, whether it involved sex or another mode of transmission) (Tarantola and Gruskin 1998). The degree to which gender factors influence the relative risk of becoming infected through various routes of transmission during childhood, and how they may influence patterns of access to care and the quality of care provided to boys and girls once HIV infection has set in, remains unknown. There has been very little attention to the general failure to differentiate by sex in the collection and analysis of epidemiological information on 'children' younger than 15. This raises a host of human rights concerns and may result in neglect of the very real differences between female and male adolescents in the prevention and care programmes that do exist.

Violations of the right to information in the context of health policies and programmes must be mentioned specifically, as these can have substantial health impacts (Freedman 1999). Examples include decisions by governments to withhold or block access to valid scientific information that would enable people to participate in the improvement of their health, avoid disease, or claim and seek better care. Such is the case for young women who become unwillingly pregnant or acquire sexually transmitted diseases because they are denied information considered too sexually explicit for them—even though they became pregnant or infected because they were sexually active (Alan Guttmacher Institute 1998; Dowsett and Aggleton 1999).

The health and human rights approach determines whether health policies, programmes, and practices are valid from both a public health and a human rights perspective (IFRCRC/FXBC 1999). The first step in this analysis will always be to determine the stated justification for the measure—and then to consider the framework set forth in the Siracusa Principles mentioned above (ECOSOC 1985). In analysing health policies and programmes, as Jonathan Mann was fond of saying: 'Assume all health policies and programmes are discriminatory or restrictive of rights until proven otherwise' (Mann 1997a).

The Impact of Neglect or Violations of Human Rights on Health

When health is understood to include physical, mental, and social well being, it seems reasonable to conclude that the violation or neglect of any human right will impact adversely on health. While this is certainly true with respect to specific rights, such as non-discrimination or education, the impact of neglect or violation of rights is also compounded by the number of rights brought into question by any particular situation. The health impacts of certain severe human rights violations, such as torture, imprisonment under inhumane conditions, summary executions, and disappearances have long been understood. Much work has been done in this field, and efforts in this regard continue to expand. Such efforts include exhumations of mass graves to ascertain how people have died, the coding and matching of genetic information to reunite families separated during war and massive political repression, examination of torture victims to bring perpetrators to justice and to assist with asylum claims, and entry into prisons and other state-run institutions, such as detention centres, to assess health conditions and the health status of confined populations. The impacts on health of these human rights violations can be both obvious and subtle. For example, torture is a violation that causes immediate and direct harm to health. Yet only recently has the full impact of torture begun to be recognized, including the lifelong injury to the victim, the effects on the health of families and of entire communities, and the transgenerational damage (Amnesty International 1983; Goldfeld 1988). There is increasing recognition of the need to assess the duration and extent of the health impacts of such human rights violations, including the direct and immediate impact of being subjected to torture oneself, but also its severe and lifelong effects on survivors and the trauma associated with being forced to witness summary executions, rape, and other forms of torture and trauma perpetrated on others (Dawes 1990).

Health practitioners can—and in most cases do—have a strong positive influence on the promotion and protection of human rights within the populations they serve. Yet violations of human rights perpetrated by health professionals regularly occur. These include not only such egregious examples as doctor participation in torture and other severe violations of human rights, but also actions in the provision of treatment and care, for example when care providers make decisions concerning patient access to available prevention services, or when children with a chronic fatal disease or disability are denied immunization against measles and other preventable childhood infections (Savage 1998; UN 1998b; Ward and Myers 1999). In many countries, rich and poor, patients with diabetes, carcinoma, chronic renal syndrome, mental disability, haemophilia, or other severe health conditions may receive a lower standard of care than others not only with respect to the health issue in question but in general because their possibility of cure is regarded as limited (UN 1992b; Crofts et al. 1997).

A less obvious impact of neglect of human rights on health concerns the many children from poor or marginalized communities, where poor nutrition and ill health prevail, that have a below-average school enrolment and attendance rate and, as a result, below-average educational attainment (Swartz and Levett 1989; Brundtland 1999). The deprivation of these children from access to basic health services, coupled with the imposition of school fees, leads to a limitation of their ability to exercise their right to education, producing lifelong effects on their health and well being.

In addition to the impact of egregious violations of rights on health, the more subtle effects of neglect or violations of rights on health can also be considered. These would include exposures to ill health resulting from violations of such rights as work, free movement, association, and participation (Daniels et al. 1990; Berlinguer et al. 1996). The impact of neglect or violation of factors considered to form the underlying preconditions for health must also be considered. In addition to medical services, these have been understood to include such factors as adequate housing, education, food, safe drinking water, sanitation, access to information, and protection against discrimination. Understood in human rights terms, neglect of these rights, particularly in combination, can have serious negative consequences on health (Mann et al. 1994). No community is fully protected from neglect or violation of rights and its detrimental consequences to individual and public health (CESR 1999; UN 1999a, b). In particular, gender-based discrimination poses a pervasive threat to health. Girls and women who are denied access to education, information, and various forms of economic, social, and political participation are particularly vulnerable to the impact of discrimination on their health. This is true when discrimination is recognized, tolerated, acknowledged, or even condoned by governments, but also when it remains insidiously hidden or deliberately ignored behind an accepted status quo (Dixon-Mueller 1990; Sullivan 1995).

One example, drawn from the world of reproductive health, dramatically illustrates this point. There is now general acknowledgement that violations of human rights, including systematic gender discrimination, create an environment of increased risk in relation to women's health (Cook 1995; Berer 1999). In this context, it is necessary to consider those factors that are understood to influence directly the reproductive health of women. Access to information, education, and quality services is critical, as are services adequately targeted to respond to the needs of women of different ages and from different communities. Underlying all this is the impact that gender roles and gender discrimination have on both health status and service delivery (Doyal 1995; WHO 1998a). The relevance of human rights to this analysis becomes clear when considering the gaps and inequalities in services and structures in relation to the social roles that construct male and female identity. Equally important is how these factors play out at the policy and programme level in terms of reproductive health research, policy, financing, and service delivery. Traditional public health focused on the need for information, education, contraception, counselling, and access to quality services. These elements of health practice were, and still are, central to improving women's reproductive health. However, even if these services are available, an individual woman has to be able to decide when and how she is going to access these services. This implies that she has to have the ability to control and make decisions about her life.

In this example, considering the impact that violation or neglect of human rights has on health highlights the societal context that would hinder or empower an individual woman's ability to make and act on the free and informed choices necessary for her reproductive health. From a broader policy and programme perspective, this insight reveals that linking the human rights framework to health implies recognizing that individual health is largely influenced by one's environment. This means that the integration of human rights in the design, implementation, and evaluation of health policies and programmes is necessary not only because of a government's human rights obligations, but also in purely pragmatic public health terms. Thus, attention to the civil, political, economic, social, and cultural factors that are relevant to a person's life, such as gender relations, racism, or homophobia, and the ways this combination of factors projects itself into who becomes ill and what is done about it, is central to sound health and human rights practice.

The process of documenting evidence on the health impacts resulting from violations or neglect of human rights must be thorough and thoughtful because of the multifarious effects on health of human rights neglect or violations. The involvement of communities that are disproportionately affected by human rights violations in the development, implementation, and monitoring of decisions affecting them is crucial to mitigating these impacts. Affected individuals working together in defence or advocacy groups—be they concerned with breast cancer, diabetes, renal syndromes, haemophilia, chronic disabilities, or other health issues—have been effective in bringing to light some of the more subtle mechanisms that come into play in linking health status with the human rights violations to which people are subjected (Steingraber 1997; UNAIDS 1999).

Optimizing Health and Human Rights in Practice

A crucial step in optimizing the relationship between health and human rights is to conduct a systematic review of how and to what extent governmental policies and programmes are respectful of human rights and of benefit to public health. Such a review, presented in Box 1.3, is proposed as a first step in improving new and existing policies and programmes through assessment of their validity, applicability, and soundness, while addressing their practical implications from both human rights and public health perspectives. The suggested questions can be used by policy-makers and public health and other government officials to help in the development, implementation, and evaluation of more effective policies and programmes, and by non-governmental organizations and other concerned actors as an advocacy tool to hold governments accountable for the ways they are and are not in compliance with their international legal obligations to promote and protect both public health and human rights.

Box 1.3 Issues to be Addressed in Assessing Policies and Programmes (Gruskin and Tarantola 2000)

The following questions may serve as starting points to help:

- What is the specific intended purpose of the policy or programme?
- What are the ways and the extent to which the policy or programme may impact positively and negatively on health?
- Using the relevant international human rights documents, what and whose rights are impacted positively and negatively by the policy or the programme?
- Does the policy or programme necessitate the restriction of human rights?
- If so have the criteria/preconditions to restrict rights been met?
- Are the health and other relevant structures and services capable of effectively implementing the policy or programme?
- What system of monitoring, evaluation, accountability, and redress exist to ensure that the policy or programme is progressing towards the intended effect and that adverse effects can be acted upon?

The importance of the human rights framework to policies and programmes is that it can provide a method of analysis and a framework for action, which can then be used to help shape specific interventions aimed at reducing the impact of health conditions on the lives of individuals and populations. This approach requires work with the international human rights documents to determine the specific rights applicable to a given situation, and then considering how and to what extent morbidity, mortality, disability, risk behaviours, and vulnerability to ill health are caused or exacerbated by insufficient realization of human rights. This analysis will be most effective if done in partnership with people with substantive knowledge of human rights.

A second level of analysis can be created by recognizing the convergence of the three health domains described above (health outcome, health systems, and underlying conditions for health) with the three levels of governmental obligations that exist for each right—respect, protect, and fulfill (Table 1.1). Health practitioners will find this table most relevant to their work if they use the suggested health domains (first column of Table 1.1) as their entry point and then move to the right, seeking to identify how each level of governmental obligation can influence health policies and action within each of the three domains. Ultimately, such an analysis could be extended to examine how those approaches recognized as best health practice in each domain could contribute to the advancement of human rights with respect to each level of governmental obligation. The issues raised in Table 1.1 are not meant to be highly detailed, but simply to serve as examples of the issues this approach brings to light.

The questions proposed in Box 3 may be used to create an agenda for action to help guide the analysis of governmental obligations for health outcomes, health systems, and the societal preconditions for health proposed in Table 1.1. Human resource development in support of health requires that health training include the skills necessary to document and measure the health effects of neglect or violations of rights. Education and training of people working in human rights should likewise provide them with the skills necessary to analyse the complex relations between neglect or violation of rights and their health impact, in such a way that the information provided can be used to monitor and ensure government accountability. This joint approach is necessary if the health and human rights framework is to be practical and useful. Only when the many dimensions necessary for health are described, measured, and named in human rights terms can the full extent of the relationship between health and human rights be realized. Such a review offers a critical approach to assessing the validity, applicability, and soundness of new and existing policies and programmes, and to addressing their practical implications from both human rights and public health perspectives. Through this approach, the disciplines of health and of human rights come together most visibly, and national capacity building to ensure reasoned and sound analysis becomes a necessity.

Another dimension of developing the health and human rights relationship is the application of mechanisms, methods, and tools to monitor progress and shortcomings in implementation of health and human rights at the national and international level. An earlier section described the role of treaty bodies in engaging in dialogue with governments on their degree of compliance with their international legal obligations. The WHO, for its part, is developing monitoring methods and indicators that, although technically not binding on governments (with the exceptions of reporting under the International Health Regulations), set out international norms by which member states commit to abide in principle after passage at the World Health Assembly. Previously, the

Table 1.1 A pathway to health and human rights

Domains of Health	Governmental Obligations with Respect to Human Rights		
	Respect	**Protect**	**Fulfill**
Health outcome	Government not to violate rights of people on the basis of their health status including in information collection and analysis, as well as in the design and provision of health and other services.	Government to prevent non-state actors (including private health-care structures and insurance providers) from violating the rights of people on the basis of their health status including in the provision of health and other services.	Government to take administrative, legislative, judicial, and other measures to promote and protect the rights of people regardless of their health status, including the generation of data concerning health outcomes for use in guiding health policies and the provision of health and other services, as well as providing legal means of redress that people know about and can access.
Health systems	Government not to violate rights directly in the design, implementation, and evaluation of national health systems, including ensuring that they are sufficiently accessible, efficient, affordable, and of good quality for all members of the population.	Government to prevent non-state actors (including private health-care structures and insurance providers) from violating rights in the design, implementation, and evaluation of health systems and structures, including ensuring that they are sufficiently accessible, efficient, affordable, and of good quality.	Government to take administrative, legislative, judicial, and other measures including sufficient resource allocation and the building of safety nets, to ensure that health systems are sufficiently accessible, efficient, affordable, and of good quality, as well as providing legal means of redress that people know about and can access.
Societal and environmental preconditions	Government not to violate the civil, political, economic, social, and cultural rights of people directly, recognizing that neglect or violations of rights impact directly on health.	Government to prevent rights violations by non-state actors, recognizing that neglect or violations of rights impact directly on health.	Government to take all possible administrative, legislative, judicial, and other measures, including the promotion of human development mechanisms, towards the promotion and protection of human rights, as well as providing legal means of redress that people know about and can access.

Adapted from Tarantola and Gruskin (1998).

WHO's attempts to measure health on the national or international level selectively used morbidity, mortality, and disability indicators (WHO 1999a). This exercise was severely constrained by incomplete national data, differences in measurement methods across countries, and, even more importantly, an inability to relate health outcomes to the performance of health systems. Furthermore, most of these indicators were applied at a national aggregate level with insufficient attempts to disaggregate the data collected to reveal the disparities that exist within nations. It has been understood that measurement indicators and benchmarks that focus on the aggregate (national) level may not reveal important differentials that may be associated with a variety of human rights violations—in particular, discrimination.

In order to improve the knowledge and understanding of health status and trends, and to relate these trends to health system performance, the WHO has developed the following five global indicators (WHO 2000c).

1. Healthy life expectancy: a composite indicator incorporating mortality, morbidity, and disability in a disability-adjusted life years measure. This indicator will reflect time spent in a state of less than full health.
2. Health inequalities: the degree of disparity in healthy life expectancy within the population.
3. Responsiveness of health systems: a composite indicator reflecting the protection of dignity and confidentiality in and by health systems, and people's autonomy (that is, their individual capacity to effect informed choice in health matters).
4. Responsiveness inequality: the disparity in responsiveness within health systems, bringing out issues of low efficiency, neglect, and discrimination.
5. Fairness in financing: measured by the level of health financing contribution of households.

The WHO has stated that it will collect this data through built-in health information systems, demographic and health surveys conducted periodically within countries, and other survey instruments. Data will thus be analysable by sex, age, race/birth (if warranted under national law), population groups (for example, indigenous populations), educational achievement, and other variables.

The WHO has also expressed its commitment to working with countries towards increasing their capacity to collect this information and also to determine additional data and targets that may be specifically suited to country-specific situations and needs. The WHO and other institutions concerned with health have stated their desire to use these data to assess trends in the performance of national health systems, inform national and international policies and programmes, make comparisons across countries, and monitor global health. This process is also intended to support the development of national benchmarks whereby targets will be set by individual governments with a view towards being able to compare their own health system performance with others, and to compare among regions and over time. These benchmarks will be chosen according to each country's set of health priorities and information needs (WHO 2000c).

The global indicators now being tested by the WHO, as well as its current efforts to enhance the capacity of member states to monitor their health performances, appear to be in line with human rights principles. These developments, coupled with the increasing attention to health by the bodies responsible for monitoring governmental compliance with their human rights obligations, are promising steps for the future development and application of the health and human rights framework.

Conclusion

This chapter has outlined the health and human rights framework as a pathway towards enhancing the value and impact of health work by health policy-makers, programme developers, practitioners, and students. It is hoped that increased attention to this fundamental relationship can open new avenues to human development, and by so doing, marshall new resources towards improving individual and population health. Keeping in mind the tools proposed in the previous section, there are three levels on which this new synergy can be recognized, applied, and monitored. The first concerns the development of adequate monitoring tools reflecting both health and human rights concerns; the second, the application of the health and human rights framework to health practice; and the third, the creation of a significant research agenda to advance our collective understanding of the health and human rights relationship.

First, on the level of health best practice and international human rights law, evidence-informed health policy and programme development can be guided by a systematic human rights analysis. This process involves significant efforts to ensure that the information that is sought, collected, and analysed brings attention to both trends and disparities, and that this information is used to address these gaps. This would include attention to the relative successes and failures of progress achieved towards global goals, such as those to which countries have subscribed in such forums as the World Health Assembly or through the international conference processes.

It is of critical importance that the WHO and the human rights treaty bodies are currently and simultaneously engaged both in the process of setting out global indicators and in defining approaches towards the development of country-specific benchmarks consistent with international knowledge, practice, and experience. The prevailing state of health and resource availability within individual countries must, nonetheless, be taken into account to allow trends and disparities to be measured in relation to individual benchmarks. While the existence of this work is encouraging, there is a need to further develop, test, and apply indicators that capture the disparities that may prevail within a population, as well as those that can begin to suggest the differences between government unwillingness and incapacity. Relevant indicators have been developed in the economics field, where the Gini coefficient, for example, is used as a measure of economic heterogeneity within a population (Kennedy et al. 1998). Disaggregation of data would allow the attributes on which discrimination is often based, including sex, age, prior health status, disability, birth, or social status, to be taken into account. Policies and programmes could then aim to advance the health of populations by setting out higher goals for the population as a whole, while bringing increased attention to reducing the gaps between those who enjoy better health and better services and those who, for political, civil, economic, social, or cultural reasons, are more vulnerable to ill health and to inadequate services and structures.

The second level on which health and human rights are beginning to converge is in ensuring that health systems and practice are sufficiently informed by human rights norms and standards. Sound formulation and implementation of health policies and programmes must seek to achieve the optimal balance between the promotion and protection of public health and the promotion and protection of human rights and dignity. Processes to arrive at this optimal balance can be built within national systems on the basis of the approach proposed in the previous sections, incorporating evidence collected in the ways suggested above and through participatory dialogues between decision-makers with expertise in public health, those with expertise in human rights, and concerned populations. The realization of such an approach requires additional efforts to create consultative mechanisms, as well as education and training in health and human rights.

Finally, the third level of convergence between health and human rights lies in the broad need for further research. Given that human rights are established, internationally agreed upon norms to which states have subscribed, the reciprocal impacts between human rights and health must be further researched and documented. There is a national and international obligation to increase research and documentation, as well as to conceptualize and implement policies and programmes that fully take these connections into account. The utility of this research will largely be predicated on the extent to which those with expertise in health collaborate with people knowledgeable about human rights in the conceptualization of their research agendas and in the steps necessary for carrying this work forward.

The challenges posed in linking health with human rights are immense. There is, however, increasing evidence that public health efforts that respect, protect, and fulfil human rights are more likely to succeed in public health terms than those that neglect or violate rights. National and international policy and decision-makers, health professionals, and the public at large all, to varying degrees, understand the fundamental links between health and human rights, and the way in which those links can provide new ways to analyse and conceive responses to health issues. To move the work of health and human rights forward will require building and strengthening the information and education available about human rights concepts and procedures. It will also require information exchange and stronger co-operation between those working on health and those working on human rights. When people are sufficiently knowledgeable about human rights, they will be able to identify the issues for which the synergy of human rights and health is critical, and to act accordingly. Human rights and health are progressing, in parallel, towards a common goal that will never be fully realized. Yet, together, they project a vision and an approach that may fundamentally and positively improve the lives of people everywhere in the world.

Notes

African [Banjul] Charter on Human and Peoples Rights (1982). OAU Document CAB/LEG/67/3 rev. 5, 21 ILM 58.

AI (Amnesty International) (1983). *Chile: evidence of torture.* AI Publications, London.

Alan Guttmacher Institute (1998). *Into a new world: young women's sexual and reproductive lives.* Alan Guttmacher Institute, New York.

Alfredsson, G. and Tomaševski, K. (1998). *A thematic guide to documents on health and human rights.* Martinus Nijhoff, Dordrecht.

Al-Mazrou, Y., Berkley, S., Bloom, B., et al. (1997). A vital opportunity for global health. *Lancet*, 350, 750–1.

Alston, P. (1991). The international covenant on social, economic, social and cultural rights. In *Manual on human rights reporting*, pp. 63–5. United Nations Centre for Human Rights. UN Document HR/PUB/91/1.

Alston, P. (1997). What's in a name: does it really matter if development policies refer to goals, ideas or human rights? *SIM Special Issue*, 22, 95–106.

Alston, P. and Quinn, G. (1987). The nature and scope of state parties' obligations under the international covenant and economic, social and cultural rights. *Human Rights Quarterly*, 9, 165–6.

Altman, D. (1998). HIV, homophobia, and human rights. *Health and Human Rights*, 2, 15–22.

Aluwihare, A.P.R. (1998). Xenotransplantation. Ethics and rights: an Interaction. *Annals of Transplantation*, 3, 59–61.

American Convention on Human Rights (1969). *OAS treaty.* Series No. 36, 1144 UNTS 123 entered into force 18 July 1978. In *Basic documents pertaining to human rights in the inter-American system.* OEA/Series LV/II.82 document 6 rev. 1 at 25.

Andrews, L.B. (1995). Genetic privacy: from the laboratory to the legislature. *Genome Research*, 5, 209–13.

Barnett, T. and Whiteside, A. (1999). HIV/AIDS and development: case studies and conceptual framework. *European Journal of Development Research*, 11, 200–34.

Barry, M. and Molyneux, M. (1992). Ethical dilemmas in malaria drug and vaccine trials: a bioethical perspective. *Journal of Medical Ethics*, 18, 189–92.

Barton Smith, D. (1998). Addressing racial inequities in health care: civil rights monitoring and report cards. *Journal of Health Politics, Policy and Law*, 23, 75–105.

Bayer, R., Dubler, N., and Landesman, S. (1993). The dual epidemics of tuberculosis and AIDS: ethical and policy issues in screening and treatment. *American Journal of Public Health*, 83, 649–54.

Beloqui, J., Chokevivat V., and Collins, C. (1998). HIV vaccine research and human rights: examples from three countries planning efficacy trials. *Health and Human Rights*, 3, 39–58.

Berer, M. (1999). Access to reproductive health: a question of distributive justice. *Reproductive Health Matters*, 7, 8–14.

Berlinguer, G., Falzi, G., and Figà-Talamanca, I. (1996). Ethical problems in the relationship between health and work. *International Journal of Health Services*, 26, 147–71.

Beyrer, C. (1998). Burma and Cambodia: human rights, social disruption, and the spread of HIV/AIDS. *Health and Human Rights*, 2, 85–97.

Bilder, R.B. (1992). An overview of international human rights law. In *Guide to international human rights practice* (ed. H. Hannum) (2nd edn), pp. 3–18. University of Pennsylvania Press, Philadelphia. PA.

Boerefon, I. and Toebes, B. (1998). Health issues discussed by the UN treaty monitoring bodies. Netherland Institute of Human Rights. *SIM Special Issue*, 21, 25–53.

Braveman, P. (1998). *Monitoring equally in health: a policy-oriented approach in low and middle class income countries*. Working Paper No. 3, WHO, Geneva.

Brenner, J. (1996). Human rights education in public health graduate schools. *Health and Human Rights*, 2, 129–39.

Brundtland, G.H. (1998). The UDHR: fifty years of synergy between health and human rights. *Health and Human Rights*, 3, 21–5.

Brundtland, G.H. (1999). Nutrition, health and human rights. *ACE/SCN Symposium on The Substance and Politics of a Human Right Approach to Food and Nutrition Policies and Programmes*. United Nations, Geneva.

Brundtland, G.H. (2000). Health in times of globalization. In *Health, the key to human development*, pp. 49–73. Campus-Verlag, Frankfurt.

Carrin, G. and Politi, C. (1996). *Exploring the health impact of economic growth, poverty reduction and public health expenditure*. Technical Paper No. 18, WHO, Geneva.

CEDAW (Committee on the Elimination of Discrimination Against Women) (1979). *Convention on the elimination of all forms of discrimination against women*. GA Resolution 34/180, UN GAOR, 34th Session, Supplement No. 46, at 193, UN Document A/34/46. UN, New York.

CEDAW (Committee on the Elimination of Discrimination Against Women) (1989). *General Recommendation No. 12 (Eighth Session). Violence against women*. UN Document A/43/38. UN, New York.

CEDAW (Committee on the Elimination of Discrimination Against Women) (1990a). *General Recommendation No. 14 (Ninth Session). Female circumcision*. UN Document A/45/38, UN, New York.

CEDAW (Committee on the Elimination of Discrimination Against Women) (1990b). *General Recommendation No. 15 (Ninth Session). Avoidance of discrimination against women in national strategies for the prevention and control of acquired immunodeficiency syndrome (AIDS)*. UN Document A/45/38, UN, New York.

CEDAW (Committee on the Elimination of Discrimination Against Women) (1999). *General Recommendation 24 on Women and Health*, EDAW/C/1999/J/WGII/WP2/Rev. 1. UN, Geneva.

CESR (Center for Economic and Social Rights) (1999). Rights violations in the Ecuadorian Amazon. The human consequences of oil development. In *Health and human rights: a reader* (ed. J. Mann, S. Gruskin, M. Grodin, and G. Annas). Routledge, New York.

Clinton, W.J. (1998). United States Executive Order on Implementation of Human Rights Treaties. US Government Printing Office. Washington, D.C..

Cohen, M.L. (1998). Resurgent and emergent disease in a changing world. *British Medical Bulletin*, 54, 523–32.

Cohen, R. and Wiseberg, L. (1990). *Double jeopardy—threat to life and human rights; discrimination against persons with AIDS*. Human Rights Internet, Cambridge, MA.

Coliver, S. (ed.) (1995). The right to information necessary for reproductive health and choice under international law. In *The right to know: human rights and access to reproductive health information*, pp. 38–82. Article 19. University of Pennsylvania Press, Philadelphia, PA.

Comite Latinoamericano para la Defensa de los Derechos de la Mujer (1999). *Nada personal: reporte de derechos humanos sobre la aplicacion de la anticoncepcion quirurgica an el Peru, 1996–1998.* Comite de America Latina y el Caribe para la Defensa de los Derechos del la Mujer, Lima.

Cook, R.J. (1992). International protection of women's reproductive rights. *New York University Journal of International Law Politics*, 24, 645–727.

Cook, R.J. (1994). *Women's health and human rights*, pp. 5–12. WHO, Geneva.

Cook, R.J. (1995). Gender, health and human rights. *Health and Human Rights*, 1, 350–66.

Cooper Well, D.E., Alibusan, A.P., Wilson, I.F., Reich, M.R., and Bradley, D.I. (1990). *The impact of the development policies on health*, WHO, Geneva.

Corporación Casa de la Mujer (1998). *Women's reproductive rights in Colombia: a shadow report.* Center for Reproductive Law and Policy (CRLP), New York.

Council of Europe (1950). *European Convention for the Protection of Human Rights and Fundamental Freedoms and Its Nine Protocol.* ETS. No. 5.

CRC (Convention on the Rights of the Child) (1989). *GA Resolution 44/25*, UN GAOR, 44th Session, Supplement No. 49, at 166, UN Document A/44/25. UN, Geneva.

Crofts, N., Louie, R., and Loff, B. (1997). The next plague: stigmatization and discrimination related to hepatitis C virus infection in Australia. *Health and Human Rights*, 2, 86–97.

Daniels, C., Paul, M., and Rosofsky, R. (1990). Health, equity, and reproductive risks in the workplace. *Journal of Public Health Policy*, 11, 449–62.

Dawes, A. (1990). The effect of political violence on children. A consideration of South African and related studies. *International Journal of Psychology*, 25, 13–31.

d'Cruz-Grote, D. (1996). Prevention of HIV infection in developing countries. *Lancet*, 348, 1071–4.

Detels, R., Holland, W., McEwen, J., and Omenn, G.S. (ed.) (1997). *Oxford textbook of public health* (3rd edn). Oxford University Press.

Dixon-Mueller, R. (1990). Abortion policy and women's health in developing countries. *International Journal of Health Services*, 20, 297–314.

Dowsett, G. and Aggelton, P. (1999). Young people and risk-taking in sexual relations. In *Sex and youth: contextual factors affecting risk for HIV/AIDS*, pp. 10–56. UNAIDS Best Practice Collection, Geneva.

Doyal, L. (1995). *What makes women sick: gender and the political economy of health.* Rutgers University Press. New Brunswick, NJ.

ECOSOC (Economic and Social Council) (1985). *The Siracusa Principles on the limitations and derogation provisions in the international covenant on civil and political rights.* UN Document E/CN.4/1985/4, Annex, UN, Geneva.

ECOSOC (Economic and Social Council (1991). *Revised general guidelines regarding the form and contents of reports to be submitted by states parties under articles 16 and 17 of the International Covenant on Economic, Social and Cultural Rights*, 17 June 1991. UN Document E/C.12/1991. UN, Geneva.

Efferen, L.S. (1997). In pursuit of tuberculosis control: civil liberty vs. public health. *Chest*, 112, 5–6.

Eide, A. (1995a). Economic, social and cultural rights as human rights. In *Economic, social and cultural rights: a textbook* (ed. A. Eide, C. Krause, and A. Rosas), pp. 1–40. Martinus Nijhoff, Dordrecht.

Eide, A. (1995b). The right to an adequate standard of living, including the right to food. In *Economic, social and cultural rights: a textbook* (ed. A. Eide, C. Krause, and A. Rosas), pp. 89–105. Martinus Nijhoff, Dordrecht.

Farmer, P., Robin, S., Ramilus, S.I., and Kim, Y.K. (1991). Tuberculosis, poverty, and 'compliance': lessons from rural Haiti. *Seminars in Respiratory Infection*, 6, 254–60.

Fenner, F., Henderson, D.A., Arita, L., Jezek, Z., and Ladugi, T.D. (1988). *Smallpox and its eradication.* WHO, Geneva.

Fluss, S.S. (1999). A select bibliography of health aspects of human rights: 1984–1999. *Health and Human Rights*, 4, 265–76.

Fluss, S.S. and Little, J. (1999). Vaccination and human rights. *Archives of Clinical Bioethics*, 2, 79–85.

Focht-New, V. (1996). Beyond abuse: health care for people with disabilities. *Issues in Mental Health Nursing*, 17, 427–38.

Freedman, L. (1999). Censorship and manipulation of family planning information: an issue of human rights and women's health. In *Health and human rights: a reader* (ed. J.M. Mann, S. Gruskin, M.A. Grodin, and G.J. Annas), pp. 145–78. Routledge, New York.

FWCW (Fourth World Conference on Women) (1995). *Action for equality, development and peace*. UN Document A/CONF.177/20/Rev. 1 (96.IV.13). UN, Geneva.

Gilmore, N. (1996). Drug use and human rights: privacy, vulnerability, disability, and human rights infringements. *Journal of Contemporary Health Law and Policy*, 12, 355–447.

Goldfeld, A., Mollica, R.F., Pesavento, B., and Faraone, S. (1988). The physical and psychosocial sequelae of torture. *Journal of the American Medical Association*, 259, 2725–9.

Gruskin, S. (1998). The highest priority: making use of UN conference documents to remind governments of their commitments to HIV/AIDS. *Health and Human Rights*, 3, 107–42.

Gruskin, S. and Tarantola, D. (2000). HIV/AIDS, health and human rights. *Handbook for the design and management of HIV/AIDS prevention and care programs in resource-constrained settings*. Family Health International, Arlington, VA.

Gruskin, S., Tomaševski, T., and Hendriks, A. (1996). Human rights and responses to HIV/AIDS. In *AIDS in the world, II* (ed. J.M. Mann and D.J.M. Tarantola), pp. 326–40. Oxford University Press.

Gubler, D. (1998). Resurgent vector-borne diseases as a global health problem. *Emerging Infectious Diseases*, 4, 442–50.

Hallack, J. (1999). *Globalization, human rights, and education*. IEP Contributions No. 33, UNESCO, Paris.

Hannum, H. (1998). The UDHR in national and international law. *Health and Human Rights*, 3, 145–58.

Heggenhougen, K. (1999). Are the marginalized the slag-heap of globalization? Disparity, health and human rights. *Health and Human Rights*, 4, 205–13.

Hendriks, A. (1995). A selected bibliography of human rights and disability. *Health and Human Rights*, 1, 212–25.

Heymann, S.J. and Sell, R.L. (1999). Mandatory public health programs: to what standards should they be held? *Health and Human Rights*, 4, 193–203.

Holder, A.R. (1992). Legal issues in adolescent sexual health. *Adolescent Medicine*, 3, 257–68.

Hossain, K. (1999). Globalization and human rights: clash of universal aspirations and special interests. In *The future of international human rights* (ed. B.H. Weston and S.P. Marks), pp. 187–99. Transnational Publishers, New York.

HRI (Human Rights Internet) (1998). *Human rights and HIV/AIDS: effective community responses*. International Human Rights Documentation Network, Ottawa.

Humphrey, J. (1976). The international bill of rights: scope and implementation. *William and Mary Law Review*, 17, 526.

Hunter, D.J. (1999). The future of molecular epidemiology. *International Journal of Epidemiology*, 28, S1012–14.

ICASO (International Council of AIDS Organizations) (1998). *The ICASO plan on human rights, social equity and HIV/AIDS*. ICASO, Toronto.

ICCPR (International Covenant on Civil and Political Rights) (1966). *GA Resolution 2200 (XXI)*, UN GAOR, 21st Session, Supplement No. 16, at 49, UN Document A/6316, UN, New York.

ICERD (1965). *Convention on the elimination of all forms of racial discrimination*. UN GA Resolution 2106A(XX) UN, New York.

ICESCR (International Covenant on Economic, Social and Cultural Rights) (1966). *GA Resolution 2200 (XXI)*, UN GAOR, 21st Session, Supplement No. 16, at 49, UN Document A/6316 UN, Geneva.

ICPD (International Conference on Population and Development) (1994). *Programme of Action of the International Conference on Population and Development*, UN Document A/CONF.171/13. UN, Geneva.

IFRCRC/FXBC (International Federal of Red Cross and Red Crescent Societies and the François-Xavier Bagnoud Center for Health and Human Rights) (1999). The public health-human rights dialogue. In *AIDS, health and human rights: an explanatory manual*, pp. 39–47. IFRCRC/FXBC, Geneva.

ILO (International Labor Organization) (1996). Occupational safety and health. In *Globalization of the footwear, textiles and clothing industries: effects on employment and working conditions*, pp. 101–2. ILO, Geneva.

Jackson, H. (1998). Societal determinants of women's vulnerability to HIV infection in southern Africa. *Health and Human Rights*, 2, 9–14.

Kennedy, B.P. Kawachi, I., Glass, R., and Prothrow-Stith, D. (1998). Income distribution, socio-economic status, and self rated health in the United States: multilevel analysis. *British Medical Journal*, 317, 917–21.

Kirby, M. (1999). The right to health fifty years on: still skeptical? *Health and Human Rights*, 4, 7–24.

Kolodner, E. (1994). *Transnational corporations: impediments or catalysts of social development?* Social Summit Occasional Paper No. 5. United Nations Research Institute for Social Development, Geneva.

Krieger, N. and Sidney, S. (1996). Racial discrimination and blood pressure: the CARDIA study of young black and white women and men. *American Journal of Public Health*, 86, 1370–8.

Krieger, N. and Zierler, S. (1997). The need for epidemiologic theory. *Epidemiology*, 8, 212–14.

Lallemant, M., LeCoeur, S., Tarantola, D., Mann, J.M., and Essex, M. (1994). Anti-retroviral prevention of HIV perinatal transmission. *Lancet*, 343, 429–30.

Leaning, J. (1997). Human rights and medical education. *British Medical Journal*, 313, 1390–1.

Leary, V. (1994). The right to health in international human rights law. *Health and Human Rights*, 1, 24–56.

Lombardo, P.A. (1996). Medicine, eugenics, and the Supreme Court: from coercive sterilization to reproductive freedom. *Journal of Contemporary Health Law and Policy*, 13, 1–25.

McMichael, A.J. (1993). *Planetary overload: global environmental change and the health of the human species*. Cambridge University Press.

Maastricht Guidelines on Violations of Economic, Social and Cultural Rights (1997). *Human Rights Quarterly*, 20, 691–705.

Mann, J. (1997a). *Human rights and health: a program designed specifically for health professionals*. Centers for Disease Control. Atlanta, GA.

Mann, J.M. (1997b). Medicine and public health, ethics and human rights. *Hastings Center Report*, 27, 6–13.

Mann, J.M. and Tarantola, D.J.M. (1996a). From vulnerability to human rights. In *AIDS in the world II*, pp. 463–76. Oxford University Press, New York.

Mann, J.M. and Tarantola, D.J.M. (ed.) (1996b). Societal vulnerability: contextual analysis. In *AIDS in the world II*, pp. 444–62. Oxford University Press, New York.

Mann, J.M. and Tarantola, D.J.M. (ed.) (1996c). Vulnerability: personal and programmatic. In *AIDS in the world II*, pp. 441–3. Oxford University Press, New York.

Mann, J.M. and Tarantola, D.J.M. (1998). Responding to HIV/AIDS: a historical perspective. *Health and Human Rights*, 2, 5–8.

Mann, J.M., Tarantola, D.J.M., and Netter, T.W. (ed.) (1992). Assessing vulnerability to HIV infection and AIDS. In *AIDS in the World*, pp. 577–602. Harvard University Press, Cambridge, MA.

Mann, J.M., Gostin, L., Gruskin, S., Brennan, T., Lazzarini, Z., and Fineberg, H. (1994). Health and human rights. *Health and Human Rights*, 1, 6–23.

Marks, S.P. (1997). Common strategies for health and human rights: from theory to practice. *Health and Human Rights*, 2, 95–104.

Miller, A.M., Rosga, A., and Satterthwaite, M. (1995). Health, human rights and lesbian existence. *Health and Human Rights*, 1, 428–48.

Moody, H.R. (1989). Age-based entitlements to health care: what are the limits? *Mount Sinal Journal of Medicine*, 56, 168–75.

Murray, C.J.L. and Lopez, A.D. (1996). The global burden of disease: a comprehensive assessment of mortality and disability from diseases, injury and risk factors in 1990 and projected to 2020. In *Global burden of diseases injury series*, Vol. I. Harvard School of Public Health on behalf of the WHO, Cambridge, MA.

Orford, A. (1999). Contesting globalization: a feminist perspective on the future of human rights. In *The future of international human rights* (ed. B.H. Weston and S.P. Marks), pp. 157–85. Transnational Publishers, New York.

Ottawa Charter for Health Promotion (1986). Presented at the First International Conference on Health Promotion, Ottawa.

Plata, M.I. and Yanuzova, M. (1993). *Los derechos humanos y la convencion sobre la eliminacion de todas las formas de discriminacion contra la mujer, 1979*. Profamilia, Bogotá.

Radhakrishna, A., Gringle, R., and Greenslade, F. (1997). Adolescent women face triple jeopardy: unwanted pregnancy, HIV/AIDS and unsafe abortion. *Women's Health Journal*, 2, 53–62.

Raviglione, M.C., Snider, D.E., and Kochi, A. (1995). Global epidemiology of tuberculosis: morbidity and mortality of a worldwide epidemic. *Journal of the American Medical Association*, 273, 220–6.

Reich, M.R. (2000). The global drug gap. *Science*, 287, 1979–81.

Roemer, M.I. and Roemer, R. (1990). Global health, national development and the role of government. *American Journal of Public Health*, 80, 1188–92.

Savage, T.A. (1998). Children with severe and profound disabilities and the issue of social justice. *Advanced Practical Nursing Quarterly*, 4, 53–8.

Schmidt, T.A. (1995). When public health competes with individual needs. *Academy of Emergency Medicine*, 2, 217–22.

Shenker, M. (1992). Occupational lung diseases in the industrializing and industrialized world due to modern pollutants. *Tubercle and Lung Disease*, 73, 27–32.

Shrader-Frechette, K. (1991). Ethics and the environment. *World Health Forum*, 12, 311–21.

Smith, S. (1911). The powers and duties of the board of health. *Social Diseases*, 2, 9.

Sonis, J., Gorenflo, D.W., Jha, P., et al. (1996). Teaching of human rights in US medical schools. *Journal of the American Medical Association*, 276, 1676–8.

South Africa Government Gazette (1999). R. 485. Draft law. *South Africa Government Gazette*.

Steiner, H. and Altston, P. (1996). *International human rights in context: law, politics and morals*. Oxford University Press.

Steingraber, S. (1997). Mechanism, proof, and unmet needs: the perspective of a cancer activist. *Environmental Health Perspectives*, 105 (Supplement 3), 685–7.

Stevens, H. (1998). AIDS, not hearing AIDS: exploring the link between the deaf community and HIV/AIDS. *Health and Human Rights*, 2, 99–113.

Sullivan, D. (1995). The nature and scope of human rights obligations concerning women's right to health. *Health and Human Rights*, 1, 368–98.

Swartz, L. and Levett, A. (1989). Political repression and children in South Africa: the social construction of damaging effects. *Social Science and Medicine*, 28, 741–50.

Tarantola, D. (1998). *Expanding the global response to HIV/AIDS through focused action*. UNAIDS Best Practice Collection, Geneva.

Tarantola, D. and Gruskin, S. (1998). Children confronting HIV/AIDS: charting the confluence of rights and health. *Health and Human Rights*, 3, 60–86.

Terrangi, F. (1993). Biotechnology patents and ethical aspects. *Cancer Detection and Prevention*, 17, 317–21.

Toebes, B. (1999). *The right to health as a human right in international law*. Intersentia-Hart, Antwerp.

Tomaševski, K. (1995a). Health rights. In *Economic, social and cultural rights: a textbook* (ed. A. Eide, C. Krause and A. Rosas), pp. 125–42. Martinus Nijhoff, Dordrecht.

Tomaševski, K. (1995b). Health. In *United Nations Legal Order*, Vol. 2 (ed. O. Schachter and C. Joyner), pp. 859–906. American Society of International Law and Cambridge University Press.

UN (United Nations) (1945). *UN charter*, adopted 26 June 1945, entered into force 24 October 1945, as amended by GA Res. 1991 (XVIII) 17 December 1963, entered into force 31 August 1966 (557 UNTS 143); 2101 of 20 December 1965, entered into force 12 June 1968 (638 UNTS 308); and 2847 (XXVI) of 20 December 1971, entered into force 24 September 1973 (892 UNTS 119). UN, New York.

UN (United Nations) (1948). *Universal declaration of human rights*. GA Resolution 217A (III), UN GAOR, Resolution 71, UN Document A/810. UN, New York.

UN (United Nations) (1981). *Declaration on the elimination of all forms of intolerance and of discrimination based on religion or belief*. GA Resolution 36/55, UN GAOR 36th Session, UN Document A/RES/36/55 (1981). UN, New York.

UN (United Nations) (1984a). *Convention against torture and other cruel, inhuman or degrading treatment or punishment*. GA Resolution 39/45, UN GAOR, 39th Session, Supplement No. 51, at 197, UN Document A/39/51. UN, New York.

UN (United Nations) (1984b). *Progressive development of the principles and norms of international law relating to the new international economic order*. Report of the Secretary General, GA, Session 39, UN Document A/39/504/Add. 1. UN, New York.

UN (United Nations) (1992a). Commission on Human Rights. SubCommission on Prevention and Discrimination and Protection of Minorities. *Discrimination against HIV-infected people or people with AIDS*. UN Document E/CN. 4/Sub.2/1992/10 (28 July 1992). UN, Geneva.

UN (United Nations) (1992b). United Nations General Assembly. *The protection of persons with mental illness and the improvement of mental health care*. Resolution Adopted by the General Assembly. UN Document A/RES/46/119, UN, New York.

UN (United Nations) (1993a). *Standard rules on the equalization of opportunities for persons with disabilities*. 85th plenary meeting 20 December 1993. UN Document A/RES/48/96. UN, Geneva.

UN (United Nations) (1993b). *Sub-commission on prevention and discrimination and protection of minorities discrimination against HIV-infected people or people with AIDS*. UN Document E/CN.4/Sub.2/1993/9 (23 August 1993), UN, Geneva.

UN (United Nations) (1993c). United Nations General Assembly. *Vienna declaration and programme of action*. World Conference on Human Rights, Vienna 14–25 June 1993. UN Document A/CONF.157/23. UN, New York.

UN (United Nations) (1994). Committee on Economic. Social and Cultural Rights (UNCESCR). *General Comment No. 5 (Eleventh Session). Persons with disabilities*. UN Document E/C.12/1194/13. UN, Geneva.

UN (United Nations) (1995a). Committee on Economic, Social and Cultural Rights (UNCESCR). *General comment No. 12 (Twentieth Session). The right to adequate food*. UN Document E/C.12/1995/5. UN, Geneva.

UN (United Nations) (1995b). *Programme of action for the world summit for social development*, Copenhagen 6–12 March, UN Document A/CONF.166/9 (96.IV.8). UN, New York.

UN (United Nations) (1995c). *World economic and social survey 1995: current trends and policies in the world economy*. UN, New York.

UN (United Nations) (1996). *Manual on human rights reporting*, UN Document HR/PUB/96/1. United Nations Centre for Human Rights, Geneva.

UN (United Nations) (1997a). *Report by the Secretary General on programme for reform*. UN Document A/51/950, UN, New York.

UN (United Nations) (1997b). Committee on Economic, Social and Cultural Rights (UNCESCR). *General Comment No. 7 (Sixteenth Session). The right to adequate housing*. UN Document E/C.12/1991/4. UN, Geneva.

UN (United Nations) (1998a). *Coordination of the policies and activities of the specialized agencies and other branches of the United Nations system related to the coordinated follow-up to and the implementation of the Vienna Declaration Programme of Action*. Report of the Secretary-General, UN Document E/1990/60, June 1998. UN, New York.

UN (United Nations) (1998b). *Report of the United Nations Consultative Expert Group Meeting on International Norms and Standards Relating to Disability*. UN, New York.

UN (United Nations) (1999a). *Committee on Economic, Social and Cultural Rights (UNCESCR). Concluding observations. Cameroon*. E/C.12/1/Add.40. UN, Geneva.

UN (United Nations) (1999b). *Committee on Economic, Social and Cultural Rights (UNCESCR). Concluding observations. Mexico*, E/C.12/1/Add.41. UN, Geneva.

UNAIDS (Joint United Nations Programme on HIV/AIDS) (1997). *The UNAIDS guide to the United Nations human rights machinery*. UNAIDS, Geneva.

UNAIDS (Joint United Nations Programme on HIV/AIDS) (1999). *From principle to practice: greater involvement of people living with or affected by HIV/AIDS (GIPA)*. UNAIDS Best Practice Collection, Geneva.

UNAIDS/IOM (Joint United Nations Programme on HIV/AIDS and the International Organization for Migration) (1998). Migration and AIDS. *International Migration*, 36, 445–68.

UNCHR (United Nations Commission on Human Rights) (1989). *Non-discrimination in the field of health*, preamble. Resolution 1989/11 (2 March 1989), UN, Geneva.

UNCHR (United Nations Commission on Human Rights) (1994). *Protection of human rights in the context of HIV and AIDS*. UN Document E/CN.4/1994/L.60 (1 March 1994). UN, Geneva.

UNDAW (United Nations Division for the Advancement of Women) with the United Nations Population Fund (UNFPA) and United Nations High Commissioner for Human Rights (UNHCHR) (1996). *Roundtable of Human Rights Treaty Bodies, with a Focus on Sexual and Reproductive Health and Rights*. UN, New York.

UNDP (United Nations Development Programme) (1998a). *Integrating human rights with sustainable development: a UNDP policy document.* UNDP, New York.

UNDP (United Nations Development Programme) (1998b). *Symposium on human development and human rights.* UN, New York.

UNDP (United Nations Development Programme) (1999). *Memorandum of understanding between the United Nations Development Programme and Office of the High Commissioner for Human Rights.* Survey of UNDP Activities in Human Rights, New York.

UNFPA (United Nations Population Fund) (1998). *Ensuring reproductive rights and implementing sexual and reproductive health programmes including women's empowerment, male involvement and human rights.* UNFPA, New York.

UNGA (United Nations General Assembly) (1997). *Renewing the United Nations: a programme for reform,* 14 July 1997, UN Document A/RE/52/12. UN, New York.

UNHCHR (United Nations High Commissioner for Human Rights) (1996). *Report of the Seventh Meeting of the Treaty Bodies.* UN Document A/51/482. UN, Geneva.

UNHCHR (United Nations High Commissioner for Human Rights) (1997). *Report of the Eighth Meeting of the Treaty Bodies.* UN Document A/52/507. UN, Geneva.

UNHCHR (United Nations High Commissioner for Human Rights) (1998a). *Report of the Ninth Meeting of Persons Chairing the Human Rights Treaty Bodies.* UN Document A/53/125. UN, Geneva.

UNHCHR (United Nations High Commissioner for Human Rights) (1998b). *Report of the Tenth Meeting of Persons Chairing the Human Rights Treaty Bodies.* UN Document A/53/432. UN, Geneva.

UNHCHR (United Nations Office of High Commissioner for Human Rights) (2000). *Business and human rights: a progress report.* UN, Geneva.

UNHRC (United Nations Human Rights Committee) (1994). *Fiftieth Session Communication,* No. 488/1992, CCPR/C/50/D/488/1992. 4 April 1994. UN, Geneva.

UNICEF (United Nations International Children's Emergency Fund) (1998). *A human rights approach to UNICEF programming in children and women: what it is, and some changes it will bring.* UNICEF, New York.

UNICEF (United Nations International Children's Emergency Fund) (2000). *Mission statement,* March 2000. UN, New York.

Ward, C. and Myers, N.A. (1999). Babies born with major disabilities: the medical-legal interface. *Pediatric Surgery International,* 15, 310–19.

Watson, R.T., Dixon, J.A., Hamburg, S.P., Janetos, A.C., and Moss, R.H. (1998). *Protecting our planet, securing our future.* United Nations Environment Programme and United States National Aeronautics and Space Administration, New York.

Weiss, E. and Gupta, G.R. (1993). Women facing the challenges of AIDS: prevention and policy concerns. In *Women at the center: development issues and practices for the 1990s,* pp. 168–81. Kumarlan Press, West Hartford, CT.

WHO (World Health Organization) (1946). *Constitution of the World Health Organization,* adopted by the International Health Conference, New York, 19 June–22 July 1946, and signed on 22 July 1946. WHO, Geneva.

WHO (World Health Organization, with UNICEF) (1979). *International conference on primary health care.* WHA 32.30. WHO, Geneva.

WHO (World Health Organization) (1987). *World Health Assembly, Resolution WHA 40.26, Global Strategy for the Prevention and Control of AIDS,* 5 May 1987. WHO, Geneva.

WHO (World Health Organization) (1992). *Our planet, our health.* Report of the WHO Commission on Health and Environment. WHO, Geneva.

WHO (World Health Organization) (1994a). *Framework for effective tuberculosis control.* Tuberculosis Programme, WHO/TB/94.179. WHO, Geneva.

WHO (World Health Organization) (1994b). *Women's health, towards a better world.* Report of the first meeting of the global commission on women's health. WHO/DGH/94.4, pp. 21–3. WHO, Geneva.

WHO (World Health Organization) (1995). *WTO: What's in it for WHO?* WHO Task Force on Health Economics Document WHO/TFHE/95.5. WHO, Geneva.

WHO (World Health Organization) (1998a). *Gender and health.* Technical Paper WHO/FRH/WHD/98.16. WHO, Geneva.

WHO (World Health Organization) (1998b). *Tobacco free initiative.* Executive Board, Provisional Agenda Item 3, 103rd Session, EB103/5. WHO, Geneva.

WHO (World Health Organization) (1998c). *WHO fact sheet,* No. 104. WHO, Geneva.

WHO (World Health Organization) (1998d). *World Health Assembly Resolution on the World Health Declaration,* WHA51/5 adopted by the fifty-first World Health Assembly, 1998. WHO, Geneva.

WHO (World Health Organization) (1999a). *Removing obstacles to healthy development.* WHO Report on Infectious Diseases, WHO/CDS/99.1. WHO, Geneva.

WHO (World Health Organization) (1999b). *WHO corporate strategy for the WHO Secretariat.* Executive Board Provisional Agenda Item 2, 105th Session, EB105/3. WHO, Geneva.

WHO (World Health Organization) (1999c). *World health report 1999—making a difference.* WHO, Geneva.

WHO (World Health Organization) (2000a). *The economic impacts of tuberculosis.* Ministerial Conference, the Stop TB Initiative 2000 Series WHO/CDS/STB/2000–5. WHO, Geneva.

WHO (World Health Organization) (2000b). *Informal consultation on mainstreaming human rights in WHO, 3–4 April 2000.* WHO, Geneva.

WHO (World Health Organization) (2000c). *World health report—2000.* WHO, Geneva.

WHO/UNAIDS (World Health Organization and the Joint United Nations Programme on AIDS) (1999). *Consultation on HIV/AIDS reporting and disclosure, 20–22 October 1999.* WHO, Geneva.

Wodak, A. (1998). Health, HIV infection, human rights, and injecting drug use. *Health and Human Rights,* 2, 25–41.

Youth Research (1997). Naked wire and naked truths: a study of reproductive health risks faced by teenage girls in Honlara, Solomon Islands. *Pacific Aids Alert Bulletin,* 16, 11–12.

Zierler, S., Cunningham, W.E., Andersen, R., et al. (2000). Violence victimization after HIV infection in a US probability sample of adult patients in primary care. *American Journal of Public Health,* 90, 208–15.

2

The UDHR

Fifty Years of Synergy Between Health and Rights

Gro Harlem Brundtland

Fifty years ago, the World Health Organization was founded on the basis of a Constitution which projects a vision of health as a state of complete physical, mental and social well-being—a definition of health that is more relevant today than ever. It recognizes that "the enjoyment of the highest attainable standard of health is one of the fundamental rights of every human being" and that "governments have a responsibility for the health of their peoples which can be fulfilled only by the provision of adequate health and social measures."

On the fiftieth anniversary of the Universal Declaration of Human Rights— a document that sets out the conditions necessary for health—the world continues to confront complex and difficult challenges with serious consequences for health and for human rights. As we seek new approaches to prevent and mitigate the impact of the unevenly distributed burden of known communicable and noncommunicable diseases, new threats to our physical, mental and social well-being continue to emerge. The expanding prevalence of microbial resistance to drugs (as is the case for tuberculosis and malaria); newly discovered infectious agents (such as those responsible for hemorrhagic fevers); increasing recognition of the negative and long lasting consequences of violence in its various forms; and many of the health issues linked to risk-taking behaviors (such as unprotected sex, and alcohol, tobacco and illicit drug use) force us to query both the evolving meaning of health and the reasons why the conditions necessary for its attainment have not been met. The Universal Declaration of Human Rights, in particular its explicit attention to discrimination, affords us a convenient frame-work to recognize, examine and address these conditions.

When the World Health Organization set out to improve health 50 years ago, there were hopes that the existence of antibiotics, and the progress achieved in the development of vaccines and in biomedical technology would provide the tools sufficient to enable individuals everywhere in the world to reach the highest attainable standard of physical, mental and social well-being. However, decades of health development have clearly shown that regardless of the effectiveness of technologies, the civil, cultural, economic, political and social conditions underlying ill-health have to be addressed as well. Indeed, we need to realize that health depends on the fulfillment of all human rights and attention to the increasingly complex relationship of people to their environment. The major determinants of better health lie outside the health system and include better education and information, and fulfillment of those rights which enable people to make and effectuate the decisions relevant to their lives. Poverty and underdevelopment, in fact, epitomize the compounding effects of ill-health and lack of realization of human rights. Poverty most severely affects the developing world which carries over 90 percent of the global disease burden—with access to only 10 percent of the resources for health. Poverty also persists in industrialized countries where the social, economic and health gaps between the haves and the have-nots relentlessly continue to grow. And as a new recession threatens the world's economies, governments and the international community are being provided with new opportunities to examine the ways in which health can best be assured, including the provision of safety nets for the most vulnerable populations. Failing this, the prospects for better health in the next century are alarmingly bleak.

Poverty and the threat of recession illustrate a situation where the neglect or the inability of governments to recognize and fulfill their human rights obligations may impact on health. Discrimination—on the basis of such factors as race, color, sex, language or religion—may further compound the adverse effects of poverty on health. Even where poverty is not a critical issue, discrimination can have a severe negative impact. No community is fully protected from discrimination and its detrimental consequences to individual and public health. In particular, gender-based discrimination poses a pervasive threat to health. Girls and women who are denied access to education, information and various forms of economic, social and political participation are particularly vulnerable to the impact of discrimination on their health. Discrimination can undermine any efforts we make towards better health and a better society. This is true when discrimination is recognized, tolerated, acknowledged or even condoned by governments, but also when it remains insidiously hidden or deliberately ignored behind an accepted status quo. Unrecognized or unattended, its burden on health surreptitiously continues to grow. Recognized, it challenges governments, both individually and collectively, to implement deep social reforms.

In this year of the fiftieth anniversary of the Universal Declaration of Human Rights, we have come to realize that there is a powerful synergy between health and rights. By design, neglect or ignorance, health policies and programs can promote and protect or conversely restrict or violate human rights. Similarly, the promotion, protection, restriction or violation of human rights can have direct impacts on health. Thus, health and rights should inform and inspire each other. Both public health and human rights recognize the ultimate responsibility of governments to create the enabling conditions necessary for people to make and effectuate choices, cope with changing patterns of vulnerability and keep themselves and their families healthy. The recognized, and yet incompletely explored, synergy between health and rights offers us a way forward.

The WHO is working to accelerate and strengthen the operational bond between its health mandate and human rights. In this context, the WHO has recognized the concept of "health security," a principle which encompasses a constellation of rights enshrined in the Universal Declaration of Human Rights. It necessitates universality in health care, access to education and information, the right to food in sufficient quantity and of good quality, and the right to decent housing and to live and work in an environment where known health risks are controlled. Knowledge, freedom of choice and, through various forms of societal and economic transformation, the empowerment of people to effect desired changes in their own lives are understood as critical to move health security from theory to reality.

The WHO of the twenty-first century is embarked on a set of challenging tasks. It aims to enhance the fight against communicable and non-communicable diseases; it strives towards sustainable health development; it is determined to roll back malaria and committed to a Tobacco Free Initiative. These priorities, and others which form the work of WHO, necessitate a health and human rights response. Diseases find fertile ground where information and education are lacking, and where the freedom of community organization is restricted. They recede when the conditions exist for individuals to acquire knowledge and to organize. Malaria spreads and kills where the right of individuals to a healthy environment is not fulfilled. The conditions for malaria transmission and reduced access to treatment also occur where massive violations of human rights result in community disintegration, population displacement and civil unrest. The pandemic of tobacco smoking is fueled by creating addiction among young people in a manner which overruns the rights of the child, as when governments allow tobacco companies to target young populations in the developing world for the dumping of their most health damaging products.

Even when governments are well-intentioned, they may have difficulty fulfilling their health and human rights obligations. Governments, the WHO and other intergovernmental agencies, should strive to create the conditions favorable to health, even in situations where the base of public finance threatens to collapse. We need to build sustainable and equitable health systems that can stand the test of changing times and economic restraints. This is a particular challenge in today's context of widespread health sector reform. These reforms are expected to bring about welcome improvements but, as they take place, we must be mindful that human rights are not undermined and inequalities in health accentuated. The reorientation of public health strategies and reallocation of resources will require us to be attentive to our obligations to all people and, consequently, to the availability of safety nets for those who are most vulnerable. Furthermore, the increasing role of nongovernmental organizations and civil society in the health field, at a time when governments are stepping back from their traditional role as care providers, creates a compelling need to reexamine the concept of partnership in health. Human rights can guide us to redefine ways in which governments and the international community as a whole are accountable for what is done and not done about the health of people.

Our continuing quest for the full attainment of health and human rights requires progressive measures defined not only by resources, but by our commitment. This concept of progressive implementation, recognized by the Universal Declaration of Human Rights 50 years ago, helps us to deal with the ever-changing complexities of our present world, as we strive towards our long term goal in a spirit of constant progress.

3

Human Rights and Health
The Universal Declaration of Human Rights at 50

George J. Annas

War, famine, pestilence, and poverty have had obvious and devastating effects on health throughout human history. In recent times, human rights have come to be viewed as essential to freedom and individual development. But it is only since the end of World War II that the link between human rights and these causes of disease and death has been recognized.[1-3] The 50th anniversary of the Universal Declaration of Human Rights—signed on December 10, 1948—provides an opportunity to review its genesis, to explore the contemporary link between health and human rights, and to develop effective human rights strategies in order to promote health and prevent and treat disease.

War and Human Rights

The modern human rights movement was born from the devastation of World War II. Nonetheless, appeals to universal human rights are at least as old as government. When Jean Anouilh staged Sophocles' *Antigone* in Nazi-occupied Paris in early 1944, the French audience applauded the performance, identifying Antigone with the French resistance. Antigone was sentenced to be buried alive for defying King Creon's order not to bury her dead brother (whom the king considered a traitor) but to leave his body to rot in public. The Nazis in the audience also applauded the performance, apparently because they identified with Creon and his difficulty in maintaining law and order in the face of seemingly fanatical resistance.[4]

Antigone, which was written more than 2400 years ago, focuses on a central moral question: Is there a higher, universal law to which all humans must answer,

63

or is simply obeying the written law of one's country sufficient? Antigone justified her defiance of the king on the basis of an unwritten, higher law:

 Nor did I think your edict had such force that you, a mere mortal, could override the gods, the great unwritten, unshakable traditions.[4]

The source of higher law has varied throughout human history and has included the mythical gods of Olympus, the God of the Old Testament, the God of the New Testament, human reason, and respect for human dignity. The multinational trial of the Nazi war criminals at Nuremberg after World War II was held on the premise that there is a higher law of humanity (derived from rules of "natural law" that are based on an understanding of the essential nature of humans) and that persons may be properly tried for violating this law. Universal criminal law concerns crimes against humanity, such as state-sanctioned genocide, torture, and slavery.[5] Obeying the orders of superiors is no defense: the state cannot shield its agents from prosecution for crimes against humanity.[5] Another major step toward incorporating human rights into international law was taken when the Universal Declaration of Human Rights was signed in a liberated Paris.[6]

The United Nations

The United Nations was formed at the end of World War II as a permanent peace-keeping organization. The charter of the United Nations, signed by the 50 original member nations in San Francisco on June 26, 1945, spells out the organization's goals. The first two goals are "to save succeeding generations from the scourge of war ... and to reaffirm faith in fundamental human rights, in the dignity and worth of the human person, in the equal rights of men and women and of nations large and small."[7] After the charter was signed, the adoption of an international bill of rights with legal authority proceeded in three steps: a declaration, a treaty-based covenant, and implementation measures.

The Universal Declaration of Human Rights

The Universal Declaration of Human Rights was adopted by the United Nations General Assembly in 1948, with 48 member states voting in favor of adoption and eight (Saudi Arabia, South Africa, and the Soviet Union together with five other countries whose votes it controlled) abstaining.[8] The declaration was adopted as a "common standard for all people and nations."[9] As Steiner notes, "No other document has so caught the historical moment, achieved the same moral and rhetorical force, or exerted so much influence on the human rights movement as a whole."[10] The rights enumerated in the declaration "stem from the cardinal axiom that all human beings are born free and equal, in dignity and rights, and are endowed with reason and conscience. All the rights and freedoms belong to everybody."[6] These points are spelled out in Articles 1 and 2. Non-discrimination is the overarching principle. Article 7, for example, is explicit: "All are equal before the law and are entitled without any discrimination to equal protection of the law."[8] Other articles prohibit slavery, torture, and arbitrary detention and protect freedom of expression, assembly, and religion, the right to own property, and the right to work and receive an education. Of special importance to health care professionals is Article 25, which states, in part, "Everyone has the right to a standard of living adequate for the health and well-being of himself and his family, including food, clothing, housing and medical care and necessary social services."[8]

Human rights are primarily rights individuals have in relation to governments. Human rights require governments to refrain from doing certain things, such as torturing persons or limiting freedom of religion, and also require that they take actions to make people's lives better, such as providing education and nutrition programs. The United Nations adopted the Universal Declaration of Human Rights as a statement of aspirations. The legal obligations of governments were to derive from formal treaties that member nations would individually sign and incorporate into domestic law.

The Treaties

Because of the Cold War, with its conflicting ideologies, it took almost 20 years to reach an agreement on the texts of the two human-rights treaties. On December 16, 1966, both the International Covenant on Civil and Political Rights and the International Covenant on Economic, Social and Cultural Rights were adopted by the General Assembly and offered for signature and ratification by the member nations. The United States ratified the International Covenant on Civil and Political Rights in 1992, but not surprisingly, given our capitalist economic system with its emphasis on private property, we have yet to act on the International Covenant on Economic, Social and Cultural Rights. The division of human rights into two separate treaties illustrates the tension between liberal states founded on civil and political rights and socialist and communist welfare states founded on solidarity and the government's obligation to meet basic economic and social needs.

The rights spelled out in the International Covenant on Civil and Political Rights include equality, the right to liberty and security of person, and freedom of movement, religion, expression, and association. The International Covenant on Economic, Social and Cultural Rights focuses on well-being, including the right to work, the right to receive fair wages, the right to make a decent living, the right to work under safe and healthy conditions, the right to be free from hunger, the right to education, and the right of everyone to the enjoyment of the highest attainable standard of physical and mental health.

Given the horrors of poverty, disease, and civil wars over the past 50 years, it is easy to dismiss the rights enunciated in these documents as empty gestures. Indeed, Amnesty International, in marking the 50th anniversary of the Universal Declaration of Human Rights, has labeled the rights it articulates "little more than a paper promise" for most people in the world.[11] It is certainly true that unadulterated celebration is not in order, but as Kunz noted almost 50 years ago in writing about the birth of the declaration, "In the field of human rights as in other actual problems of international law it is necessary to avoid the Scylla of a pessimistic cynicism and the Charybdis of mere wishful thinking and superficial optimism."[6]

Human Rights and Health

The Universal Declaration of Human Rights and the two subsequent treaties form a global human rights framework for action and have a special relevance for global health.[1-3] In recent years, the relation between health and human rights has been most persuasively articulated and tirelessly championed by Dr. Jonathan Mann, the first director of the World Health Organization's Global Program on AIDS, whose life was tragically cut short in the September 1998 crash of Swissair flight 111. The strongest predictor of health is income—that is, poverty is strongly correlated with disease and disability—and one way to attack disease and improve health internationally is to redistribute income.[12] This seems a hopeless goal to most people in developing nations. Reliance on income redistribution as a single or primary strategy can lead to pessimism about the possibility that anything can be done or cynicism about the likelihood that anything will be done.[12,13] Equality of income may be unattainable. But it is not unreasonable to expect the rich to share their wealth with the poor, and thereby help create the conditions necessary for good health for all. The United Nations has noted, for example, that the cost of universal access to basic education, health care, food, and clean water is only $40 billion a year—less than 4 percent of the combined wealth of the 225 richest people in the world.[14] This figure seems too low (if 2 billion people needed additional resources, it would provide only $20 for each); nonetheless, it focuses on proper global goals and suggests that not much redistribution is required to have a major impact on the lives of most people in the world.

Multinational corporations should be actively involved in promoting human rights as well, because they control much of the wealth of the world. This has become evident in the global environmental movement in the areas of pollution, resource conservation, and global warming, and should be evident in the area of health care as well. Much of the agenda for research on drugs and vaccines, for example, is controlled by large multinational corporations, not by governments.

By broadening our perspective, the language of human rights highlights basic needs, such as equality, education, nutrition, and sanitation. Improvement in each of these areas can have a major role in improving health. Over the past decade, the World Bank has become involved in international health. In 1993, the World Bank issued a report entitled *Investing in Health*.[15] Although not stated in the language of human rights, the report's agenda for action implicitly acknowledged that only the recognition of basic human rights could improve the health status of most of the world's population. In low-income countries, for example, the World Bank's two primary recommendations for improvement of health were "increased investment in schooling for girls" and the financing and delivery of a basic package of public health programs, including AIDS prevention.[15] The other major recommendations included increasing the income of the poor, promoting the rights and status of women through "political and economic empowerment and legal protection against abuse," and delivering essential clinical services to the poor.[15] These recommendations directly address the human rights issues of access to education, access to health care, and discrimination against women.

Human Rights and Public Health

World War II, arguably the first truly global war, led many nations to acknowledge the university of human rights and the responsibility of governments to promote them. Mann perceptively noted that the AIDS epidemic can be viewed as the first global epidemic, because it is taking place at a time when all countries are linked both electronically and by easy transportation.[16] Like World War II, this tragedy requires us to think in new ways and to develop effective methods to prevent and treat disease on a global level. Globalization is a mercantile and ecologic fact; it is also a reality in health care. The challenge facing medicine and health care is to develop a global language and strategy to improve the health of all the world's citizens.[17]

Clinical medicine is practiced one patient at a time. The language of medical ethics is the language of self-determination and beneficence: doing what is in the best interests of the patient with the patient's informed consent. This language is powerful, but often has little application in countries where physicians are scarce and medical resources very limited.

Public health deals with populations and prevention of disease—the necessary frame of reference in the global context. In the context of clinical practice, the treatment of human immunodeficiency virus infection with a combination of antiviral medicines makes sense. In the context of worldwide public health, however, such treatment may be available to less than 5 percent of people with AIDS.[18] To control AIDS, it has become necessary to deal directly with discrimination, immigration status, and the rights of women, as well as with the rights of privacy, informed consent, education, and access to health care. It is clear that population-based prevention is required to address the AIDS epidemic effectively on a global level (as well as, for example, tuberculosis, malaria, and tobacco-related illness). Nonetheless, it has been much harder to articulate a global public health ethic. The field of public health itself has had an extraordinarily difficult time developing its own ethical language.[19,20] This problem of language has two basic causes: the incredibly large array of factors that influence health at the population level, and the emphasis by contemporary public health professionals on individualism and market forces rather than on the collective responsibility for social welfare.[19,21] Because of its universality and its emphasis on equality and dignity, the language of human rights is well suited to public health.

On the 50th anniversary of the Universal Declaration of Human Rights, I suggest that the declaration itself sets forth the ethics of public health, since its goal is to provide the conditions under which people can flourish. This is also the goal of public health. The unification of public health and human rights efforts throughout the world could be a powerful force to improve the lives of every person. In my view, the declaration is a much more powerful public health document in 1998 than it was in 1948, because global interdependence and human equality are better recognized today.

Human Rights and Physicians

Both medical ethics and human rights represent aspirations that are difficult to enforce.[21] Over the past two decades, medical ethics has been transformed into medical law, with more litigation and regulation. In the United States, for example, medical organizations, hospitals, and health plans often emphasize avoiding legal liability rather than doing the best or right thing.[22] The domain of medical ethics is shrinking.

The domain of human rights, on the other hand, is growing. Not only are human rights being taken more seriously by governments, but they are also becoming a major driving force in private, nongovernmental organizations. Of course, there are different kinds of rights and different ways to enforce them, some of which are more effective than others. Earlier this year, for example, at a meeting in Rome held under the auspices of the United Nations, the countries in attendance voted overwhelmingly (120 to 7) to propose the establishment of a permanent International Criminal Court with jurisdiction over war crimes, crimes against humanity, genocide, and aggression.[23,24] The United States refused to support the establishment of the court unless it could, among other things, veto trials of Americans, especially American troops acting abroad.[23] [The Statute of the International Criminal Court entered into force on July 1, 2002. Eds.]

But this condition, of course, is incompatible with the entire purpose of the court: to punish violations of basic human rights regardless of the perpetrator.

Individuals and nongovernmental organizations can use the language and concepts of human rights to energize their own activities. Many groups of physicians have taken the lead in promoting human rights, including International Physicians for the Prevention of Nuclear War and its U.S. affiliate, Physicians for Social Responsibility, Physicians for Human Rights, Médecins sans Frontières (Doctors without Borders), and Médecins du Monde (Physicians of the World). Global Lawyers and Physicians (of which I am a cofounder) broadens the base by providing an opportunity for physicians and lawyers to work together to promote human rights in health care.[2,16,17] The Consortium for Health and Human Rights has provided a new forum for co-operative action among health-related nongovernmental organizations. Other groups, such as Amnesty International and the National Academy of Sciences Committee on Human Rights, have developed very effective letter-writing campaigns on behalf of persons who have been arbitrarily detained and imprisoned. Physicians interested in promoting human rights thus have many organizations they can support. Most of these organizations have concentrated on the medical consequences of wars, torture, abuses of prisoners, and arbitrary detention, as well as the threats to health posed by nuclear, chemical, and biologic weapons, land mines, and other means of killing and maiming.[2]

The fact that the Universal Declaration of Human Rights is a declaration, not a treaty, need not limit its reach to human rights violations involving crimes against humanity any more than the reach of the Declaration of Independence has been limited by this fact. Although the Declaration of Independence started a war and the Universal Declaration of Human Rights was drafted to prevent war, it is the power of the concepts and language that matters most. As Maier has noted, the Declaration of Independence "rests less in law than in the minds and hearts of the people, and its meaning changes as new groups and new causes claim its mantle."[25] Lincoln, for example, claimed to be upholding the "all men are created equal" pronouncement of the declaration both when he spoke at Gettysburg and when he issued the Emancipation Proclamation.[25,26] And a century later, Martin Luther King, Jr. stood at the site of the Lincoln Memorial and invoked the words of the Declaration of Independence in calling for a new birth of the freedom Lincoln had promised, by which he meant "an end to the poverty, discrimination, and segregation that left black citizens 'languishing in the corners of American society,' exiles in their own land."[26] The meaning of the Universal Declaration of Human Rights will also be invoked and reinterpreted to meet the changing challenges of the times. The agenda for human rights should be broad; it should include efforts to make basic health care available to everyone and to prevent disease and injury and promote health worldwide. Fifty years after the signing of the Universal Declaration of Human Rights, the language of human rights pervades international politics, law, and morality. The challenge now is to make the promise of the Universal Declaration of Human Rights a reality.

Notes

1. Mann, J., Gruskin, S., Grodin, M., and Annas, G.J. *Health and Human Rights: A Reader.* New York: Routledge (1999).
2. The Writing Group for the Consortium for Health and Human Rights. Health and human rights: a call to action on the 50th anniversary of the Universal Declaration of Human Rights. *JAMA* 1998; 280:462–4.
3. Mann, J., Gostin, L., Gruskin, S., Brennan, T., Lazzarini, Z., and Fineburg, H. Health and human rights. *Health Hum Rights* 1994; 1:6–23.
4. Knox, B. Introduction. In: *Sophocles: The Three Theban Plays: Antigone, Oedipus the King, Oedipus at Colonus.* New York: Viking Penguin, 1984.
5. Bassiouni, M. C. *Crimes against Humanity in International Criminal Law.* Dordrecht, the Netherlands: Martinus Nijhoff, 1992.
6. Kunz, J.L. The United Nations Declaration of Human Rights. *Am J Int Law* 1949; 43:316–22.
7. Simma, B., ed. *The Charter of the United Nations: A Commentary.* New York: Oxford University Press, 1994.
8. Universal Declaration of Human Rights. *JAMA* 1998;280:469–70.
9. Steiner, H. J. and Alston, P. *International Human Rights in Context: Law, Politics, Morals.* New York: Oxford University Press, 1996.
10. Steiner, H.J. Securing human rights: the first half-century of the universal declaration, and beyond. *Harvard Magazine.* September/October 1998; 45–6.
11. Palmer, J. Hollow celebration of 50 years of human-rights campaiguing. *Lancet* 1998; 351:1940.
12. Benatar, S.R. Global disparities in health and human rights: a critical commentary. *Am J Public Health* 1998; 88:295–300.
13. Somerville, M.A. Making health, not war – musings on global disparities in health and human rights. *Am J Public Health* 1998; 88:301–3.
14. Kofi Annan's astonishing facts! *New York Times*, September 27, 1998; 16.
15. World Bank. *World Development Report, 1993: Investing in Health.* New York: Oxford University Press, 1993.
16. Mann, J. Human rights and AIDS: the future of the pandemic. *John Marshall Law Rev* 1996; 30:195–206.
17. Annas, G.J. *Some Choice: Law, Medicine and the Market.* New York: Oxford University Press, 1998.
18. Stephenson, J. International AIDS Conference faces "new realism" of advances, obstacles. *JAMA* 1998; 280:587–8, 590.
19. Beaglehole, R. and Bonita R. *Public Health at the Crossroads.* Cambridge, England: Cambridge University Press, 1997.
20. Mann, J.M. Medicine and public health, ethics and human rights. *Hastings Cent Rep* 1997; 27(3):6–13.
21. Petersen, A. and Lupton, D. *The New Public Health: Health and Self in the Age of Risk.* London: Sage, 1996.
22. Annas, G.J. *Standard of Care: The Law of American Bioethics.* New York: Oxford University Press, 1993.
23. Podgers, J. War crimes court under fire. *Am Bar Assoc J.* September 1998; 64–9.
24. Meron, T. War crimes law comes of age. *Am J Int Law* 1998; 92:462–8.
25. Maier, P. *American scripture: Making the Declaration of Independence.* New York: Vintage Books, 1997.
26. Wills, G. *Lincoln at Gettysburg: The Words that Remade America.* New York: Simon & Schuster, 1992.

II
Health and Human Rights in Development

Development, health, and human rights—as policy objectives of governments, international institutions, and civil society—all refer to policies and programs aimed at the betterment of the human condition. They differ in that the objectives of development focus primarily on the material conditions that allow people to benefit from economic processes, while those of health concentrate on the requirements of physical, mental, and social conditions for human existence, and those of human rights deal with normative demands on power relations, including the elimination of repressive and oppressive processes.

The literature on development's relevance to health is vast, covering most studies on poverty reduction (if the broad definition of health is used) and all work on health systems and primary or basic health care in developing countries (if a narrower definition is used). The literature on human rights in development is growing as scholars, international and national development agencies are increasingly adopting "rights-based approaches to development." Currently, few studies deal with human rights and development with an explicit focus on health. The selections in this part illustrate the place of health in the theory and practice of human rights in development.

It is widely accepted that development is not limited to the economic parameters characterized by economic growth, construction of infrastructure, expansion of industry, and increased production and consumption of goods and services. Most scholars and agencies concerned with development have adopted a framework, often referred to as "human development," that embraces human needs and social goals beyond material well-being, such as higher standards of education and health care, wider opportunities for work and leisure, and increased capabilities and choices for the individual. Thus the United

71

Nations Development Programme (UNDP) has stressed capabilities and choices since its first *Human Development Report* (HDR) in 1990. According to UNDP, "the most basic capabilities for human development are leading a long and healthy life, being educated, having access to the resources needed for a decent standard of living and being able to participate in the life of one's community."[1] The capability of leading a healthy life is central to this understanding of human development. UNDP, in its *Human Development Report 2000*, the theme of which was human rights, proposed ways to make international human rights part of national development policy and practice, drawing heavily on health-related examples.

The human rights perspective on health and development is sometimes confused with social justice. Indeed, the social change implied by a commitment to human rights is consistent with most definitions of social justice. The chapter by Paul Farmer that follows is a powerful statement of the social justice perspective, which reveals unjust structures that are responsible for poverty and proposes strategies, including human rights, for dealing with those structures. There are other approaches to human rights in development that are relevant to health, some of which are explained in the second chapter, by Stephen Marks. He reviews three theoretical approaches and three strategies for action to include human rights in development, noting in each case how they relate to improvements in health.

Specific problems of development for health and human rights run the gamut from unequal impacts of market forces, to trade and investment policy and practice, to rural-urban migration, and myriad other aspects of efforts to promote growth and meet human needs. One major area of concern is the power of major international financial institutions to decide on gigantic infrastructural projects without adequate participation of affected populations. Another is the vulnerability that characterizes marginalized populations, such as indigenous peoples, whose suffering from high morbidity and mortality is reinforced by their powerlessness due to the denial of human rights. The chapter by Claudio González-Parra brings out both issues by describing how a hydroelectric dam project in Chile affected an indigenous population and the related efforts to harmonize development and human rights during a transition to democracy.

Notes

1. UNDP, *Human Development Report 2002* (New York: Oxford University Press, 2002) p. 13.

4

Rethinking Health
and Human Rights
Time for a Paradigm Shift
Paul Farmer with Nicole Gastineau

*From the perspective of a preferential option for the poor, the right to
health care, housing, decent work, protection against hunger, and other
economic, social, and cultural necessities are as important as civil and
political rights and more so.*

– Leigh Binford, The El Mozote Massacre

Medicine and its allied health sciences have for too long been peripherally involved in work on human rights. Fifty years ago, the door to greater involvement
was opened by Article 25 of the Universal Declaration of Human Rights, which
underlined social and economic rights. "Everyone has the right to a standard of
living adequate for the health and well-being of himself and his family, including
food, clothing, housing, and medical care and necessary social services, and the
right to security in the event of unemployment, sickness, disability, widowhood, old age or other lack of livelihood in circumstances beyond his control."[1]

But the intervening decades have seen too little progress in the push for
social and economic rights, even though we may point with some pride to gains
in civil and political rights. That these distinctions are crucial is made clear by
a visit to a Russian prison. With its current political and economic disruption,
Russia's rate of incarceration—644 per 100,000 citizens are currently in jail or
prison—is second only to that of the United States, where there are 699 prisoners
per 100,000 in the population. Compare this to much of the rest of Europe,
where the figure is about one-fifth as high.[2]

In the cramped, crammed detention centers where hundreds of thousands of Russian detainees await due process, many fall ill with tuberculosis. Convicted prisoners who are diagnosed with tuberculosis are sent to one of more than fifty "TB colonies." Imagine a Siberian prison in which the cells are as crowded as cattle cars, the fetid air thick with tubercle bacilli. Imagine a cell in which most of the prisoners are perpetually coughing and all are said to have active tuberculosis. Let the mean age of the inmates be less than 30 years old. Finally, imagine that many of these young men are receiving ineffective treatment for their disease—given drug toxicity, worse than receiving placebo—even though they are the beneficiaries of "directly observed therapy" with first-line anti-tuberculous agents, delivered by European humanitarian organizations and their Russian colleagues.

If this seems hard to imagine, it shouldn't be. I have seen this situation in several prisons; there are still prisoners receiving directly observed doses of medications that cannot cure them. For many of these prisoners, the therapy is ineffective because the strains of tuberculosis that are epidemic within the prisons are resistant to the drugs being administered. Various observers, including some from international human rights organizations, have averred that these prisoners have "untreatable forms" of tuberculosis, and few have challenged this claim even though treatment based on the standard of care used elsewhere in Europe and in North America *can* cure the great majority of such cases.[3] "Untreatable," in these debates, really means "expensive to treat." For this and other reasons, tuberculosis has again become the leading cause of death among Russian prisoners – even among those nominally receiving treatment. Similar situations may be found throughout the former Soviet Union.

Are human rights violated in this dismal scenario? If we look only at civil rights without taking social and economic rights into consideration, we would focus on a single violation: prolonged pretrial detention. Those arrested are routinely detained for up to a year before making a court appearance. In many documented cases, young detainees have died of prison-acquired tuberculosis before their cases ever went to trial. Such detention clearly violates not only Russian law, but several human rights charters to which the country is signatory. Russian and international human rights activists have focused on this problem, demanding that all detainees be brought quickly to trial. An impasse is quickly reached when the underfunded Russian courts wearily respond that they are working as fast as they can. The Ministry of Justice agrees with the human rights people, and is now interested in amnesty for prisoners and alternatives to imprisonment. But these measures, helpful though they may prove, will not save those already sick.

What of social and economic rights violations? Examining these yields a far longer list of violations—but, importantly, also a longer list of possible interventions. Prison conditions are deplorable; the directors of the former gulag do not dispute this point. The head of the federal penitentiary system, speaking to Amnesty International, described the prisoners as living in "conditions amounting to torture."[4] Detainees are subjected to conditions that guarantee increased exposure to drug-resistant strains of *M. tuberculosis*, and to make matters worse, they are denied adequate food and medical care. In the words of one physician: "I have spent my entire medical career caring for prisoners with tuberculosis. And although we complained about shortages in the eighties, we had no idea how good we had it then. Now it's a daily struggle for food, drugs, lab supplies, even heat and electricity."[5]

These prisoners are dying of ineffectively treated multidrug-resistant tuberculosis (MDRTB). Experts from the international public health community, have argued that it is not necessary to treat MDRTB—the "untreatable form" in question—in this region. These experts have argued that all patients should be treated with identical doses of the same drugs and that MDRTB will disappear if such strategies are adopted.[6] Cost-efficacy arguments against treating drug-resistant tuberculosis almost always fail to note that most of the drugs necessary for such treatment have been off-patent. for years. And it is simply not true that MDRTB is untreatable—Partners In Health has done work in Peru and Haiti showing that MDRTB can be cured in resource-poor settings.[7] All the prison rights activism in the world will come to naught if prisoners are guaranteed the right to treatment but given the wrong prescriptions. A civil and political rights perspective does not allow us to grasp the full nature of these human rights violations, much less attempt to fix all of them.

So what does a focus on health bring to the struggle for human rights? A narrow legal approach to health and human rights can obscure the nature of violations, thereby enfeebling our best responses to them. Casting prison-based tuberculosis epidemics in terms of social and economic rights offers an entry point for public health and medicine, an important step in the process that could halt these epidemics. Medicine enters the picture and can respond to the past-neglected call for action. Conversely, of course, failure to consider social and economic rights can prevent the allied health professions and the social sciences from making their fullest contribution to the struggle for human rights.

Pragmatic Solidarity: A Synergy of Health and Human Rights

Public health and access to medical care are social and economic rights. They are at least as critical as civil rights. One of the ironies of our global era is that while public health has increasingly sacrificed equity for efficiency, the poor have become well-informed enough to reject separate standards of care. In our professional journals, these subaltern voices have been well-nigh blotted out. But snatches of their rebuke have been heard recently with regard to access to antiretroviral therapy for HIV disease. Whether we continue to ignore them or not, the destitute sick are increasingly clear on one point: Making social and economic rights a reality is the key goal for health and human rights in the twenty-first century.

Although trained in anthropology, I, like most anthropologists, do not embrace the rigidly particularist and relativist tendencies popularly associated with the discipline.[8] That is, I believe that violations of human dignity are not to be accepted merely because they are buttressed by local ideology or long-standing tradition. But anthropology—in common with sociological and historical perspectives in general—allows us to place both human rights abuses and the discourses (and other responses) they generate in broader contexts. Furthermore, these disciplines permit us to ground our understanding of human rights violations in broader analyses of power and social inequality. Whereas a purely legal view of human rights tends to obscure the dynamics of human rights violations, the contextualizing disciplines reveal them to be pathologies of power. Social inequalities based on race or ethnicity, gender, religious creed, and—above all—social class are the motor force behind most human rights violations. In other words, violence against individuals is usually embedded in entrenched structural violence.

In exploring the relationships between structural violence and human rights, I draw on my own experience serving the destitute sick in settings such as Haiti and Chiapas and Russia, where human rights violations are a daily concern (even if structural violence is not always seen as a human rights issue). I do this not to make over-much of my personal acquaintance with other people's suffering, but rather to ground a theoretical discussion in the very real experiences that have shaped my views on health and human rights. Each of these situations calls not only for our recognition of the relationship between structural violence and human rights violations, but also for what we have termed "pragmatic solidarity": the rapid deployment of our tools and resources to improve the health and well-being of those who suffer this violence.

Pragmatic solidarity is different from, but nourished by, solidarity—the desire to make common cause with those in need. Solidarity itself is a precious thing: people enduring great hardship often remark that they are grateful for the prayers and good wishes of fellow human beings. But when sentiment is accompanied by the goods and services that might diminish unjust hardship, surely it is enriched. To those in great need, solidarity without the pragmatic component can seem like abstract piety. The goal of our partnerships with sister organizations in Haiti, Peru, Mexico, Russia, and the United States is neither charity nor development. Rather, these relationships reflect a commitment to struggle along-side the poor, and against the economic and political structures that create their poverty. We see pragmatic solidarity as a means to synergize health and human rights—when the destitute sick can fulfill their human right to health, the door may be opened to more readily achieve other economic, social, cultural, and political rights.[9] One telling example comes from Haiti, where HIV-positive patients placed on antiretroviral therapy repeatedly inform us that they can now return to daily life and caring for their children.[10] When we move beyond sentiments to action, we incur risks, and these deter many. But it is possible, clearly, to link lofty ideals to sound analysis. This linkage does not always occur in human rights work, in part because of a reluctance to examine the political economy of suffering and brutality.

I will not discuss, except in passing, the covenants and conventions that constitute the key documents of the human rights movement here. The goal of this article is to raise, and to answer, some questions relevant to health and human rights; to explore the promise of pragmatic solidarity as a response to structural violence; and to identify promising directions for future work in this field. It is my belief that the conclusions that follow are the most important challenges before those who concern themselves with health and human rights.

How Far Has the Human Rights Movement Come?

The field of health and human rights, most would agree, is in its infancy. Attempting to define a new field is necessarily a treacherous enterprise. Sometimes we appear to step on the toes of those who have long been at work when we mean instead to stand on their shoulders. Human rights law, which focuses on civil and political rights, is much older than human rights medicine. And if vigor is assessed in the typical academic style—by length of bibliography— civil and political rights law is the more robust field, too. That legal documents and scholarship dominate the human rights literature is not surprising (note Steiner and Alston), given that the human rights movement has "struggled to assume so law-like a character."[11]

But even in legal terms, the international human rights movement is essentially a modern phenomenon, beginning, some argue, with the Nuremberg trials. It is this movement that has led, most recently, to the creation of international tribunals to judge war crimes in the Balkans and in Rwanda. Yet 50 years after the Universal Declaration of Human Rights, and 50 years after the four Geneva Conventions, what do we have to show for these efforts? Do we have some sense of outcomes? Aryeh Neier, former executive director of Human Rights Watch, recently reviewed the history of various treaties and covenants from Nuremberg to the Convention Against Torture and Other Cruel, Inhuman or Degrading Treatment or Punishment. He said, "Nations have honored these obligations largely in the breach."[12]

Few could argue against Neier's dour assessment, but the past few years have been marked by a certain amount of human rights triumphalism. The fiftieth anniversary of the Universal Declaration has led to many celebrations, but to few careful assessments of current realities. Even those within the legal community acknowledge that it would be difficult to correlate a steep rise in the publication of human rights documents with a statistically significant drop in the number of human rights abuses. Rosalyn Higgins says pointedly:

> No one doubts that there exists a norm prohibiting torture. No state denies the existence of such a norm; and, indeed, it is widely recognized as a customary rule of international law by national courts. But it is equally clear from, for example, the reports of Amnesty International that the *great majority* of states systematically engage in torture. If one takes the view that noncompliance is relevant to the retention of normative quality, are we to conclude that there is not really any prohibition of torture under customary international law?[13]

Whether these laws are binding or largely hortatory constitutes a substantial debate in the legal literature, but such debates seem academic in the face of overwhelming evidence of persistent abuses.

When we expand the concept of rights to include social and economic rights, the gap between the ideal and reality is even wider. Local and global inequalities mean that the fruits of medical and scientific advances are stockpiled for some and denied to others. The dimensions of these inequalities are staggering, and the trends are adverse. To cite just a few examples—in 1998, Michael Jordan earned from Nike the equivalent of 60,000 years' salary for an Indonesian footwear assembly worker; Haitian factory workers, most of them women, made 28 cents per hour sewing Pocahontas pajamas, while Disney's U.S.-based chief executive officer made $97,000 for each hour he toiled.[14]

The pathogenic effects of such inequality are now recognized.[15] Many governments, including our own, refuse to redress inequalities in health, while others are largely powerless to address them.[16] But although the reasons for failure are many and varied, even optimists allow that human rights charters and covenants have not brought an end to—and may not even have slowed—egregious abuses, however they are defined. States large and small violate civil, economic, and social rights, and inequality both prompts and covers these violations. In other words, rights attributed on paper are of little value when the existing political and social structures do not afford all individuals the ability to enjoy these rights, let alone defend them.

There are, of course, exceptions; victories have been declared. But not many of them are very encouraging on close scrutiny. Haiti, the case I know best, offers a humbling example. First, the struggle for social and economic rights—food, medical care, education, housing, decent jobs—has been dealt crippling blows in Haiti. Such basic entitlements, the centerpiece of the popular movement that in 1990 brought the country's first democratically elected president to power, were buried under an avalanche of human rights violations after the military coup of 1991. And although human rights groups were among those credited with helping to restore constitutional rule in Haiti, this was accomplished, to a large extent, by sacrificing the struggle for social and economic rights.[17] In recent years, it has sometimes seemed as if the steam has run out of the movement to bring to justice those responsible for the murder and mayhem that have made Haiti such a difficult place to live. There are notable exceptions—for instance, the sentencing of military officials responsible for a 1994 civilian massacre—but both the legal and socioeconomic campaigns have slowed almost to a standstill.[18]

Or take Argentina. The gruesome details of the "dirty war" are familiar to many.[19] Seeking what Aryeh Neier has chillingly termed "a better "mousetrap of repression," the Argentine military government began disappearing" (as Latin Americans said in the special syntax crafted for the occasion) people it identified as leftists.[20] Many people know, now, about the death flights that took place every Wednesday for two years. Thousands of citizens the government deemed subversive, many of them students and most of them just having survived torture, were flown from a military installation out over the Atlantic, stripped, and shoved out of the plane. A better mousetrap, indeed.

What happened next is well-documented, although it is a classic instance of the half-empty, half-full glass. Those who say the glass is half full note that an elected civilian government subsequently tried and convicted high-ranking military figures, including the generals who shared, in the fashion of runners in a relay, the presidential office. Those who say the glass is half empty note that the prompt pardoning and release of the criminals meant that, once again, no one has been held accountable for thousands of murders.[21] Similar stories abound in Guatemala, El Salvador, the state of Chiapas in Mexico, and elsewhere in Latin America.[22]

These painful experiences are, of course, no reason to declare legal proceedings ineffective. On the contrary, they remind us that some of what was previously hidden away is now out in the open. Disclosure is often the first step in the struggle against impunity, and human rights organizations—almost all of them nongovernmental—have at times forced unwilling governments to acknowledge what really happened. These efforts should serve as a rallying cry for those who now look to constitute international criminal tribunals.

Still, the results to date suggest that we would be unwise to place all our hopes on the legal-struggle approach. This approach has proved insufficient in preventing human rights abuses, and all the civil and political rights ever granted will provide little comfort to the starving and the sick if they are not enforced by the state, as they so often are not. Complementary strategies and new openings are critically needed. The health and human rights "angle" can provide new opportunities and new strategies at the same time that it lends strength and purpose to a movement sorely in need of buttressing.

Can One Merely Study Human Rights Abuses?

A few years ago, the French sociologist Pierre Bourdieu and his colleagues pulled together a compendium of testimonies from those the French term "the excluded" in order to bring into relief *la misère du monde*. Bourdieu and colleagues qualified their claims for the role of scholarship in addressing this misery: "To subject to scrutiny the mechanisms which render life painful, even untenable, is not to neutralize them; to bring to light contradictions is not to resolve them."[23] It is precisely such humility that is needed, and rarely exhibited, in academic commentary on human rights.

It is difficult merely to study human rights abuses. We know with certainly that rights are being abused at this very moment. And the fact that we can study, rather than endure, these abuses is a reminder that we too are implicated in and benefit from the increasingly global structures that determine, to an important extent, the nature and distribution of assaults on dignity.

Ivory-tower engagement with health and human rights can, often enough, reduce us to seminar-room warriors. At worst, we stand revealed as the hypocrites that our critics in many parts of the world have not hesitated to call us. Anthropologists have long been familiar with these critiques; specialists in international health, including AIDS researchers, have recently had a crash course.[24] It is possible, usually, to drown out the voices of those demanding that we stop studying them, even when they go to great lengths to make sure we get the message. But social scientists with more acute hearing have documented a rich trove of graffiti, songs, demonstrations, tracts, and broadsides on the subject. A hit record album in Haiti was called *International Organizations*. The title cut includes the following lines: "International organizations are not on our side. They're there to help the thieves rob and devour. . . . International health stays on the sidelines of our struggle."

In the context of long-standing international support for sundry Haitian dictatorships, one can readily see the gripe with international organizations. But "international health?" The international community's extraordinary largesse to the Duvalier regime has certainly been well-documented.[25] Subsequent patterns of giving, addressed as they were to sundry Duvalierist military juntas, did nothing to improve the reputation of U.S. foreign aid or the international organizations, though they helped greatly to arm murderous bands and line the pockets of their leaders. Haitians saw international health, if not from within institutions such as the United States Agency for International Development (USAID), then as part of the same dictator-buttressing bureaucracy. Such critiques are not specific to Haiti, although Haitians have pronounced them with exceptional frankness and richness of detail. Their accusations have been echoed and amplified throughout what some are beginning to call the global geoculture.[26] A full decade before the recent AIDS research debates,[27] it was possible to collect a bookful of such commentary.[28]

It is in this context of globalization, "mediatization," and growing inequality that the new field of health and human rights emerges. Contextual factors are particularly salient when we think about social and economic rights, as Steiner and Alston have noted: "An examination of the concept of the right to development and its implications in the 1990s cannot avoid consideration of the effects of the globalization of the economy and the consequences of the near-universal embrace of the market economy."[29] This context defines our research agenda and directs our praxis. We are leaving behind the terra firma of double-blind, placebo-controlled studies, of cost effectiveness, and of sustainability. Indeed, many of these concepts end up looking more like strategies for managing, rather than challenging, inequality.

What, then, should be the role of the First World university, of researchers and health-care professionals? What should be the role of students and others lucky enough to be among the "winners" in the global era? We can agree, perhaps, that these centers are fine places from which to conduct research, to document, and to teach. A university does not have the same entanglements or constraints as an international institution such as the United Nations, or as organizations such as Amnesty International or Physicians for Human Rights. Universities could, in theory, provide a unique and privileged space for conducting research and engaging in critical assessment.

In human rights work, however, research and critical assessment are insufficient—analysis alone cannot curb human rights violations. No more adequate, for all their virtues, are denunciation and exhortation, whether in the form of press conferences or reports or harangues directed at students. To confront, as an observer, ongoing abuses of human rights is to be faced with a moral dilemma: Does one's action help the sufferers or the system? The increasingly baroque codes of research ethics generated by institutional review boards will not help us out of this dilemma, nor will medical ethics, which are so often restricted to the quandary ethics of the individual. But certain models of engagement are not irrelevant. If the university-based human rights worker is in a peculiar position, it is not entirely unlike that of the clinician researcher. Both study suffering; both are bound to relieve it; neither is in possession of a tried-and-true remedy. Both the human rights specialist and the clinician researcher have blind spots, too.

To push the analogy further, it could be argued that there are, in both lines of work, obligations regarding the standard of care. Once a reasonably effective intervention has been identified, it—and not a placebo—is considered the standard against which a new remedy must be tested. In the global era, is it wise to set, as *policy goals*, double standards for the rich world and the poor world, when we know that these are not different worlds but in fact the same one? Can we treat the rich with the "gold standard," while offering the poor an essential "placebo?" Are the acrid complaints of the vulnerable necessary to remind us that they invariably see the world as one world, riven by terrible inequality and injustice? A placebo is a placebo is a placebo.

That we have failed to meet high goals does not imply that the next step is to lower our sights, although this has been the default logic in many instances. The next step is to try new approaches and to hedge our bets with indisputably effective interventions. Providing pragmatic services to the afflicted is one obvious form of intervention. But the spirit in which these services are delivered makes all the difference. Service delivery can be just that or it can be pragmatic solidarity, linked to the broader goals of equality and justice for the poor. Again, my own experience in Haiti, which began in 1983, made this clear. The Duvalier dictatorship was then in power, seemingly immovable. Its chief source of external financial aid was the United States and various international institutions, many of them ostensibly charitable in nature. The local director of USAID at the time had often expressed the view that if Haiti was underdeveloped, the causes were to be sought in Haitian culture.[30] The World Bank and the International Monetary Fund seemed to be part of the same giant blur of international aid organizations that Haitians associated, accurately enough, with U.S. foreign policy.

Popular cynicism regarding these transnational institutions was at its peak when my colleagues and I began working in Haiti, and that is precisely why we chose to work through nascent community-based organizations and for a group of rural peasants who had been dispossessed of their land. Although we conducted research and published it, research did not figure on the wish list of the people we were trying to serve. Services were what they asked for, and as people who had been displaced by political and economic violence, they regarded these services as a rightful remedy for what they had suffered. In other words, the Haitian poor themselves believed that social and economic rights were central to the struggle for human rights. As the struggle against the dictatorship gathered strength in the mid-eighties, the language was explicitly couched in broad human rights terms. *Pa gen lapè nan tèt si pa gen lapè nan vant*: There can be no peace of mind if there is no peace in the belly.[31] Health and education figured high on the list of demands as the Haitian popular movement began to swell.

The same has been true of the struggle in Chiapas. The Zapatista rebellion was launched on the day the North American Free Trade Agreement was signed, and the initial statement of the rebellion's leaders put their demands in terms of social and economic rights:

We are denied the most elementary education so that they can use us as caunon fodder and plunder our country's riches, uncaring that we are dying of hunger and curable diseases. Nor do they care that we have nothing, absolutely nothing, no decent roof over our heads, no land, no work, no health, no food, no education. We do not have the right to freely and democratically elect our own authorities, nor do we have peace or justice for ourselves and our children.[32]

It is in settings such as these that we are afforded a rare clarity about choices that are in fact choices for all of us, everywhere. There's little doubt that discernment is a daily struggle. We must decide how health professionals might best make common cause with the destitute sick, whose rights are violated daily. Helping governments shore up failing public health systems may or may not be wise. As mentioned earlier, pragmatic solidarity on behalf of Russian prisoners with tuberculosis included working with their jailors. But sometimes we are warned against consorting with governments. In Haiti in the eighties, it made all the difference that we formed our own nongovernmental organization far from the reach of the governments of both Haiti and the United States. In Chiapas, the situation was even more dramatic, and many poor communities simply have refused to use government health services. In village after village, we heard the same story. In some "autonomous zones," the Mexican Army—again, as many as 70,000 troops are now stationed in Chiapas—entered these villages and destroyed local health records and what meager infrastructure had been developed. To quote one health worker: "The government uses health services against us. They persecute us if they think we are on the side of the rebels." Our own investigations have been amply confirmed by others, including Physicians for Human Rights:

> At best, [Mexican] Government health and other services are subordinate to Government counter-insurgency efforts. At worst, these services are themselves components of repression, manipulated to reward supporters and to penalize and demoralize dissenters. In either case, Government health services in the zone are discriminatory, exacerbate political divisions, and fail utterly to address the real health needs of the population.[33]

It's not acceptable for those of us fortunate enough to have ties to universities, and to be able to do research, to throw up our hands and bemoan the place-to-place complexity. Underlying this complexity are a series of very simple first principles regarding human rights, as the liberation theologians remind us. Our commitments, our loyalties, have to be *primarily* to the poor and vulnerable. As a reminder of how unique this commitment is, remember that the international agencies affiliated with the United Nations, including the World Health Organization, are called to work with governments. Think, once again, of Chiapas. The individual member of any one of these international institutions may have loyalties to the Zapatistas, but have no choice in his or her agency's primary interlocutor: This will be the Mexican government. Membership in a university (or hospital or local church) permits us more flexibility in making allegiances. This flexibility is a gift that should not be squandered by mimicking mindlessly the choices of the parastatal international organizations. Close allegiance with suffering communities reminds us that it is not possible to merely study human rights abuses. But part of pragmatic solidarity is bringing the real story to light.

Merely telling the truth often calls for exhaustive research. In the current era, human rights violations are usually both local and global. Telling who did what to whom and when becomes a complicated affair. The chain of complicity, I have learned, reaches higher and higher. At the time of the Haitian military coup, U.S. officialdom's explanation of human rights abuses in Haiti, including the torture and murder of civilians, focused almost exclusively on local actors and local factors. One heard of the "culture of violence" that rendered this and other similarly grisly deaths comprehensible. Such official analyses, constructed through the conflation of structural violence and cultural difference, were distancing tactics.

Innumerable immodest claims of causality, such as attributing a sudden upsurge in the torture of persons in police custody to long-standing local custom, play into the convenient alibi that refuses to follow the chain of events to their source, that keeps all the trouble local. Such alibis obscure the fact that the modern Haitian military was created by an act of the U.S. Congress during our 20-year occupation (1915–1934) of Haiti. Most official analyses did not discuss the generous U.S. assistance to the post-Duvalier military: over $200 million in aid passed through the hands of the Haitian military in the 18 months after Jean-Claude Duvalier left Haiti on a U.S. cargo plane in 1986. Bush administration statements, and their faithful echoes in the establishment press, failed to mention that many of the commanders who issued the orders to detain and torture civilians were trained in Fort Benning, Georgia. At this writing, human rights groups in the United States and Haiti have filed suit against the U.S. government in order to bring to light over 100,000 pages of documents revealing links between Washington and the paramilitary groups that held sway in Haiti between 1991 and 1994.[34]

The masking of the mechanisms of human rights violations has occurred elsewhere. In El Salvador, the massacres of entire villages could not in good conscience be considered unrelated to U.S. foreign policy, since the U.S. government was the primary funder, advisor, and supporter of the Salvadoran government's war against its own people. Yet precisely that fiction of deniability was maintained by officialdom, even though we were also the primary purveyors of armaments, as physical evidence was later to show. It was years before we could read accounts, such as that by Mark Danner, who, on investigating the slaughter of every man, woman, and child in one village, concluded: "of the two hundred and forty-five cartridge cases that were studied—all but one from American M16 rifles—'184 had discernable headstamps, identifying the ammunition as having been manufactured for the United States Government at

Lake City, Missouri.'"[35] The fiction of local struggles (ethnic, religious, historical, or otherwise picturesque) is exploded by any honest attempt to understand. Paramilitary groups linked tightly with the Mexican government were and are responsible for the bulk of intimidation and violence in the villages of Chiapas. But, as in Haiti, federal authorities have insisted that such violence is due to "local inter-community and interparty tension" or to ethnic rivalries.[36]

Immodest claims of causality are not always so flagrantly self-serving as those proffered to explain Haiti's agony, or the violence in El Salvador and Chiapas. But only careful analysis allows us to rebut them with any confidence. Physicians, when fortunate, can alleviate the suffering of the sick—but explaining the distribution and causes of suffering requires many minds and resources. To explain each individual's suffering, one must embed individual biography in the larger matrix of culture, history, and political economy. We cannot *merely* study human rights abuses, but we must not fail to study them.

What Can a Focus on Health Bring to the Struggle for Human Rights?

Scholarship is not always readily yoked to the service of the poor. Medicine, I have discovered, can be. At its best, medicine is a service much more than a science, and the latest battery of biomedical discoveries, in which I rejoice, has not convinced me otherwise. Medicine and public health, and also the social sciences relevant to these disciplines, have much to contribute to the great, often rancorous debates on human rights. But what, precisely, might be our greatest contribution? Rudolph Virchow saw doctors as "the natural attorneys of the poor."[37] A "health angle" can promote a broader human rights agenda in unique ways. In fact, the health part of the formula may prove critical to the success of the human rights movement. The honor in which public health and medicine are held affords us openings—again, a space of privilege—enjoyed by few other professions. For example, it is unlikely that my colleagues and I would have been welcomed so warmly into Russian prisons if we were social scientists or human rights investigators. We went instead as TB specialists, with the expectation that a visiting group of doctors might be able to do more for the rights of these prisoners than a delegation from a conventional human rights organization. It is important to get the story straight: the leading cause of death among young Russian detainees is tuberculosis, not torture or starvation. Prison officials were opening their facilities to us, and asking for pragmatic solidarity. (In Haiti and Chiapas, by contrast, we were asked to leave when we openly espoused the cause of the oppressed.)

Medicine and public health benefit from an extraordinary symbolic capital that is, so far, sadly underutilized in human rights work. No one made this point more clearly and persistently than the late Jonathan Mann. In an essay written with Daniel Tarantola, Mann noted that AIDS "has helped catalyze the modern health and human-rights movement, which leads far beyond AIDS, for it considers that promoting and protecting health and promoting and protecting human rights are inextricably connected."[38]

But have we gone far beyond AIDS? Is it not a human rights issue that Russian prisoners are exposed, often during illegally prolonged pretrial detention, to epidemic MDRTB and then denied effective treatment? Is it not a human rights issue that international expert opinion has mistakenly informed Russian prison officials that treatment with second-line drugs is not cost-effective or just plain unnecessary? Is it not a human rights issue that, in wealthy South Africa, where participants at the XIIIth International AIDS Conference were reminded in the glossy program that "medical care is readily available in South Africa," antiretroviral therapy that could prolong millions of (black) lives is declared "cost ineffective?" Is it not a human rights issue that villagers in Chiapas lack access to the most basic medical services, even as government medical facilities stand idly by? Is it not a human rights issue that thousands of Haitian peasants displaced by a hydroelectric dam end up sick with HIV after working as servants in Port-au-Prince?

Standing on the shoulders of giants—from the authors of the Universal Declaration to Jonathan Mann—we can recognize the human rights abuses in each of these situations, including epidemic tuberculosis within prisons. But what, precisely, is to be done? Russian penal codes already prohibit overcrowding, long pretrial detention, and undue risk from malnutrition and communicable disease. Prison officials already regard the tuberculosis problem as a top priority; that's why they have let TB specialists in. In a 1998 interview, one high-ranking prison official told me that the ministry saw their chief problems as lack of resources, over-crowding, and tuberculosis.[39] And the *pièce de résistance* might be that Boris Yeltsin had already declared 1998 "the year of human rights."

Passing more human rights legislation will not be a sufficient response to these human rights challenges, because many of the (nonbinding, clearly) instruments have already been disregarded by those in charge. The Haitian military coup leaders were beyond the pale. But how about Chiapas? Instruments to which Mexico is already signatory include the Geneva Conventions of 1949; the International Covenant on Civil and Political Rights; the International Covenant on Economic, Social and Cultural Rights; the International Labor Organization Convention 169; the American Convention on Human Rights; the Maastricht Guidelines on Violations of Economic, Social and Cultural Rights; and the Convention on the Elimination of All Forms of Discrimination Against Women. Each one of these is flouted every day in Chiapas.

As the Haitians say, "Laws are made of paper; bayonets are made of steel." Law alone is not up to the task of relieving such immense suffering. Louis Henkin has reminded us that international law is fundamentally a set of rules and norms designed to protect the interests of states, not their citizens. "Until recently," he observed in 1989, "international law took no note of individual human be-ings."[40] And states, as we have seen, honor human rights law largely in the breach—sometimes through intention and sometimes through sheer impo-tence. This chief irony of human rights work—that states will not or cannot obey the treaties to which they are signatory—can lead to despair or to cynicism, if all of one's eggs are in the international law basket.

Laws are not science; they are normative ideology and tightly tied to power.[41] Biomedicine and public health though also vulnerable to ideological deforma-tions serve different imperatives, ask different questions. Physicians practice triage and referral daily. What suffering needs to be taken care of first and with what resources? Medicine and public health do not ask whether an event or process violates an existing rule; they ask whether that event or process can be shown to have ill effects on a patient or on a population. They ask whether such events can be prevented or remediated. Thus medicine and public health, so directly tied to human outcomes, give us an immediate sense of impact and a means of measuring progress – because health fields are well-versed in marry-ing the analysis of problems with practical solutions. And when medicine and public health are explicitly placed at the service of the poor, there is even greater insurance against their perversion.

To return to the case of prisoners with MDRTB, the best way to protect their rights is to cure them of their disease. And the best way to protect the rights of other prisoners, and of those who take care of them, is to prevent transmission by treating the sick. Thus, after years of equivocation, all parties involved are being forced to admit that the right thing to do in Russia's prisons is also the *human rights* thing to do. A variety of strategies, from human rights argu-ments to epidemiologic scare tactics, have been used to make head-way in rais-ing the funds necessary to treat these and other prisoners. In the end, then, the health angle on human rights may prove more pragmatic than approaching the problem as one of penal reform alone, in part because the health angle focuses less on public blame and more on finding solutions. This is not to say that human rights advocates should not strive for policy reform, but rather that we need a fast, non-controversial solution that attacks the root of many human rights violations. Previously closed-door institutions have invited in-ternational collaboration designed to halt prison epidemics. This approach—pragmatic solidarity—may, in the end, lead to penal reform as well.

New Agendas for Health and Human Rights

Is it grandiose to seek to define new agendas? When one reads the powerfully worded statutes, conventions, treaties, and charters stemming from interna-tional revulsion over the crimes of the Third Reich, it seems pointless to call for better instruments of this sort. More recent events in the former Yugoslavia and in Rwanda serve as a powerful rebuke to undue confidence in these legalistic approaches: "That it should nevertheless be possible for Nazi-like crimes to be repeated half a century later in full view of the whole world," remarks Aryeh Neier, "points out the weakness of that system – and the need for fresh approaches."[42] Steiner and Alston, similarly call for "heightened attention to the problems of implementation and enforcement of the new ideal norms. The old techniques," they conclude, "simply won't work."[43]

A corollary question is whether a coherent agenda springs from the critique inherent in the answers to the questions presented here. If so, is this agenda compatible with existing approaches and documents, including the Universal Declaration of Human Rights? To those who believe that social and economic rights must be central to the health and human rights agenda, the answers to these questions are "Yes." This agenda, inspired by the notion of a preferential option for the poor, is coherent, pragmatic, and informed by careful scholarship. In large part because it focuses on social and economic rights, this agenda, though novel, builds on five decades of work within the traditional human rights framework: Articles 25 and 27 of the Universal Declaration inspire the vision of this emerging agenda, which could rely on tighter links between universities, medical providers, and both non-governmental and community-based organizations. The truly novel part of the alliance comes in subjugating these networks to the aspirations of oppressed and abused people.

How might we proceed with this effort if most reviews of the effects of international laws and treaties designed to protect human rights raise serious questions of efficacy, to say the least? What can be done to advance new agendas of health and human rights? In concluding, we offer six suggestions, which are intended to complement ongoing efforts.

Make Health and Healing the Symbolic Core

If we make health and healing the symbolic core of a new agenda, we tap into something truly universal – concern for the sick – and, at the same time, engage medicine, public health, and the allied health professions, including the basic sciences. Put another way, we need to throw the full weight of the medical and scientific communities behind a noble cause. The growing outcome gap between the rich and the poor constitutes both a human rights violation and a means of tracking the efficacy of our interventions. In brief, reduction of the outcome gap will be the goal of our pragmatic solidarity with the destitute sick.

Make Provision of Services Central to the Agenda

We need to listen to the sick and abused and to those most likely to have their rights violated. They are not asking for new centers of study and reflection.

That means we need new programs in addition to the traditional ventures of a university or research center. We need programs designed to remediate inequalities of access to services that can help all humans lead free and healthy lives. It everyone has a right "to share in scientific advancement and its benefits," where are our pragmatic efforts to improve the spread of these advances? How can we make the rapid deployment of services to improve health—pragmatic solidarity—central to the work of health and human rights programs? Our own group, Partners In Health, has worked largely with community based organizations in Haiti, Peru, and Mexico, with the express goal to remediate inequalities of access. This community of providers and scholars believes that "the vitality of practice" lends a corrective strength to our research and writing.[44] The possibilities for programmatic collaboration range, we have learned, from Russian prison officials to peasant collectives in the autonomolous zones of Chiapas. Novel collaborations of this sort are certainly necessary if we are to address the increasing inequalities of access here in wealthy, inegalitarian countries such as the United States. Relying exclusively on nation-states' compliance with a social-justice agenda is naïve at best.

Fifteen years of work in the most difficult field conditions have taught our group that it is hard—perhaps impossible—to meet the highest standards of health care in every situation. But it is imperative that we try to do so. Projects striving for excellence and inclusiveness—rather than, say, "cost-effectiveness" or "sustainability," which are often at odds with social justice approaches to medicine and public health—are not merely misguided quests for personal efficacy. Such projects respond to widespread demands for equity in health care. The din around AIDS research in the Third World is merely the latest manifestation of a rejection of low standards as official policy. That such standards are widely seen as violating human rights is no surprise for those interested in social and economic rights. Efficiency cannot trump equity in the field of health and human rights.

Establish New Research Agendas

We need to make room in the academy for serious scholarly work on the multiple dynamics of health and human rights, on the health effects of war and political-economic disruption, and on the pathogenic effects of social inequalities, including racism, gender inequality, and the growing gap between rich and poor. By what mechanisms, precisely, do such noxious events and processes become embodied as adverse health outcomes? Why are some at risk and others spared?

We require a new level of cooperation between disciplines ranging from social anthropology to molecular epidemiology. We need a new sociology of knowledge that can pick apart a wide body of commentary, and scholarship: complex international law; the claims and disclaimers of officialdom;

postmodern relativist readings of suffering; clinical and epidemiologic studies of the long-term effects of, say, torture and racism. But remember, none of the victims of these events or processes are asking us to conduct research. For this reason alone, research in the arena of health and human rights is necessarily fraught with pitfalls:

> Imperiled populations in developing countries include extraordinarily vulnerable individuals ripped from their cultures and communities and victimized by myriad forms of abuse and violence. Public health research on violence and victimization among these groups must vigilantly guard against contributing to emotional and social harm.[45]

The fact that research is and should remain a secondary concern does not mean that careful documentation is not critical to both our understanding of suffering and our ability to prevent or allay it. And because such research would be linked to service, we need operational research by which we can gauge the efficacy of interventions quite different from those measured in the past.

Assume a Broader Educational Mandate

If the primary objective is to set things right, education is central to our task. We must not limit ourselves to teaching a select group of students with an avowed interest in health and human rights, nor must we limit ourselves to trying to teach lessons to recalcitrant governments. Jonathan Mann signaled to us the limitations of the latter approach: "Support for human rights-based action to promote health . . . at the level of declarations and speeches is welcome, and useful in some ways, but the limits of official organizational support for the call for societal transformation inherent in human rights promotion must be recognized."[46] A broader educational mandate would mean engaging students from all faculties, but also, as noted, engaging the members of these faculties. Beyond the university and various governmental bodies lies the broader public, for whom the connections between health and human rights have not even been traced. It is doubtful that the destitute sick have much to learn from us about health and human rights, but there is little doubt that, as their students, we can learn to better convey the complexity and historicity of their messages.

Achieve Independence from Governments and Bureaucracies

We need to be untrammeled by obligations to powerful states and international bureaucracies. A central irony of human rights law is that it consists largely of appeals to the perpetrators. After all, most crimes against humanity are committed by states, not by rogue factions or gangs or cults or terrorists. That makes it difficult for institutions accountable to states to take their constituents to task. None of this is to say that international organizations have little to offer to those seeking to prevent or assuage human rights abuses. Rather, we need to remember that their supposed "neutrality" comes at a great cost, and that cost is usually paid by people who are not represented by official advocates in places like New York, Geneva, Washington, London, or Tokyo. Along with the efforts of nongovernmental organizations, university- and hospital-based programs have the potential to be independent, well-designed, pragmatic, and feasible. The imprimatur of medicine and public health would afford even more weight and independence. And only a failure of imagination has led us to ignore the potential for collaboration with community-based organizations and with communities in resistance to ongoing violations of human rights.

Although we must maintain independence from powerful institutions, this is not to say that collaboration should never happen. If these institutions team up with health and human rights practitioners to facilitate the pragmatic delivery of services, substantial gains can be made. While policy reform is certainly worth striving for, and can be an extraordinary tool, we cannot necessarily rely on institutional bodies to enforce the policies they may adopt under pressure. In short, pragmatic solidarity should be our goal—and any collaborations among health professionals, human rights activists, and governing bodies should strive toward this end.

Secure More Resources for Health and Human Rights

Of course, it's easy to demand more resources, harder to produce them. But if social and economic rights are acknowledged as such, then foundations, governments, businesses, and international financial institutions—many of them now awash in resources – may be called to prioritize human rights endeavors that reflect the paradigm shift advocated here.

Regardless of where one stands on the process of globalization and its multiple engines, these processes have important implications for efforts to promote health and human rights. As states weaken, it is easy to discern an increasing role for nongovernmental institutions, including universities and medical centers. But it's also easy to discern a trap: states' withdrawal from the basic business of providing housing, education, and medical services usually means further erosion of the social and economic rights of the poor. Our independent involvement must be quite different from current trends, which have nongovernmental organizations relieving the state of its duty to provide basic services, thus becoming witting or unwitting abettors of neoliberal policies that declare every service and every thing to be for sale.

The experience of Partners In Health suggests that ambitious goals can be met even without a large springboard. Over the past decade and against a steady current of naysaying, we have channeled significant resources to the destitute sick in Haiti, Peru, Mexico, and Boston. We didn't argue that it was "cost-effective," nor did we promise that such efforts would be replicable. We argued that it was the right thing to do. It was the human rights thing to do.

Conclusion

Some of the problems born of structural violence are so large that they have paralyzed many who want to do the right thing. But we can find resources, and we can find them without sacrificing our independence and discernment. We will not do this by adopting defensive postures that are tantamount to simply managing inequality with the latest tools from economists and technocrats. Utopian ideals are the bed-rock of human rights. We must set our sights high and reject a double standard between rich and poor.

Claims that we live in an era of limited resources fail to mention that these resources happen to be less limited now than ever before in human history. Arguing that it is too expensive to treat MDRTB among prisoners in Russia sounds nothing short of ludicrous when this world contains roughly 497 billionaires.[47] Arguments against treating HIV in precisely those areas in which it exacts its greatest toll warn us that misguided notions of cost-effectiveness have already trumped equity. Arguing that nominal civil and political rights are the best we can hope for will mean that members of the healing professions will have their hands tied. In implementing a paradigm shift that focuses on solidarity with victims of structural violence, and the provision of pragmatic services to those in need, we can begin to address these large problems of inequality and human rights violations. Otherwise, we will be forced to stand by as the rights and dignity of the poor and marginalized undergo further sustained and deadly assault.

Notes

1. *Universal Declaration of Human Rights*, G.A. Res. 217 A (III), U.N. Doc. A/810 (1948): at Article 25, available at <http://www.un.org/Overview/rights.html>.
2. The Sentencing Project, "U.S. Continues to be World Leader in Rate of Incarceration," at <http://www. sentencingproject.org/news/usno1.pdf> (revised August 2001).
3. E.E. Telzak et al. "Multidrug-Resistant Tuberculosis in Patients Without HIV Infection," *N. Engl. J. Med.*, 333 (1995): 907–11; C. Mitnick et al. "Treatment Outcomes in 75 Patients with Chronic Multidrug-Resistant Tuberculosis Enrolled in Aggressive Community-Based Therapy in Urban Peru," *International Journal of Tuberculosis and Lung Disease*, 5, no. 11, suppl. 1 (2001): S156; P.E. Farmer et al. "Preliminary Results of Community-Based MDRTB Treatment in Lima, Peru," *International Journal of Tuberculosis and Lung Disease*, 2, no. 11, suppl. 2 (1998): S371; P.E. Farmer et al. "Responding to Outbreaks of MDRTB: Introducing 'DOTS-Plus,'" in L.B. Reichman and E.S. Hershfield, eds., *Tuberculosis: A Comprehensive International Approach*, 2d ed. (New York: Marcel Dekker Inc., 1999): 447–69; K. Tahao•lu et al. "The Treatment of Multidrug-Resistant Tuberculosis in Turkey," *N. Engl. J. Med.*, 345 (2001): 170–74.
4. Amnesty International, *Torture in Russia: "This Man-Made Hell"* (London: Amnesty International, 1997): at 31.

5. Dr. Natalya Vezhina, Medical Director; TB Colony 33, Mariinsk, Kemerovo, Russian Federation; interview by author (Farmer), Mariinsk, September 1998.
6. A. Alexander, "Money Isn't the Issue; It's (Still) Political Will," *TB Monitor*, 5, no. 5 (1998); 53.
7. See Farmer et al. (1998), *supra* note 3.
8. See D. Campbell, "Herskovits, Cultural Relativism and Metascience," in M. Herskovits, ed., *Cultural Relativism: Perspectives in Cultural Pluralsim* (New York: Random House, 1972): 289–315; C. Geertz, "Anti-anti-relativism," *American Anthropologist*, 86 (1984): 263–78; E. Hatch, *Culture and Morality: The Relativity of Values in Anthropology* (New York: Columbia University Press, 1983); A.D. Renteln, "Relativism and the Search for Human Rights," *American Anthropologist*, 90 (1988): 56–72; P.F. Schmidt, "Some Criticisms of Cultural Relativism," *Journal of Philosophy*, 70 (1955): 780–91.
9. *The Right to the Highest Attainable Standard of Health: General Comment 14*, United Nations, Economic and Social Council, E/C 12/2000/4 (2000), *available at* <http://www.unhchr.ch/tbs/doc.nsf/Master Frame View/40d009901358b0e2c125691500 5090be? Opendocument>.
10. See P.E. Farmer et al. "Community-Based Approaches to HIV Treatment in Resource-Poor Settings," *Lancet*, 358 (2001): 404–09.
11. H. Steiner and P. Alston, *International Human Rights in Context: Law, Politics, Morals* (New York: Oxford University Press, 1996): at *vi*.
12. A. Neier, *War Crimes: Brutality, Genocide, Terror, and the Struggle for Justice* (New York: Times Books, 1998): at 75.
13. Cited in Steiner and Alston, *supra* note 11, at 141 (emphasis in the original).
14. J.V. Millen and T.H. Holtz, "Dying for Growth, Part I: Transnational Corporations and the Health of the Poor," in J.Y. Kim et al. eds., *Dying for Growth: Global Inequality and the Health of the Poor* (Monroe, Maine: Common Courage Press, 2000): 177–223, at 185.
15. See P.E. Farmer, "Cruel and Unusual: Drug Resistant Tuberculosis as Punishment," in V. Stern and R. Jones, eds., *Sentenced to Die? The Problem of TB in Prisons in East and Central Europe and Central Asia* (London: International Centre for Prison Studies, 1999): 70–88; R.G. Wilkinson, *Unhealthy Societies: The Afflictions of Inequality* (London: Routledge, 1997); I. Kawachi et al. "Social Capital, Income Inequality, and Mortality," *American Journal of Public Health*, 87 (1997): 1491–98; A. Leclerc et al. eds., *Les Inégalités Sociales de Santé* (Paris: Editions la Découverte et Syros, 2000).
16. See M. Whitehead et al. "Setting Targets to Address Inequalities in Health," *Lancet*, 351 (1998): 1279–82.
17. P.E. Farmer, "The Significance of Haiti," in North American Congress on Latin America, ed., *Haiti: Dangerous Crossroads* (Boston: South End Press, 1995): 217–30.
18. See B. Concannon, "Beyond Complementarity: The International Criminal Court and National Prosecutions, A View from Haiti," *Columbia Human Rights Law Review*, 32, no. 1 (2000): 201–50.
19. See Oficina de Derehos Humanos del Arzobispado de Guatemala (ODHAG), *Guatemala: Nunca Más* (Guatemala: Informe del Proyecto Interdiocesano de Recuperación de la Memoria Historica, 1998).
20. See Neier, *supra* note 12, at 33.
21. See A. Neier, "What Should be Done About the Guilty?," *The New York Review of Books*, February 1, 1990, at 32–35.
22. See A. Guillermoprieto, *The Heart that Bleeds: Latin America Now* (New York: Alfred A. Knopf, 1994); N. Chomsky, *Turning the Tide: U.S. Intervention in Central America and the Struggle for Peace* (Boston: South End Press, 1985); W. LaFeber, *Inevitable Revolutions: The United States in Central America* (New York: W.W. Norton, 1984).
23. P. Bourdieu, ed., *La Misère du Monde* (Paris: Seuil, 1993): at 944.
24. See T. Asad, ed., *Anthropology and the Colonial Encounter* (London: Ithaca Press and Humanities, 1975); D. Hymes, "The Uses of Anthropology: Critical, Political, Personal," in D. Hymes, ed., *Reinventing Anthropology* (New York: Random House, 1974): 3–79; G.D. Berreman, "Bringing It All Back Home: Malaise in Anthropology," in D. Hymes, ed., *Reinventing Anthropology* (New York: Random House, 1974): 83–98.
25. See P.E. Farmer, *The Uses of Haiti* (Monroe, Maine: Common Courage Press, 1994); G. Hancock, *The Lords of Poverty: The Power, Prestige, and Corruption of the International Aid Business* (New York: Atlantic Monthly Press, 1989).

26. See I. Wallerstein, "The Insurmountable Contradictions of Liberalism: Human Rights and the Rights of Peoples in the Geoculture of the Modern World-System," *South Atlantic Quarterly*, 46 (1995): 1161–78.

27. T. Quinn et al. "Viral Load and Heterosexual Transmission of Human Immunodeficiency Virus Type 1," *N. Engl. J. Med.*, 342 (2000): 921–29; M.S. Cohen, "Preventing Sexual Transmission of HIV — New Ideas from Sub-Saharan Africa," *N. Engl. J. Med.*, 342 (2000): 970–72; M. Angell, "Investigators' Responsibilities for Human Subjects in Developing Countries," *N. Engl. J. Med.*, 342 (2000): 967–69; D. Greco, "The Ethics of Research in Developing Countries," *N. Engl. J. Med.*, 343 (2000): 362.

28. P.E. Farmer, *AIDS and Accusation: Haiti and the Geography of Blame* (Berkeley: University of California Press, 1992).

29. See Steiner and Alston, *supra* note 11, at 1110.

30. L. Harrison, "Voodoo Politics," *The Atlantic Monthly*, 271, no. 6 (1993): 101–08.

31. Haitian proverb.

32. S. Marcos and the Zapatista Army of National Liberation, *Shadows of Tender Fury: The Letters and Communiqués of Subcomandante Marcos and the Zapatista Army of National Liberation* (New York: Monthly Review Press, 1995): at 54.

33. Physicians for Human Rights, *Health Care Held Hostage: Human Rights Violations and Violations of Medical Neutrality in Chiapas, Mexico* (Boston: Physicians for Human Rights, 1999): at 4.

34. See Concannon, *supra* note 18.

35. M. Danner, "The Truth of El Mozote," *The New Yorker* (December 6, 1993): 50–133, at 132. Danner quotes from the Truth Commission's report, *From Madness to Hope: The Twelve-Year War in El Salvador* (New York: United Nations, 1993).

36. See Physicians for Human Rights, *supra* note 33, at 4.

37. R.L.K. Virchow, *Die Einheitsrebungen in der Wissenschaftlichen Medicin* (Berlin: Druck und Verlag von G. Reimer, 1849); L. Eisenberg, "Rudolf Ludwig Karl Virchow, Where Are You Now That We Need You?," *American Journal of Medicine*, 77 (1984): 524–32.

38. J. Mann and D. Tarantola, "Responding to HIV/AIDS: A Historical Perspective," *Health and Human Rights*, 2, no. 4 (1998): 5–8, at 8.

39. Ivan Nikitovich Simonov, Chief Inspector of Prisons (now with the Chief Board of Punishment Execution), Ministry of Internal Affairs, Russian Federation; interview by author (Farmer), Moscow, June 4, 1998.

40. L. Henkin, *International Law: Politics, Values and Functions: General Course on Public International Law* (Boston: M. Nijhoff Publishers, 1990): at 208.

41. See O. Schachter, *International Law in Theory and Practice* (Boston: M. Nijhoff Publishers, 1991): at 6.

42. See Neier, *supra* note 12, at xiii.

43. See Steiner and Alston, *supra* note 11, at viii.

44. See P.E. Farmer, *Infections and Inequalities: The Modern Plagues* (Berkeley: University of California Press, 1999): at 18.

45. R. Neugebauer, "Research on Violence in Developing Countries: Benefits and Perils," *American Journal of Public Health*, 89, no. 10 (1999): 1473–74, at 1474.

46. J. Mann, "AIDS and Human Rights: Where Do We Go From Here?," *Health and Human Rights*, 3, no. 1 (1998): 143–49, at 145–46.

47. L. Kroll and L. Goldman, "The World's Billionaires" (February 28, 2002), at <http://www.forbes.com/home/2002/02/28/billionaires.html>.

5

Human Rights in Development
The Significance for Health

Stephen P. Marks

While human rights, health, and human development have emerged in the final decades of the twentieth century as significant international concerns, they have generally advanced on parallel and non-intersecting tracks. The purpose of this chapter is to explore their intersection and, in particular, the ways in which the theory and practice of human rights in development can advance health.

At the conceptual level, health, human rights, and development have all been defined in similar abstract terms relating to the betterment of the human condition. The World Health Organization (WHO) defines *health* as "a state of complete physical, mental and social well-being and not merely the absence of disease or infirmity."[1] Such a broad definition—which some consider too broad to be meaningful[2]—embraces virtually the same content as development and human rights. *Human rights* are about creating conditions in which people can develop their full potential and lead creative lives by assuring "the dignity and worth of the human person" and promoting "social progress and better standards of life in larger freedom," in the words of the Universal Declaration of Human Rights.[3] The United Nations Development Programme (UNDP) explains that *human development* is "about creating an environment in which people can develop their full potential and lead productive, creative lives in accord with their needs and interests [and is] thus about expanding the choices people have to lead lives that they value."[4] The goals of health concentrate on the requirements of physical, mental, and social dimensions of human existence; development goals tend to focus on the material conditions and distributional arrangements that allow people to benefit from economic processes in ways

95

that improve their condition; and human rights goals tend to deal with normative constraints on power relations to ensure human dignity and the elimination of repressive and oppressive processes. Thus, health, development, and human rights have in common human well-being—or, as philosophers would say, the "good life"—but approaches this meta-goal through human existence, economic processes, and normative constraints, respectively.

The relationship among health, development, and human rights will be explored here through three theoretical rationales for introducing human rights into development and three strategies for action in development practice. Each of these rationales and strategies offers a way of understanding how human rights and development contribute to health.

Rationales for a Human Rights Framework in Development

At the theoretical level, the introduction of human rights into development can be justified in various ways. Three such rationales—namely, social justice, capabilities, and responsibilities—will be explored here. They are by no means the only bases but are discussed here to illustrate the significance for health of human rights in development.

Social Justice

Many in the public health field attach primary importance to eliminating social disparities and inequalities in access to health, the moral justification of which is often expressed in terms of social justice. Human rights sometimes become a surrogate for social justice, the assumption being that what contributes to social justice in the context of development is also a contribution to human rights.

Tomas Pogge understands social justice as the justice of social institutions or a criterion "which assesses the degree to which the institutions of a social system are treating the persons and groups they affect in a morally appropriate and, in particular, even-handed way."[5] He explains the relation between social justice and human rights in this way: "A complex and internationally acceptable core criterion of basic justice might best be formulated, I believe, in the language of human rights [understood] primarily as claims on coercive social institutions and secondarily as claims against those who uphold such institutions."[6]

Paul Farmer, coming from public health and social medicine, is another voice for social justice who uses human rights as a privileged normative instrument. Drawing on the insights of liberation theology, which "argues that genuine change will be most often rooted in small communities of poor people,"[7] he uses the methodology "observe, judge, act" to challenge unjust structures and to understand how a social justice approach can be used to address disease and suffering. He explains, "For me, applying an option for the poor has never implied advancing a particular strategy for a national economy. It does not imply preferring one form of development, or social system, over another . . . A truly committed quest for high-quality care for the destitute sick starts from the perspective that health is a fundamental human right."[8] He is critical of "liberal" development theory and practice based on ideas of reformism that seek to bring the technological advances of modernity to the poor ("developmentalism"). He warns, "As international health experts come under the sway of the bankers and their curiously bounded utilitarianism, we can expect more and more of our services to be declared 'cost-ineffective' and more of our patients to be erased. In declaring health and health care to be a human right, we join forces with those who have long labored to protect the rights and dignity of the poor."[9]

Social justice captures an important feature of the human rights framework for development, namely, the emphasis on the moral imperative to eliminate glaring social inequality within societies and structurally imbedded patterns of international support for those inequalities.[10] Since the Universal Declaration of Human Rights affirmed that everyone has the right to "a social and international order in which the rights and freedoms set forth in this Declaration can be fully realized," that imperative is part of human rights discourse. However, the human rights framework goes beyond a commitment to social justice in that it supports other dimensions of a life people value that are not focused exclusively on reducing the suffering of the poor. It is also different from social justice insofar as it does not rely on a subjective sense of outrage at the suffering of the poor and excluded within society—however admirable such sentiments may be—but rather on a set of agreed upon standards that limit what governments can do that would contribute to social injustice and defines what they must do to redress such injustice. Applied to health, the human rights framework goes beyond the commitment to the "destitute sick" or to eliminating health inequalities. It embraces the full range of normative prescriptions of the right to health and related rights, the realization of which implies the achievement of social justice. In many ways, social justice suggests a *general* commitment to eliminating inequality and poverty, while human rights define the *specific* norms to achieve that result.

Capabilities

A second theoretical basis for human rights in development is the capabilities approach as articulated by the Nobel Prize–winning economist Amartya Sen and the philosopher and jurist Martha Nussbaum. In his chapter entitled "Poverty as Capability Deprivation" in *Development as Freedom*,[11] Sen argues that development is not the acquisition of more goods and services but the enhanced freedom to choose, the freedom to lead the kind of life one values. These enhanced choices are called capabilities.[12] Poverty, he explains, is the deprivation of basic capabilities, and he urges that attention be focused on aspects of life other than income to understand what poverty is and how to respond to it in places like South Asia and sub-Saharan Africa, where extreme poverty is concentrated. These two regions "stand out as the regions where short and precarious lives [measured in terms of life expectancy] are concentrated in the contemporary world."[13] He uses three focal features of deprivation of basic capability—premature mortality, undernourishment, and illiteracy—to compare and contrast these two regions, although he is the first to admit that these indicators do not "provide a comprehensive picture of capability-poverty in these regions."[14] In the capabilities discourse, "capability" is the option available to the individual to partake of some valued dimension of life; "functioning" is the exercise of that option.[15]

Public policy tends to focus on functionings, like food consumption or health care delivery, for example. Sen and Nussbaum propose that public policy should instead focus on capabilities. Capabilities in relation to food refer to the conditions that make it possible for a farmer to produce adequate food, for a worker to purchase it, and for the entire population to have adequate nourishment. Similarly, health is the capability of leading a healthy life in terms of accessibility, affordability, and appropriateness and quality of care, as defined in the General Comment on the Right to Health,[16] as well as other human rights considered as "integral components of the right to health."[17] This focus on capabilities also underscores the "common vision" and mutually reinforcing nature of human development and human rights, in that both seek human freedom, that is, the freedom of people "to exercise their choices and to participate in decision-making that affects their lives."[18]

Duties and Responsibilities

A third theoretical rationale for human rights in development relates to duties and responsibilities. Specifically, development discourse frequently stresses "duties" of individuals to contribute to development, "obligations" of governments to eliminate corruption and waste, and "responsibilities" of the international community to aid developing countries to reach their development objectives. Some assert that duties to the community are the essence of the role of the individual in society and that such duties should prevail over any attempts by individuals to use human rights to challenge the cultural foundations of society, presumed to be based on duties, or the decisions of leaders, presumed to be based on wisdom.

Understanding the legitimate role that duties and responsibilities have in the realization of human rights is essential to understanding the relevance of human rights to development. There are three types of duties under international human rights standards that establish direct and indirect responsibilities.[19] First is the general proposition that for every right there is a corresponding duty of the state or other duty-holder. The second is the social contractarian concept of duties owed by every individual to the community in exchange for the individual freedoms and security protected by society. The third is the recognition in the major international human rights texts that legitimate limitations on and derogations from certain rights may be made in certain circumstances, thus tempering the absolute character of those rights by the constraints of governance.

The difficulty with the *correlation of rights and duties* lies in the notion that human rights, such as the right to health, are only rights properly speaking if they involve "perfect obligations" of an identified duty-holder to perform a specific act or abstain from certain acts vis-à-vis an identified right-holder, as in the performance of a contract or in not committing an assault. However, the realization of the right to health involves many obligations that are not "perfect" in this sense, especially considering that it is subject to progressive implementation as set out in the International Covenant on Economic, Social and Cultural Rights (ICESCR). The right to health does not imply that anyone has the right to be healthy or that the state must provide the most advanced health care to everyone who is sick or injured. It does imply a set of state obligations to maximize health outcomes over time through the best combination of state, community-based, and private health services.

These imperfect obligations are nonetheless legal and not just moral. In an essay introducing a "rights-inclusive consequentialism," Sen asks, "Why insist on the absolute necessity of co-specified perfect obligation for a putative right to qualify as a real right? Certainly, a perfect obligation would help a great deal toward the realization of rights, but why cannot there be *unrealized* rights, even rights that are hard to realize?"[20] He answers by explaining that he "would resist the claim that any use of rights except with co-linked perfect obligations must lack cogency. . . . Human rights are seen as rights shared by all—irrespective of citizenship—and the benefits of which everyone *should* have. The claims are addressed generally . . . to anyone who can help. Even though no particular person or agency has been charged with bringing about the fulfillment of the rights involved, they can still be very influential."[21] Indeed, the language of the main human rights treaties does not lack cogency because it refers, as in Article 2 of the ICESCR, to the obligation of states parties "to take steps, individually and through international assistance and co-operation . . . to the maximum of its available resources, with a view to achieving progressively the full realization of the rights recognized in the present Covenant by all appropriate means, including particularly the adoption of legislative measures." That text is a catalogue of imperfect obligations and nevertheless establishes duties to specify, without undue delay, what steps will be taken, and when; what forms of assistance will be sought and from whom; what resources will be allocated; and at what pace the right will be progressively realized. The general comments adopted by the various treaty bodies have sought to clarify these "imperfect obligations of others to help in a general way" not only by providing guidelines on specific steps but by outlining distinctions between obligations to respect, protect, and fulfill, sometimes subdividing the latter into obligations to facilitate, to promote, and to provide.[22]

The second type of duty concerns the *duties individuals have to others and to the community.* As the Universal Declaration of Human Rights recalled in 1948, "Everyone has duties to the community in which alone the free and full development of his personality is possible." More elaborate versions of this principle were inserted into the major UN human rights instruments,[23] as well as in the regional human rights treaties.[24] To these general human rights texts should be added a set of specific duties defined in normative instruments applying to certain professions, including health. The World Medical Association adopted the Declaration of Helsinki to guide doctors and other participants in medical research involving human subjects, including research on identifiable human material or identifiable data.[25] Physicians are thus duty-bound to give priority to the health of their patients in such research. The UN has also adopted Principles of Medical Ethics relevant to the Role of Health Personnel, particularly Physicians, in the Protection of Prisoners and Detainees against Torture and Other Cruel, Inhuman or Degrading Treatment or Punishment.[26] The core principle of this document is that "Health personnel, particularly physicians, charged with the medical care of prisoners and detainees have a duty to provide them with protection of their physical and mental health and treatment of disease of the same quality and standard as is afforded to those who are not imprisoned or detained." International documents have defined duties for other professions, in particular law enforcement officials, the judiciary, lawyers, prosecutors, and other professions involved in the administration of justice.[27]

The third type of duty recognized in international human rights law is the *duty to exercise rights responsibly.* Human rights texts regularly contain *derogation* and *limitation clauses* that allow the state to restrict the enjoyment of certain rights in order to ensure that they are exercised responsibly, such as restrictions on freedom of movement and residence under emergency health measures designed to halt the spread of an epidemic. The principal general text on this principle is Article 29(2) of the Universal Declaration, which reads: "In the exercise of his rights and freedoms, everyone shall be subject only to such limitations as are determined by law solely for the purpose of securing due recognition and respect for the rights and freedoms of others and of meeting the just requirements of morality, public order, and the general welfare in a democratic society." Such limitation clauses are contained in the International Covenant on Civil and Political Rights (ICCPR) with respect to six rights[28] to allow the rights in question to be limited as long as they are prescribed by law and necessary in a democratic society to protect public order, public health, public morals, national security, public safety, or the rights and freedoms of others. The ICCPR and regional human rights treaties also allow states to derogate from certain rights in time of public emergency threatening the life of the nation.

Because duties are often cited as critical to furthering development and sometimes as incompatible with human rights and even with public health, it is important to keep the human rights perspective in mind when considering the various duties and obligations relating to development and, in particular, to development goals in the field of health. The above reflections show that the right to health often involves imperfect obligations of the state; that human rights standards include specific duties of health professionals; and that needs of health policy are usually accommodated by, rather than clash with, the human rights framework. These theoretical perspectives have implications for the strategies of applying that framework to health problems in the context of development.

Strategies for Promoting Health Through Human Rights in Development

Numerous strategies are aimed at improving health outcomes through the application of human rights in the development context. Three strategies will be discussed here. The first is the so-called "human rights-based approach to development," which has become common to bilateral and multilateral development agencies. The second is the right to development, which has broad but not unanimous political support and little application in practice. The third is human rights education, which is a community-based approach to empowering people to advance social change.

The Human Rights-Based Approach to Development

Perhaps the most frequent linking of human rights and human development in policy has been the so-called "rights-based" approach to development, affirming that development should be pursued in a "human rights way" or that human rights must "be integrated into sustainable human development." The "rights way to development" is the shorthand expression for "the human rights approach to development assistance," as articulated by, among others, André Frankovits of the Human Rights Council of Australia. The essential definition of this approach is "that a body of international human rights law is the only agreed international framework which offers a coherent body of principles and practical meaning for development cooperation, [which] provides a comprehensive guide for appropriate official development assistance, for the manner in which it should be delivered, for the priorities that it should address, for the obligations of both donor and recipient governments and for the way that official development assistance is evaluated."[29]

Julia Häusermann, writing for the Department for International Development of the United Kingdom, defined the human rights approach to development as one that "puts people first and promotes human-centered development, recognizes the inherent dignity of every human being without distinction, recognizes and promotes equality between women and men, promotes equal opportunity and choices for all, . . . promotes national and international systems based on economic equity, equity in the access to public resources, and social justice, and promotes mutual respect between people . . ."[30] She uses the example of health to demonstrate how the human rights approach addresses the structural causes of poverty: "Economic and social inequalities and inequities are observable through differential health status. Poor health frequently reflects poverty and social marginalization. In turn, poor health exacerbates impoverishment and disadvantage. Health status indicators...are thus frequently an indication of the denial of the human rights that are so vital for survival and development in dignity."[31] Frankovits and Häusermann are typical of NGO advocates for a human rights-based approach.[32]

The human rights-based approach to development has become policy of the principal human rights office of the UN and has been adopted by several UN development agencies.[33] The Office of the High Commissioner for Human Rights uses the expression "rights-based approach to development," which it defines as follows:

> A rights-based approach to development is a conceptual framework for the process of human development that is normatively based on international human rights standards and operationally directed to promoting and protecting human rights.
>
> Essentially, a rights-based approach integrates the norms, standards and principles of the international human rights system into the plans, policies and processes of development.
>
> The norms and standards are those contained in the wealth of international treaties and declarations. The principles include equality and equity, accountability, empowerment and participation. A rights-based approach to development includes the following elements:
> • Express linkage to rights
> • Accountability
> • Empowerment
> • Participation
> • Non-discrimination and attention to vulnerable groups[34]

UNDP, for its part, also uses a "human rights approach to development," which it defines as a new approach that "focuses on the realization of human rights through human development rather than through a violations policy, and finds resonance in the majority of human rights covenants, declarations and treaties." However, UNDP explains, "the successful implementation of this strategy depends on the ability of countries to progressively and systematically mainstream human rights concerns into national legislation and governance programmes, and base them on human development goals."[35]

The growing trend among scholars, development NGOs, and international institutions to use the human rights-based approach to development both integrates concepts that already had currency in development theory—such as accountability and transparency in the context of good governance—and adds a dimension with which development practitioners were less familiar—especially the explicit reference to government obligations deriving from international human rights law and procedures.

For the practitioner in the field of public health, several steps may be taken to move from human rights theory to development practice, beginning with the following elements of a rights-based approach:

1. ***Define socioeconomic issues in terms of rights.*** Issues of health, education, food, shelter, labor, vulnerability, marginalization, equity, gender, and similar matters are constant concerns of the development practitioner. The ICESCR and other human rights treaties have formulated them all in normative terms. The challenge is to learn the similarities and differences in the understanding of these issues in the context of development planning and implementation, on the one hand, and human rights, on the other. For example, the typical public health approach to improving health outcomes would be enhanced by introducing policies that simultaneously optimize human rights protections, such as non-discrimination and respect for privacy.

2. ***Use the General Comments issued by the treaty bodies.*** The treaty monitoring committees, especially the Committee on Economic, Social and Cultural Rights, have issued thoughtful interpretations of the content of specific rights, with examples of what they expect States parties to do to fulfill their obligations with respect to those rights.[36] The public health practitioner would benefit from a careful reading of General Comment 14 on the right to health and other General Comments of direct relevance to health, such as General Comments 18, 19, and 24 of the Committee on the Elimination of Discrimination Against Women,[37] or General Comment 3 of the Committee on the Rights of the Child.[38] It is especially important to reflect on the concept of "core minimum obligations."[39]

3. ***Refer to treaty obligations of the main human rights treaties.*** The six main human rights treaties contain commitments that States parties have made in areas directly affecting development. It is appropriate—and even mandated by the Memorandum of Understanding between the High Commissioner for Human Rights and the Administrator in the case of UNDP—to draw on these obligations in discussion with governments regarding their development plans and priorities. One need not consider

it too political or controversial, for example, to draw a government's attention to a project that acquiesces to, or results in some form of, discrimination in access to health care. In that case, explicit reference to that government's obligations under human rights treaties should be part of the discussion.

4. ***Focus on obligations to respect, protect, and fulfill.*** The General Comments have tended in recent years to focus on these different types of obligations implied by governmental agreement to realize fully the treaty rights. It is sometimes useful to make a table indicating what the state should do to respect, to protect, and fulfill (promote, facilitate, and provide for each issue or sub-issue, for example by indicating government obligations with respect to children infected with HIV, affected by HIV/AIDS, and vulnerable to HIV/AIDS).[40]

5. ***Apply the participatory method.*** Participation is part of most development strategies. The human rights framework enhances this dimension of development and surrounds it with certain guarantees, such as freedom of association and expression, the right to information, and protection from arbitrary treatment of persons who express critical views. The Declaration on Human Rights Defenders, the resolutions on the UN Decade for Human Rights Education, and the Declaration on the Right to Development provide useful reference points for advocating participation.

In addition to these five elements of a human rights approach, development practitioners need to be conscious of two aspects of this approach that often create confusion if not controversy, namely, reference to human rights violations and reference to indicators. Many development professionals tend to shy away from human rights because it conjures up a confrontational "naming and shaming" approach used by organizations like Amnesty International and Human Rights Watch. While these organizations do use pressure on states by calling attention to their shortcomings, human rights advocacy is not at all limited to that mode of interaction. The cooperative mode, often readily observed in the practice of the treaty monitoring bodies, offers ample opportunity for both foreign development partners (bilateral and multilateral) and domestic civil society organizations to interact productively with ministerial officials and other government agents of development. Explanations, information, indications of best practices, and the like are often more effective than threats of publicity or prosecution. Understanding the nature of government responsibilities, as well as those of individuals and non-state actors, is essential to knowing when and how to shift from the cooperation to the accountability mode. For example, ministries of health often welcome discussion with and support from development partners to apply human rights towards the achievement of better health outcomes and, with such ministries, it would be counter-productive to argue that the public health officers are responsible for "violations" of the right to health.

With respect to indicators, development practitioners often assume that the development indicators with which they are familiar provide the best answer to whether rights to education, health, food, and the like are being fulfilled. There are serious methodological problems with this assumption, and there are no easy answers. Sometimes some typical development indicators are relevant; other times they are not relevant, or only partially so. These methodological problems have been discussed in the literature[41] and by the United Nations Development Programme.[42] The development practitioner needs to understand the limitations of indicators and to contribute to the ongoing discussion within the agencies and the treaty monitoring bodies on how this situation can be improved.

A critical moment in applying the human rights approach to development is the discussions within the Ministry of Health and the Planning Commission or its equivalent. This approach may be completely new to the partners with which the practitioner is used to working. It may be contrary to expectations of bilateral donors, international financial institutions (IFIs), and other funding partners who continue planning that excludes the human rights approach. It should also be noted that the Common Country Assessment (CCA) and UN Development Assistance Framework (UNDAF) guidelines may be inadequate in terms of references to key human rights texts. These guidelines have been improved, but more work is needed for the systematic integration of human rights into the analysis. The same is true for the Poverty Reduction Strategy Papers (PRSPs), about which a team of experts has produced human rights guidelines published by the High Commissioner's Office.[43]

It is equally important to monitor implementation of development projects for compliance with the human rights criteria identified during the planning phase and to correct unanticipated human rights problems that may arise. This vigilance requires sensitivity to local government inexperience with the human rights approach and the involvement of civil society. Many bilateral donors have explicit mandates for human rights in development. Their experience can be valuable in developing the skills needed for human rights monitoring of development projects. Some UN agencies are slower than UNDP in integrating human rights into development, especially the international financial institutions (IFIs) and the specialized agencies. WHO has developed policies and issued papers on health and human rights but has not yet made the human rights framework a systematic reference point for its development practice. More could be done to work with agencies like WHO to provide monitoring and to develop progressively the habits that both reflect and generate a common commitment to the official policy, which comes with experience with integrating human rights into human development across the UN system.

The human rights approach to development requires attention to the habits of local NGOs and other elements of civil society. They may engage in or acquiesce to traditional practices harmful to health (such as female genital cutting) or contrary to equity (such as ethnic or gender discrimination). The development practitioner should identify the human rights constituency within the civil society that can take the lead in dealing with traditional practices. Most intractable among these is entrenched corruption in government and civil society, which runs directly counter to attention to equity concerns and participatory aspects of the human rights approach. Certain types of human rights work, such as working with civil society groups, especially women, to facilitate a bottom-up approach to the elimination of harmful traditional practices, requires a high degree of cultural sensitivity.

The Right to Development

A second strategy for applying human rights in development is to consider development itself as a human right. In the early 1970s the right to development was publicly proposed as a human right,[44] and the UN General Assembly proclaimed development as a human right in its 1986 Declaration on the Right to Development.[45] The United States cast the only negative vote; eight other countries abstained. A considerable body of commentary has appeared in support of the declaration, mainly in legal and human rights publications,[46] but critical and skeptical views have also emerged in legal and political writings.[47] The challenge from the beginning has been to translate the hopeful but ambiguous language of the Declaration on the Right to Development into concepts that are meaningful to economists and useful to the rethinking of the development process. It is unfortunate indeed that after thirty years of scholarly writing and diplomatic efforts to propose ways of implementing the right to development, and almost 20 years after the Declaration was adopted, the debate remains polarized and confused. On the positive side, one thing is clear today: any claim that development takes priority over respect for human rights, and that the realization of human rights must await a certain level of development, is contrary to the principle that all human rights, including civil and political rights, must be respected in development planning and implementation.[48] It is less well understood that the Declaration precludes states from determining whatever development policy suits them. In fact, the Declaration establishes the duty of states "to formulate appropriate national development policies that aim at the constant improvement of the well-being of the entire population and of all individuals, on the basis of their active, free and meaningful participation in development and the fair distribution of the benefits resulting therefrom."[49] The right to development thus implies that development policies should be revised to meet the human-centered and participatory elements of the definition contained in the Declaration. The UN Independent Expert on the Right to Development, Arjun Sengupta, has stressed that development is a process in which developing countries integrate human rights, and development partners (donor governments, international financial and trade institutions, and Specialized Agencies) provide enhanced resources to assist them in this effort.[50] The World Bank, the IMF, UNCTAD, ILO, UNDP, UNESCO, and several donor governments have expressed interest in participating in such a new approach to implementing the right to development.

Little attention has been given to identifying the extent to which the concept of the right to development and a human rights–based approach to development overlap or differ. Expressed simply, the right to development is broader than the human rights–based approach, encompassing a critical examination of the overall development process, including planning, participation, allocation of resources, and priorities in international development cooperation. The human rights–based approach to development is part of the right to development, but it may also involve isolating a particular issue, such as health, and applying to that issue a clear understanding of the state's obligations under the relevant international human rights instruments and the insights applicable to project implementation derived from authorized interpretations of those obligations, such as General Comment 14. Thus, the right to development implies both a critical review of the development process in a given country and a program of action to integrate a human rights approach within all aspects of that process.

The right to development has at least three advantages for the promotion of health in the context of development. First, it is a concept that developing countries have enthusiastically supported as one of the highest priorities in human rights and that donor countries are beginning to include in their aid policies. Therefore, invoking it should be a politically acceptable means of advocating the allocation of increased resources for health. Second, it provides further justification for focusing on the human rights implications of health policy in light of the obligations of the ICESCR and other human rights treaty provisions on the right to health. Third, the right to development offers a means of drawing attention to the ways that many human rights, besides the right to health, in both the categories of civil and political right and of economic, social and cultural rights, contribute to health outcomes, since the right to development implies that governments integrate all human rights into development.

These advantages are only useful to the extent that the right becomes part of government policy. However, as the Independent Expert noted, this has not happened "because appropriate policies for realizing the right to development have rarely been adopted."[51] He recommends remedying this situation by coordinating national policies in such a way that specific rights to food, health, etc., can be part of policies aimed at sustainable and participatory development.[52]

The absence of clear national and international policies is a sign that the commitment to this right is essentially rhetorical and that governments and intergovernmental organizations do not genuinely expect their support for the concept to have consequences. To the extent that countries change their policies, as recommended by the Independent Expert and the Commission on Human Rights, health goals can be advanced by the right to development. The political will to do so is further supported by the commitment of the Millennium Summit "to making the right to development a reality for everyone and to freeing the entire human race from want."[53]

Human Rights Education

A third approach to including human rights in the practice of development is that of human rights education (HRE). As understood here, HRE is close to the concept of community-based development work or participatory action research (PAR). The essence of these ideas is that the most effective means of enhancing people's capabilities is to facilitate their own social transformation through participation in the decisions that affect their development.

When the United Nations General Assembly proclaimed the UN Decade for Human Rights Education (1995–2004) in 1994, it stated that human rights education was "more than providing information." It should be understood, rather, "as a comprehensive lifelong process by which people at all levels of development and in all strata of society learn respect for the dignity of others and the means and methods of ensuring that respect within a democratic society."[54] Government acceptance of HRE is further reflected in the Declaration on Human Rights Defenders, which was adopted on the occasion of the fiftieth anniversary of the Universal Declaration of Human Rights.[55] That Declaration covers human rights training and education, including the duty to facilitate human rights education at all levels of schooling, and in particular in the training of lawyers, law enforcement officials, members of armed forces, and public officials.[56] The Declaration recalls various human rights treaties establishing the duty of States parties to adopt measures to promote human rights through teaching, education, and training; to ensure the widespread dissemination of information about national and international human rights laws; to report to UN treaty bodies; and to encourage states to support the establishment of independent human rights institutions, such as human rights commissions and ombudspersons. These are useful commitments on which development practitioners can build when working with governments on integrating the HRE approach into their human rights agenda.

The most salient feature of HRE is the concept and practice of a transformative pedagogy of human rights, which holds the potential for altering the power structure behind most forms of oppression and repression. Indeed, it is based on the assumption that the space for abuse of public trust, violence against the physical and mental integrity of others, and exploitation of the vulnerable will contract if people everywhere commit to building a political culture based on the right and responsibility of everyone to respect, ensure, and fulfill human rights for all. Clarence Dias has listed five ways HRE contributes to development: by helping monitor development activities; by mobilizing support for victims' struggles for rehabilitation, redress, and justice; by promoting understanding of the rationale for development; by securing more effective participation in the development process; and by securing accountability for those responsible for misuse of public resources.[57] Each of these ways holds considerable potential for health promotion. For example, part of the response to communal violence is to mobilize support for rehabilitation through treatment of the physical and mental health consequences of violence. Participation of health workers and those served by the health system in setting the priorities for development projects in the health sector is another example.

Human rights education, as defined here, is promoted by NGOs such as the People's Movement for Human Rights Education[58] and Human Rights Education Associates,[59] and has been adopted in part by the Office of the High Commission for Human Rights[60] and by the World Health Organization in the area of reproductive health and rights.[61] Moreover, support by international agencies like UNDP for international and local NGO projects based on such an approach is consistent with the resolutions and plan of action of the UN Decade for Human Rights Education, which governments have accepted. Extensive information is available on the various approaches to conducting HRE activities in a wide range of settings[62] and on resources and contacts.[63]

The basic precepts of HRE give content to the participation concept in development. In practical terms, HRE as a development strategy focuses on non-formal human rights education in which the human rights educator's role is that of "facilitator" rather than "teacher." More specifically, it is "goal-oriented non-formal education," that is, organized, systematic educational activity outside the school system that is designed to reach any of the following six goals:[64]

- Enhance knowledge
- Develop critical understanding
- Clarify values
- Change attitudes
- Promote solidarity
- Alter behavior or practice

When all six are met, the most important goal can be achieved: *empowerment*, which Richard Claude defines as "a process through which people and/or communities increase their control or mastery over their own lives and the decisions that affect their lives."[65] A constant concern of the human rights educator is to make the learners aware of their right to know their rights and especially their right to claim them. It is in this sense that we refer to human rights education as transforming beggars into claimants, that is, shifting from development as charity to development as the realization of capabilities. It is therefore essential that HRE apply "participatory methodologies" to provide an experiential foundation for learning. The learning process, according to this methodology, is not memorization of information communicated by the instructor, but an experience through which learners acquire understanding by doing, that is, by "experiential" or "hands-on" learning. It is democratic as opposed to traditional methodologies in which the educated elite tend to dominate, thus maintaining social hierarchies. In experiential work, there exists a leveling mechanism, which assures greater democratic participation. Finally, experiential methods are open-ended. While the facilitator may have a predetermined goal, the exercises emphasize process; therefore, the participants determine the practice to a great extent.

The principles of HRE can be applied in the context of development in a six-step strategy of community-based HRE. In enumerating these steps below, an example is provided of an actual health-related intervention launched in 2001 by the Legal Resources Center (LRC) in Ghana, an NGO located in Nima, a sprawling enclave of very low income rural migrants near the center of Accra.[66] LRC leadership was quite familiar with the HRE model and developed the strategy for its health and sanitation project based on its capacity to bring the critical perspective of the local community to people placed at high levels of political, administrative, and bureaucratic responsibility. As explained by the project director, Raymond Atuguba, "through this we hoped to draw them into a . . . localized space for learning . . . mediated and facilitated by grass roots level operatives. The synergies and learning thereby produced would then be harnessed for broader reforms . . ."[67] The stages LRC followed correspond roughly to the six steps in the HRE model, although they overlap in practice rather than following a strict sequence.

1. *The group, after leaning to work democratically, engages in its own analysis of their situation of human rights deprivation.* In the LRC example, the research team, with participation of the local population, compiled information on individuals affected by the failure of the local health care providers to respect the exemption from user fees for the poor population. Its legal team surveyed 161 households and convened fifteen grassroots workshops. They also gathered testimony from community residents about health impacts of inadequate sanitation.

2. *The group begins to develop a strategy to change that situation.* In the LRC case, the users mobilized to challenge the hospital that required fees from the poor, bringing health providers together to discuss steps how the user-fee exemptions could be effectively enforced. The team presented

at a public hearing and community workshops a list of eight administrative practices to be followed.

3. *The facilitator provides information on relevant human rights means and methods that appear relevant to the strategy chosen by the participants.* In Ghana, the team used the human rights provisions of the constitution and international law on the right to health to plan interventions to challenge the government's failure to enforce the exemption law. Community-based groups mobilized to monitor the local government's compliance with its obligations to provide toilets, garbage collection, and sanitation services.

4. *The group, with the facilitator's help if needed, implements first phase of action plan to change reality.* LRC filed a lawsuit in September 2001 with the Ghana High Court. They also educated community-based "mothers' groups" about their right to user-fee exemptions and organized meetings with community leaders to strategize on how to challenge the government's failure to provide adequate sanitation.

5. *The group assesses the impact of its action and moves to higher level of intervention, dealing with structures of oppression and repression.* In the Ghana case, persons detained for not paying the fee were released notwithstanding the absence of a final judgment by the court. This experience allowed LRC to document the functioning of the fee system and the government policy vis-à-vis the World Bank. LRC reported on its efforts on health-financing and sanitation to public hearings of the community, attended by representatives of the Ghanaian and donor governments. Community residents gave public testimony and were invited to participate in the campaigns to protect and advance their right to health.

6. *The group carries out higher-level intervention and evaluates the results with a view to enlarging the process of claiming human rights.* In Ghana, LRC, sent a memorandum to the World Bank challenging the Bank's report on the implementation of Ghana's exemption law and recommending monitoring loans to Ghana's health sector to ensure better enforcement of the exemption law, and also sent a repot the World Bank's Inspection Panel. LRC also worked with the parliamentary standing Committee on Health to ensure funding and equitably administration of the user-fee exemption. Finally, it sent a report to the African Commission on Human and People's Rights. For the sanitation component of the project, LRC sent a letter to the Accra Metropolitan Assembly demanding compliance with environmental health and sanitation regulations. The project has continued its advocacy with Parliament and the Ministry of Health, its training of Mothers' Clubs and other community-based organizations and research and consultation with local opinion leaders about strategies for community participation in a health insurance program.

The HRE approach can take many forms, from small-group community task forces to the creation of human rights cities or communities. The concept of human rights communities, as promoted by PDHRE, is based on the idea of members of a community accepting human rights obligations in all aspects of community life, whether in the family (for example, agreeing to respect the rights of women and children as defined in CEDAW and CRC regardless of contrary traditional practices), in professional life (for example, judges agreeing to apply national and international human rights law in their courts), or as citizens (for example, reviewing local authority use of financial resources).

The principal effort to apply this approach to HRE systematically is through "sustainable human rights cities." These communities are selected on the basis of a demonstrated commitment to human rights among civil society and local authorities, as well as the willingness of all to apply the expansive definition of human rights learning as a tool for political, economic, and social change. The process of creating a human rights city usually involves representative segments of the society (workers, teachers, youth, municipal officials, religious groups, advocates and persons responsible for food, health, housing, and water, women's organizations, etc.) who create a steering committee to coordinate human rights learning and the drafting of a charter or other statement of the principles by which the human rights goals of the city will be met. The idea has been implemented in several cities in different parts of the world[68] and is being expanded with the assistance of UNPD. The method lends itself well to local participation in improving access to and quality of health.

From Human Rights Theory to Development Practice

The rationales in theory and the approaches in practice to applying human rights to development discussed above are by no means exhaustive; rather, they cover some of the main ways in which human rights can be applied to human development, with special reference to health. *Social justice* is a particularly appealing concept for public health practitioners because it captures their concern for poverty, inequality, and exclusion. These concerns are also part of the human rights perspective and relevant to the priority in development for poverty reduction. However, human rights define specific obligations of conduct and result, the realization of which is necessary for the achievement of social justice. The idea of *capabilities* underscores the critical role of freedom of people to choose and to participate in decisions affecting their lives, including making choices that reduce morbidity and extend life expectancy. Such an understanding of development as freedom is inseparable from the freedoms covered by the human rights framework. *Duties and responsibilities* are often invoked in the context of development and have often been misinterpreted as being opposed to human rights, whereas human rights theory actually accords a significant place to them. The conclusion of the brief remarks concerning these three conceptual approaches to development is that their relation to human rights deepens the potential for practical strategies to promote health in the development process.

The health practitioner, whether holding positions of responsibility in government, working for an NGO, or representing an international agency, is likely to be skeptical of human rights-based strategies unless and until they demonstrate a value added compared to more traditional approaches to primary health care, health sector reform or community-based health promotion. That value added is proposed through so-called *human rights-based development,* the implementation of the *right to development* and programs of *human rights education* focusing on social change. Such strategies do not claim to replace sound health promotion in development but rather to focus their objectives and methods on meeting priority human needs defined through the language of human rights. Such development practices can transform the human rights framework from the theory of academics or the rhetoric of resolutions adopted in New York and Geneva into practice that affects people's lives and health.

Notes

1. Preamble to the Constitution of the World Health Organization as adopted by the International Health Conference, New York, June, 19–22, 1946; signed on July 22, 1946 by the representatives of 61 States (Official Records of the World Health Organization, no. 2, p. 100) and entered into force on April 7, 1948.
2. See Gian Luca Burci and Claude-Henri Vignes, *World Health Organization.* The Hague: Kluwer Law International, Intergovernmental Organizations – Suppl. 14 (July 2003), para. 208, at p. 109.
3. The brief allusion here to definitional issues of health and development have their counterpart with respect to human rights, especially the problem some philosophers (and the United States government) have with the inclusion of positive rights, i.e., those that imply more than government refraining from interfering with individual freedom. However, there is a wide consensus, officially endorsed by all governments at the International Conference on Human Rights in Vienna in 1993, that the Universal Declaration and related instruments define universal human rights.
4. UNDP, *Human Development Report 2002,* p. 9. Without the qualifier "human", "development" is often used to mean economic growth. However, as UNDP pointed out in launching the HDR, the human development "way of looking at development differs from the conventional approach to economic growth, human capital formation, human resource development, human welfare or basic human needs." *Human Development Report 1990,* p. 11.
5. Thomas Pogge, *World Poverty and Human Rights* (Cambridge: Polity Press, 2002), p. 31.
6. Id., p. 44.
7. Paul Farmer, *Pathologies of Power. Health, Human Rights and the New War on the Poor* (Berkeley: University of California Press, 2003), p. 140.
8. Id. p. 152.
9. Id., p. 159.
10. An example of a social justice analysis applied to international health issues is Jim Young Kim, Joyce V. Millen, Alec Irwin, and John Gershman, *Dying for Growth. Global Inequality and the Health of the Poor* (Monroe, ME: Common Courage Press, 2000).
11. Amartya Sen, *Development as Freedom* (New York: Knopf, 1998), pp. 87–110.

12. The concept of capabilities has also been articulated by Martha Nussbaum, who has collaborated with Sen, in numerous writings. See, for example, M. Nussbaum, "Nature, Function and Capability: Aristotle on Political Distribution," in *Oxford Studies in Ancient Philosophy*, Supplementary Volume 1 (1988), pp. 145–84; M. Nussbaum, "Non-Relative Virtues: An Aristotelian Approach," in M. Nussbaum and A. Sen (eds.), *The Quality of Life* (Oxford: Clarendon Press, 1993). See also A. David Crocker, "Functioning and Capability: The Foundation of Sen and Nussbaum's Development Ethics," *Political Theory*, vol. 20:4, pp. 584–612.

13. Amartya Sen, *Development as Freedom*, p. 99.

14. Id., p. 103.

15. A more technical analysis of capabilities and functioning in relation to personal well-being and advantage is provided in Amartya Sen, *Commodities and Capabilities* (Oxford University Press, 1999). See also, Martha Nussbaum, "Capabilities, Human Right, and the Universal Declaration," in Weston & Marks, *The Future of International Human Rights*, Transnational Publishers, 1999.

16. ICESCR, *General Comment 14: The right to the highest attainable standard of health*, UN doc. E/C.12/2000/4, July 4, 2000, paras. 34–37.

17. The related rights enumerated in the General Comment are: "the rights to food, housing, work, education, human dignity, life, non-discrimination, equality, the prohibition against torture, privacy, access to information, and the freedoms of association, assembly and movement." *Id.*, para. 3

18. UNDP, *Human Development Report 2001*, p. 9.

19. This analysis draws in part on that provided by the International Council on Human Rights Policy in *Taking Duties Seriously: Individual Duties in International Human Rights Law. A Commentary*, 1999.

20. Amartya Sen, "Consequential Evaluation and Practical Reason," *The Journal of Philosophy*, vol. xvii, no. 9 (September 2000), p. 496.

21. Id., p. 497.

22. In a comment on types of state duties imposed by human rights treaties, Steiner and Alston extend this list to five obligations: "respect the rights of others," "create institutional machinery essential to realization of rights," "protect rights/prevent violations," "provide goods and services to satisfy rights," and "promote rights." Steiner and Alston, *International Human Rights in Context: Law, Politics, Morals*, 2nd ed. (2000), pp. 182–84.

23. See, for example, International Covenants on Human Rights (1966), Preamble; Declaration on the Right to Development (1986), Article 2(2); Declaration on Human Rights Defenders (1998), Article 18; Convention on the Rights of the Child (1989), Articles 5, 18(1) and 27(2).

24. American Convention on Human Rights (1969), Article 32(1) (See also American Declaration on the Rights and Duties of Man (1948)); African Charter of Human and Peoples' Rights (1961), Article 27 (See also Preamble and Articles 28–29).

25. The text is reproduced in Stephen P. Marks (ed.), *Health and Human Rights: Basic International Documents*, Cambridge, MA: Harvard Series in Health and Human Rights, distributed by Harvard University Press, 2004, pp. 11–14.

26. General Assembly Resolution 37/194 of 18 December 1982.

27. United Nations, *Compendium of United Nations Standards and Norms in Crime Prevention and Criminal Justice*, ST/CSDHA/16, New York, 1992.

28. Article 12(3) (movement), Article 14(1) (public trial), Article 18(3) (religion), Article 19(3) (opinion), Article 21 (assembly), and Article 22(2) (association).

29. The Human Rights Council of Australia, Inc., *The Rights Way to Development: A Human Rights Approach to Development Assistance* (Sydney, Australia, 1995). The same organization has produced a manual on the subject. See André Frankovits and Patrick Earle, *The Rights Way to Development: Manual For a Human Rights Approach to Development Assistance* (Marrickvill, Australia, 1998).

30. Julia Häusermann, *A Human Rights Approach to Development* (London: Rights and Humanity, 1998), p. 32.

31. Id., p. 33.

32. Another example of such an NGO is ActionAid, which has published a book on this approach: Anita Cheria, Sriprapha Petcharamesree and Edwin, *A Human Rights Approach to Development: Resource Book* (Banglore, India: Books for Change, 2004).

33. See Urban Jonsson, *Human Rights Approach to Development Programming*, Nairobi: UNICEF, 2003.
34. http://www.unhchr.ch/development/approaches-04.html.
35. http://www.undp.org/rbap/rights/Nexus.htm.
36. They are available on the Web site of the UN High Commissioner for Human Rights; see http://www.unhchr.ch/tbs/doc.nsf. See also Part IX of this volume.
37. These deal respectively with disabled women, violence against women and women and health.
38. This comment deals with HIV/AIDS and the rights of the child.
39. See, for example, Committee on Economic, Social and Cultural Rights, General Comment No. 3 (1990), UN Doc. E/1991/23, Annex III, para. 10.
40. This example of the charting of human rights obligations was pioneered by Daniel Tarantola and Sofia Gruskin in "Children Confronting HIV/AIDS: Charting the Confluence of Rights and Health," *Health and Human Rights*, vol. 3, no. 1 60–86 (1998).
41. See, for example, Kate Raworth, Measuring Human Rights, *Ethics and International Affairs*, vol. 15, no. 1, pp. 111–131; Craig Mokhiber, Toward a Measure of Dignity: Indicators of Rights-based Development, manuscript, September 2000, both of which are reproduced in Part VI of this volume.
42. See *Human Development Report 2000,* chapter 5, Using indicators for human rights accountability, pp. 89–111.
43. Draft Guidelines: A Human Rights Approach to Poverty Reduction Strategies, available at http://www.unhchr.ch/development/povertyfinal.html.
44. Various starting dates have been proposed. A significant inaugural moment was Judge Kéba M'Baye's lecture at the International Institute of Human Rights in 1972, published as "Le droit au développement comme un droit de l'homme," *Human Rights Journal*, vol. V, no. 2–3, pp. 505–34.
45. UN GA Res. 41/128. The Commission referred to the right to development in resolutions before the General Assembly adopted the Declaration. See, for example, Commission resolutions 4 (XXXIII) of February 21, 1977, 4 (XXXV) of March 2, 1979, 36 (XXXVII) of March 11, 1981, and 1985/44 of March 14, 1985.
46. In this abundant literature, the following are particularly useful: George Abi-Saab, "The Legal Formulation of a Right to Development," in *The Right to Development at the International Law* (Hague Academy of International Law, 1980), p. 163 ff; Philip Alston, "Revitalizing United Nations World on Human Rights and Development," *Melbourne Univ. Law Review*, vol. 18 (1991), p. 216 ff; P. Alston, "Making Space for Human Rights: The Case of the Rights to Development," *Harvard Human Rights Yearbook*, vol. 1 (1988) p. 1 ff.; Upendra Baxi, "The Development of the Right to Development," in Baxi, *Mambrino's Helmet?: Human Rights for a Changing World* (Har-Anand Publication, New Delhi, 1994), p. 22 ff (reproduced in Janusz Symonides, *Human Rights: New Dimensions and Challenges*, Ashgate and Unesco, 1998, pp. 99–116); I. Brownlie, *The Human Right to Development*, Commonwealth Secretariat, 1989; Y. Ghai and Y. R. Rao, *Whose Human Right to Development*, Commonwealth Secretariat, 1989; M. Bedjaoui, "The Right to Development," in Bedjaoui, *International Law: Achievements and Prospects* (UNESCO, 1991), p. 1177 ff; Subrata Roy Chowdhury, Erik M. G. Denters, and Paul J. I. M. de Waart, *The Right to Development in International Law*, Nijhoff, 1992; Ahmed Mahiou, "Le droit au développement," in *International Law on the Eve of the Twenty-first Century: Views from the International Law Commissio* (United Nations, 1997), pp. 217–36; Kéba M'Baye, "Le droit au développement comme un droit de l'homme," *Revue internationale des droits de l'homme*, vol. 5, p. 505 ff (1972); Alain Pellet, "Note sur quelques aspects juridiques de la notion de droit au développement," in Flory, Mahiou, and Henry, *La formation des norms en droit international du développement,* 1984, p. 71 ff; James C. N. Paul, "The Human Right to Development: Its Meaning and Importance," *The John Marshall Law Review*, vol. 25, pp. 235–64.
47. See, for example, J. Donnelly, "In Search for the Unicorn: The Jurisprudence and Politics of the Right to Development," *Calif. Western International Law Journal*, vol. 15 (1985), p. 4723 ff.
48. Declaration on the Right to Development (DRD), Article 6(3).
49. DRD, Article 2 (3).
50. See Arjun Sengupta, "On the Theory and Practice of the Right to Development," *Human Rights Quarterly*, vol. 24 (2002), pp. 848–52.

51. *Preliminary study of the independent expert on the right to development, Mr. Arjun Sengupta, on the impact of international economic and financial issues on the enjoyment of human rights*, submitted in accordance with Commission resolutions 2001/9 and 2002/69, UN doc. E.CN.4/2003/WG.18/2, December 10, 2002, para. 39.
52. Id., para. 42.
53. General Assembly Resolution 55/2. United Nations Millennium Declaration adopted on September 8, 2000.
54. GA Res. 48/127, 48th Sess. Supp No.49 at 246 UN Doc. A/48/49 (vol.1) (1993).
55. The Declaration is officially known as the "Declaration on the Right and Responsibility of Individuals, Groups and Organs of Society to Promote and Protect Universally Recognized Human Rights and Fundamental Freedoms." See General Assembly resolution 53/144 of December 9, 1998.
56. See Declaration cited in note 46, Articles 14 and 15. A similar provision can be found in the Convention on Torture: "Each State party shall ensure that education and information regarding the prohibition against torture are fully included in the training of law enforcement personnel, civil or military, medical personnel, public officials and other persons who may be involved in the custody, interrogation or treatment of individuals subjected to any form of arrest, detention or imprisonment." Convention Against Torture and Other Cruel, Inhuman or Degrading Treatment or Punishment, GA Res. 39/46 of December 10, 1984, Article 10.
57. Clarence Dias, "Human Rights Education as a Strategy for Development," in Andreopoulos and Claude, *Human Rights Education for the Twenty-First Century* (Philadelphia: University of Pennsylvania Press, 1997), pp. 52–53.
58. See its Web site at www.pdhre.org. The organization's former name was People's Decade for Human Rights Education (PDHRE).
59. See its Web site at www.hrea.org.
60. See, for example, Report of the SecretaryGeneral, *Guidelines for national plans of action for human rights education*, UN doc. A/52/469/Add.1 (October 20, 1997).
61. See, for example, WHO, *Transforming Health Systems: Gender and Rights in Reproductive Health. A Training Curriculum for Health Programme Manager* (Geneva: WHO, 2001). WHO/RHR/01.29.
62. See, in particular, George J. Andreopoulos and Richard Pierre Claude, *Human Rights Education for the Twenty-First Century* (Philadelphia: University of Pennsylvania Press, 1997). PDHRE is planning to publish a world report on human rights education containing many more examples and theories of HRE.
63. Frank Elbers, *Human Rights Education Resourcebook* (Cambridge, MA: Human Rights Education Associates. 2000). Available online at http://www.hrea.org/pubs/HREresourcebook/resourcebook.pdf.
64. These goals of HRE were articulated in Richard Claude's *Methodologies for Human Rights Education.*
65. *Popular Education for Human Rights: 24 Participatory Exercises for Facilitators and Teachers* (Cambridge, MA: Human Rights Education Associates, 2000), p. 6.
66. The health and sanitation project of LRC is described at http://www.lrc-ghana.org/what/health.asp.
67. Information communicated to the author.
68. The strategy has been applied in Rosario, Argentina; Graz, Austria; Dinajpur, Bangladesh; The People of Abra, Philippines; Elfasher City, Sudan Thies, Senegal; Nima/Mamobi, Ghana; Nagpur, India; and Kati, Mali. More on these cities and on the strategy for creating them is set out http://www.pdhre.org/projects/hrcommun.html.

6

Indigenous Peoples and Mega-Projects

Hydroelectric Dams in the Land of the Pehuenches in the Highlands of the Bío Bío River, Chile, Utopia of Development and Human Rights

Claudio González-Parra

In the last 500 years of occidental cultural domination, the indigenous peoples of Latin America have become the poorest sectors (in socio-economic terms) of the continent, and constitute today a large percentage of the Latin American and Chilean indigent. Despite the incessant efforts of different governments to relieve the situation of poverty and marginality of the indigenous peoples, there remain many obstacles to their autonomous social, economic and political participation.[1] In the last 20 years, however, the indigenous peoples have become better organized and capable of expressing their demands in both national and international forums and are today searching for solutions to their poverty and marginality in order to overcome the historic, obstacles to their socio-economic development. At the same time, there is a greater, although limited, awareness at the international level of the need to find new ways to solve the problems of the indigenous people, especially with respect to the recognition of their legitimate ancestral rights to land.[2]

The improvements in indigenous peoples' organizations and the greater national and international awareness of their rights is, however, not sufficient. At the international level, human rights and indigenous peoples' commissions have created innumerable documents which describe the historical and daily violations of their rights by governments in particular. These violations extend from the basic right of association through to genocide and ethnocide in order to obtain access to the natural resources in the ancestral territories of indigenous people.[3]

117

There is also a growing pressure from the business sector on indigenous people to integrate themselves and their resources into the development process. In the case of Chile, the government and private electricity sector have built and want to continue building hydroelectric dams in the highlands of the Bío Bío river, the ancestral lands of the Pehuenche Indians.[4]

In *Mapudungún* 'Pehuenche' means 'people of the Pehuen tree'. For the Pehuenches, the Pehuen tree is holy, and in the winter their principal food is its pine nut. The Pehuenches were originally nomadic hunters who lived in the Andes mountains. With the arrival of the Spanish *conquistadores* in the seventeenth century, the Pehuenches mixed with the Mapuches. At present, the two communities are a loosely organized group held together by a shared culture, a symbolic system (including language) and their relationship to the dominant Chilean (*huinka*) society.

Dam Construction in the Highlands of the Bío Bío River

The construction of hydroelectric dams in the highlands of the Bío Bío river, hereafter sometimes referred to as the Alto Bío Bío, is a development where the recognition of the rights of the Pehuenches is presented as a prerequisite for the eradication of their poverty. Those who support the construction of the dams affirm that the dams will generate development in a needy sector and that the actions of the Pehuen Foundation will mitigate the Pehuenches' poverty, heralding a system of social well-being that will change the situation. Those who are against the dam argue that the dams violate the basic rights of the two communities and that their implementation will result in the destruction of the Pehuenches' way of life and the disappearance of the Pehuenche culture in a very short period.[5]

The fallacy is not, however, in the equation that the dam will create development.[6] It lies in the belief that development can be created without the active participation of the Pehuenches. Two independent researchers have evaluated the Pehuen Foundation. Both evaluations were critical, and ENDESA, the most important Chilean electricity company, and the International Financing Corporation (IFC) have striven to keep them from publication. According to the evaluation reports several issues need to be addressed in order to reduce the cultural and environmental damage wrought by the dams.

Powerful external actors are negotiating the future of the Pehuenche communities, constituting a violation of the rights of these communities freely to decide their future.[7] Innumerable meetings have been held in Santiago and Washington, without either the participation or knowledge of the group. Withholding publication of the evaluation reports prevents the Pehuenches and the general public from understanding the development plans for these communities. The following section presents a brief history of ENDESA's projects and their ramifications amongst the Pehuenche.

The Pangue Project

ENDESA's first project which directly affected the Pehuenches was the building of the Pangue hydroelectric dam, 113 metres high and 103 metres wide. The lake resulting from the dam holds 175 million m³ and covers 500 hectares. The average annual generated energy is expected to be 2,156Wh, which is 55 per cent of full capacity. The IFC controls 2.5 per cent of the assets and contributed US$120 million of the US$450 million total cost. The president of both ENDESA and the Pangue project is the same person.

During the construction of the dam, the IFC and Pangue agreed to the establishment of the independent Pehuen Foundation, among whose objectives were to be the following:

- make the foundation into a vehicle to create sustainable development for the long-term benefit of the Pehuenche communities;
- work with those communities to mitigate the possible negative effects of the Parigue project during and after construction;
- preserve and reinforce the cultural identity of the Pehuenche;
- bring electricity to the communities.

In pursuance of these objectives, the Pangue project allocates approximately 0.3 per cent of its net gains, approximately US$130,000 per year, to the Pehuen Foundation until 2001.

According to the independent evaluations, however, the Pehuen Foundation has not pursued these objectives. ENDESA has instead used the foundation[8] to address the problems of extreme poverty in the communities as an example of the benefits to be received from the construction of the Pangue and Ralco dams.[9]

The families affected live and survive in extremely vulnerable conditions of poverty. They are below Chile's official poverty line and a third are considered to be indigent. There is little state assistance present in the area. Not surprisingly, the Pehuenches are extremely vulnerable to offers to better their living conditions, by, for example, ENDESA.

To illustrate this point, we can examine the case of the Calpan family, affected by the Ralco dam. The son, Eleuterio Calpan Quipaiñan, who works for ENDESA, wants to relocate himself to the El Barco lands. His father, Segundo Calpan Lepiman, says that if it were up to him he wouldn't move. It appears that in the majority of cases where families accept relocation, the wife or head of the household works for ENDESA and that it is that person who decides to relocate, accepting the conditions imposed by the company without the consent of the other family members.

One can also observe a lack of a sense of cultural community amongst the affected group, a product of the process of acculturation transmitted by the schools and the churches. At this time, for example, there does not exist a clear awareness that relocation is a decision that affects the community as a whole.

ENDESA utilizes this weakness to its benefit in the process of convincing individual after individual to accept its proposals. One has to understand that these families perceive living areas only as places to survive in given that there are no alternatives on offer, either for living or for stable work.

The Role of the Pehuen Foundation

The two independent evaluations of the Pehuen Foundation were made by anthropologists hired by the IFC.[10] Their critical report presented evidence about the activities of the Pehuen Foundation with respect to:

- environmental damage and deforestation which remain to be corrected;
- multiple and confirmed threats of involuntary resettlement;
- practices which constitute a dramatic assault on the Pehuenche cultural customs and traditions;[11]
- cover-ups of vital information which would permit the discussion of alternatives that would mitigate the cultural, economic and environmental damage.

The fact that these are the result of actions by the Pehuen Foundation is especially important considering that the Pehuen Foundation is the institution set up to mitigate the possibly damaging cultural, social and environmental effects of ENDESA's projects, and the resettlement of approximately 1,000 Pehuenches. It is necessary to analyse the points raised by ENDESA's latest plan, while pointing out that the Chilean Environmental Protection Corporation (CONAMA) approved the plan with a few corrections. One of the changes CONAMA requested was a change in foundation membership to include the community of Ralco Lepoy. This led to the accusation that IFC and ENDESA executives tried to organize the foundation in such a way as to hide information from its indigenous directors and the affected communities.[12]

Is it possible for ENDESA and the World Bank Group to design a resettlement plan without the advice of independent experts who would ensure that the rights of the communities are respected? Is it possible that this plan would ignore the World Bank's own standards for resettlement or that ENDESA and the World Bank would approve this plan without prior discussion with, and the participation and approval of, the communities involved? In practice, the Pehuen Foundations has not recognized the traditional leaders of the communities affected by the dams, Los Avellanos, Malla, and Quepuca Estadio.

The implementation of mega-projects and the process of resettlement without the active participation of the affected communities is a violation of these communities' rights and of indigenous law. But many argue that the development which the dam will bring will justify whatever human rights violations have occurred in the process, or is another equilibrium possible? Are there minimum conditions of resettlement which would respect the Pehuenches' human rights and facilitate sustainable development in the highlands of the Bío Bío river? Will the Pehuenches benefit from the development of the dam or will they subsidise the hydroelectric development of Chile as a whole at the expense of their local economy, natural resources and culture?

The Ralco Project

The second dam planned by ENDESA on the Bío Bío river is the Ralco, which will result in the resettlement of 88 families from the communities of Quepuca-Ralco and Ralco-Lepoy. Since the land on which the dam is to be built is indigenous land, the property cannot be sold according to Chilean Indigenous Law. The Chilean government agency of Indian development, CONADI, must approve any transfer of indigenous lands to third parties. The official position of the Chilean, government is in support of dam construction.

To this end, during August 1997 a group of government functionaries together with consultants to CONADI carried out personal interviews with the Pehuenche family communities of Quepuca-Ralco and. Ralco-Lepoy. The objective was to determine the number of families willing to be resettled and to identify the reasons for their decision. Amongst the families interviewed were those six families that had already requested resettlement. CONADI had access to 68 families, who were visited in their homes, a significant opinion sample to compare with ENDESA's assertions about the acceptability of their scheme amongst the affected communities.[13]

This CONADI initiative constitutes a systematic effort to implement the agreement on the support policies of CONADI's Southern Region to the area affected by the flooding of the dams. The objective in this case is to make known the official position of CONADI to the families that will be directly affected by

Table 6.1 Opinions with respect to resettlement

	Willing to relocate	Unwilling to relocate	Undecided	Total
Total	25	38	5	68
Percentage	37	56	7	100

Source: CONADI Regional.

Table 6.2 Results of the interviews from home visits in Quepuca-Ralco and Ralco-Lepoy

Would relocate	Would not relocate	Undecided	Not interviewed
28.4%	43.2%	6%	22.4%

Source: Empress Focus Limitada, 13–16 August 1997

the construction of the Ralco dam. This signifies the beginning of a new mode of work for CONADI, given the difficult challenge that the Pehuenche population confronts in the Development Area of the Alto Bío Bío.

CONADI states that 37 per cent of the families favour relocation. Underlying this percentage, however, is a clear ignorance by the families of their rights and those accorded by Chile's Indigenous Law. It is also clear that the families believed that the dam will go ahead and that there are no alternatives to relocation to the El Barco lands, reflecting the policy and stance of ENDESA that no other solutions are possible.

The families that have sought relocation have been thoroughly instructed by ENDESA personnel and realize that they are under pressure to accept. The role played by the Pehuen Foundation has also directly supported ENDESA's objectives and the construction of the dam. The families believe that they will lose their lands and everything they possess below the rising water, as well as a year's benefits from the Pehuen Foundation, if they reject ENDESA's argument. In this area there is no clear difference between the functions and roles of the Pehuen Foundation and those of ENDESA.

Seven per cent of the families are undecided. These families lack knowledge of the protection which the law offers them and a belief that CONADI has little or no ability to defend their rights. There is a clear lack of confidence with respect to what CONADI can do, given ENDESA's power in this area. Against this, a small majority of 56 per cent of the Pehuenche families reject relocation, a significant number of which believe in their right to their ancestral lands and identify clearly with their traditions. In spite of everything, this important group refuses to move, convinced that it must defend its lands against the enemy.

Mapuche Claims before the UN Human Rights Commission

The Chilean government supported ENDESA's plans until August 1998, when it asked for the resignation of CONADI director Domingo Namuncura and two board members of the CONADI council. These individuals had actively intervened in the interactions between the Pehuenche community and ENDESA. At the same time, it became clear that the indigenous members of the CONADI council had become increasingly critical of ENDESA's resettlement proposals. Mapuche communities filed an official complaint to the UN Commission on Human Rights, calling attention to the severity of the human rights violation committed against the Mapuches as people of an ethnic, religious and linguistic minority.

The complaint was presented by the International Peace Bureau to the fifty-fourth session of the commission, held between 16 March and 24 April 1998, and reads as follows:

Just over 100 years ago, the Mapuche nation, spread across the present-day states of Argentina and Chile, possessed a vast territory which, on the Chilean side, stretched from the Bío Bío river down to the south. This territory was recognized first by treaties with the Spanish Crown and then by a series of treaties and parliaments held with the newly established Republic of Chile. With the military defeat of the Mapuche people in 1883, the Chileans took possession of the Mapuche territory by conquest; territory which the Mapuche communities still claim as theirs today. Despite the loss of national sovereignty and annexation to the Republic of Chile, the Mapuche have by no means renounced their claims to possession of their land and resources.

Without the recovery of these lands, and the inalienable right of property over them, the survival of the Mapuche communities and of their culture is under threat. Deprived of their lands, the Mapuche communities suffer growing social instability, with the evident danger of outbreaks of violence, which could have unforeseeable consequences for the peace and stability of the Chilean state as a whole.

We demand, therefore, the recognition of the fundamental rights of the Mapuche people, as guaranteed by legal instruments both national and international, such as the International Covenant on Economic, Social and Cultural Rights, Article 1.

With regard to the situation of its indigenous population, Chile theoretically took an important step forward with the passing of Law No. 19.253 in 1993. This law establishes norms for the protection, promotion and development of that population and recognizes a number of basic rights, such as the recognition of the Mapuche as a people. It guarantees the protection of ownership of land and water, and the introduction of multicultural and bilingual education. It also prohibits manifest and malicious discrimination. Under this law, the government must consult the indigenous peoples of Chile on all issues affecting them directly. In reality, however, this law is not implemented. With the return to democracy and the rule of law in Chile, and with the strengthening of its legal institutions and its ratification of international treaties in the field of human rights, Chile presents a normal and civilized face to the rest of the world. But if we look at recent events, it becomes clear that the treatment of the Mapuche people has not improved since the days of Pinochet's regime. Injustice, violations of human rights, usurpation of ancestral lands, inhuman and humiliating treatment, discrimination and racism are still very much the order of the day.

Between October 1997 and March 1998, 85 Mapuches, among them women and children, were detained in Temuco, Malleco, Arauco, Angol and Santiago. This was the result of the introduction of the Law of State Security and the

Anti-Terrorist Law in five communes in the Mapuche region. Using these legal instruments, the Chilean police carried out a massive military operation in the entire region. Together with anti-terrorist forces, and using military vehicles and helicopters, the police patrolled the area, entering homes and threatening the inhabitants. Detentions took place at any hour of the day or night. According to the statement of one of the detained, he was held incommunicado for seven days (Chilean law stipulates five days), during which he suffered inhuman and degrading treatment.

In a confrontation between security guards from the logging company Arauco S.A. and Mapuche families from the Pichi Lonkollan and Pilin Mapu communities of the Lumaco sector of Malleco Province, who were trying to halt the exploitation of their traditionally held forest land, two trucks were burnt. These incidents can, however, hardly be considered to have constituted a 'threat to the interior security of the state'. The reaction of the Chilean state towards the Mapuche population in this case has been irresponsible and totally exaggerated.

Projects for the improvement of the country's infrastructure, such as the building of new roads and dams, are being carried out without the prior consent of the affected communities, in violation of the Indigenous Law No. 19.253 of October 1993. Not only has the Chilean government not implemented this law, due, it says, to a 'lack of economic resources' (at the very moment in which Chile is buying weapons worth hundreds of millions of dollars), it has manifestly violated it. For example, the imminent construction of a series of hydroelectric power stations on the Bío Bío river in the Mapuche Pehuenche region, without the consent of communities affected, is in direct contradiction with Article 13 of the Indigenous Law, which provides that 'indigenous lands, as national interest demands, shall enjoy the protection of this law. They shall not be alienated, seized, nor acquired by limitation, except between communities or indigenous persons belonging to the same ethnic group'.

A large number of indigenous communities are facing such situations, due to the implementation of a number of mega-projects such as the Coast Road, the Temuco By-Pass, urban expansion, exploitation of forest and privatization of coastal areas and their waters. All these projects plunge Chile's most needy ever deeper into poverty, leading to enormous social and cultural problems amongst them. The disastrous environmental consequences of the projects barely need mention.

Although the Mapuche people are not opposed to progress, they want fair, sustainable and harmonious development, with full respect for their rights and ancestral values, and a development process from which they are not absolutely excluded. Development depends, however, on the recognition of the country's cultural diversity in order to begin an historic reparation which the indigenous peoples are anxiously awaiting, and which sooner or later the Chilean state will have to consider. Only in this way will a solid base of coexistence with the country's original inhabitants be created. The demands of the Mapuches are based on full respect for the Chilean legal order, which includes the common law norms which traditionally governed them, reserving their right to self-determination as the basis for their protection and development in their ancestral territory. It is important that the Mapuche people are recognized by the Chilean Constitution and that Chile ratifies ILO Convention 169, one of the few texts, if not the only one, that recognizes the inalienable rights of indigenous peoples.

ENDESA's Quality of Life Plan

On 25 October 1998, ENDESA and all the families affected by the Ralco project signed the Resettlement Plan in support of dam construction. CONADI, the provincial government of Los Angeles and the Catholic Church participated in reaching the agreement. CONADI met with all the individuals, communities and indigenous organizations in the Quepuca-Ralco and Ralco-Lepoy areas. It carried out social surveys to determine the number of families affected by the Ralco project as well as their needs and desires. The community organizations Comunidad de Ralco-Lepoy, Organización Pehuenche Quepuca Estadio and Junta de Vecinos de Palmucho represented the 184 affected families in designing the resulting Quality of Life Improvement Plan, which reflects their concerns and aspirations.

The Quality of Life Improvement Plan will strengthen the actions contemplated in the resettlement plan and the transfer of land for the families directly affected. At the time of writing ENDESA had reached an agreement with 83 of the families. This agreement states:

- that the benefits provided by the resettlement plan for the (91) families do not generate differences or conflicts between the families of the two communities, so that the community ties remain unbroken;
- that there is full collaboration with government plans in the Development Area of the Alto Bío Bío in order to be more efficient in resource administration. It is believed that a coordinated effort will best improve the quality of life of the Pehuenches;
- that the Ralco dam is part of the solution rather than the problem of the Alto Bío Bío. The construction of the dam creates positive externalities for the Pehuenche communities that had been forgotten and isolated for years.

The Quality of Life Improvement Plan contemplates actions on several fronts to benefit the communities affected by Ralco:

- *Soil Conservation.* Collaboration in plans to achieve three forested hectares for each family. This project also includes training in plantation and soil conservation as well as temporary jobs in reforestation, conservation and soil-recovery programmes.
- *Rural Housing Subsidies.* Once land titles are established, ENDESA promises to add complementary financing to the government subsidy for rural housing as well as financing for other infrastructure projects.
- *Rural Electrification.*[14] ENDESA will provide financing for a Rural Electricity Programme whose objective is to provide electricity to all housing in the communities affected.
- *Roads.* ENDESA will construct a new road in the Alto Bío Bío to replace the one that will be flooded by the lake created by the Ralco dam. It will be 50 kilometres long, between the Pangue bridge and the El Barco Plantation (proposed resettlement location). ENDESA will also assist in the creation of paths to connect the different community farms.
- *Education.* ENDESA promises to collaborate in the development to expand and improve the existing Frontier Elementary School in Ralco to become a Technical–Professional High School.
- *Cultural Programmes and Encouragement of Tourism.* The Pehuen Foundation promises to continue supporting the development of cultural and productive activities in the two communities. ENDESA will contact the Chile Foundation to prepare a holistic design of the tourist potentials for the two communities affected as well as the proposed resettlement location, incorporating Pehuenche feedback. Additionally ENDESA promises to finance complementary studies on tourism.
- *Community Centre.* ENDESA promises to construct a community centre for the communities of Quepuca-Ralco and Ralco-Lepoy.
- *Pehuen Foundation.* ENDESA will study the reorganization of the executive committee in order to ensure Pehuenche pre-eminence.
- *Employment Opportunities.* In order to ensure employment opportunities for the Pehuenches, ENDESA guarantees important quotas for the women and men of the affected communities.
- *Implementation and Supervision of the Improvement Programme.* By express petition of the communities, this programme will be incorporated into the Long-Run Development Resettlement Plan. In this way, the programme will be implemented and supervised according to the procedures established by the government's environmental protection agency CONAMA in its approval of the Ralco project.
- *Using Dialogue to Continue.* Several families still refuse to transfer their lands. ENDESA has stated its desire to continue a dialogue with them in order to reach a fair agreement, rather than ask for judicial intervention to determine the situation.

Recognizing Human Rights to Achieve Development

How can power be distributed in a manner which allows the fulfillment of human rights, in this case the defence of the rights of the Pehuenches of the Alto Bío Bío?[15] How can guarantees to respect the human rights of the Pehuenche organizations be phrased? There is a general state of impunity with respect to the systematic violation of essential, basic and historic rights of the Pehuenche communities, which has placed them in a position of being forced to accept the construction of the Pangue[16] and Ralco Dams as the sole paradigm of development and the sole means of alleviating the generalized poverty of their communities.

On paper, the creation of a private foundation as an instrument for mitigating the environmental impact of the dams while at the same time ensuring that the indigenous communities share in the profits of the Pangue project and not simply suffer the harmful effects of development that hydroelectric dams generate looks promising.[17] In this case, however, good intentions and declared goals are far from the crude realities in the communities where there is no understanding of what indigenous rights are supposed to guarantee.

The construction of the dams in the highlands of the Bío Bío river need not result in the impoverishment of the Pehuenche.[18] The following proposals for the reorientation of the relationship between ENDESA, the Pehuen Foundation and the affected communities were presented by Theodore Downing, co-author of the evaluation report on the Pehuen Foundation:

- realign the Pehuen Foundation according to the agreement between the IFC and Pangue;
- reorganize Pehuen Foundation policies to satisfy the requisites about conflicts of interest, cultural information, and to promote pluralism and diversity;
- recognize the Pehuenche language, *Mapudungún*, as the second official language of the Pehuen Foundation and look for experts in indigenous issues to be independent consultants;
- make an emergency plan which would stop the indiscriminate cutting of the forests, ensure that all indigenous land is protected, and design and follow a plan to mitigate the possible social, economic and environmental effects of the present and proposed project;
- have the Pehuen Foundation prepare and implement a sustainable strategic and participatory project which emphasizes the administration of natural resources controlled by the Pehuenche, especially the virgin forests;
- ensure the full participation in a culturally adequate form of the *lonkos* (traditional leaders) who represent the affected communities;
- establish Pehuenche groups to monitor the affected communities;

- increase on-site supervision of the IFC, including assistance to the future leaders of the communities;
- have the Pehuen Foundation and the IFC publicize the independent evaluations to the affected parties.

Conclusion

A strengthening of indigenous organizations, finally culminating in the 1993 Indigenous Law, arose from the grave abuse of the rights of indigenous communities documented in Chile during the years 1973 to 1990, which resulted in political ethnocide.

With the transition to democracy in Chile, a number of indigenous peoples' demands were added to the 1993 law, but conditions were not yet ready for these demands to be recognized. The fact that the Pehuen Foundation, a private entity created by the World Bank Group, continues to exercise important influence over the Pehuenche communities in a way that is contrary to their interests and destructive of their culture has not been addressed. For example, in 1993 the Pehuen Foundation chose and donated books to the libraries of three schools in the Alto Bío Bío.[19] The donation represented 57 per cent of the funds allocated by the foundation to educational projects. The book collection was composed of a selection of great literary works of western civilization, including Homer, Shakespeare, Cervantes, and books on the history of Chile, written at a level beyond the understanding of Pehuenche students in the primary grades. Some of the books had pictures of the dismemberment of Indians at the hands of Euro-Chileans. The communities were terrorized by the books and they were hidden by the teachers. This would not have happened had the Foundation been aware of the specific needs of these communities.

The actions of external actors have broken the historic internal power equilibrium in these communities into multiple parts, as illustrated by the duplication of the various offices in the communities. It is also reinforced by the Indigenous Law.

To initiate a development process that does not result in the destruction of the Pehuenche way of life demands the harmonization of development and human rights. Any responsible person should meditate on the answers to the following questions and only then attempt to construct a new paradigm for a more just society; this is the least we can do if we are to rescue and restore a culture that will be lost due to the irreversible effects of mega-projects on the Alto Bío Bío today.[20] Is it possible to speak of democratizing the concepts of human rights in a form that makes us appreciate how our decisions can generate irreversible damage in communities? What is the relationship between power and human rights? Is the answer to the last question an example of the generalized impunity of Chilean society when the basic rights of Chile's indigenous communities are violated?

Notes

1. Salomon Nahmad (ed.) (1996) 'La perspectiva de etnias y naciones: los pueblos indios de América Latina', *Colección Biblioteca Abya-Yala*, No. 33, Ediciones Abya-Yala, Quito, Ecuador.
2. José Bengoa, *Globalización, distribución de los ingresos y los derechos económicos, sociales y culturales*, paper presented to the CROP and ALOP Workshop in Santiago de Chile, 24–26 September 1997.
3. Briefing on the Pehueche Human Rights situation at the Conference of the American Anthropological Association (AAA) in Washington, D.C. by Dr Theodore Downing, University of Arizona and Dr Claudio González-Parra, University of Concepción, 21 November 1997
4. Washington, D.C., 17 December 1992: 'The Board of Directors of the International Finance Corporation (IFC) today approved an investment in the Pangue hydroelectric power generation . . . IFC's insistence on the creation of the Pehuen Foundation, funded by the project's income to enhance the quality of life for the local indigenous population . . . The power generated will be clean and economically produced, for the use of 93 per cent of the Chilean population who live in Santiago and Central Chile'.
5. 'The sacrifice of human rights and the cultural survival of an indigenous group is an unacceptable cost of doing business or of economic development', Theodore Downing's letter to Tom Greaves, 1997.
6. Michael M. Cernea (1997) 'The Social Side of Hydropower: Forging a New Alliance', *Hydro Review Worldwide*, Vol. 5, Nos 1–6.
7. On 18 December 1996, Theodore Downing, in a letter to Jannik Lindbaek, Executive Vice-President of IFC, accused the 'IFC staff of joining its client in these violations, once it had been made aware of them, instituting a cover up and then, in an "in your face" response to human and indigenous rights, arrogantly forging a secret agreement with the company over the future of an ethnic group'.
8. William Ryrie, Executive Vice-President of IFC, noted IFC's 'sensitivity to the impact of this project on the indigenous communities near the project site'. IFC Press release No. 93/32.
9. 'These steps include the establishment of an Ecological Station to monitor environmental conditions in the project area, a watershed management protection plan, development of a construction impact minimization plan, and an equitable resettlement plan including housing and land ownership for 53 people displaced by the reservoir.' Press release No. 93/32. The IFC failed to resettle the Sotomayor family (CONADI, No. 0006067) who lived in the area south of the Pangue dam.
10. Theodore Downing, Research Professor of Social Development, University of Arizona, and Jay Hair, former President of the National Wildlife Federation, made the evaluations.
11. Letter from Theodore Downing, 18 December 1996, to Jannik Lindbaek, Executive Vice-President of IFC: 'Officers of IFC responsible for the Pangue Project are involving the institution in an unacceptable, racial-discrimination practice and withholding information from certain members of the Pehuen Foundation Board of Directors on the basis on their race and ethnicity. My efforts to convince three of the officers—Martyn Riddle, Denis Koromsay, and their legal Counsel Motoko Aizawa—that IFC's actions violate Pehuenche human rights have failed.'
12. 'This racial discrimination is intended to cover up the time-sensitive findings and deprive the Pehuenche people of important knowledge which has a direct bearing on the Pehuenche economic and cultural future. The ageing interim evaluation contains evidence of on-going extensive, unmitigated environmental damage including deforestation, multiple threats of involuntary resettlement, and a misguided assault on the Pehuenche culture. Most seriously, the cover up is delaying constructive actions to mitigate on-going cultural, economic and environmental damages which had been identified' (*ibidem*).
13. The interviews were carried out by the following CONADI officials: Mr. Luis, Huincache, Regional Director; Carlos Vargas, Treasurer; Juan Nanculef, Chief of Personnel, National Office; Gonzalo Toledo, Chief of Development; Manuel Namuncura, Chief of Personnel,

Office of the Southern National Region; Lucy Traipe, Secretariat, Office of the Southern National Region; Cecilia Neculpan, Program for Development Fund, Office of the Southern National Region; Horacio Cheuquelaf, Programme on Lands, Office of the Southern National Region; and Luis Luszinger, Driver, National Office.

14. 'The generic lessons, however, should not distract from the tragedy in the Alto Bío Bío. I am haunted by the image of impoverished Pehuenche freezing to death in El Barco as urban Chileans are heated by the electrical power which the Pehuenches subsidized with their culture and forest.' Theodore Downing's letter to Tom Greaves, 1997.

15. Michael M. Cernea (1998) 'Impoverishment or Social Justice? A Model for Planning Resettlement', in *Development Projects and Impoverishment Risks. Resettling Project-affected People in India*, Hari Mohan Mathur and David Marsden (eds), Oxford University Press, Delhi.

16. Washington, D.C., 17 December 1992: 'The Board of Directors of the International Finance Corporation (IFC) today approved an investment in the Pangue hydroelectric power generation project located on the Bío Bío river in Chile. Board ratification of the proposed investment followed a comprehensive environmental review of the project by IFC . . . Board members voiced strong approval of the work done by IFC in setting high environmental and social standards with respect to the Pangue project.' Press Release No. 93/32.

17. 'It is equally unacceptable that a small, indigent Indian culture must pay the tuition for the valuable lessons learned by IFC ... students in the classroom, and ENDESA. Nor can I believe that an institution with such plentiful resources, and her sister institutions in the World Bank family, are helpless to act.' Theodore Downing's letter to Tom Greaves, 1997.

18. Michael M. Cernea (1997) 'The Risk and Reconstruction Model for Resettling Displaced Populations', *World Development*, Vol. 25, No. 10, October, pp. 1569–88.

19. Micheal M. Cernea (1996) 'Social Organization and Development Anthropology', the 1995 Malinowski Award Lecture, *Environmentally Sustainable Development Studies and Monographs Series No. 6*, World Bank, Washington, D.C.

20. For more information, see the Arizona *Daily Star* Online at: http://www.azstarnet.com/downing.

III
Health and Human Rights in Emerging Technologies

The right to participate in the fruits of scientific advancement is a human right that has particular resonance in the health and human rights field. The extreme inequalities in access to basic health care, even to "essential drugs," around the world brings particular salience to the idea that new, cheaper, better, and more accessible drugs, vaccines, and health-related goods could vastly improve health. This idea is reflected, for example, in the work of the Gates Foundation and other international actors focusing on the availability of drugs and new vaccines for malaria, tuberculosis, and HIV/AIDS. These and similar efforts are in sharp contradistinction to the so-called "10/90 gap," which describes the funding of medical research dollars: 90 percent are spent on health problems that affect only 10 percent of the world's population.[1]

As we strive to craft better mechanisms to develop and distribute essential drugs and vaccines to the world's population who need them, others are deeply concerned with the human rights consequences of medical "progress" and human experimentation. The rights of individuals in human experimentation, including issues of informed consent, have been well spelled out in the Nuremberg Code, and subesequent human rights documents, and have been the subject of an extensive and growing literature. Much less has been written on two related questions: deciding which areas of research should be pursued, and distributing the benefits of research to those who need them. These are the two areas on which the chapters in this part focus.

The first two chapters deal with the question of whether a particular line of research should be pursued at all because of its potential human rights implications. The example that these chapters explore is the genetic manipulation of human embryos for the purpose of producing a child with specific traits: human

131

cloning and inheritable genetic alterations. The first chapter, by George Annas, Lori Andrews, and Rosario Isasi, suggests that these genetic manipulations will always involve unjustified human experimentation on the child-to-be for both safety and human dignity reasons. "Successful" genetic alteration leading to "superior" children could be an even worse disaster for human rights protection, leading to the division of the human species into two or more subspecies, each of which may see the other as unfit—and therefore a fit object of genocide. To avoid immediate, unjustified human experimentation, as well as the long term risk of "genetic genocide," the authors propose a treaty to prohibit such research. In December 2004, work on a more limited human cloning treaty proposal at the United Nations was abandoned because of the inability of countries to agree on a plan simply to outlaw reproductive cloning (even as a large number wanted to outlaw research cloning as well in the same treaty)[2] and it is likely that a more modest declaration on the subject will be proposed. In the second chapter, on the same subject, Stephen Marks argues that the relevant human rights documents and doctrines are ambiguous on the issue of human cloning, and could even be read to justify labeling a ban on cloning as itself a human rights violation.

The overall reason to include both articles, of course, is to underline the point that new medical and scientific technologies, not specifically considered within the relevant human rights texts, can produce difficult questions of interpretation. It can also be noted, as it has been in the areas of tobacco and gun control, that both sides of a public policy debate on a potentially danger- ous product or research agenda may attempt to cloak their arguments in terms of human rights terms because the rhetoric of human rights is so powerful.

The final two chapters in this part deal with the issue of affordability and access to new medical technologies, such as drugs. Once a new drug or other medical technology is developed and proven safe and effective, can attention to human rights help ensure that it will actually be available to those who need it? In the first piece, Philippe Cullet examines the highly contentious issue of the relationship between the Agreement on Trade-Related Aspects of Intellectual Property Rights (TRIPS) and the availability of patented drugs in resource- poor countries. He situates the discussion firmly within the health and human rights framework and explains why the much publicized Doha Declaration is insufficient to assure access to essential drugs to all those who need them, and how it is that making essential drugs available only to those people who can afford to pay market price for them is a violation of the right to health. His analysis remains timely. Although the World Trade Organization (WTO) an- nounced in Cancún in August 2003 that agreement had been reached to operationalize the Doha Declaration and promote "access to essential medi- cines," in fact it remains highly uncertain how this goal will actually be met.

One of the most vocal critics of the Doha approach to ensuring access to essential drugs is Ellen 't Hoen of Médecins sans Frontères, the author of the last chapter in this part. She has said, for example, that the Cancún agreement offers little comfort for poor patients. Global patent rules will continue to drive up the price of medicines. In the piece reprinted here, she examines the issue of drug access from a practical perspective, looking briefly at the situation in South Africa and Brazil, and exploring how NGOs and the United Nations can take action to help make patented drugs more accessible to those who need them. The issues are complex, but there is increasing international agreement that ways must be found to deliver life-saving and life-prolonging drugs to those who need them, or the entire rationale for developing such drugs in the first place will collapse.

Notes

1. Global Forum for Health Research, *10/90 Report on Health Research 2003–2004*, GFHR, Geneva, Switzerland, 2004.
2. Rosario Isasi and George J. Annas, "Arbitrage, Bioethics, and Cloning: The ABCs of Gestating a United Nations Cloning Convention," *Case Western Reserve Journal of International Law* (2003) 35:397–414.

7

Protecting the Endangered Human

Toward an International Treaty Prohibiting
Cloning and Inheritable Alterations

George J. Annas, Lori B. Andrews, and Rosario M. Isasi

We humans tend to worry first about our own happiness, then about our families, then about our communities. In times of great stress, such as war or natural disaster, we may focus temporarily on our country but we rarely think about Earth as a whole or the human species as a whole. This narrow perspective, perhaps best exemplified by the American consumer, has led to the environmental degradation of our planet, a grossly widening gap in living standards between rich and poor people and nations, and a scientific research agenda that focuses almost exclusively on the needs and desires of the wealthy few. Reversing the worldwide trends toward market-based atomization and increasing indifference to the suffering of others will require a human rights focus, forged by the development of what Vaclav Havel has termed a "species consciousness."[1]

In this chapter we discuss human cloning and inheritable genetic alterations from the human species perspective, and suggest language for a proposed international "Convention of the Preservation of the Human Species" that would outlaw all efforts to initiate a pregnancy by using either intentionally modified genetic material or human replication cloning, such as through somatic cell nuclear transfer. We summarize international legal action in these areas over the past five years, relate these actions to arguments for and against a treaty and conclude with an action plan.

Human Rights and the Human Species

The development of the atomic bomb not only presented to the world for the first time the prospect of total annihilation, but also, paradoxically, led to a renewed emphasis on the "nuclear family," complete with its personal bomb shelter. The conclusion of World War II (with the dropping of the only two atomic bombs ever used in war) led to the recognition that world wars were now suicidal to the entire species and to the formation of the United Nations with the primary goal of preventing such wars.[2] Prevention, of course, must be based on the recognition that all humans are fundamentally the same, rather than on an emphasis on our differences. In the aftermath of the Cuban missile crisis, the closest the world has ever come to nuclear war, President John F. Kennedy, in an address to the former Soviet Union, underscored the necessity for recognizing similarities for our survival:

> [L]et us not be blind to our differences, but let us also direct attention to our common interests and the means by which those differences can be resolved. . . . For, in the final analysis, our most basic common link is that we all inhabit this small planet. We all breathe the same air. We all cherish our children's future. And we are all mortal.[3]

That we are all fundamentally the same, all human, all with the same dignity and rights, is at the core of the most important document to come out of World War II, the Universal Declaration of Human Rights, and the two treaties that followed it (together known as the "International Bill of Rights").[4] The recognition of universal human rights, based on human dignity and equality as well as the principle of nondiscrimination, is fundamental to the development of a species consciousness. As Daniel Lev of Human Rights Watch/Asia said in 1993, shortly before the Vienna Human Rights Conference:

> Whatever else may separate them, human beings belong to a single biological species, the simplest and most fundamental commonality before which the significance of human differences quickly fades. . . . We are all capable, in exactly the same ways, of feeling pain, hunger, and a hundred kinds of deprivation. Consequently, people nowhere routinely concede that those with enough power to do so ought to be able to kill, torture, imprison, and generally abuse others. . . . The idea of universal human rights shares the recognition of one common humanity, and provides a minimum solution to deal with its miseries.[5]

Membership in the human species is central to the meaning and enforcement of human rights, and respect for basic human rights is essential for the survival of the human species. The development of the concept of "crimes against humanity" was a milestone for universalizing human rights in that it recognized that there were certain actions, such as slavery and genocide, that implicated the welfare of the entire species and therefore merited universal condemnation.[6] Nuclear weapons were immediately seen as a technology that required international control, as extreme genetic manipulations like cloning and inheritable genetic alterations have come to be seen today. In fact, cloning and inheritable genetic alterations can be seen as crimes against humanity of a unique sort: they are techniques that can alter the essence of humanity itself (and thus threaten to change the foundation of human rights) by taking human evolution into our own hands and directing it toward the development of a new species, sometimes termed the "posthuman."[7] It may be that species-altering techniques, like cloning and inheritable genetic modifications, could provide benefits to the human species in extraordinary circumstances. For example, asexual genetic replication could potentially save humans from extinction if all humans were rendered sterile by some catastrophic event. But no such necessity currently exists or is on the horizon.

As a baseline, if we take human rights and democracy seriously, a decision to alter a fundamental characteristic in the definition of "human" should not be made by any individual or corporation without wide discussion among all members of the affected population. No individual scientist or corporation has the moral warrant to redesign humans (any more than any individual scientist or corporation has the moral warrant to design a new, lethal virus or bacteria that could kill large numbers of humans). Altering the human species in a way that could endanger it is an issue that directly concerns all of us, and should only be decided democratically, by a body that is representative of everyone on the planet.[8] It is the most important decision we will ever make.

The environmental movement has adopted the precautionary principle to help stem the tide of environmental alterations that are detrimental to humans. One version of this principle holds that "when an activity raises threats of harm to human health or the environment . . . the proponent of that activity, rather than the public, should bear the burden of proof [that the activity is more likely to be beneficial than harmful]."[9] The only way to shift the burden of proof is to outlaw potentially lethal activities, thus requiring proponents to change the law before proceeding. This can be done nation by nation, but can only be effective (because scientists and laboratories can move from country to country) by an internationally-enforceable ban. The actual text of a treaty banning human replicative cloning and inheritable modifications will be the subject of debate. We suggest the following language, obviously subject to future negotiations as well as added details, as a basis for going forward:

Convention on the Preservation of the Human Species

The Parties to this Convention,

Noting that the Charter of the United Nations affirms human rights, based on the dignity and worth of the human person and on equal rights of all persons;

Noting that the Universal Declaration of Human Rights affirms the right of every person not to be discriminated against;

Realizing that human dignity and human rights derive from our common humanity;

Noting the increased power of genetic science, which opens up vast prospects for improving health, but also has the power to diminish humanity fundamentally by producing a child through human cloning or by intentionally producing an inheritable genetic change;

Concerned that human cloning, which for the first time would produce children with predetermined genotypes, rather than novel genotypes, might cause these children to be deprived of their human rights;

Concerned that by altering fundamental human characteristics to the extent of possibly producing a new human species or subspecies, genetic science will cause the resulting persons to be treated unequally or deprived of their human rights;

Recognizing the history of abuses of human rights in the name of genetic science;

Believing that no individual, nation or corporation has the moral or legal warrant to engage in species-altering procedures, including cloning and genetic alteration of reproductive cells or embryos for the creation of a child;

Believing that the creation of a new species or subspecies of humans could easily lead to genocide or slavery; and

Stressing the need for global cooperation to prevent the misuse of genetic science in ways that undermine human dignity and human rights;

Have agreed on the following:

Article 1

Parties shall take all reasonable action, including the adoption of criminal laws, to prohibit anyone from initiating or attempting to initiate a human pregnancy or other form of gestation using embryos or reproductive cells which have undergone intentional inheritable genetic modification.

Article 2

Parties shall take all reasonable action, including the adoption of criminal laws, to prohibit anyone from utilizing somatic cell nuclear transfer or any other cloning technique for the purpose of initiating or attempting to initiate a human pregnancy or other form of gestation.

Article 3
Parties shall implement systems of national oversight through legislation, executive order, decree or other mechanism to regulate facilities engaged in assisted human reproduction or otherwise using human gametes or embryos for experimental or clinical purposes to ensure that such facilities meet informed consent, safety, and ethical standards.

Article 4
A Conference of the Parties and a Secretariat shall be established to oversee implementation of this Convention.

Article, 5
Reservations to this Convention are not permitted.

Article 6
For the purpose of this Convention, the term "somatic cell nuclear transfer" shall mean transferring the nucleus of a human somatic cell into an ovum or oocyte. "Somatic cell" shall mean any cell of a human embryo, fetus, child or adult, other than a reproductive cell. "Embryo" shall include a fertilized egg, zygote (including a blastomere and blastocyst) and preembryo. "Reproductive cell" shall mean a human gamete and its precursors.[10]

Perhaps the most difficult challenge in implementing this treaty is setting up the monitoring and enforcement mechanisms. Article Four would have to address these in detail. Although the specifics are beyond the scope of this article, some general comments are needed. Monitoring and compliance bodies must be broadly representative, possess authority to oversee activities related to human cloning and human genetic modification, and be able to enforce bans by announcing and denouncing potential violators. Moreover, we believe the commission (and the countries themselves) should support, through the Convention and through their national criminal laws, the establishment of two new international crimes: initiation of a pregnancy to create a human clone and initiation of a pregnancy using a genetically-altered embryo.[11]

An International Convention: Why Now?

More than five years after the announcement of the cloning of Dolly the sheep it is time to ask not whether cloning and inheritable alterations should be regulated, but *how*. Had a five-year moratorium for further thought and discussion been placed on cloning humans, as the National Bioethics Advisory Commission (NBAC) recommended in 1997, for example, the time would now have expired.[12] What new have we learned?

First, virtually every scientist in the world with an opinion believes it is unsafe to attempt a human pregnancy with a cloned embryo.[13] This is, for example, the unanimous conclusion of a 2002 report from the U.S. National Academy of Sciences, which recommended that human "reproductive" cloning be outlawed in the United States following a study that included the viewpoints of the only two scientists in the world who publicly advocate human cloning today.[14] Although scientists seldom like to predict the future without overwhelming data to support them, many believe that human cloning or inheritable genetic alternations at the embryo level will never be safe because they will always be inherently unpredictable in their effects on the children and their offspring. As Stuart Newman has noted, for example, it is unlikely that a human created from the union of "two damaged cells" (an enucleated egg and a nucleus removed from a somatic cell) could ever be healthy.[15] Of course, adding genetic modification to the somatic cell's nucleus just adds another series of events that could go wrong, because genes seldom have a single function, but will usually interact in complex and unpredictable ways with other genes.[16] It is worth underlining that the dangers are not just physical, but also psychological. Whether cloned children could ever overcome the psychological problems associated with their origins is unknown and perhaps unknowable.[17] In short, the safety issues, which inherently make attempts to clone or genetically alter a human being unethical human experiments, provide sufficient scientific justification for the treaty alone.

If and when safety can be assured, assuming this will ever be possible, two primary arguments have been set forth in favor of proceeding with cloning (and its first cousin, inheritable genetic alterations). First, cloning is a type of human reproduction that can help infertile couples have genetically-related children. Second, cloning is a part of human "progress" that could lead to a new type of genetic immortality, therefore, to prevent it is to be anti-scientific.

The infertility argument is made by physiologist Panos Zavos and his former Italian colleague, infertility specialist Severino Antinori. They argue that the inability of a sterile male to have a genetically-related child is such a human tragedy that it justifies human cloning.[18] This view not only ignores the rights and interests of women and of children (even if only males are to be cloned, eggs must be procured from a woman, the embryos must be gestated by a woman and the child is the subject of the experiment), but also contains a highly-contested assertion: that asexual genetic replication or duplication should be seen as "human reproduction."[19] In fact, humans are a sexually reproducing species and have never reproduced or replicated themselves asexually.

Asexual replication may or may not be categorized by future courts as a form of human reproduction, but there are strong arguments against it. First, asexual reproduction changes a fundamental characteristic of what it means to be human (i.e., a sexually reproducing species) by making sexual reproduction involving the genetic mixture of male and female gametes optional. Second, the "child" of an asexual replication is also the twin brother of the male "parent," a relationship that has never existed before in human society. The first clone, for example, will be the first human being with a single genetic "parent" (unless the biological grandparents are taken to be the actual "parents" of the clone).[20] Third, the genetic replica of a genetically sterile man would be sterile himself and could only "reproduce" by cloning. This means either that infertility is not a major problem (because if it were, it would be unethical for a physician to intentionally create a child with this problem), or that the desire of existing adults should take precedent over the welfare of children. We find neither conclusion persuasive, and this is probably why, although some ethicists believe that cloning could be considered a form of human reproduction, infertility specialists have not joined Antinori's call for human cloning as a treatment for infertile males. In fact the organization that represents infertility specialists in the United States, and is generally opposed to the regulation of the infertility industry, the American Society of Reproductive Medicine, has nonetheless consistently opposed human cloning.[21]

There are, nonetheless, legal commentators who believe that human cloning should be classified as a form of human reproduction, and protected as such, at least if it is the only way for an individual to have a "genetically-related child." The strongest proponent of this view is probably John Robertson,[22] although Ronald Dworkin[23] shares his enthusiasm as well. Suffice it to say here that it is very unclear that human reproduction or procreation of a kind protected by principles of autonomy and self-fulfillment can be found in a "right to have a genetically-related child." It cannot be just the genetic tie that is important in human reproduction, because if it were, this could be accomplished by having one's twin brother have a child with one's wife[24]—the genetic tie would be identical, yet few, if any, would argue that this method of reproduction should satisfy the twin's right to have a "genetically-related child." Genes are important, but there is more to human reproduction, as protected by the U.S. Constitution, than simple genetic replication.

The second major argument in favor of human cloning is that it can lead to a form of immortality. This is the premise of the Raelian cult that has chartered its own corporation, Clonaid, to engage in human cloning. The leader of the cult, who calls himself Rael (formerly Claude Vorilhon, the editor of a French motor sport magazine), believes that all humans were created in the laboratories of the planet Elohim and that the Elohims have instructed Rael and his followers to develop cloning on Earth to provide earthlings with a form of immortality.[25] The Raelians, of course, can believe whatever they want to; but just as human sacrifice is illegal, experiments that pose a significant danger to women and children can also be outlawed,[26] and the religious beliefs of this cult do not provide a sufficient justification to refrain from outlawing cloning.

Just as two primary arguments in favor of cloning and inheritable genetic alterations have emerged over the past five years, so have two basic arguments about the future regulation of these technologies. The first, exemplified by Lee Silver, is that these technologies, while not necessarily desirable, are unstoppable because the market combined with parental desire will drive scientists and physicians to offer these services to demanding couples.[27] Similar to the way parents now seek early educational enrichment for their children, he believes that parents of the future will seek early genetic enhancement to give them a competitive advantage in life. Silver thinks this will ultimately lead to the creation of two separate species or subspecies, the GenRich and "the naturals."[28]

A related "do nothing" argument is that regulation may not be needed because the technologies will not be widely used. The thought is that humans may muddle through, either because the science of human genetic alterations may never prove possible, or because it will be used by only a handful of humans because most will instinctively reject it. Colin Tudge, a proponent of this argument, also accepts Silver's argument that the market is powerful and often determinative, but nonetheless believes that the three fundamental principles of all religions—personal humility, respect for fellow humans and reverence for the universe as a whole—could lead the vast majority of humans to reject cloning and genetic alterations.[29] In his words:

> The new technologies, taken to extremes, threaten the idea of humanity. We now need to ask as a matter of urgency who we really are and what we really value about ourselves. It could all be changed after all—we ourselves could be changed—perhaps simply by commercial forces that we have allowed to drift beyond our control. If that is not serious, it is hard to see what is.[30]

We agree with Tudge that the issues are serious. We think that they are too serious to be left to religions or human instinct, or even to individual national legislation, to address.

In this regard, we find a second approach, that of a democratically-formed regulatory scheme more reasonable. Indeed, in our view the widespread condemnation of human replicative cloning by governments around the world means that cloning provides a unique opportunity for the world to begin to work together to take some control over the biotechnology that threatens our very existence.[31]

The primary arguments against cloning and inheritable genetic alterations, which we believe make an international treaty the appropriate action, have been summarized in detail elsewhere. In general, the arguments are that these interventions would require massive dangerous and unethical human experimentation,[32] that cloning would inevitably be bad for the resulting children by restricting their right to an "open future,"[33] that cloning would lead to a new eugenics movement for "designer children" (because if an individual could select the entire genome of their future child, it would seem impossible to prohibit individuals from choosing one or more specific genetic characteristics of their future children),[34] and that it would likely lead to the creation of a new species or subspecies of humans, sometimes called the "posthuman."[35] In the context of endangering the species, the last argument has gotten the least attention, and so it is worth exploring.

Specifically, the argument is that cloning will inevitably lead to attempts to modify the somatic cell nucleus not to create genetic duplicates of existing people, but "better" children.[36] If this attempt fails, that is the end of it. If it succeeds, however, something like the scenario envisioned by Silver and others such as Nancy Kress,[37] will unfold: a new species or subspecies of humans will emerge. The new species, or "posthuman," will likely view the old "normal" humans as inferior, even savages, and fit for slavery or slaughter. The normals, on the other hand, may see the posthumans as a threat and if they can, may engage in a preemptive strike by killing the posthumans before they themselves are killed or enslaved by them. It is ultimately this predictable potential for genocide that makes species-altering experiments potential weapons of mass destruction, and makes the unaccountable genetic engineer a potential bioterrorist. It is also why cloning and genetic modification is of species-wide concern and why an international treaty to address it is appropriate.[38] Such a treaty is necessary because existing laws on cloning and inheritable genetic alterations, although often well-intentioned, have serious limitations.

International Restrictions on Cloning and Genetic Modifications

Despite the fact that no children have been born as a result of these species-altering interventions, policymakers around the world have expressed concerns about the use of these technologies. Some countries' lawmakers have enacted bans on these proposed experimental technologies, while others have assumed that existing laws apply to the techniques. However, both categories of laws have shortcomings.

Moratoria

Some countries have approached species-altering procedures with caution, instituting moratoria in order to consider the wide range of impacts of the technologies. Israel, for example, has stated that the purpose of such moratoria is to have time "to examine the moral, legal, social and scientific aspects of such types of intervention and their implication on human dignity."[39] In 1998, Israel adopted a five-year moratorium on cloning a human being, defining cloning as "the creation of an entire human being, who is genetically identical to another person or fetus, alive or dead."[40] The same law banned interventions to create a child through the use of reproductive cells that have undergone a permanent intentional genetic modification.[41] Some countries are using that same time period to consider the wealth of issues involved in species-altering procedures.[42] Others, though, have already determined that such technologies are inimical to human values and human dignity.[43]

Limitations in Human Cloning Bans

Some countries have attempted to ban human cloning, but have used language that inadvertently creates ambiguities. In other countries, policymakers may believe that their laws ban human cloning, but that may not be the case. Japan, for example, explicitly and clearly bans cloning.[44] Germany bans attempts to bring to birth a human embryo having the same genetic information as another embryo.[45] Spain, Victoria, Australia and Western Australia prohibit cloning and other procedures that bring about the birth of an identical human being.[46] But because cloning includes mitochondrial DNA from the woman whose egg is used, the clone will not have a completely identical genome (unless a woman clones herself and uses her own egg) and thus the practice of cloning may not be adequately banned.

Some countries ban embryo research,[47] but cloning through the Dolly technique of somatic cell nucleus transfer (SCNT) may not be viewed as embryo research. The SCNT technique utilizes an experimental procedure involving an egg to create an embryo.[48] Once the embryo has been created, no experimental technique is necessary. The resulting embryo can be implanted into a woman using the same standard clinical technique as is used in the *in vitro* fertilization (IVF) process.

British lawmakers thought they had a ban in place to prevent human cloning. The British have created a regulatory structure for IVF and related technology under the Human Fertilisation and Embryology Act of 1990 (HFEA).[49] The statute requires that activities falling within the act, such as the creation, storage, handling and use of human embryos outside of the body, must only be undertaken in licensed facilities.[50] Only activities enumerated in the Act, or approved by the Human Fertilisation and Embryology Authority, may be undertaken.[51] Certain activities, such as placing a human embryo in an animal, are completely prohibited. The British Act defines an "embryo" as a "live human embryo where fertilisation is complete" or "an egg in the process of fertilisation."[52] British lawmakers assumed human reproductive cloning was prohibited under the Act because it was not listed as an allowable activity with human embryos.[53]

In November 2000, the Pro-Life Alliance brought suit claiming that embryos created through cloning are not covered by HFEA. On November 15, 2001, the British High Court of Justice, Queen's Bench Division, Administrative Court, ruled in favor of the Pro-Life Alliance. The judge said, "With some reluctance, since it would leave organisms produced by CNR [cell nuclear replacement] outside the statutory and licensing framework, I have come to the conclusion that to insert these words would involve an impermissible rewriting and extension of the definition."[54] In response, Parliament passed new legislation just two weeks after the ruling making it an offense, punishable by up to ten years in prison, for a person to place "in a woman a human embryo which has been created otherwise than by fertilisation."[55] Ultimately, a higher court ruled that a human embryo created by cloning was in fact covered by HFEA.[56]

Bans on Inheritable Genetic Interventions

Internationally, the bans on inheritable or germline genetic interventions are general enough to reach a wide range of technologies. These laws reflect a profound understanding of the need to avoid the social pressures to engineer a "better" race, as occurred in the Nazi era. German law understandably forbids germline intervention.[57] Victoria, Australia, in its Infertility Treatment Act of 1995, has comprehensive language prohibiting germline genetic alterations.[58] The law prohibits altering the genetic constitution of gametes[59] or altering the genetic, pronuclear or nuclear constitution of a zygote.[60] A Western Australia law prohibits the alteration of the genetic structure of an egg in the process of fertilization or an embryo.[61] In Norway, a 1994 law provides that the "human genome may only be altered by means of somatic gene therapy for the purpose of treating serious disease or preventing serious disease from occurring."[62] Sweden prohibits research that attempts to modify the embryo.[63] France, too, prohibits such interventions.[64] Costa Rica bans any manipulation or alternation of an embryo's genetic code.[65]

The Legal Status of Human Cloning and Germline Genetics Intervention in the United States

In 1997 President Clinton issued an executive order banning the use of federal funds for human cloning.[66] However, such a ban has little effect on private fertility clinics. For twenty years, the federal government has refused to provide funds for research on IVF, but that has not stopped the hundreds of privately-financed IVF clinics from creating tens of thousands of babies. The ban on federal funding of embryo research and human cloning does not, of course, apply to scientists who wish to undertake either activity with private funds.

The Application of U.S. Laws Banning Embryo Research
to Human Cloning and Inheritable Genetic Intervention

Existing U.S. laws banning embryo research, dating back in some states to the mid-1970s, could potentially be used to prohibit certain species-altering technologies at the experimental stage.[67] Eleven states have laws regulating research and/or experimentation on conceptuses, embryos, fetuses or unborn children that use broad enough language to apply to early embryos.[68] It should be noted, however, that these bans would not apply once the techniques are no longer considered to be research and instead are thought of as standard practice.

Several arguments could be made to suggest that most of the embryo research statutes should be construed narrowly so as not to apply to cloning. Eight of the eleven states prohibit some form of research on some product of conception, referred to in the statutes as a conceptus,[69] embryo,[70] fetus[71] or unborn child.[72] With cloning, an argument could be made that the experimentation is being done on an egg, not the product of conception, and thus these statutes should not apply.[73] By the time the egg is re-nucleated, the experiment or research has already been completed and the resulting embryo could be implanted under standard practices, as with IVF.

Moreover, two of the eleven states define the object of protection—the conceptus (Minnesota) or unborn child (Pennsylvania)—as the product of fertilization. If transfer of nucleic material is not considered fertilization (as was the case in the initial court decision in England), then these laws would not apply. In addition, at least eight of the states banning embryo research are sufficiently general that they might be struck down as unconstitutionally vague.[74]

Under New Hampshire's embryo research law, a researched-upon pre-embryo may not be transferred to a uterine cavity.[75] Thus, if a re-nucleated oocyte is considered to be a pre-embryo and if cloning is considered to be research, it would be impermissible in New Hampshire to implant the resulting conceptus to create a child. Possibly as a result of the deficiencies in the embryo research laws, three of the states with embryo research bans have new laws banning cloning.[76]

The embryo research bans could potentially affect the practice of inheritable genetic alterations. Under these laws, research attempts to insert genes into embryos would be prohibited if undertaken strictly to gain scientific knowledge. If the genes were added in an attempt to "cure" a particular embryo that was destined to go to term, however, it is likely to be permissible in most states. Maine might still ban it, because it prohibits "any form of experimentation."[77] But several of the other embryo research bans explicitly allow procedures for the purpose of providing a health benefit to the fetus or embryo, and therefore might not affect gene alterations.[78] In some states, the embryo research bans might forbid the use of evolving or insufficiently-tested therapies if such therapies were not necessary to the preservation of the life of the fetus. However, these laws or related laws generally require the protection and preservation of viable fetuses. Therefore, it seems unlikely that the embryo research laws in these states would be invoked to enforce the withholding of gene therapy as a form of treatment if doctors argued that the procedure held out some actual promise of a health benefit to the embryo and prospective child.

The New Hampshire and Louisiana laws have unique twists. New Hampshire's law might ban creating a child with inheritable alterations because it prohibits the transfer of any embryo donated for research to a uterus.[79] Louisiana's law has the opposite effect, prohibiting farming or culturing embryos solely for research purposes,[80] but apparently allowing research as long as the embryo is implanted.

We do not believe there is any constitutional prohibition that would limit the legal authority of the federal government to enter into an international treaty banning human cloning and inheritable genetic alterations, although this question has been the subject of wide discussion in the legal literature.[81]

The United States itself currently has no federal law on either cloning or inheritable genetic modification, even though both President George W. Bush and former President Bill Clinton are in favor of outlawing human "reproductive" cloning.[82] In August 2001, the House of Representatives voted to outlaw both research and reproductive cloning, and this proposal, known as the Weldon bill, has reached the Senate.[83] When the Senate takes up the issue, it will have to decide whether to agree with the Weldon bill (in which case it will be signed by the President and become law), or to try to craft a bill that outlaws reproductive cloning, but permits research cloning, as recommended by the National Academy of Sciences. In this case, the Senate bill will be sent to a conference committee where, unless the politics of the issue changes radically, it will likely die.[84] Of course, unless the United States passes legislation outlawing reproductive cloning, it cannot take any meaningful leadership role in the international treaty area on this issue.

Promulgating an International Treaty

The adoption of an international treaty is the most appropriate approach to prohibit species-altering interventions. A rogue doctor or scientist who wishes to offer the procedure can easily move across borders if a particular nation bans the procedure. When the American physicist Richard Seed announced he intended to clone human beings and U.S. lawmakers threatened to clamp down on the procedure, he responded that he would open up a clinic in Mexico[85] or join a Japanese-based project.[86] Restrictions on European biotechnology companies have stimulated some to move to Africa.[87]

Various international declarations and laws already oppose human cloning or inheritable genetic interventions, either directly or indirectly. As summarized above,[88] many of these existing legal documents have shortcomings. Some are mere moratoria, set to expire in 2003. Some are limited in the type of species-altering technologies they ban, covering only cloning and not inheritable genetic interventions, or even just applying to cloning via a limited range of techniques.

Some of the existing laws have also been outpaced by technology and do not comprehensively ban all forms of reproductive cloning and inheritable interventions. Others are ambiguous as to what they cover. In some cases, potentially relevant laws were adopted more than two decades ago to deal with a different set of technologies and concerns; it is unclear whether their expansive prohibitions will be applied to the newer technologies of reproductive cloning and inheritable interventions. Moreover, many of the existing declarations and laws do not include sanctions. Thus, there is a need for an international treaty to encourage participating nations to clarify what is prohibited and have them commit to effective criminal penalties for breaches.

The treaty we propose takes a strong human rights perspective. This approach comports with international human rights traditions because it conceptualizes medical research issues as human rights matters.[89] It also comports with people's concerns about cloning and inheritable intervention. For example, in a survey of 2,700 Japanese doctors and academics, ninety-four percent of respondents found cloning to be ethically unacceptable, primarily because it insulted human dignity.[90] In Portugal, the National Ethics Council for Human Sciences deemed human cloning unacceptable due to concerns about human dignity and about the equilibrium of the human race and social life.[91] Human rights language is also evident in calls for a prohibition on cloning, such as one by the Council of Europe's Parliamentary Assembly, emphasizing that "every individual has a right to his own genetic identity."[92]

Concerns about human cloning run sufficiently deep that even those who would make money on the procedure have come out against it. Ian Wilmut, the scientist whose team cloned Dolly the sheep, might benefit financially if humans were cloned because his group holds a patent on a cloning process. But he has testified around the world against human cloning.[93] Similarly, BIO (the Biotechnology Industry Organization, a U.S. trade association of biotechnology companies) opposes human reproductive cloning.[94]

Numerous entities have called for an enforceable international ban on species-altering interventions. The World Health Organization (WHO) at its fifty-first World Health Assembly reaffirmed that "cloning for replication of human beings is ethically unacceptable and contrary to human dignity and integrity."[95] WHO urges member states to "foster continued and informed debate on these issues and to take appropriate steps, including legal and juridical measures, to prohibit cloning for the purpose of replicating human individuals."[96]

The European Union's Council of Europe adopted the Council of Europe Protocol, prohibiting the cloning of human beings. Twenty-nine countries have signed the treaty.[97] Similarly, the European Parliament has adopted a Resolution on Human Cloning. The Resolution indicates that people have a fundamental human right to their own genetic identity.[98] It states that human cloning is "unethical, morally repugnant, contrary to respect for the person and 'a grave violation of fundamental human rights which cannot under any circumstances be justified or accepted.' "[99] The Resolution calls for member states to enact binding national legislation banning cloning and also urges the United Nations to secure an international ban on cloning.[100]

UNESCO's Universal Declaration on the Human Genome and Human Rights specifically addresses cloning.[101] Like the treaty we propose, the Declaration is based on "universal principles of human rights."[102] The Declaration specifically refers to UNESCO's constitution, which underscores "the democratic principles of the dignity, equality and mutual respect of men."[103] Article 11 of the Declaration states, "Practices which are contrary to human dignity, such as reproductive cloning of human beings, shall not be permitted."[104] However, the Declaration does not have an enforcement mechanism. Rather, it calls upon nations and international organizations to enact national and international policies to prohibit cloning and to identify and prohibit those genetic practices that are contrary to human dignity.[105]

On August 7, 2001, France and Germany urged the U.N. Secretary-General to add an International Convention against reproductive cloning of human beings to its agenda.[106] The French-German initiative is focused on banning only reproductive cloning apparently because there is an international consensus on this issue. It is worth noting that the laws of both countries ban research cloning and other forms of inheritable genetic interventions as well, and that political leaders in both countries have spoken out publicly in favor of imposing a broader ban. Nonetheless, both of these countries seem content to pursue a two-step process at the United Nations: securing as soon as possible a ban on reproductive cloning, and leaving negotiations on other issues, including inheritable genetic alterations and research cloning, for a second round of international negotiations. This may in fact be the only practicable way to proceed.

In November 2001, the Legal Committee of the United Nations added its support to a ban on reproductive cloning,[107] and the first meeting on the treaty was held in February 2002. There was virtual unanimous support for the treaty among the approximately 80 countries that attended, although the United States took the position that it would only support the treaty if it also outlawed research cloning. The issues of reproductive cloning discussed in this chapter can, of course, be separated from those involved in research cloning, and will likely have to be if a treaty on reproductive cloning is to be adopted.[108] Whether the U.S. position will change remains to be seen. It seems likely that this U.N. treaty process is the only way a cloning treaty is likely to be achieved.[109] The treaty we propose is an attempt to provide language that could be used in both stages of a two stage process, or in one process if they are combined. It is drafted in a way to reflect the broad social concerns against species-altering technologies and to close loopholes in existing legal documents and declarations. Like the U.N. Legal Committee, we believe that the time is ripe for a flat-out international ban on human cloning. We also advocate a similar ban on inheritable genetic interventions.

Biotechnology, especially human cloning and inheritable genetic alteration, has the potential to permit us to design our children and to literally change the characteristics of the human species. The movement toward a posthuman world can be characterized as "progress" and enhancement of individual freedom in the area of procreation; but it also can be characterized as a movement down a slippery slope to a neo-eugenics that will result in the creation of one or more subspecies or superspecies of humans. The first vision sees science as our guide and ultimate goal. The second is more firmly based on our human history as it has consistently emphasized differences, and used those differences to justify genocidal actions. It is the prospect of "genetic genocide" that calls for treating cloning and genetic engineering as potential weapons of mass destruction, and the unaccountable genetic researcher as a potential bioterrorist.

The greatest accomplishment of humans has not been our science, but our development of human rights and democracy. Science cannot tell us what we should do, or even what our goals are, therefore, humans must give direction to science. In the area of genetics, this calls for international action to control the species-endangering techniques that could lead us to commit species suicide. We humans clearly recognized the risk in splitting the atom and developing nuclear weapons; and most humans recognize the risk in using human genes to modify ourselves. Because the risk is to the entire species, it requires a species response. Many countries have already enacted bans, moratoria and strict regulations on various species-altering technologies. The challenge, however, is global, and action on the international level is required to be effective.

We believe that the action called for today is the ratification of an international convention for the preservation of the human species that outlaws human cloning and inheritable genetic alterations. This ban would not only be important in itself, but it would also mark the first time the world worked together to control a biotechnology. Cloning and inheritable genetic alterations are not bioweapons per se, but they could prove just as destructive to the human species if left to the market and individual wants and desires.

We think an international consensus to ban these technologies already exists, and that countries, non-governmental organizations and individual citizens should actively support the treaty process, as they did with the recent Convention on the Prohibition of the Use, Stockpiling, Production and Transfer of Anti-Personnel Mines and their Destruction (Land Mine Treaty).[110]

Cloning may not seem as important as landmines, as no clone has yet been born and thus no children have been harmed by this technique. Nonetheless, cloning has the potential to harm all children, both directly by physically and mentally harming them, and indirectly by devaluing all children—treating them as products of their parents' genetic specifications. Likewise, inheritable genetic alteration carries the prospect of developing a new species of humans that could turn into either destroyers or victims of the human species. Opposition to cloning and inheritable genetic alteration is "conservative" in the strict sense of the word: it seeks to conserve the human species. But it is also liberal in the strict sense of the word: it seeks to preserve democracy, freedom and universal human rights for all members of the human species.*

Notes

1. "We still don't know how to put morality ahead of politics, science and economy. We are still incapable of understanding that the only genuine backbone of all our actions, if they are to be moral, is responsibility—responsibility to something higher than my family, my country, my company, my success." Vaclav Havel, "Excerpts from Czech Chief's Address to Congress," *N.Y. Times*, Feb. 22, 1990, at A14. See also Amartya Sen, *Development as Freedom* (1999); George J. Annas, "Mapping the Human Genome and the Meaning of Monster Mythology," 39 *Emory L.J.* 629, 661–64 (1990).
2. See *The Charter of the United Nations: A Commentary* 49 (Bruno Simma et al. eds., 1995).
3. Commencement Address at American University in Washington, *Pub. Papers* 459, 462 (June 10, 1963).

   President George W. Bush echoed Kennedy's words almost forty years later:

   All fathers and mothers, in all societies, want their children to be educated and live free from poverty and violence. No people on earth yearn to be oppressed or aspire to servitude or eagerly await the midnight knock of the secret police. . . . America will lead by defending liberty and justice because they are right and true and unchanging for all people everywhere.

   No nation owns these aspirations and no nation is exempt from them. We have no intention of imposing our culture, but America will always stand firm for the non-negotiable demands of human dignity: the rule of law; limits on the power of the state; respect for women; private property; free speech; equal justice; and religious tolerance.

   Address Before a Joint Session of the Congress on the State of the Union, 38 *Weekly Comp. Pres.* DOC 133, 138 (Jan. 29, 2002).
4. See Henry J. Steiner and Philip Alston, *International Human Rights in Context: Law, Politics, Morals* 137–41 (2d ed. 2000).
5. Quoted in Mary Ann Glendon, *A World Made New: Eleanor Roosevelt and the Universal Declaration of Human Rights* 223 (2001).
6. See generally M. Cherif Bassiouni, *Crimes Against Humanity in International Criminal Law* (1992) (exploring the history and evolution of "crimes against humanity"). See also George J. Annas, "The Man on the Moon, Immortality, and Other Millennial Myths: The Prospects and Perils of Human Genetic Engineering," 49 *Emory LJ*, 753, 778–80 (2000)

---

*For a summary of the laws enacted on human cloning and germline genetic engineering by individual countries, see www.glphr.org/genetic.htm.

(discussing the possibility of species-alteration becoming a new category of "crimes against humanity").

7. See e.g., Francis Fukuyama, *Our Postuman Future: Consequences of the Biotechnology Revolution* (2002). Of course, these actions have not yet been recognized as crimes against humanity or any other type of international crime, and this is one reason why some still see these activities as legitimate.

8. Obviously, the only current candidate is the United Nations.

9. *Protecting Public Health and the Environment: Implementing the Precautionary Principle 354* (Carolyn Raffensperger & Joel A. Tickner eds., 1999).

10. This proposed Convention is the product of many people, including the participants at a September 21–22, 2001 conference at Boston University on "Beyond Cloning: Protecting Humanity from Species-Altering Procedures." The treaty language was the subject of a roundtable that concluded the conference. The authors, together with others, most especially Patricia Baird and Alexander Morgan Capron, had drafted language to be considered at the conference, and revised it after the conference based on the discussion that occurred there and comments on the draft by others.

The original draft also included the following codicil to encourage individual countries to examine broader issues as well:

ISSUES FOR NATIONS TO CONSIDER IN FURTHERANCE OF THE CONVENTION ON THE PRESERVATION OF THE HUMAN SPECIES

In the course of discussions about the Convention on the Preservation of the Human Species, countries may desire to expand the provisions to deal in greater detail with other matters. Perhaps there will be a desire to add a moratorium on the creation of cloned human embryos for research. It may also be thought useful to include provisions that deal more comprehensively with assisted reproduction and life-science patents. Such provisions could take into consideration the following issues:

Assisted Human Reproduction

Potential Regulation:
The regulation of the practice of assisted human reproduction could include such provisions as requirements of a license for any healthcare professional who or healthcare facility that:

• Facilitates assisted human reproduction, e.g., via donor insemination or *in vitro* fertilization;
• Undertakes research or treatment using an *in vitro* embryo;
• Collects, stores, transfers, destroys, imports or exports sperm, ova or *in vitro* embryos for reproduction or research purposes; or
• Undertakes genetic screening on an *ex utero* embryo.

The regulation of the practice of assisted human reproduction could also include provisions to ensure:

• Free and informed consent of prospective parents and gamete donors as a prerequisite to the use of the techniques;
• Quality assurance and proficiency testing for labs;
• Reporting to a governmental entity the outcomes (including births per attempt and data about morbidity and mortality of the resulting children for the first five years) and disclosure to the public of this information;
• Non-misleading advertising (to the extent that advertising is permitted at all); and
• Confidentiality of individually identifiable health information.

Other prohibitions beyond those on human cloning and germline intervention might include bans on:

• Extracorporeal gestation of a human being;
• Transfer of a human embryo into an animal;

- Creation of embryos solely for research purposes; or
- Transplanting reproductive material (including gametes, ovaries or testes) from animals into humans.

Gene Patents

The purpose of the patent system is to encourage innovation and the development of products by providing the holder of a patent with a twenty-year monopoly over the use of an invention. Patenting genes runs counter to this purpose because gene patents are stifling innovation and impeding access to genetic diagnostic and treatment technologies. Many researchers who are searching for genes that predispose individuals to diseases are reluctant to share information and tissue samples with other researchers because they want to discover the gene themselves and to reap the financial rewards of discovery. These rewards can be high. For example, one particular gene patent in the United States is worth $1.5 billion annually.

Once a gene is discovered, the patent holder can prevent any doctor or laboratory from even checking a person's body to see if he or she has a mutation of the gene. Alternatively, the patent holder can collect a very high royalty from the doctors and laboratories that examine the gene. The patent holder can even stop any use of the patented gene. One patent holder, for example, will not permit the use of its gene in prenatal screening because of the controversy surrounding abortion. Another patent holder, a major European pharmaceutical company, will not allow anyone to use its patented gene to develop a test which shows which patients will benefit from one of the company's drugs and which will not. Another biotechnology company has a patent on the genetic sequence of a particular infectious disease and is stopping another company from instituting inexpensive public health screening to determine if people are infected.

On the other hand, patent holders themselves may encourage premature adoption of genetic diagnostic tests and unsafe efforts at gene transfer experiments to benefit the patent holder rather than patients or research subjects. Moreover, special issues are raised in the case of patenting human tissue, including the ethical and legal propriety of ownership of one person's genetic information by another.

Potential regulation:

No patents shall be granted on human genes, parts of human genes or unaltered products of human genes, nor on the genes of bacteria, viruses or other infectious agents that cause disease in humans.

Work on a national regulatory scheme for the new reproductive technologies will, of course, be most relevant to countries that have an in-vitro fertilization (IVF) industry. We also believe that the best existing guidance for approaching such regulation is contained in the final report of Canada's Royal Commission on New Reproductive Technologies. Patricia Baird, *Proceed with Care: Final Report of the Royal Commission on New Reproductive Technologies,* 564–76 (1993). Also, to the extent that a country wants to proceed with research cloning (e.g., for the purpose of making stem cells or studying embryonic growth), regulation of the infertility industry will be needed to prevent a cloned embryo from being implanted in a woman's uterus. Such regulation could include, for example, the prohibition of freezing cloned embryos, and the prohibition of any physician or embryologist involved in IVF from making or possessing a cloned embryo.

11. While we believe these crimes should be subject to the jurisdiction of the International Criminal Court, this may not be possible in the near future, and it is more important to establish them as international crimes than to broaden the definition of "crimes against humanity" as it applies to the International Criminal Court at this time.

12. Nat'l Bioethics Advisory Comm'n, *Cloning Human Beings 109* (1997), available at http://bioethics.georgetown.edu/nbac/pubs.html.

13. For example, during the 1998 debate on cloning in the U.S. Senate, more than sixteen scientific and medical organizations, including the American Society of Reproductive Medicine and the Federation of American Societies for Experimental Biology (which includes more than sixteen scientific and medical organizations), believed that there should be a moratorium on the creation of humans by cloning. See 144 *Cong. Reg.* S434–38 (1998); 144 *Cong. Reg.* S661 (1998). None of these organizations has since changed their position.

See, e.g., Press Release, *Am. Soc'y Reproductive Med.*, "ASRM Statement on Attempts at Human Cloning" (Apr. 5, 2002) ("[W]e caution policy makers not to be rushed into approving over-reaching legislation that will criminalize valid scientific and medical research and the therapies they might lead to.") available at http://www.asrm.org/Media/Press/cloningstatement4–02; Letter from Carl B. Feldbaum, President, Biotechnology Ind. Org., to President George W. Bush (Feb. 1, 2002) ("The current moratorium on cloning humans should remain until our nation has had time to fully explore the impact of such cloning."), available at http://www.bio.org/bioethics/cloning_letter_bush.html. See also Rudolf Jaenisch & Ian Wilmut, "Don't Clone Humans!," 291 *Science* 2552 (2001) ("We believe attempts to clone human beings at a time when the scientific issues of nuclear cloning have not been clarified are dangerous and irresponsible."); Editorial, "Reasons to be Cloned," 414 *Nature* 567 (2001) ("[T]he health risks to mother and child inherent in [cloning] . . . demand that it be banned.").

14. Nat'l Research Council, *Scientific and Medical Aspects of Human Reproductive Cloning* (2002).

> Human reproductive cloning . . . is dangerous and likely to fail. The panel therefore unanimously supports the proposal that there should be a legally enforceable ban on the practice of human reproductive cloning . . . The scientific and medical considerations related to this ban should be reviewed within 5 years. The ban should be reconsidered only if at least two conditions are met: (1) a new scientific and medical review indicates that the procedures are likely to be safe and effective and (2) a broad national dialogue on the societal, religious, and ethical issues suggests that a reconsideration of the ban is warranted.

> *Id.* at ES-1 to ES-2. See also *Nat'l Research Council, Stem Cells and the Future of Regenerative Medicine* (2001).

15. Stuart A. Newman, Speech at the "Beyond Cloning" Conference, Boston University (Sept. 21, 2001).
16. See, e.g., Jon W. Gordon, "Genetic Enhancement in Humans." 283 *Science* 2023, 2023 (1999).
17. Hans Jonas, for example, argued that it is a crime against the clone by depriving the cloned child of his or her "existential right to certain subjective terms of being." Hans Jonas, *Philosophical Essays: From Ancient Creed to Technological Man* 160 (1974). Jonas believes that a clone will not have a "right to ignorance" or the "right . . . to a unique genotype." *Id.* Instead, a clone knows:

> [Altogether too much about himself and is known . . . altogether too well by others. Both facts are paralyzing for the spontaneity of becoming himself . . . [T]he clone is antecedently robbed of the freedom which only under the protection of ignorance can thrive: and to rob a human-to-be of that freedom deliberately is an inexplicable crime that must not be committed even once.

> *Id.* at 161. Human reproductive cloning poses both physical and psychological risks to children who might be conceived using this technique. In animals, cloning currently only results in a successful pregnancy three to five percent of the time. And, even in those rare instances, many of the resulting offspring suffer—one-third die shortly before or right after birth. Other cloned animals seem perfectly healthy at first and then suffer heart and blood vessel problems, underdeveloped lungs, diabetes, immune system deficiencies and severe growth abnormalities. The mothers who gestate clones are also at risk, due to the often abnormally large size of the offspring produced—some cattle clones for example, are born up to twice the normal weight expected for calves.

18. Tim Adams, "Interview: The Clone Arranger," *The Observer*, Dec. 2, 2001, at 3 (comments of Severino Antinori).

> Male infertility grows . . . My invention of ICSI has helped. I have helped men whose sperm are misformed or too slow. I have helped men whose sperm does not come out from their testes! And the next step [cloning] is to help men who—traumatico!—have lost their ability to produce any sperm at all. Through war or accident or cancer. I will help only stable, loving couples. Some doctors say this is a step too far, but those same doctors have said that about all the other steps too. Very few doctors are pioneers! Very few have

both the knowledge and the, the, the . . . courage. *Id,* See also Robert Winston, "The Promise of Cloning for Human Medicine," 314 *Brit.Med.J.* 913 (1997) (advocating for the use of cloning to help infertile men have genetically-related children). Zavos and Antinori dissolved their partnership in 2002. David Brown, "Human Clone's Birth Predicted," *Wash. Post,* May 16, 2002, at A8.

19. See generally, Michael H. Shapiro, "I Want a Girl (Boy) Just Like the Girl (Boy) that Married Dear Old Dad (Mom): Cloning Lives," 9 *S. Cal. Interdisc. L.J.* I (arguing, in part, that cloning should be considered reproduction, for the essence of reproduction is the creation of a new person).

   A variety of personal desires may interest people in creating a child through cloning or germline genetic engineering. The NBAC report suggests it would be "understandable, or even, as some have argued, desirable" to create a cloned child from one adult if both members of the couple have a lethal recessive gene; from a dying infant if his father is dead and the mother wants an offspring from her late husband; or from a terminally ill child to create a bone marrow donor. *Cloning Human Beings, supra* note 12, at 78–80. Some of the experts testifying before the NBAC suggested that cloning should be appropriate in exceptional circumstances. Rabbi Elliot Dorff opined that it would be "legitimate from a moral and a Jewish point of view" to clone a second child to act as a bone marrow donor so long as the "parents" raise that second child as they would any other. *Id.* at 55. Rabbi Moshe Tendler raised the scenario of a person who was the last in his genetic line and whose family was wiped out in the Holocaust. "I would certainly clone him," said Tendler. *Id.* For other Jewish perspectives supporting cloning, see Peter Hirschberg, "Be Fruitful and Multiply and Multiply and Multiply," *Jerusalem Rep., Apr.* 16, 1998, at 33. In contrast, the Catholic viewpoint is that cloning "is entirely unsuitable for human procreation even for exceptional circumstances." *Cloning Human Beings, supra* note 12, at 55.

20. Before a U.S. Senate Committee, which also heard from Ian Wilmut shortly after he had announced the birth of Dolly, one of us made the argument that a human clone would be the first human being with one genetic parent. *Testimony on Scientific Discoveries and Cloning: Challenges for Public Policy, Before the Sen. Subcomm. on Public Health and Safety. Sen. Comm. on Labor and Human Resources,* 105th Cong. 25 (1997) (statement of George J. Annas), available at http://www.bumc.bu.edu/www/sph/lw/pvl/Clonetest.htm. Population geneticist Richard Lewontin challenged this assertion, writing:

   A child by cloning has a full set of chromosomes like anyone else, half of which were derived from a mother and half from a father. It happens that these chromosomes were passed through another individual, the cloning donor, on the way to the child. The donor is certainly not the child's "parent" in any biological sense, but simply an earlier offspring of the original parents. R.C. Lewontin, "Confusion over Cloning," *N.Y. Rev. Books,* Oct. 23, 1997, at 20.

   It should be noted that Lewontin's position takes genetic reductionism to its extreme: people become no more than containers of their parent's genes, and their parents have the "right" to treat them not as individual human beings, but rather like embryos—entities that they can "split" or "replicate" without consideration of the child's choice or welfare. Children, even adult children, under this view have no say as to whether or not they are replicated because it is their "parents," not them, who are "reproducing." This radical redefinition of reproduction and the denial to children of the choice to procreate or not turns out to be an even stronger argument against cloning children than its biological novelty. George J. Annas, *Some Choice: Law, Medicine & the Market* 13 (1998).

21. See, e.g., Ethics Comm., Am. Soc'y Reproductive Med., "Human Somatic Cell Nuclear Transfer (Cloning)," 74 *Fertility & Sterility* 873, 873–76 (2000).

22. John A. Robertson, "Two Models of Human Cloning," 27 *Hofstra L. Rev.* 609 (1999).

23. Ronald Dworkin, *Sovereign Virtue: The Theory and Practice of Equality* 437–42 (1997).

24. Leon Kass made this point in another context, Leon R. Kass, *Toward a More Natural Science: Biology and Human Affairs* 110–111 (1985).

25. See Rael, *The True Face of God* (Int'l Raelian Movement 1998).

26. *See* Jay Katz, *Experimentation with Human Beings* (Russell Sage Found. 1972).

27. Lee Silver, *Remaking Eden: Cloning and Beyond in a Brave New World* 123 (1997).

28. *Id.* at 4.

29. Colin Tudge, *The Impact of the Gene: From Mendel's Peas to Designer Babies,* 4 (2000).

30. *Id.* at 342. See also Ian Wilmut et al. *The Second Creation: Dolly and the Age of Biological Control* 267–98 (2000) (discussing the implications of cloning for humankind).

31. See www.glphr.org/genetic/genetic.htm for current national laws on human cloning and inheritable modifications.

32. See generally *The Nazi Doctors and the Nuremberg Code* (George J. Annas & Michael A. Grodin eds., 1992) (exploring the "history, context, and implications of the Doctor's Trial at Nuremberg and the impact of the Nuremberg Code on subsequent codes of research ethics and international human rights").

33. Jonas, *supra* note 17, at 161–62.

34. It is in this sense that children become "manufactured" products. See Kass, *supra* note 24, at 71–73.

35. See Annas, *supra* note 6, at 776–780; Fukuyama, *supra* note 7, at 22; Francis Fukuyama, "Natural Rights and Human History," *Nat'l Interest*, Summer 2001, at 19, 30. For arguments favoring inheritable genetic modifications, see, for example, *Engineering the Human Germline* (Gregory Stock & John Campbell eds., 2000); Gregory Stock, *Redesigning Humans* (2002) (arguing, among other things, that it is inherent in our human nature to want to change our human nature, and that an international treaty would be unenforceable because every nation would have an economic incentive to defect and capture the market for inheritable modifications).

36. See, e.g., Wilmut et al., *supra* note 30, at 5–6 (discussing how the post-Dolly experiments were designed to use cloning techniques to make "better animals," which was always Ian Wilmut's and Keith Campbell's plan for cloning technology). See also Angelika E. Shnieke et al. "Human Factor IX Trans-gene Sheep Produced by Transfer of Nuclei from Transplanted Fetal Fibroblasts," 278 *Science* 2130 (1997).

37. See, for example, Nancy Kress's Beggars series: *Beggars in Spain* (1993); *Beggars and Choosers* (1994); and *Beggar's Ride* (1996).

38. See Annas, *supra* note 6, at 778–81. An alternative scenario, that sees equal access to genetic "improvement" by all seems like pie in the sky to us in a world where fewer than ten percent of the population has access to contemporary medical care, and even in the world's richest country, more than forty million people lack health insurance. We do not think it is reasonable to even discuss equal access to genetic alterations until all members of the species have access to current medical technologies as a matter of right.

39. Prohibition of Genetic Intervention Law No. 5759 (1998).

40. *Id.* §3(1).

41. *Id.* § 3(2).

42. See Ania Lichtarowicz, "*Scientist Warns on Human Cloning*," *BBC News, at* http://news.bbc.co.uk/hi/English/world/Europe/newsid_1719000/1719195.htm (Dec. 21, 2001) (noting that Spain and Belgium are still considering different types of legislation for adoption).

43. "Britain to Ban Human Cloning." CNN.com, *at* http://www.cnn.com/2001/WORLD/europe/UK/04/19/cloning.legislation/index.html (Apr. 19, 2001). *See also* Human Reproductive Cloning Act 2001, U.K. Stat. 2001, ch. 23, Enactment Clause (Eng.), (stating that the law "prohibit[s] the placing in a woman of a human embryo which has been created otherwise than by fertilisation").

44. "Ministry Bans Cloning Technology for Humans," *Daily Yomiuri*, July 29, 1998, at 2.

45. Gesetz zum Schutz von Embryonen (Embryonenschutzgesetz), v. 13.12.1990 (BGBI. I S.2747). [Federal Embryo Protection Law].

46. Manipulacion Gentica y Reproduccion [Genetic Manipulation and Reproduction]; Victoria Infertility Treatment Act, 2000; Human Reproductive Technology Act, 1991, § 7(1)(d)(i) (W. Austl.).

47. See, e.g., "The Logical Next Step? An International Perspective on the Issues of Human Cloning and Genetic Technology," 4 *ILSA J. Int'l & Comp.L.* 697, 721–25 (1998).

48. See, e.g., Valerie S. Rup, "Human Somatic Cell Nuclear Transfer Cloning, the Race to Regulate, and the Constitutionality of the Proposed Regulations," 76 *U. Det. Mercy L. Rev.* 1135, 1138–39 (1999); Christine Willgoos, Note, "FDA Regulation: An Answer to the Questions of Human Cloning and Germline Gene Therapy," 27 *Am. J.L. & Med.* 101, 103 (2001).

49. Human Fertilisation and Embryology Act, 1990, ch. 37, Enactment Clause (Eng.). See generally Ruth Deech, "The Legal Regulation of Infertility Treatment in Britain," in

Crosscurrents: Family Law and Policy in the U.S. and England 165–86 (Sanford Katz et al. eds, 2000).

50. Human Fertilisation and Embryology Act. ch. 27, §§ 3, 12.
51. *Id.* ch. 37, § 41.
52. *Id.* ch. 37, Enactment Clause.
53. The Act also had a ban, predating Dolly, on the replacement of the nucleus of a human embryo cell with that of any person or embryo, but that prohibition does not cover somatic cell nucleus transfer into a human egg.
54. Pro-Life Alliance v. Sec'y State for Health, CO/4095/2000 (Q.B. 2001), available at 2001 *WL* 1347031.
55. Human Reproductive Cloning Act, 2001, U.K. Stat. 2001 ch. 23 § 1.
56. *R (Quintavalle) v. Sec'y of State for Health*, 2 *WLR* 550 (C.A. 2002), reprinted at "Cell Nuclear Replacement Organism is 'Embryo'" *The Times* (London), Jan. 25, 2002.
57. Federal Embryo Protection Law, 1990 (Eng.)
58. Victoria Infertility Treatment Act, 1995.
59. Federal Embryo Protection Law, 1990 (Eng.), at Part 5, § 39(1).
60. Federal Embryo Protection Law, 1990 (Eng.), at Part 5, § 39(2).
61. Human Reproductive Technology, 1991, § 7(l)(j) (Austl.).
62. The Act Relating to the Application of Biotechnology in Medicine, ch. 7.
63. Law No. 115 of March 14, 1991, Act Concerning Measures for the Purposes of Research or Treatment in Connection with Fertilized Human Oocytes (1993).
64. Law No. 94–654 of July 29, 1994, on the Donation and Use of Elements and Products of the Human Body, Medically Assisted Procreation, and Prenatal Diagnosis.
65. Decree No. 24029-S: A Regulation on Assisted Reproduction, Feb. 3, 1995.
66. *See* Memorandum on the Prohibition on Federal Funding for Cloning of Human Beings, 33 *Weekly Com.? Pres. Doc.* 281 (Mar. 4, 1997); see also "Transcript of Clinton Remarks on Cloning," *U.S. Newswire,* Mar. 4, 1997, available at 1997 *WL* 5711155.
67. Yet despite the risks, only six states—California, Iowa, Louisiana, Michigan, Rhode Island and Virginia—have passed legislation that prohibits human reproductive cloning. *Cal. Health & Safety Code Ann.* § 24185 (West 2002); *Iowa Code* § 707B, CSB 218 (S.F. 2118) (2002); *La. Rev. Stat.* 40:1299.36.2 (West 2002); *Mich. Comp. Laws Ann.* § 750.430a (West 2001); *R.I. Gen. Laws* § 23–16.4 (2001); *Va. Code Ann.* §§ 32.1–162.21, 162.22 (Michie 2002). In addition, Missouri prohibits the use of any state funds to bring about the birth of a child via cloning techniques. *Mo. Ann. Stat.* § 1.217 (West 2002). The U.S. House of Representatives in July 2001 voted to ban human cloning. *See* The Human Cloning Prohibition Act of 2001, H.R. 2505, 107th Cong. (2001). See also Sheryl Gay Stolberg, "House Backs Ban on Human Cloning for any Objective," *N.Y. Times,* Aug. 1, 2001, at Al. At the time of this writing, the U.S. Senate was scheduled to consider this issue in 2002.
68. *Fla. Stat. Ann.* § 390.0111(6) (West 2002); *La. Rev. Stat. Ann.* § 9:121–129 (West 2002); *Me. Rev. Stat. Ann.* tit. 22, § 1593 (2002); *Mass. Gen. Laws Ann.* ch. 112, § 12J West (2002); *Mich. Comp. Laws Ann.* § 333.2685–2692 (West 2002); *Minn. Stat.* § 145.421 (2001); *N.D. Cent. Code* § 14-02.2-01 (2001); *N.H. Rev. Stat. Ann.* § 168–B:15 (2002); 18 *Pa. Cons. Stat.* § 3216 (2001); *R.I. Gen. Laws* § 11–54–1 (2001). A South Dakota law bans research that destroys an embryo, when such research has not been undertaken to preserve the life and health of the particular embryo. *S.D. Codified Laws* § 34–14–18 (Michie 2001).
69. *Minn. Stat. Ann.* § 145.421.
70. *Mich. Comp. Laws Ann.* § 333.2685.
71. *Fla. Stat. Ann.* § 390.0111(6); *Me. Rev. Stat. Ann.* tit. 22, § 1593; *Mass. Gen. Laws Ann.* ch. 112, § 12J; *Mich. Comp. Laws Ann.* § 333.2685–.2692; *N.D. Cent. Code* § 14–02.2–01; *R.I. Gen. Laws* § 11–54–1.
72. 18 *Pa. Cons. Stat.* § 3216.
73. See Ronald M. Green, "The Ethical Considerations," 286 *Scientific Am.* 4850, 4850 (Jan. 2002) (arguing that when Advanced Cell Technology created what the company called the "world's first human cloned embryo," all it had really done was create an "activated egg"). The company's president, Michael West, had previously argued that the company's work did not violate the Massachusetts Federal Research statute, and we believe he is correct in this argument.

74. Four states' fetal research bans—those of Arizona, Illinois, Louisiana, and Utah—have already been struck down on those grounds. *Forbes v. Napolitano,* 236 F.3d 1009 (9th Cir. 2000); *Margaret S. v. Edwards,* 794 F.2d 994, 998–99 (5th Cir. 1996); *Jane L. v. Bangerter,* 61 F.3d 1493, 1499–1502 (10th Cir. 1995); *Lifchez v. Hartigan,* 735 F. Supp. 1361, 1363–66 (N.D. 111, 1990).

75. *N.H. Rev. Stat. Ann.* § 168–8:15(11) (2002).

76. *La. Rev. Stat. Ann.* § 40:1299.36.2 (West 2002); *Mich. Comp. Laws Ann.* §§ 333.16275, 750.430(a) (West 2001); *R.I. Gen. Laws* § 23–16.4–2 (2001).

77. *Me. Rev. Stat. Ann.* tit. 22, § 1593 (2002).

78. See, e.g., *Fla. Stat. Ann.* § 390.0111(6) (West 2002); *Mass. Gen. Laws Ann.* ch. 112, § 12J (West 2002); *Mich. Comp. Laws Ann.* § 333.2685–2692 (West 2002); *Minn. Stat.* § 145.421 (2001); *N.D. cent. code* § 14–02.2–01 (2001); 18 *Pa. Cons. Stat.* § 3216 (2001); *R.I. Gen. Laws* § 11–54–1.

79. *N.H. Rev. Stat. Ann.* § 168-B:15(11).

80. *La. Rev. Stat. Ann.* § 9:122 (West 2002).

81. The right to make decisions about whether or not to bear children is constitutionally protected under the constitutional right to privacy. See, e.g., *Eisenstadt v. Baird,* 405 U.S. 438 (1972); *Griswold v. Connecticut,* 381 U.S. 479 *(1965).* The constitutional right to liberty also affords such protection. See *Planned Parenthood of S.E. Pa. v. Casey,* 505 U.S. 833, 857 (1992). The U.S. Supreme Court in 1992 reaffirmed the "recognized protection accorded to liberty relating to intimate relationships, the family, and decisions about whether to bear and beget a child." *Id.* at 857. Early decisions held that the right to privacy protected married couples' ability to make procreative decisions, but later decisions focused on individuals' rights as well. The U.S. Supreme Court has stated, "If the right of privacy means anything, it is the right of the individual, married or single, to be free from unwarranted governmental intrusion into matters so fundamentally affecting a person as the decision whether to bear or beget a child." *Eisenstadt,* 405 U.S. at 453.

A federal district court has indicated that the right to make procreative decisions encompasses the right of an infertile couple to undergo medically-assisted reproduction, including IVF and the use of a donated embryo. *Lifchez v. Hartigan,* 735 F. Supp. 1361, 1367–69. (N.D. 111. 1990). *Lifchez* held that a ban on research on concepteses was unconstitutional because it impermissibly infringed upon a woman's fundamental right to privacy. *Id.* at 1363. Although the Illinois statute banning embryo and fetal research at issue in the case permitted IVF, it did not allow embryo donation, embryo freezing or experimental prenatal diagnostic procedures. *Id.* at 1365–70. The court stated, "It takes no great leap of logic to see that within the cluster of constitutionally protected choices that includes the right to have access to contraceptives, there must be included within that cluster the right to submit to a medical procedure that may bring about, rather than prevent, pregnancy." *Id.* at 1377. The court also held that the statute was impermissibly vague because of its failure to define "experiment" or "therapeutic." *Id.* at 1376.

Some commentators argue that the Constitution similarly protects the right to create a child through cloning. See John Robertson, "Views on Cloning: Possible Benefits, Address Before the National Bioethics Advisory Commission" (Mar. 14, 1997), available at http://bioethics.georgetown.edu/nbac/transcripts/index.html. This seems to be a reversal of Robertson's earlier position that cloning "may deviate too far from prevailing conception of what is valuable about reproduction to count as a protected reproductive experience. At some point attempts to control the entire genome of a new person pass beyond the central experiences of identity and meaning that make reproduction a valued experience." John Robertson, *Children of Choice: Freedom and the New Reproductive Technologies* 169 (1994).

However, cloning is sufficiently different from normal reproduction and the types of assisted reproduction protected by the *Lifchez* case that constitutional protections should not apply. In even the most high-tech reproductive technologies available, a mix of genes occurs to create an individual with a genotype that has never before existed. In the case of twins, two such individuals are created. Their futures are open and the distinction between themselves and their parents is acknowledged. In the case of cloning, however, the genotype already exists. Even though it is clear that the individual will develop into a person with different traits because of different social, environmental and generational influences, there is evidence that the fact that he or she posses an existing genotype will affect how the resulting clone is treated by himself, his family and social institutions.

In that sense, cloning is sufficiently distinct from traditional reproduction or alternative reproduction to not be considered constitutionally protected. It is not a process of genetic mix, but of genetic duplication. It is not reproduction, but a sort of recycling, where a single individual's genome is made into someone else. This change in kind in the fundamental way in which humans can "reproduce" represents such a challenge to human dignity and the potential devaluation of human life (even comparing the "original" to the "copy" in terms of which is to be more valued) that even the search for an analogy has come up empty. *Testimony on Scientific Discoveries and Cloning: Challenges for Public Policy, Before the Sen Subcomm. on Public Health and Safety. Sen. Comm. on Labor and Human Resources*, 105th Cong. 25 (1997) (statement of George J. Annas). Gilbert Meilaender, in testifying before NBAC, pointed out the social importance of children's genetic independence from their parents: "They replicate neither their father nor their mother. That is a reminder of the independence that we must eventually grant to them and for which it is our duty to prepare them." *Cloning Human Beings, supra* note 12, at 81.

Even if a constitutional right to clone were to be recognized, any legislation which would infringe unduly upon this fundamental right would be permissible if it furthered a compelling interest in the least restrictive manner possible in order to survive this standard of review. *See Lifchez*, 735 F. Supp. at 1377. Along those lines, the NBAC raised concerns about physical and psychological risks to the offspring, as well as about "a degradation of the quality of parenting, and family if parents are tempted to seek excessive control over their children's characteristics, to value children according to how well they meet every detailed parental expectation, and to undermine the acceptance and openness that typify loving families." *Cloning Human Beings, supra* note 12, at 77. The NBAC also noted how cloning might undermine important social values, such as opening the door to a form of eugenics, or by tempting some to manipulate others as if they were objects instead of persons, and exceeding the moral boundaries of the human condition. *Id.*

The potential physical and psychological risks of cloning an entire individual are sufficiently compelling to justify banning the procedure. The notion of replicating existing humans seems to fundamentally conflict with our legal system, which emphatically protects individuality and uniqueness. Banning procreation through nuclear transplantation is justifiable in light of common law and constitutional protection of the sanctity of the individual and personal privacy. Francis C. Pizzulli, Note, "Asexual Reproduction and Genetic Engineering: A Constitutional Assessment of the Technology of Cloning," 47 *S. Cal. L. Rev.* 476, 502 (1974).

In the United States, couples' constitutional arguments regarding a privacy right or liberty right to use inheritable genetic interventions would appear to be stronger than those regarding access to cloning. In decisions construing the Americans with Disabilities Act, including one before the U.S. Supreme Court, individuals with AIDS were judged to be disabled because their disease was seen as interfering with a major life function—reproduction. *Bragdon v. Abbott*, 524 U.S. 624, 631 (1998). The argument seems to be that "normal" reproduction involves the creation of children without diseases.

Couples who both have sickle cell anemia or some other recessive genetic disorder might argue that a ban on germline interventions deprives them of reproductive liberty because it is the only way they can have healthy children. (There are several fallacies in that argument. The children born may have other diseases. And the genetic modification intervention itself might harm the children or be ineffective.) Forbidding the use of the techniques, it would be argued, forces them to go childless.

The couple might bolster their argument with a reference to another aspect of the *Lifchez* holding. The court in that case also held the ban on embryo research unconstitutional because it forbade parents from using experimental diagnostic techniques to learn the genetic status of their fetus. See *Lifchez*, 735 F. Supp. at 1366–67. The court reasoned that, if the woman has a constitutional right to abort, she has a right to genetic information upon which to make the decision. *See id.* Using an expansive interpretation, *Lifchez* could be understood as saying that it was understandable that couples would choose to have only children of a certain genetic makeup and that such a decision was constitutionally protected. However, even if there were a constitutional right to use inheritable genetic interventions, such interventions could be banned if they posed compelling physical, psychological or social risks. To be constitutional, the ban would also need to be narrowly focused to operate in the least restrictive manner possible.

82. See Kaiser Family Found., "Lawmakers Vow to Introduce Cloning Restrictions, Bush Signals He Will 'Work to Pass' Ban," *Kaiser Daily Reprod. Health Rep.*, Mar. 29, 2001, available at http://report.kff.org/archive/repro/200173/kr010329.2.htm.

83. As of June, 2002, the Senate had three bills to consider. S. 790, introduced by Senator Brownback of Kansas, is substantially the same as the Weldon bill passed by the House of Representatives in August, 2001. Human Cloning Prohibition Act, S. 790, 107th Cong. (2001). It would ban both the creation of human embryos by cloning as well as attempts to create a human child by cloning. *Id.* at § 3. S. 1758, introduced by Senator Dianne Feinstein of California bans attempts at human cloning, defined as "asexual reproduction by implanting or attempting to implant the product of nuclear transplantation into a uterus." Human Cloning Prohibition Act, S. 1758, 107th Cong. (2001). It also specifically permits certain activities, including "nuclear transplantation to produce human stem cells." *Id.* at § 4. It was slightly modified on May 1 and reintroduced as S. 2439 with the endorsement of Senator Orin Hatch. 148 Cong. Rec. S36,633 (2002) Finally, S. 1893, introduced in late January, 2002 by Senator Harkin of Iowa would simply ban cloning as defined as "asexual human reproduction by implanting or attempting to implant the product of nuclear transplantation [defined as "introducing the nuclear material of a human somatic cell into a fertilized or unfertilized oocyte from which the nucleus has been or will be removed or inactivated"] into a woman's uterus or a substitute for a woman's uterus." S. 1893, 107th Cong. § 498C (2002). For more details, see George J. Annas, "Cloning and the U.S. Congress," 346 *New Eng. J. Med.* 1599 (2002). [As of January 2005 the U.S. Senate has not voted on any of these bills. Ed. note]

84. The outstanding question is whether abortion politics will permit members of Congress to outlaw so-called reproductive cloning (which they all agree should be done) without also outlawing research cloning (a prohibition included in the Weldon and Brownback bills because some supporters object to any creation of human embryos in the laboratory, and others believe that once created by cloning, it is inevitable that a cloned human embryo will be introduced into a woman's uterus and eventually result in the birth of a cloned child). The slippery slope from research to reproductive cloning is real, of course, but could be made much less likely by adding restrictions to what physicians involved in infertility treatment could do (e.g., no creation or use of cloned embryos by infertility specialists). Three further steps would virtually eliminate the danger: creation of a federal oversight panel that would have to approve any research projects involving the creation of cloned embryos; outlawing the purchase and sale of human eggs (as is done now for organs and tissues for transplant); and outlawing the freezing or storage of cloned human embryos, eliminating the potential for stockpiling human embryos, and making it almost impossible for a research embryo to be used for reproduction in practice. George J. Annas, "Cell Division," *Boston Globe*, Apr. 21, 2002, E1.

85. Gene Weingarten, *"Strange Egg,"* *Wash. Post*, Jan. 25, 1998, at F1.

86. "Radical Scientist to Help Open Cloning Clinics in Japan," *Japan Sci. Scan*, Dec. 7, 1998, *available at* 1998 WL 8029927.

87. Thomas Hirenee Atenga, "Africa: Biotech Firms Have Their Eyes on Africa, Euro MPs Say," *Int'l Press Serv.*, Oct. 14, 1998.

88. *See supra* notes 39 to 56 and accompanying text.

89. Brit. Med. Ass'n, *The Medical Profession and Human Rights* 205–40 (2001), see also sources cited *supra* note 32.

90. "Most Doctors, Academics Oppose Human Cloning," *Japan Econ. Newswire*, Nov. 7, 1998.

91. Conselho Nacional de Etíca para as Ciencias de Vida [National Council on Ethics for the Life Sciences], Opinion on Embryo Research and the Ethical Implications of Cloning, No. 21/CNEV/97 (1997).

92. Resolution on Human Cloning, European Parliament, Jan. 15, 1998, O.J. (C 34) 164 (1998).

93. See Ian Wilmut, "Cloning for Medicine," *Scientific Am.*, Dec. 1998, at 58:

None of the suggested uses of cloning for making copies of existing people is ethically acceptable to my way of thinking, because they are not in the interests of the resulting child. It should go without saying that I strongly oppose allowing cloned human embryos to develop so that they can be tissue donors.

Id. Wilmut has testified around the world against human cloning. See, e.g., Christine Corcos et al. "Double-Take: A Second Look at Cloning, Science Fiction and Law," 59 *La. L. Rev.* 1041, 1051 (denouncing cloning human beings at a talk at Princeton University); "Creator of Dolly Stresses Benefits of Further Research on Cloning," *Daily Yomiuri,* June 7, 1997, available at 19997 WL 1211052 (advocating a worldwide prohibition against human cloning); "Cult in the First Bid to Clone Human," *Espress,* Oct. 11, 2000, available at 2000 WL 24217743 (responding to a British couple's plan to clone their deceased daughter, stating that "it is absolutely criminal to try this [cloning] in a human."); Curt Suplee, "Top Scientists Warn Against Cloning Panic; Recreating Humans Would Be Unethical Experts Say," *Wash. Post,* Mar. 13, 1997, at A03 (testifying against human cloning before the NBAC).

94. Press Release, *Biotechnology Ind. Org.,* "BIO Reiterates Unequivocal Opposition to Reproductive Cloning; Support for Therapeutic Applications," Nov. 25, 2001, available at http://www.bio.org/newsroom/news.asp. See also Frances Bishop, "11th Annual Bio Conference: Ethical Issues in Genetics Create Challenges for Biotech Industry," 8 *Bioworld Today* 112 (1997), available at 1997 WL 11130296.

95. Press Release, W.H.O., *World Health Assembly,* "World Health Assembly States its Position on Cloning Human Reproduction" (May 14, 1997), available at http://www.who.int/archives/inf-pr-1997/en/97 wha9.html.

96. WHO, *World Health Assembly,* 51st Sess., "Ethical, Scientific and Social Implications of Cloning in Human Health," WHA51, 10, (1998).

97. 1) Croatia, 2) Cyprus, 3) Czech Republic, 4) Denmark, 5) Estonia, 6) Finland, 7) France, 8) Georgia, 9) Greece, 10) Hungary, 11) Iceland, 12) Italy, 13) Latvia, 14) Lithuania, 15) Luxembourg, 16) Moldova, 17) Netherlands, 18) Norway, 19) Poland, 20) Portugal, 21) Romania, 22) San Marino, 23) Slovenia, 24) Slovenia, 25) Spain, 26) Sweden, 27) Switzerland, 28) the former Yugoslav Republic of Macedonia and 29) Turkey. See also *Additional Protocol (Explanatory Report) to the Convention of Human Rights and Biomedione,* Jan. 12, 1998, available at http://conventions.coe.int/Treaty/en/Reports/Html/168.htm.

98. Resolution on Human Cloning, Eur. Parliament, Jan. 15, 1998 O.J. (C34) 164 (1998).

99. *Id.*

100. *Id.*

101. UNESCO, *Universal Declaration on the Human Genome and Human Rights,* 29th Sess., 29 C/Res. 16 (1997), available at http://www.unesco.org/human_rights/hrbc.htm. The declaration was adopted by the General Assembly in 1999. G.A. Res. 152, U.N. GAOR, 53rd Sess., U.N. Doc. A/53/152 (1999).

102. *Universal Declaration on the Human Genome and Human Rights,* Introduction.

103. *Id.*

104. *Id.* art. 11.

105. *Id.*

106. "Request for the Inclusion of a Supplementary Item in the Agenda of the 56th Session, International Convention Against the Reproductive Cloning of Human Beings," *U.N. GAOR,* 56th Sess., U.N. Doc. A/56/192 (2001).

107. "United Nations Calls for a Treaty to Ban Human Cloning." *Birmingham Post,* Nov. 21, 2001, at 8.

108. *See supra* note 84. The next meeting of the ad hoc committee is scheduled at the United Nations for September 23–27, 2002. It is anticipated that the mandate to guide subsequent treaty negotiations will be adopted at this meeting, and that treaty language may be agreed upon a year or so later. [As of December 2004 work on a treaty seems to have been abandoned. Ed. note]

109. Stephen P. Marks, "Tying Prometheus Down: The International Law of Human Genetic Manipulation," 3 *Chi. J. Int'l L.* (2002). The other U.N. treaty method is known as a framework convention, which is used when countries agree that a particular field needs to be regulated (such as the environment), but do not yet agree on the specifics of how the regulation should work. Because there is basic international agreement on human reproductive cloning, the framework convention is inappropriate. See, e.g., Daniel Bodansky, "The United

Nations Framework Convention on Climate Change: A Commentary," 18 *Yale J. Int'l L.* 451, 494 (1993). See also Anthony, *Aust. Modern Treaty Law and Practice* 97 (2000); Donald M. Goldberg, "Negotiating the Framework Convention on Climate Change," 4 *Touro J. Transnat'l L.* 149 (1993); Lee A. Kimball, "The Biodiversity Convention: How to Make it Work," 28 *Vand. J. Transnat'l L.* 763 (1995).

110. Convention on the Prohibition of the Use, Stockpiling, Production and Transfer of Anti-Personnel Mines and on their Destruction, G.A. res. 47/39, 47 *U.N. GAOR Supp.* (No. 49) at 54, U.N. Doc. A/47/49 (1992).

8
Tying Prometheus Down
Human Rights Issues of Human Genetic Manipulation

Stephen P. Marks

Human rights are frequently alluded to or mentioned explicitly in the existing instruments of international law on human genetic manipulation. International instruments relating to human rights provide ambiguous standards by which the human impact of biotechnological applications may be judged and are invoked to support the conflicting assumptions regarding genetic manipulations. The impact of genetic engineering on human rights was anticipated decades ago. In 1971, George Brand catalogued the possibilities, warning that "[i]t is easy, but dangerous, to dismiss all of these possibilities as science fiction."[1] The scientific complexity of the issues, the uncertainty of the technology, the limited number of governments with an interest in regulation, and the divergent philosophical assumptions of those governments contribute to the difficulty of adopting international norms in this area. The following broad-brush reflections on the human rights implications of human genetic manipulation illustrate that difficulty. They will show that most international human rights standards lend themselves to both sides of the argument. To facilitate analysis of the fifteen rights involved, I have grouped them—somewhat arbitrarily—into three broad categories.

Rights Relating to the Nature and Autonomy of the Human Person

The rights in this category (dignity; life, identity, non-discrimination, privacy, information, free consent, and intellectual property) refer to elements of the essential nature of human beings or to the basic freedom to act as an autonomous agent.

The human right to dignity has been treated as the cornerstone of human rights. Echoing the Universal Declaration's reference to "the inherent dignity . . . of all," (a 1997) UNESCO Declaration affirms that "dignity makes it imperative not to reduce individuals to their genetic characteristics and to respect their uniqueness and diversity,"[2] and characterizes human reproductive cloning as one of the "practices which are contrary to human dignity [and which] shall not be permitted."[3] The aim of the European Biomedicine Convention is "to safeguard human dignity and the fundamental rights and freedoms of the individual with regard to the application of biology and medicine."[4] States parties agree to "protect the dignity and identity of all human beings."[5] The protocol adds that "[t]he deliberate creation of genetically identical human beings is contrary to human dignity and thus constitutes a misuse of biology and medicine."[6]

Dignity is not well defined in international law but, in its normal meaning as the state of being worthy of honor or respect and not subjected to humiliation, it would not necessarily be violated in the case of a cloned individual any more than it would in the case of a "natural" twin. The first successful clones would probably suffer a lack of dignity by being the object of much curiosity, publicity, and even scorn. However, such attitudes might diminish, as they have with respect to "test tube babies" since *in vitro* fertilization (IVF) technology has become more widely used. Stereotyping by race and sexual orientation often violates the dignity of the targeted persons; however, education and other means of influencing social behavior used to eliminate such stereotyping could also be used to protect the dignity of humans produced by asexual reproduction. Experience with IVF also raises doubts as to the dangers of the "instrumentalization" of human reproduction by cloning.[7] A human being does not necessarily lose dignity merely because a complex technique was used in his or her creation. However, should cloning or germline genetic manipulation result in physical or behavioral traits perceived by the general population as "freakish," then the application of these forms of biotechnology may indeed violate human dignity.

The right to identity, frequently invoked along with dignity, does not relate in positive international law to the existential meaning of identity, but rather to civil status.[8] Name and nationality are not likely to be denied people whose genome has been modified by biotechnology. "Family relations" of a clone are more problematic; a clone would be both a sibling and a child of its "parent." However, as a matter of legal identity, the clones would be the children of those who take legal responsibility for their upbringing.

Evelyne Shuster supports the existential sense of identity when she affirms that cloning threatens "rights to personal identity, individuality, and uniqueness."[9]

Genetic independence comes . . . from a unique genetic identity. Because it makes impossible the child's genetic independence, cloning holds that child genetic prisoner of another person's genome. The child is robbed of the freedom to become who he/she is . . . the one unique person who lives and dies. . . . In short, cloning violates the child's right to an open future.[10]

Because there are no recognized rights to "uniqueness" (although it is mentioned in the UNESCO Declaration) or "an open future" in positive human rights law, Shuster makes recourse to the right to dignity and the prohibition of slavery and cruel, inhuman, or degrading treatment, as well as the child's right to identity and to education directed to the development of the child's personality. Unfortunately, none of these recognized human rights contains an explicit reference to uniqueness or an open future. It has also been argued that there is a human right "of each newborn child to be a complete surprise to its parents."[11] This idea, like "uniqueness" and existential "identity," may be emotionally appealing but it is not part of current international human rights law.

The rights to non-discrimination and to equal protection of the law are a concern of both the UNESCO and Council of Europe texts, as well as the Charter of Fundamental Rights of the European Union (European Charter). Discrimination issues arise primarily with respect to genetic testing or screening, the results of which could induce prospective or current employers or insurers to exclude persons from employment or coverage whose propensity to disease or other health conditions is high as revealed by their gene sequencing. Such concerns would extend to persons created through reproductive cloning or modified by germline engineering, since their particular genetic heritage would have been identified, and the dangers represented by the known genes or by unknown side effects may lead employers or insurers to consider them too great a risk.[12] This issue is already the subject of litigation in the United States.

Persons created or altered through genetic manipulation might also be regarded as benefiting inequitably from positive discrimination. Their genes may have been selected in order to make them smarter, stronger, faster, or more creative, thereby giving them advantages over people who result from normal sexual reproduction. The ban against discrimination would thus favor them over persons with lesser mental or physical capabilities. Moreover, in most cases, they would have benefited from a form of discrimination by having had access to expensive biotechnology (boutique medicine), medicine that less well-off people could not afford and that is unlikely to be offered through public health services.

The right to privacy and the related right to seek, receive, and impart information, have both been included in the emerging international law of human genetic manipulation. The UNESCO Declaration provides that "[g]enetic data associated with an identifiable person and stored or processed for the purposes of research or any other purpose must be held confidential in the conditions set by law."[13] The European Biomedicine Convention at Article 10 provides that "[e]veryone has the right to respect for private life in relation to information about his or her health . . . [and] to know any information collected about his or her health. However, the wishes of individuals not to be so informed shall be observed."

The protection of privacy already includes health-related information. Human genetic data collection only increases the need for protection. People whose DNA is analyzed also have a right to know who is collecting the information, why, where it is stored, and who has access to it. Sometimes their rights are protected by the destruction of the genetic information.[14]

Experimental and therapeutic interventions for the purpose of genetic engineering raise special problems regarding "free consent to medical or scientific experimentation."[15] The UNESCO Declaration and the European Biomedicine Convention require a risk-benefit assessment with prior, free, and informed consent. However, most decisions will require informed consent even where the risk-benefit assessment is impossible. Buchanan and others remind us that "genetic interventions leave room for many unintended genetic effects with unknown risks."[16] They insightfully point out that uncertainty can only be removed by human experimentation, which would be ethically impossible with germline therapy "since consent cannot be obtained from future offspring who might be affected, nor from the embryos upon whom the intervention would be performed."[17]

Paradoxically, intellectual property rights appear to protect biotech companies against the claims that their patents violate human rights, even though they derive from a human right, namely "the right of everyone . . . to benefit from the protection of the moral and material interests resulting from any scientific . . . production of which he is the author."[18] In practice, of course, biotechnology companies rely on intellectual property rights to protect their inventions and patents, including methods of human genetic manipulation and even genotypes, and use them for commercial gain. But, is the "human right" to ownership in patents compatible with the human rights principle of Article 4 of the UNESCO Declaration and Article 21 of the European Biomedicine Convention that bar economic gain from the exploitation of the human genome and the patenting of life forms?[19] The researcher who makes great strides in stem cell research and discovers a means of genetic engineering to eliminate a gene linked to Alzheimer's disease, would, from a human rights perspective, deserve protection of his or her "moral and material interests." What if the patient suffered from terrible health consequences as a result? The deterioration in the patient's health, including premature death, could be considered the "destruction" of rights to life and to health, contrary to the principle that no provision of the Covenants, such as the right to intellectual property, may be used to justify "any State, group or person . . . engag[ing] in any activity or . . . perform[ing] any act aimed at the destruction of any of the rights or freedoms recognized herein."[20]

The TRIPS agreement allows World Trade Organization (WTO) members to exclude from patentability inventions "to protect human, animal, or plant life or health" as well as "diagnostic, therapeutic and surgical methods for the treatment of humans."[21] The ambiguities of such language can only be removed by further standard-setting or by case law, assuming the Dispute Settlement Body and the Appellate Body will be able to balance intellectual property and other human rights as cases arise.

Rights Relating to Physical and Mental Integrity and Well-Being

At least four other rights concern human well-being, both physical and mental. The European Charter of Fundamental Rights includes a general provision on physical and mental integrity, which captures the essentialist assumptions that DNA should not be altered.[22]

The claim that human genetic manipulation threatens the right to life implies, in the language of the international human rights texts, the arbitrary taking of life. This would not be the case if human reproductive cloning and germline gene therapy were understood as processes to create and protect life. However, the Council for Responsible Genetics (CRG) proposes a different understanding of this right, namely the claim that "all people have the right to have been conceived, gestated, and born without genetic manipulation."[23] That is a rather odd twist on the right to life, since it is a right retroactively to have been born a certain way, which suggests a concomitant remedy for "wrongful life" or "wrongful disability." It is not unlike a recent French award of substantial damages to the mother of a child with Down Syndrome because the doctor had not informed her of the likelihood of the disease and the possibility to abort the fetus, thus establishing a legal right never to have been born and to sue doctors that attended the pregnancy.[24]

The matter takes on greater complexity in the context of the duty of states, under the inherent right to life of the child, to "ensure . . . the survival and development of the child."[25] Some—including the Roman Catholic Church—will argue that a gamete or embryo has the right to survival and development. This argument is behind the efforts to ban stem cell research and the highly unsettled question of what constitutes life. But, one could also argue that parents should be able to choose any means, including gene therapy, to protect the survival and development of their child.

International human rights law includes the prevention and repression of a growing number of large-scale human rights violations qualified as international crimes, including torture, slavery, terrorism, genocide, and crimes against humanity. Even if suffering that might result from cloning or germline genetic manipulation did not reach the threshold of torture, one can imagine physical or mental conditions of a cloned individual or genetically altered person that would make their life "cruel." Cruelty might also arise from stigmatizing of disability by others who see special needs as "deformities" to be ridiculed or pitied. Paradoxically, such attitudes could reinforce the contention that physical and mental "abnormalities" resulting from human genetic manipulation constitute "cruel treatment," in violation of human rights.

George Annas points out that genetic manipulation of embryos could be viewed as "inhuman" treatment. He refers to the danger of creating a person who would be "viewed as a new species or a subspecies of human and thus not necessarily a possessor of human rights." If the physical traits were altered to a sufficient degree and (as suggested by Annas) the altered individual were not able to reproduce other humans, then some would regard the clone as inhuman, making it more difficult to accuse those who authorized or carried out the procedures as responsible for "inhuman treatment."

As for slavery, one could imagine the extreme scenario frequently portrayed in science fiction of a well-funded group or government insane enough to attempt to clone large numbers of specially gifted humans for military, labor, or other tasks. Such armies could reasonably be considered slaves or persons subjected to forced labor, in violation of human rights law. Annas goes further, arguing that human replication cloning, and other forms of genetic engineering "fit into a new category of 'crimes against humanity.'"[26] Unless a democratic world body agreed that such experiments should go forward, he argues, carrying them out would be "a terrorist act."[27] He fears genocide either through the mass killing of genetically altered "posthumans" (because "we will see them as a threat to us") or by the posthumans deciding that we should be "slaughtered preemptively."[28] Qualifying scientifically hazardous experiments and possible disregard for human welfare by the biotech industry in the pursuit of profits as international criminal behavior is perhaps a useful attention-grabbing metaphor, but a questionable application of international criminal law. However, Annas—whose path-breaking insights I generally applaud—intends it literally, as he suggests referral to the International Criminal Court.[29] Applying a standard of criminal negligence appears more plausible and absolute liability for such ultra-hazardous activity might offer a deterrent to such abuses.

The right to health is clearly the most ambiguous human right at issue. The Committee on Economic, Social and Cultural Rights (CESCR) considered, in its General Comment 14, that the right of everyone to the enjoyment of the highest attainable standard of physical and mental health must be "conducive to living a life of dignity."[30] In fact, the Committee enumerated fourteen rights related to the right to health and on which that right depends. Most human rights treaties, including the European Biomedicine Convention, include a formulation of this right. General Comment 14 notes that the provision in the International Covenant on Economic, Social, and Cultural Rights (ICESCR) on the reduction of the stillbirth rate and of infant mortality, as well as the healthy development of the child, "may be understood as requiring measures to improve child and maternal health, sexual and reproductive health services, including access to family planning, pre- and post-natal care, emergency obstetric services and access to information, as well as to resources necessary to act on that information."[31] It is a matter of opinion whether gene modification can be classified among such services. The General Comment also acknowledges that genetic factors play a role in determining an individual's health, but does not address specifically genetic manipulation or cloning.

Following the Committee's three types or levels of obligations of States parties,[32] one could argue that a state's obligation to respect the right to health requires that no government agency participate in or fund dangerous genetic manipulation; that the obligation to protect includes preventing the biotech industry from engaging in such activity; and that its obligation to fulfill means that its legislative, executive, and judicial branches act to suppress such activities, and inform the health professions and the population of the dangers. Using contrary assumptions about the risks and moral implications, these same obligations could be invoked to engage the national health system and other organs of the state in tolerating, promoting, and practicing genetic manipulation. At the current stage of knowledge and ethical debate, national policies and legislation show a wide divergence of laws and practice.[33]

A significant sub-area of the right to health concerns reproductive rights.[34] Regarding the threat to women's reproductive rights, Marcy Darnovsky writes,

[h]uman cloning and germline engineering would move decisions about reproduction further away from women, not only toward doctors and technicians but also toward marketers proffering the 'enhancements' developed by biotech companies. Women could find themselves simultaneously losing ever more control of their own childbearing experiences, and subject to vastly increased pressures to produce 'the perfect baby.'[35]

The CESCR includes within the right to health "the right to control one's health and body, including sexual and reproductive freedom, and the right to be free from interference, such as the right to be free from torture, non-consensual medical treatment, and experimentation."[36] A parent's decision to create a child asexually or to use germline genetic engineering is arguably part of such sexual and reproductive freedom. It could also be argued that the parent provides the requisite consent of the resultant child to the experiment. The European Biomedicine Convention would limit the parent's choice of treatment by requiring that "[a]n intervention seeking to modify the human genome may only be undertaken for preventive, diagnostic or therapeutic purposes and only if its aim is not to introduce any modification in the genome of any descendants."[37]

The authors of *From Chance to Choice* place this issue in the broader context of the conflict between liberty and intergenerational harm prevention. They posit the situation in which "the obligation to prevent genetically transmitted harms is strong enough to justify limiting or interfering with reproductive freedom,"[38] especially when the harm is transmitted over generations. They leave open the moral possibility of coercive non-conception (sterilization), germline therapy, and abortion to prevent cumulative harm to future generations, but tend to favor reproductive freedom over such coercion because the benefit to any one individual in the future is very small compared to the importance of reproductive freedom.[39]

Rights Dealing with Social Relations and Participation

Finally, five rights are concerned with the participation of humans in social relations, such as the right to education, children's rights, the right to found a family, the right to enjoy the benefits of scientific progress, and the right to scientific research.

The right to education includes the directive that "education shall be directed to the full development of the human personality and the sense of its dignity"[40] and that "education of the child shall be directed to the development of the child's personality, talents and mental and physical abilities to their fullest potential."[41] These texts refer to traditional notions of child development in psychology, not the particular development problem that might arise if a child's genetically determined development potential is selected by the parent. The challenge to the right to education comes both from efforts to improve the "personality" of the child (such as friendly disposition, intellectual capacity to master complex tasks) through successful germline genetic engineering and from failed interventions resulting in unexpected psychological responses (such as increased anxiety or even psychotic reactions). It is, of course, highly speculative whether genes related to personality can be transmitted through germline therapy. Assuming it is possible, the human rights framework does not—and understandably so—indicate whether the "human personality" to be developed is different in a genetically altered individual than it is in a child resulting from sexual reproduction without genetic manipulation. If the genetic manipulation fails, one might consider that the right to education has been violated by the parents and the medical team involved because the potential has been negatively altered. The intention may have been to create a happy and well-adjusted child with enhanced physical and mental talents, but if those enhanced qualities are not attained, then the criterion of "fullest potential" is clearly not met. Similarly, the creation of a person with genetically enhanced physical and mental capabilities may have a negative effect on the education of "normally" endowed people.

Most of the human rights discussed so far concern the rights of offspring and therefore are children's rights, the underlying idea of which is the best interest of the child and special protection, because children do not have the capacity to ensure the realization of their rights in the same way as adults. The Convention on the Rights of the Child requires parents "to provide direction and guidance in the exercise by the child of the rights [in the Convention]."[42] One may query whether this duty is met when a parent decides for the child what physical and mental traits it will have or—where the procedure produces unintended results—creates for the child a lifelong dependency. These voluntary acts by the parents are not directly related to the child's exercise of rights in the Convention but they certainly influence the child's range of choices in exercising those rights, particularly with respect to the "right of the child to . . . the highest attainable standard of health and to facilities for the treatment of illness and rehabilitation of health."[43] Proponents of genetic manipulation might argue that intervention in a child's genetic makeup raises the standard of the child's health or constitutes a facility for the treatment of illness.

Another children's rights issue is the alleged right to life of the unborn. Some who oppose voluntary termination of pregnancy argue that a gamete or embryo has the right to survival and development, and therefore, producing numerous embryos in order to remove the nucleus from one and destroy the others would violate the rights of all those potential children. However, this is a rather radical theological position, unsupported by the current interpretation of the right to life and children's rights in international human rights law.

In a different vein, an uncompromising argument against cloning as a violation of children's rights has been made by Evelyne Shuster.[44] She argues that cloning is fundamentally destructive of the rights of children and their human dignity. Specifically, she claims that cloning robs children of their rights to personal identity, individuality, and uniqueness, commodifies children by treating them as interchangeable, and changes the way we think about sexuality and mortality in disruptive and destructive ways. She proposes a world summit on the future of the human species to protect the integrity of the human species to prevent the powerful biotechnological industries, venture capitalists, and self-serving scientists from deciding for us what is best for our future and the future of our children.

Article 23 of the International Covenant on Civil and Political Rights (ICCPR) recognizes the right of men and women of marriageable age to marry and to found a family. It is widely recognized that IVF is an acceptable means of implementing this right. One might extend that argument to cloning as a means of founding a family. The covenant does not establish any conditions on the method for founding a family. In fact, cloning may be a means of allowing same-sex couples—where such partnering is recognized as a legitimate arrangement for marriage and founding a family—to produce children having traits of one of the parents without the need—in the case of lesbian couples—of male sperm. Hilary Putnam sees in human cloning a problem for the "moral images of the family," which should "reflect our tolerant and pluralistic values."[45] We should value such an image of the family, he says, rather than designing our children out of "narcissistic and xenophobic" values.

One of the principal arguments in favor of human genetic manipulation is that it constitutes an advance in science and technology that benefits humankind. The internationally recognized right of everyone to enjoy the benefits of scientific progress and its applications supports such an argument. Article 12 of the UNESCO Declaration provides that benefits from advances in biology, genetics, and medicine that concern the human genome, shall be made available to all, with due regard for the dignity and human rights of each individual, and that applications in these fields shall seek to offer relief from suffering, and improve the health of individuals and humankind as a whole.

Consumers wishing to avail themselves of techniques of genetic manipulation and companies proposing to market them can claim such a right. This right is not, on its face, contrary to patent protection since one could argue that patents are designed to encourage advances in biotechnology, and that the benefits therefrom will be made "available to all" after the expiration of the patent. In fact, TRIPS, the principle instrument supporting patents in international trade, states that "the protection and enforcement of intellectual property rights should contribute to the promotion of technological innovation and to the transfer and dissemination of technology, to the mutual advantage of producers and users of technological knowledge and in a manner conducive to social and economic welfare, and to a balance of rights and obligations."[46] The TRIPS Agreement appears to favor the international transfer of technology. However, the bioethics texts establish a clear hierarchy between human well-being and the interests of science.[47] According to this principle, potential harm to individuals of experiments on genetic manipulation should be adequate to justify measures to limit or halt such experimentation in the interest of science.

Closely related to the right to benefit from scientific progress is the undertaking by States "to respect the freedom indispensable for scientific research and creative activity."[48] A 1974 UNESCO text provides some elements of the definition of freedom of scientific research by recognizing "that open communication of the results, hypotheses and opinions—as suggested by the phrase 'academic freedom'—lies at the very heart of the scientific process and provides the strongest guarantee of accuracy and objectivity of scientific results."[49] With respect to publicly supported scientific research, UNESCO recommends that member states allow researchers to enjoy "the degree of autonomy appropriate to their task and to the advancement of science and technology" and to take fully into account "that creative activities of scientific researchers should be promoted in the national science policy on the basis of utmost respect for the autonomy and freedom of research necessary to scientific progress."[50] This freedom suggests non-interference by the state in research on human genetic manipulation, although restriction on funding of embryonic stem cell research and banning of human cloning may be consistent with the Recommendation's reference to member states' duty to encourage researchers to determine methods which should be humanely, socially, and ecologically responsible.

US legislation banning cloning sometimes specifies that the ban:

> shall not be construed to restrict biomedical and agricultural research or practices unless expressly prohibited herein, including research or practices that involve the use of: (i) somatic cell nuclear transfer or other cloning technologies to clone molecules, including DNA, cells, or tissues; (ii) gene therapy; or (iii) somatic cell nuclear transfer techniques to create animals other than humans.[51]

Lori Andrews has noted that a lower federal court suggested that scholars have a right "to do research and advance the state of man's knowledge" although other federal courts "have refused to recognize a First Amendment right to scientific inquiry."[52] She concludes, "the government could regulate to protect against compelling harms . . . so long as the regulation is no more restrictive on speech than is necessary to further that intent."[53]

The World Health Assembly recognized, in the context of cloning in human reproduction, "the need to respect the freedom of ethically acceptable scientific activity and to ensure access to the benefits of its applications."[54] Similarly, the European Biomedicine Convention acknowledges freedom of scientific research and testing for health related research. Both the European Biomedicine Convention and the UNESCO Declaration make an exception to freedom of research where human welfare or human rights would suffer.

Toward a New International Treaty?

The preceding discussion should have made evident the tension that exists between two principles of international law, each with underlying philosophical assumptions. The first is the restrictive principle, which draws support from a half century of development of international human rights law, to which proponents of the position that the human species must be preserved appeal in order to place such technology beyond the pale. The opposing principle is the permissive principle, supported by international trade and intellectual property law, and justified by ideas of free markets, free trade, freedom of scientific research, and freedom of choice of consumers. This perspective calls for minimal limitations on the developing and marketing of technologies of human genetic manipulation.

At the governmental level, the Franco-German initiative at the UN has become mired in debates. At the same time, the Secretary-General has proposed ways to coordinate activities and thinking on bioethics across the UN system and the Sub-commission on the Promotion and Protection of Human Rights has appointed a Special Rapporteur to study human rights and the human genome. The Commission on Human Rights, for it part, drew:

> the attention of Governments to the importance of research on the human genome and its applications for the improvement of the health of individuals and mankind as a whole, to the need to safeguard the rights of the individual and his/her dignity, as well as his/her identity and unity, and to the need to protect the confidentiality of genetic data concerning a named person.[55]

The non-governmental initiatives are unlikely to advance unless they join forces with the European initiative at the UN. If the eventual treaty appeals to a large number of states, it may be because it will not satisfy either the essentialist/welfare state or the utilitarian/neoliberal camp and will not constrain governments beyond what they have already accepted. The convergence of the political left and right, as well as the religious and secular advocates on the issue of human cloning, may bring enough pressure for the treaty to be ratified and adopted.

Scholars, scientists, and science fiction writers have predicted for generations that advanced genetic and medical technology could modify the genetic makeup of humans as a means of alleviating human suffering and improving the quality of life. Progress in reproductive health technology has already allowed thousands of people to make choices affecting the genetic heritage of their offspring. Embryonic stem cell research holds out hope for other advances. At the same time, the prospects for altering inheritable genes through human reproductive cloning and germline gene therapy have raised fears that such tampering with the gene pool would result in profound and irreparable harm to human existence. The most authoritative consultative bodies, such as those convened by the World Health Organization and the now defunct National Bioethics Advisory Commission, have acknowledged that it is premature to regulate beyond a moratorium on human cloning or, for the successor President's Council on Bioethics, a moratorium on cloning for biomedical research.

In the meantime, specific issues that call for the application of international law will be settled by reconciling human rights and intellectual property law. The latter is supported by the dominant neoliberal paradigm, while the former builds on an international regime of human dignity. Although, as this article argues, international human rights law does not go as far as the species preservation advocates sometimes claim, where it does provide guidance, it should prevail in case of conflict with the international trade or intellectual property regimes. This conclusion is supported both by positive law and by elementary moral considerations.

Thirty years ago, a leading international lawyer predicted that:

> [t]he regulation of technological innovation and scientific progress will have to be undertaken in relation to the values of human dignity. . . . Genetic engineering will soon permit the creation and modeling of men to take place in scientific laboratories. Such breakthroughs have a fundamental bearing on the place of man in the world and should be evaluated by men as beneficial or harmful. The tradition of scientific freedom needs to be reconsidered from the viewpoint of human capacity to put discoveries about forces of nature to constructive social and ecological use.[56]

He added an allusion to mythology: "We may discover that Olympian gods exhibited a reluctant wisdom by chaining Prometheus—the bearer of progress and technology—to a rock so that he might suffer under public scrutiny."[57] International law provides a tool for tying the biotech Prometheus down. The chain is being tightened now to restrain his propensity to clone human beings reproductively, but it remains uncertain for the moment which other potential Promethean developments in human genetic manipulation require the restraining effect of international law.

Notes

1. Brand referred to:

    artificial inovulation; *in vitro* fertilization; parthenogenesis; choice of sex of offspring; creation of human beings by an asexual process called cloning; manipulation of the DNA molecule so as to interfere with the processes of heredity ('genetic surgery'); the improvement, by procedures adopted before birth, of the future intelligence of a child, and the creation of part-human chimeras.

    George Brand, *Human Rights and Scientific and Technological Developments*, 4 Hum Rts J 351, 354 (1971).

2. UNESCO, Universal Declaration on the Human Genome and Human Rights, Records of the General Conference, UNESCO, 1997, vol. 28, pp. 41–46 (UNESCO Declaration), Article 2, reproduced in Stephen P. Marks (ed.), *Health and Human Rights: Basic International Documents*, Cambridge, MA: Harvard Series in Health and Human Rights, distributed by Harvard University Press, 2004 (Marks, *Basic Documents*), pp. 281–285.

3. Id., Article 11.

4. Council of Europe, Convention for the Protection of Human Rights and Dignity of the Human Being with regard to the Application of Biology and Medicine: Convention on Human Rights and Biomedicine (European Biomedical Convention), Preamble, reprinted in Marks, *Basic Documents*, pp. 285–290.

5. Id., Article 1. The drafters' intention is clear on the central value of dignity: "The concept of human dignity, which is also highlighted, constitutes the essential value to be upheld. It is

the basis of most of the values emphasized in the Convention." Explanatory Report to the Convention for the Protection of Human Rights and Dignity of the Human Being with Regard to the Application of Biology and Medicine, reprinted in 36 ILM 817, 828 (1997).

6. Council of Europe, Additional Protocol to the Convention for the Protection of Human Rights and the Dignity of the Human Being with regard to the Application of Biology and Medicine on the Prohibition of Cloning Human Beings, Preamble, reprinted in 36 ILM 1417 (1997).

7. See Council of Europe, Explanatory Report to the Draft Additional Protocol to the Convention for the Protection of Human Rights and Dignity with Regard to the Application of Biology and Medicine on the Prohibition of Cloning Human Beings, para 3, reprinted in 36 ILM 1419 (1997).

8. See International Covenant on Civil and Political Rights ("ICCPR"), Article 24, 999 UNTS 171 (1967) ("Every child shall be registered . . . and have a name . . . [and] the right to acquire a nationality."); United Nations Convention on the Rights of the Child, Article 8, General Assembly Res No 44/25, UN Doc No A/RES/44/25 (1990) (asserting "[t]he right of the child to preserve his or her identity, including nationality, name and family relations").

9. Evelyne Shuster, *My Clone, Myself, My Daughter, My Sister: Echoes of Le Petit Prince*, Proceedings of the International Symposium AMADE-UNESCO on Bioethics and the Rights of the Child 39 (Monaco 2000).

10. Id., para. 40.

11. Justine Burley, ed, *The Genetic Revolution and Human Rights* (Oxford 1999) (Putnam, *Cloning People*), p. 13.

12. In an editorial in *Science* in 1989, Daniel Koshland wrote:

A genome sequence should not be a precondition of employment, and legislation might be needed if that problem were to arise. However, less accurate data of the same type would be available today from family histories, and that does not seem to be part of current employment forms. If more accurate information provides temptation for abuse, action will be needed.

Daniel E. Koshland, Jr., *Sequences and Consequences of the Human Genome*, 246 Science 189 (Oct 13, 1989).

13. UNESCO Declaration, Article 7.

14. In a US case in 1998, a Boston court found that taking DNA samples as part of routine blood testing of prisoners without permission was a clear violation of human rights. See *Landry v Harshbarger*, 1998 Mass Super LEXIS 479. See also Martine Jacot, *DNA in the Dock*, 53 UNESCO Courier 37, 39 (April 2000) (noting that Germany, Austria, Finland, Sweden, Denmark, and the Netherlands have all ordered the destruction of the DNA samples held in police databases and laboratories once the suspect's identity has been established; though, the UK places no limit on how long that data can be kept and periods vary among states in the US).

15. International Covenant on Civil and Political Rights (ICCPR), Article 7.

16. Buchanan, et al. *From Chance to Choice: Genetics and Justice* 192 (Cambridge University Press, 2000).

17. Id., para. 194.

18. International Covenant on Economic, Social and Cultural Rights (ICESCR) Article 15.

19. See Council for Responsible Genetics (CRG), 13 *Gene Watch: A Bulletin of the Council for Responsible Genetics* 3 (April 2000) (proposing a Genetic Bill of Rights, in which Article 2 provides "[a]ll people have the right to a world in which living organisms cannot be patented, including human being . . . and all their parts.").

20. ICCPR, Article 7.

21. Agreement on Trade-Related Aspects of Intellectual Property Rights, April 15, 1994, Marrakesh Agreement Establishing the World Trade Organization, Annex 1C, 1869 U.N.T.S. 299, 33 I.L.M. 1197 (1994), (TRIPS Agreement), Article 27.

22. See Charter of Fundamental Rights of the European Union, art 3, 2000 OJ (C 364) 10 (prohibiting "eugenic practices, in particular those aiming at the selection of persons . . . [and] reproductive cloning of human beings").

23. See CRG, 13 *Gene Watch* at 3 (asserting such a right at Article 10 in its Genetic Bill of Rights).

24. See *French Court Confirms Handicapped's Right not to be Born*, Agence France Presse (Nov 28, 2001); Nanette van der Laan, *France Debates Right not to be Born*, Christian Science Monitor (Dec 7, 2001). On wrongful life suits in general; see Buchanan, et al. *From Chance to Choice* at 232–33.

25. Convention on the Rights of the Child at Article 6.

26. See George J. Annas, *Some Choice: Law, Medicine, and the Market* 23–24 (Oxford 1998). See also George J. Annas, *The Man on the Moon, Immortality, and other Millennial Myths: The Prospects and Perils of Human Genetic Engineering*, 49 Emory LJ 753, 778 (2000).

27. Annas, 49 Emory LJ at 778.

28. See George J. Annas, *Genism, Racism, and the Prospect of Genetic Genocide*, paper prepared for presentation at UNESCO 21st Century Talks: The New Aspects of Racism in the Age of Globalization and the Gene Revolution at the World Conference against Racism, Racial Discrimination, Xenophobia and Related Intolerance (Durban) (Sept 3, 2001), available online at <http://www.bumc.bu.edu/www/sph/lw/pvl/genism.htm> (visited Mar 24, 2002).

29. Annas, 49 Emory LJ at 771, 780.

30. CESCR General Comment 14 (2000) (General Comment 14), UN doc E/CN. 12/2000/4, para. 1.

31. Id., para. 14.

32. Id., para. 33.

33. See Global Lawyers and Physicians, *Database of Global Policies on Human Cloning and Germline Engineering*, available online at <http://www.glphr.org/genetic/genetic.htm> (visited Mar 24, 2002) (a systematic compilation of these national laws, as well as a complete collection of national and international references on both human cloning and germline engineering).

34. See Convention on the Elimination of All Forms of Discrimination Against Women, art 16(1)(e), (1981) (asserting the right of "men and women . . . to decide freely and responsibly on the number and spacing of their children"); Report of the International Conference on Population and Development, para 7.2, UN Doc No A/CONF.171/13 (1994) (asserting a right of people "to be informed and to have access to safe, effective, affordable and acceptable methods of family planning of their choice").

35. Marcy Darnovsky, *Human Germline Engineering and Cloning as Women's Issues*, 14 Gene Watch 1 (July 2001).

36. General Comment 14, para. 8.

37. European Biomedicine Convention, Article 13.

38. Buchanan, et al. *From Chance to Choice*, p. 213.

39. See id pp. 204–57.

40. ICESCR, Article 12.

41. Convention on the Rights of the Child, Article 29(1).

42. Id., Aricle 5.

43. Id., Article 24(11).

44. See Evelyne Shuster, *My Clone, Myself*, pp. 37–45.

45. Putnam, *Cloning People*, p. 12.

46. TRIPS Agreement, Article 7.

47. See European Biomedicine Convention, Article 2 ("The interests and welfare of the human being shall prevail over the sole interest of society or science.").

48. ICESCR, Article 15(3).

49. See *Recommendation on the Status of Scientific Researchers preamble (1974)*, reprinted in *UNESCO and Human Rights: Standard-Setting Instruments and Major Meeting Publications*, available online at <http://www.unesco.org/human_rights/htcf.htm> (visited Mar 24, 2002).

50. Id., para. 8.

51. Va Code Ann § 32.1–162.22 (2001).

52. Lori B. Andrews, *Cloning Human Beings: The Current and Future Legal Status of Cloning* F-6 (National Bioethics Advisory Commission 1997) (quoting *Henley v Wise*, 303 F Supp 62 (ND Ind 1969)). The Charter of the National Bioethics Advisory Commission expired on October 3, 2001.

53. Andrews, *Cloning Human Beings* at F-36.

54. World Health Assembly, *Cloning in Human Reproduction*, WHA Res No 50.37 (1997).
55. UN Commission on Human Rights Resolution 2001/71 of 25 April 2001, para. 6.
56. Richard Falk, *This Endangered Planet: Prospects and Proposals for Human Survival 307* (Random House 1971)
57. Id.

9

Patents and Medicines

The Relationship between TRIPS and the Human Right to Health

Philippe Cullet

The link between medical patents and the human right to health has become a subject of central concern at the international level, as exemplified by the debates at the 2001 World Trade Organization (WTO) ministerial conference.[1] International attention to the issue has focused in large part on the HIV/AIDS crisis and the question of access to drugs for patients in developing countries, which are the most severely affected by the epidemic.[2] The issue of access to drugs is acute in the case of HIV/AIDS but is of general concern in most developing countries.

From a legal perspective, two main areas of law are relevant in current debates. First, the question of access to medicines is a central issue in any consideration of the human right to health. Human rights law, in particular through the Convenant on Economic, Social and Cultural Rights, has made a significant contribution to the codification of the human right to health and our understanding of its scope.[3] Second, debates on access to drugs are now strongly linked to the questions of whether drugs can, and should, be patentable. The increasing scope of patentability in the health sector, codified in the Agreement on Trade-Related Aspects of Intellectual Property Rights (TRIPS), constitutes one of the most significant changes in law for developing countries that are WTO members.[4]

Intellectual property law and human rights law have largely evolved independently. However, with the broadening scope of patents in areas related to basic needs such as health, and recent developments in the health sector itself, the links between the two fields are becoming increasingly obvious and direct, necessitating further consideration of the relationship between the right to health and patents on medicines, in particular in the case of developing countries. While human rights documents have given some consideration to the position of intellectual property in relation to human rights, there has been no similar effort in the field of intellectual property.

This article starts by examining the conceptual framework in which the debate over access to drugs is taking place. The first section looks at the intellectual property perspective and examines in particular the situation as it is developing in the context of the TRIPS Agreement. The second section focuses on human rights and examines in particular the development of the links between human rights and intellectual property. Finally, the third section examines some of the possible solutions to the problem of access to drugs in developing countries, focusing on the contribution that human rights can make to the debate in the case of inconsistencies between intellectual property and human rights.

Access to Drugs and the International Intellectual Property Rights Regime

General Considerations

Intellectual property rights, in particular patents, are deemed to provide the necessary incentives for research and technological development. Patents are time-bound monopoly rights. They constitute a derogation from the principle of free trade by offering exclusive rights to an inventor to exploit the invention and stop others from using it without his/her consent. The rationale for granting patents is the need to reward an inventor. In practice, this translates mainly into a right to commercialize the invention and simultaneously to stop others from doing so. The exception to the free trade rule is balanced by limiting the duration of the right and by forcing the inventor to disclose the invention so that society at large benefits from scientific advancement.

Human rights protect the fundamental rights of individuals and groups. Fundamental rights can be defined as entitlements that belong to all human beings by virtue of their being humans.[5] This is in direct contrast to property rights, which can always be ceded in voluntary transactions.[6] As codified in the two UN covenants and other relevant instruments,[7] human rights constitute the basic framework guiding state actions at the domestic and international levels.[8] As a result, states must bear in mind their human rights obligations when they negotiate and implement international rules on intellectual property rights or trade liberalization.[9]

Health Concerns in the Intellectual Property Rights System

Patents generally constitute an incentive for the development of the private sector in areas where they are granted. In the pharmaceutical sector, the private sector health industry finds them indispensable.[10] Industry representatives argue that the pharmaceutical industry spends more than any other industry on R&D and that, while the development of new drugs is a costly process, it is relatively easy to copy an existing drug.[11] The patent system thus allows firms to charge prices that are higher than the marginal price of production and distribution for the first generations of patients, who are expected to absorb the cost of developing the drug. It is only after the patent protection for the product expires that competition among generic versions can bring the price closer to the marginal cost. Compared to products in other sectors, however, the marginal price of drugs tends to be higher due to the relative inelasticity of demand for medicines.[12]

Despite the pharmaceutical industry's plea for patent protection, a number of countries traditionally put restrictions on the patentability of drugs on public policy grounds.[13] While patents on drugs are now the norm in developed countries, even those with significant interests in the pharmaceutical sector, such as Switzerland, introduced product patents on drugs relatively recently.[14] As far as developing countries are concerned, a number of them provided either no patent protection or only partial protection in the pharmaceutical sector before the Uruguay Round of the world trade negotiations, in large part because they took the view that the health sector met a basic need and thus should be protected from full commercialization.[15] India characteristically endorsed this position with its strict patent legislation which did not recognize product patents on pharmaceuticals.[16]

In recent years there have been wide-ranging debates concerning the potential contribution of the introduction of patents in developing countries to the development of drugs related to specific tropical diseases. One of the perceived advantages is that it should give incentives to the private sector pharmaceutical industry to undertake more R&D in finding cures for diseases common in developing countries.[17] However, if patent protection has the capacity to raise incentives marginally, it may also support considerably higher prices.[18] Further, it is uncertain whether the redistribution of resources to the private sector which accompanies the introduction of patents will trigger the development of more drugs specifically related to the needs of the poor.[19] In fact, as noted by the World Health Organization (WHO), of the 1,223 new chemical entities developed between 1975 and 1996, only 11 were for the treatment of tropical diseases.[20]

The issue of patent protection in the health sector has proved increasingly divisive. This is in part attributable to the fact that there is a significant tension between the pharmaceutical industry's aim to recoup its investments and governments' interest in containing the costs of health care. Further, from a theoretical point of view, it remains uncertain whether the intellectual property rights system does in fact provide an incentive to invent.[21] Controversies at the theoretical and practical levels concerning patents on drugs have led to the search for alternatives. A number of proposals look at making the patent system more 'health friendly' by keeping the existing system in place and seeking new arrangements within it, focusing for example on some of the 'traditional' exceptions allowed in patent law such as compulsory licensing. In recent times, significant attention has also been given to differential pricing.

Access to Drugs and Medical Patents

Access to drugs is one of the fundamental components of the human right to health.[22] It is of specific importance in the context of the introduction of patents on drugs, because patents have the potential both to improve access, by providing incentives for the development of new drugs, and to restrict access, because of the comparatively higher prices of patented drugs. Accessibility generally refers to the idea that health policies should foster the availability of drugs, at affordable prices, to all those who need them.[23] This implies a strong link between lack of access to drugs and poverty. About one-third of the world's population does not have access to basic drugs, a proportion which rises above one-half in the most affected regions of Africa and Asia.[24] Furthermore, a large proportion of people in developing countries do not have access to medical insurance and more often than not pay for drugs themselves.[25] Since price is a major issue in access, it is significant that patented drugs are more expensive than generics.[26] However, patents are not the only factor influencing access,[27] since even cheap generic drugs may not be affordable for people below the poverty line. In these situations access can be ensured only through further measures such as public subsidies or price control measures. The sheer scale of the problem of access to drugs is only too clear in the context of HIV/AIDS. A consortium of international organizations has estimated that fewer than 10 per cent of the people living with HIV/AIDS in developing countries have access to antiretroviral therapy. This proportion goes down to about 0.1 per cent in Africa.[28]

The links among patents, the price of medicines and access to drugs have been taken into consideration by various countries in developing their legal and policy framework in the health sector. India is particularly noteworthy in this respect. As noted above, India adopted patent legislation which prohibited product patents for medicines, and this constituted one of the major incentives for the development of a relatively strong pharmaceutical industry.[29] In the first 25 years after independence, the domestic pharmaceutical industry remained relatively small, and by 1970 (the year in which the Patents Act was passed) accounted for only about 25 per cent of the domestic market; but thereafter the restrictions on product patents, prices and foreign investment contributed to the rapid development of the industry, which now accounts for 70 per cent of bulk drugs and meets nearly all the demand for formulations.[30] One of the most important impacts of the Indian Patents Act, prior to its recent TRIPS-related amendments, and the resulting development of a generic pharmaceutical industry has been significantly lower prices for drugs compared to other countries. Indeed, while drug prices in India were among the highest in the world in the initial stages of development, they are now among the lowest.[31] This is not to say that access to drugs is universal—millions still cannot afford basic generic medicines—but the trend since 1970 has definitely been in the right direction.[32] Apart from the exclusion of product patents, the Indian Patents Act introduced further measures to foster access to drugs. With regard to the duration of patent protection, the Act provided specific restrictions in the health sector. While normal patents were granted for 14 years, process patents on drugs or food were granted for only seven years.[33] The Act also provided a strict compulsory licensing regime which included not only compulsory licences but also licences of right.[34]

The TRIPS Agreement and Access to Drugs

The main vehicle for the introduction of medical patents in developing countries is the TRIPS Agreement. TRIPS generally seeks to provide minimum levels of intellectual property protection in all WTO member states. In other words, all WTO member states must accept standards of protection which are generally equivalent to a consensus position among developed countries. In the field of patents, the final agreement stipulates the patentability of inventions, whether products or processes, in all fields of technology.[35] The TRIPS Agreement is, as its name implies, concerned mainly with the interests of intellectual property rights holders. Further, intellectual property rights in the TRIPS Agreement are seen mainly as a vehicle to foster international trade and not as a moral recognition for scientific or technological prowess. Despite the very 'technical' nature of the agreement, TRIPS has significant impacts beyond the trade and intellectual property areas. However, the linkages among intellectual property, environmental management and human rights are not given much prominence in the WTO framework.

The TRIPS Agreement is by any account a treaty of major importance. For developing countries, TRIPS was part of the broader package deal of the GATT agreements of 1994. Even though TRIPS was never understood by these countries as being a good bargain, the agreement includes at least some broad safeguard provisions. The objective clause of the TRIPS Agreement provides, for instance, that intellectual property rights should 'contribute to the promotion of technological innovation *and* to the transfer and dissemination of technology'.[36] The implementation of this provision requires a certain level of flexibility in implementing the substantive clauses of the TRIPS Agreement—or, in other words, differential treatment for developing countries.[37] TRIPS will have significant impacts on the realization of fundamental human rights, such as the right to food and health in developing countries. As far as health is concerned, TRIPS will be an important agent of change in the health sector, especially in countries which previously rejected product and/or process patents on drugs. Indeed, the introduction of such patents in the pharmaceutical sector implies a fundamental change of orientation for countries like Brazil where no patents were available in this field prior to the Uruguay Round.[38] In particular, the new regime will have important implications in countries like India where, as noted above, the domestic pharmaceutical industry owes its current status largely to the existing legal framework.

The TRIPS Agreement introduces a strict legal regime for intellectual property protection, but provides some exceptions and qualifications which can be used to foster certain public policy goals, such as access to essential drugs. TRIPS first reminds signatory states that the intellectual property rights regime put in place should contribute to the promotion of technological innovation and to the transfer and dissemination of technology in a manner conducive to social and economic welfare.[39] It also recognizes that the rights and obligations of patent holders should be balanced, thus acknowledging that limitations on intellectual property rights are a fundamental component of the regime. The agreement specifically indicates that states can adopt measures necessary to protect public health and to promote the public interest in sectors of vital importance to their socioeconomic and technological development.[40] The potential of these provisions has not been lost on developing countries, as is clear from a statement by India to the WTO that articles 7 and 8.2 of the TRIPS Agreement are overarching provisions that should qualify other provisions of TRIPS meant to protect intellectual property rights.[41]

Apart from the general qualificatory clauses in articles 7 and 8, a number of important exceptions are found in the patents section itself. First, some exceptions to the scope of patentability are allowed.[42] Article 27.2 allows states to restrict the patentability of inventions, for instance, if they pose a threat to human life or health. However, the restriction on patentability is not acceptable if the law simply bans the exploitation of the invention. This would, for instance, prohibit a blanket restriction on product patents on pharmaceuticals. Additionally, article 30 permits states to limit the exclusive privilege granted through patent rights. The major difference between article 27.2 and article 30 is that the latter does not allow states to reject the patentability of a given drug or other invention but only to regulate its use. The exception provided at article 30 is also bound by several qualificatory provisions. First, there can be only 'limited exceptions' to monopoly rights. Second, the exceptions should not 'unreasonably conflict' with the exploitation of the patent; and third, the exceptions should not 'unreasonably prejudice the legitimate interests' of the patent owner. While the exceptions provided by article 30 are bound by these qualificatory statements, there is no definition of what the 'limited exceptions' can be. This provision can thus be used by countries to pursue public health goals. Indeed, that is exactly what the objectives clause of article 7 requires by calling for a balance between the promotion of innovation and the transfer and dissemination of innovation, and for a balance of rights and obligations on the part of the patent holder. This analysis is confirmed by a reading of the last part of article 30, which provides that states must both avoid 'unreasonably' prejudicing the interests of patent owners and at the same time take into account the legitimate interests of third parties. On this basis, it may even be possible to argue that article 30 permits states facing a severe HIV/AIDS crisis to make exceptions to patent rights to meet the 'legitimate interests of third parties'—in other words, of HIV/AIDS patients who need access to existing life-saving drugs.

The general exceptions provided for in articles 27.2 and 30 are supplemented by article 31, which sets out a regulatory framework for compulsory licensing. Compulsory licensing is permissible under TRIPS but under strict conditions.[43] These include the following: states can allow compulsory licensing only on a case-by-case basis; they must first try to secure authorization on commercial terms unless it is a situation of national emergency or the state wants to make public non-commercial use of the invention; further, the term of the licence must be limited in time to the purpose for which it is authorized, must be non-exclusive, and must be mainly to supply the domestic market; the patent holder is entitled to 'adequate' remuneration and the decisions taken are subject to judicial review.

The compulsory licensing framework offers developing countries tools with which to control some of the impacts of the introduction of patents even where they are forced to extend patentability to new areas under article 27. The positive features from the perspective of public health include the fact that there is no limitation on the purposes for which compulsory licences can be granted, thus giving member states significant leeway in framing public health and other public policy goals.[44] This remains limited in so far as article 31 allows the licensing only of individual inventions. Clauses permitting the compulsory licensing of a whole class of products, such as drugs, would therefore be unacceptable.[45]

Other important features of article 31 include the provisions concerning remuneration of the patent holder. While article 31(h) stipulates adequate remuneration, the context of article 31 implies that this remuneration is necessarily below the cost of a normal licence, since there would be no need for compulsion otherwise.[46] Article 31 also leaves states free to determine what constitutes a national emergency, as confirmed by the Doha declaration of

2001.[47] This is one of the clauses which may foster significant flexibility in TRIPS in the case of health emergencies. Indeed, African heads of state have proclaimed HIV/AIDS to represent a state of emergency across the whole continent.[48] They have also specifically stated their intention to use international trade regulations to ensure the availability of drugs at affordable prices.

Article 31(f) also addresses issues related to the exercise of patent rights and importation. As specified under article 28, the patent holder is not forced to produce the protected invention industrially in the country where it is registered. Commercial use through imports is also possible.[49] However, article 6 specifically indicates that the question of parallel imports is not dealt with under TRIPS.[50] This leaves countries free to decide whether to take advantage of existing price differences in countries around the world. In the case of compulsory licensing, countries can still take advantage of these provisions if they do not have the capacity to manufacture or can find cheaper alternatives elsewhere. However, article 31(f) restricts countries from compulsorily licensing an invention to manufacture it mainly for export. Articles 6 and 31(f) read together can thus be used by countries that have relatively high drug prices in their domestic market or no manufacturing capacity to buy elsewhere. In practice, the usefulness of compulsory licences for developing countries remains a matter of debate, partly because they have not been applied, having at most been used as a bargaining chip in negotiations with pharmaceutical companies.[51]

The International Human Rights Regime and Access to Drugs

Until recently, intellectual property law has been only very loosely linked to human rights law. This is because the intellectual property system has traditionally not been informed by socioeconomic concerns. The extension of patentability to sectors directly linked to the fulfilment of basic needs, such as health, requires renewed analysis of the linkages between intellectual property and human rights. This section focuses specifically on the human right to health and its relationship to the intellectual property rights system.

Health as a Human Right

The importance of a healthy life has generally been acknowledged at both national and international levels. Health as a human right has been included in a number of international instruments but, like other economic and social rights, it remains subject to frequent criticism for being vague in content and intersecting with too many other rights.[52] One of the most detailed pronouncements of this right is found in the International Covenant on Economic, Social and Cultural Rights (ESCR Covenant) which recognizes everyone's right to the 'enjoyment of the highest attainable standard of physical and mental health'.[53] The right to health implies, like other economic and social rights, obligations to respect, protect and fulfil that right. States are to refrain from interfering directly or indirectly with the enjoyment of the right; they should take measures to prevent third parties from interfering with the guarantees provided; and they should adopt appropriate legislative, administrative and other measures towards the full realization of the right.[54]

The Covenant generally requires members states to take all feasible steps to the maximum of their available resources progressively to achieve the full realization of the protected rights. It also indicates that these measures should be taken both by individual states and through international assistance and cooperation.[55] The Covenant thus recognizes that the full realization of the rights may require more than domestic measures. It is symptomatic that the Committee on Economic, Social and Cultural Rights (ESCR Committee) has indicated in its authoritative interpretation of the right to health that states have an obligation to facilitate access to essential health facilities, goods and services in other countries and to provide the necessary aid when required.[56] Further, states are to ensure that other international agreements to which they accede do not adversely impact on the right to health. These are indications that states must, for instance, cooperate in making drugs available at affordable prices.

As expounded by the ESCR Committee, the core obligations of the right to health include the imperative to ensure the right of access to health facilities, especially for vulnerable or marginalized groups.[57] In the case of primary health care, this includes the promotion of a safe and adequate food supply and proper nutrition; an adequate supply of safe water and basic sanitation; immunization against the major infectious diseases; appropriate treatment of common diseases and injuries; and provision of essential drugs.[58] In the case of HIV/AIDS more specific elaborations of these obligations have been given. The World Health Assembly has, for instance, called on its member states to increase access to treatment and prevention of HIV-related illnesses through measures such as ensuring provision and affordability of drugs.[59] The UN Human Rights Commission has taken the same direction with its resolution on HIV/AIDS stating that access to medication in this context is one fundamental element for achieving the full realization of the right to the enjoyment of the highest attainable standard of physical and mental health.[60]

Apart from emphasizing the importance of accessibility and affordability, the ESCR Committee has also indicated some circumstances in which the right to health is said to be violated. This includes, for instance, the repeal of legislation which is necessary for the continued enjoyment of the right to health, or the adoption of legislation or policies manifestly incompatible with pre-existing domestic or international legal obligations in relation to the right to health.[61] Similarly, the obligation to respect the right to health is violated if a state fails to take into account its legal obligations when entering into bilateral or multilateral agreements.[62]

Links between Intellectual Property and Human Rights

From the point of view of human rights instruments, the relationship between the intellectual property rights system and the realization of human rights has been given only limited consideration. References to the links between the two fields seem to have surfaced mainly in two distinct periods, namely at the time of the drafting of the ESCR Covenant and the Universal Declaration of Human Rights,[63] and more recently following the adoption of TRIPS and the growing importance of intellectual property rights in the realization of some human rights.

In treaty law, the core human rights provision dealing with intellectual property is found in the ESCR Covenant. Article 15.1(c) recognizes everyone's right 'to benefit from the protection of the moral and material interests resulting from any scientific, literary or artistic production of which he is the author'.[64] The context within which intellectual property was included in human rights treaties is of direct relevance, given the lack of state practice. First, sub-paragraph (c) was not present in the original draft covenant of 1954. Article 15.1 included only two sub-paragraphs, which recognized everyone's right to take part in cultural life and the right 'to enjoy the benefits of scientific progress and its application'.[65] Article 15.1 was thus conceived mainly from the point of view of the 'end users' of scientific inventions or cultural development. The original article did not include even an indirect reference to the interests of inventors or authors. Article 15.1(c) must thus be read as an addition and should not be given precedence over the first two sub-paragraphs of the article.[66] Further, article 15.1(c) refers only to 'authors'. Indeed, the rationale for the introduction of the amendment, by Costa Rica and Uruguay, was to protect authors against improper action on the part of publishers.[67] Uruguay argued that the lack of international protection allowed the piracy of literary and scientific works by foreign countries which paid no royalties to authors.[68] The intention was not to qualify the first two sub-paragraphs but rather to highlight one specific problem.[69]

Article 15.1(c) directly derives from article 27.2 of the Universal Declaration.[70] The drafting history of the declaration brings some more useful elements to the fore. First, the original article 27 did not include a second paragraph.[71] This was added following an amendment proposed by Mexico on the basis of a similar provision included in the 1948 Bogota Declaration.[72] In support of its submissions, Mexico argued that there was a need to add to the rights already protected in the draft declaration the rights of the intellectual worker, scientist or writer, so that all forms of work, manual and intellectual, would be protected on an equal basis.[73] Mexico and the other Latin American countries viewed the introduction of an intellectual property clause as a safeguard against predatory moves by foreign publishing houses. While some countries made reference to scientific development and patents in the course of the deliberations, statements show that state representatives usually analysed the clause from the perspective of copyright only.[74]

Following the adoption of TRIPS, UN human rights bodies have progressively given more attention to the question of the impacts of intellectual property rights on the realization of human rights. Among the political organs, the Sub-Commission on Human Rights adopted, for instance, a resolution in 2001 which recognizes the existence of potential conflicts between the implementation of TRIPS and the implementation of economic, social and cultural rights.[75] Further, the ESCR Committee has embarked on the task of adopting a General Comment on the relationship between human rights and intellectual property. As an intermediary measure, a statement on the matter was adopted in 2001.[76] Though not binding on member states, this statement constitutes an important guide for an understanding of the human right to health in the TRIPS era. Specific elements of this statement are highlighted below.

The TRIPS Agreement and the Human Right to Health

In most developing countries, the introduction of process and product patents on drugs is likely to influence access to drugs to a significant extent. There will be abrupt rises in price, impacts on local pharmaceutical industries and a greater emphasis on private sector research and development. Together, these are likely to create a situation where drugs become both less accessible and less affordable. There is therefore a direct link between the patentability of drugs on the one hand and, on the other, the availability of medicines, the realization of the right to health and ultimately of the right to life. In other words, it is necessary to analyse closely the relationship between intellectual property rights and the human right to health.[77]

Since human rights instruments mention intellectual property, it is germane to examine whether intellectual property rights qualify as human rights. The debates of 1948 and 1957 indicate that basic human rights treaties did not intend to recognize the interests of authors or inventors as fundamental human rights.[78] Both the Universal Declaration and the first covenant recognize as a basic claim everyone's right to enjoy the fruits of cultural life and scientific development; the right of the individual author is subsidiary in the balancing of priorities. The implication is that human rights put the emphasis on societal benefits.[79] This approach is opposed to that of intellectual property rights instruments, which focus mainly on the rights of authors, inventors and other legal entities to claim exclusive rights over an intellectual creation. The question of the balance of rights and obligations is addressed by the TRIPS Agreement, but here the interests of society at large figure more as an addition to—or even as an exclusion from—the rights provided than as an integral part of the treaty. Human rights treaties require the balance to be attempted from the perspective of society at large.

Overall, there appears to be a substantive difference between intellectual property rights, and the fundamental and universal entitlements called human rights. The former are temporary rights granted by the state that can be revoked and transferred, while the latter are inalienable and timeless.[80]

Access to Drugs after Doha

To date, only scant attention has been given to the relationship between TRIPS and the human right to health. This is due in part to the sectoral nature of international law but also to the unresolved issues raised by potential conflicts between different areas of international law. The general principle remains that developing countries should do their utmost to implement both the ESCR Covenant and TRIPS in such a way as to minimize conflicts. However, there are situations where conflicts may remain. This section starts by examining developing countries' options within the TRIPS framework as they are understood after the Doha meeting. It then goes on to examine ways in which conflicts between intellectual property rights and the human right to health could be resolved under international law.

Fostering Access to Drugs through the Intellectual Property System

Some of the avenues that developing countries can use within the TRIPS context to foster better access to drugs and the realization of the right to health in general have been outlined above. So far, the emphasis has been on finding acceptable interpretations of TRIPS from the point of view of access to drugs rather than examining the broader relationship between TRIPS and the right to health. This latter line of enquiry must, however, be pursued given that developing countries are obliged to implement TRIPS taking into account the existence of the ESCR Covenant and other relevant international treaties.

A number of recent developments at the international level indicate that developing countries can explore different possible interpretations of the TRIPS provisions or decide to act on the margin of TRIPS. This situation has been brought about largely by the scale of the HIV/AIDS crisis and the extremely high price of existing medicines used to alleviate the disease. In fact, the extent of the crisis has been sufficient to trigger the adoption of a U.S. executive order which directs that measures taken by countries to promote access to HIV/AIDS medicines should not be challenged.[81] The failed challenges to the South African and Brazilian Acts also indicate that even if the measures adopted are not strictly compliant with TRIPS, they are unlikely to be challenged again in the near future.[82] This is likely to be the case with most laws seeking to foster better access to drugs for major epidemics but not necessarily for other diseases or in other sectors.[83]

The question of the margin of manoeuvre that countries have in implementing TRIPS can be approached first from the perspective of the Doha Declaration. In effect, the Doha Declaration restates and increases the mechanisms that states can use within the TRIPS context to foster public health goals. The Declaration confirms, for instance, that member states can interpret their TRIPS obligations in such a way that they contribute to and do not work against their health policies.[84] In other words, it reaffirms the importance of articles 7 and 8 in so far as they provide member states with a clear legal basis in TRIPS for taking measures that may diverge from generally accepted interpretations of the agreement.

The Declaration is important for developing countries in that it strengthens the position of countries that want to take advantage of the existing flexibility within TRIPS.[85] The Declaration does not open up new avenues within TRIPS, but confirms the legitimacy of measures seeking to use to the largest extent possible the flexibility already built into the agreement. In other words, it constitutes a confirmation of the position of countries like South Africa and Brazil which sought to go beyond a narrow interpretation of TRIPS in their search for ways to tackle health crises.

While the Doha Declaration has contributed to softening the tone of international debates concerning access to medicines in the context of TRIPS, it stops short of addressing the most significant issues in this field. Recent debates have focused mostly on the extent to which developing countries should be able to adapt the intellectual property rights system in situations where major problems have arisen. This does not address the question of whether the introduction of process and product patents in all WTO member states is generally reconcilable with the measures that states must take to foster the realization of the right to health.

The Declaration also fails to provide answers to more practical questions, such as the prohibition on a country such as India compulsorily licensing a drug mainly to export it to other countries that do not have a manufacturing base of their own. If exports are not permitted in this context, most sub-Saharan African countries will not be able to take advantage of alternative sources of medicines.[86] This problem points to one of the major challenges that all developing countries will face in the future. If existing manufacturing capacity in countries like India were to be substantially reduced, this would have an impact not only on India but also on a number of other countries which do not have the capacity to manufacture drugs themselves and would therefore become totally dependent on supplies from developed country manufacturers.[87]

Since the Doha meeting, there seems to be an international consensus that countries trying to deal with health emergencies will not be questioned in terms of their obligations under TRIPS. This, however, leaves completely open a number of other issues. As far as Brazil is concerned, while the United States halted the dispute settlement proceedings, it is not at all clear whether there is an international consensus that Brazil is free to grant compulsory licences for any 'reasons related to the public health, nutrition, protection of the environment or to the technological or social and economic development of the country.'[88] In the case of South Africa, article 15C(a) of the Medicines Act provides that patent rights can be overruled in some circumstances.[89] While the Act entered into force as adopted, it is unclear whether it will be fully implemented and, if so, whether implementation will go unchallenged. The theoretical acceptability of the Brazilian and South African laws thus does not indicate that all countries are entitled to deviate to such an extent from TRIPS.

From a broader perspective, even if deviation from TRIPS is allowed as an exception in the case of some health emergencies, this remains an unsatisfactory response from the perspective of human rights. It is not possible to distinguish the realization of the right to health from the eradication of poverty in general or the realization of the right to food and water. If exemptions are warranted in the case of health, they should be extended to all sectors related to the fulfilment of basic needs.

In other words, the fact that developing countries can use loopholes or unclear language in TRIPS to pursue the realization of the right to health is unsatisfactory in so far as the central concern of health is consistently framed as an exception to a property right. Thus the Doha Declaration on health is inadequate in so far as it merely extends the possibilities for granting compulsory licences and does not amend the TRIPS Agreement.

From the perspective of the right to health and access to drugs, the TRIPS Agreement needs to be revised to include principles in favour of access to drugs in the main provisions of the agreement rather than as exceptions.[90] However, an amendment to article 27 of TRIPS that would compulsorily reduce the scope of patentability is not very likely in the near future, while a strengthening of TRIPS in the context of forthcoming WTO negotiations is possible. There is, therefore, a need to analyse TRIPS in its present form and examine the extent to which states can fully implement their TRIPS obligations together with their human rights commitments.

Fostering Access to Drugs: Linking Human Rights and Patent Rights

As noted, there are potential tensions between TRIPS and the ESCR Covenant. In trying to find a solution to the latent conflicts, it is of paramount importance to set the overall framework that should guide the more technical legal analysis. From the narrow perspective of access to medicines, the challenge is to find ways to make sure that existing drugs are available at little or no cost to people who need them. More generally, the central concern that should guide the implementation of all international treaties concerning health directly or indirectly is the promotion of better health care.

From the standpoint of TRIPS, the question of health can be tackled through some of the exceptions provided in section 5 of the agreement or through the two general qualificatory clauses of articles 7 and 8. This, however, falls short of an adequate resolution of the relationship between TRIPS and human rights. From the point of view of human rights, the link between the two fields was considered in the drafting of human rights treaties, when, as noted above, it was concluded that the interests of the community at large should generally prevail over those of individual authors. This does not imply a rejection of the interests of the author but rather their subordination to broader goals.[91]

A human rights perspective on health neither entails an *a priori* rejection of all intellectual property rights in the field of health nor provides another avenue for developing countries to claim preferential treatment. However, it does call into question some of the tenets of intellectual property law. As noted, patent protection does not ensure that the most common diseases will attract the most research even though it entails higher drug prices. This implies that even if patent protection can be justified in markets where all consumers can afford to pay (directly or indirectly) the price of patented drugs, this is not so in other situations. While there is a general divide between developed and developing countries with regard to the issues of drug prices and the development of medicines directly related to developing country diseases, a human rights approach to health is not strictly concerned with the level of economic development of countries. What is more fundamental from a human rights perspective is a focus on the most disadvantaged and marginalized individuals and communities. While human rights are universal entitlements, their effective realization is to be judged against the level of implementation among the most disadvantaged. The issue is therefore not whether developing countries can afford patent rights in general, but whether the majority of their poor population will benefit.[92] One of the first steps in tackling the problems faced by the most disadvantaged sections of society would be to make sure that all essential medicines remain free from patent protection. This conceptual framework is what informed the 1970 Indian Patents Act, which rejected product patents on drugs, and, to a more limited degree, the Brazilian decree on compulsory licensing, which seeks to provide an extensive definition of the public interest.[93]

From a practical point of view, patents on medicines in developing countries are fraught with other difficulties. In a number of countries, most people pay for their own health care. Since a large part of the population does not have access to existing drugs today, any price rise tends to limit access for more people. The Indian example is useful. Today, millions of Indian people cannot afford drugs under a regime which denies product patents on pharmaceuticals. If prices are allowed to go even higher under TRIPS-mandated product patents, even fewer people in India will have access to drugs. From this perspective, there is a need not for patent rights that lead to price rises but for even lower prices to facilitate broader access to drugs.

If compliance with TRIPS leads to reduced access to drugs, this might imply a substantive violation of the ESCR Covenant. Indeed, while article 2 of the covenant does not require immediate full implementation of the right to health, it requires states to take positive measures towards the fulfilment of that right.[94] The introduction of product patents could be construed as a 'deliberately retrogressive' step if no measures are taken to limit the impacts of TRIPS compliance on access to medicines.[95] From a health perspective, TRIPS is justified because, while it protects the interests of the private sector pharmaceutical industry, it also promotes increased R&D in the health sector. Going beyond controversies over the actual nature of the increases in R&D fostered by the patent system, it has become clear over time that, at the very least, the incentives provided by the patent system do not lead the private sector to invest preferentially in the most common diseases of the poor. As a result, one of the few possibilities open to developing countries to make sure that the introduction of medical patents does not constitute a retrogressive step in the implementation of the right to health is to provide significant public resources for R&D directed towards diseases of the poor and increased subsidies to facilitate access to drugs for the poorest.[96]

Avoiding Conflicts between Human Rights and Intellectual Property

The previous paragraphs highlight some of the problems that exist when trying to reconcile patents and the right to health but do not yet address the way in which international law would solve a conflict in practice if it occurred.[97] While most conflicts can be avoided with an interpretation that bridges the gaps between the different treaties, some further problems arise in the case of the relationship of WTO treaties and human rights treaties.

In case of conflict, states should first refer to treaty law, which provides broad rules of interpretation and reviews the question of conflicts between different treaties. At a general level, states must attempt to the maximum extent possible to reconcile all their international obligations, or at least to minimize conflicts, to comply with their duty to implement all their obligations.[98] International treaties are often sufficiently vaguely drafted to allow states significant room for manoeuvre in implementing them, and this provides an important tool enabling them simultaneously to implement fully all their international obligations.

Previous sections of this article show that patents on drugs and the right to health can be reconciled only to a certain extent. In other words, simultaneously meeting the different commitments under TRIPS and the ESCR Covenant seems feasible only if states are allowed to adopt broad interpretations of TRIPS. Concerning the question of the relationship of the two treaties with each other, it is significant that neither specifically provides rules of interpretation.[99] However, it is not improbable that they may be on a collision course. TRIPS obligations tend to be precisely drafted and are backed by an effective dispute settlement mechanism.[100] The ESCR Covenant is drafted in much broader terms and there is no enforcement mechanism. The ESCR Committee has nevertheless indicated that a violation of the right to health can occur if states agree to international measures which are manifestly incompatible with their previous international legal obligations, an interpretation which clearly puts TRIPS in a lower position than the covenant in the hierarchy of obligations.[101] The ESCR Covenant could also be seen as providing more specific norms in the field of the right to health, given that TRIPS addresses health concerns only peripherally.

While treaty law provides a number of rules to adjudicate conflicts between conventional norms,[102] it is improbable that a conflict between human rights and other treaties can be satisfactorily addressed in this way. International law is to a large extent based on the principle that there is no hierarchy between sources of law and different areas of the law.[103] However, international law is not free from all forms of hierarchy. First, the UN Charter states that it prevails over any other treaty signed by its member states.[104] The Charter does not, however, provide a clear answer to the question of conflicts between human rights and other treaty obligations.[105] Beyond the hierarchy recognized in the Charter, the notion of *jus cogens* is noteworthy.[106] It is today largely agreed that there are some fundamental principles and norms that states are not free to modify or abrogate.[107] These include, for instance, the prohibition of slavery and crimes against humanity. The peremptory status of some other norms, such as the primacy of the respect for all human rights, remains controversial.[108] At the time of the drafting of the Vienna Convention on the Law of Treaties, a number of states mentioned human rights in their enumeration of peremptory norms. Further, human rights treaties recognize the peremptory status of some specific rights.[109] However, while regional legal regimes such as the European Convention on Human Rights indicate an increasing recognition of the special nature of human rights, in general international law it is not yet possible to argue that all human rights are peremptory norms.[110] The human right to health is clearly not a non-derogable right under present international law. However, if a hierarchy had to be established between human rights and intellectual property rights, it is likely that human rights would generally take precedence. This concurs with the conclusions of the UN Sub-Commission on Human Rights in its recent resolution on intellectual property and human rights, in which it noted 'the primacy of human rights obligations under international law over economic policies and agreements' and called on states to ensure that the implementation of TRIPS should not negatively impact on the enjoyment of human rights.[111]

Overall, there seem to be a number of ways to resolve conflicts between the right to health and intellectual property rights without resorting to a prioritization between the two, for instance by guaranteeing the 'social dimensions of intellectual property.'[112] Similarly, international judicial bodies have shown that they can go a long way towards resolving potential conflicts between different norms of international law. The concept of evolutionary approach—used, for instance, by the International Court of Justice—under which an old treaty can be interpreted in light of further developments in other fields of international law, is a case in point.[113] However, in cases where prioritization is necessary, human rights should be given more weight than intellectual property rights. This is a situation that a number of countries may face. If the introduction of patents on medicines, which implies higher prices for drugs, is not counter-balanced with measures to offset price hikes and the shift in R&D away from diseases afflicting the poor, this is likely to lead to reduced access to drugs for most people in developing countries who have to pay for their own drugs. This situation is particularly in evidence in countries like India, which had formerly adopted specific restrictions on the patentability of drugs with a view to fostering better access to drugs. In this case, the dismantlement of a legal regime intended to foster better access to medicines is a step backwards in terms of the progressive realization of the human right to health. Unless these changes are offset by other measures such as subsidies to promote better access to drugs, this may amount to a violation of the ESCR Covenant which requires states at least to take positive measures towards implementation.[114]

Conclusion

TRIPS is without doubt one of the most significant international treaties of the late twentieth century. In the field of health, it has had and will have sweeping impacts in most developing countries. One of the complications from an international law point of view is that TRIPS is being applied not in a vacuum but in a context where the right to health is a well-established human right codified in one of the two main international human rights treaties.

The introduction of patents on drugs has provoked a significant outcry in a number of developing countries where access to medicines is already abysmally low. The justifications offered for the existence of patents as incentives to innovation often do not appear convincing to patients in developing countries, who see that hardly any R&D is being invested in diseases specific to those countries. In other cases, such as HIV/AIDS, where drugs to alleviate the condition exist, the prices of these—for all practical purposes, life-saving—drugs have been so high as to render them unaffordable for all but the wealthiest in developing countries.

The legal arguments concerning the relationship between human rights and intellectual property rights, and the practical debates concerning access to drugs in developing countries, both point towards the existence of potential conflicts between the introduction of patents on drugs in developing countries and the realization of the right to health. While states must endeavour as far as possible to reconcile their different international obligations, there seem to be some cases where the implementation of TRIPS directly implies a reduction in access to drugs and thus a step back in the implementation of the right to health. This appears to be unacceptable under the ESCR Covenant and countries in this situation would be expected to give priority to their human rights obligations. This solution, which gives primacy to human rights, is unlikely to meet with the approval of all states and would probably not stand if it came for adjudication in a WTO context. It nevertheless seems adequate from a legal and ethical point of view.

Notes

1. See WTO, Declaration on the TRIPS Agreement and Public Health, Ministerial Conference, Fourth Session, WTO Doc. WT/MIN(01)/DEC/2 (2001) [hereafter Doha Health Declaration].
2. Over 95% of people living with HIV/AIDS are in developing countries. See UNICEF-UNAIDS-WHO/HTP/MSF, *Sources and prices of selected drugs and diagnostics for people living with HIV/AIDS* (May 2001) [hereafter Drug Price Report].
3. International Covenant on Economic, Social and Cultural Rights, New York, 16 Dec. 1966, repr. in *International Legal Materials* 6: 360, 1967 [hereafter ICESCR].
4. Agreement on Trade-Related Aspects of Intellectual Property Rights, Marrakesh, 15 Apr. 1994, repr. in *International Legal Materials* 33: 1197, 1994 [hereafter TRIPS Agreement].
5. See e.g., Martha C. Nussbaum, 'Capabilities, human rights and the universal declaration', in Burn H. Weston and Stephen P. Marks, eds, *The future of international human rights* (Ardsley, NY: Transnational, 1999).
6. See e.g., Guido Calabresi and A. Douglas Melamed, 'Property rules, liability rules, and inalienability: one view of the cathedral,' *Harvard Law Review* 85, 1972, p. 1089.
7. ICESCR; International Covenant on Civil and Political Rights, New York, 16 Dec. 1966, repr. in *ILM* 6, 1967, p. 368 [hereafter ICCPR].
8. Cf., preamble of the ICESCR.
9. See article 1 of the Vienna Declaration and Programme of Action, Vienna, 25 June 1993, UN Doc. A/CONF.157/24 (Part I), which states that '[h]uman rights and fundamental freedoms are the birthright of all human beings; their protection and promotion is the first responsibility of Governments.'
10. See e.g., Frédéric M. Scherer, 'Le système des brevets et l'innovation dans le domaine pharmaceutique,' *Revue internationale de droit économique* 110: 1, 2000. Note also that intellectual property protection is also considered essential in influencing investment decisions, including in developing countries. See Ida Madieha Azmi and Rokiah Alavi, 'TRIPS, patents, technology transfer, foreign direct investment and the pharmaceutical industry in Malaysia,' *Journal of World Intellectual Property* 4, 2001, p. 948, concerning Malaysia.
11. See e.g., Harvey E. Bale, Jr, 'The conflicts between parallel trade and product access and innovation: the case of pharmaceuticals,' *Journal of International Economic Law* 1, 1998, p. 637; Thomas B. Cueni, 'Industrial property protection: lifeline for the pharmaceutical industry,' in Thomas Cottier and Peter Widmer, eds, *Strategic issues of industrial property management in a globalizing economy: abstracts and selected papers* 13 (Oxford: Hart, 1999).

12. See e.g., John H. Barton, *Differentiated pricing of patented products.* Commission on Macroeconomics and Health Working Paper Series no. WG4: 2, 2001.

13. See e.g., Carlos Correa, *Integrating public health concerns into patent legislation in developing countries* (Geneva: South Centre, 2000).

14. For Switzerland, see Loi fédérale sur les brevets d'invention, 25 June 1954, *Recueil officiel des lois fédérales* 1955, p. 893 and amendment of 17 Dec. 1976, *Recueil officiel des lois fédérales* 1977, p. 1997. Note also that the trigger for this change in some European countries was the adoption of the European Patent Convention more than internal pressure to change the laws. See Friedrich-Karl Beir, 'The European patent system,' *Vanderbilt Journal of Transnational Law* 14, 1981, p. 1.

15. World Health Organization, *Globalization, TRIPS and access to pharmaceuticals*, WHO Policy Perspectives on Medicines no. 3, 2001 [hereafter WHO Policy Perspectives].

16. See India Patents Act 1970. See also Justice N. Rajagopala Ayyangar, *Report on the Revision of the Patents Law*, Sept. 1959.

17. Pradeep Agrawal and P. Saibaba, 'TRIPS and India's pharmaceuticals industry,' *Economic and Political Weekly* 36, 2001, p. 3787.

18. See e.g., World Bank, *Global economic prospects 2002* (Washington, D.C.: World Bank, 2001).

19. The Commission on Intellectual Property Rights, *Integrating intellectual property rights and development policy* (London: CIPR, 2002) [hereafter CIPR Report] notes at p. 33 that all the evidence examined concerning the role that intellectual property protection plays in stimulating R&D on diseases prevalent in developing countries 'suggests that it hardly plays any role at all, except for those diseases where there is a large market in the developed world.'

20. WHO Policy Perspectives.

21. See e.g., John H. Barton, 'Intellectual property rights and innovation,' in Nicholas Imparato, ed., *Capital for our time: the economic, legal, and management challenges of intellectual capital* (Stanford, CA: Hoover Institution Press, 1999), pp. 123 at p. 132, arguing that the intellectual property rights system generally favours large firms over small ones and in the final analysis stifles innovation rather than promotes it. As a result, the intellectual property system may contribute to an unnecessarily concentrated industrial structure.

22. See e.g., Commission on Human Rights, Resolution 2001/33, 'Access to medication in the context of pandemics such as HIV/AIDS,' in *Report on the 57th Session*, 19 March-27 April 2001, UN Doc. E/2001/23-E/CN.4/2001/167.

23. See e.g., Germán Velásquez and Pascale Boulet, 'Globalization and access to drugs: implications of the WTO/TRIPS Agreement,' in *Globalization and access to drugs – perspectives on the WTO/TRIPS Agreement* 2, WHO doc. WHO/DAP/98.9 (1998). See also United Nations Development Programme, *Human development report 2001* (Oxford: Oxford University Press, 2001), p. 3, estimating that about 2 billion people do not have access to low-cost essential drugs.

24. See e.g., Germán Velásquez, 'Médicaments essentiels et mondialisation,' *Revue internationale de droit écononique* 37: 1, 2000.

25. See e.g., World Health Organization and World Trade Organization Secretariats, *Report of the workshop on differential pricing and financing of essential drugs*, Høsbjør, Norway, 8–11 April 2001.

26. See e.g., Jérome Dumoulin, 'Les brevets et le prix des médicaments,' *Revue internationale de droit économique* 45: 1, 2000. In the case of Malaysia, see Azmi and Alavi, 'TRIPS, patents.'

27. See e.g., Drug Price Report, p. 5, indicating that factors related to affordability include patents, limited volume, limited competition, import duties and tariffs, local taxes and mark-ups for wholesaling, distribution and dispensing.

28. Drug Price Report.

29. See e.g., Jean O. Lanjouw, *The introduction of pharmaceutical product patents in India: 'Heartless exploitation of the poor and suffering'?*, NBER Working Paper no. 6366, 1999.

30. Government of India, Department of Chemicals and Petrochemicals, *Annual Report 1999–2000*.

31. Shekhar Chaudhri, 'The evolution of the Indian pharmaceutical industry,' in Greg Felker et al. eds., *The pharmaceutical industry in India and Hungary: policies, institutions, and technological development* (Washington, D.C.: World Bank, 1997), p. 6.

32. Note also that the Patents Act 1970 was not the only element in the Indian health policy aimed at containing health costs. It was supplemented by other important tools such as the Drug Prices Control Order. The latest version of the latter is the Drug (Price Control) Order, 1995.

33. See section 53 of the Indian Patents Act 1970.

34. See sections 86ff. of the Indian Patents Act 1970, which authorized the government to force patent holders to provide licences to any applicant who made an application. While licences of right were to be authorized only in specific cases for normal patents, the Act provided that process patents for inventions relating to medicines were automatically subjected to these provisions.

35. Article 27.1 of the TRIPS Agreement.

36. Article 7 of the TRIPS Agreement (emphasis added).

37. Cf., statement by the Committee on Economic, Social and Cultural Rights on Human Rights and Intellectual Property, in Committee on Economic, Social and Cultural Rights, *Report on the 25th, 26th and 27th Sessions*, UN Doc. E/2002/22–E/C.12/2001/17, Annex XIII [hereafter CESCR IP Statement].

38. See Brazil, Industrial Property Code, Law 5772/71, 21 Dec. 1971.

39. Article 7 of the TRIPS Agreement.

40. Article 8 of the TRIPS Agreement. However, it would be difficult to justify an exception not foreseen in TRIPS under article 8 unless it were an exception to a right which is not protected under TRIPS.

41. World Trade Organization, *Communication from India*, WTO Doc.IP/C/W/195 (2000).

42. In principle, all inventions, whether product or processes, in all fields of technology are patentable. See article 27 of the TRIPS Agreement.

43. See article 31 of the TRIPS Agreement.

44. As confirmed by the Doha Health Declaration.

45. Cf., section 87 of the Indian Patents Act 1970 providing in derogation of the general regime that all food-and medicine-related inventions should be deemed to be endorsed with the rubric 'licence of right'.

46. See e.g., Jayashree Watal, *Intellectual property rights in the WTO and developing countries* (New Delhi: Oxford University Press, 2001); Robert Weissman, 'A long, strange TRIPS: the pharmaceutical industry drive to harmonize global intellectual property rules, and the remaining WTO legal alternatives available to Third World countries,' *University of Pennsylvania Journal of International Economic Law* 17, 1996, p. 1069. cf.. Daniel Gervais, *The TRIPS Agreement: drafting, history and analysis* (London: Sweet & Maxwell, 1998).

47. See Section 5(c) of the Doha Health Declaration.

48. Organization of African Unity, *Abuja Declaration on HIV/AIDS, tuberculosis and other related infectious diseases*, 27 April 2001, OAU Doc. OAU/SPS/ABUJA/3 (2001).

49. The understanding of what amounts to 'working' the patent has changed over time and industrial use is not required any more. cf.. Carlos M. Correa, *Intellectual property rights and the use of compulsory licenses: options for developing countries*, Working Paper no. 5 (Geneva: South Centre, 1999).

50. On parallel imports, see generally Frederick M. Abbott, 'First report (final) to the Committee on International Trade Law of the International Law Association on the subject of parallel importation,' *Journal of International Economic Law* 1, 1998, p. 607.

51. See e.g., Frederick M. Abbott. 'The TRIPS Agreement, access to medicines, and the WTO Doha ministerial conference,' *Journal of World Intellectual Property* 5, 2002, p. 15.

52. Cf., David P. Fidler, *International law and infectious diseases* (Oxford: Oxford University Press, 1999).

53. See article 12 of the ICESCR. On the right to health, see generally Brigit C. A. Toebes, *The right to health as a human right in international law* (Antwerp: Intersentia, 1999).

54. See Committee on Economic, Social and Cultural Rights, General Comment no. 14, *The right to the highest attainable standard of health*, UN Doc. E/C.12/2000/4 (2000) [hereafter General Comment 14].

55. ICESCR.
56. General Comment 14.
57. General Comment 14.
58. See article VII of the Declaration of Alma-Ata, 12 Sept. 1978, repr. in *Report of the International Conference on Primary Health Care* (Geneva: World Health Organization, 1978).
59. World Health Assembly, 'HIV/AIDS: confronting the epidemic,' Resolution WHA53:14 (Genoa: World Health Organization, 2000).
60. Commission on Human Rights, 'Access to medication in the context of pandemics such as HIV/AIDS,' Resolution 2001/53 (23 April 2001).
61. General Comment 14.
62. See e.g., CESCR IP Statement, para, 12, which states specifically that 'any intellectual property regime that makes it more difficult for a State party to comply especially with its core obligations in relation to health, food, education or any other right set out in the Covenant, is inconsistent with the legally binding obligations of the State party.'
63. Universal Declaration of Human Rights, 10 Dec. 1948, UN General Assembly Resolution 217 (III) A, *Official Records of the Third Session of the General Assembly*, Part I, 21 Sept.–12 Dec. 1948, Resolutions.
64. Article 15.1(c) of the ICESCR.
65. Draft Covenant on Economic, Social and Cultural Rights, Commission on Human Rights, Report of the 10th Session, ECOSOC, 18th Session, Suppl. 7, Doc E/2573-E/CN.4/705 (1954). Note that article 15 was article 16 in the 1954 draft. References in this article are all to article 15.
66. For the text of the proposed amendment, see UN Doc. A/C.3/L.636/Rev.1 (1957).
67. Draft International Covenant on Human Rights, Report of the 3rd Committee, UN Doc. A/3764 (1957).
68. United Nations, Third Committee Summary Record of Meetings, UN Doc. A/C.3/SR.797 (1957).
69. Note that the amendment was accepted by 39 states, including most west European and Latin American countries, and rejected by nine countries from the communist bloc. Twenty-four countries abstained, including the United States. See Draft International Covenant on Human Rights, Report of the 3rd Committee, UN Doc. A/3764 (1957).
70. United Nations, Third Committee Summary Record of Meetings, UN Doc. A/C.3/SR.796 (1957).
71. See United Nations, Report of the 3rd Session of the Commission on Human Rights, UN Doc. E/800 (1948). Note that article 27 of the final text was article 25 in the draft Declaration, References in this article are all to article 27.
72. See article 13 of the American Declaration of the Rights and Duties of Man, repr. in *United Nations, human rights: a compilation of international instruments*, vol. II: *Regional instruments*, UN Doc. ST/HR/1/Rev. 5 (Vol. II), 1997; United Nations, *Draft International Declaration of Human Rights – Mexico; amendment to article 25 of the draft declaration*, UN Doc. A/C.3/266 (1948).
73. United Nations, Third Committee Summary Record of Meetings, UN Doc. A/C.3/SR.150 (1948).
74. See e.g., the statements of the Dominican Republic supporting the amendment, UN Doc. A/C.3/SR.799 (1957), and India, which abstained, UN Doc. A/C.3/SR.798 (1957).
75. See Resolution 2001/21, 'Intellectual property and human rights,' United Nations Sub-Commission on Human Rights, UN Doc. E/CN.4/Sub.2/RES/2001/21 (2001).
76. CESCR IP Statement.
77. cf.. United Nations Development Programme, *Human development report 2000* (Oxford: Oxford University Press, 2000), which mentions that TRIPS raises issues of compatibility with human rights and international environmental law.
78. Sub-Commission on the Promotion and Protection of Human Rights, *The impact of the Agreement on Trade-Related Aspects of Intellectual Property Rights on human rights*, UN Doc. E/CN.4/Sub.2/2001/13 (2001).
79. Cf., ibid.
80. See CESCR IP Statement, section 6.
81. US Executive Order no. 13,155, 'Access to HIV/AIDS pharmaceuticals and medical technologies,' *Federal Register 65*, 2000, p. 30,521. Note, however, that under this executive

order, beneficiary countries can benefit from its provisions only if they provide adequate and effective intellectual property protection.

82. In South Africa, the dispute concerned the Medicines and Related Substances Control Amendment Act, 1997 (Republic of South Africa, Government Gazette, 12 Dec. 1997). See *The Pharmaceutical Manufacturers' Association of South Africa et al.* v. *The President of the Republic of South Africa et al.* Notice of Motion, High Court of South Africa (Transvaal Provincial Division), 18 Feb. 1998 and *The Pharmaceutical Manufacturers' Association of South Africa et al.* v. *The President of the Republic of South Africa et al.* Joint Statement of Understanding (2001). In Brazil, the dispute concerned the Industrial Property Law, Law No 9.279 of 14 May 1996. See *Brazil: measures affecting patent protection—notification of mutually agreed solution*, WTO Doc. WT/DS199/4 (2001).

83. The United States indicated as it was challenging Brazil in the WTO that it made a clear distinction between the health and other sectors. See United States Trade Representative, *2001 Special 301 Report* (Washington, D.C.: USTR, 2001).

84. Para. 4 of the Doha Health Declaration. See also Paul Vandoren, 'Médicaments sans frontières? Clarification of the relationship between TRIPS and public health resulting from the WTO Doha ministerial declaration,' *Journal of World Intellectual Property 5*, 2002, p. 4.

85. Cf., Abbott, 'The TRIPS Agreement,' p. 38, suggesting more generally that measures adopted by developing and least developed countries to address public health should be presumed to be consistent with TRIPS and that any member challenging them should bear the burden of proof.

86. See e.g., CIPR Report, p. 35.

87. The Doha Health Declaration has not tackled this problem but required the TRIPS Council to provide a solution within a limited time frame (see para. 6 of the declaration).

88. This constitutes the definition of 'public interest' under article 1 of the Brazilian Presidential Decree on Compulsory Licensing, Decree no. 3,201, 6 Oct. 1999. On this point, see also Paul Champ and Amir Attaran, 'Patent rights and local working under the WTO TRIPS Agreement: an analysis of the US-Brazil patent dispute,' 27 *Yale Journal of International Law* 27, 2002, p. 365.

89. See Medicines and Related Substances Control Amendment Act 1997, Republic of South Africa, *Government Gazette*, 12 Dec. 1997.

90. As argued by the World Bank; see *Global economic prospects 2002*, p. 148.

91. See above, p. 136.

92. Similarly, the fact that developed countries in general can 'afford' the costs involved in patent-protected drug research does not imply that all individuals in those countries are in a position to benefit from the system.

93. See Indian Patents Act 1970 and Brazilian Presidential Decree on Compulsory Licensing, Decree no. 3,201, 6 Oct. 1999.

94. Committee on Economic Social and Cultural Rights, General Comment no. 3. 'The nature of states parties obligations (art. 2, para. 1 of the covenant),' in *Compilation of general comments and general recommendations adopted by human rights treaty bodies*, UN Doc. HRI/GEN/1/Rev.4 (2000).

95. Ibid.

96. Cf., World Bank. The Bank would rather see public funds used to purchase drugs or licences than essential drugs removed from patentability; see *Global economic prospects 2002*, p. 148.

97. Note that a conflict occurs if the fulfilment of one obligation leads to the violation of another commitment. A conflict can also arise where the only way to reconcile two treaties is to apply the one providing stricter obligations. On this point see Joost Pauwelyn, 'The role of public international law in the WTO: How far can we go?', *American Journal of International Law* 95, 2002, p. 535.

98. See article 26 of the Convention on the Law of Treaties, Vienna, 23 May 1969, repr. in *International Legal Materials* 8, 1969, p. 679 [hereafter Vienna Convention 1969].

99. This makes reliance on the intention of the parties difficult. cf.. Pauwelyn, 'The role of public international law in the WTO,' p. 543.

100. See article 22 of the Understanding on Rules and Procedures Governing the Settlement of Disputes, Marrakesh, 15 April 1994, repr. in *International Legal Materials* 33, 1994, p. 1226.

101. See also Pauwelyn, 'The role of public international law in the WTO,' p. 549, who concludes that the modification of human rights treaties by WTO treaties may have difficulties passing the test required by article 41.1(b) of the Vienna Convention 1969.
102. See Vienna Convention 1969.
103. See e.g., Dominique Carreau, *Droit international*, 7th edn (Paris: Pédone, 2001).
104. See article 103 of the UN Charter.
105. Cf., Jean-Pierre Cot and Alain Pellet, eds, *La charte des Nations Unies: Commentaire article par article*, 2nd edn (Paris: Economica, 1991).
106. See e.g., Lauri Hannikainen, *Peremptory norms (jus cogens) in international law; historical development, criteria, present status* (Helsinki: Finnish Lawyers' Publishing, 1989). See also Teraya Koji, 'Emerging hierarchy in international human rights and beyond: from the perspective of non-derogable rights,' *European Journal of International Law* 12, 2001, p. 917.
107. Article 53 of the Vienna Convention 1969.
108. Carreau, *Droit international*.
109. See e.g., article 4 of the ICCPR.
110. Some authors agree, however, that human rights are *jus cogens*. See e.g., Hannikainen, *Peremptory norms*, p. 429, noting that '[i]n my view there is no doubt that contemporary international law has reached a stage in which it has the prerequisites for the existence of peremptory obligations upon States to respect basic human rights.'
111. Paras 3 and 5 of Resolution 2001/21, 'Intellectual property and human rights.'
112. Para. 18 of the CESCR IP Statement.
113. On this point, see e.g., Louise de la Fayette, 'United States: import prohibition of certain shrimp and shrimp products; recourse to article 21.5 of the DSU by Malaysia,' *American Journal of International Law* 96, 2002, p. 685.
114. See text accompanying note 94 above, p. 140–41.

10

TRIPS, Pharmaceutical Patents, and Access to Essential Medicines

A Long Way From Seattle to Doha

Ellen 't Hoen

Infectious diseases kill over 10 million people each year, more than 90 percent of whom are in the developing world.[1] The leading causes of illness and death in Africa, Asia, and South America—regions that account for four-fifths of the world's population—are HIV/AIDS, respiratory infections, malaria, and tuberculosis.

In particular, the magnitude of the AIDS crisis has drawn attention to the fact that millions of people in the developing world do not have access to the medicines that are needed to treat disease or alleviate suffering. Each day, close to eight thousand people die of AIDS in the developing world.[2] The reasons for the lack of access to essential medicines are manifold, but in many cases the high prices of drugs are a barrier to needed treatments. Prohibitive drug prices are often the result of strong intellectual property protection. Governments in developing countries that attempt to bring the price of medicines down have come under pressure from industrialized countries and the multinational pharmaceutical industry.

The World Trade Organization (WTO) Trade-Related Aspects of Intellectual Property Rights Agreement (TRIPS or Agreement), which sets out the minimum standards for the protection of intellectual property, including patents for pharmaceuticals, has come under fierce criticism because of the effects that increased levels of patent protection will have on drug prices. While TRIPS does offer safeguards to remedy negative effects of patent protection or patent abuse, in practice it is unclear whether and how countries can make use of these safeguards when patents increasingly present barriers to medicine access.

The Fourth WTO Ministerial Conference, held in 2001 in Doha, Qatar, adopted a Declaration on TRIPS and Public Health (Doha Declaration or Declaration) which affirmed the sovereign right of governments to take measures to protect public health. Public health advocates welcomed the Doha Declaration as an important achievement because it gave primacy to public health over private intellectual property, and clarified WTO Members' rights to use TRIPS safeguards. Although the Doha Declaration broke new ground in guaranteeing Members' access to medical products, it did not solve all of the problems associated with intellectual property protection and public health.

The Access Problem and Intellectual Property

A number of new medicines that are vital for the survival of millions are already too costly for the vast majority of people in poor countries. In addition, investment in research and development (R&D) towards the health needs of people in developing countries has almost come to a standstill. Developing countries, where three-quarters of the world population lives, account for less than 10 percent of the global pharmaceutical market. The implementation of TRIPS is expected to have a further upward effect on drug prices, while increased R&D investment, despite higher levels of intellectual property protection, is not expected.[3]

One-third of the world population lacks access to the most basic essential drugs and, in the poorest parts of Africa and Asia, this figure climbs to one-half. Access to treatment for diseases in developing countries is problematic either because the medicines are unaffordable, have become ineffective due to resistance, or are not sufficiently adapted to specific local conditions and constraints.

Many factors contribute to the problem of limited access to essential medicines. Unavailability can be caused by logistical supply and storage problems, substandard drug quality, inappropriate selection of drugs, wasteful prescription and inappropriate use, inadequate production, and prohibitive prices. Despite the enormous burden of disease, drug discovery and development targeted at infectious and parasitic diseases in poor countries has virtually ground to a standstill because drug companies in developed and developing nations simply cannot recoup the cost of R&D for products to treat diseases that abound in developing countries.[4] Of the 1,223 new drugs approved between 1975 and 1997, approximately one percent (13 drugs) specifically treat tropical diseases.[5]

TRIPS sets out minimum standards and requirements for the protection of intellectual property rights, including trademarks, copyrights, and patents. The implementation of TRIPS, initially scheduled for 2006 by all WTO Members, is expected to impact the possibility of obtaining new essential medicines at affordable prices.

Médecins sans Frontières (MSF), together with other non-governmental organizations (NGOs), formulated the following concerns related to TRIPS:

- Increased patent protection leads to higher drug prices.[6] The number of new essential drugs under patent protection will increase, but the drugs will remain out of reach to people in developing countries because of high prices. As a result, the access gap between developed and developing countries will widen.
- Enforcement of WTO rules will have a negative effect on local manufacturing capacity and will remove a source of generic, innovative, quality drugs on which developing countries depend.
- It is unlikely that TRIPS will encourage adequate R&D in developing countries for diseases such as malaria and tuberculosis, because poor countries often do not provide sufficient profit potential to motivate R&D investment by the pharmaceutical industry.
- Developing countries are under pressure from industrialized countries and the pharmaceutical industry to implement patent legislation that goes beyond the obligations of TRIPS. This is often referred to as "TRIPS plus." TRIPS plus is a non-technical term which refers to efforts to extend patent life beyond the twenty-year TRIPS minimum, to tighten patent protection, to limit compulsory licensing in ways not required by TRIPS, or to limit exceptions which facilitate prompt introduction of generics.[7]

Industrialized countries and World Intellectual Property Organization (WIPO) offer expert assistance to help countries become TRIPS-complaint. This technical assistance, however, does not take into account the health needs of the populations of developing countries. Both of these institutions are under strong pressure to advance the interests of large companies that own patents and other intellectual property rights.

Important Developments in the Debate on Access to Drugs and Intellectual Property

A number of factors have shaped the debate on TRIPS and access to medicines, directly or indirectly impacting the content of the Doha Declaration.

Big Pharma vs. Nelson Mandela: Trade Dispute in South Africa

In February 1998, the South African Pharmaceutical Manufacturers Association and forty (later thirty-nine, as a result of a merger) mostly multinational pharmaceutical manufacturers brought suit against the government of South Africa, alleging that the Medicines and Related Substances Control Amendment Act,

No. 90 of 1997 (Amendment Act) violated TRIPS and the South African constitution.[8]

The Amendment Act introduces a legal framework to increase the availability of affordable medicines in South Africa. Provisions included in the Amendment Act are generic substitution of off-patent medicines, transparent pricing for all medicines, and the parallel importation of patented medicines.[9]

At the start of the litigation, the drug companies could rely on the support of their home governments. For its part, the US had put pressure on South Africa by withholding trade benefits and threatening further trade sanctions, aiming to force the South African government to repeal the Amendment Act.[10] In 1998, the European Commission joined the US in pressuring South Africa to repeal the legislation.[11] AIDS activists effectively highlighted these policies, profoundly embarrassing then-presidential candidate Al Gore. Confronted at election campaign rallies about his personal involvement in the dispute, demonstrators accused him of killing babies in Africa.[12] As a result of increasing public pressure, the U.S. changed its policies at the end of 1999. By the time the case finally reached the courtroom in May 2000, the drug companies could no longer count on the support of their home governments.

Demonstrators in major cities asked the companies to drop the case; several governments and parliaments around the world, including the European Parliament, demanded that the companies withdraw from the case. The legal action turned into a public relations disaster for the drug companies.[13]

During the course of the trial it became clear that the most contentious section of the Amendment Act was based on a draft legal text produced by the WIPO Committee of Experts,[14] a fact that made it difficult for the drug companies to maintain the position that the Amendment Act violated South Africa's obligations under international law. Eventually, the strong international public outrage over the companies' legal challenge of a developing country's medicines law and the companies' weak legal position caused the companies to unconditionally drop the case in April 2001.

The widely publicized South African court case brought two key issues out into the international arena. First, the interpretation of the flexibilities of TRIPS and their use for public health purposes needed clarification to ensure that developing countries could use its provisions without the threat of legal or political challenge. Second, it became clear that industrialized countries that exercised trade pressures to defend the interest of their multinational industries could no longer exert pressure without repercussions at home.

US vs. Brazil: The Brazilian AIDS Program

Since the mid-1990s, Brazil has offered comprehensive AIDS care, including universal access to antiretroviral (ARV) treatment. An estimated 536,000 people are infected with HIV in Brazil, with 203,353 cases of AIDS reported to the Ministry of Health from 1980 through December 2000. In 2001, 105,000 people with HIV/AIDS received ARV treatment. The Brazilian AIDS program has reduced AIDS-related mortality by more than 50 percent between 1996 and 1999.[15] In two years, Brazil saved $472 million in hospital costs and treatment costs for AIDS-related infections.

At the core of the success of Brazil's AIDS program is the ability to produce medicines locally. In Brazil, the price of AIDS drugs fell by 82 percent over five years as a result of generic competition.[16] The price of drugs that had no generic competitor remained relatively stable, falling only nine percent over the same period. Brazil has also been able to negotiate lower prices for patented drugs by using the threat of production under a compulsory license.[17] Article 68 of the Brazilian patent law allows for compulsory licensing, which allows a patent to be used without the consent of the patent holder.[18] The Brazil AIDS program serves as a model for some developing countries that are able to produce medicines locally, and Brazil has offered a cooperation agreement, including technology transfer, to developing countries for the production of generic ARV drugs.[19]

In February 2001, the US took action against Brazil at the WTO Dispute Settlement Body (DSB) over Article 68 of the Brazilian intellectual property law. Under that provision, Brazil requires holders of Brazilian patents to manufacture the product in question within Brazil—a so-called "local working" requirement. If the company does not fulfill this requirement, the patent shall be subject to compulsory licensing after three years, unless the patent holder can show that it is not economically feasible to produce in Brazil or can otherwise show that the requirement to produce locally is not reasonable. If the company is allowed to work its patent by importation instead of manufacturing in Brazil, parallel import by others will be permitted.

The US argued that the Brazilian law discriminated against US owners of Brazilian patents and that it curtailed patent holders' rights. The US claimed that the Brazilian law violated Article 27.1 and Article 28.1 of TRIPS.[20] Brazil argued that Article 68 was in line with the text and the spirit of TRIPS, including Article 5.4 of the Paris Convention, which allows for compulsory licensing if there is a failure to work a patent. Article 2.1 of TRIPS incorporates relevant articles of the Paris Convention.

The US action came under fierce pressure from the international NGO community, which feared it would have a detrimental effect on Brazil's successful AIDS program.[21] Brazil has been vocal internationally in the debates on access to medicines, and on several occasions, including the G-8, the Roundtable of the European Commission, and WHO meetings, Brazil has offered support to developing countries to help them increase manufacturing capacity by transferring technology and know-how. NGOs feared that the US action could have a negative effect on other countries' ability to accept Brazil's offer of assistance. On June 25, 2001, in a joint statement with Brazil, the US announced that it would withdraw the WTO panel against Brazil.[22]

The Role of NGOs

NGOs have played a key role in drawing attention to provisions of TRIPS that can be used to increase access to medicines. One such provision pertains to compulsory licensing, which enables a competent government authority to license the use of an invention to a third-party or government agency without the consent of the patent holder. The patent holder, however, according to Article 31 of TRIPS, retains intellectual property rights and "shall be paid adequate remuneration" according to the circumstances of the case. The first international meeting specifically on the use of compulsory licensing to increase access to AIDS medicines took place in March 1999 at the Palais de Nations in Geneva and was organized by Consumer Project on Technology, Health Action International, and MSF. Later that year, the same group of NGOs organized the Amsterdam Conference on Increasing Access to Essential Drugs in a Globalized Economy, which brought together 350 participants from 50 countries on the eve of the Seattle WTO ministerial conference. The statement drawn up at this conference (Amsterdam Statement) focused on establishing a working group in the WTO on TRIPS and access to medicines, considering the impact of trade policies on people in developing and least-developed countries, and providing a public health framework for the interpretation of key features of WTO agreements. The working group was to address questions related to the use of compulsory licensing to increase access to medicines, mechanisms to allow production of medicines for export markets to a country with no or insufficient production capacity, patent barriers to research, and overly restrictive and anticompetitive interpretations of TRIPS rules regarding protections of health registration data. In addition, the working group was to examine "burden sharing" approaches for R&D that permit countries to consider a wider range of policy instruments to promote R&D and to consider the practical burdens on poor countries of administrating patent systems. The Amsterdam Statement also urged national governments to develop new and innovative mechanisms to ensure funding for R&D for neglected diseases.

The Amsterdam Statement has served as a guide for the work of NGOs and other advocates on TRIPS and public health. Many international and national NGOs, such as the Oxfam campaign, "Cut the Cost," the South African Treatment Action Campaign, and Act Up, are now involved in campaigning for access to medicines.

The WTO Ministerial 1999 in Seattle

Though public health and access to medicines did not form part of the official agenda in Seattle in the way it would two years later in Doha, the issue did receive attention for a number of reasons. First, in Seattle a Common Working Paper section on TRIPS contained the following proposal: "to issue . . . compulsory licenses for drugs appearing on the list of essential drugs of the World Health Organization."[23] Since only about 11 of the 306 products on the WHO Model List of Essential Drugs are patented drugs in certain countries,[24] this proposal could have limited the use of compulsory licensing, rather than making sure it became a useful tool to overcome access barriers, such as prohibitive pricing, caused by patent abuse.

Then-US President Clinton chose Seattle as the venue to declare a change in US policy with regard to intellectual property rights and access to medicines. The US government had come under fierce attack from AIDS activists because of its policies in South Africa. Under the new policy, the US Trade Representative and the Department of Health and Human Services would together establish a process to analyze health issues that arise in the application of US trade-related intellectual property law and policy. In his speech, President Clinton referred specifically to the situation in South Africa and the HIV/AIDS crisis, saying that "the United States will henceforward implement its health care and trade policies in a manner that ensures that people in the poorest countries won't have to go without medicine they so desperately need."[25]

In May 2000, President Clinton confirmed the change in US policy by issuing an Executive Order on Access to HIV/AIDS Pharmaceuticals and Medical Technologies, supporting the use of compulsory licenses to increase access to HIV/AIDS medication in sub-Saharan Africa.[26] Although this policy change contributed to breaking the taboo on the use of compulsory licensing in the health field, attention to TRIPS and medicines at the WTO was diverted by the collapse of the WTO conference in Seattle.[27] However, outside the WTO, the debate on access to medicines, TRIPS, and compulsory licensing became more intense.

Changing Attitudes among Global Players

A number of international institutions and UN agencies contributed to the debate on access to medicines and looked into the consequences of stronger intellectual property protection for developing countries as a result of TRIPS.

The World Health Organization

The public health community first raised concerns about the consequences of globalization and international trade agreements with respect to drug access during the 1996 World Health Assembly. A resolution on the Revised Drug

Strategy (RDS) set out the WHO's medicines policy.[28] The WHO resolution on the RDS requested the WHO in paragraph 2(10) "to report on the impact of the work of the World Trade Organization (WTO) with respect to national drug policies and essential drugs and make recommendations for collaboration between WTO and WHO, as appropriate." This resolution gave the WHO the mandate to publish, in 1998, the first guide with recommendations to Member States for implementing TRIPS while limiting the negative effects of higher levels of patent protection on drug availability.[29] The US and a number of European countries unsuccessfully pressured the WHO in an attempt to prevent publication of the guide.[30]

At that time, the WHO's involvement in trade issues was highly controversial. The emphasis on public health needs versus trade interest was seen as a threat to the commercial sector of the industrialized world. For example, in 1998, in response to the draft World Health Assembly's resolution on the RDS and in reference to "considerable concern among the pharmaceutical industry," the European Directorate General for Trade (DG Trade) of the European Commission concluded: "No priority should be given to health over intellectual property considerations."[31]

However, subsequent resolutions of the World Health Assembly have strengthened the WHO's mandate in the trade arena. In 2001, the World Health Assembly adopted two resolutions in particular that had a bearing on the debate over TRIPS.[32] The resolutions addressed 1) the need to strengthen policies to increase the availability of generic drugs, and 2) the need to evaluate the impact of TRIPS on access to drugs, local manufacturing capacity, and the development of new drugs. As a result, the WHO's work program on pharmaceuticals and trade now includes the provision of policy guidance and information on intellectual property and health to countries for monitoring and analyzing the effects of TRIPS on access to medicines.[33]

The UN Sub-Commission for the Promotion and Protection of Human Rights

The UN Sub-Commission for the Promotion and Protection of Human Rights passed a resolution, pointing out the negative consequences for human rights to food, health, and self-determination if TRIPS is implemented in its current form. The resolution was an initial effort to monitor the implications of TRIPS on human rights concerns. Reminding governments of the primacy of human rights obligations over economic policies and programs, the resolution states that there are "apparent conflicts between the intellectual property rights regime embodied in TRIPS, on the one hand, and international human rights law, on the other."[34] Referring specifically to pharmaceutical patents, the resolution stresses the need for intellectual property rights to serve social welfare needs.

The United Nations Development Program

In 1999, the United Nations Development Program's (UNDP's) Human Development Report made a plea for re-writing the rules of globalization to make them work "for people—not just profits."[35] The report, in particular, draws attention to the high cost of the patent system for developing countries compared to the unequal distribution of the system's benefits. 97 percent of the patents held worldwide are held by individuals and companies of industrialized countries, and 80 percent of the patents granted in developing countries belong to residents of industrial countries. UNDP called for a full and broad review of TRIPS and called upon countries not to create an unsustainable burden by adding new conditions to the intellectual property system. The report suggested that countries present frameworks for alternatives to the provisions of TRIPS and that the room for manoeuvring granted in TRIPS be respected in practice.

The European Union

In February 2001, the EU adopted the Program for Action, a program which accelerates action on HIV/AIDS, malaria, and tuberculosis in the context of poverty reduction. The EU program recognized the potential problems of TRIPS and the need to rebalance its priorities. In addition, several European Parliament resolutions reflected a shift in support of a pro-public health approach to TRIPS.[36] As part of this approach, DG Trade changed its policy to acknowledge the concerns of developing countries. Reflecting this change, DG Trade dropped its objections to the use of compulsory licensing to overcome patent barriers to medicine access and became an advocate for a global tiered pricing system for pharmaceuticals.[37] These policy changes are in stark contrast to previous European Commission policies, which closely track the pharmaceutical industry's agenda.

Other Organizations

Other organizations, such as UNAIDS, the World Bank, the Group of 77, and regional organizations such as the Organization of African Unity, added their voice to the debate on TRIPS and access to medicines.

Unable to turn a deaf ear to the growing chorus of critics of TRIPS and its effects on access to medicines, the WTO changed course. In April 2001, when proposing a special TRIPS Council session on access to medicines, Zimbabwe—chair of TRIPS Council—said that the WTO could no longer ignore the access to medicines issue, an issue that was being actively debated outside the WTO but not within it.[38] The voices had been heard; public health would be featured as a key subject at the Doha Conference.

A Brief History of the Doha Declaration on TRIPS and Public Health

The Fourth Ministerial Conference of the WTO took place in Doha in 2001 and was a breakthrough in international discussions on TRIPS and access to medicines. The WTO Ministerial adopted a Declaration on TRIPS and Public Health, which put public health before commercial interests and offered much needed clarification in the field of TRIPS and public health.

The African Proposal for a Special TRIPS Council Meeting in June

Zimbabwe's statement on behalf of the "African Group" about the need to confront the access to medicines issue initiated preparations for the Declaration. Just two months later, in June 2001, the TRIPS Council held its first session devoted to TRIPS and access to medicines. It was the first time that the TRIPS Council discussed intellectual property issuing in the context of public health. At that meeting, the African Group proposed issuing separate declarations on access to medicines.[39] Referring to the devastating AIDS crisis in Africa and mounting public concern, Zimbabwe stated: "We propose that Members issue a special declaration on the TRIPS Agreement and access to medicines at the Ministerial Conference in Qatar, affirming that nothing in the TRIPS Agreement should prevent Members from taking measures to protect public health."[40]

In September 2001, the TRIPS Council devoted another full day of discussion to the topic of access to medicines. At this meeting, the African Group, joined by nineteen other countries, presented a draft text for a ministerial declaration on TRIPS and Public Health. A comprehensive text, this proposal addressed political principles to ensure that TRIPS did not undermine the legitimate right of WTO Members to formulate their own public health policies. The text also provided practical clarifications for provisions related to compulsory licensing, parallel import, data protection, and production for export to a country with insufficient production capacity. In addition, the draft included a proposal for evaluating the effects of TRIPS on public health, with particular emphasis on access to medicines and R&D for the prevention and treatment of diseases predominantly affecting people in developing and least-developed countries.

At the meeting, the US, Japan, Switzerland, Australia, and Canada circulated an alternate draft, stressing the importance of intellectual property protection for R&D, arguing that intellectual property contributes to public health objectives globally. The text was aimed at limiting the flexibilities of TRIPS during crisis and emergency situations. The EU circulated its own draft, which proposed a solution to the problem of production for exports to fulfill a compulsory license in a country with insufficient or no production capacity by allowing production under the TRIPS Article 30 exception.

From the onset of the pre-Doha negotiations, the main point of contention was the text proposed by the developing countries: "Nothing in the TRIPS Agreement shall prevent Members from taking measures to protect public health."[41] Some developed countries saw this wording as a new rule that would override the present rules of TRIPS, which do not allow for health exceptions that are inconsistent with TRIPS.[42]

The text drafted by the chair of the WTO General Council, Mr. Stuart Harbinson, that was the basis for the negotiations in Doha left the issue unresolved and instead offered two options for Paragraph 4. The first option read:

> Nothing in the TRIPS Agreement shall prevent Members from taking measures to protect public health. Accordingly, while reiterating our commitment to the TRIPS Agreement, we affirm that the Agreement shall be interpreted and implemented in a manner supportive of WTO Members' right to protect public health and, in particular, to ensure access to medicines for all. In this connection, we reaffirm the right of WTO Members to use, to the full, the provisions in the TRIPS Agreement which provide flexibility for this purpose.

Whereas the second option offered was:

> We affirm a Member's ability to use, to the full, the provisions in the TRIPS Agreement which provide flexibility to address public health crises such as HIV/AIDS and other pandemics, and to that end, that a Member is able to take measures necessary to address these public health crises, in particular to secure affordable access to medicines. Further, we agree that this Declaration does not add to or diminish the rights and obligations of Members provided in the TRIPS Agreement. With a view to facilitating the use of this flexibility by providing greater certainty, we agree on the following clarifications.

In Doha, for three days the discussions on TRIPS and public health dominated the trade talks. Early on in the meeting it became clear that a majority of Members preferred the first option of the Harbinson draft, making it the basis for further negotiation. The core supporters of the second option included the US, Japan, Australia, Switzerland, Canada, and Korea. The EU, at this stage, did not take a clear position and claimed it was playing the role of "honest broker." After three days of negotiation among the participating Members, a compromise was reached. The compromise text, which resulted from negotiations primarily between Brazil and the US, read:

> We agree that the TRIPS Agreement does not and should not prevent Members from taking measures to protect public health. Accordingly, while reiterating our commitments to the TRIPS Agreement, we affirm that the Agreement can and should be interpreted and implemented in a

manner supportive of WTO Members' right to protect public health and, in particular, to promote access to medicines for all.[43]

This text acknowledges the unmitigated right of countries to take measures to protect public health. Thus, if intellectual property rules should stand in the way of doing so (for example, in the case of high prices associated with patented medicines), countries are allowed to override the patent.

In Paragraph 5, the Declaration lays out the key measures and flexibilities within TRIPS that can be used to overcome intellectual property barriers to access to medicines. The discussions at Doha and the Doha Declaration itself make it unambiguously clear that the use of compulsory licenses is in no way confined to cases of emergency or urgency; in fact, the grounds for issuing a compulsory license are unlimited. Members who proposed language that would have limited measures like compulsory licensing to emergency situations, pandemics, or specified diseases such as HIV/AIDS were unsuccessful. In addition, the Declaration leaves Members free to determine for themselves what constitutes a national emergency or urgency, in which cases the procedure for issuing a compulsory license becomes easier and faster. The Declaration also resolves the question of whether TRIPS authorizes parallel trade once and for all by noting: "The effect of the provisions in the TRIPS Agreement that are relevant to the exhaustion of intellectual property rights is to leave each Member free to establish its own regime for such exhaustion without challenge."[44]

In addition, the Declaration grants least-developed country (LDCs) Members an extra ten-year extension—until 2016, instead of 2006—to the implementation deadline for pharmaceutical product patent protection. The negotiating history illustrates that this outcome was not predetermined. Pre-Doha, the U.S. proposed two operative paragraphs, which included this extension of transition periods until 2016 for patents on pharmaceutical products, as well as offering a moratorium on dispute settlement action to sub-Saharan African countries, which do not fall within the LDC grouping. The moratorium covered laws, regulations and other measures that improve access to patented medicines for HIV/AIDS and other pandemics. These proposals were viewed as a "divide and conquer" strategy employed by the US to break the cohesion of the developing countries[45] and the proposal for a moratorium on dispute settlement actions was rejected at Doha. The proposals to extend the deadlines for LDCs were accepted. The extended deadlines are important because they extend the timeframe (until 2016) in which countries may rethink the kind of pharmaceutical intellectual property law they want while still being able to import and produce generic medicines.

The Declaration also refers to the as-yet unfulfilled commitment of developed-country Members to provide incentives to their enterprises and institutions to promote technology transfer to LDCs pursuant to Article 66.2.

The ten-year extension might be of limited value because only LDCs will be able to benefit from this provision. Of the 143 WTO members, only 30 are LDCs, representing 10 percent of the world's population. The ten-year extension is also limited to Sections 5 (patents) and 7 (undisclosed information) of TRIPS; the extension does not apply to other provisions of the Agreement relevant to pharmaceuticals, notably Article 70 (exclusive marketing rights). Though there seemed to be an understanding among the negotiators in Doha that Paragraph 7 implied that LDCs are not required to provide "mail box" protection or "exclusive marketing rights," this is not clear from the text of the declaration. Paragraph 7 of the declaration refers to pharmaceutical products, which means that LDCs still are under the obligation to provide process patents.

Other Areas of Debate

1. *Public Health*: Most of the language aimed at narrowing the scope of the Declaration to health crises and pandemics[46] was replaced with language that referred generally to public health. Indeed, the title itself—Doha Declaration on Public Health—reflects this shift.

2. *Access for All*: Some countries objected to the text that countries have the right "to ensure access to medicines *for all.*"[47] In particular, Switzerland objected to the wording, but had difficulty defending a position that advocated access to medicines for some but not for others.

3. *Scope*: A point of strong contention was how far-reaching the Declaration would be. Some WTO Members feared that the negotiations could lead to changes in TRIPS and wanted to include a confirmation that the Declaration was purely a clarifying exercise. They borrowed language from the WTO Dispute Settlement Process Rules to indicate that the Ministerial Declaration would have no formal legal effect to change the rights and obligations TRIPS established.

The text did not, however, make it into the final version of the Declaration. As a result, one could argue that the Declaration actually does go beyond clarifying the already existing rules. A Member can appeal to the Declaration and its negotiating history in the event that a Member's legislation, particularly relating to patents in the health field, is challenged on the grounds that it is incompatible with TRIPS.

Why Doha Came to Pass

Why was it possible to achieve a declaration on such a contentious issue considering that public health hardly played a part in the trade talks two years ago? Mike Moore, WTO Director-General, made it clear on the opening day of the conference that the TRIPS and health issue could be the deal-breaker for a new trade round. Observers point to a number of factors that contributed to the success of the negotiations.[48] First, the developing country Members were extremely well prepared and operated as one bloc. Second, the uncompromising positions of western countries such as the US and Canada were hard to maintain in light of the anthrax crisis and the threat that a shortage of Ciprofloxacine (Cipro) might occur. Both the US and Canada rapidly expressed their willingness to set aside the patent held by the German company Bayer if other solutions could not be found.[49] The anthrax scare and the threatened shortage of Cipro forced all WTO Members to ask how much of a prisoner they want to be of their own patent systems. Third, a growing and active international NGO movement ensured the issue would be high profile, and that NGOs would monitor different countries' positions.

Drug Industry Response to the WTO Declaration on TRIPS and Public Health

The multinational pharmaceutical industry argued from the beginning that a declaration was not necessary because: a) patents are not a problem,[50] and b) weakening patent protection would have devastating effects on the R&D capabilities of the research-based industry. Although the International Federation of Pharmaceutical Manufacturers (IFPMA) officially welcomed the Declaration on TRIPS and Public Health, individuals in the industry expressed their concerns. Indeed, the US pharmaceutical companies asked the USTR to re-open the negotiations even after an agreement on the text of the Declaration was reached.

For more than two years, IFPMA has warned against the dangers of compulsory licensing—ever since NGOs started to propose compulsory licensing systems to overcome patent barriers. IFPMA's position has not changed. "[C]ompulsory licensing is a threat to good public health by denying patients around the world the future benefits of R&D capabilities of the research-based industry from which new therapies come."[51]

The generic drug industry welcomed the Declaration, in particular the freedom of countries to decide the grounds for compulsory licensing. The generic drug industry did express concern about possible unilateral pressure to influence countries not to make full use of the Declaration. The industry suggested that the advanced WTO Members should commit to the Declaration in practice by refraining from exerting unilateral pressure. The generic drug contingent expressed disappointment that there was no resolution of the issue that arises when a country with limited production capacity that issues a compulsory license for a medicine cannot find an efficient, affordable, and reliable source of medicines, due to TRIPS restrictions on production and export of medicines. After 2005, production of affordable medicine will increasingly become dependent on compulsory licensing. However, production under a compulsory license is restricted to production "predominantly for the supply of the domestic market."[52] The problem is not the compulsory license itself, but the need to allow exports from a country where the drug is under patent to a country that has issued the compulsory license.

The genetic drug industry expressed further disappointment that the Declaration did not offer an interpretation of the data protection issue addressed in Article 39.3 of TRIPS.[53] The concern here is that an overly restrictive interpretation of Article 39.3 will lead to delays in introduction of generic medicines, may provide exclusive marketing rights beyond the patent protection term and increase barriers to the registration of generic medicines including those produced under a compulsory license.

The Post-Doha Agenda

A key issue that remained unresolved in Doha is how to ensure that production for export to a country that has issued a compulsory license, but does not have manufacturing capacity, can take place within a country that provides pharmaceutical patents. Since Article 31(f) of TRIPS limits compulsory licensing to uses which are predominantly for the supply of the domestic market, further clarification is necessary to ensure that countries without production capacity can make use of compulsory licensing provisions to the same extent that countries with manufacturing capacity can use these provisions. The Doha Declaration acknowledges the problem in Paragraph 6:

> We recognize that WTO Members with insufficient or no manufacturing capacities in the pharmaceutical sector could face difficulties in making effective use of compulsory licensing under the TRIPS Agreement. We instruct the Council for TRIPS to find an expeditious solution to this problem and to report to the General Council before the end of 2002.

It is increasingly urgent that the production for export issue be resolved. Implementation deadlines for some important producing countries are quickly approaching, thus further limiting the possibilities of producing generic versions of medicines that are protected by patent elsewhere.

Another flaw of the Doha Declaration is that it does not resolve the problem of production for export from markets that provide patents to countries that do not grant pharmaceutical patents (and subsequently do not grant compulsory licenses). This is of particular importance now that the least-developed WTO Members can delay the granting of pharmaceutical product patents until 2016. These countries need to have access to sources of affordable medicines, which threaten to dry up as the 2005 deadline for TRIPS implementation is nearing for producing countries.

Another challenge will be to find ways to make the Doha Declaration on TRIPS and Public Health operational at the regional and national levels. A classic example is the Bangui Agreement, the regional intellectual property agreement for francophone Africa, which was adopted in 1977 and revised in 1999 to ensure TRIPS compatibility, but includes typical TRIPS plus provisions that are not in line with the Doha Declaration.

At the national level, countries should be encouraged to make full use of the Doha Declaration in the process of adjusting national intellectual property laws to become compliant with TRIPS. This will require substantial advice and technical assistance from institutions like WIPO and WTO. While the spirit of the Doha Declaration is to go slowly and to tailor intellectual property laws to national needs, the practice has been to encourage developing countries to go beyond the minimum requirements and speed up the process to become TRIPS-compliant. It will require a "culture change" at WIPO and WTO to adjust the type of technical assistance to developing countries' needs. In addition to increasing their interaction with countries, WIPO and WTO will have to increase their level of collaboration with the public health community, including the WHO, which has become heavily involved in trade discussions as a result of the process that led to the Doha Declaration.

The very fact that public health and access to medicines have been singled out as major issues needing special attention in TRIPS implementation indicates that health care and health care products need to be treated differently from other products. By giving countries broad discretion in deciding how to counter the negative effects of TRIPS, the Doha Declaration may stand for the proposition that public health concerns outweigh full protection of intellectual property.

In fact, the Doha Declaration takes a large step toward ensuring that intellectual property protection actually serves the public interest, an interest broader than that of the commercial sector. In the years to come, it will be important to scrutinize closely whether the results of intellectual property protection serve the poor as well as the rich. The Doha Declaration lays out the options countries have available when prices of existing patented drugs are too high for their populations. But Doha did not solve every problem: the lack of R&D investment in new drugs for the particular health needs of the poor remains to be addressed.[54]

In the Doha process, developing countries and NGOs pointed to commercial and public sector neglect of the R&D needs of developing countries. Recent studies claim that the R&D cost of a commercial drug company per new pharmaceutical product is $802 million.[55] The Global Alliance for Tuberculosis Drug Development, a non-profit entity for R&D of tuberculosis drugs, estimated that the total R&D cost for a new tuberculosis drug, including the cost of failure, is between $115 million and $240 million.[56] These high R&D costs claimed by the commercial pharmaceutical sector pose some key questions that need to be resolved. Is the present system for funding R&D the most efficient, and is it sufficient to rely on the present intellectual property systems to fuel innovation? Clearly, in the area of neglected diseases, the answer is no.

In an increasingly globalized economy, additional international mechanisms need to be developed to address health needs in developing countries. MSF and others have proposed a radical shift in the way health R&D is financed in particular for drugs for neglected diseases. For example, health R&D could be financed based on burden sharing between countries, or obligating companies to complete essential medical research. Such a proposal might be incorporated into an international treaty on essential health R&D. In the end, the challenge for the coming years will be to encourage essential health R&D not only for the benefit of some, but for the benefit of all.

Notes

1. World Health Organization, *The World Health Report* 2001, 144 (WHO 2000).
2. See UNAIDS, *Report on the Global HIV/AIDS Epidemic* 125, 129, 133 (UNAIDS 2000), available online at <http://www.unaids.org/epidemic_update/report/Epi_report.pdf> (visited Mar 24, 2002) (outlining the statistics utilized to reach the generally recognized figure of eight thousand deaths per day due to AIDS in the developing world).
3. See MSF Access to Essential Medicines Campaign and The Drugs for Neglected Diseases Working Group, *Fatal Imbalance: The Crisis in Research and Development for Drugs for Neglected Diseases* 10–18 (Sept 2001), available online at <http://www.msf.org/source/access/2001/fatal/fatal.pdf> (visited Mar 24, 2002).
4. See Bernard Pécoul, et al. Access to Essential Drugs in Poor Countries. A Lost Battle?, 281 JAMA 361 (1999).
5. See Parrice Trouiller and Piero Olliaro, *Drug Development Output from 1975 to 1996: What Proportion for Tropical Diseases?*, 3 Intl J Infect Diseases 61 (1999).
6. See F. Michael Scherer and Jayashree Watal, *Post TRIPS Options for Access to Patented Medicines in Developing Countries* 11 (WHO Jan 2001), available online at <http://www.cmhealth.org/docs/wg4_paper1.pdf> (visited Mar 24, 2002) (reporting on three independent studies that found a mean price increase of well over 200 percent with the introduction of product patents).
7. See World Health Organization, *Globalization, TRIPS and Access to Pharmaceuticals* 4 (March 2001), available online at <http://www.who.int/medicines/library/edm_general/6pagers/PPMO3%20ENG.pdf> (visited Mar 24, 2002).
8. See Pharmaceutical Manufactures' Association of South Africa v President of the Republic of South Africa, Case No 4183/98 (filed Feb 18, 1998).
9. Parallel imports are cross-border trade in a patented product, without the permission of the manufacturer or publisher. Parallel imports take place when there are significant price differences for the same good in different markets. For more information, *see Health Care and Intellectual Property: Parallel Imports*, available online at <http://www.cptech.org/ip/health/pi/> (visited Mar 24, 2002).
10. See Omnibus Consolidated and Emergency Supplemental Appropriations Act, Pub L No 105–277, 112 Stat 2681 (1999):

    [N]one of the funds appropriated under this heading may be available for assistance for the central Government of the Republic of South Africa, until the Secretary of State reports in writing to the appropriate committees of the Congress on the steps being taken by the United States Government to work with the Government of the Republic of South Africa to negotiate the repeal, suspension, or termination of section

15(c) of South Africa's Medicines and Related Substances Control Amendment Act No. 90 of 1997.

Simon Barber, *U.S. Withholds Benefits over Zuma's Bill*, Bus Day 13 (S Africa) (Jul 15, 1998).

11. See Letter from Sir Leon Brittan, Vice-President of the European Commission, to Thabo Mbeki, Vice-President of South Africa (Mar 23, 1998) ("Section 15c of the [medicines] law in question would appear to be at variance with South Africa's obligations under the TRIPS and its implementation would negatively affect the interest of the European pharmaceutical industry.") [Letter on file with *CJLL*].

12. See Simon Barber, *Activists Accuse the US of Blocking Access to Drugs*, Bus Day 6 (S Africa) (Apr 19, 1999).

13. See Helene Cooper, Rachel Zimmerman, and Laurie McGinley, *Patents Pending: AIDS Epidemic Traps Drug Firms In a Vise: Treatments vs. Profits*, Wall St J A1 (Mar 2, 2001) ("Can the pharmaceutical industry inflict any more damage upon its aling public image? Well, how about suing Nelson Mandela?").

14. See Pat Sidley, *Silent Trump Card Gives State Winning Hand*, Bus Day 2 (S Africa) (Apr 20, 2001).

15. See Tina Rosenberg, *Look at Brazil*, NY Times § 6 at 26, 28 (Jan 28, 2001) ("The treatment program has cut the AIDS death rate nationally by about 50 percent so far.").

16. See Ellen 't Hoen and Suerie Moon, *Pills and Pocketbooks: Equity Pricing of Essential Medicines in Developing Countries* (MSF Jul 11, 2001), available online at <http://www.accessmed-msf.org/prod/publications.asp?sentid=318200146197&contenttype=PARA> (visited Mar 24, 2002).

17. See Brazil Ministry of Health, Official Note, *Ministry of Health Announces Compulsory Licensing of Nelfinavir Patent* (Aug 22, 2001) [on file with author]: Jennifer L. Rich, *Rache Reaches Accord on Drug with Brazil*, NY Times C1 (Sept 1, 2001).

18. Law No 9,279 of May 14, 1996.

19. See Brazil Ministry of Health, *National AIDS Drug Policy* (May 2001), available online at <http://www.aids.gov.br/assistencia/aids_drugs_policy.htm> (visited Mar 24, 2002) (discussing the Horizontal Technical Co-operation Program in Latin America).

20. See World Trade Organization, Request for the Establishment of a Panel by the United States, *Brazil Measures Affecting Patent Protection*, WTO Doc No WT/DS199/3 (Jan 9, 2001).

21. See, for example, MSF, *US Action at WTO Threatens Brazil's Successful AIDS Programme*, Press Release (Feb 1, 2001), available online at <hrtp://www.accessmed.msf.org/prod/publications.asp?senrid=2182001228232&contenttype=PA RA> (visited Mar 24, 2002).

22. See Helene Cooper, *U.S. Drops WTO Complaint Against Brazilian Patent Law*, Wall St J Eur A2 (June 26, 2001).

23. Common Working Paper of the EC, Hungary, Japan, Korea, Switzerland, and Turkey to the Seattle Ministerial Declaration 3 (Nov 29, 1999), available online at <http://europa.eu.int/comm/trade/2000_round/friends.pdf> (visited Mar 24, 2002).

24. High cost or price of a drug in general excludes a drug from the WHO Essential Drug List.

25. William J. Clinton, *Remarks at a World Trade Organization Luncheon in Seattle*, 35 Weekly Comp Pres Doc 2494, 2497 (Dec 1, 1999).

26. Exec Order No 13,155, 65 Fed Reg 30,521 (2000).

27. See Kevin Gopal, With Chaos, A Reprieve. The Collapse of the WTO Talks in Seattle Has, for the Time Being Diverted Attention from the Issue of Compulsory Licensing, Pharmaceutical Executive 32 (Jan 2000) ("Unlikely as it seems the pharmaceutical industry may have reason to thank the demonstrators who brought Seattle and the ministerial meeting of the World Trade Organization (WTO) to a standstill. Had the demonstrators not disrupted the gathering, the forecast for global pharma might be much cloudier.").

28. See World Health Organization, *Revised Drug Strategy Resolution*, World Health Assembly Resolution WHA 49.14 (1996).

29. See Germán Velasquez and Pascale Bouler, Globalization and Access to Drugs: Perspectives on the WTO/TRIPS Agreement (WHO 2d ed. 1999).

30. See Paul Benkimoun, Agressions et Menaces contre un Responsable de l'OMS Defenseur de l'Accès du Tiersmonde aux Médicaments, Le Monde (Aug 23, 2001).

31. European Commission (DGI), *Note on the WHO's Revised Drug Strategy*, Doc No 1/D/3/BW D (98) (Oct 5, 1998), available online at <http://www.cptech.org/ip/health/who/eurds98.html> (visited Mar 24, 2002).

32. See World Health Organization, *Scaling up the Response to HIV/AIDS*, World Health Assembly Resolution WHA 54.10 (2001); World Health Organization, *WHO Medicines Strategy*, World Health Assembly Resolution WHA 54.11 (2001).

33. See World Health Organization, Technical Cooperation Activities: Information from Other Intergovernmental Organizations, WHO Doc No IP/C/W/305/Add 3 (Sept 25, 2001).

34. United Nations Economic and Social Council Commission on Human Rights Sub-Commission on the Promotion and Protection of Human Rights Resolution 2000/7, para 2, UN Doc No E/CN.4/SUB.2/RES/2000/7 (2000).

35. United Nations Development Program, *Human Development Report 1999*, 2 (Oxford 1999).

36. See, for example, European Parliament Resolution on Access to Drugs for HIV/AIDS Victims in the Third World, 2001 OJ (C 343) 300.

37. See *World AIDS Day: Lamy Calls for More Action on Access to Medicines After Progress in Doha*, Press Release of Pascal Lamy's speech marking World AIDS Day, European Union Trade Commissioner (Nov 30, 2001), available online at <http://europa.eu.int/comm/trade/speeches_articles/spla87_en.htm> (visited Mar 24, 2002).

38. See Statement by Zimbabwe to the WTO TRIPS Council (Apr 5, 2001) ("Our intention is to bring into this Council an issue that has aroused public interest and is being actively debated outside this organisation, but one which we cannot afford to ignore.") [on file with *CJIL*].

39. Compare *TRIPS and Public Health*, WTO Doc No IP/C/W/296 (June 29, 2001) (working paper submitted by the African group, joined by seventeen developing countries) with *The Relationship Between the Provisions of the TRIPS Agreement and Access to Medicines*, WTO Doc No IP/C/W/280 (June 12, 2001) (working paper submitted by the European Communities).

40. See WTO Council for Trade-Related Aspects of Intellectual Property Rights, *Special Discussion on Intellectual Property and Access to Medicines* 4, WTO Doc No IP/C/M/31 (Restricted) (July 10, 2001) [on file with *CJIL*].

41. *TRIPS and Public Health* at summary (cited in note 39).

42. See Agreement on Trade Related Aspects of Intellectual Property Rights, art 8(1), Marrakesh Agreement Establishing the World Trade Organization, Annex 1C, 33 ILM 81 (1994) ("TRIPS Agreement").

43. World Trade Organization, Doha Ministerial Declaration on the TRIPS Agreement and Public Health, para 4, WTO Doc No WT/MIN(01)/DEC/2 (2001) ("Doha Declaration" or "Declàration").

44. Id at para 5(d).

45. See Third World Network Info Service on WTO Issues, *Update on Ministerial Declaration on TRIPS and Public Health*, available online at <http://www.twnside.org.sg/title/info3.htm> (visited Mar 24, 2002) (discussing this and other points of contention between the developed and developing WTO states).

46. Pandemics refer to diseases, mostly of infectious nature, that travel across borders.

47. Doha Declaration at para 4 (cited in note 43) (emphasis added).

48. See David Banta, *Public Health Triumphs at WTO Conference*, 286 JAMA 2655, 2655–65 (2001).

49. See Amy Harmon and Robert Pear, A Nation Challenged: The Treatment; Canada Overrides Patent for Cipro to Threat Anthrax, NY Times A1 (Oct 19, 2001).

50. At Doha, the International Federation of Pharmaceutical Manufacturers ("IFPMA") distributed Amir Attaran and Lee Gillespie-White, *Do Patents for Antiretroviral Drugs Constrain Access to AIDS Treatment in Africa?*, 286 JAMA 1886 (2001).

51. IFPMA, *Access to Medicines: The Right Policy Prescription* (distributed at the WTO 2001) [on file with *CJIL*].

52. TRIPS Agreement at art 31(f) (cited in note 42).

53. See Jayanta Ghosh, *No Gains from Doha, Say Pharma Firms*, Times (India) (Nov 27, 2001).

54. See World Trade Organization, Doha General Ministerial Declaration, para 17, WTO Doc No WT/MIN(01)/DEC/1 (Nov 14, 2001) ("We stress the importance we attach to implementation and interpretation of the Agreement on Trade-Related Aspects of Intellectual Property Rights (TRIPS Agreement) in a manner supportive of public health, by promoting both access to existing medicines and research and development into new medicines and, in this connection, are adopting a separate declaration.").

55. See Tufts Center for the Study of Drug Development, *Tafts Center for the Study of Drug Development Pegs Cost of a New Prescription Medicine at $802 Million*, Press Release (Nov 30, 2001), available online at <http://www.tufts.edu/med/csdd/images/NewsRelease113001 pm.pdf> (visited Mar 24, 2002). See also James Love, *How Much Does it Cost to Develop a New Drug*, available online at <http://www.cptech.org/ip/health/econ/howmuch.html> (visited Mar 24, 2002).

56. For details see The Global Alliance for TB Drug Development, *Drug Development Costs*, available online at <http://www.rballiance.org/3_costs.cfm;rm=economics&sub=costs> (visited Mar 24, 2002).

IV
Health and Human Rights in Sexual and Reproductive Health

The HIV epidemics helped to draw attention to the differences among individuals and to the fact that policies and programs, if they are to be effective, must take into account the differences in gender, age, and the economic, social, cultural, and political context in which people live. The first human rights document to focus specifically on the rights of children—the Convention on the Rights of the Child (CRC)—was opened to signature in 1990 as the devastating impact of the HIV/AIDS epidemics on the lives of children was becoming more apparent. The 1993 International Conference on Population and Development held in Cairo and the 1994 Beijing Fourth World Conference on Women also brought attention to the impact of these factors on reproductive and sexual health—most notably with respect to conceptual and operational work on reproductive and sexual rights. Not only did these events bring new strength and resources to previously existing efforts but, as a result of these international meetings, attention to the intersection of human rights and health began in corners previously unimaginable, including the organs and agencies of the United Nations system, national governments, and nongovernmental organizations. In large part, the range of government and civil society organizations that have integrated a health and human rights approach into their HIV/AIDS, reproductive, sexual, and adolescent health work have lead the way to more general awareness of the structural connections between health and human rights. Human rights advocacy and approaches have proven key to identifying of challenges and strategies for action in these fields. Framing HIV/AIDS and reproductive and sexual health strategies in human rights terms has also highlighted the importance of the public accountability that governments and intergovernmental organizations have for their actions toward people in the context of health issues.

Conceptual thinking has advanced considerably in this field; yet, while a review of efforts made toward implementation of reproductive and sexual rights in the past decade shows some successes at the global, regional, and national levels, full translation of these concepts into reality have unfortunately been few and far between. The pieces gathered here explore the status of reproductive and sexual rights with respect to both their conceptual development and their implementation. In this part, the chapter by Tarantola and Gruskin proposes an approach to systematically analyze the relation of HIV/AIDS to the rights of the child, creating opportunities for synergy between those involved in HIV prevention, care and research, and those engaged in the promotion and protection of the rights of the child. They argue that this lens is critical to analysis and action in relation to children who are themselves HIV-infected, children affected by the pandemic because their families, communities and the societies within which they grow are strained by its consequences, and as relates to children's vulnerability to becoming infected or being denied adequate care and support once they are infected. This piece has proven useful for moving conceptual thinking forward in HIV/AIDS and reproductive and sexual health and rights more generally, even as it does not grapple with the practical implications of trying to operationalize these linkages. The other two chapters by Bonnie Shepard and Barbara Klugman each consider the practical implications, as well as the obstacles, to realization and implementation of reproductive and sexual rights. Shepard uses the example of the "double discourse" in Latin America, under which repressive policies on reproductive and sexual rights coexist with unofficial and often illegal mechanisms that expand reproductive and sexual choices in practice. She then explores the ways in which this double discourse impacts negatively on the rights and health of the poorest members of society. Barbara Klugman focuses on concrete examples of how sexual rights have come to be implemented in southern Africa. She uses the example of HIV/AIDS policies and educational materials to consider the extent to which the concepts of sexual rights have translated into practice in the region, with opportunities for building a concrete practice of sexual rights internationally.

What these chapters have in common is that each points to both the public health responsibilities of governments and their human rights obligations under the human rights documents to which they have agreed to be bound. Unfortunately, reproductive and sexual health remain the ideological battleground for the integration of human rights into public health work. The experience of the past decade has shown the value of integrating thinking about rights into the policy and program responses to these health issues, but additional work is needed to provide hard evidence of the effectiveness of these approaches.

11

Children Confronting HIV/AIDS

Charting the Confluence of Rights and Health

Daniel Tarantola and Sofia Gruskin

In 1990, as the devastating impact of HIV/AIDS epidemics on the lives of children was becoming more apparent, the first human rights document to focus specifically on the rights of children—the Convention on the Rights of the Child (CRC)—came into being.[1] The availability of this document, ratified within a few years by almost every nation in the world, shed new light on government responsibility for ensuring that children no longer be the objects of decisions affecting them, but subjects taking an increasing role in these decisions as their capacity to do so evolves.[2]

Every day around the world 1,500 children are born with HIV infection, 90 percent of them in the developing world.[3] In addition, an unknown number of children through the age of 18 acquire HIV infection from unsafe blood and blood products, unsterile medical injections performed inside and outside formal health care settings, the sharing of needles in illicit drug use, and through sex, including sexual abuse. Although these modes of HIV transmission are the same as those affecting adults, the very construct of childhood forces us to consider them from another perspective.

The complex relationship of children to adult support and decision-making has often been hidden by a tendency to regard children as a homogeneous entity, regardless of sex, age, and evolving intellectual capacity. The CRC defines the child as every human being below the age of 18 years.[4] From a child rights perspective, HIV/AIDS serves to illuminate how cultural norms and legal precepts facilitate or constrain the capacity of the child to decide. From a health perspective, the relationship between childhood and HIV/AIDS must take into account the evolving capacity of boys and girls to participate, at different stages of their physical and intellectual development, in decisions relevant to the future course of their lives. This is crucial not only to promoting and protecting children's rights but to a dynamic understanding and response to their needs in the face of the HIV/AIDS epidemics, and in the broader context of child health and development.

HIV/AIDS in the lives of children may impact negatively on the extent to which their rights are respected, protected, or fulfilled, and, conversely, violations or neglect of their rights may increase children's vulnerability to HIV/AIDS.[5] The work presented here is an attempt to raise some questions and to map out issues relevant to children in the context of HIV/AIDS from the perspective of the CRC. The CRC provides the basic framework for analyzing the impact of HIV/AIDS on children, the response to the epidemic, and the tools for evaluating governmental response which follow.

Children Confronting HIV/AIDS: Infected, Affected, and Vulnerable

As the pandemic pursues its course, its impact on the lives of children in the developing world and in marginalized communities in the industrialized world is increasingly felt. Infected by HIV, affected by the impact of the HIV epidemics, and vulnerable to acquiring HIV infection, infants, young children, adolescent girls and boys are confronting new challenges to their health and development.[6,7]

Children *infected* with HIV/AIDS, girls and boys diagnosed with HIV or presumed to be living with HIV, suffer the physical consequences of infection through increased morbidity, stunted growth, disability, and premature death. Furthermore, their condition creates psychological stress and may expose them to stigma and discrimination, including loss of entitlements to educational, health, and social services.

The Joint United Nations Programme on HIV/AIDS (UNAIDS) estimates that, of the 30.6 million people who were living with HIV in December 1997, 1.1 million were children born with HIV infection.[8] Of these children, the majority are in Africa and in Asia. While the number of children infected around birth can be estimated, there is an enormous gap in data on the incidence of infection among children as they grow into adulthood. There is an acute lack of information on how, when, and to what extent girls and boys become infected, and whether this is through early sexual activity, sexual abuse, substance use, or exposure to unsterile blood, blood products, and skin-piercing instruments.[9] Insufficient research on children living with HIV/AIDS has translated into a lack of information about effective care and support programs for these children.

A first step in fulfilling their obligations to children is for governments to design prevention, care, and research programs in light of appropriately collected information. Governmental obligations extend to ensuring that all children, including those living with HIV/AIDS, have access to health services, treatment, education, and social programs. Some governments have achieved considerable progress in this direction; others have yet to respond adequately to rising needs. Children's quality of life can be improved if the coping capacity of families is enhanced, either by increasing their abilities to support themselves, or through direct social support.

Children are *affected* when their close or extended family, their community, and, more broadly, the structures and services which exist for their benefit are strained by the consequences of the HIV/AIDS pandemic.[10] The most devastating impact on children is when their immediate family environment and support system is challenged by the sickness, disability, and premature death from AIDS of one or both of their parents.[11] The emotional impact of such a trauma, including living through the deprivation of parental support and loss of childhood, creates serious obstacles to the child's development. Furthermore, as a result of the reduced ability of infected parents and extended families to sustain their livelihood, children may have to be removed from their homes, leave school, enter employment, or seek a life on the streets. Finally, children of parents living with HIV/AIDS are often marginalized or discriminated against because they too are assumed to be infected.

The impact of HIV/AIDS on children also results in diminished access to the services and structures needed for their survival and development. For example, schools may be forced to reduce the number of school hours, merge several classes, or even close after having lost teachers to AIDS. Health services may be so overwhelmed by growing demands for HIV/AIDS care, which consumes ever increasing amounts of staff-time and financial resources, that the coverage and quality of routine child health programs may suffer.

Governments must strive to prevent and alleviate some of the impact of HIV/AIDS on these children. This entails providing assistance to affected families so that, to the maximum extent possible, children remain within existing family structures and receive needed care. It is also the responsibility of governments to ensure that children are supported through alternative systems of protection and assistance when their family's coping capacity has been exhausted, and that they are protected against all forms of abuse and exploitation.

Children are *vulnerable* to HIV/AIDS to the extent that they are born, grow, and become sexually active in a world which has added the risk of acquiring HIV infection to many of the situations which mark their childhood.[12] Children's capacity to modulate this risk depends on the degree of their awareness and their ability to minimize behaviors that may result in their exposure to HIV infection, such as unprotected sex or injecting drug use. Behaviors resulting in HIV infection are influenced by the environment in which children evolve and the availability of, and access to, services intended for their benefit. In many countries, children's vulnerability to HIV/AIDS is increased because they are denied access to information and to sexual and reproductive health services and, even when these are available, they are seldom designed to meet children's specific needs.

But vulnerability to HIV is even more acute for children in exceptionally difficult circumstances. These children suffer not only the direct consequences of physical or mental abuse, negligent treatment, exploitation, survival on the street, inadequate alternative systems of protection, violence, armed conflict, and resulting population displacements, but as a result of these situations, their vulnerability to HIV/AIDS is amplified.[13]

Every governmental effort towards realizing the enabling conditions necessary for children's harmonious and safe development is a step towards reducing children's vulnerability to HIV/AIDS. Governments must offer children access to quality services and work to create a friendlier environment for them—so that they can become true participants in our collective response to HIV/AIDS.

The Advent of the Rights of the Child: The Four General Principles

Violations of the rights of children can be the result of their real or perceived HIV status or that of their family members or communities, and can also make those not already infected more vulnerable to infection. Discrimination, exploitation, and abuse point to just some of the human rights violations which have exacerbated the effects of the pandemic on the lives of children around the world. Nonetheless, governmental attention and commitment to the rights of children has permeated international fora in recent years.

International human rights documents ranging from the International Covenant on Civil and Political Rights (ICCPR) to the CRC contain legally binding provisions specifically detailing the human rights of children, and nearly every article in the general human rights instruments apply equally to children and to adults.[14,15] While none of the human rights treaties contain specific elaborations of the rights of adults or children in the context of HIV/AIDS, the treaty monitoring bodies have, to varying degrees, expressed their commitment to explore the implications of HIV/AIDS for governmental obligations under their treaties.[16] In addition, governments have stated their responsibility for both ensuring the rights, health, and well-being of children and for reducing the impact of HIV/AIDS on individuals and communities in the political commitments contained in the declaration and programs of action from recent international conferences.[17] Relevant conference documents include the 1990 World Summit for Children, the 1993 World Conference on Human Rights, the 1994 International Conference on Population and Development, the 1995 World Summit for Social Development and Fourth World Conference on Women, and the 1996 World Congress on the Sexual Exploitation of Children.[15] The commitments are there. Yet both the pandemic and the violations continue to grow. Recognition of the applicability of the human rights framework to the design and implementation of HIV/AIDS policies and programs could go a long way toward reducing the impact of the pandemic on the lives of children.

The four general principles of the CRC, *non-discrimination, best interests of the child, survival and development,* and *participation* are useful for conceptualizing the complex nature of the rights of children and their relation to HIV/AIDS: they are rights-holders and active agents in their own lives and are at the same time vulnerable and in need of special protection.[18] These principles are set forth as ordinary articles in the CRC but acquired a special status during the first session of the Committee on the Rights of the Child (the Convention's monitoring body). The Committee determined that these rights should be used as the lens through which realization of all rights in the Convention are analyzed, implemented, and evaluated.[19] This concept is unique to the CRC; no other human rights treaty contains rights which are meant to be discussed both in and of themselves, and as a means to analyze governmental progress towards implementation of other rights. A brief summary of the content of the four general principles follows:

- *Non-Discrimination* requires that all children are protected from discrimination of any kind.[20] Children are protected on the same grounds laid out in other human rights instruments, but additional general protections are specified based on ethnic origin and disability, as well as the status of parents or legal guardians. Adverse discrimination relating to refugee or minority status is also explicitly forbidden with respect to certain articles. Confronting the stigma which remains attached to HIV/AIDS, children may benefit from specific protections from discrimination, for example based on disability, or on their own or their parent's real or perceived health status.

- *Best Interests of the Child* gives the child's interests equal footing with the interests of parents, families, communities, and the state.[21] The Convention explicitly identifies the few instances when it considers the best interests of the child to be the primary consideration, but as a general principle the child's best interests are equal to the interests of others. It is understood that this concept is flexible and will respond to the evolving capacities of the child, living conditions, cultural norms, and expectations. Concern for the best interest of the child is of paramount importance in devising and implementing HIV/AIDS prevention, care, and research programs.

- *Survival and Development* is understood as the precondition of all other rights.[22] This concerns not only children's right not to be killed arbitrarily at the hands of the state, but also their right to benefit from economic and social policies which will allow them to survive into adulthood and to develop in the broadest sense of the word.[23] Born to the world in the time of AIDS, children have a right to survival and development which includes their ability to benefit from governmental policies which will help them to progress into adulthood.

- *Participation* concerns the child's right to express an opinion, have it heard, considered, and given due weight.[24] This is perhaps the most radical provision of the Convention in that it requires adults, who normally wield power in affairs which concern children, to make it possible for children to express their views, and obliges adults to adequately consider these views with respect to all matters, whether within the family or the broader community. The child's right to express an opinion and have it heard must be given due weight in devising and implementing HIV/AIDS prevention, care, and research programs.

Governments on the Forefront: Respect, Protect, and Fulfill Rights

These four general principles—non-discrimination, best interest of the child, survival and development, and participation—have direct implications for HIV/AIDS as it impacts on children. The interplay of these principles should guide governments with respect to any actions they have taken or may be considering taking that may impact on child health and development. These obligations may go far beyond policies and programs directly and consciously targeted at children. For example, a governmental decision concerning the reallocation of public space may result in the closing of a socially secure environment in which children had been able to play, thereby pushing them toward unsafe gathering sites. From an HIV/STD perspective, this suppression of conditions favorable to the enhancement of social skills in children may increase their likelihood of engaging in unsafe behaviors which, in turn, may expose them to a higher risk of acquiring HIV/STD infection. While from a CRC perspective the right of the child to rest and leisure (Article 31) is the only right immediately and directly applicable, recognition of the four general principles can help mediate this process and lead to a decision best for all concerned.

The Example of Education

States are responsible for not violating rights directly, as well as for ensuring the conditions which enable the realization of our rights as fully as possible. This is understood as an obligation on the part of governments to *respect, protect,* and *fulfill rights.* While these principles can be applied to governmental obligations as they relate to every right, every person, adult or child, and every action taken, the following analysis uses these obligations to consider the right to education as it applies to governmental action that may concern children infected, affected, or vulnerable to HIV/AIDS.

Respect: The duty to respect requires governments to refrain from directly violating rights.[25] For example, for children infected with HIV, the right to education would be respected if access to primary school education were ensured. In contrast, this right would not be respected if a government barred children from attending school on the basis of their HIV status. For children affected by HIV, the extent to which governments respect the right to education may be reflected in a government's choice to sustain or close a primary school in a community hard-hit by HIV/AIDS. For children vulnerable to HIV, respect of the right to education means that, for example, the government must provide and not withhold education to incarcerated children.

Protect: The duty to protect points to governmental obligations regarding private action, in that the government is responsible for preventing rights violations by non-state actors, including individuals, groups, and organizations, and if a violation does occur, ensuring that there is a legal means of redress that people know about and can access.[26] For infected children, protecting the right to education would impose an obligation on the government to take action against a private school which excluded children on the basis of their HIV status. A situation concerning children affected by HIV could include orphans who have lost both parents to AIDS and whose surviving relatives want to remove them from primary school in order for them to work in a factory. Their right to education would be protected if the government ensured that these children were able to pursue their primary education. The vulnerability of adolescents to HIV can increase if they are denied access to reproductive health education. In protecting the right to education of adolescents in the context of HIV, the government should ensure that, for example, extremist religious groups do not successfully oppose that such education be made available.[27]

Fulfill: The duty to fulfill requires governments to take administrative, legislative, budgetary, judicial, and other measures towards the full realization of rights.[28] With respect to children infected with HIV, governments must fulfill their right to education by enacting laws that ensure that, for example, in the development of vocational education, this education is available and accessible to children with HIV on an equal basis with other children.[29] In the case of children affected by HIV/AIDS, governments must work to fulfill the right to education by taking measures which ensure that strains on the economic capacity of HIV-affected communities do not result in children being withdrawn from school. The vulnerability of children to HIV/AIDS can be exacerbated if government fails to fulfill its obligation to develop an educational program realistically targeted to the needs of children.

Government Action

An agenda for governmental action can be created by recognizing the convergence of the three situations in which children are confronting a world with AIDS (children infected, affected, and vulnerable) and the three levels of government obligations which exist for every right (respect, protect, and fulfill). This approach incorporates the promotion and protection of the rights of the child into the diversity of responses needed to bring the pandemic under control and mitigate its impact. Table 11.1 summarizes the three situations and three levels of obligations which should be considered when identifying children's specific needs and related rights in the context of HIV/AIDS.

A human rights framework can help identify when governmental action is abusive, whether intentionally or unintentionally. Recognition of human rights

Table 11.1 Governmental obligations with respect to the rights of the child in the context of HIV/AIDS

	Children infected with HIV	Children affected by HIV/AIDS	Children vulnerable to HIV/AIDS
Respect	Government to refrain from directly violating rights of children on the basis of their HIV status.	Government to refrain from directly violating rights of children affected by the HIV/AIDS pandemic.	Government to refrain from directly violating rights of children which impact on their vulnerability.
Protect	Government is responsible for preventing rights violations by non-state actors against children living with HIV/AIDS, and for providing some legal means of redress.	Government is responsible for preventing violations by non-state actors that would increase the burden of HIV/AIDS on affected children, and for providing some legal means of redress.	Government is responsible for preventing rights violations by non-state actors that may increase children's vulnerability to HIV/AIDS, and for providing some legal means of redress.
Fulfill	Government to take administrative, legislative, judicial and other measures towards realization of the rights of children living with HIV/AIDS.	Government to take administrative, legislative, judicial and other measures towards the realization of the rights of children affected by HIV/AIDS.	Government to take administrative, legislative, judicial and other measures towards the realization of the rights of children in order to minimize their vulnerability to HIV/AIDS.

in the design, implementation, and evaluation of governmental policy can point the way toward actions which are not only necessary but, in public health terms, most effective. These actions may, under specific circumstances, include restrictions on human rights if strictly necessary to ensure the public's health.[30,31] Several criteria have to be met, however, for these decisions to be acceptable under international human rights law: the action has to be taken in accordance with the national law; the action has to be in the interest of a legitimate objective; it has to be strictly necessary to achieve this goal; it must be the least restrictive alternative; and it must not be imposed in an unreasonable or discriminatory way.[32] A clear example of where restrictions have been regarded by governments as necessary for public health and consistent with human rights is routine childhood immunization, a mandated public health measure equally applicable to all eligible children in a society.

Is There an Age for Childhood and an Age for HIV?

There is inconsistency between the age range used by the CRC to define "children" and the age groupings used to analyze HIV epidemic trends. This impacts on the ways population subsets targeted for prevention are defined and, therefore, on the ways services are delivered. While the CRC maintains that the term "children" includes every individual under the age of 18, for the purpose of epidemiological surveillance, 0–14 year-olds are considered "children" and those 15–18 are included in the 15–49 "adult" category. The arbitrariness of this grouping categorizes all boys and girls in the 0–14 age group as "children," regardless of the age at which they become sexually aware, initiated, and active. The assumption inherent in this grouping is that individuals over the age of 15 are equally as likely to be sexually active as all those between the ages of 19 and 49, and thus equally at risk of acquiring HIV (or other STDs) through sexual contacts. However, retrospective analysis of reported AIDS cases for which age-specific information is available suggests that the majority of all HIV infections acquired by "adults" occur in the 15–24 year-old age group.[33]

It is possible to collect age-specific information in research and prevention intervention projects conducted in well-defined study populations, but few national epidemiological surveillance systems currently have the capacity to collect and analyze such data with the degree of accuracy required to make such an analysis meaningful to policy and program design or evaluation.[34] Recognition that countries around the world were seldom able to provide such detailed information led the World Health Organization (WHO), on the global level, to decide in the late 1980s to collect information from countries for the 0–14 and 15–49 year age groups for the purpose of global AIDS surveillance. The WHO reinforced the implications of this decision when they used this 0–14 "child" and 15–49 "adult" categorization in the development of the ten

HIV/AIDS "Priority Prevention Indicators" in 1993–1994.[35] These indicators, which have been further elaborated by UNAIDS, are meant to enable the monitoring of HIV/STD trends around the world, and to facilitate comparison between countries and over time.

The aggregation of age groups into the two "children" and "adult" categories for epidemiological purposes at the national and global levels is further carried through in the delivery of health and social services. From a rights perspective, the fact that this epidemiological information is used for the targeting and monitoring of services and programs is problematic. One can see that using the 0–14 and 15–49 age groupings has the potential to obscure relevant developmental, psychological, sexual, and societal factors which affect children's lives differently than adults. For example, a young person of 14 with an STD runs the risk of being referred to pediatric services and, only a few months later, to an adult STD clinic, neither of which is well-equipped to meet young people's needs.

The collection of information on children in a manner consistent with the CRC would not only recognize that those under 18 are children with different levels of understanding and needs, but would bring into focus sexual and epidemiological factors which have not received sufficient attention. For example, from both an epidemiological and a rights perspective, the fact that children under 18 have not yet attained "the age of majority" could help underscore HIV/STD infection trends which may be due to rights violations, including sexual abuse. This recognition would, in turn, call for targeted HIV prevention and care interventions combined with human rights protections, which might not occur under the current categories. Different age cut-offs also exist for the legal "age of consent" for consensual sex.[36] In many countries, there is a difference between the age of consent for females and for males, in addition, in countries where same-sex sex is legal, there is a difference in the age of consent for engaging in sexual activity with a person of the same or different sex. The arbitrariness of the application of these cut-off ages to the analysis of sexual behaviors and HIV/STD trends is pertinent to those working on HIV/AIDS, and those more directly concerned with the promotion and protection of the rights of the child, in interpreting epidemiological trends and the extent to which the rights of the child are fulfilled.

The inconsistency in age groupings and in the targeting of programs will probably remain for years to come. It is essential that studies be conducted to explore the dynamics and determinants of HIV/STD infection and of situations and behaviors leading to infection in girls and in boys, from their birth through the age of 18. Estimates of the number of children born with HIV infection acquired perinatally are usually extrapolated from HIV prevalence rates among pregnant women. However, little is known about the number of children who become infected through breast-feeding in their first years of life and through unsterile skin-piercing medical or other practices, blood transfusion, sexual contacts, or injecting drug use as they grow older. The invisibility of "adolescents . . . caught between childhood and adulthood, in terms of both their social status and physical development" is detrimental to the protection of the rights of the child, both concerning recognition of actions that jeopardize their health and development, such as sexual abuse, but also to the development of effective prevention strategies realistically targeted to their needs.[37]

Ignoring Gender?

Epidemiological data from countries where heterosexual transmission of HIV predominates show that teenage girls have higher rates of HIV-infection than boys of the same age.[38] As adolescent girls and boys grow through early adulthood, this difference tends to narrow so that by their mid-thirties, about as many men as women live with HIV infection. The differential in HIV incidence in younger age groups has been attributed in part to patterns of sexual partnership (adolescent girls having sexual contact with older males who are more likely than younger ones to be HIV-infected), as well as to the biological and physiological vulnerability of younger girls to HIV infection and other STDs. Furthermore, societal and cultural norms defining female and male gender roles may make it difficult for younger women to impose safer sex practices on their sexual partners.[39] Differentials determined by sex or gender roles in relation to HIV/STD infection are not systematically considered in the collection and analysis of HIV/STD epidemiological data, nor are they sufficiently studied or built into the design of prevention and care programs.

In countries where the HIV/AIDS pandemic has matured, some 15–16 year-old girls attending antenatal clinics for their first pregnancy are already infected with HIV, but no information is available as to the cause of this infection (i.e., whether it involves sex or another mode of transmission).[40] The degree to which gender factors influence the relative risk of becoming infected through various routes of transmission during childhood, and how it may influence patterns of access to care and to the quality of care provided to boys and girls once HIV infection has set in, remains unknown. There is increasing recognition that the collection and analysis of epidemiological and prevention information concerning adults must be disaggregated by sex. Yet there has been little attention given to the fact that the information collected on "children" younger than 15 generally fails to differentiate by sex. In addition to obscuring such differences as may occur in the natural history of HIV infection, this may result in neglect of the very real differences between female and male adolescents and calls into question the efficacy of prevention programs which have failed to recognize these differences.

On the global level, it is worth noting that, of the ten WHO Prevention Indicators (PI) mentioned earlier, seven call for the collection of data on "people" or "individuals," and of the remaining three, two are specific for females (PI 8 and 10: prevalence of positive serology for syphilis and HIV, respectively, in women attending antenatal clinics), and one for males (PI 9: incidence of urethritis in men). The first seven indicators which call for data on "people" or "individuals" concern such issues as knowledge of preventive practices (PI 1), condom availability (PI 2 and PI 3), reported number of non-regular sexual partners (PI 4), reported condom use in the most recent sexual intercourse at risk (PI 5), and STD case management (PI 6 and PI 7).[41] Although these seven indicators may have been applied to males and females separately in studies validating population surveys for the measurement of these indicators, the lack of attention to gender in the way they have been set out remains of concern. This is particularly the case since these indicators are used to monitor progress in HIV prevention and to influence HIV/AIDS-related policy development and program design.

These prevention indicators should require separate measuring and reporting for males and for females, and possibly the inclusion of additional indicators to monitor the sex-differentials in rates and in trends. In line with the recommendations made at the 1995 UN Fourth World Conference on Women, these indicators should be reformulated to reflect gender specificity.[42] Drawing attention to gender differences is important and urgent as their recognition may enhance the impact of national responses to HIV/AIDS.

From an HIV/STD prevention and care perspective, policies and programs must recognize the different needs, and expression of these needs, among boys and girls. Gender sensitivity should extend to the identification of information equally useful and accessible to girls and to boys, as well as attention to the ways in which assumptions about gender roles may impact on the design of prevention strategies and services. Different treatment of girls and boys in the context of HIV prevention and care, and more broadly as concerns their health and development, draws attention to the specter of gender-based discrimination. Examples of discrimination in this context include the provision of contraception to young boys which is denied to young girls, with the stated rationale that access might prompt girls to be sexually active. Each of the major human rights documents prohibits distinctions which are made against a person which results in their being treated unfairly and unjustly on the basis of their sex. The prohibition of discrimination does not mean that differences should not be acknowledged, only that different treatment must be based on reasonable and objective criteria. Therefore, applying different approaches to information collection, analysis, and use in policy and programs affecting girls and boys should be based on the valid recognition of gender-related differentials in risk and vulnerability and minimize the influence of prescribed gender roles and cultural norms.

From Concept to Practice

The work presented here is an initial attempt to make explicit the confluence of issues affecting children living in a world with AIDS. Using a simple analytical framework in the form of a three-by-three table, this work began by recognizing the obligations of governments with respect to the three situations in which the AIDS pandemic can impact on the health and development of children, where they are infected with, affected by, and/or vulnerable to HIV/AIDS. This proposed approach to exploring the relationship between rights and health in children extends beyond HIV/AIDS, and can be used to explore a broad range of infectious diseases affecting children, as well as other challenges to their health and development such as malnutrition or physical and mental abuse.

The Annex provides a different level of analysis of the convergence between the response to HIV/AIDS and the rights of the child. This table is intended only to serve as a methodological illustration of the linkages between HIV and the rights of the child, and is by no means intended to be exhaustive. For each of the three situations confronted by children living in a world with AIDS, selected issues relevant to HIV/AIDS prevention, care, and related research are detailed and the immediately relevant CRC provisions provided. The four general principles of the CRC should be understood as applicable to any analysis of the issues presented in this Annex.

Application of the three-by-three table presented earlier (Table 11.1) to each of the situations set out in the Annex may help to determine the specific actions needed to respect, protect, and fulfill the rights of children infected with, affected by, or vulnerable to HIV/AIDS. A reverse analysis could also be conducted where, using the issues detailed in the Annex and taking CRC articles as entry points, it would be possible to suggest how the respect, protection, and fulfillment of rights may impact on the survival and development of children confronting HIV/AIDS.

Linking human rights to HIV/AIDS in these ways may contribute not only to increased awareness of some of the manifest health consequences of the lack of respect, protection, or fulfillment of the rights of the child, but also to improved strategies for alleviating the impact of HIV/AIDS on the lives of children. However, the likelihood of successful action is dependent on the willingness and capacity of those concerned with HIV/AIDS and those engaged in human rights work at the local, national, and international levels to realize the potential synergy of their respective actions and the benefits of combining efforts.

Conclusions

The synergistic relationship between the promotion and protection of rights and sound public health policies and programs is increasingly being recognized.

Far more attention than in times past is also being given to the meaning and implications of the rights of children to their health and development, as well as to the roots and consequences of the HIV/AIDS epidemics. However, to translate this awareness into effective actions will require the involvement of young people and the combined efforts of governments, intergovernmental and nongovernmental institutions, the private sector, and communities. This approach could then be used to stimulate governmental accountability on what is being done—and not done—for children living a world with AIDS.

Much work lies ahead to establish and promote the links between the rights of the child and child health and development—with respect to HIV/AIDS as well as other diseases and health conditions. Empirical knowledge and experience acquired through community-based work, linked to policy and program-based research, will be necessary to better shape the governmental and other responses necessary for the survival and development needs of children.

Notes

1. Convention on the Rights of the Child, GA Res 44/25, UN GAOR, 44th Sess., 41st plen. mtg., Annex, UN Doc A/44/25 (1989).
2. G. Van Bueren, *The International Law on the Rights of the Child* (Dordrecht: M. Nijhoff, 1995).
3. UNAIDS and WHO, *Report on the Global HIV/AIDS Epidemic* (Geneva, 1997): p. 3.
4. The Convention on the Rights of the Child defines more fully the child as "Every human being under the age of 18 unless, under the laws of the country, majority is attained earlier," CRC, see note 1, art. 1.
5. The Maastricht Guidelines on Violations of Economic, Social and Cultural Rights were developed by a group of more than 30 experts in international law, January 22–26, 1997. See, for example, A. Eide, "The Right to an Adequate Standard of Living, Including the Right to Food," in: *Economic, Social and Cultural Rights: A Textbook*, A. Eide, C. Krause, A. Rosas (eds.) (Dordrecht: M. Nijhoff, 1995), pp. 89–105.
6. UNAIDS and UNICEF launched the "Children in a World With AIDS" initiative at the XI International Conference on AIDS in Vancouver, British Columbia, July 8, 1996.
7. UNAIDS, "Children Living in a World with AIDS," World AIDS Campaign, Media Briefing document, June 27, 1997.
8. UNAIDS, see note 3, p.3.
9. D. Tarantola, B. Schwartländer, "HIV/AIDS Epidemics in Sub-Saharan Africa: Dynamism, Diversity and Discrete Declines?" *AIDS* 11(suppl B) (1997):S15.
10. UNAIDS, see note 6.
11. C. Levine, D. Michaels, S.D. Back, "Orphans of the HIV/AIDS Pandemic," in: J.M. Mann, D. Tarantola (eds.), *AIDS in The World II* (New York: Oxford University Press, 1996), pp.278–286.
12. UNAIDS, see notes 6 and 7, "Vulnerability of Young People to HIV/AIDS: a Proposed Analytical Framework," Box 40–4, see note 11, pp. 454–457.
13. Joanna Santa Barbara, "The Psychological Effects of War on Children," in: *War and Public Health*, B. S. Levy, V. W. Sidel (eds.), (New York: Oxford University Press, 1997), pp. 12, 168–185.
14. *Universal Declaration on Human Rights*, adopted and proclaimed by UN General Assembly Resolution 217A(III) (December 10, 1948), art. 1.
15. S. Gruskin, K. Pflaker, "Are the Rights of the Child Relevant to Women's Human Rights?" in: *Women's International Human Rights*, D. Koenig, K. Askin (eds.), (Transnational Publishers, 1997).
16. S. Gruskin, A. Hendriks, K. Tomasevski, "Human Rights and Responses to HIV/AIDS," see note 11, pp. 330–331.

17. World Summit for Children, 1990, World Conference on Human Rights, 1993; International Conference on Population and Development, 1994; The World Summit for Social Development, 1995, Fourth World Conference on Women, 1995; World Congress on the Sexual Exploitation of Children, 1996.

18. G. Van Bueren, see note 2.

19. Committee on the Rights of the Child, General Guidelines, CRC/C/5, paragraph 14.

20. CRC, see note 1, art. 2.

21. CRC, see note 1, art. 3.1.

22. CRC, see note 1, art. 6.

23. Thomas Hammarberg, "Children," in: *Economic, Social and Cultural Rights: A Textbook*, A. Eide, C. Krause, A. Rosas (eds.) (Dordrecht: M. Nijhoff, 1995), pp. 289, 292.

24. CRC, see note 1, art. 12.

25. A. Eide et al. see note 5.

26. Ibid.

27. United Nations Population Fund, Programme of Action, adopted at the International Conference on Population and Development, September 5–13, 1994, Cairo, Egypt, paragraph 7.46.

28. A. Eide et al. see note 5.

29. CRC, see note 1, art. 28.1.b., which provides that vocational education must be made "available and accessible to every child."

30. United Nations Economic and Social Council, "The Siracusa Principles on the Limitation and Derogation Provisions in the International Covenant on Civil and Political Rights," UN Doc. E/CN.4/1985/4, Annex.

31. S. Gruskin, A. Hendriks, K. Tomasevski, "Human Rights and Responses to HIV/AIDS," see note 11, pp. 326–340.

32. Ibid.

33. UNAIDS and WHO, see note 3.

34. Ideally, HIV incidence data (i.e., the proportion of those infected over a given period, usually a year) should be collected by single-year age groups so as to provide information which reflects the dynamics of HIV spread. Incidence data are commonly derived from annual differences in the prevalence (i.e. proportion of children/young adults in a specific age category who are infected at a given point in time). This extrapolation is possible for younger age groups whose exposure to HIV is likely to be recent, but is increasingly problematic as adults grow older, since the age at which they became infected can no longer be ascertained.

35. T. Mertens, M. Caraël, et al. "Prevention Indicators for Evaluating the Progress of National AIDS Programmes," *AIDS* 8 (1994):1359–1369.

36. The arbitrariness of what determines who is a child and who is an adult in society is noted in the work of the Committee on the Rights of the Child. See M. Santos Pais, "The Convention on the Rights of the Child," in: *Manual on Human Rights Reporting*, Revised Version (United Nations, International Training Centre of the ILO, & United Nations Centre for Human Rights, 1996), pp. 1–75.

37. Report of the Expert Group Meeting on Adolescent Girls and their Rights (Addis Ababa, Ethiopia, October 13–17, 1997) EGM/AGR/1997/Rep. 1, November 6, 1997. United Nations Division for the Advancement of Women, (DAW), UNICEF, UNFPA, and the United Nations Economic Commission for Africa (ECA), paragraph 22.

38. A.J. Nunn, J.F. Kengeya-Kayondo, S.S. Malamba, et al. "Risk Factors for HIV-1 Infection in Adults in a Rural Ugandan Community: a Population Study," *AIDS* 8 (1994):81–86.

39. M. Caraël, A. Buvé, K. Awusabo-Asare, "The Making of HIV Epidemics: What Are the Driving Forces?" *AIDS* 11(suppl B) (1997):S23–S32.

40. K. Fylkesnes, Z. Kasumba, Z. Ndhlovu, R. Musonda, "Box II: Comparing Sentinel Surveillance and Population-based HIV Prevalence Rates in Zambia," *AIDS* 11(suppl B) (1997):S12.

41. T. Mertens et al. see note 34.

42. In fact, the Platform for Action calls for data that is "collected, analyzed and disaggregated by . . . sex and age." See Fourth World Conference on Women, *Report of the Fourth World Conference on Women*, Beijing, September 4–15, 1995, UN Doc. A/Conf. 177/20, October 17, 1995, Annex II, para. 109(a).

Annex 11.1

1. The Child Infected With HIV

Issues in HIV/ AIDS prevention, care, and research	Specific issues relevant to this population	Immediately relevant CRC articles* (by key words)
Care and support issues	Knowledge of HIV status	13: Information 16: Privacy 17: Access to information sources
	Participation in and exclusion from research and consent issues	13: Information 16: Privacy 17: Access to information sources 19: Protection against all forms of abuse, including negligent treatment 24: Highest attainable standard of health and facilities for treatment 25: Periodic review of treatment
	Psychological and social support from family and services	18: Common responsibility of parents 19: Protection against all forms of abuse, including negligent treatment 20: Care if deprived of family environment 23: Disability 24: Highest attainable standard of health and facilities for treatment 26: Social insurance 27: Standard of living 39: Reintegration after exploitation
	Access to and quality of care	24: Highest attainable standard of health and facilities for treatment 25: Periodic review of treatment 26: Social insurance
	Prevention and treatment of opportunistic infections	24: Highest attainable standard of health and facilities for treatment 25: Periodic review of treatment
	Access to prescription drugs	24: Highest attainable standard of health and facilities for treatment 26: Social insurance
	Immunization	24: Highest attainable standard of health and facilities for treatment
Child growth and development	Access to educational, vocational, and recreational opportunities	28: Education 29: Personality and abilities 31: Rest and leisure (engage in play) 32: Child labor and economic exploitation

*The four general principles (Article 2, Article 3, Article 6, Article 12) should be brought into the analysis for each issue presented.

1. The Child Infected With HIV (cont.)

Issues in HIV/ AIDS prevention, care, and research	Specific issues relevant to this population	Immediately relevant CRC articles (by key words)
	Sexuality, sexual health and reproductive health	13: Information 15: Freedom of association 16: Privacy 17: Access to information sources 19: Protection against all forms of abuse, including negligent treatment 24: Highest attainable standard of health and facilities for treatment 29: Personality and abilities 39: Reintegration after exploitation
	Nutrition, including infant feeding	23: Disability 24: Highest attainable standard of health and facilities for treatment 27: Standard of living
Children in difficult circumstances	Adoption	9: No forced separation 11: Illicit transfer and non-return of children 19: Protection against all forms of abuse, including negligent treatment 20: Care if deprived of family environment 21: Adoption 24: Highest attainable standard of health and facilities for treatment

2. The Child Affected by HIV/AIDS

Impact on family and community	Children whose parents or siblings are living with HIV/AIDS	9: No forced separation 18: Common responsibility of parents 20: Care if deprived of family environment 27: Standard of living
	Children orphaned by AIDS	19: Protection against all forms of abuse, including negligent treatment 20: Care if deprived of family environment 21: Adoption
	Exhaustion of extended family's coping capacity	18: Common responsibility of parents 19: Protection against all forms of abuse, including negligent treatment 26: Social insurance 27: Standard of living 32: Child labor and economic exploitation 36: Protection against all other forms of exploitation 39: Reintegration after exploitation

2. The Child Affected by HIV/AIDS (cont.)

Issues in HIV/ AIDS prevention, care, and research	Specific issues relevant to this population	Immediately relevant CRC articles (by key words)
Impact on services	Loss of educational and vocational opportunities	28: Education 32: Child labor and economic exploitation 39: Reintegration after exploitation
	Diminished access to prevention, care, and social services	18: Common responsibility of parents 24: Highest attainable standard of health and facilities for treatment 26: Social insurance 27: Standard of living
Exploitation of children	Greater likelihood of family reliance on child labor	19: Protection against all forms of abuse, including negligent treatment 27: Standard of living 28: Education 31: Rest and leisure (engage in play) 32: Child labor and economic exploitation 36: Protection against all other forms of exploitation 39: Reintegration after exploitation
	Greater risk of sexual exploitation	19: Protection against all forms of abuse, including negligent treatment 27: Standard of living 28: Education 29: Personality and abilities 31: Rest and leisure (engage in play) 34: Protection against sexual exploitation and sexual abuse 36: Protection against all other forms of exploitation 39: Reintegration after exploitation

3. The Child Vulnerable to HIV/AIDS

Growth and development	Physical and mental development	9: No forced separation 10: Family reunification 13: Information 17: Access to information sources 18: Common responsibility of parents 19: Protection against all forms of abuse, including negligent treatment 24: Highest attainable standard of health and facilities for treatment 27: Standard of living 28: Education 29: Personality and abilities 31: Rest and leisure (engage in play) 32: Child labor and economic exploitation

3. The Child Vulnerable to HIV/AIDS (cont.)

Issues in HIV/ AIDS prevention, care, and research	Specific issues relevant to this population	Immediately relevant CRC articles (by key words)
		33: Protection from illicit use of narcotic drugs
		34: Protection against sexual exploitation and sexual abuse
		36: Protection against all other forms of exploitation
		39: Reintegration after exploitation
	Recognition of sexuality, sexual orientation, and sexual and reproductive health	13: Information
		15: Freedom of association
		16: Privacy
		17: Access to information sources
		19: Protection against all forms of abuse, including negligent treatment
		24: Highest attainable standard of health and facilities for treatment
		29: Personality and abilities
		34: Protection against sexual exploitation and abuse
		39: Reintegration after exploitation
Personal characteristics and social role	Recognition of risk-taking behavior	13: Information
		17: Access to information sources
		29: Personality and abilities
	Autonomy	7: Right to acquire nationality
		8: Preservation of identity
		14: Freedom of thought, conscience, and religion
		15: Freedom of association
		18: Common responsibility of parents
		28: Education
		29: Personality and abilities
Awareness and skills	Ability to modulate risk of acquiring HIV infection (negotiation, sexual practices, condoms, other preventive behaviors)	13: Information
		17: Access to information sources
		24: Highest attainable standard of health and facilities for treatment
		29: Personality and abilities
		34: Protection against sexual exploitation and sexual abuse
Livelihood: exploitation of children	Child labor	19: Protection against all forms of abuse, including negligent treatment
		27: Standard of living
		28: Education
		31: Rest and leisure (engage in play)
		32: Child labor and economic exploitation
		36: Protection against all other forms of exploitation
		39: Reintegration after exploitation

3. The Child Vulnerable to HIV/AIDS (cont.)

Issues in HIV/ AIDS prevention, care, and research	Specific issues relevant to this population	Immediately relevant CRC articles (by key words)
	Sexual exploitation	19: Protection against all forms of abuse, including negligent treatment 27: Standard of living 28: Education 29: Personality and abilities 31: Rest and leisure (engage in play) 34: Protection against sexual exploitation and sexual abuse 36: Protection against all other forms of exploitation 39: Reintegration after exploitation
Services and programs	Access to education	13: Information 17: Access to information sources 27: Standard of living 28: Education 29: Personality and abilities
	Access to health services (including sexual and reproductive health)	18: Common responsibility of parents 23: Disability 24: Highest attainable standard of health and facilities for treatment. 26: Social insurance
	Access to social services	18: Common responsibility of parents 23: Disability 24: Highest attainable standard of health and facilities for treatment 26: Social insurance 27: Standard of living
Children in difficult circumstances	In times of conflict and internally displaced	23: Disability 24: Highest attainable standard of health and facilities for treatment 38: Protection and care 39: Reintegration after exploitation
	Institutionalization (prison, mental institutions, etc.)	23: Disability 24: Highest attainable standard of health and facilities for treatment 25: Periodic review of treatment 37: Appropriate assistance 40: Special concerns/privacy
	Homelessness	20: Care if deprived of family environment 23: Disability 24: Highest attainable standard of health and facilities for treatment 26: Social insurance 27: Standard of living

3. The Child Vulnerable to HIV/AIDS (cont.)

Issues in HIV/ AIDS prevention, care, and research	Specific issues relevant to this population	Immediately relevant CRC articles (by key words)
	Exposure to violence	18: Common responsibility of parents
		19: Protection against all forms of abuse, including negligent treatment
		27: Standard of living
		31: Rest and leisure (engage in play)
		32: Child labor and economic exploitation
		36: Protection against all other forms of exploitation
		37: Special protections
		39: Reintegration after exploitation
	Injecting drug use by children	33: Protection from illicit use of narcotic drugs
		39: Reintegration after exploitation
	Asylum seekers and refugees	8: Preservation of identity
		10: Family reunification
		11: Illicit transfer and non-return of children
		20: Care if deprived of family environment
		22: Refugee status
		23: Disability

12

The "Double Discourse" on Sexual and Reproductive Rights in Latin America

The Chasm between Public Policy and Private Actions

Bonnie Shepard

The international policy arena today is marked by strong clashes of values with regard to sexuality and reproduction. This chapter will examine how political controversies affect citizens' ability to exercise sexual and reproductive rights in Latin America, with examples from several countries, but focusing mainly on Chile. This is not a comprehensive overview of the variety of sexual and reproductive rights abuses in the region, but rather an analysis of the social and political dynamics associated with contested policy issues in sexual and reproductive rights. The chapter will argue that societies accommodate conflicting views on sexuality and reproduction via a "double discourse system," which maintains the status quo in repressive or negligent public policies while expanding private sexual and reproductive choices behind the scenes. Two specific examples—divorce law in Chile and abortion advocacy in Colombia and Chile—will highlight how this breach between public discourse and private actions operates in practice, and who is harmed by it. The chapter will conclude by discussing the implications of this system for rights advocacy.

In Latin America and worldwide, general consensus exists among governments on the now-standard phrases that summarize reproductive rights in the Programme of Action of the International Conference on Population and Development (ICPD), held in Cairo in 1994:

> . . . the basic right of all couples and individuals to decide freely and responsibly the number, spacing and timing of their children, and to have

the information and means to do so, and the right to attain the highest standard of reproductive and sexual health. [Reproductive rights] also includes [couples and individuals'] right to make decisions concerning reproduction free of discrimination, coercion and violence, as expressed in human rights documents.[1]

In Latin America, as in many other regions, certain concrete implications of these principles of consensus are vehemently disputed at all levels, from the family to the central government. Do these rights extend to adolescents—that is, do adolescents count as "couples and individuals?" In the recent UN meetings on Cairo+5, many delegations argued that parents' rights supersede those of adolescents. Also, if women have the right to decide freely on the number and spacing of their children, doesn't that entail the right to safe abortion services? This is certainly the most publicized conflict in the reproductive rights field, so much so that all too often the term "reproductive rights" is reduced to the issue of abortion in the public mind. Finally, the term "sexual rights" has never made its way into any conference document or international convention. For the purposes of this chapter, sexual rights include the right to sexual health, "which is the enhancement of life and personal relations, and not merely . . . care related to reproduction and STDs," as well as the "individual's right to have control over and decide freely in matters related to his or her sexuality, free of coercion, discrimination, and violence," provided that one's sexual behaviors do not harm others.[2] It should also be noted that, while there finally appears to be some consensus that sexual violence and coercion are violations of basic human rights, many conservative groups remain opposed to the term "sexual rights," which they believe will lead, among other things, to recognition of freedom of sexual orientation as a right.

Repressive Public Laws and Expanded Private Options: Sexual and Reproductive Rights in Latin America

The political climate surrounding sexual and reproductive rights is characterized by a worldwide increase in religious fundamentalism on the one hand and cultural globalization on the other, which has exacerbated preexisting political and cultural divisions. In Latin America, the majority of citizens identify as Roman Catholic, and the Church is the main force against full recognition of sexual and reproductive rights. As in European countries with a dominantly Catholic tradition and among Catholics in the United States, most studies show that in practice Latin American Catholics do not follow the official teachings of the Church on the use of contraception and abortion.[3] The increasing strength of hard-line factions over the past 20 years has resulted in growing rigidity in the Church positions on these issues and increasing repression of dissident views within Catholic institutions.[4] While the channels through which the Roman Catholic hierarchy exercises its political influence are often hidden from public view, the visible result is policies that deny reproductive and sexual rights to citizens—policies that seem to become ever more deeply entrenched in a polarized political climate.

How do Latin American countries accommodate the sharp divisions in public opinion on these issues and the universal and often pressing need for individuals and couples to exercise freedom of decision-making in sexuality and reproduction? In many cultures, escape valves allow private accommodations to repressive policies, leaving the official legal and/or religious norms untouched while reducing the social and political pressure for policy advances.

This type of societal rift between public stands and private actions also operates at the level of the individual. In a recent book, Rosalind Petchesky discusses women's private strategies to expand their reproductive choices:

> As our fieldwork progressed, . . . we found that the two extremes of outright resistance and passive accommodation are much rarer than the kinds of complicated, subtle reproductive and sexual strategies that most of our respondents adopt in order to achieve some degree of autonomy and at the same time maintain their place in the family and community. . . . [A woman] may see no contradiction whatsoever in both acting against a particular norm and speaking in deference to it. Indeed, accommodation in practice often means a nonconfrontational or conciliatory way of achieving one's wishes or sense of right.[5]

A recurrent theme within the Latin American countries with which the author is most familiar—Colombia, Peru, Chile, and Argentina—is the "double discourse" (*doble discurso*).[6] This phrase, usually applied to individuals, is widely understood to signify the art of espousing traditional and repressive sociocultural norms publicly, while ignoring—or even participating in—the widespread flouting of these norms in private. I expand the use of the term "double discourse" in this chapter to signify a political and cultural system, not just an agglomeration of individuals privately "sinning." Thanks to the ubiquity of the double discourse, in most Latin American countries the reproductive and sexual choices open to citizens are much wider than the official policies would lead one to believe. At the heart of this system lies the chasm between public discourse, upholding traditional religious precepts that limit individual choices, and unofficial private discourses—in conversations, interior monologues, and the confessional—that rationalize or ask forgiveness for transgressions. These private individual discourses are complemented by social and political mechanisms—laws or interpretations of laws providing escape valves, common practices, clandestine services, etc.—that make expanded choices possible. The primary features of the double discourse system, then, are the following:

- For historical and political reasons, the hierarchies of a hegemonic religion exercise considerable influence over state policies, imposing the religion's moral codes on legal norms. The distinction between immorality and criminality is blurred.
- The official discourse and policies uphold highly restrictive norms, based in religious doctrine, which violate citizens' sexual and reproductive rights. These norms assume a sacred and inviolable character.
- There are always political costs attached to espousing a change in the norm, which is sacred. Public officials and civil society organizations come under attack when they publicly defend the legitimacy of the sexual or reproductive right in question or when they attempt to reform the policies. There may or may not be political costs attached to publicly recognizing the ubiquity of infractions of the law (as in the case of abortion) or the use of legal loopholes that subvert the intent of the law (as in the case of annulments).
- Individual practices that flout the norm are widespread, as are the social and political mechanisms that make them possible. These mechanisms constitute an escape valve that expands citizens' sexual and reproductive choices, but because they are makeshift, illegal, or unofficial, neither availability, safety (in the case of services), nor protections of basic rights are guaranteed.
- The worst consequences of the restrictive policies fall on low-income sectors and on groups that are disadvantaged, discriminated against, or marginalized in other ways, e.g., ethnic minorities, single mothers, inhabitants of rural areas, and homosexual men and women. Political elites usually do not suffer the worst consequences of the restrictive laws.
- The combination of high political costs attached to efforts for reform and the political disenfranchisement of the groups that feel the worst consequences of the restrictive policies leads to a lack of political will for reform. Public debate can lead to increased repression and limits on the informal mechanisms that expand choice, creating ethical dilemmas for advocates of reform.

Clearly, this chasm between public norms restricting individual rights and private discourses and mechanisms expanding them is not limited to the area of sexual and reproductive rights. So many sociocultural taboos and restrictions lie in this realm, however, that in Latin American popular usage *el doble discurso* generally refers to sexual and reproductive matters. In fact, the term "double discourse" is somewhat misleading, because its essence is that private actions deviating from the norm, even if they are almost universally practiced, are not favored with any *public* discourse at all that defends their legitimacy. The *private* discourse does not usually defend the sexual and reproductive rights that contravene these traditional norms; rather, it rationalizes individual actions or explains them in terms of weakness and sin.

Doble discurso is a fitting non-judgmental label arising from these predominantly Catholic cultures, since the closest words in English for this phenomenon—for example, "hypocritical," "deceptive," "two-faced," and "duplicitous"—are harsh in their judgments. The polarized debates that often co-exist with double discourse systems beget severe judgments. For example, in the debates about sex education in Chile, the reformers believe that they are simply recognizing the reality and risks of adolescent sexual behavior, while their opponents are "hypocrites" who hide their heads in the sand. Likewise, those opposing the public health approach to sex education accuse the reformers of being "permissive" and promoting "promiscuity."[7] It might be fair to say that a double discourse system is built into Catholic cultures in those countries where for a variety of historical and political reasons the Church has great influence on the state. In these countries, many of which are in Latin America, public officials often feel compelled to uphold the Church's teachings publicly although they know that actions at variance with the teachings are common.[8] Catholics view this attitude not as hypocritical, but rather as upholding an ideal to which many, including oneself, fail to measure up, for reasons that God will understand and forgive.

Like the women described above in the IRRRAG studies, both Catholic women and the clergy make their personal peace with private choices that flout official norms. Clergy at the grassroots level are often more empathetic and flexible than the hierarchy. Since the hierarchy often "silences" clergy who speak out publicly against the Church's repressive norms on sexuality and reproduction, their support for individuals' forbidden reproductive and sexual behaviors usually takes place in the private realm of conversations and the confessional.[9] A little-known study in Colombia on the attitudes of Catholic women and Catholic priests on abortion showed that most priests give absolution in the confessional to women who have had abortions, despite recent edicts urging priests to excommunicate women who have had abortions. For their part, Catholic women interviewed in abortion clinics made a *de facto* distinction between the public notion of mortal sin and the private spiritual notion of an understanding deity. While they recognized that abortion is a sin, they stated that their relationship with God was not in any way ruptured by their actions, which arose from extreme hardship and necessity.[10]

Examples of the Double Discourse System

The examples of divorce law in Chile and abortion advocacy in Colombia and Chile will demonstrate these features of the double discourse system. Both illustrate how policy-makers are willing to turn a blind eye to private actions and social institutions that flout the official norm, despite a perceived obligation to defend the norm. In both cases, disadvantaged groups have suffered disproportionately from the current policies, and individuals and groups advocating for reform have encountered multiple roadblocks.

The Catholic Church and Divorce Law in Chile[11]

During the 17 years of military dictatorship from 1973 to 1990, the Catholic Church played a progressive role in Chile as the main proponent of respect for human rights and social justice. The Church's *Vicaría de Solidaridad* (Vicariate of Solidarity), which defended victims of human rights abuses during the years of the military dictatorship, saved the lives of countless opposition politicians and activists who are now officials in the civilian government and leaders in the center-left government coalition, the *Concertación*. Furthermore, historically the Church has been an important wellspring and source of support for efforts to increase socioeconomic justice in Chile. The progressive origins of the Christian Democratic Party, the majority party in the *Concertación*, have their roots in liberation theology movements in the Catholic Church. For these reasons, the Church now enjoys a great deal of political influence in Chile, more than in most Latin American countries.[12]

Coincident with this increase in the Church's political influence has been the worldwide growth in power of the conservative wing of the Church, noted above. The Church's increasingly repressive focus on sexual and reproductive rights issues intensified during the 1990s in Chile, strengthening partnerships with the socially conservative opposition parties.[13] The Church is thus in the enviable position of having strong alliances with socially conservative politicians of all political tendencies—both from the *Concertación* and from the rightist opposition parties—on policies related to the family, gender, reproduction, and sexuality. As a result, the public discourses in the Congress and in the media regarding proposed legal reforms on issues such as adultery, divorce, same-sex sexual relationships, new reproductive technologies, and abortion are all remarkably uniform in Chile in comparison with other Latin American countries.[14] There is a notable lack of lively public debate on these policies, although most Chileans acknowledge that the private flouting of the policies is widespread. The *doble discurso* is nowhere so amply recognized and commented on as in this socially conservative country.

The countries without a divorce law can be counted on the fingers of one hand, although there is no official United Nations convention that explicitly sanctifies the right of individuals to separate definitively from their spouses and remarry.[15] The powerful influence of the Church on the two civilian governments of the '90s may explain why Chile is one of these countries, although, according to a recent survey, 70% of Chilean women are in favor of a divorce law.[16] As in most modern industrialized countries, Chilean couples separate and pair up with new partners quite frequently. Many people simply live with a new partner and remain legally separated; others take the precaution of never getting married in the first place. During the 1990s, the courts granted almost 7,000 annulments per year.[17] Most analysts recognize that the Chilean legal framework for civilian annulment is a fraudulent safety valve that allows for the absence of a divorce law. The ground most frequently used is that one of the spouses (backed up by two witnesses) swears that s/he gave the wrong address at the time of the wedding ceremony and thus did not fall under the jurisdiction of the official who performed the ceremony.[18] Unfortunately, lawyers' fees make this option unavailable to most low-income people. Certainly one could argue that the lack of the option of divorce results in many second unions—especially for low-income families—that are never formalized, thus violating the recognized human right to contract marriage and form a family. One clear result of this situation is a high and increasing rate of births out of wedlock, which has climbed from 30% in 1985 to 46% in 1999.[19] The annulment means that legally the marriage never existed, and any division of marital assets is completely up to negotiations between the couple.[20]

Therefore, the annulment leaves the custodial parent—usually a woman with fewer assets than her husband and no independent income—without the usual protections regarding rights to assets accumulated during marriage that are incorporated into legal divorces in most countries. While biological fathers are supposed to pay child support (*pensión alimenticia*), the inefficient justice system cannot guarantee compliance, so that the mothers and children often suffer economically under this arrangement.[21] In this sense, the lack of a divorce law can be argued to constitute discrimination against women, as well as a violation of equality of rights in marriage.[22]

It is clear, then, which social sectors are harmed by the lack of a divorce law. It is less clear why there is so little political will to lead efforts for reform, although there have been several attempts. First of all, it is emotionally and politically possible for Chilean legislators with annulled marriages or legal separations to be vehement opponents of the passage of a divorce law, in the name of the Chilean family and Catholic values. Private transgressions and public defense of norms coexist quite peacefully in a double discourse system. Second, the punitive power of the Catholic Church is probably a major factor in the failure of legislative efforts for reform. The Church is willing to throw its considerable influence behind successful campaigns to elect socially conservative legislators, and to unseat legislators who lead the efforts to pass divorce laws and other laws expanding sexual and reproductive rights. The label of "*divorcista*" has been attached to reformers.[23] A divorce law did pass the Chamber of Deputies in 1997, however, thanks to a rare coalition of supporters that included an influential faction within the majority Christian Democratic Party and three legislators from the rightist parties. The bill passed the Chamber with 10 votes from rightist parties.[24] While the bill was defeated in the more conservative Senate, additional legislative developments since then give some cause for hope that the political will to act on contentious social issues related to sexuality and reproduction is increasing.[25]

One factor that may weaken the political will to push for reform is that professionals with political influence come primarily from middle-class and upper-class backgrounds and can afford the lawyer's fees for an annulment. Although all classes certainly suffer inconveniences and difficulties from the lack of a divorce law, those in a position to affect political decisions do not suffer personally from the most negative consequences of the current laws.

The lack of strong civilian pressure to pass a divorce law is more puzzling. Even from the women's movement, there has been little active pressure on legislators. One feminist legislator who helped lead recent efforts to push a divorce law through Congress remarked sadly that there were no supporters in the galleries during discussions of the bill. "It seems that [the women's movement] is extremely demobilized, and sometimes I feel very isolated in my efforts," she said.[26]

One study hypothesized that a factor in the relative failure of Chilean feminists to address such issues might be the dispersion of Chilean feminists into NGOs that depend on government contracts for a substantial portion of their income. This dependence would lead to "self-censorship" regarding family law and those sexual and reproductive rights issues that cannot be addressed by the government due to Church opposition.[27] Finally, there is widespread recognition, especially among NGOs that engage in community-level work, of the decreased level of mobilization of popular-sector women's organizations since the advent of democracy.[28]

As we have seen, the case of divorce law reveals some of the main features of the double discourse system. Because of the escape valves in marriage laws, most of those Chileans who might have any influence on the political process are able to secure an annulment, thus weakening political will for reform. So long as the rule of official silence is respected, political equilibrium is maintained. This equilibrium, however, is also profoundly inequitable toward low-income couples who cannot afford annulments and mothers with custody of their children who are not able to privately negotiate a fair settlement regarding marital assets with their spouse.

Abortion Advocacy in Colombia and Chile: When to Break the Silence?[29]

As mentioned in the introduction, there is perhaps no issue related to reproductive rights so hotly contested as the right to safe and legal interruption of unwanted pregnancies. Most reproductive rights advocates hold that this right derives logically from "the right of couples and individuals to decide freely and responsibly the number, spacing and timing of their children."[30] While there are many other arguments in favor of this right, the most widely used are public health and equity arguments, which recognize that the practice of abortions is widespread and that illegality causes maternal morbidity and mortality through unsafe abortions, mainly among low-income women.[31] Middle- and upper-income women generally can pay for access to relatively safe clandestine abortion services, so that the clandestine mechanisms to expand reproductive choice discriminate against the poor. In UN forums and in Catholic countries, public health and equity arguments are gaining ground, but the double discourse system mandates that abortion cannot be officially made legal, even if it is widespread.

El Salvador and Chile share the dubious distinction of being the only countries in the world where all abortions, even to save the mother's life, are illegal and penalized, a legal situation that can be seen to violate the mother's right to life.[32] These laws are even stricter than the Canonical Code of the Catholic Church, which allows abortions in cases of ectopic pregnancies and reproductive cancers.[33] Because of the clandestine nature of induced abortions, the statistics on its prevalence are based on hospital data. The 1994 studies by the Alan Guttmacher Institute estimate that there are about 288,400 abortions annually in Colombia and 159,650 in Chile (with total populations of roughly 36 million and 14 million respectively).[34] Other estimates for Colombia range as high as 400,000 per year.[35] A nationwide Colombian urban household survey by Lucero Zamudio of the Universidad Externado found that one out of three women who had ever been pregnant had had an abortion.[36] In Chile, 35 of every 100 pregnancies end in abortion. In Colombia, it is estimated that almost 600 women a year die from complications of abortion, which account for 67% of all hospitalizations for gynecological causes.[37] In both countries, it is mainly low-income women who end up in public hospitals due to complications of unsafe abortions. Health providers in the public hospitals who disapprove of abortion often take punishing attitudes toward these patients. There are many accounts not only of hostile remarks, but also of providers performing D&Cs without anesthesia on women with incomplete abortions and forcing women to take medications designed to halt spontaneous abortions.[38]

Nevertheless, in both countries, public opinion regarding abortion is much more progressive than the official policies. A 1997 poll of Colombian women in union (married or in a permanent relationship) found that 20% of the respondents had had an abortion, and 48% thought that it should be legal under certain circumstances. Much larger majorities thought that abortion should be legal "if the mother was in danger" (88%), if the fetus had severe physical or mental defects (78%), or in cases of rape (76%).[39] The electorate in Chile is perhaps only slightly more conservative on this issue. A 1999 national survey found that high percentages of women favored legal abortion in cases of rape or incest (59%), danger to mother's life (78%), and fetal problems (70%). Fully 30% of women thought that abortion should be available "upon the woman's request."[40] These results in Chile are remarkable given the almost complete lack of media coverage of rights-affirming views on abortion.

Despite these similar results, however, the public reactions to the Alan Guttmacher studies in the two countries were startlingly different. There is generally less public debate on the issue of abortion in Chile than in Colombia. In Chile, the publicity surrounding the publication of the Alan Guttmacher statistics was seen to be an intolerable flouting of the *doble discurso* system, according to which infractions are tolerated so long as they remain out of the public view. "*De eso no se habla*" (one doesn't speak of such matters) is the key phrase applied to topics such as abortion. In this case, considerable media coverage and debate following the release of the study made the findings impossible to ignore. While progressive Catholic legislators and officials responded by advocating increased support for family planning services to prevent abortions, conservative legislators revived their attempts to increase the criminal penalties for abortion. In fact, the most tangible result was an unusually comprehensive crackdown on clandestine abortion clinics that continued sporadically over the next few years. Not even the best-known high-cost clinic in the upper-class neighborhood of Providencia was exempt from the police raids. Those who publicized the study did so to point out the futility of penalizing such a widespread practice and the public health consequences of its continued illegality. The consequences of the publicity, however, seem to have been mainly negative and punitive, depriving many women of access to needed services.[41]

Colombian society, on the other hand, is less conservative, and the Catholic Church has less influence on public policy there than in Chile. Colombian law provides for legal divorce, freedom of religious instruction in the schools, and mandatory sex education in the schools; the new Health Law 100 guarantees the right to family planning methods.[42] However, in both countries public officials still feel compelled to espouse the Catholic norms, while the Church publicly exercises influence to block changes in the abortion laws and to censor AIDS prevention television messages that include condom use.

Abortion services, a few of which are operated safely and ethically, are generally much more available in Colombia than in Chile. In the mid-1990s, the author saw full pages of ads in the daily papers advertising clinics where women could go if they were nervous about "menstrual delays."[43] In addition, many clinics legally provide treatment for incomplete abortions, which are generally started by women in their homes through unsafe methods. Nevertheless, these (or other similar) clinics are raided periodically by the police and shut down. The public reaction to the findings of the Alan Guttmacher study was much more muted in Colombia than in Chile, which may reflect a more widespread knowledge and acceptance of the availability of abortions. The Zamudio study, however, which was released at a regional conference for abortion researchers in Bogotá in November 1994, gained much more media attention, perhaps because the conference itself was a high-profile event attended by legislators throughout the region. Furthermore, the findings were firmer than the estimates in the Guttmacher study, and therefore less easily ignored. It is not clear whether this media attention was causally linked to a subsequent increase in raids and shutdowns of abortion clinics or whether the raids resulted from other dynamics in the political establishment. At any rate, many of the clinics reopened after a prudent lapse in time.

One Colombian official spoke frankly to the media about how the double discourse system (also called "*doble moral*" or double morality in Colombia) operates with regard to abortion in Colombia: "Abortion is not a problem of legal sanctions, but of collective double morality. There is not a single person who doesn't know where at least one of these medical centers operates, and probably has had occasion to recur to their services. Abortion is an egregious case of clandestine practices that won't disappear."[44]

One explanation for the differences in the level of repression exercised against clandestine providers in the two countries may be the differences in the rule of law. Chile is renowned for its legalistic culture and is known as "the Switzerland of Latin America." Throughout Chilean history, laws and rules in general have been taken very seriously.[45] However, this legalism is selective and arbitrarily applied in the case of laws such as those on abortion that are generally viewed as repressive or as requiring a breach of medical ethics by health providers. While there are a significant number of women who have been in jail in Chile for having undergone an abortion, as documented in a study by lawyer Lidia Casas, most of these women were not caught in raids, but rather denounced by a small minority of health providers.[46] Providers are enjoined by law to turn over to the authorities women who come to hospitals with complications from induced abortion, thus ostensibly forcing them to breach the confidentiality of the health provider/client relationship. The Casas study, however, suggested that most health providers in Chile respect the confidentiality of this relationship, since the bulk of the denunciations come from a handful of public hospitals serving low-income populations. Furthermore, they tend to cluster on days when certain doctors are on duty.[47] In this instance, the double discourse system operates by creating a public policy that is privately disregarded, thus saving most women from one of the worst consequences of the policy. However, the unlucky few who fall into the hands of providers who obey the letter of the law are imprisoned. Furthermore, both the risk of mortality/morbidity and the risk of imprisonment fall inequitably on low-income women, who disproportionately end up in public hospitals with complications from unsafe abortions. Middle and upper class women, who have access to safer private services, usually escape with impunity. One could argue, as in the case of divorce, that this escape valve weakens the will of political actors in both official and civil society to address this issue in an effective and unified manner.

Colombia, on the other hand, is renowned for widespread impunity for a variety of legal infractions due to its fragile, disorganized, and ineffective system of justice and citizen security/policing.[48] In this country, there is more tolerance for provision of abortion services than in Chile, so long as it remains private and behind-the-scenes, with occasional crackdowns that give a nod to the rule of law and the official discourse condemning abortion. As with other double discourse mechanisms that expand choice, there are no guarantees of accessibility and safety. There seem to be proportionately fewer women who end up in jail in Colombia for abortions than in Chile, although there are no definitive statistics.[49]

The women's and reproductive rights movements in Colombia have suffered from divisions about the best strategy to pursue to decriminalize abortions. Whether the crackdowns that followed the 1994 Zamudio study were coincidental or not, in recent years, nearly every time the issue of abortion has gained prominence in public debates, the repression and crackdowns on clandestine clinics increase, thus incurring negative consequences for women seeking abortions.[50] Thus, there are real advantages to continuing the silence. Furthermore, networks on reproductive rights understand that it is not to their advantage to be solely identified in the public mind with the issue of abortion, which is much more controversial than other sexual and reproductive rights issues in equal need of attention. Like legislators, they run political risks if they identify too strongly with this issue.[51]

Unfortunately, another source of division on the issue of abortion in Colombia comes precisely from the efforts of the reproductive rights movement to expand its reach beyond explicitly feminist organizations. There is some evidence that the level of disagreement on the issue of abortion rises as membership in sexual and reproductive rights networks expands to include grassroots low-income women's organizations, which tend to have a much more diverse social base than the feminist NGOs.[52]

Faced with these divisions, the Colombian Sexual and Reproductive Rights Network, which operates in six cities, decided to focus its campaigns in 1997–98 on the issue of sexual violence, in particular on inequities in the laws and the culture and in the judicial treatment of victims. Through this campaign, the network addressed the issue of abortion in the context of advocating for elimination of criminal penalties in cases of rape. In this way, they managed to forge a broader coalition, momentarily solving the problems of dissension on abortion within their ranks. In general, the network had more success in gaining coverage in the local media than in national organs.[53] One could hypothesize that in a double discourse system, the more national (and therefore semi-official) the media outlet, the harder it is to gain exposure for alternative viewpoints that flout semi-sacred norms on reproduction and sexuality.

In Chile, the silencing of those who are in favor of depenalizing abortion, or introducing exceptions under which abortion would not be penalized, is much more thorough.[54] Abortion for health reasons or in case of severe fetal defects was legal until 1989, when one of the last acts of the military government was to make it illegal. Yet groups and legislators wishing simply to restore the civil code to its pre-1989 state are vilified in the conservative press. Early in the democratic period, when Congresswoman Adriana Munozñ proposed to restore the clauses allowing therapeutic abortion, she was branded an "abortionist" and defeated on that basis in her re-election campaign in 1993.[55] In general, socially conservative politicians take the lead on this issue, having introduced repeated initiatives since 1990 to increase the criminal penalties for women who undergo induced abortions. Fortunately, there is just enough awareness in the legislature of the inequitable burden of the criminal penalties for low-income women, and these proposals have all been defeated.

Lately the women's movement has helped to defeat these proposals, although the overall dynamic is still defensive. The Open Forum on Reproductive Rights and Health has been especially active. Formed in 1991, it is a network of organizations in several provinces that has slowly gained more legitimacy, and is valued by feminists as the only entity within the Chilean women's movement that dares to openly advocate less repressive laws on abortion.[56] Despite this strength, the outreach and effectiveness of the Forum are hampered by several factors. The self-censorship among women's NGOs in Chile in the case of divorce operates even more strongly in the case of abortion advocacy, so that some of the major women's NGOs are not willing to join the Forum or its campaigns. Furthermore, as in Colombia, the Forum has encountered diversity of opinion within its ranks on the topic of abortion as their network expands to provincial cities and to more diverse and grassroots women's organizations. In practice, the network is forced to maintain a policy of voluntary adherence to its campaigns on this issue. For example, only some regional chapters participate in the Forum's main public strategy on abortion, which is to stand with banners advocating decriminalization of abortion and hand out educational materials in the main city plaza on one Friday of every month. In the tradition of the human rights movement during military dictatorships (most notably the Mothers of the Plaza de Mayo in Argentina), this is a symbolically public statement, bringing a prohibited and ostracized discourse into the most officially public space in the city. It brings citizen disagreement with official policies on taboo topics having to do with reproduction and sexuality out into the open, breaking the logic of the double discourse system. Recently, the Forum has complemented this strategy, which mainly targets public opinion, with alliances with other NGOs and communications with legislators or government officials when urgent needs for political action arise, as in the case of the most recent bill that proposed increases in the criminal penalties for abortion.[57] It is puzzling indeed that there is more political activity among Chilean women's NGOs on the much more taboo issue of abortion than on the continuing legislative efforts to pass a divorce law.

The dynamics affecting advocacy for safe and legal abortions in these two countries demonstrate the main features of the double discourse system: the heavy influence of religious dogma on public policy; the violation of women's reproductive rights to voluntary maternity, the existence of informal or illegal mechanisms to expand private choices; the discrimination against low-income women, both in access to these mechanisms and in the arbitrary and haphazard application of punitive laws and practices; divisions within the political class and citizen movements on the issue; and the lack of sufficient political will among both legislators and the women's movement to provide redress.

Implications for Advocacy: A Discussion

The above examples demonstrate how semi-official, clandestine, and private mechanisms subvert the limitations on exercise of sexual and reproductive rights imposed by repressive policies and deep societal polarization of opinion. One can only applaud human ingenuity in finding so many circuitous ways to expand individual choices in such contexts. The disadvantages of such a system, however, cannot be ignored, because the consequences lead to irreparable harm to so many individuals and families. When solutions that expand sexual and reproductive choices are unofficial, clandestine, and/or dependent on the judgment of professionals such as health providers, no one is guaranteed access to these solutions, no one can oversee their quality, and the health and legal risks fall disproportionately on low-income or marginalized individuals. The informal mechanisms that expand choice generally are safer and more commonly available as one climbs the socioeconomic ladder, thus softening the consequences of repressive policies for members of those very sectors that influence policy decisions, whether from the side of the state or of civil society. This mitigation of consequences, along with the political risks associated with advocacy for sexual and reproductive rights, is linked to the lack of political will to defend these rights. This article has pointed out the risks for legislators. The risks are also considerable for NGOs and those within Catholic institutions.

Political Costs

Those within Catholic institutions who believe in the principle of free conscience in sexual and reproductive matters suffer disproportionately from repression. The Latin American regional network of Catholics for Free Choice has many clandestine supporters who would lose their jobs if they openly declared themselves to be members. The increasing repression of dissident voices within the Church has crippled attempts to foster dialogue among the hierarchy; between the hierarchy and clergy (including nuns), who are generally much more flexible and progressive on these issues; and between lay believers and the hierarchy. Several brave clergy who have voiced their pro-rights views publicly in publications and in the media have been "silenced," with well-known examples in Colombia and Brazil.[58] Recently, a prominent endocrinologist from the Catholic University in Chile lost his professorship when he published an article in the newspaper *El Mercurio* using arguments from Catholic theology to oppose the Larrain bill, which would have increased criminal penalties for abortion.[59] In the face of this repression, Catholics for Free Choice has used research (for example, using focus groups of Catholic women on these issues) and public opinion polls to demonstrate the mismatch between the private reality and opinions of lay Catholics and the public discourse of the hierarchy. Through publications and speaking tours, they have publicized the views of dissident Catholic theologians to legitimate their point of view. Unfortunately, the Catholic Church is not a democracy, and these strategies have less power to sway Church leaders than they would when used by lay advocates to influence elected legislators. Nevertheless, such research and media exposure still serves a key purpose by helping to legitimize a pro-rights discourse in countries whose public policies are heavily influenced by the Church.

Citizen advocacy groups, many of whom are women's NGOs, are often unable to be as persistent and as effective as anti-rights activists. In the cases cited above in Chile and Colombia, citizen activists were insufficiently mobilized on these issues for a variety of political, economic, and cultural reasons. On the economic side, due to dramatic decreases in foreign aid, many Latin American NGOs have been suffering from such a precarious financial situation that their ability to be a consistent and independent voice in public debates is in peril. Not only are the few remaining staff completely overextended, but in such precarious situations, it is a big risk to make an organizational decision to carry the banner for controversial issues. Lacking foreign aid and private national donors for often-controversial programs, the NGOs have begun to depend on local and national government contracts, or on bilateral and multilateral contracts that must be approved by governments, for a significant portion of their funding. In several cases in the region, opposing the government's official position on sexual and reproductive rights issues has made an NGO persona non grata with some government agencies. As a result, the NGO is then unofficially excluded from winning government contracts or consulting jobs, no matter how unrelated to the NGO's stand on sexual and reproductive rights.

Possible Strategies

An analysis of the logic of the double discourse system leads to three possible strategies to increase the political will for change: using both public health and ethical arguments, decreasing the political risks for various political actors, and eliminating the safety valves. The latter path would be greatly mistaken and would only increase suffering and harm. It would produce the same effects as the Chilean crackdowns on illegal abortion providers, narrowing the choices for thousands of desperate women and couples and probably leading them to take more unsafe measures to end their pregnancies.[60] The safety valves exist because there is a demand for them that will not be denied, no matter what the official policies.

How then can advocacy strategies address the double discourse system? On issues from divorce to abortion, the main strategies have been to point out the obvious epidemiological facts in lobbying efforts: adolescents are sexually active, women are having abortions, mothers are dying, and couples are separating. Armed with information on the negative consequences for public health of rights-denying policies, advocates lobby behind the scenes and in professional conferences to sway policymakers.

In all advocacy strategies, it is important to study one's audience and to tailor approaches to diverse groups within the ranks. There is a more or less hidden diversity within the corps of legislators and public officials on these issues in most countries. The most vehement defenders of rights, on the one hand, and of semi-sacred norms limiting rights, on the other, are only the most visible and obvious audiences. Using audience analysis, there is a key flaw in the strategy that depends on public health and equity arguments with regard to the subset of legislators who strongly defend limits to rights on religious grounds: the epidemiological facts will not sway someone who is defending a sacred norm. In Christian religious thinking, the fact that people transgress or sin does not mean that the Ten Commandments should be thrown out the window. In this view, suffering as a result of transgression does not constitute an injustice. Morality is conflated with the law, so that making divorce or abortion or adultery legal is tantamount to giving them moral approval.

Besides the public health and equity arguments, there is another argument that may be more effective with these most intransigent opponents of sexual and reproductive rights, and more compelling to believers in all religions: the principle of religious diversity. A group of religious leaders from all of the world's major religions, including a representative from the socially conservative sector of the Catholic Church hierarchy, was convened before the ICPD to discuss reproductive rights issues. A key principle that they all agreed on was that no religion should have the power, through the state or by other means, to impose its precepts on the believers of any other religion. Religious diversity has increased significantly in Latin America and in most traditionally Catholic countries, making this an important argument for advocates.[61] One complementary advocacy strategy would thus be to forge alliances with believers in religions other than Catholicism to demand that state policies not be linked to the doctrines of any one religion.[62]

Advocates of sexual and reproductive rights do not face arguments based only in religious doctrine. Increasingly, opponents of reform are also using the discourse of human rights, citing the fetus's right to life, or the parents' right to control the education of their adolescent children. Unfortunately, this type of argument falsely pits rights against rights, resulting in stalemated discussions: adolescents' rights against those of parents, and women's rights against those of fetuses. In Latin America, however, the Catholic doctrines of human life and rights beginning at conception and the inadmissibility of premarital sex are embedded in these arguments, so that it is useful for sexual and reproductive rights advocates to deconstruct them to show their basis in one dominant religion's doctrines.

While it is important to understand the belief system of the most committed opponents of sexual and reproductive rights, the use of public health information and equity arguments is still an effective strategy with other policymakers who may be more open to rights perspectives. This discussion will focus on two less visible audiences present in many legislatures and government agencies: (1) those who have not given the issues much attention and take the traditional stance as the path of least resistance, and (2) those who are already in favor of sexual and reproductive rights but voice these opinions only behind the scenes.

The first audience may not have seriously examined the issues or may have little information, being politicians, they have taken the safe road, which is usually to espouse the traditional norms. This group may be more open to persuasion by information on the inequitable and public health consequences of repressive laws and norms, especially if public opinion seems to be leaning in the direction of reform. One advocate discussed this group as follows:

> Lack of information plays an important role among decision-makers with regard to reproductive issues in many countries. I have interviewed legislators who have no idea of the implications of passing restrictive laws and have never heard different points of view on abortion. . . . The Catholic Church steps into this information vacuum, bringing their lobbyists to the Congress with sensationalist videos on abortion. Unfortunately, the women's groups don't have the same capacity for reaction and mobilization in any [Latin American] countries.[63]

In this quotation may also be seen the importance of the role of the media in airing diverse points of view and the imbalance in the mobilizing capacity between anti-rights and pro-rights lobbyists. The second audience consists of those legislators and public officials who take rights-affirming stances on sexual and reproductive health issues in private. There are fierce behind-the-scenes disagreements within governmental agencies, political parties, and committees, too often resulting in bland and meaningless consensus statements, or simply in inaction. Anecdotes about these controversies in private conversations are as common as weeds, but how rare it is that such disagreements come into the public light so that the citizenry can somehow weight into the debate! Within most agencies and political parties, the appearance of public consensus is an unquestioned value. As a result, the "legitimate" discourse with guaranteed access to the media is still that of the Catholic Church hierarchies or public figures who agree with them, while the proactive voices in defense of sexual and reproductive rights rarely reach the public eye and ear except when the Church is attacking them. This dynamic accords unequal footing to pro-rights discourses in policy debates, perpetuates the political marginalization of rights advocates, and keeps disagreements among political actors safely behind the scenes.

As long as the political costs of espousing controversial pro-rights proposals remain so high, the most effective short-term political strategy for advocates is to obey the logic of the double discourse system by conducting all negotiations and lobbying behind the scenes, out of the public eye. In both Colombia and Chile, most current advocacy efforts for abortion law reform are low-key and effectively out of sight. Advocates defend this strategy on ethical grounds: in both countries, public debates on abortion have resulted in increased repression of clandestine clinics. This strategy might result in some legal gains, but in the long term it fails to solve the problem of the perceived illegitimacy and immorality of pro-rights stances on these controversial issues in the public realm.

How can the political culture be changed so that bringing these debates into the public view is less costly, both for the advocates and for the men and women who most suffer from the double discourse system? How can the defensive dynamic be turned around, so that the pro-rights forces could play a proactive role in national debates, rather than responding to initiatives that would erode rights even further? It is clear that various advocacy strategies must focus on reducing political risks for potential advocates. One such strategy could be to present rights-affirming voices in the mass media, bringing hitherto private opinions into the open. Increased exposure to the arguments on both sides helps to legitimize the debate itself as well as pro-rights positions, and to reduce the political costs of engaging in debate and taking such positions publicly.

With the same aim, groups in Colombia, Peru, and Chile have used public opinion surveys to legitimize rights perspectives. Surveys can help to persuade politicians that defending rights accords with the views of their constituents and thus might come with fewer political costs than they fear.[64] Complementing these surveys with those conducted by Catholics for the Right to Free Choice might be doubly effective in showing politicians the extent of the distance between the laity and hierarchy within the Church.

In both countries, one of the sources of division within the women's movement on abortion has been precisely their effort to broaden their social base by including more grass-roots and low-income women's organizations. Broadening the coalition that is pro-rights, however, is indeed a promising strategy for civil society groups. The more diverse and broad-based the groups that are supporting rights, the lower the political risk of defending those rights. Although such organizations are much more apt to be ideologically diverse than the feminist NGOs, it is precisely these low-income sectors that suffer the brunt of the negative consequences of rights-denying policies and have the most to gain from policy reform. Therefore, it would be advantageous to create partnerships with subgroups within these organizations, if not with the organization as a whole. In the last six years, many women's organizations and pro-rights public officials have followed the strategy of using the language of consensus documents and conventions signed by the leaders of their country and monitoring the country's progress towards the implementation of the accords. While the Programme of Action from the ICPD and the Platform for Action from the UN Conference on Women in Beijing reflect compromises on some sexual and reproductive rights issues, their recommendations have still proved to be invaluable instruments for advocacy. This strategy is so useful precisely because it legitimates sexual and reproductive health and rights as key policy issues, thus reducing the political risks of advocacy.

For all potential advocates for sexual and reproductive rights, whether in government, civil society, or the Church, the political risks of publicly defending these rights are probably the key obstacle to attaining a critical mass of supporters. It is one thing to agree privately that sexual and reproductive choices should be a matter of personal conscience rather than law and to privately avail oneself of all of the mechanisms to expand such choices. It is a completely different thing to take on the political costs associated with committing oneself wholeheartedly to advocacy on behalf of controversial issues such as depenalization of abortion. Before designing strategies, an important exercise for advocates is to analyze the nature of the risks, as well as the sources, the arguments, and the tactics of attacks. Multifaceted strategies that use a combination of tactics to reduce these risks and effectively counter attacks—e.g., public opinion polls, alliances on other issues, international agreements, partnerships with media, and education of policymakers—are most effective, since such tactics are mutually reinforcing. Analyzing the differences among potential allies is also important in order to approach each of them appropriately. While the double discourse system poses important obstacles to advocacy efforts on behalf of sexual and reproductive rights in many Latin American countries, progress has still been made on key issues such as violence against women and sexual violence. It is to be hoped that rigorous analysis of the nature of political risks, adapting approaches to the diverse audiences for advocacy, and determined outreach to potential partners will bring successes in protecting the full range of sexual and reproductive rights. In the long run, as modern societies become ever more diverse in belief systems and in cultural/religious traditions, there may be less and less acceptance of the undue influence of one religious doctrine on the State. The blurring of the distinction between what is considered immoral and what should be illegal greatly hampers efforts in Latin America to protect sexual and reproductive rights. Acceptance of diversity of opinions and belief systems among citizens of a country, and indeed among the believers in any religion, is one cornerstone of defense of sexual and reproductive rights. Respect for human rights is the other. Sexuality and reproduction are key aspects of human life and welfare, in relation to which governments should carry out their positive duty to promote comprehensive physical, emotional, and social health and well-being. As democratic cultures deepen and take hold, states may not be able to sustain repressive norms that deny essential choices to an ever-diversifying citizenry. In the long run, in democracies, policies that deny the sexual and reproductive rights of all citizens are not sustainable.

Notes

1. Programme of Action of the International Conference on Population and Development, Report of the International Conference on Population and Development, 5–13 September 1994, UN Doc. A/CONF.171/13, para. 7.3. The reservations expressed by Argentina in the recent "Cairo+5" meetings coordinated by UNFPA represent an exception to the general consensus in Latin America.
2. The first quotation is from the ICPD Programme of Action (see note 1), para. 7.3. The second is draft "bracketed" language for the Platform for Action of the Fourth World Conference on Women, September 1995, UN Doc. A/CONF, 177/20 (October 17, 1995), note 22, para. 97.
3. Catholics for Free Choice, *Catholics and Reproduction: A World View* (Washington, D.C.: CFFC, 1994).
4. L. Haas. "The Catholic Church in Chile," in C. Smith and J. Prokopy (eds), *Latin American Religion in Motion* (New York and London: Routledge, 1999), M. Htun, "Democracy, Dictatorship and Gender Rights: Divorce, Abortion and Women's Rights in Argentina, Brazil and Chile," unpublished Ph.D. dissertation, Harvard University, 1999. See also Htun's chapter on divorce in Chile and M. Blofield, The Politics of Abortion in Chilean and Argentina: Public Opinion, Social Actors and Discourse, and Political Agendas, presented at Latin American Studies Association conference, Chicago, September 1998.
5. R. Petchesky, and K. Judd (eds) for the International Reproductive Rights Action Group (IRRRAG), *Negotiating Reproductive Rights* (New York and London: Zed Books, 1998), p. 17.
6. The author worked in these countries from 1992 to 1998 as the Program Officer in charge of the Ford Foundation's Sexual and Reproductive Health Program, based in the Andean Region and Southern Cone office in Santiago, Chile.
7. I am indebted to Mari Luz Silva, Director in the 5th Region of the Ministry of Education in Chile and one of the designers of the government's sex education program, for her thoughts

on Catholic cultures and the double discourse.

8. The Philippines and the Vatican are other notable examples of states heavily influenced by Catholicism. It would be interesting to analyze whether the double discourse system operates in other countries with a hegemonic religion as well.

9. From the author's conversations with members of Católicos por el Derecho a Decidir (Latin American affiliates of Catholics for Free Choice) in six Latin American countries.

10. Koinonia [organization of theologians], *Problemática Religiosa de la Mujer que Aborta* (Bogotá: Universidad Externado de Colombia, 1996). Also presented at a World Health Organization meeting of Latin American researchers on abortion at the Universidad Externado de Colombia, Bogotá, Colombia, November 1994.

11. For an excellent in-depth analysis of the issue of divorce in Chile, see M. Htun (note 4).

12. L. Haas (see note 4) describes how Church officials "collect the bill" (*cobran la cuenta*) in their lobbying of representatives of the Left who received protection from the Church (p. 60).

13. John Paul II's conservative appointments of bishops started during the military dictatorship, strengthening the faction of the Church that was allied with the military government even as progressive sectors of the Church led the efforts to protect human rights. See L. Haas (note 4) and M. Htun (note 4) for a full discussion.

14. The ownership of Chilean newspapers and television stations is concentrated in two large conglomerates and the Catholic Church, all of which tend to have socially conservative editorial policies. See M. Blofield (note 4), p. 22. Uca Silva of Sur Profesionales, Santiago, also analyzes the effect on public debates of this concentration in an unpublished 1996 report to the Ford Foundation's Andean and Southern Cone office.

15. Chile, Malta, and Andorra are the only countries with no divorce law. See M. Htun (note 4).
    The Universal Declaration of Human Rights, G.A. Res. 217A (III), UN GAOR, Res. 71, UN Doc. A/810 (1948), art. 16.1 states that "Men and women of full age, without any limitation due to race, nationality or religion, have the right to marry and to found a family. They are entitled to equal rights as to marriage, during marriage and at its dissolution," thus implicitly recognizing dissolution as part of the right to marriage. Articles 23.2 and 23.4 of the International Covenant on Civil and Political Rights, G. A. Res. 2200 (XXI), U.N. GAOR, 21st Sess., Supp. No. 16, at 49, UN Doc. A/6316 (1966) contain similar language. Applying the logic of implicit recognition, the most recent report of the UN Committee on Human Rights on Chile (CCPR/C/79/Add.104, para. 17) said that the lack of a divorce law might constitute a violation of Article 23. Thanks to Luisa Cabal of the Center for Reproductive Law and Policy and Gaby Oré Aguilar of the Ford Foundation for thoughts and references.

16. Grupo Iniciativa Mujeres; "Encuesta Nacional: Opinión y Actitudes de las Mujeres Chilenas sobre la Condición de Género," January 1999, carried out by Quanta Sociología Aplicada, using a nationally representative urban sample of 1,800 women in 22 cities.

17. M. Aylwin and I. Walker, *The Chilean Family: Aspirations, Realities, and Challenges* (1996), p. 121, quoted in M. Htun (see note 4).

18. This provision has its basis in canon law, in which it was assumed priests would know the situation of couples residing in the same neighborhood well enough to prevent them from being married if there were important impediments, such as too close a relation or an existing spouse. The opinion in the Supreme Court case of Sabioncello con Haussman (March 28, 1932) reads: "It is legitimate to prove the lack of competence of the Official of the Civil Registry by means of the witnesses' testimony [that neither of the spouses lived within the jurisdiction of that official] during the annulment proceedings." Quoted in H. Corral, "Iniciativas Legales sobre Familia y Divorcio," in *Controversia sobre Familia y Divorcio* [Santiago: Ediciones Universidad Católica de Chile, 1997), p. 172.

19. This high rate is explained by both nonformalized unions and adolescent pregnancies. A new law giving children born inside and outside of marriage equal rights and benefits took effect in 1999; see C. Gutierrez, "46% de niños chilenos nacen fuera del matrimonio," 27 October 1999, *La Tercera* [newspaper].

20. M. Htun (see note 4).

21. Meeting with Instituto de la Mujer in Chile in 1996, reporting on research on pensión alimenticia.

22. As established in Article 23.2.4 of the ICCPR (see note 15).

23. There is definitely less stigma attached to advocating for a divorce law, however, than for a law on "therapeutic" abortion, which in current debates in Chile would include legality of abortion in cases of rape, incest, and severe fetal problems.

24. L. Haas (see note 4), p. 60, and M. Htun (see note 4). Htun's chapter on divorce in Chile provides an in-depth analysis of the "reformist coalitions" promoting divorce in the 1990s and of the dynamics within the corps of Christian Democrat legislators.

25. See C. Kraus, "Victoria Would Not Be Amazed by Chile Today," 24 October 1999, New York Times. The new law abolishing legitimacy and a resolution abolishing the law against sodomy were both passed recently. L. Haas (see note 4) also agrees with this assessment, quoting several rightist deputies to document her perception that members of the political right are defecting from their formerly uniform support for the Church's lobbying efforts.

26. María Antonieta Saa, deputy to the Congress, quoted in an unpublished 1997 study by Peruvian sociologist Maruja Barrig, "De Cal y Arena: ONGs y Movimiento de Mujeres en Chile," p. 17.

27. M. Barrig (see note 26), p. 16.

28. Many personal communications from Chilean colleagues between 1992 and 1999.

29. The main sources for this section on Colombia and Chile are the NGO shadow reports for the 20th session of the CEDAW Committee for both countries. Both are available in English and Spanish. For Colombia, see Center for Reproductive Law and Policy (CRLP) and Corporación Casa de la Mujer, Derechos Reproductivos de la Mujer en Colombia: Un Reporte Sombra (New York and Bogotá: CRLP and Corporación Casa de la Mujer, 1998). The Chilean NGO shadow report, The Rights of Women in Chile (New York and Santiago, 1999) was co-written by CRLP, the Comité Latinoamericano y del Caribe para la Defensa de los Derechos de la Mujer (CLADEM), the Foro Abierto de Salud y Derechos Sexuales y Reproductivos, and the Corporación de la Mujer, La Morada.

30. ICPD Programme of Action (see note 1), para. 7.3.

31. Although hospital data on abortion are widely acknowledged to be under-reported, abortion still figures in official data as the first cause of maternal moxtality in seven Latin American Countries, including Chile. See FLACSO (Chile) and Instituto de la Mujer (Spain), Mujeres Latinoamericanas en Cifras: Tomo Comparativo (Santiago, Chile: FLACSO, 1995), p. 131.

32. The list of countries and restrictions is available from the Center for Reproductive Law and Policy at http://www.crlp.org/icpdabortionl.html. In this list, Colombia is counted as a country allowing abortion in cases of threat to the woman's life or physical health, but in fact the law is ambiguous. No. 5, Article 29 in the Colombian Penal Code can be interpreted as depenalizing interruptions of pregnancy in "estado de necesidad" (state of necessity) to protect the life or health of the mother. Protection in these cases is open to interpretation by individual judges and thus is not guaranteed. For a full discussion of the legal situation of abortion in Colombia, see D. Arcila, "El Aborto Voluntario en Colombia: Urgencia de un Abordaje Jurídico Integral," in Perspectivas en Salud y Derechos Sexuales y Reproductivos (Medellín: CERFAMI, 1999), pp. 14–22.

33. Personal communication from Dr. José Barzelatto, Center for Health and Social Policy.

34. Alan Guttmacher Institute, An Overview of Clandestine Abortion in Latin America (New York: Alan Guttmacher Institute, 1996).

35. "Aborto: Informe Especial," Cambio 16, February 1997, 20–23, quoted in D. Arcila (see note 32).

36. L. Zamudio, presentations to the Meeting of Researchers on Induced Abortion in Latin America and the Caribbean at the Universidad Externado, Bogotá, November 1994, and the Latin American and Caribbean Parliamentarians' Meeting on Abortion, Bogotá, October 1998.

37. D. Arcila (see note 32), p. 8.

38. D&C stands for dilation and curettage—that is, the scraping of all remains of the fetus from the uterus in cases of incomplete abortion. The account of forced medication comes from a conversation with the Medellín, Colombia chapter of the National Network for Sexual and Reproductive Rights in the mid-1990s. In the author's experience, the accounts of hostile remarks are almost universal when talking with researchers and activistis who work with the health sector and community groups on the issue of abortion.

39. January 29, 1997 survey by the Centro Nacional de Consultoría, quoted in D. Arcila (see note 32), p. 22.

40. See Grupo Iniciativa Mujeres (note 16).

41. I was first alerted to this issue in a conversation with anthropologist Monica Weisner, the researcher for the Alan Guttmacher study. Most informants in the Chilean women's movement believe that safe clandestine abortion services became scarcer after 1994 than they were previously, and now the clandestine referral networks often have no referrals to offer.

42. In Chile, the author's personal experience shows that a course on Catholic religion is mandatory in all schools, public and private, and can only be taught by instructors certified by a Catholic institute. Parents of children of other faiths must request to be excused from the class and cannot organize an alternative class on, say, world religions.

43. Examples of these ads can also be found in the article "Aborto: ¿Hora de legalizar?" *Semana*, 9–16 February 1993, 41.

44. "Aborto; ¿Hora de legalizar?" (see note 43).

45. The glaring exception to this trend has been the amnesty for the human rights abuses committed during the dictatorship. This amnesty is now, however, subject to serious legal challenges both within Chile and from abroad—most notably in England, where legal proceedings to extradite General Pinochet to Spain have set new precedents in the enforcement of international human rights standards.

46. Lidia Casas, *Women Behind Bars* (New York: Center for Reproductive Law and Policy and Santiago: Open Forum on Reproductive Health and Rights, 1998). A Spanish language edition is also available.

47. Personal communication from José Barzelatto.

48. 98% of all court cases do not result in a sentence. In cases of homicide, 95% of the cases are never solved. Source: Mauricio Rubio, *Crimen sin sumario. Análisis Geoeconómico de la Justicia Colombiana* [Bogotá: Centro de Estudios para el Desarrollo de la Universidad de los Andes (CEDE), 1996]. The *Consejo Superior de Judicatura* disputes this figure and estimates impunity at 60%, which is still extremely high. Personal communication from Carmen Posada, lawyer and Executive Director of CERFAMI (Center of Integrated Resources for Families) in Medellín.

49. In 1991, there were 137 court cases and 29 people imprisoned for abortion in Colombia, see "Aborto: ¿Hora de legalizar?" (note 43). In comparison, the Chilean study (see note 46) shows that 57% of the women who had abortions and whose cases were reviewed spent time in prison, and 36% were held for more than two weeks. The study also reports that 22 women in the small provincial city of Puerto Montt were in jail for abortion at the time of a visit by the Open Forum, a reproductive health NGO network (p. 21). Given that Colombia has 2.6 times the population of Chile, the level of repression in Chile is clearly much higher. Given the high levels of impunity for other crimes in Colombia, however, it is telling that so many women end up in jail for abortion.

50. Many personal communications from Colombian colleagues over the years, most recently from Carmen Posada (see note 48).

51. Author's personal experience through meetings with reproductive and sexual rights groups in Colombia, 1992–1998.

52. Preliminary finding from the author's study of reproductive and sexual rights networks.

53. This campaign took many forms in different cities, since the network is decentralized. The network in Medellín achieved much national press coverage and an outpouring of support from diverse sources for their campaign on the case of Alba Lucia, a poor peasant woman and the victim of a rape that was never proved in court, who accidentally killed her newborn while giving birth in a latrine. Unfortunately, the case suffered a defeat in the higher court, partially because she had never had access to a proper lawyer until the later stages of her case, and also because it was legally a homicide rather than an abortion or rape case. (Personal communications from the network members and Carmen Posada.)

54. Current proposals would allow abortion to save the woman's life and health or in cases of severe fetal defects or rape and incest, under the misnomer of "therapeutic abortion."

55. She regained her seat in the next elections in 1997, however, Mala Htun (personal communication) notes that other sponsors of the bill were not defeated. It would be interesting to analyze what circumstances made her more vulnerable.

56. M. Barrig (see note 26).

57. This was known as the Larrain bill. Personal communication from Josefina Hurtado of the Forum, October 1999.

58. The best-known example from Brazil is that of Sister Yvone Gerbara, who gave an interview to the national magazine *Veja* in which she advocated depenalization of abortion. In Colombia, Alberto Munera, a prominent Jesuit theologian, was deprived of his teaching post in 1995 after he defended ICPD principles on a national television program.

59. This was Dr. Horacio Croxatto from the Instituto Chileno de Medicina Reproductiva (ICMER). Personal communications from Dr. José Barzelatto and several other Chilean colleagues.

60. It would be important to conduct a follow-up study to the 1994 Guttmacher study to verify whether in fact there are fewer providers than before and whether, as a consequence, abortion-related morbidity and mortality has risen.

61. I am indebted to Dr. José Barzelatto for consistently pointing out the importance of this agreement. See "World Religions and the 1994 UN International Conference on Population and Development: A Report on an International and Interfaith Consultation" (Chicago: Park Ridge Center for the Study of Health, Faith, and Ethics, 1994). For a full discussion of increased religious-diversity in Latin America, see C. Smith and J. Prokopy (note 4).

62. According to the 1992 census, about 13.4% of the Chilean population are Evangelical/Protestant, while 76.7% are Catholic. Atheists make up 5.8% of the population, and "other religions" (probably mainly Jewish and Muslim) make up 4.24%. See F. Kamstee.g., "Pentecostalistm and Political Awakening in Pinochet's Chile and Beyond," in C. Smith and J. Prokopy (note 4). More recent studies show an increase in the percentage of Evangelicals to 16% and a decrease in the percentage of Catholics to 72%. See *Diario El Segundo*, 17 December 1998, quoted in a personal communication from Josefina Hurtado.

63. Personal communication from Luisa Cabal, staff attorney, Center for Reproductive Law and Policy.

64. Calandria, a communications NGO in Peru, promoted this strategy, which has also been adopted by the Grupo Impulsora in Peru and the Grupo Iniciativa in Chile, two post-Beijing NGO networks.

13

Sexual Rights in Southern Africa
A Beijing Discourse or a Strategic Necessity?

Barbara Klugman

At the 1995 Fourth World Conference on Women (FWCW) in Beijing, the international community agreed that human rights include the right of women to control over their sexuality.[1] Although the terminology is contested, this principle is frequently encapsulated as "sexual rights." Using the southern African region as a case study, this chapter explores varying interpretations of sexual rights and the extent to which the concept has significance beyond the rhetorical agreement reached in Beijing. The chapter is written from the perspective that sexual rights ought to encompass the conditions that allow for gender equality to be present in sexual relationships and for sexuality to become a positive and pleasurable component of human experience. Sexual rights matter because they are central to the achievement of social justice. The achievement of sexual rights requires gender equality in cultural and social systems, as well as in economic systems. Thus, they frequently serve as a pivot around which civil, political, social, and economic rights interact.

While sexual rights are relevant to a wide range of health and human rights issues, this chapter focuses on HIV/AIDS because HIV/AIDS policies and informational materials provide a targeted opportunity to interrogate international, regional, and national approaches to gender equality, sex, and sexuality. In addition, as HIV/AIDS has become a threat to the economic and social functioning of many countries, it provides an entry point for bringing questions of sexuality and sexual power relations into the public arena.

The chapter draws on the author's personal experience as a participant in the debates on sexual rights at the 1994 International Conference on Population and Development (ICPD) in Cairo, the FWCW, and the ICPD+5 review

271

process, and as the director of an NGO that focuses on rights and health.[2] It also draws upon the relevant policies of the Southern African Development Community (SADC) and policies and information, education, and communication (IEC) materials of various member states. It focuses particularly on Botswana, South Africa, and Swaziland, since the very diverse political histories of these countries—Botswana is a long-standing democracy, South Africa has recently emerged from a human rights struggle, and Swaziland is a monarchy with government straddling traditional and parliamentary systems—offer some insight into the policy differences within the region.

The drafting of consensus language of international agreements is frequently and incorrectly presumed to be a one-way process controlled by international players. In fact, however, it is individual countries or alliances that bring the issues to the agenda at the outset. Therefore, it is important to ask not to what extent the debates and agreements regarding sexual rights in Beijing were later taken up in the SADC region, but rather to what extent the concept and terminology of sexual rights are part of SADC policy and of the policy and practice of its member states, and to what extent this practical experience can contribute to further processes of consensus development at an international level.

HIV/AIDS and Sexual Rights in Southern Africa

Women in general, especially young women, are particularly vulnerable to HIV/AIDS in the region. This results to some extent from biology but predominantly from the interaction of poverty and culture, an interaction that is consolidated within the dynamic of sexual interaction. We see in Southern African countries a "traditional" cultural practice in which men have the right to make all decisions regarding sexual relations. If a husband initiates sex, his wife may not refuse him; the same applies in relationships outside of marriage. This makes it impossible for women to protect themselves from HIV/AIDS by initiating non-penetrative sex, for example, or insisting on fidelity or condom use. Women are, of course, also products of this culture and may themselves have internalized ideas of manhood that make it appropriate for men to have many partners and to manage sexual relations while they accept their partners' dominance and remain faithful. Within the economic system, women have unequal access to ownership of productive resources in the form of land, credit, or jobs within the formal sector—particularly jobs beyond the unskilled level. This reinforces their dependence on men and their inability to refuse unsafe sex. At times it leads women to engage in transactional sex—one man providing food, another clothing, and so on—to make financial ends meet.

Young people, too, tend to believe that men have a need for sex and the right to coerce women into sex. There is little discourse about women's sexual needs or rights.[3] Young women are pushed to engage in sexual relationships not only by male coercion, but also at times by their own need for resources. The "sugar daddy" syndrome epitomizes this dynamic, but it is not the only expression of it. For example, a study of in- and out-of-school youth in the Manzini and Lubombo regions of Swaziland found that 38.3% of boys said that they believed that in sexual relationships girls expected money, 18.1% said girls expected sex, and only 5.5% said girls expected fidelity. When girls were asked what they believed were the reasons girls have sexual relations, 29.9% said that "girls want money from their boyfriends," while 13.9% said girls "cannot refuse proposals."[4] Here, too, a complex interaction of economic subordination and cultural subordination in sexual relations places women at greater risk of HIV than men.

The absence of sexual rights within a society reflects a fundamental failure within that society. Fraser argues that women in cultures around the world are a "despised gender."[5] To address the cultural domination of women by men, manifested in a lack of civil and political rights, women would have to be revalued. However, civil and political recognition alone is not enough to achieve sexual rights. Also necessary would be the redistribution of access to such necessities as credit and inheritance, as well as of responsibility for such activities as domestic work and childcare, so that they are shared equally between women and men.[6]

The remainder of this chapter is composed of three sections, the first exploring the different assumptions underlying the positions of major interest groups on the language and content of sexual rights in the negotiations at the ICPD and the FWCW, focusing particularly on the positioning of Africa in this debate.[7] The second section explores to what extent the principles of sexual rights are embedded in SADC policies and the practices of member states. This approach will help to illuminate the interactive process through which international, regional, and national policy and practice develop over time, and to explore how experience at one level may be used to push forward consensus at other levels. These two sections explore similar categories of issues but focus on diverse content within each category, given the different nature of the arguments and policies surrounding complex issues at the international, regional, and national levels. The second section also includes an examination of the implementation of specific portions of Paragraph 96 of the Beijing Platform for Action. The third section briefly addresses prospects for moving from the current focus on absence of rights toward acceptance of sexual pleasure as a component of sexual rights.

Assumptions Underlying Sexual Rights at the International Level

Gender Equality

As already discussed, gender inequality is at the base of inequality in heterosexual relationships. The countries of the world accepted this principle and the need to promote equality between men and women in all sectors at the ICPD and the FWCW. Yet despite this recognition of the impact of gender inequality on sexual relations, there was no attempt to further conceptualize or develop action plans in this area. There is still a critical need to conceptualize and elaborate actions to promote sexual rights.

The Language of Sexual Rights

The term "sexual rights" was first put on the international agenda by advocates from the international women's health movement during the preparations for the ICPD. Although it was ultimately not incorporated into the ICPD Programme of Action, the consensus reached on the existence and meaning of reproductive rights as including the "right to make decisions concerning reproduction free of discrimination, coercion and violence" was an achievement in itself.[8] The conference also reached consensus on the existence and meaning of sexual health, and the Programme of Action alludes to sexual rights, although arguably it does not specify that sexual relations themselves should be free of discrimination, coercion, and violence. The ICPD Programme of Action also contains detailed descriptions and proposals regarding sexual rights. For example, in relation to violence, it promotes sexual rights by committing countries to "take full measures to eliminate all forms of exploitation, abuse, harassment and violence against women, adolescents and children."[9] In relation to HIV/AIDS and violence, it talks about the need for "integral sexual education and health services for young people."[10]

It is not surprising that consensus could be achieved at the ICPD regarding the language of reproductive rights but not sexual rights. The victory for reproductive rights was won through a complex alliance between women's rights and health advocates and the population establishment. Despite divergences in the meanings attributed to reproductive rights and the disclaimers that implementation would be guided by national laws and cultural and religious contexts, the coalition was broad enough to win international consensus for this terminology.[11]

Having achieved consensus on reproductive rights and sexual and reproductive health at the ICPD, delegations won agreement that the language of the Cairo document could not be renegotiated at the FWCW. Country delegations, both independently and as a result of NGO input, seized this opportunity to cover new ground and once again tabled the terminology of "sexual rights" in the preparations for the FWCW. At the FWCW itself, sexual rights became the focus of one of the central debates. After a lengthy and heated discussion, consensus was reached on a wording that encapsulated the content of sexual rights without using the actual terminology:

> The human rights of women include their right to have control over and decide freely and responsibly on matters related to their sexuality, in-

cluding sexual and reproductive health, free of coercion, discrimination and violence. Equal relationships between women and men in matters of sexual relations and reproduction, including full respect for the integrity of the person, require mutual respect, consent and shared responsibility for sexual behaviour and its consequences.[12]

What did different countries mean by this language, and why did they take positions for and against? The following broad categorizations cover some of the main debates at Beijing.

Talking about Sex and Sexuality

Some countries held that the term "sexual rights" implied the right to sex, meaning promiscuity, the right of people to have sex with whomever they desired (including children), and, at moments of tension in the negotiations, bestiality. In part this interpretation was the result of conceptual problems in the translation process, since the nuances of meaning are different across languages. However, it was also the result of discomfort with discussing sex and sexuality. This position was held predominantly by countries with governments espousing fundamentalist religious values and was linked to the doctrinal base underlying these countries' approach to sexual relations. Every effort was made by the group advocating this position, both in Cairo and later during the ICPD+5 process, to ensure that the documents referred only to sexual health services or care.

Impact of Religion

The approach discussed above was based on interpretations of religious texts, rather than on an assessment of current issues faced by women and children in their countries. Fears were expressed from a religious perspective that sexual rights might undermine family relations. This position built on earlier debates on reproductive rights in which these countries favored the rights of the couple, but not those of the individual, to decide on matters of reproduction. At the heart of this debate is the question of whether women should be allowed the right to make decisions regarding their sexual and reproductive capacity independently of their partners and, indeed, their families. Freedman argues that in this position, women's desire for these rights is seen not as a normal aspiration but rather as a rebellion against national, ethnic, or religious identity.[13]

Development Priorities

The other substantive argument against sexual rights at the FWCW was that such issues were Western constructs out of touch with the immediate reality of poverty in developing countries. For example, in a small group discussion among countries holding opposing positions on sexual rights, the ambassador of Benin argued that in developing countries people were concerned with the burning issues of poverty and unemployment, not with issues such as violence against women. Other delegations—for example, from Morocco—argued that some problems in countries arguing for sexual rights, such as high rates of teenage pregnancy, incest, and violence against women, were not found in their countries, and hence were not high on their agenda. Their argument was that, since international agreements need to be responsive to the reality of all countries, sexual rights issues should therefore not be addressed.

On the other hand, the official African position—generated in an Organisation of African Unity (OAU) meeting of African ministers in preparation for the FWCW, and represented by Senegal, the leader of the OAU at the time—argued on the basis of national realities and priorities in favor of the language of sexual rights. African ministers had accepted the terminology of sexual rights on the basis of its importance in the context of HIV/AIDS and violence on the continent. They recognized that addressing unequal sexual power relations between men and women was a central pre-requisite for preventing HIV/AIDS and responding to violence against women and, further, that both HIV/AIDS and violence placed substantial constraints on Africa's development goals. As a result, although some African countries, such as Benin and Morocco, argued vocally against sexual rights, the official African position was for sexual rights. Delegates from a number of African countries, most notably Ghana, Cameroon, and some SADC member states, consistently supported the Senegalese delegate on this point.

Ultimately, sexual rights took prominence in Beijing as a topic of serious negotiation because so many non-Western groups supported the language. The African position in support of sexual rights, the willingness of many delegates from other southern countries at the Conference (particularly from the Caribbean) to speak explicitly for this position, and the presence of an organized lobby for sexual rights made up of NGOs from both North and South, such as Health, Empowerment, Rights and Accountability (HERA), undermined the fundamentalist argument that sexual rights was a Western construct irrelevant to developing countries. If the sexual rights language had been supported only by the European Union and Western NGOs, with a few other Western allies, global support would have been much weaker.

Addressing Discrimination on the Basis of Sexual Orientation

Another position during the FWCW debates, held by the countries of the European Union in particular, was to support the language of sexual rights because it implied freedom from discrimination on the basis of sexual orientation. At the start of negotiations in Beijing, freedom from discrimination on the basis of sexual orientation was made explicit in the text, but few believed it would remain there after negotiations. In the end, it was taken out despite eloquent and emotional arguments for its retention from a number of governments—predominantly, however, from the West. South Africa was the only African country to speak for its inclusion. Thus, while commitment to the terminology of sexual rights was shared by the majority of delegates, interpretation as to its meaning differed. Had the African delegations understood sexual rights to mean rights to gay relationships, they would have retracted their support as a result of their own prejudices. The European delegates, on the other hand, unable to conceptualize sexual rights beyond the limited aspect of discrimination on the basis of sexual orientation, could not provide substantive support to the other delegations supporting this language. As a result, the pro-sexual rights delegates could not muster adequate support to get the terminology of sexual rights retained in the document. The extent of support for sexual rights did, however, allow delegates to negotiate a paragraph outlining the broad content of sexual rights that is loose enough to allow different interpretations.[14]

Are Sexual Rights a New Human Right?

In addition to substantive arguments, the debate also included a procedural argument: that including the concept of sexual rights in the text would mean creating a new right. Those against the concept used this as their fallback position. This position, however, was weak, given the agreement in Cairo that the use of the language of reproductive rights did not create new rights within the UN system, but rather worked to ensure that the interpretation of existing rights extended into the areas of family and reproductive relations. In Beijing, sexual rights advocates extended this principle to argue that sexual rights would not create any new rights, rather, the concept would extend international human rights protection to the terrain of sexuality.

From International to Regional: A Case Study of Southern Africa

This section takes up the diverse interpretations and concerns regarding sexual rights expressed in Beijing, as presented in the above categories, to consider their relevance and meanings both in SADC as a legal entity and in member states, using examples from different member states. In doing so, it attempts to assess the linkages between international and national concerns, as well as between policy and implementation. It examines both the use of the words "sexual rights" and the extent to which the diverse meanings of the phrase are addressed in policy and practice. As indicated above, any discussions of sexual rights must be premised on an understanding of the need for gender equality. Since interest in gender equality cannot be assumed in any country, it is necessary to begin this exploration of SADC policy regarding sexual rights by looking at its approach to gender equality.

Gender Equality

SADC policies generally promote gender equality and require member states to do the same. In February 1997, the SADC Council of Ministers passed a Declaration on Gender and Development that established a policy framework for mainstreaming gender in all SADC activities and strengthening the efforts of member countries to achieve gender equality.[15] The Declaration stipulates that "gender equality is a fundamental human right" and resolves to "ensure the eradication of all gender inequalities in the region."[16] It includes a redistributive component, including a commitment to improving women's access to and control over productive resources.[17] It also contains a revaluation or recognition component, including commitments to ensure women's equal political representation and to change laws and social practices that discriminate against women.[18]

On September 14, 1997, SADC passed an addendum to this Declaration entitled The Prevention and Eradication of Violence Against Women and Children, which commits to eradication of "norms, religious beliefs, practices and stereotypes which legitimize and exacerbate the persistence and tolerance of violence against women."[19]

While all SADC states accept the discourse of gender equality, in some states the law nonetheless continues to consider women as minors.[20] For example, Swaziland's National Development Strategy recognizes that minority status puts women in a position where they "cannot decide about their lives, which includes reproductive health and sexuality," but the country continues to retain minor legal status for women.[21] This contradiction between broad policy declarations of gender equality and laws that retain women as minors is found in a number of SADC member states. Partly it is due to a time lag, since most SADC countries have re-evaluated or are currently re-evaluating laws and policies that deny women's human rights, but it also demonstrates contradictions within government structures, with some sectors and machineries giving priority to gender equality and others ignoring or avoiding it.

Some countries use the language of gender equality more explicitly than others. Mozambique, for example, is implementing programs to institutionalize government capacity to promote gender equality. Many countries have or are developing specific policies on gender. The translation of gender equality concerns into health concerns is not, however, very systematic. This can be seen in a comparison of South African and Botswanan policies on the one hand and Namibian policies on the other. The first two commit to gender equality, the former in its overall development policy and the latter in its Policy on Women in Development.[22] Both extrapolate from these commitments to their HIV/ AIDS policies.[23] In contrast, the Namibian gender policy commits to addressing the linkages between gender inequality and health, but its National Strategic Plan on HIV/AIDS fails to note the need to approach men and women in different ways or to challenge gender inequality, even in its sections on IEC.[24]

These inconsistencies (sometimes between and often within countries) reflect the ongoing realities concerning policymaking and implementation. In the case of Namibia, for example, a policy analysis would likely reveal that activists on gender equality, both within and outside of the government, had been engaged in the development of Namibia's gender policy, whereas more traditional health professionals had been responsible for developing the HIV/AIDS strategic plan. Identifying and understanding the sources of contradictions in policy is important for developing strategies to promote change.

Talking about Sex and Sexuality

In Beijing, a number of SADC member states were uncomfortable with references to sex or sexuality which went beyond the context of provision of sexual health services. It seems, however, that the architects of SADC member states' policies and IEC materials are comfortable using this language in a number of ways, although contradictions abound. Botswana's National Action Plan for Youth mentions a need for "culture sensitive health information dissemination" and recognizes the reality of secrecy and discomfort in communicating on health issues, especially between parents and children, but offers no guidance on the extent to which such cultural sensitivities should be accommodated or challenged.[25] Awareness of the need to approach sensitive matters in a culturally acceptable style can be seen clearly in such IEC materials as the Lesotho government pamphlet "Women and AIDS," which provides necessary information but also opens with a letter addressing women as "My children" and signed "from Granny (Nkhono)," drawing on the tradition that elders' voices have greater authority and credibility.[26]

Outside of government, religious discomfort with talking about sex has been a major barrier to the realization of sexual rights. The HIV/AIDS pandemic is, however, beginning to challenge this problem. For example, Reverend Nangula Kathindi, a member of the Namibian National Multi-Sectoral AIDS Co-ordination Committee (NAMA-COC) by virtue of her recent appointment as general-secretary of the Council of Churches in Namibia, stated publicly: "People are dying of AIDS because we are not willing to discuss sex. We cannot hide behind the Bible. Encouraging member churches to open up to new teachings on sexuality and HIV/AIDS is a priority. We cannot afford to condemn anyone because everyone is made in the image of God, whether or not they go to Church."[27] The cultural influence of the churches renders this recognition significant. Increasing the ability to talk about sex is but one of many challenges facing organized religion in addressing HIV/AIDS in the SADC countries.

Impact of Religion

Most populations of SADC countries are religious. Christianity is the predominant organized religion, although many citizens simultaneously hold to traditional spiritual frameworks. The discomfort of Christianity with sex and sexuality has meant that governments have understood HIV/AIDS prevention from the very beginning in terms of moral fundamentalism, although ironically this has not prevented them from promoting condom use. The message of "ABC: abstain, be faithful, and condomize" is the central conceptual framework for IEC in the SADC member states, as elsewhere in Africa, found on billboards, in pamphlets, and on the radio. For example, South African President Mbeki's call for a Partnership Against AIDS, argues: "You have the right to live your life the way you want to. But I appeal to the young people, who represent our country's future, to abstain from sex for as long as possible. If you decide to engage in sex, use a condom. In the same way, I appeal to both men and women to be faithful to each other, but otherwise to use condoms."[28] The Botswana HIV and AIDS Plan provides for IEC covering "delay of sex initiation and adoption of abstinence," to be achieved in part through strengthening "the provision of moral education" and "empowering adolescents through Family Life Education to resist early sexual activities and practice safer sex."[29]

We may assume that, in the absence of this religious context, the approach to HIV/AIDS prevention would be directed more to the actual causes of current sexual behaviors, at both economic and cultural levels. The Swaziland strategic plan, however, notes: "Condoms are by far the only available device that could help this country to reduce the spread of HIV/AIDS/STDs. The use of condoms is not acceptable to the majority of people. Culture and religion are cited as the driving force that makes people reject condom use."[30] IEC messages throughout the region continue to promote abstinence and faithfulness messages simultaneously with condom messages. There seems to be no attempt to understand the social norm that religious populations have sexual relationships in violation of religious mores. Further, there has been very little recognition of the internal contradiction within the "ABC" message, which in one sentence tells people to abstain or be faithful and in another tells them to use a condom, recognizing that they are in fact unlikely to abstain or be faithful. It seems that lip-service to the moral values of abstaining or being faithful must be maintained in order to avoid acknowledging the reality of extensive premarital and extramarital sexual relations. Since the IEC messages have not even attempted to understand the factors motivating sexual behavior, it should come as no surprise that there is a high awareness of HIV in most SADC countries, but inadequate behavior change.

Development Priorities

In Beijing, some SADC member states questioned the relevance of sexual rights to developing countries. On the other hand, the SADC and its member states have recognized HIV/AIDS, and the sexual behaviors that are the immediate cause of transmission, to be both the result of poverty and a threat to the maintenance of development achievements.[31]

The HIV/AIDS plans of most member states recognize the need to address both poverty and HIV/AIDS because poverty, within a context of gender inequality, has catalyzed the rapid spread of the disease. For example, the Botswana HIV/AIDS plan includes attention to provision of credit facilities and income-generating activities for both youth and women, as well as the need to support projects which give commercial sex workers alternative sources of income.[32] IEC materials identify a range of contexts and activities that highlight the lack of sexual rights, such as peer pressure, exposure to "situations such as gang rapes," and the fact that "girls living in a poor family can have relationship [sic] with older men for economic reasons."[33] One IEC pamphlet produced by the government of Lesotho exhorts women to help other women who are jobless and to initiate programs to prevent teenage pregnancies and unemployment for girls.[34]

Thus, to return to Fraser's analysis, HIV/AIDS strategies in SADC countries are often redistributive, recognizing the need to redress women's poor economic position because it makes them vulnerable to exploitative sexual relations and thus increases their risk of HIV transmission. This approach has become increasingly institutionalized. The SADC Health Ministers' meeting in Maputo in 1999 reoriented the SADC institutional response to HIV/AIDS, directing that its existing task force, which comprises only health sector representatives, be broadened to include other relevant sectors. This move may foster greater recognition of the need to address women's economic empowerment as part of an HIV/AIDS prevention strategy, thereby helping to promote an inclusive sexual rights approach. At the level of member states, some countries already have detailed plans to be executed by different sectors of government, others are in the process of reorienting towards a multisectoral strategy.

Addressing Discrimination on the Basis of Sexual Orientation

In Beijing, the issue of sexual orientation remained a subtext in the discussion on sexual rights, since so many countries—particularly the African bloc—would have withdrawn their support for the language of sexual rights if the phrase had been explicitly interpreted as including freedom from discrimination on the basis of sexual orientation. Nevertheless, Paragraph 96, construed broadly, can be understood to allow this interpretation. How, then, have the SADC countries approached the question of sexual orientation?

Of all SADC member states, only South Africa explicitly guarantees against discrimination on the basis of sexual orientation.[35] There is full legal recognition of gay and lesbian identity, and gay and lesbian groups have mobilized around a human rights discourse. Recently, the economic discrimination faced by gay and lesbian people has been recognized, leading to attempts towards redistribution—for example, to grant same-sex partners the same medical and life insurance benefits as heterosexual married partners. This reorientation has extended into certain parts of the religious community; Nobel Peace Prize winner Archbishop Desmond Tutu, for example, has advocated internationally for the ordination of gay priests in the Anglican church. Nonetheless, South African HIV/AIDS IEC materials make no effort to explicitly address gay people or to promote acceptance of gay relationships.

In other SADC countries, the battle for legal recognition of gay men and lesbians is ongoing.[36] In recent years there has been a spate of pronouncements by African politicians against homosexuality.[37] In Zimbabwe, one activist sums up President Mugabe's position as follows: he does not mind if homosexuals "do it in private, it's when they try to organize themselves that he objects."[38] This raises the question of to what extent the vitriol against homosexuals is a response to the public mobilization of gay people around recognition of gay identity in the past decade. The presence of gay rights organizations in these countries is a challenge to the policy-level denial that gay people live in these countries. Stigmatization is not, however, the whole picture in SADC countries. A review of some HIV/AIDS materials from a number of countries indicates substantial differences in practical approaches to homosexuality in relation to HIV/AIDS prevention. For example, although the president of Namibia has argued that homosexuals should be condemned, materials in the Namibian life skills program directed at children in the school system acknowledge homosexuality and argue that ". . . you are born with these attractions. Gay people face different life style choices than heterosexual people and their choices should be accepted and respected."[39] To some extent, this definition recognizes homosexual identity, in that it does not describe homosexuality as a matter of choice. This contrast suggests that, despite the public position of the President, Namibian policymakers are open to recognizing different sexual orientations.

Occasionally, HIV/AIDS prevention activities in SADC countries recognize same-sex sexual practice as distinct from homosexual identity—for example, a Botswanan pamphlet describing why anal sex is risky, presumably predominantly a reference to homosexual practice.[40] On the other hand, other materials further stigmatize homosexual relationships. For example, a pamphlet on women and HIV/AIDS from Lesotho fails to specify why anal sex can be dangerous, instead suggesting that it is homosexual relations themselves that are dangerous.[41]

This brief review shows that public statements by political leaders in the SADC countries do not always accord with actual policy. When they provide information about homosexual identity or about anal sex, countries are acknowledging the reality that their populations include people having sex with same-sex partners.[42] Just as HIV/AIDS has pushed many countries to break the barriers around discussion of sex and sexual relations with young people, so it may provide an entry point for recognizing homosexuality within countries of the region.

Are Sexual Rights a New Human Right?

SADC states did not engage in the debates in Cairo and Beijing about whether the terminology of sexual rights was creating a new right. The SADC Declaration on Gender and Development, however, does use the wording of "sexual rights" once, committing SADC and member states to "Recognising, protecting and promoting the reproductive and sexual rights of women and the girl child."[43] The use of this language is significant in that it indicates that the language itself is acceptable to the SADC community. The language is not, however, common currency within all SADC countries, and it may be used differently by different actors. This policy was developed by human rights and women's rights activists, while health policies continue to be framed by health professionals whose discourse does not include rights language.[44] However, the fact that those in the health field are wholeheartedly promoting reproductive rights just five years after Cairo is an achievement in itself.[45]

SADC member states do not use the term "sexual rights" in their policies, and not all refer to "reproductive rights." Yet, as will be discussed below, all promote some dimensions of sexual rights. Thus the oblique language of Beijing's Paragraph 96 parallels the situation on the ground in Southern Africa: there is commitment to the concept of sexual rights in broad terms but little use of the term. Since many SADC countries are currently revisiting their HIV/AIDS policies, it will be interesting to monitor the extent to which the words "sexual rights" appear in future policy and programmatic work.

The Relevance of Paragraph 96

This section examines policy at the SADC level and in diverse SADC member states in relation to various components of the "sexual rights" paragraph in the Beijing Platform of Action.

"Free of Coercion, Discrimination and Violence"

The SADC Declaration on Gender and Development and the Addendum on violence both require interventions at the legislative, social service, and educational levels to remove discrimination against women, to empower them, to promote and protect their human rights, and to take action against perpetrators of gender-based violence while providing support to those who have been abused.[46] The Strategic Plan of the SADC AIDS and STD Programme likewise recognizes the linkages between women's position and violence as contributing factors to the rapid spread of HIV, as well as the need to review cultural issues to inform further action, although specific details are not provided.[47]

Most SADC countries have or are currently considering legislation regarding women's legal status and specific issues concerning violence against women and children. HIV/AIDS policies throughout the SADC region recognize the linkage between coercion, discrimination, and violence and women's vulnerability to HIV transmission. However, while there is a broad commitment to ensuring that women are "free of coercion, discrimination and violence," the depth of this commitment varies among countries, as does its link to sexual relations of different kinds. Swaziland, for example, provides no actions to address women's vulnerability.[48] On the other hand, Botswana distinguishes between obligatory, coercive, commercial, and recreational sex and provides policy, institutional, and service-related interventions in relation to each.[49]

"Equal Relationships and Shared Responsibility"

Less clear is the position of SADC countries on "equal relationships between women and men in matters of sexual relations and reproduction, including full respect for the integrity of the person" and the "mutual respect, consent and shared responsibility for sexual behaviour and its consequences" that these require.[50] The policies and IEC materials of member states are generally very ambivalent in this regard, and there are vast differences between countries, particularly in the extent of gaps between policy and action.

Swaziland and Lesotho, for example, identify the problem of unequal power relations between men and women but provide no strategies to address it.[51] Botswana's plan, in contrast, can be read as a sexual rights strategy in that it identifies the linkages between poverty, sexual behavior patterns, and women's lack of power and specifies prevention strategies to address these problems, including an explicit recommendation to empower women "for more effective participation in decision-making about safer sex."[52]

"Mutual Respect and Consent"

While in many ways Botswana seems to be further along than other member states with regard to sexual rights, its approach is not entirely consistent. Its plan also presents the strategy of "encouraging men to use their authority and power in sexual and family relationships responsibly and positively to protect themselves, their partners and families from infection, through targeted education activities."[53] Conspicuously absent is the goal of building mutuality in sexual decision-making. One might argue that this strategy is designed to be pragmatic in that it promotes responsibility without attempting to challenge the more fundamental human rights abuse of gender inequality. The juxtaposition of the two strategies does indicate that the focus is on limiting the spread of HIV rather than on promoting sexual rights overall—that sexual rights are being promoted only to facilitate prevention of the spread of HIV. In fact, there is an unresolved ambivalence regarding the role of men and culture, relative to the problem of inequality in sexual relations, in most SADC-country policies. The South African policy, for example, strives to offer "facts," leaving cultural norms unchallenged: "While such education will endeavour to be sensitive to the moral and cultural ethos of different communities, it will, nevertheless, ensure that factual information is provided to the youth."[54] It fails to offer an alternative cultural ethos that would promote equality in sexual decision-making. In the Botswana plan, strategies for addressing "obligatory sex" in marriage and established relationships focus on strengthening the family and traditional values and on promoting men's role and responsibilities in reproductive health.[55] Nowhere does it specify that women's subordinate roles in traditional practice must also be challenged. Thus the plan unrealistically proposes contradictory strategies to promote women's status and participation in politics and the economy, on the one hand, and to strengthen men's traditional role in the family, on the other. Many other policies and materials promote a focus on men and men's access to services without attempting to redress the unequal power relations between men and women in Southern Africa. Most interventions are "gender-blind"—for example, the South African policy, which addresses youth without specifying the differential experiences and power of young men and women.[56] Likewise, in Botswana, HIV/AIDS pamphlets describe the right to say no and the importance of "you and your partner" working together to prevent HIV/AIDS or sharing responsibility for using condoms.[57] They fail, however, to acknowledge women's vulnerability or to warn that it is common for men to abuse or beat up their female partners for suggesting condom use. Some IEC materials do discuss the different experiences of men and women, but generally they too fail to address the ability of men and women to promote mutual respect and equality and shared responsibility. For example, a Swazi NGO pamphlet contains a case study that encourages a woman to leave her relationship if her boyfriend won't use a condom, but fails to suggest ways of building mutual communication and shared responsibility.[58] In general, such pamphlets neither promote nor build skills to move towards gender equality in sexual relations.

Some peer education materials assert rights in this context.[59] For example, one brochure states that "women have the right to protect their health by having safer sex"—although they usually fail to advocate explicitly for a change in men's behavior and in power relations between women and men.[60] One exception is a South African training manual on sexual rights, which explicitly guides participants through a process of exploring their experience of "saying no" or of having been refused sex and identifying steps that they could take to prevent negative outcomes.[61] This approach indicates a recognition that mutual respect and equality cannot be achieved solely by asserting the right to equality or women's right to protect their health—that, in fact, all individuals need opportunities to explore how to claim these rights.

Beyond Beijing: The Right to Sexual Pleasure

From the above review, it is clear that the dominant discourse on sexuality within southern Africa attempts to deny it, avoid it, cover it in latex, or protect women from coercion, rather than recognizing it as a dimension of human experience—a dimension that can and should provide richness and fulfillment in addition to satisfying a reproductive function. This latter approach would allow enjoyment of sexuality to replace anti-sex morality as the entry point for addressing HIV prevention. It would promote women's right to sexual decision-making as part of this approach.

The international consensus has gone as far in its definition of reproductive health as including a statement that "people are able to have a safe and satisfying sex life."[62] Sexual pleasure for its own sake, however, is not yet on the international agenda. HERA, one of the international NGOs that lobbied for the sexual rights terminology in Cairo and Beijing, has provided a definition of sexual rights that reaches much farther than simply protecting women from harm, toward creating the conditions in which sexuality and sexual experience can be positive and pleasurable. HERA's approach is positive rather than negative. Rather than seeking a commitment to sexual rights solely to avoid discrimination or prevent the spread of HIV/AIDS, HERA argues that sexual rights are valuable in their own right. In their definition, "[s]exual rights are a fundamental element of human rights. They encompass the right to experience a pleasurable sexuality, which is essential in and of itself and, at the same time, is a fundamental vehicle of communication and love between people. Sexual rights include the right to liberty and autonomy in the responsible exercise of sexuality."[63] To what extent, then, is this perspective on the agenda in Southern Africa?

Currently in SADC countries the discourse of sexuality requires men to show their masculinity by having sex at a young age and with many women. Women, in contrast, are not expected to flaunt their sexuality, but rather to satisfy men. This principle is most graphically demonstrated in the common practice of using vaginal drying agents, which dry the vagina to simulate virginity and provide men with a tight sheath.[64] A wet vagina has been constructed as a sign of promiscuity rather than of normal sexual desire. The drying agents not only mean that sex is painful for women, but they also damage the vaginal walls, thus increasing women's vulnerability to transmission of STDs, including HIV. Jackson points out that both men and women may be ignorant of the signs of female arousal or about female orgasm and that women may not feel entitled to pleasure.[65] Yet IEC materials provide no information on pleasurable sexual relations, nor do they challenge the sexual power relations implicated in the practice of dry sex and the consequences for women's experience of sex. The Botswanan pamphlet for youth on HIV/AIDS lists as one explanation of why women are particularly vulnerable "the use of drying or tightening agents into the vagina in order to increase male sexual pleasure."[66] It makes no attempt to challenge men's expectations of a dry vagina or women's concern to please men in this way.

Some SADC countries are beginning to table the question of sexual pleasure. Namibia's National Gender Policy and Plan of Action on Gender uses the Cairo language, saying that "[r]eproductive health means that women and men are able to have a safe and satisfying sex life."[67] Just as significantly, Swaziland's strategic plan includes "poor quality of sexual experience" as a problem in its analysis of factors causing the HIV/AIDS epidemic. However, it presents no strategies or interventions to address this issue.

The absence of a chapter on sexuality in the Swaziland training guide for teachers on HIV/AIDS highlights this gap. This potentially useful guide covers biological development and substantial information on HIV/AIDS and discusses to a limited extent the reality of gender inequality. The chapter on sexuality describes the physical, psychological, and social changes associated with adolescence but does not provide teachers with any information on sexuality itself. The diagram in that chapter on female reproductive organs is a case in point. While ovary, vagina, and even urethra are marked, the clitoris is not.[68]

A South African government pamphlet on HIV/AIDS and relationships redefines sex as not being limited to penetration, although its purpose is only to promote safer sex by presenting sex without penetration or "contact with body fluids" as alternatives to condom use. It instructs readers to "find out other ways to have safer sex," but does not encourage finding other safe ways to enjoy sexual pleasure or to explore other ways of enjoying each others' bodies—a step that would have begun to challenge current approaches to sex. Despite an overall tendency within the region to avoid addressing sex as it relates to pleasure and to focus instead on danger, there are some positive approaches. For example, an HIV/AIDS prevention training manual targeting women in Botswana provides a diagram that includes the position of the clitoris and a short explanation of its role in sexual pleasure.[69] Namibia's life skills training material acknowledges masturbation as "a normal sexual behaviour and the safest form of sex."[70] In the section on condoms, it says that "It is important that girls know how to assist boys with putting on a condom. The idea is to make condom use part of the sexual play rather than a step which interrupts the sex play."[71]

The existence of these materials suggests that there are openings that could be used to help redefine assumptions about the nature and purpose of sex. One initiative explicitly promoting such a change in paradigm is the Sexual Rights Campaign being run by a consortium of NGOs in South Africa, which seeks to bring together mutuality, choice, and pleasure in sexual relations.[72] It suggests "love play—that is, having sex without penetration. Examples are 'ukusoma' or thigh sex, masturbating each other, hugging and cuddling, body massage, kissing or stroking."[73] It also offers case studies that explore diverse negative experiences, including not only sexual violence but also discrimination on the basis of sexual orientation. Finally, it engages participants in a process of articulating their own responses to these issues in order to develop a rights-based consensus on a positive and respectful approach to sexual expression.

Conclusion

This review of the policies and materials of the SADC and some of its member states suggests that, while the words "sexual rights" are not present in the general discourse, the issues underlying sexual rights and a commitment to human rights—in particular, the impact of the interaction of poverty, culture, and gender inequality on sexual relations—are generally reflected in the problem analyses presented and in the commitments made. Nevertheless, their implications for action are not spelled out in great detail, and it is therefore possible for SADC, as well as the relevant sectors and officials in member states, to avoid addressing gender inequality in sexual relationships. In the final analysis, these countries remain ambivalent about women's rights. While they argue for the right of women to say "no," they nonetheless avoid undermining cultural values regarding roles and responsibilities that privilege men.

In relation to HIV/AIDS prevention, this has translated into a focus on technical fixes to the HIV/AIDS problem—in particular, condom use—with no attempt to redress the social and economic injustices that often make condom use impossible. Rhetoric aside, this approach is not dissimilar to that of the old population paradigm that existed prior to the development of the ICPD Programme of Action and the Beijing Platform for Action. In the population context, exhortations to use contraception failed because they did not address the structure of women's identity and the social and economic reality of those targeted by the messages. Attempts to prevent the spread of HIV/AIDS should be informed by this experience.

SADC countries are all beginning to take action to promote women's economic and social status, both for its own sake and for the overall development of their countries—two areas that are fundamental to the achievement of sexual rights. Countries are also increasingly aware of how women's subordination makes them more vulnerable to transmission of HIV/AIDS. This recognition provides an entry point for promoting actions focusing specifically on the sexual dimension of sexual rights—on building a new culture of sexuality that allows individuals to take responsibility for their actions, and that promotes mutual respect as well as individual choice, expression, and pleasure.

It is not the case, as is frequently argued, that women who assert their rights to control their bodies and their sexuality are acting in opposition to their own national, religious, or ethnic identities.[74] A sexual rights approach allows individuals to develop to their full potential and experience themselves fully within their own family and society. Gupta has stated that arguing for individual empowerment is important not only for the sake of the individual, but for the collective social and economic good.[75] As this chapter has indicated, there are some openings for progress in countries in the region, including a number of contradictions between policy and practice that reflect changing contexts, as well as the roles of diverse actors in influencing the discourse surrounding sexuality. As the debates taken to Cairo and Beijing continue to play themselves out at country, regional, and international levels, the opportunities to push for a paradigm shift continue to grow. It may seem instrumental to argue for sexual rights in order to avoid a further escalation of the HIV/AIDS pandemic. However, HIV/AIDS is placing the economic and social functioning of countries fundamentally under threat. This disaster may provide the opportunity for a fundamental shift in paradigm, in which sexual rights will become a means not only to defeat the spread of HIV/AIDS, but to promote social justice.

Notes

1. Platform for Action of the Fourth World Conference on Women, September 1995, para. 96, UN Doc. A/CONF.177/20 (October 17, 1995).
2. The author was on the South African delegations to the ICPD, the FWCW, the Hague Forum, and the final Preparatory Committee and United Nations General Assembly review of the implementation of the ICPD.
3. The SADC member states are Angola, Botswana, Lesotho, Malawi, Mauritius, Mozambique, Namibia, South Africa, Swaziland, Tanzania, Zambia, and Zimbabwe.
4. K. Wood and R. Jewkes, "'Love Is a Dangerous Thing:' Micro-dynamics of Violence in Sexual Relationships of Young People in Umtata" (Pretoria: Medical Research Council, 1998).
5. T. P. Maphalala, "In and Out of School Youth Family Health Needs Assessment and Sexual Behaviors, Attitudes and Family Planning Practices: Manzini and Lubombo Regions" (Family Life Association of Swaziland, 1995), p. 20.
6. N. Fraser, *Justice Interruptus: Critical Reflections on the "Postsocialist" Condition* (New York: Routledge, 1997), p. 20.
7. Achievement of sexual rights requires access to sexual health services, as well as the processes of recognition and redistribution discussed here. The health services dimension of implementation, however, is beyond the scope of this article.
8. SADC did not operate as a tight caucus at the ICPD, since it had not prepared substantially beforehand. In Beijing, however, it did operate as a unit for much of the time, focusing particularly on issues pertaining to the girl child and inheritance rights for women. It also promoted the concept of sexual rights.
9. Programme of Action of the International Conference on Population and Development, Report of the International Conference on Population and Development, 5–13 September 1994, para. 7.3, UN Doc. A/CONF.171/13.
10. ICPD Programme of Action (see note 9), para. 4.9.
11. ICPD Programme of Action (see note 9), para. 7.37.
12. On the reproductive rights context, see L. Freedman, "Reflections on Emerging Frameworks of Health and Human Rights," *Health and Human Rights* 1995, 1(4): 314–48. For the disclaimers, see ICPD Programme of Action (note 8), ch. II, para. 1.
13. FWCW Platform for Action (see note 1), para. 96.
14. Freedman (see note 12).
15. FWCW Platform for Action (see note 1), para. 96.

16. SADC Gender Unit, "Gender Mainstreaming at SADC: Policies, Plans and Activities" (Botswana, 1999).

17. SADC Gender Unit (see note 16), para. B.i.

18. SADC Gender Unit (see note 16), para. H.iii.

19. SADC Gender Unit (see note 16), para. H.ii and H.iv.

20. SADC Gender Unit (see note 16), para. H.ii and iv.

21. Ministry of Health and Social Welfare, *Strategic Planning Document 1998–2000* (The Kingdom of Swaziland National AIDS Programme/World Health Organization, 1998), p. 6, sec. 2.2.

22. Ministry of Health and Social Welfare (see note 21), p. 8, sec. 2.3.

23. For South Africa, see African National Congress, *The Reconstruction and Development Programme* (Johannesburg: Umanyano Publications, 1994), p. 9. For Botswana, see Women Affairs Division, *Policy on Women in Development* (Gaborone: Department of Culture and Social Welfare, Ministry of Labour and Home Affairs, Government of Botswana, 1995).

24. Department of Health, "White Paper for the Transformation of the Health System in South Africa," General Notice 667, Government Gazette 17910, 16 April 1997, para. 9.2.le; AIDS/STD Unit, *Botswana HIV and AIDS Second Medium Term Plan, MTP II, 1997–2002* (Ministry of Health, Republic of Botswana, 1997), p. 15.

25. Department of Women Affairs, *Summary: National Gender Policy and National Plan of Action on Gender* (Windhoek: Republic of Namibia, 1998), p. 9. Republic of Namibia, *The National Strategic Plan on HIV/AIDS (Medium Term Plan II) 1999–2004* (Windhock: Republic of Namibia, 1999).

26. Republic of Botswana, *National Action Plan for Youth*, Draft 1999–2005 (abridged version) (Gaborone: Government Printer, 1999), p. 22.

27. Health Education Division of the Department of Health, "Women and AIDS" (Maseru: National AIDS Prevention and Control Programme), p. 2.

28. E. Kalondo and H. Rushways, "Heading the Churches: A Portrait of Nangula Kathindi," *Sister Namibia 1999*, 11(2): 4–6.

29. HIV/AIDS and STD Directorate, *Partnership Against AIDS: The South African Declaration on AIDS* (Pretoria: Department of Health, 1998).

30. AIDS/STD Unit (see note 24), p. 51.

31. Ministry of Health and Social Welfare (see note 21), p. 8.

32. SADC, *AIDS and STD Programme, Strategic Plan, 1999–2003* (Southern African Development Community, 1999), p. 1, sec. 2.

33. SADC (see note 32), p. 2.

34. AIDS/STD Unit (see note 24), p. 41.

35. IEC Sub-unit, *Youth Decisions In Preventing HIV/AIDS* (Gaborone: AIDS/STD Unit, Ministry of Health, 1999).

36. Health Education Division of the Department of Health (see note 27).

37. Constitution of the Republic of South Africa, Act No. 108 of 1996.

38. M. Gevisser, "Subtle Art of Being Gay the African Way," *Sunday Dispatches, The Sunday Independent* (Johannesburg), 26 September 1999, p. 15.

39. Gevisser (see note 38).

40. Keith Goddard of Gays and Lesbians of Zimbabwe, cited in Gevisser (see note 38).

41. Youth Health and Development Programme, *My Future Is My Choice: Participants' Work Book, Life Skills Education Training* (Windhoek: Government of the Republic of Namibia and UNICEF, 1999), p. 34. On the president of Namibia's statements, see Gevisser (note 38).

42. IEC Sub-unit (see note 35), p. 13.

43. Health Education Division of the Department of Health (see note 27), p. 6.

44. No explicit references to lesbianism were found in this review.

45. SADC Gender Unit (see note 16), p. 18, para. H.viii.

46. SADC (see note 32), p. 4, sec. 4.

47. The Southern African Ministers' Conference on Population and Development, held in May 1999, adopted a resolution that "members who are yet to develop Reproductive Health Policy are encouraged to do so and ensure that issues of Reproductive Rights are explicitly addressed." This marks a significant shift in focus within the population establishment. See Population in Development Department, *Report of the Southern African Ministers' Conference on Population and Development (SAMCPD), 11–14 May 1999, Lusaka, Zambia*

(Lusaka: Ministry of Finance and Economic Development, Republic of Zambia, 1999), p. 28.

48. SADC Gender Unit (see note 16), pp. 18, 21–22.
49. The SADC AIDS and STD Programme's Strategic Plan also recognizes the linkages between the position of women and violence in the rapid spread of HIV, see SADC (note 32), p. 2, sec. 2. On cultural issues, see p. 6, para. 8.1.1.
50. Ministry of Health and Social Welfare (see note 21), p. 10.
51. AIDS/STD Unit (see note 24), pp. 44–46.
52. FCWC Platform for Action (see note 1), para. 96.
53. For Lesotho, see Ministry of Health and Social Welfare, *Strategic Plan for MTP II* (Maseru: Ministry of Health and Social Welfare), p. 26.
54. AIDS/STD Unit, *Botswana National Policy on HIV/AIDS* (Gaborone: Ministry of Health, 1993), p. 3, para. 2.2, and p. 6, para. 4.4.
55. AIDS/STD Unit (see note 54), p. 6, para. 4.4.
56. Department of Health (see note 24), para. 9.1.1.ci.
57. AIDS/STD Unit (see note 24), p. 46.
58. Department of Health (see note 24), para. 9.1.1.ci.
59. HIV/AIDS and STD Directorate, *HIV/AIDS and Relationships* (Pretoria: Department of Health, 1998); HIV/AIDS and STD Directorate, *Male Condoms* (Pretoria: Department of Health, 1998).
60. Brochure reprinted in TASC, *Annual Report 1998* (Manzini: AIDS Information and Support Centre, 1998).
61. AIDS/STD Unit, *Information, Education and Communication for AIDS/STD Prevention: A Manual for Those Involved in AIDS/STD Education* (Gaborone: Ministry of Health, 1994), NACP 23, K. Norr, B. McElmurry, and S. Tlou, *Women and HIV/AIDS Prevention Peer Education Program: A Global Approach, Training Manual* (Chicago: WHO Collaborating Centres for Nursing Development in Primary HealthCare, University of Illinois at Chicago and University of Botswana, 1997); P. Bardsley, *Act on AIDS: A Manual for AIDS Trainers/Educators Using Participatory Training Methods* (Gaborone: AIDS Action Trust, 1995).
62. The quotation is from Norr (see note 61).
63. N. Christofides, M. Russell, and D. Conco, *Sexual Rights Workshop Manual* (Johannesburg: Women's Health Project, Department of Community Health, University of the Witwaterstand, 1999), p. 12.
64. ICPD Programme of Action (see note 9), para. 7.2.
65. Health, Empowerment, Rights and Accountability (HERA), "Sexual Rights," in *Women's Sexual and Reproductive Rights and Health: Action Sheets* (New York: HERA, 1999).
66. E. Boikanyo, "So Much for Women-Sensitive Sexual Relations: The Use of Vaginal Potions," *Agenda* 1992, 15: 3–7.
67. H. Jackson, "Societal Determinants of Women's Vulnerability to HIV Infection in Southern Africa," *Health and Human Rights* 1998, 2(4): 9–14.
68. IEC Sub-unit (see note 35).
69. Department of Women Affairs (see note 25), p. 8.
70. School Health Education to Prevent STDs (SHAPE), *HIV/AIDS: Training Guide* (Schools HIV/AIDS and Population Education).
71. Norr (see note 61).
72. Youth Health and Development Programme (see note 41), p. 21.
73. Youth Health and Development Programme (see note 41), p. 25.
74. Joint Enrichment Project, NACOSA, NAPWA, National Network Against Violence Against Women, PPASA, and Women's Health Project, *Sexual Rights Campaign for Equality and Mutual Respect in Sexual Decision Making* (Johannesburg: Women's Health Project, University of the Witwatersrand, 1999).
75. "Ukosoma" refers to sex with the man's penis between the woman's thighs rather than in the vagina, a technique originally promoted in order to avoid premarital pregnancy. See Christofides (note 63), p. 15.
76. Freedman (see note 12).
77. G. R. Gupta, "Strengthening Alliances for Sexual Health and Rights," *Health and Human Rights* 1997, 12(3): 55–63.

V

Health and Human Rights in Understanding and Responding to Violence

Violence is the oldest and most obvious threat to health and human rights. Violence prevention in civil society requires that human rights be respected, protected, and fulfilled. Violence prevention in times of war and conflict requires that humanitarian law be respected and obligations fulfilled. Emerging issues in the relationship of violence and health and human rights focus on new methods of action.

The publication of the *World Report on Violence and Health* by the World Health Organization in October 2002 represents the first comprehensive report to address violence as a global public health problem. Violence is one of the leading causes of death for people aged 14–44 years of age. In the twentieth century, over 191 million people have been killed directly or indirectly in war or armed conflict. Before World War I, 90 percent of casualties were military, but by the end of the twentieth century 90 percent of casualties in war were civilian. Health care expenditures related to violent injuries may account for as much as 5 percent of the Gross Domestic Product in many countries.[1]

The first chapter in this part, by Joan LeGraw and Michael Grodin, focuses on state-sponsored violence in the form of the death penalty. The United States is one of the few resource-rich countries in the world that maintains a death penalty. Over the past decades, within the United States the practice of capital punishment has moved from the use of firing squads, the gas chamber, and the electric chair to sanitized and medicalized killing by lethal injection involving health professionals. This chapter addresses the efforts of medical professionals in the United States to stop executions by refusing to participate in lethal executions on the grounds that they violate medical ethics.

Effective human rights advocacy starts with good and effective compilation of facts. Data grounds the effective use of human rights strategies for change. The second piece, by Physicians for Human Rights, uses a cross sectional survey on maternal mortality and human rights in the Herat Province of Afghanistan. This study of the violation of women's human rights demonstrates the importance of collecting accurate public health data to document abuses and the ways in which these efforts can lay the groundwork for advocacy. It is not only well established that decreasing maternal and newborn mortality depends on human rights monitoring and protection, but rates of maternal mortality can also serve as an important indicator of the status of women in particular societies. As this piece demonstrates, empirical data collection can inform priority setting and short and long term planning for women's health and human rights.

The third chapter in this part, by Claude Bruderlein and Jennifer Leaning, identifies emerging problems in international humanitarian law, including distinguishing the military from civilians, ongoing civil wars, the protection of medical and aid workers, and the provision of "neutral spaces." The authors argue that new strategies are needed to expand protections through the strengthening of international judicial institutions. Three paradigmatic examples of the need for protections are discussed, including protecting civilians through the landmine treaty, protecting internally displaced persons, and prohibiting the recruitment of child soldiers.

The fourth and final piece in this part, by Stephen Marks, examines the use of sanctions as a means to pressure governments to conform to international law. Although sanctions themselves do not directly employ violence, the ways in which they are carried out may nonetheless result in human rights violations. The piece explores humanitarian exceptions to sanctions, especially those permitting humanitarian aid. The author suggests that alternatives to sanctions might include arms embargoes, the severing of communication lines, and the increased use of international criminal prosecution, as these alternatives target the regime rather than the people living within the country.

The chapters in this part reflect important emerging strategies to address the enduring problems of violence in global society. The next challenge will be to move to a prevention model. This will require a better understanding of the nature, antecedents, and causes of human violence as well as the promotion and protection of human rights.

Note

1. *World Report on Violence and Health*, eds. E. Krug, L. Dahlberg, J. Mercy, A. Zwi, and R. Lozano (World Health Organization, Geneva 2002).

14

Health Professionals and Lethal Injection Execution in the United States

Joan M. LeGraw and Michael A. Grodin

He was strapped down . . . we couldn't get the intravenous line in to his arm . . . Then the doctor got the line in; he used an alcohol swab to sterilize the skin and I said "What's the point."
    – Burl Cain, Warden of Angola Penitentiary (Louisiana, 1996)[1]

When the state of Texas executed Charlie Brooks, Jr. with an overdose of drugs in 1982, it was the first time that a prison medical staff was utilized to carry out a death sentence in the United States. Because for many Americans, the focus of the debate regarding the death penalty was simply that the Eighth Amendment required that an "execution be imposed more humanely than it had in the past,"[2] this lethal injection was viewed by some as a victory. Many abolitionists, however, feared that the use of simple injection as a method of execution could make the death penalty more palatable to juries[3] and easier for the public to accept,[4] which would increase the incidence of capital punishment. Current statistics illustrate that such fears and predictions regarding the far-reaching implications of this new "humane" method of execution were well-founded. Of the 143 executions from 1976 to 1990, only fifty-four, or roughly 38 percent, were by lethal injection.[5] In contrast, in the next ten years, 606 people were executed. Lethal injection was the method used in 530, or about 87 percent, of these cases.[6] To date, all executions in 2002 have been by lethal injection.[7]

While the U.S. Supreme Court has been actively involved in judicially regulating the death penalty since 1976, ostensibly to ensure a "fair" determination that an execution was properly decided upon, a review of several of the more significant judicial decisions[8] supports the conclusion that the Supreme Court's death penalty jurisprudence has evolved into a "pro-death penalty self-fulfilling constitutional construct."[9] Nevertheless, the evidence indicates that the popularity of the death penalty and the dramatic increase in the number of executions in recent years has been "driven largely by the increase in lethal injection execution"[10] and not the decisions of the high court. In fact, it is more likely that the availability of lethal injection, and its perception of painless efficiency, has catalyzed many recent pro-capital punishment judicial decisions.[11]

A state cannot execute anyone by lethal injection, however, without utilizing medical knowledge, techniques, equipment, and, if not licensed people, then people trained by licensed professionals. In fact, although most health professions have issued position statements that officially denounce the participation of their members,[12] physicians, nurses, and other medically trained personnel continue to play a vital role in lethal injection executions in the United States.[13] Perhaps this is because after more than twenty years of expert opinions and official denunciations, there is still no agreed upon definition of what constitutes "participation in an execution," nor any effective means of monitoring health professionals and enforcing ethical standards.

For example, during the first execution by lethal injection, Dr. Ralph Gray, medical director of the Texas Department of Corrections, examined Charlie Brooks' arms in order to ascertain whether his veins were adequate and then supervised the technicians who administered the injection.[14] The drugs used to kill Brooks came from Dr. Gray's "prison drug supply."[15] Nevertheless, despite the fact that the American Medical Association (AMA) issued an opinion in 1980 that physicians should not participate in capital punishment, under the AMA's own interpretation of its position paper, Dr. Gray did nothing wrong or unethical. According to a statement issued at the time, because Dr. Gray did not "compound the substance or inject the medication," he did not "participate in the execution."[16] Likewise, the Oklahoma Corrections Department medical director's interpretation of participation also did not include ordering the drugs necessary for the execution or having physicians employed by the state inspect the IV equipment. In an ironic statement, the director stated that "our medical people are not going to be involved except to see that highest standards of medicine are followed."[17]

Certainly it is true that the Position Statements issued by these professional organizations, as well as scholarly interpretation and expert opinions, have helped to clarify the ethical principles at issue. It is equally true, however, that guidelines regarding the limits or ethical parameters of physician participation in executions by lethal injection have been ignored by state legislatures, have been ineffective in influencing public opinion, and have been largely unenforced because professional associations have neither the power to revoke a health professional's license nor the ability to prevent its members from violating its guidelines. In addition, there are broader ethical implications in the use of an overdose of drugs to effectuate the death penalty, and "merely invoking professional ethics"[18] by refusing to participate does not address such issues.

Lethal injection execution is a violation of medical ethics because it utilizes medical skills and knowledge to give judicial homicide the appearance of painless clinical competence and humanity, which in turn has insulated such executions from constitutional scrutiny and public attack. We maintain that, because all other methods have routinely been acknowledged to be painful and cruel, without lethal injection, the death penalty in the United States would be unlikely to survive.[19] Therefore, the complicity of the health professions in this continued violation of human rights extends beyond the actual participation of licensed practitioners.

Furthermore, because other countries have begun to use lethal injection to justify judicial homicide, the human rights violations encouraged and facilitated by this method of execution are likely to become a major concern of the international community.[20] Therefore, the efforts of human rights activists and other abolitionists should be focused on eliminating the use of drugs in executions. In addition, all health professionals must be encouraged to take an unambiguous stance against lethal injection executions as a violation of medical ethics.

Although this chapter primarily concerns the ethics and consequences of lethal injection as a method of execution and not the death penalty in general, we make no attempt to disguise our opinion that capital punishment is always, regardless of the method used, a violation of the most basic human right, the right to life. Furthermore, it is our position that, as practiced in the United States, capital punishment violates U.S. constitutional law, customary international law, and international covenants and treaties that the United States has signed and ratified. Therefore, in order to place this discussion in context, we briefly discuss the international movement toward the abolition of the death penalty in contrast to the increasing escalation of executions in the United States.

We then trace the evolution of capital punishment in the United States from a violent public event to the medically sanitized and invisible procedure that it is today. We discuss the historical use of drugs in executions and the complicity of the medical profession. Finally, we explore the reasons why lethal injection has become virtually the sole method of execution in the United States.

Next we discuss the Supreme Court's interpretation of American "standards of decency." We suggest that, based upon the Court's recent opinions and its tendency to minimize, if not ignore, international norms, state legislative enactments and jury sentencing behavior have become the most important indicator of American "standards of decency." Based upon the overwhelming legislative trend toward lethal injection execution as the only "humane" method of execution and a review of recent court decisions in methodology cases, we suggest that the gas chamber, electrocution, hanging, and the firing squad will soon become "de facto" unconstitutional. Furthermore, because in the near future lethal injection will be the only method of execution in the United States, any opposition to the use of lethal injection as a method of execution is effectively opposition to the death penalty.

We then summarize the opinions and attitudes of individual health professionals and the official Position Statements of various professional organizations. We suggest that although health professionals should continue to refuse to participate, this mere refusal is no longer sufficient. Because capital punishment has flourished in this country through the use of medical technology, we argue that execution is not simply a legal issue, as the AMA recently announced, but a continued violation of medical ethics by the state.

We report on the current involvement of health professionals in capital punishment in the United States. We reviewed all state statutes detailing the method of execution, as well as pending legislation, in order to ascertain the extent to which states are requiring, expecting or encouraging the cooperation and participation of physicians and other health professionals. We found that despite the objections of professional organizations, the involvement of health professionals in executions has increased.

Finally we offer recommendations for action, which seek to ensure that health professionals are not involved in capital punishment on any level. The ultimate goal, however, is the demise of lethal injection execution in the United States, and eventually, the practice of judicial homicide.

International Law and the Death Penalty in the United States

Since the signing of the Universal Declaration of Human Rights after World War II,[21] the international community has progressively moved toward the recognition that capital punishment is a violation of human dignity and our most basic human right, the right to life.[22] Currently there are three major international protocols and covenants calling for its worldwide abolition.[23] New members of the Council of Europe are now required to ratify Protocol 6 to the European Convention on Human Rights, which has led to the virtual abolition of the death penalty in Europe. South Africa's parliament voted to abolish the death penalty, after it had been declared unconstitutional by the Constitutional Court.[24] The United Nations Commission on Human Rights recently renewed its call for a worldwide moratorium on executions with the goal of completely abolishing capital punishment.[25] As of February 2002, 109 countries have abolished the death penalty in law or practice, and although eighty-six other countries retain the death penalty, the number which actually execute prisoners is much smaller.[26]

The United States is the last industrialized Western democracy that retains the death penalty.[27] This country has also refused to honor the minimal safeguards of the rights of the accused as established by international law,[28] as well as the restrictions of the international covenants and treaties that it has signed and ratified.[29] In addition, the United States is the leading executioner of juvenile defendants in the world.[30]

Despite the above as well as evidence that capital punishment does not deter future criminals,[31] that execution is more expensive than life imprisonment,[32] and that many innocent people have been executed,[33] the majority of Americans still support capital punishment.[34] In fact, while the rest of the world has moved progressively toward the abolition of the death penalty as a violation of human rights, in the United States, executions have increased nearly every year.[35] According to a 31 March 2000 report from the Economic and Social Council of the United Nations, between 1994 and 1998 only China, the Islamic Republic of Iran, and Saudi Arabia executed more people than the United States.[36]

The Evolution of Capital Punishment in the United States from a Violent Public Event to a Private, Medically Sanitized Procedure

The Connection Between Private Executions and the Use of Drugs

Historically state killing was a deliberate spectacle designed to be public and violent.[37] In the United States, executions were well attended by all social classes.[38] By 1820, however, the upper class of society found executions distasteful and refused to attend.[39] Ministers, legislators, editors, and other commentators at the time proclaimed that public executions subverted morals and "brutalized people by the barbarity of the example."[40] It is not entirely clear why public executions, which were essentially unchanged for two centuries, became unacceptable and even revolting at this time.[41] According to R.J. Lifton, when an execution "inspires 'revulsion'. . . it has lost its power to affirm social mores."[42] Therefore, it could have been, as some have suggested, that there was a "civilizing process" in the nineteenth century and a "beginning of a greater sensibility about what constitutes cruelty."[43]

Whatever the reason for the rather sudden distaste for public executions, legislators at the time were "not willing to advocate the abolition of capital punishment entirely," and the private execution was put forth as a solution to the problem.[44] The idea was welcomed with "no acute political conflict," and by 1845, public executions were outlawed in many states.[45] Executions were held behind prison walls with only limited and authorized witnesses in attendance.[46] Therefore, because the violence of the death penalty was now "invisible,"[47] it became unnecessary to deal with the underlying reasons for society's "disaffection with the killing spectacle."[48] In fact, unlike the "unpredictable spectacles that could unfold on the public scaffold," the appeal of the private execution was that it could be "a simple, quiet, uncontroversial, almost collaborative execution."[49]

It is not surprising, therefore, that soon commentators began suggesting it may be helpful[50] or humane to use drugs to anesthetize the inmate before the execution.[51] Anesthesia was introduced in 1846 and was quickly incorporated into medical practice. By 1849[52] one reporter wrote that "ether or chloroform is now universally used by surgeons in painful operations, shall not the convict share also the advantage of this benign discovery."[53] Most commentators were not abolitionists but nevertheless questioned whether "now that science has found a means of alleviating extreme physical suffering [shouldn't we allow] the benefit of it to the miserable wretches whom we simply wish to cast contemptuously out of existence?"[54] Ultimately, these opinions were not translated into policy, and there is no evidence that inmates were medicated before being executed.

The issue of giving anesthesia to the condemned was occasionally revived, however, as commentary arose on the desire to find the "'easiest mode of taking life' " and regarding "'motives of humanity.' "[55] Louis Masur noted that "the use of anesthesia, like private executions, [would help] to sustain the illusion that, though the hanging occurred, decorum, propriety, and civility were preserved, the control of vicious passions effectuated."[56] Likewise, the current preference for the lethal injection can be explained by its "ease, cleanliness, and relative lack of drama . . . and in the overall numbing surrounding capital punishment."[57]

Lethal injections have privatized the execution experience more thoroughly than hiding the scaffold did for prior generations: While a private execution allowed the public to avoid seeing the actual killing, a painless overdose of drugs encourages the illusion that we are not "killing strictly speaking [just] putting-to-sleep."[58] Clearly then the motivations that led to the demise of the public execution are the roots "in a slightly roundabout way to the wonderful appeal of the lethal injection."[59]

Nevertheless, while killing by a lethal dose of medicine may have removed the physical revulsion in witnessing an execution,[60] many people still recoil at the thought of the executioner.[61] As states began enacting legislation to adopt lethal injection as a method of execution, the medical profession became "worried that [it would] drag them into the role of executioner."[62] Because executioners have "always been shunned by society," the concern was that society would begin to mistrust physicians "if they were seen as accomplices."[63]

This concern was real because, even when executions were public and well attended, executioners were often seen as "evil" and "contaminated by the death work that was their livelihood."[64] Since they often faced the real danger of physical violence from the angry crowd or relatives of the condemned, "they were often afforded a hood or cloak while at work to protect their identities, which would offer them a token shield against harm."[65] Currently, although executions are still technically private, the voluminous amount of information regarding many aspects of modern executions that is now available on the Internet or through other sources has made them more quasi-public events. Furthermore, there is an even greater effort than in the past to keep the identity[66] and activities of the executioner a secret.[67] Health professionals who participate or assist are afforded a modern "executioner's cloak . . . official anonymity."[68]

The Historical Involvement of Physicians in Judicial Homicides

Despite the higher visibility of the role of medical science in capital punishment inherent in the use of the lethal injection, proponents of the death penalty are correct in noting that the involvement and participation of physicians in capital punishment is not a recent phenomenon.[69] Physicians have historically been involved in many distinct areas,[70] including assisting with the actual execution process and supervising nonprofessional personnel. In addition to lending a scientific and sanitizing aura of acceptability,[71] medical personnel are often on hand "to make sure that the procedure [goes] smoothly."[72] For example, at the first judicial exection by electrocution, when the condemned man, William Kemmler, was found to be still alive, one of the physicians who had advised the warden regarding how long the contact should be maintained shouted "This man is not dead. Turn on the current instantly."[73] A physician provided the same type of assistance at the execution of Charlie Brooks, Jr. in 1982. At one point, the doctor who was monitoring the vital functions of the prisoner advised the executioner to continue administering the poison for a "couple more minutes."[74]

Physicians also contribute to the continued public support for the death penalty by offering their expert medical opinions on pain and suffering to the media. After Charlie Brooks, Jr. was executed, two doctors who had been in attendance commented to the press that he "did not experience his own death . . . and . . . death by injection is more humane [than other methods]."[75] In 1997, when the execution of Pedro Medina in Florida's electric chair was "botched" and "a foot long blue and orange flame shot from the mask covering his head . . . filling the execution chamber with the odor of charred human flesh,"[76] the public may have been shocked by its brutality. News reports at the time, however, also contained the opinion of the medical director of the Florida State Prison that "I saw no evidence of pain or suffering . . . in my professional opinion, he died a very quick, humane death."[77]

Perhaps the area in which physicians have been most intimately involved, however, has been through the application of their "expertise in mathematics, physics and medicine [to increase] the effectiveness and efficiency of executions."[78] The French guillotine was named after its doctor-inventor, and was later perfected by a French Surgeon named Dr. Antoine Louis "who redesigned the blade to make a cleaner cut."[79] An army medical corps officer invented the gas chamber in 1924.[80]

The search for a better method of killing continued with the work of a Buffalo, New York dentist Alfred Porter Southwick. Southwick made two notable contributions to society, both of which apparently were motivated by humanitarian concerns. First, he is known to have contributed to the understanding and treatment for cleft palate, a congenital deformation of the mouth and palate that make it difficult for a person to eat and talk. Second, history refers to him as the "father of electrocution" for his work on perfecting and promoting the use of electricity in judicial homicides.[81] Southwick was fascinated after listening to the account of an accidental electrocution in which the victim died immediately and without apparent pain. He speculated that electricity could be useful to medicine as a dental anesthetic or by providing anesthesia for medical operations.[82] In addition, he thought that electricity could be used as a form of euthanasia for unwanted animals.[83] Eventually it was suggested that electrocution may be useful in the execution of humans as a "humane replacement for the gallows."[84] Though initially dismissed as cruel, due to Southwick's diligence, the idea gradually gained acceptance.

Although the actual electrocution of a human being could just as easily have taken place standing or lying down on a gurney, as a dentist "Southwick was most familiar with a particular way of treating his patients [and he knew that] a chair had many advantages when dealing with a patient who had mixed feelings about the procedure that was about to take place."[85] So the use of electricity as a method of execution became synonymous with "chair," and early photographs indeed show that the chair "resemble[d] a dentist's chair."[86]

Although the physicians and medical personnel who invented these machines may have honestly believed that they were humanitarians, the fact that members of the medical profession were responsible for the design of a "machine to decapitate people,"[87] a chamber for asphyxiating people, and a chair to electrocute people was a "spectacular perversion of medical sciences."[88] Physicians justify their involvement in the methodology of the death penalty by claiming that their goal is to "reduce the pain for the prisoner."[89] Experience has suggested, however, that such efforts are more often successful in reducing the suffering of the executioner by eliminating any "intimate contact with the inmate."[90] In fact, above any consideration for the condemned, the effect, if not the intent, of these inventions, including the lethal injection, has been to relieve society's guilt over an act of obvious brutality.[91]

The Rise of the Lethal Injection as the Execution Method of Choice in the United States

Because physicians had been involved for many years in the development and design of new technologies to facilitate a "humane execution," it is not surprising that eventually it would again be suggested that the actual tools of medicine should be utilized. Lethal injection was first considered in the United States over 100 years ago when New York was researching the most humane method of execution because of the number of botched hangings.[92] Hanging and the guillotine were rejected, but the proposal for a lethal injection of prussic acid (cyanide) was initially regarded favorably.[93] New York ultimately rejected lethal injection because "the medical profession strongly opposed the use of the hypodermic needle for executions fearing that the public would associate the practice of medicine with death."[94]

Great Britain considered lethal injection in 1953 when the Royal Commission on Capital Punishment Report detailed its investigation into the question as to whether there were methods of execution that "could inflict death as painlessly and certainly as hanging but with greater decency."[95] Apparently, the British Medical Association had expressed the opinion (without offering suggestions) that an alternative to hanging should be found. After dismissing the electric chair, the gas chamber, and the gas mask, the Royal Commission considered a lethal injection from a hypodermic syringe and noted that this method would satisfy "humanity, decency and certainty."[96] Nevertheless, Parliament ultimately rejected this approach because, among other reasons, the British Medical Association was opposed to "a method of execution which would require the services of a medical practitioners either in carrying out the actual process of killing or in instructing others in the technique of the process."[97]

The idea of using drugs in judicial killing resurfaced in the United States in 1973[98] when Ronald Reagan, then the governor of California, suggested:

> Being a former farmer and horse raiser, I know what it is like to try and eliminate an injured horse by shooting him. Now, you call the veterinarian and the vet gives it a shot and the horse goes to sleep—that's it. I myself have wondered it maybe this isn't part of our problem [with capital punishment]; if maybe there aren't even more humane methods now—the simple shot or tranquilizer.[99]

When Oklahoma Senator Bill Dawson sought to change the state's method of execution, however, his motivation was economic not humanitarian. He wanted to avoid the cost of replacing the state's electric chair or building an expensive gas chamber.[100] The senator asked Dr. Stanley Deutsch, the Chairman of Oklahoma Medical School Anesthesiology Department, if he could recommend a method of execution through the intravenous administration of drugs.[101] Dr. Deutsch apparently did not recognize any ethical violation in his recommendation that "the intravenous method would be a rapid and painless way to produce unconsciousness and ensuing death."[102] Dr. Deutsch's suggestions were used to draft the first lethal injection statute, which was signed into law in Oklahoma on 11 May 1977.[103] Dr. Roy Chapman, the state medical examiner testified for the passage of the bill stating that execution by lethal injection would be like "drawing a curtain" and that the "only pain inflicted . . . would be the prick of the needle used to sedate the recipient."[104] Texas adopted similar legislation the following day.[105]

Although the most common stated rationale for the use of the lethal injection is that it is the "most humane method of execution,"[106] less noble reasons are probably more responsible for its popularity. Although it is less expensive than the gas chamber or electrocution,[107] economics does not appear to be the only, or even the main, motivation given the overall expense of the execution process in general.[108] It is more likely that the motivation is the vitality of capital punishment.[109] Supporters of the death penalty realize that "for capital punishment to be acceptable it must also be made palatable."[110] In that regard, one reason that lethal injection has become the preferred method of execution is the belief that juries are more likely to vote for the death penalty if they believe that the method is humane.[111] For example, according to Thomas H. Paterniti, author of the New Jersey lethal injection bill: "if you're on the jury, the thought of some guy in that chair sizzling is going to bother them. . . . This way, with lethal injection, it might ease their conscience when they come up with the verdict."[112]

A 1978 law review article suggested that lethal injection was "clearly the most humane of the present methods," and involved "little more indignity than attends an ordinary surgical operation."[113] Although the indignity of execution is clearly more grave than that of an operation, the procedure does mimic a medical intervention so much that the medical technicians typically swab the prisoner's arm with alcohol before inserting the needle. Richard Peabody, the deputy warden at Louisiana State Penitentiary, explained the contradiction by stating that "our people are trained to start IV lines in a professional manner. It's just good procedure."[114] And when commenting upon the actions of one doctor who participated in an execution by lethal injection, the AMA referred to the lethal substance as "medication" in a statement given to the press.[115] This reference was understandable, however, because the drugs used to kill the prisoner are given to thousands of patients each day.[116]

These comments illustrate the blurring line between healing and killing that is inevitable with lethal injection as a method of execution. The above history also illustrates a fact that is at times disputed: a lethal injection is a medical procedure—a relatively simple medical procedure, but still a medical procedure,[117] that is utilized, however, to accomplish a goal other than the practice of medicine. Perhaps because the goal of lethal injection is not within the definition of ethical medical practice, some have suggested that an "[e]xecution by lethal injection is no more a medical procedure than execution by firing squad is a military procedure."[118] The analogy, which is similar to many others that have been made, is flawed, however, because in addition to the fact that the purpose of a gun is to kill, the U.S. military has no legitimate use for a firing squad outside of capital punishment. In contrast, the "technology of rapid anesthetic [which is the procedure used in lethal injection execution] was introduced for healing purposes"[119] and continues to be used by anesthesiologists every day. What is true is that the procedure is not "normal medical practice" but rather a "perversion of biomedical knowledge and skill for a nonmedical purpose."[120]

The focus of the debate, however, has not been whether the lethal injection is a medical procedure but rather the ethics of physician or medical personnel participation. This focus makes some sense because, after all, if lethal injection is not a medical procedure, then "what business can a professional society have advising its members not to participate."[121] In fact, although doctors have assisted the state with executions for centuries, it was only when states began using lethal injection, a medical procedure, that the medical profession issued a position statement forbidding physician participation. Nevertheless, the issue also is not whether licensed health care workers should be allowed to inject the drug or monitor the execution because even if doctors or nurses refuse to participate directly in executions "the fact remains that someone plays the role of executioner and that person has to apply medical knowledge and have some medical training in order to carry out the task."[122]

Evolving Standards of Decency and Lethal Injection Execution

The Eighth Amendment states that "excessive bail ought not to be required nor excessive fines imposed nor cruel and unusual punishments inflicted."[123] The exact meaning of the words is elusive, however, and the Supreme Court has acknowledged that "the exact scope of the constitutional phrase cruel and unusual has not been detailed by this Court."[124] In *Gregg v. Georgia*, the Court held that although the Eighth Amendment was initially concerned with proscribing torture and other barbarous methods of punishment, execution methods that were outlawed at the time of the signing of the Constitution are not the only punishments that may be prohibited.[125] In fact, "the clause forbidding cruel and unusual punishments is not fastened to the obsolete but may acquire meaning as public opinion becomes enlightened by humane justice."[126] Ultimately, the Supreme Court held that the Eighth Amendment must draw its meaning from the "evolving standards of decency that mark the progress of a maturing society."[127] The Court indicated that it would look to objective indicia, such as legislative enactments[128] that reflect public attitude toward a government sanction, to define the "standards of decency." The *Gregg* plurality noted, however, that although the legislative measures adopted by the people's chosen representatives are one important means of ascertaining contemporary values, legislation alone cannot be determinative of Eighth Amendment standards because the Eighth Amendment itself was intended to safeguard individuals from legislative power.[129] In addition, although the jury is a reliable indicator of society's values, "public perceptions of standards of decency are not conclusive."[130]

In *Gregg* the Court also held that the sanction must be in accord with the dignity of man.[131] As a result, the punishment must not be excessive.[132] By contrast, the punishment must be proportional to the severity of the crime and must not "involve the unnecessary and wanton infliction of pain."[133] Unnecessary pain was defined as "something inhumane and barbarous, something more than the mere extinguishment of life."[134]

Since the *Gregg* case, however, conservatives on the Court have rejected the role of a proportionality review and penological justification as unnecessary to an Eighth Amendment constitutional analysis. In *Stanford v. Kentucky*,[135] writing the plurality opinion (joined by Justices White, Kennedy and Chief Justice Rehnquist), Justice Scalia considered the only relevant test to be legislative enactments and jury sentencing behavior.[136] In addition, the Court, in the past, "often consulted the standards of other nations."[137] Justice Scalia rejected this practice in his opinion in *Stanford* where he wrote that "we emphasize that it is American conceptions of decency that are dispositive [and we reject] the contention of the petitioners . . . that the sentencing practices of other countries are relevant."[138]

Because some new members of the Court, such as Justice Thomas, are likely to hold similar views, "legislative enactments [may soon] become the sole determinate of constitutionality,"[139] and "legislative trends away from a particular punishment" are considered relevant evidence of whether the punishment is cruel and unusual,[140] lethal injection may soon be the only "constitutional method" of execution in the United States. For example, in a recent decision, the Georgia Supreme Court held that because the legislature adopted lethal injection (for sentences after May 2000), its decision to abolish electrocution as cruel and unusual punishment was founded on "the clearest and most objective evidence of a prevailing condemnation of the people of Georgia of that particular punishment" and that the adoption of lethal injection reflects a "societal consensus 'that the science of the present day' has provided a less barbarous means of taking the life of condemned prisoners."[141] Furthermore, the Georgia Court held that "the fact that a method involving less pain and mutilation exists . . . clearly must play an important factor in the determination of whether an older method is cruel and unusual punishment."[142]

A Review of Methodology Cases and the Current Judicial Interpretation of the "Standards of Decency Test"

The Supreme Court has never reviewed evidence regarding whether a particular method of killing violates the Constitution.[143] Despite this fact, states have frequently changed their methods of execution. Although humanity and greater standards of decency are often the stated rationale, a review of case law and legislative history indicates that it is more likely that states change an execution method "to stay one step ahead of a constitutional challenge."[144] This trend can easily be illustrated by reviewing several recent methodology cases.

In 1995, in *Fierro v. Gomez*, the Ninth Circuit Court of Appeals held that, because of the factual findings of pain, "execution by lethal gas is cruel and unusual," and therefore violates the Eighth Amendment.[145] Because the findings of pain were dispositive, "there was no need for the district court to turn to a consideration of legislative trends."[146] Presumably, if the findings of pain were not dispositive, then the court would undertake a review of legislative enactments.[147]

Nevertheless, most legislatures are not leaving anything to chance, and are enacting lethal injection statutes in order to ensure the constitutionality of the death penalty. For example, subsequent to the decision in *Fierro*, the California legislature amended the state's death penalty statute to provide for lethal injection as the method of inflicting death unless the defendant requests that the state use the gas chamber. On appeal, the Supreme Court vacated the judgment of the Ninth Circuit Court of Appeals and remanded the case in light of the new statute.[148] On remand, the Ninth Circuit held that the inmates lacked standing to challenge the constitutionality of lethal gas because neither had elected to be executed by that method.[149]

In *Rupe v. Wood*, a 409-pound inmate alleged that hanging him would be cruel and unusual punishment. The Washington statute allowed the prisoner to choose lethal injection, but because he would not choose, he was to be executed by hanging.[150] The District Court for the Western District of Washington agreed that executing Rupe by hanging would be cruel and unusual punishment. After the state's appeal was argued, however, Washington amended its death penalty law, reversing the prior presumption in favor of hanging. The state assured the court that if no choice was made, Mr. Rupe would be executed by lethal injection. The appeal regarding the constitutionality of hanging was dismissed as moot.[151]

In 1999, the Supreme Court granted certiorari to hear arguments in *Bryan v. Moore*,[152] concerning whether execution by electrocution violated the Eighth Amendment.[153] In direct response to the appeal, the Florida legislature added the option of lethal injection to the death penalty statute. On 24 January 2000, the Supreme Court held that:

> In light of the representation by the State of Florida, through its Attorney General, that petitioner's 'death sentence will be carried out by lethal injection, unless [he] affirmatively chooses electrocution' pursuant to the recent amendments . . . to the Florida Statutes, the writ of certiorari is dismissed as improvidently granted.[154]

In *LaGrand v. Stewart*,[155] the Ninth Circuit Court of Appeals issued a certificate of appealability and enjoined the state of Arizona from executing the inmate, or anyone similarly situated, by means of lethal gas. On appeal, the. Supreme Court held that *because he elected* to be executed by lethal gas, LaGrand "waived his claim" that this method is unconstitutional.[156] Arizona provided a choice of lethal gas or lethal injection, with the default in favor of lethal injection. Therefore, by affirmatively choosing lethal gas, LaGrand could not challenge its constitutionality. Recall, however, that in *Fierro*, the Ninth Circuit Court of Appeals held that the petitioners lacked standing to challenge the constitutionality of lethal gas because they had *not elected* to be executed by that method.[157]

Therefore, if a state has a statute that allows the inmate to choose lethal injection, there appears to be no way to challenge, at the federal level, the constitutionality of any other method (such as electrocution or the gas chamber). If the condemned chooses an alternative method, the Supreme Court has held that the prisoner has waived his right to adjudicate the constitutionality of that method by such a choice. At least one federal circuit court has held that, in order to challenge a method as unconstitutional, an inmate must choose that method. Even if an inmate elects lethal injection, however, he may also have no case. Because the inmate will never face the alternative method of execution, he actually has no case in controversy, and the Court refuses to hear such cases. Therefore, based on the holding in *LaGrand*, only if a state forced a method of execution on an inmate could that method be challenged.[158]

Only two states, Alabama and Nebraska, do not provide for lethal injection under any circumstance; the sole method of execution in both states is electrocution.[159] In Arkansas, any defendant sentenced to death prior to 4 July 1983 may elect to be executed by lethal injection by requesting so in writing within one week of the execution. Failure to do so is construed as a waiver of the "right" to be executed with lethal injection, and the defendant would be electrocuted.[160] In Utah, the statute states that execution will be by lethal injection or firing squad with the method to be specified in the warrant.[161] In New Hampshire, the statute states that, if lethal injection is "impractical to carry out," the sentence may be carried out by hanging.[162] All other death penalty jurisdictions provide for lethal injection as the main method of execution or offer a choice to the condemned, with the default method being lethal injection.

It is technically possible for a small minority of inmates to challenge electrocution as unconstitutional. There is an even smaller possibility that shooting or hanging, if utilized in Utah or New Hampshire, could be challenged in court. It is more likely, however, that if an Eighth Amendment claim were filed, the state legislature would simply amend its statute rendering the constitutional challenge moot. Alternatively, if challenged, states may follow the recent decision of the Georgia Supreme Court, which held that electrocution was unconstitutional as a matter of state constitutional law.[163] Therefore, based upon an analysis of recent case law, it is more likely that no inmate will ever have the standing or opportunity to challenge hanging, shooting, lethal gas, or electrocution as unconstitutional in the Supreme Court.

Opposition of Health Professionals in the United States to Participation in Capital Punishment

In a well-known article published in 1980 in the *New England Journal of Medicine*, William J. Curran and Ward Casscells outlined the major arguments against the participation of medical personnel in executions by lethal injection.[164] The authors cite the Hippocratic Oath and a more modern version of the oath, the World Medical Association's Declaration of Geneva, as well as international ethical principles in condemning the participation of physicians in executions.[165] They also note that "the physician should not escape moral responsibility by ordering a subordinate to do what he or she may not properly do directly," specifically referring to a nurse or medical technician.[166]

Curran and Casscells touch only indirectly upon the issue of the morality of the death penalty in general. It is no secret that the authors are abolitionists by their reference to the "grievous expansion of medical condonation of and participation in capital punishment," to capital punishment as "inhumane treatment," and their observation that a "medical presence gives the impression of moral sanction by the healing professions."[167] Although they recognized that lethal injection is a procedure which "requires the direct application of biomedical knowledge and skills," and they urged the medical profession to "condemn all forms of medical participation in this method of capital punishment," they did not specifically condemn the method itself as a violation of medical ethics.[168] At the time of their article, only four states had lethal injection statutes.

By 1993, Robert Truog and Troyen Brennan noted that, despite the objection of professional organizations, "the participation of doctors and nurses continues and is likely to become more common."[169] The authors discuss different stages of participation in detail and parallel this discussion with the American Medical Association's (AMA) guidelines.[170] Of the six stages of participation by doctors in executions, Truog and Brennan condone only the first. This stage involves caring for the medical needs of death row prisoners, such as providing sedatives and tranquilizers. They consider any further involvement to be in violation of medical ethics. Their analysis is not solely based upon the principle in the Hippocratic Oath that physicians should "do no harm" because, as they observe, the involvement of the physician in some of the early stages of the execution process may even "minimize the likelihood of suffering."[171] Interestingly, the authors also opine that the harm of a physician participating in an execution is not necessarily related to the actual physical participation or the fact that capital punishment involves killing. "Instead the context of the act is the critical feature. . . . medicine defines a moral sphere within which medical activities have special meaning. The execution of a criminal lies far outside the medical sphere. A physician's participation in that execution does nothing to promote the moral community of medicine."[172] According to Truog and Brennan, it is crucial to develop arguments against the participation of physicians in the execution process independent of the argument against the morality of capital punishment itself, presumably because the death penalty "enjoys overwhelming support in the United States."[173]

Most health care professions agreed with Truog and Brennan and have issued Position Statements individually and jointly stating that participation in capital punishment is inconsistent with the ethics of their professions.[174] But all health care professions, however, have avoided taking a position on the morality of capital punishment.[175] The AMA's Council on Ethical and Judicial Affairs stated that "an individual's opinion on capital punishment is the personal moral decision of the individual. A physician, as a member of a profession dedicated to preserving life when there is hope of doing so, should not be a participant in a legally authorized execution."[176] In a joint statement, the AMA, American Nurses' Association (ANA), and the American Public Health Association (APHA) indicated a specific objection to participation in an execution process that "employs the same medical knowledge, devices and methods used by health professionals to heal and preserve life. When a health professional serves in an execution under circumstances that mimics care the healing purpose of the health services and technology is perverted."[177] Nevertheless, the joint statement also indicates that "this statement is directed to the issue of health professional involvement in capital punishment . . . [t]his statement is not a statement on the rightness or wrongness of capital punishment in our society."[178] Both the AMA and the ANA have noted that "the endorsement of the death penalty remains a personal decision."[179]

Although these statements were an important first step towards the abolition of lethal injection executions, they offer no real defense to the argument that if the endorsement of the death penalty is a personal decision, then the participation in executions[180] should also be "a moral choice that an individual health care provider must make."[181] In fact, some health care professionals disagree with the basic premise that "a physician's participation in an execution does nothing to promote the moral community of medicine."[182] They argue that to deny the physician a role is to "introduce even more brutality in the execution process."[183] Certain physicians would be willing to accept the responsibility of participating in an execution due to their duty to their patients, in this case the condemned man, to "try to make the remaining life as comfortable and painless as possible."[184] Furthermore, who could deny that, generally, if a competent physician or nurse were to insert the IV and administer the lethal injection or train the person who did so, the chance of botching the execution and causing the inmate pain would decrease. The truth is that with lethal injection, unless health professionals are willing to take the position that the death penalty is inherently immoral or wrong, it becomes difficult, if not impossible, to argue against the position of the physician or nurse who believes that it is ethical to participate in order to "ensure that the ... murderer's sufferings are not prolonged."[185]

Clearly, the actual participation of the individual in lethal injection execution is not the primary issue. With other methods of execution, it may have been possible to focus only on health professionals' participation in executions. Because lethal injection utilizes medical skills and procedures to sanitize and legitimize the death penalty, this method of execution involves the entire medical community by implication, even those who personally refuse to participate. In addition, although it is true that if "doctors and nurses will not serve as executioners there are technicians who will,"[186] states still require the assistance of the health professions in other less obvious capacities. For example, at least seven states have incorporated into law the explicit statement that the person administering the injection need not be a licensed person, or that the state may not compel a licensed person to participate.[187] The presence of the health professional is still evident, however, by certain statements in statutes in these states, such as: the executioner should be "trained to administer a lethal injection"[188] or "qualified to administer injections and . . . familiar with medical procedures."[189] Therefore, the vitality of lethal injection executions and because it is virtually the sole method of execution, the death penalty itself, is related to the extent to which assistance is provided by the health professions.[190]

More importantly, however, the death penalty is related to the extent to which health care professionals continue to allow the state to appropriate their skills and procedures for the purposes of judicial killing. Therefore, the true objection to participation of health professionals in lethal injection executions is an objection to the method itself as a violation of medical ethics. In this regard, however, "the voice of organized medicine is all but silent."[191]

Current Involvement of Health Professionals in Capital Punishment in the United States

In 1994 Physicians for Human Rights along with other authors published a report entitled *Breach of Trust: Physician Participation in Executions in the United States*.[192] At that time there were twenty-five states with lethal injection statutes, fourteen of which prescribed lethal injection as the sole method of execution and eleven of which listed it as an option.[193] The report found that physicians were involved in all methods of executions but especially in executions by lethal injection. Physicians consulted on lethal dosages, examined veins, witnessed executions, and pronounced death.[194] The authors discovered that state laws and regulations were often in direct conflict with ethical standards, and that the majority of the death penalty states designed a specific role for physicians.[195] The report concluded that the "threat posed to the moral standing of physicians, and to the public trust that physicians hold, is great. It warrants immediate and decisive action to assure the public, and each patient, that physicians will not use their skills to cause immediate and irreparable harm."[196] The report recommended lobbying for legislative changes to state laws in order to incorporate the AMA guidelines on physician participation, as well as changes to laws mandating physician presence and pronouncement of death. Furthermore, the report argued that laws that "facilitate violations of medical ethics," such as anonymity clauses, should not be enacted because the profession would be unable to police itself. Finally, the report suggested that state medical societies should take an active role in defining ethical violations and that licensing boards should take action against physicians who violate ethical standards.[197]

Since 1994, the use of medicine to execute the death penalty has become even more entrenched and health professionals continue to play an active role in such executions.[198] As of June 2001, in addition to the federal government and the U.S. military, there were thirty-six states with lethal injection statutes, twenty-two as the sole method,[199] thirteen as an option,[200] and one with lethal injection as an option after a specified date with the default method prior to that date being electrocution.[201] The two remaining death penalty states, Alabama[202] and Nebraska,[203] have legislation pending that would change the method of execution to lethal injection.

Twenty-eight death penalty states specifically mention the presence of a physician in various capacities. In at least nine states, the law requires that the prisoner be injected until "death is pronounced by a licensed physician according to accepted medical practice."[204] Two states require only that death be pronounced by a licensed physician.[205] In seventeen other states one or more physicians either "shall," "must," or "may" be invited or required to attend the execution.[206] In New Jersey, the law also requires that, prior to the execution, the defendant be sedated "by a licensed physician, registered nurse or other qualified personnel."[207]

One state does not mention a physician, but requires that death be pronounced "according to accepted standards of medical practice."[208] Utah deleted the requirements that a physician may attend the execution and that death be pronounced by a physician. The statute, however, still requires the lethal injection to be administered by "two or more persons trained in accordance with acceptable medical practices," and certification of death by a physician.[209]

Although certain statutes of the remaining eight states have been written to give the appearance of limited participation by health care professionals, it is clear that health professionals are still involved in executions in these states. In

Louisiana, for example, the statute provides that "no health care professional shall be compelled to administer the lethal injection."[210] The Department of Corrections regulations, however, lists "a physician as one of the four witnesses to be present in the execution room during the execution."[211] Nevertheless, this does not conflict with state law because one of the four people to be present must be a person "competent to administer lethal injections."[212] The implication is that the nonlicensed person will administer the injection and the physician will supervise. Furthermore, although the Delaware statute does not mention a physician, there is also a role for a medical doctor in the Department of Correction regulations.[213] Likewise, although Missouri deleted the requirement that a physician "shall be invited" to the execution, there is no indication that the regulations of the Department of Corrections, which indicate that "the IV is placed by medical staff. . . . vital signs monitored by medical staff . . . and inmate pronounced dead by a physician," have been altered.[214] Montana and Arizona both amended their death penalty statutes to delete any reference to a physician. In Montana, however, although the executioner "need not be a physician, nurse or LPN," that person must be "trained to administer a lethal injection." Furthermore, the "identity of the executioner must remain anonymous," and "facts pertaining to the selection and training of the executioner must remain confidential."[215] In Arizona, the identity of the executioner and "other persons who participate" to perform ancillary functions is confidential. Furthermore, the statute forbids any licensing board from suspending or revoking a license "as a result of a person's participation in an execution."[216] Similarly, in Kansas there is no mention of the role of a healthcare practitioner, but the "identity of the executioner and other persons designated to assist shall be confidential," and the drugs to be used must be certified by the Secretary of Health and Environment as certain to result in "a swift and humane death."[217]

In two states, Pennsylvania and Nebraska, it is unclear from available information, whether physicians or other health professionals participate in executions. Proposed legislation in both states provides some indication, however, that health professionals must be involved on some level. Pennsylvania deleted the reference to a physician in its death penalty statute in 1998 and now death is pronounced by a coroner. Although no information regarding the procedure of the Pennsylvania Department of Corrections was available, there is some indication that the Pennsylvania legislature would like to make anyone who "participates in the administration of an execution" confidential.[218] If the executioner were not in some way connected to health professionals, this secrecy would not be necessary. Nebraska's current statute provides for execution by electrocution, and the role of the healthcare professional is unclear. Nevertheless, several bills have been filed in the Nebraska legislature to change the execution method to lethal injection. In this regard, the proposed new law states that the "assistance with, participation in, or performance of ancillary functions pursuant to the administration of the substance or substances . . . shall not be construed to be the practice of medicine."[219]

Currently, eleven states have legislation that declares, in some version, that the participation in an execution is not the practice of medicine, and two of those statutes also include other professions relating to health care.[220] Presumably, therefore, a health care professional in these states cannot be subject to disciplinary action for participating in an execution. At least one state is more explicit, stating that a licensing board shall not "suspend or revoke" a license as a result of a person's participation in an execution,[221] while other states have amended professional practice acts to state that participation in an execution is not a violation.[222] In six states, the law requires that the identity of the executioner and others who participate in the execution remain confidential.[223] In ten states statutes specifically state that no prescription is necessary in order to obtain the drugs necessary for the execution.[224]

In their article, two scholars observed that these laws, which redefine medical practice by offering anonymity to participating health care professionals and otherwise attempting to encourage and protect those who violate professional ethics, are a "corruption of medical ethics to suit the convenience of lawmakers and bureaucrats."[225] The practical effect of these laws is that it becomes impossible for professional organizations to gain access to any information regarding who took part in an execution, thereby making it impossible to censure the individuals involved.[226]

We agree with Truog and Brennan that "state medical societies should take the position that involvement in capital punishment is grounds for revoking a physician's license."[227] Nevertheless, their argument that, even though many states grant anonymity to the physician performing or participating in executions, "the risk of losing one's license should [still] serve as a deterrent."[228] This argument, however, rings hollow. There is virtually no such risk. At present, the state will not take away the licenses of health care professionals for participating in executions and the professional societies do not have the power to do so. Therefore, there is no practical way to "enforce ethical behavior from within the profession," or to revoke the licenses of individual doctors or nurses who participate in executions.[229]

The fact that the medical profession has little ability to police its members in the current system is evidenced by a recent suit in California, *Thorburn v. Department of Corrections.*[230] In *Thorburn*, thirteen physicians licensed in California filed suit alleging that physician participation in executions constituted "unprofessional conduct" within the meaning of the California Business and Professions Code. The *Thorburn* lawsuit was not attempting to take away the license of or to censure any individual who may have already participated in an execution. Instead, the plaintiffs sought only an injunction against such conduct in the future. This case represents one of the first organized attempts by physicians "to enforce ethical behavior from within the profession"[231] by using the existing law to stop physicians from participating in any future executions.

The court was asked to take judicial notice that the medical profession and other health professions accept that participation in capital punishment is always unethical conduct.[232] The court refused to do so. In fact, while the court acknowledged that "ethical rules serve ... a vital purpose" of guaranteeing trust between physicians and their patients, it held that "we do not agree that physicians' participation in executions is likely to erode trust."[233] As a rationale, the court noted that physicians had participated in executions for many years and that the plaintiffs had presented no evidence that this participation had eroded trust in physicians in the general population. In others words, despite the "views of the American Medical Association, the California Medical Association, the American College of Physicians, the World Medical Association, the American Public Health Association, as well as medical ethicists, all agreeing that participation in lethal injection executions violates ethical principles,"[234] it was not accepted by the court as fact.

It is not surprising that the *Thorburn* court did not accept the universal opinion of the medical profession and medical ethicists that physician participation in executions is unethical. If it had done so, the court could not have justified the result in the case. The court held that "it is reasonable to assume that by enacting [the lethal execution statute] the legislature contemplated the direct participation of physicians in the execution process."[235] Therefore, the court had to reject the premise that participation was a violation of medical ethics unless it was also prepared to hold that the legislature had authorized "unethical conduct." And that is true of every state that utilizes lethal injection execution.

Recommendations

The utilization of lethal injection as a method of execution humanizes "executions so that they are as quick, painless, and reliable, and as little disfiguring as possible [which] is an essential aspect of preserving capital punishment in any society that regards itself as civilized."[236] In the near future, it is likely that lethal injection will be the sole method of execution in the United States. Since it is unlikely that states will revert back to hanging, asphyxiation, electrocution, or the firing squad after the extensive legislative history, court decisions, and public opinion declaring lethal injection as the humane alternative to more traditional methods, the vitality of judicial homicide in the United States is dependent upon the continuation of this perversion of medicine.

The *Thorburn* case and other efforts of the medical profession to "enforce ethical behavior from within the profession" have consistently failed. Primarily, this is because the participation of health professionals, which has been an unfortunate reality for as long as there has been capital punishment, is not the real issue. The real issue is that the use of a medical procedure to execute human beings is, by itself, a violation of medical ethics and human rights. Therefore, despite the importance of political action to limit the involvement of health professionals, an unambiguous stance against capital punishment by organizations representing health professionals, as well as individuals, is important (maybe more important) because of the effect it would have on public opinion, and ultimately, the Supreme Court's evaluation of the death penalty in general, and more specifically, the "evolving notions of decency in a civilized society."[237]

Therefore, while it may be true that "an individual's opinion on capital punishment is the personal moral decision of the individual,"[238] because the death penalty and lethal injection execution are inseparable issues, arguments against one have evolved, by default, into arguments against the other. In other words, while we agree with Truog and Brennan that the unacceptability of participation of health professionals in capital punishment should be recognized as a mature principle of medical ethics despite any divergent views of the individual, because of the use of lethal injection, we believe that this can no longer be accomplished without condemning the death penalty in general.

In the United States, the efforts of human rights activists, health professionals, and others who oppose the death penalty should be focused on the elimination of the lethal injection as a method of execution. In that regard, certain suggestions and recommendations for action include the following:

1. The Position Statements of the AMA, the ANA, and all other professional associations representing health care professionals should be revised to acknowledge that, while the participation of health professionals in any form of capital punishment is a violation of medical ethics, as a *method* of capital punishment, lethal injection is a violation of medical ethics. In line with rejection of lethal injection by the British Medical Association over fifty years ago, we suggest that the new Position Statements state that, because lethal injection is a method of execution that utilizes medical skills and knowledge and always "requires the services of [medical personnel] either in carrying out the actual process of killing, *or in instructing others in the technique of the process*," the method is a violation of medical ethics, independent of the participation of licensed professionals.[239]

2. The cooperation of health professionals is necessary in order for a state to implement lethal injection as a method of execution (even if such cooperation consists only of assistance with policies, procedures, or training). It is critically important, therefore, that the lethal injection protocol, including all policies and procedures, the training of executioners, as well as the names of all participants and their professional affiliations, be made

public. Publicity is necessary because as long as there are no real consequences, health professionals will continue to participate, and lethal injection execution will continue. Currently, however, participants in executions are allowed to wear the "black hood" of anonymity through legislation that seeks to limit information regarding "the selection and training of the executioners"[240] or the identity of "other persons who participate."[241] Furthermore, even in states without such laws, it is difficult to obtain the identity of the execution team. These laws and policies of confidentiality not only limit the enforcement of ethical standards by the medical profession, they also protect health professionals from the damage to their practices and reputations that may result if the public were aware of their participation in executions. For reasons stated above, legislatures and courts are unlikely to recognize the participation by licensed professionals in executions as unprofessional conduct or a violation of medical ethics. Therefore, efforts to reverse these laws by legal redress will almost certainly be futile. Consequently, there is a need for investigative human rights reporting, which will then be made available to the public and filed with the state medical boards and national and state professional associations. We predict that the lifting of the "executioner's hood" will be far more effective in limiting the involvement of health professionals than any effort to date.

3. It is inappropriate for states to amend practice acts to exclude participation in executions as outside the practice of medicine or any other profession relating to health care. There are currently eleven states that have such legislation in some form.[242] The effect of such laws is that professionals are not "doctors" or "nurses" when participating in an execution, and therefore, are outside the jurisdiction of professional organizations' ability to issue sanctions. By enacting these laws, the state has asserted the right to control physicians by defining, not only parameters of medical ethics, but also what it means to practice medicine. Even physicians who do not oppose lethal injection executions should be wary of attempts by the state to define their practice and encourage or limit their professional actions.

4. In the eleven states[243] that require that death be pronounced by a physician (most according to accepted medical practice), individual physicians should encourage (insist that) the state medical society lobby for legislative changes that would remove the requirement of their pronouncing death. In the seventeen states[244] that also specially mention the presence of a physician without mentioning a specific role, legislative changes should be advocated. For example, laws should be enacted that specifically state that doctors are not required to be present at an execution. Because these actions are already considered a violation of medical ethics under

the AMA guidelines, it does not represent a controversial action and should not be difficult to accomplish, even if the result is more symbolic than practical.

5. Except for a few articles, individual accounts,[245] and the brief Position Paper by the ANA, the voice of the nursing profession has been conspicuously absent in this debate. For example, the 1995 edition of a famous treatise on nursing ethics fails to mention the issue of capital punishment in any respect, much less discuss the participation of nurses.[246] It is vital, however, that nurses make a commitment to end their silence and get involved. It is recognized by doctor-members of Amnesty International that they cannot do it alone. "If nurses are willing to undertake executions, much of the doctors' campaigning to limit physician involvement is ineffective."[247] The International Council of Nurses (INC) is a nongovernmental organization representing nurses in more than 120 countries. The INC Code for Nurses is considered the "foundation for ethical nursing practice throughout the world."[248] The INC "considers the death penalty to be the ultimate form of inhumanity" and has condemned the participation of nurses in executions. It also "fully supports the UN Universal Declaration of Human Rights . . . and calls on national nurses associations to lobby for the abolishment of the death penalty in all countries still practicing this form of punishment."[249] The ANA is a member of the INC, and therefore, a signatory on INC policy. State nurses associations should actively encourage the ANA to issue a Position Statement consistent with INC policy and the above recommendations, which condemn the death penalty under all circumstances as a violation of human rights, as well as challenge the AMA to follow its example.

6. In a 1998 survey regarding the opinions of a random sample of practicing physicians regarding the ethics of participation in executions, 43 percent of physicians who answered the questionnaire saw no ethical violation when a physician acts as an executioner by directly injecting lethal drugs. Seventy-four percent agreed that it is not an ethical violation for a physician to be present to pronounce an inmate dead even if the doctor is then placed in the position of asking the executioner to inject more drugs because the inmate is still alive.[250] While the sample was admittedly small, of the physicians who responded it was clear that many either did not care about, or misunderstood, the basis for the ethical objection to medical involvement in executions. Medical schools, nursing schools, and other professional schools should incorporate into the curriculum information regarding the death penalty in general, and specifically, the basis for the ethical objections to medical involvement in lethal injection executions. Furthermore, the publication of articles on the ethical issues involved in lethal injection execution should be actively recruited by professional

journals. In addition, there is also a need for continuing education for working professionals in order to increase the level of awareness of the seriousness of this issue.

7. The death penalty is largely driven by public support and the impact of that support on the political process. Health professionals, through their state agencies or other organizations, could form a committee to educate the lay public about the inequality and unfairness of the judicial system and other issues discussed in this article.

8. The skills, knowledge, and techniques of the health professions have been appropriated by the state to give judicial homicide the appearance of humanity and a veneer of competence and painlessness. It is this façade that has protected the death penalty from constitutional scrutiny and has ensured that executions are not unpalatable to the public. Because most of the other methods of execution have been acknowledged to be painful and cruel, either explicitly by some courts as in the case of lethal gas and electrocution or implicitly in the legislative history of death penalty statutes, capital punishment in the United States would be unlikely to survive without the lethal injection. Furthermore, because the method is a violation of medical ethics, even if a licensed professional does not participate, health professionals have a moral obligation to end the tacit acceptance of the states' utilization of the tools and techniques of healing in the service of state killing. Physicians, nurses, and all allied health professionals must acknowledge a collective responsibility for their complicity as a profession in this continued violation of human rights and actively work for the abolition of capital punishment by lethal injection in the United States.

Notes

1. Amnesty International (AI), *Lethal Injection: The Medical Technology of Execution* (Jan. 1998), ACT 50/001/1998 (quoting a press interview regarding the execution of Antonia James March 1996) [hereinafter AI, *Lethal Injection*].
2. Martin Gardner, "Executions and Indignities-An Eighth Amendment Assessment of Methods of Inflicting Capital Punishment," 39 *Ohio State L.J.* 96, 130 (1978).
3. See Michael Reese & Stryker McGuire, "The First Humane Execution," *Newsweek*, 20 Dec. 1982.
4. See Ronald Kotulak, "Execution by Injection: The Doctor's Dilemma," *Chicago Tribune*, 12 Dec. 1982, quoting Dr. Mark S. Frankel.
5. Death Penalty Information Center (DPIC), "Executions in the U.S. 1976–1986 and 1987–1990," available at <http://www.deathpenaltyinfo.org/facts.html#Executions> (visited 19 Feb. 2002).
6. Id. at "Executions in 1991 to 2001."
7. Id. at "Executions in 2002." All executions in 2001 were also by lethal injection. Id. at "Executions in 2001."
8. For example, the Supreme Court has held that:
    (i) a potential juror may be excused for cause if opposed to the death penalty, resulting in a pro-death penalty jury; Lockhart v. McCree, 476 U.S. 162 (1986);
    (ii) capital sentences need not be compared to similar capital cases in order to determine proportionality; Pully v. Harris, 465 U.S. 37 (1984);

(iii) juvenile offenders may be put to death; Stanford v. Kentucky, 492 U.S. 361 (1989);

(iv) mentally retarded people can legally be put to death; Penry v. Lynaugh, 492 U.S. 302 (1989);

(v) a trial judge may impose a sentence of death over a jury's recommendation of life in prison; Spaziano v. Florida, 468 U.S. 447 (1984).

9. Susan Raeker-Jordan, "A Pro-Death, Self-Fulfilling Constitutional Construct: The Supreme Court's Evolving Standards of Decency for The Death Penalty," 23 *Hastings Const. L.Q.* 455, 456–57 (1996); see also Carol S. & Jordan M. Steiker, "Sober Second Thoughts: Reflections on Two Decades of Constitutional Regulation of Capital Punishment," 109 *Harv. L. Rev.* 357 (1995). "The Supreme Court has in fact turned its back on regulating the death penalty and no longer even attempts to meet the concerns about the arbitrary and discriminatory imposition of death . . . " Id. at 358.

10. Deborah W. Denno, "Adieu to Electrocution," 26 *Ohio N.U.L. Rev.* 665, 678 (2000).

11. See *infra* notes 143–63 and accompanying text.

12. See "Professional Societies Oppose Health Care Professionals Participation in Capital Punishment, A Joint Statement by the American Medical Association, the American Nurses Association, and the American Public Health Association," Press Release 13 Sept. 1994, available at <http://www.nursingworld.org/1996/execut1.htm>. (visited 15 Feb. 2002).

13. See *infra* notes 192–224 and accompanying text.

14. Dr. Gray was not at all concerned that his actions may have been unethical as he "glibly argued that physicians routinely cut living flesh out of patients for therapeutic reasons and that by analogy, he is entitled to help society try to cure itself of crime by killing a criminal." Henry Schwarzchild, "Homicide By Injection," *N.Y. Times*, 23 Dec. 1982.

15. Marcia Cohen, "Execution by Injection, A Texas Killer's 'Death by Needle' Sparks a Medical and Ethical Furor," US, 14 Feb. 1983, at 18.

16. Id. at 20.

17. Patrick Malone, Death Row and the Medical Model, Hastings Center, Oct. 1979. In 1993 the AMA detailed specific actions that would be prohibited and under the new standard the above actions would be considered unethical. Council on Ethical and Judicial Affairs, American Medical Association, "Physician Participation in Capital Punishment," 270 J. *Am. Med. Ass'n* 365–68 (1993).

18. J.K. Boehnlein, et al. "Medical Ethics, Cultural Values, and Physician Participation in Lethal Injections," 23(1) *Bull. Am. Acad. Psychiatry & L.* 129–34 (1995).

19. This can be illustrated by the recent decision of the Georgia Supreme Court declaring that *compared with lethal injection*, "electrocution with its specter of excruciating pain and its certainty of cooked brains and blistered bodies, violates the prohibition of cruel and unusual punishment [in the Georgia Constitution.]" *Dawson v. State*, 554 S.E.2d 137 (Ga. 2001).

20. Until recently, the United States was the only country that utilized lethal injection as an execution method. This was true until 1997, when China followed our example and became the second country to medicalize the execution of human beings. There are indications that, in China, there is the potential for "massive use of this form of execution." AI, *Lethal Injection, supra* note 1. In fact, recently the Chinese government has said that it will increase the use of the lethal injection. *See* Amnesty International Online, available at <http://www.amnesty.org> (visited 22 Jan. 2002). "News for Health Professionals," ACT 8 Sept. 2000 84/018/2000, dated 9 Aug. 2000. The first execution by lethal injection in Guatemala took place on 10 February 1998. Prior to the execution the Guatemalan press and authorities said that lethal injection was being introduced because it was more humane. See also "Lethal Injection, Guatemala," *AMR* 17 Jan. 2002 34/14/1998. The Philippines also has a lethal injection execution law. AI, *Lethal Injection, supra* note 1. In Thailand, the Prime Minister recently endorsed a bill to replace the shooting of condemned prisoners with the more "humane" lethal injection. "Amnesty Int'l News for Health Professionals," 4 AI *Bull.* 2 Feb. 2001, AI *Index: ACT* 84/03/01 (2 Feb. 2001).

21. See generally "Universal Declaration of Human Rights," 1948, in *Basic Documents on Human Rights* (Ian Brownlie ed., 3d ed., 1992). The issue of the abolition of the death penalty was promoted as a goal for civilized nations during the drafting of the Universal Declaration of Human Rights. Although not explicitly mentioned in the document, aboli-

tion was crucial in the drafting of Article 3, the "right to life." See also William A. Schabas, *The Abolition of the Death Penalty in International Law* 24 (2d ed. 1997).

22. Despite considerable progress toward abolition, there is no international consensus that capital punishment should be condemned as a violation of human rights. See Toni M. Fine, "Moratorium 2000: An International Dialogue Toward a Ban on Capital Punishment," 30 *Colm. Hum. Rts. L. Rev.* 421 (1999); see also Richard Dieter, "International Perspectives on the Death Penalty: A Costly Isolation for the U.S." (Oct. 1999), available at <http://www.deathpenaltyinfo.org/internationalreport.html> (visited 4 Feb. 2002).

23. See "Second Optional Protocol to the International Covenant on Civil and Political Rights (ICCPR)," adopted 15 Dec. 1989, *G.A. Res.* 44/128 (entered into force July 11, 1991), available at <http://www.unhchr.ch/html/menu3/b/a_opt2.htm> (visited 15 Feb. 2002) (ratified by forty-six states and signed by seven); "Sixth Protocol to the Convention for the Protection of Human Rights and Fundamental Freedoms Concerning the Abolition of the Death Penalty," E.T.S. 114, entered into force 1 Mar. 1985, available at <http://www1.umn.edu/humanrts/euro/z25prot6.htm> (visited 25 Feb. 2002) (this protocol agrees to abolish the death penalty in peacetime and has been ratified by thirty-nine states and signed by three); "Protocol to the American Convention on Human Rights to Abolish the Death Penalty," available at <http://www.oas.org/juridico/english/Treaties/a-53.htm> (visited 25 Feb. 2002) (ratified by eight states and signed by one). See also Amnesty International, Website Against the Death Penalty, "Facts and Figures on the Death Penalty," available at <http://web.amnesty.org/rmp/dplibrary.nst/index? openview> (visited 25 Feb. 2002) (hereinafter AI "Death Penalty Web site").

24. DPIC, "History of the Death Penalty, Part II," available at <http://www.deathpenaltyinfo.org/history3.html> (visited 26 Apr. 2001).

The Ukraine, one of the leaders in executions, has stopped utilizing capital punishment in order to be admitted to the Council of Europe, and Russian President Boris Yeltsin signed a decree commuting the death sentences of all convicts on death row in 1999. See *id.*

Therefore, there is good reason to believe that the Russian Federation will soon become an abolitionist state. See generally "Crime Prevention and Criminal Justice, Capital Punishment and the Implementation of Safeguards Guaranteeing Protection of the Rights of Those Facing the Death Penalty," *Report of the Secretary General*, ECOSOC, U.N. Doc. E/2000/3, 31 Mar. 2000, at 9 (hereinafter "Crime Prevention and Criminal Justice").

25. See AI, *"Death Penalty News," AI Index ACT* 53/03/99 (1. June 1999). Because it was clear from the outset that the absolute prohibition of the death penalty would necessarily be a gradual process, international standards and covenants that sought to limit the scope of the practice were developed for those countries that retained capital punishment. See AI, *United States of America "A Macabre Assembly Line of Death, Death Penalty Developments in 1997,"* AI Index AMR 51/20/98.

26. See AI Death Penalty Web site, *supra* note 23 (Abolitionist and Retentionist Countries).

27. See id. Although Japan has not abolished the practice, capital punishment is utilized infrequently in that industrialized country. *See* Stephen Thaman, "Is America a Systematic Violator of Human Rights in the Administration of Criminal Justice?" 44 *St. Louis L.J.* 999, 1000 (2000).

28. The Economic and Social Council of the United Nations by resolution 1996/15 of 23 July 1996, called upon retentionist states to apply effectively the safeguards guaranteeing the protection of the rights of those facing the death penalty. These safeguards call upon states to ensure: (a) that the death penalty is reserved for only the most serious crimes; (b) capital punishment should only be imposed if the penalty was in place before the crime was committed and the defendant should benefit from changes in the law after which would warrant a lesser penalty after the commission of a crime; (c) juvenile defendants never ever face the death penalty; (d) there should be no remaining question of guilt, (e) a defendant is entitled to a fair trial in accordance with article 14 of the ICCPR; (f) appellate rights should be mandatory; (g) the condemned have the right to seek pardon or commutation of their sentence; (h) the sentence of death shall not be carried out while an appeal or other procedure is pending; (i) capital punishment shall inflict the least possible suffering. See *Crime Prevention and Criminal Justice, supra* note 24, at 17 and Annex II.

29. For example, the International Covenant on Civil and Political Rights, *adopted* 16 Dec. 1966, G.A. Res. 2200 (XXI), U.N. GAOR, 21st Sess., Supp. No. 16, art. 14, § 3 (b), U.N. Doc. A/6316 (1966), 999 U.N.T.S. 171 (*entered into force* 23 Mar. 1976) art. 14, § 3(b) states that defendants should have adequate time and facilities for the preparation of a defense. In addition, legal assistance should be provided free to those who cannot afford to hire an attorney. Although under U.S. law each state is required to provide indigent defendants with an attorney, there is no requirement that the attorney be competent, have adequate resources to prepare a defense, or even that the attorney be awake and sober. A 1984 Supreme Court opinion held that a defendant not only had to prove that his lawyer's performance was deficient, but that it had affected the outcome of the trial. See *Strickland v. Washington*, 466 U.S. 668, 687 (1987). The *Strickland* decision instructed appeals court judges that in reviewing a defense lawyer's performance they must "indulge a strong presumption that counsel's conduct falls within the wide range of reasonable professional assistance." *id.* at 689. As Justice Ruth Bader Ginsburg recently said, 'People who are well represented at trial do not get the death penalty. I have yet to see a death penalty case among the dozens coming to the Supreme Court on the eve of execution stay applications in which the defendant was well represented at trial." DPIC, "What's New: Last Updated April 24, 2001," quoting *Associated Press,* 10 Apr. 2000. In its application of the death penalty, the United States is also in violation of the Race Convention, the Torture Convention, and the Vienna Convention on Consular Relations. See DPIC, "Discrimination, A Response to the Initial Report of the United States to the United Nations," *Ford Foundation Symposium*, 12 Nov. 1998; DPIC, Richard Dieter, "The U.S. Death Penalty and international Law: the Compliance with the Torture and Race Conventions," *Ford Foundation Symposium*, 12 Nov. 1998. See also "International Convention on the Elimination of All Forms of Racial Discrimination," adopted 21 Dec. 1965, 660 U.N.T.S. 195 (entered into force 4 Jan. 1969), reprinted in *5 I.L.M.* 352 (1966); "Convention Against Torture and Other Cruel, Inhuman or Degrading Treatment or Punishment," adopted 10 Dec. 1984, *G.A. Res.* 39/46, U.N. GAOR 39th Sess., Supp. No. 51, U.N. Doc. A/39/51 (1985) (entered into force 26 June 1987), reprinted in 23 *I.L.M.* 1027 (1984), substantive changes noted in 24 *I.L.M.* S35 (1985); "Vienna Convention on Consular Relations," adopted 24 Apr. 1963, 596 U.N.T.S. 261.

30. Between 1994 and 1998, the United States executed four people who were below the age of eighteen at the time that they committed their crime. Only three other countries executed child defendants during the same time period, including the Islamic Republic of Iran, Nigeria, and Pakistan. See "Crime Prevention and Criminal Justice," *supra* note 24, at 21 ¶ 90. In fact, since 1990, although seven countries have been known to execute juvenile offenders, the United States has executed fourteen juvenile offenders, more than any other country. AI Death Penalty Website *supra* note 23, at ¶ 5 (AI Index: *ACT* 50/002/2001) (5 Apr. 2001). The other countries are Congo (Democratic Republic), Iran, Nigeria, Saudi Arabia, and Yemen. *Id.* As of February 2001, seventy-three juvenile offenders await execution in the United States. Twenty-six are on death row in Texas. DPIC, "Case Summaries for Current Death Row Inmates Under Juvenile Death Sentences" <http://www.deathpenalty info.org/juvcases.html> (visited 15 Feb. 2002).

31. The argument that the death penalty deters crime has been consistently discredited by a lack of scientific evidence and it negates the internationally accepted goal of rehabilitation by replacing it with revenge and retribution. See "Crime Prevention and Criminal Justice," *supra* note 24, at 17. See also *America's Experiment With Capital Punishment–Reflection on the Past Present, and Future of the Ultimate Penal Sanction* (James Acker, Robert Bohm, & Charles Lanler eds., 1998).

32. See DPIC, "Costs of the Death Penalty" <http://www. deathpenaltyinfo.org/costs2.html> (visited 15 Feb. 2002).

33. A recent statistical study that reviewed capital appeals in the United States from 1973 to 1995 found the "overall Prejudicial error rate in the American capital punishment system was 68%." James Liebman, et al. *A Broken System: Error Rates in Capital Cases, 1973–1995* The Justice Project <http://www.ThejusticeProject.org> (visited 23 May 2001). Capital trials produce so many mistakes that "there is grave doubt as to whether we do catch [all of the errors]" and that "high error rates put many individuals at risk for wrongful execution." *Id.* at 2. It has been estimated that "for every six prisoners executed since the reinstatement of

the death penalty the USA, one innocent person was condemned to die and later exonerated." AI Press Release, "USA: No Getting Away From it the Risk of Lethal Error in Death Penalty Cases," AI Index: *AMR* 51/88/98, 3 Nov. 1998. In fact from 1973 to 1 June 2001, ninety-five people on death row have been exonerated and released. *See* <http://www.deathpenaltyinfo.org> (last updated June 1, 2001). Less fortunate prisoners, who may be equally blameless "have gone to their deaths." *Id.*

34. ̆ Although it is true that public support has decreased recently, abolitionists remain in the minority. See M. Kranish, "McVeigh Case Defies Views on Death, In General Support For Executions Drops," *Boston Globe*, 11 June 2001, at A1 and A11 (referring to a recent poll that indicated that support for the death penalty is at a twenty-year low. Support dropped from 80 percent in 1995 to 66 percent in 2001.).

35. The United States has executed 760 people since 1976. *See* DPIC, *supra* note 5, at *Executions in 2002*. There are approximately 3,709 inmates on death row. See DPIC, "Death Row Inmates by State" <http://www.deathpenaltyinfo.org/DRowlnfo.html> (visited 20 Feb. 2001).

36. See "Crime Prevention and Criminal Justice," *supra* note 24, at 13 ¶ 60. Although it is true that the United States, due to its size, actually had one of the lowest rates per capita of executions, two thirds of the executions in the United States between 1994 and 1998 took place in only six of the thirty-eight states with the death penalty. *Id.* at 13–15 ¶ 61.

37. See David J. Rothman, "Physicians and the Death Penalty," 4 *J. L. & Pol'y* 151 (1995).

38. Because capital punishment was justified by its alleged ability to deter crime, public executions were ostensibly a warning to others of the power of the state over a criminal. In theory, this threat would deter future criminal conduct. See *Capital Punishment, Cruel and Unusual?* 58 (Nancy R. Jacobs et al. eds., 1998).

39. See John P. Rutledge, "The Definitive Inhumanity of Capital Punishment," 20 *Whittier L. Rev.* 283, 290 (1998).

40. Louis P. Masur, *Rites of Execution: Capital Punishment and the Transformation of American Culture* 22, 96–97 (1989).

41. See *id.* at 94–95 (this question was initially posed by Masur in his study of capital punishment in America).

42. R.J. Lifton & G. Mitchell, *Who Owns Death, Capital Punishment, The American Conscience, And The End of Eexcutions* 30 (2000).

43. Rothman, *supra* note 37, at 155.

44. See Masur, *supra* note 40, at 96–97.

45. See *id.* at 94.

46. See *id.* at 21.

47. Rothman, *supra* note 37, at 154.

48. See "Lifton & Mithell," *supra* note 42, at 30. According to Lifton, such disaffection "always reflects a decline in confidence in society's policy of execution." *Id.*

49. Robert Johnson, *Death Work: A Study of the Modern Execution Process* 29–31 (2d ed. 1998), citing Masur, *supra* note 40, at 22.

50. See id.

51. See Masur, *supra* note 40, at 21.

52. The debate regarding the potential use of drugs in capital punishment appears to have begun with the murder trial of Washington Goode in 1849, an African-American sailor. It is interesting to note that this debate began during a time of national debate over capital punishment. *Id.* at 9–14.

53. *Id.* at 20.

54. *Id.* at 21.

55. *Id.* at 20 (citing Wendell Phillips, *Speeches, Lectures and Letter, Liberator,* 29 June 1849, at 108–09).

56. *Id.* at 21–22.

57. Lifton & Mitchell, *supra* note 42, at 62.

58. R.J. Lifton, *The Nazi Doctors: Medical Killing and the Psychology of Genocide* 57 (1986). In Hitler's Germany the medicalization of state killing was considered an indispensable part of the direct euthanasia program and the Final Solution. And while the Nazis believed that "the syringe belongs in the hands of the physician" some also believed that "only doctors should carry out the gassings." *Id.* at 71–72. This was because as Karl Brandt stated

"this whole question can only be looked at from a medical point of view." *Id.* at 72.

59. Rothman, *supra* note 37, at 154.
60. One of the most important decisions that the judge in the trial of Oklahoma bomber Timothy McVeigh faced was whether to allow the execution to be televised. See Ausyon Sarat, *When the State Kills, Capital Punishment and the American Condition* 188 (2001). The judge allowed 232 surviving victims and their families to watch by closed circuit television, and one witness noted that McVeigh was "allowed to die quietly by lethal injection compared to the bloody horror of the Alfred P. Murrah Federal Building." See also D. Jackson, "McVeigh Gone But Pain Lingers," *Boston Globe*, 13 June 2001, at A19.
61. See Johnson, *supra* note 49, at 125. See generally, 1. Solotaroff, *The Last Face You Will Ever See* (2001).
62. Ronald Kotulak, "Execution by Injection: The Doctor's Dilemma," *Chicago Tribune*, 12 Dec. 1982, at 4.
63. *Id.*
64. Johnson, *supra* note 49, at 125.
65. *Id.*
66. At least six states have laws that require that the identity of the executioner and his assistants remain confidential. These states are Arizona, Florida, Illinois, Kansas, Montana, and New York. See *Ariz. Rev. Stat.* § 13–704 (2000); *Fla. Stat. Ann.* § 9222.10 (West 2000); 725 *Lu. Comp. Stat.* 119–5 (2001); *Kan. Stat. Ann.* § 22–4001 (1999); *Mont. Code Ann.* § 46–19–103 (2000); *N.Y. Correction Law* § 660 (McKinney 2000).
67. For example, shortly after the federal government executed Oklahoma bomber Timothy McVeigh in June 2001, the fifty-four page Bureau of Prisons "protocol manual" was available on the Internet. This manual addressed everything from the purchase of the chemicals that were used to kill McVeigh to the post-mortem site clean-up. Upon inspection however, the portions of the document that were "blacked out by Bureau of Prison lawyers," were among others, those portions regarding the "execution checklist." Because there is no indication of the training, identity, and educational background of the execution team it is reasonable to assume that this information was contained within the ablated sections of the document. See "Federal Bureau of Prisons Execution Protocol Manual, The Smoking Gun Archive" available at <http://www.thesmokinggun.com/archive/bopprotocol1.shtml> (visited 26 July 2001).
68. Johnson, *supra* note 49, at 125.
69. See Kotulak, *supra* note 62.
70. There are many ethical dilemmas surrounding the psychiatric treatment of death row inmates and the general use of medical testimony in the criminal justice system. Medical doctors are asked to certify that a defendant is mentally fit to stand trial and/or that the defendant was sane at the time of the commission of the crime. In addition, the Supreme Court has placed medical doctors in the untenable position of certifying that a prisoner is sane enough to be killed or treating him until he is well enough to be killed. See *Ford v. Wainwright,* 477 U.S. 399 (1986). See generally W.J. Curran, "Medical Intelligence, Law-Medicine Notes, Psychiatric Evaluations and Mitigating Circumstances in Capital Punishment Sentencing," 307 *New Eng. J. Med.* 1431–32 (1982); Christina Michalos, "Medical Ethics and the Execution Process in the United States of America," *Med. Law* 16 (1997). The ethical issues raised by the above are complex and are beyond the scope of this work and will therefore not be addressed.
71. For example, during William Kemmler's execution, many physicians were in attendance. In fact, among twenty witnesses, there were fourteen doctors. See Lifton & Mitchell, *supra* note 42, at 94.
72. AI, *Lethal Injection, supra* note 1.
73. American College of Physicians et al. Breach of Trust: Physician Participation in Executions in the United States (1994) [hereinafter Breach of Trust].
74. AI, *Lethal Injection, supra* note 1 (citing Amnesty International, "The Execution by Lethal Injection of Charles Brooks in Huntsville Texas," 7 Dec. 1982, AI Index: *AMR* 51/10/82).
75. Marcia Cohen, "Execution by Injection, A Texas Killer's 'Death by Needle' Sparks a Medical and Ethical Furor," US, 14 Feb. 1983, at 18–19.
76. Sarat, *supra* note 60, at 61–62.
77. *Id.*

78. S. Ragon, A Doctor's Dilemma: Resolving the Conflict Between Physician Participation in Executions and the AMA's Code of Medical Ethics, 20 *U. Dayton L. Rev.* 975 (1995).

79. *Breach of Trust, supra* note 73.

80 See Meghan S. Skelton, "Lethal Injection in the Wake of *Fierro v. Gomez*," 19 *Thomas Jefferson L. Rev.* 1, 8 (1997).

81. See Craig Brandon, *The Electric Chair, An Unnatural American History* 22 (1999).

82. See *id.* at 14.

83. Dr. Southwick and various colleagues actually spent a considerable amount of time experimentally executing stray animals with electricity in order to ascertain the correct voltages and techniques. After hundreds of animals were electrocuted and Southwick got consistent results he published articles stating that electrocution was the "safest and kindest method of killing" animals. *Id.* at 21.

84. *Id.* at 22.

85. *Id.* at 24.

86. *Id.*

87. Lifton & Mitchell, *supra* note 42, at 93, citing Daniel Arasse.

88. *Id.* at 93.

89. *Id.*

90. *Id.*

91. For example, the representative who introduced the lethal injection bill into the Texas house said that electrocution is "a very scary thing to see. Blood squirts out of the nose. The eyeballs pop out. The body almost virtually catches fire." Scott Christianson, "Corrections Law Developments, Execution by Lethal Injection," 15 *Crim. L. Bull.* 69, 73 (1979).

92. See AI, *Lethal Injection, supra* note 1.

93. *See id.*

94. Deborah Denno, "Execution and the Forgotten Eighth Amendment, in America's Experiment with Capital Punishment: Reflections on the Past, Present, and Future of the Ultimate Penal Sanction" 561 (James R. Acker, Robert M. Bohm & Charles S. Lanier eds., 1998); AI, *Lethal Injection, supra* note 1. The committee appointed to consider the issue included as one of its three members, Dr. Southwick, the father of electrocution. They came out in favor of electrocution in 1889. See AI, *Lethal Injection, supra* note 1.

95. Royal Commission on Capital Punishment 1949–1950 Report, Presented to Parliament by Command of Her Majesty, Sept. 1953, London, Her Majesty's Stationery Office, Reprinted 1973, at 256.

96. *Id.* at 257.

97. *Id.* at 258.

98. This was prior to the Supreme Court case in 1976 that held that the punishment of death does not violate the Constitution. See *Gregg v. Georgia,* 428 U.S. 153 (1976).

99. Deborah Denno, "Getting to Death: Are Executions Constitutional," 82 *Lowa L. Rev.* 319, 374 n.315 (1997) quoting Henry Schwarzschild, "Homicide By Injection," *N.Y. Times,* 23 Dec. 1982, at A15. See also Christianson, *supra* note 91, at 69, 78.

100. See Patrick Malone, "Death Row and the Medical Model," 9 *Hastings Center Report* 5 (1979). Lawmakers were told that the electric chair would have cost $62,000 to repair and a new gas chamber about $200,000. However, "death by injection would cost only about $10 to $15 per event." *Id.*

101. See Denno, *Getting to Death, supra* note 99, at 374–75, n.321.

102. *Id.* (letter from Dr. Stanley Deutsch to the Honorable Bill Dawson dated 28 Feb. 1977).

103. See Christianson, *supra* note 91, at 69, 71.

104. *Id.* at 72.

105. See AI, *Lethal Injection, supra* note 1.

106. Letter from Edgar J. Dunn Jr., Chairman of the Florida Corrections Commission, to the Governor, Senate President and Speaker of the House of Representatives, 20 June 1997 (quoting the explanation that numerous states had given for changing their execution method to lethal injection), in *Florida Corrections Commission, Supplemental Report: Execution Methods Used by States*, available at <http://www.fcc.state.fl.us/fcc/reports/exmeth.pdf> (visited 26 Feb. 2002).

107. See Denno, *Getting to Death, supra* note 99, at 374.

108. See Richard C. Deiter, "Millions Misspent: What Politicians Don't Say About the High Costs of the Death Penalty," in *The Death Penalty in America* 401 (Hugo A. Bedau ed., 1997).

109. See Denno, *Getting to Death, supra* note 99, at 374.

110. Ronald Bayer, "No Nice Face for Death," *N.Y. Times*, 15 July 1983, at A23.

111. See William J. Curran & Ward Casscells," Sounding Board, The Ethics of Medical Participation in Capital Punishment by Intravenous Drug Injection," 302 *N. Eng. J. Med.* 226 (1980), citing "Changing the Execution Law," *Oklahoma City Times* 3 Feb. 1977, at 36.

112. Denno, *Getting to Death, supra* note 99 at 389, n.426, citing Michael Norman, "Why New Jersey is Leaning to Executions by Injection," *N.Y. Times*, 18 May 1983, at B6.

113. Martin Gardner, *Executions and Indignities-An Eighth Amendment Assessment of Methods of Inflicting Capital Punishment*, supra note 2, at 129.

114. David C. Anderson, "Who Wears the Blindfold at Executions?," *The Nation*, 26 Feb. 1996.

115. Cohen, *supra* note 75, at 20.

116. See Kotulak, *supra* note 62.

117. In order to add a frame of reference to the discussion, it is helpful to review the actual procedure. The Arkansas procedure is typical of most of the procedures in the states that use this method of execution. (There are some differences from state to state, but these variations are not significant.) The execution team consists of administrative staff, tiedown, and an IV team. The IV team consists of volunteer community-based medical personnel qualified to insert IV lines or to perform a cut down, which is a surgical incision to locate a vein, and security staff. Two separate IV lines are inserted into the prisoner. Although the IV team inserts the IV, the executioner actually administers the drugs and his identity is unknown. The executioner has a private meeting with the medical administrator prior to the execution. The prisoner is placed on a standard sized hospital gurney with his arm extended. The medical administrator wears a low-frequency headset and stands next to the condemned prisoner. The headset allows communication with the executioner so he can direct which IV line to use if problems arise. Three drugs are used in a particular sequence and a specific concentration to cause death: (1) sodium pentothal, which is supposed to render the prisoner unconscious, is given in a toxic but not lethal amount, followed by a saline flush to clean the IV line; (2) pancuronium bromide "pavulon," a smooth muscle paralytic which renders the inmate unable to breathe, is administered in a toxic but not lethal amount and is also followed by a saline flush of the line; and (3) potassium chloride, which stops the inmate's heart. It is important that the drugs be administered in the correct amounts and in sequence. Some of the drugs cannot be mixed or they will crystallize and become ineffective. The EKG of the prisoner is monitored to determine when he is dead. See *Florida Corrections Commission Reports, supra* note 106, at 12–14.

118. Michael Davis, *Justice in the Shadow of Death, Rethinking Capital and Lessor Punishments* 80 (1996). While raising this argument, the author does state that the lethal injection is "indisputably a medical procedure" but that it "lies at the outer margin of medical practice." *Id.* While we agree that it is a medical procedure, we disagree that it is encompassed within legitimate medical practice when used to kill.

119. Dan Colburn, "Death by Prescription 'Humane' Punishment Raises Ethical Questions," *The Herald*, 23 Jan. 1985 (quoting Dr. Michael Nelson, a Massachusetts psychiatrist and cofounder of Physicians Against the Death Penalty).

120. Curran & Casscells, *supra* note 111, at 229.

121. Davis, *supra* note 118, at 80.

122. AI, *Lethal Injection, supra* note 1.

123. *Furman v. Georgia*, 408 U.S. 288 (1972) (Douglas, J., concurring).

124. *Id.* at 360 (Brennan, J., concurring) (citing *Trop v. Dulles*, 356 U.S. 86, 99 (1958)).

125. See *Gregg v. Georgia*, 428 U.S. 153 (1976).

126. *Id.* at 171.

127. *Id.* (citing *Trop v. Dulles*, 356 U.S. 86, 101 (1958)).

128. For example, the *Gregg* plurality held that the legislative response to *Furman* (thirty-five states had enacted capital punishment statutes) indicated that society continued to endorse the death penalty. See *Gregg*, 428 U.S. at 179.

129. See *id.* at 174, n.19.

130. *Id.* at 173. It is interesting to note that when confronted with the infrequency with which juries imposed the death penalty, the Court held that it may well "reflect the humane feeling for this most irrevocable of sanctions" and not a rejection of capital punishment. *Id.* at 182.

131. See *id.* at 170.

132. Therefore, there must be some justification for the death penalty or it would be excessive. In the opinion written by Justice Stewart in the *Gregg* case, he named two social purposes or justifications for the death penalty: retribution and deterrence. He acknowledged that evidence that the death penalty actually deters crime is inconclusive but insisted that federalism would not allow the Court to override the voted representatives of the people by judicial activism. He wrote, "the value of capital punishment as a deterrent of crime . . . rests with the legislatures." *Gregg*, 428 U.S. at 186. He also noted that, although "'retribution is no longer the dominant objective of the criminal law,' *Williams v. N.Y.*, 337 U.S. 241, 248 (1949), . . . neither is it a forbidden objective nor one inconsistent with our respect for the dignity of men." *Id.* at 183–84.

133. *Id.* at 173.

134. *Id.* at 178 (citing *In re Kemmler*, 136 U.S. 436, 447 (1890)).

135. Stanford v. Kentucky, 492 U.S. 361 (1989).

136. See Raeker-Jordan, *supra* note 9, at 455, 486.

137. *Id.* at 455, 477.

138. *Stanford*, 492 U.S. at 370 n.1. Justice Scalia's legal analysis is not only a departure from the Supreme Court's previous jurisprudence—it is contrary to the opinion of many influential legal analysts. For example in the Brief of the Amici Curiae in *McCarver v. North Carolina*, which was before the Supreme Court on the issue of the constitutionality of the execution of people with mental retardation, many distinguished diplomats and scholars stated that the "amici believe that under the jurisprudence of the Eighth and Fourteenth Amendments, [the] Court cannot meaningfully evaluate "'evolving standards of decency that mark the progress of a maturing society', without weighing international as well as domestic opinion." "Brief of the Amici Curiae Diplomats Morton Abramowitz, Stephen W. Bosworth, Stuart E. Eizenstat, John C. Kornblum, Phyllis E. Oakley, Thomas R. Pickering, Felix G. Rohatyn, J. Stapleton Roy, and Frank G. Wisner," in *Support of Petitioner*, at 6, from *McCarver v. North Carolina*, Supreme Court of the United States, 2000 Term (No-00–8727) (citations omitted).

139. Raeker-Jordan, supra note 9, at 495–97 & n. 210 & n. 219. Furthermore, only states with death penalty legislation are considered relevant such that the standards of decency in abolitionists states are ignored. *Id.* at 497.

140. See *Trop v. Dulles*, 356 U.S. 86, 102 (1958). See also Gardner, *supra* note 113, at 96.

141. *Dawson v. State*, 274 Ga. 327, 335 (2001).

142. *Id.*

143. See Denno, *Getting to Death, supra* note 99, at 319, 321. In *In re Kemmler*, the Court found the Eighth Amendment inapplicable to the states. See *In re Kimmler*, 136 U.S. 436, 442 (1890). Although this decision is frequently misquoted, the Court did not hold that electrocution was constitutional under the Eighth Amendment but rather deferred to New York state law. See *In re Kremmler*, 136 U.S. at 447; Deborah W. Denno, "Adieu to Electrocution," 26 *Ohio N.U.L. Rev.* 665 (2000).

144. Denno, *Getting to Death, supra* note 99, at 389. For example, in Maryland when a death row inmate requested that his lethal gas execution be videotaped to support the petition of another inmate's constitutional challenge to the lethal gas statute, lawmakers introduced the lethal injection bill. See *Id.*

145. See *Fierro v. Gomez*, 77 F.3d 301, 309 (9th Cir. 1995).

146. *Id.* at 309.

147. In an earlier case, the same court had discounted the necessity of ever reviewing legislative trends in a methodology case. See *Campbell v. Wood*, 18 F.3d 662 (9th Cir. 1994), cert. denied, 511 U.S. 1119 (1994) (Blackmun, J., dissenting). But the *Campbell* Court's analysis was "surprising given that the Supreme Court has never held that pain is the exclusive consideration under the eighth amendment nor has it distinguished between proportionality and method of punishment cases." *Id.* (Blackmun, J., dissenting). Because legislative

enactments and jury sentencing behavior are the only (agreed upon) indicators of standards of decency, it appears unlikely that the Supreme Court would follow the Campbell Court's analysis and disregard legislative trends.

148. See *Gomez v. Fierro*, 519 U.S. 918 (1996); see also *Cal. Penal Code S.* 3604 (2001).
149. See *Fierro v. Terhune*, 147 F.3d 1158 (9th Cir. 1998).
150. See *Rupe v. Wood*, 863 F. Supp. 1307 (W.D. Wash. 1994).
151. See *Rupe v. Wood*, 93 F.3d 1434 (9th Cir. 1996).
152. *Byran v. Moore*, 528 U.S. 960 (1999).
153. See Denno, "Adieu to Electrocution," supra note 143.
154. *Bryan v. Moore*, 528 U.S. 1133 (2000). Furthermore, in a subsequent case the Florida Supreme Court held that retroactive application of the new statute did not violate federal and state Ex Post Facto clauses because, among other things, the "legislative switch to lethal injection merely changes the manner of imposing the sentence of death to a method that is arguably more humane." See *Sims v. State*, 754 So.2d 657, 665 (Fla. 2000).
155. See *LaGrand v. Stewart*, 173 F.3d 1144 (9th Cir. 1999).
156. See *Stewart v. LaGrand*, 526 U.S. 115 (1999).
157. See *Fierro*, 147 F.3d at 1158. Although the ruling of the Supreme Court in *LaGrand* overrules *Fierro*, it is interesting to note the extent to which the availability of lethal injection has been utilized by courts to manipulate legal theories to avoid deciding methodology cases.
158. The U.S. Supreme Court is prohibited by the Constitution from issuing advisory opinions. In order for a case to be justifiable under the U.S. Constitution, there must be an actual dispute between litigants and there must be a substantial likelihood that a federal court decision in favor of a claimant will bring about some change or have some effect. See Erwin Chemerinsky, *Constitutional Law: Principles and Policies* 53 (1997).
159. See *Ala. Code* § 15–18–82 (2000); *Neb. Rev. Stat.* § 29–2532 (2000).
160. See *Ark. Code Ann.* § 5–4–617 (Michie 1999).
161. See *Utah Code Ann.* § 77–19–10 (2000).
162. See *N.H. Rev. Stat. Ann.* § 630.5 (2000).
163. See *Dawson v. State*, 554 S.E.2d 137 (Ga. 2001).
164. See Curran & Casscells, *supra* note 111, at 226–30.
165. For a critical review of the Curran & Casscells article, see *Davis, supra* note 118.
166. See Curran & Casscells, *supra* note 111, at 229.
167. *Id.* at 228–29.
168. See *id.* at 230. This may be because they assumed that if participation was defined to include (as they put it) "all forms," such true resistance by the medical profession would make lethal injection impractical if not impossible as a method of execution. *Id.*
169. Robert Truog & Troyen Brennan, "Participation of Physicians in Capital Punishment," 329 *N. Eng. J. Med.* 1346–49 (1993).
170. The six stages of participation, defined by Truog & Brennan, are as follows: Stage one is the provision of medical care to prisoners on death row. Stage two includes activities that are necessary for the preparation of the execution, such as procuring or preparing the lethal drugs. Stage three involves the participation in the execution itself, such as the administration of the injection or the placing of IV lines. Stage four involves monitoring the vital signs, and pronouncing the prisoner dead. Stage five is the certification of death as opposed to the pronouncement of death. Stage six involves the harvesting of the dead prisoner's organs for transplantation. Only stage one is considered ethical according to the authors. *Id.* at 1347–48.
171. Truog & Brennan, *supra* note 169, at 1348.
172. *Id.*
173. *Id.*
174. See Position Statements, "Nurses' Participation in Capital Punishment, American Nurses Association" (8 Dec. 1994). See also *Press Release, supra* note 12; Alfred M. Freedman & Abraham L. Halpern, "The Erosion and Morality in Medicine: Physician Participation in Legal Execution in the United States," 41 *N.Y.L. Sch. L. Rev.* 169, 172–73 (1996).
175. See Position Statements, "Nurses' Participation in Capital Punishment," *supra* note 174.
176. American Medical Association, Code of Medical Ethics, Opinion 2.06, Current Opinions with Annotation, Council on Ethical and Judicial Affairs (1996–1997 ed).

177. Press Release, *supra* note 12.

178. *Id.*

179. Position Statements, "Nurses' Participation in Capital Punishment," *supra* note 174. Recently, while acting on a resolution from the American Association of Public Health Physicians, the AMA declined to endorse a national moratorium on executions. The AMA delegates characterized the death penalty as a legal, and not a medical, issue. In effect what the AMA was saying was that, however flawed, capital punishment was "not the AMA's business." "U.S. Physicians Reject Moratorium on Capital Punishment," *CMAJ Today*, 14 June 2000; available at <http://www.cma.ca/cmaj/cmaj_today/06_14.htm> (visited 11 Jan. 2001) (citing delegate Dr. Steven Thorson, AMA). The most that the AMA would endorse is the appropriate use of medical forensic techniques. *See* House of Delegates, 149th Annual Meeting, Chicago Illinois, 11–15 June 2000, Resolution 4.

180. According to one physician's opinion "doctors should not mount their moral high horse setting their actions above their fellow citizens . . . until the time that it is wrong for any citizen to participate in an execution, . . . let doctors participate if they so choose." "Is This Medicine, Physician Participation in North Carolina," 55 *N.C. Med. J.* (Dec. 1994) (Commentary by Francis A. Neelon, M.D. at 586).

181. Ann E. Aprile, "Ethical Issues Involving Medical Personnel and the Administration of Lethal Injection in Capital Punishment Cases," 7 *CRNA: The Clinical Forum for Nurse Anesthetists* 116–17 (Aug. 1996). According to this author, "the physician's responsibility for this type of *patient* is to ensure that death comes smoothly and painlessly." *Id.* at 117 (emphasis added).

182. Truog & Brennan, *supra* note 169, at 1348.

183. *Is This Medicine, supra* note 180 (Commentary by Walter L. Floyd, M.D. at 584).

184. Dennis S. Hsieh, "Physicians Should Give Injections," 261 *J. Am. Med. Assn.* 1, 132 (1989).

185. Arnold H. Greenhouse, "Doctors and the Death Penalty," *B. Med. J.* (June 1987). Other health professionals are not concerned with the humanity of the execution process but claim that "their duty lies in supporting a just sentence of those committing mass murders." They argue that certain doctors, are "self righteously turning private opinions into rules for the whole profession." *Id.*

186. Bayer, *supra* note 110, at A23.

187. Georgia, Louisiana, Maryland, Montana, New Hampshire, New Jersey (excludes only licensed physicians), South Dakota. See *GA. Code Ann.* § 17–10–38 (2000); *La. Rev. Stat. Ann.* § 15:569 (West 2000); *Md. Code Ann.* § 3–906 (2000); *Mont. Code Ann.* § 46–19–103 (2000); *N.H. Rev. Stat. Ann.* § 630.5 (2000); *N.J. Stat Ann.* § 2C: 49–3 (West 2000); *S.D. Codified Laws* § 23 A-27A-32 (Michie 2000).

188. *Mont. Code Ann.* § 46–19–103 (2000).

189. *N.J. Stat. Ann.* § 2C: 49–3 (West 2000).

190. Now that our society appears to have accepted the use of medical technology in judicial homicide the degree to which commentators have suggested that physicians and nurses become involved in capital punishment should not be surprising. It has been suggested that since many states, the federal government and society have sanctioned physician participation in executions as well as the harvesting of organs from cadaver donors "the next logical step is for physicians to combine these two individually condoned and accepted activities and to participate in the procurement of viable organs from the executed prisoner." Because current methods of execution, including lethal injection, destroy organs this would be accomplished by a "medically feasible and viable alternative: Execution by anesthesia-induced brain death and subsequent organ removal." The argument is that this would be ethical because just "as the medical community and society have accepted brain death, death could be similarly be expanded to include those who are . . . 'legally dead.'" The author of this article does not claim to support the death penalty, she states however, that since capital punishment is accepted and well entrenched in our society organ donation would be a "net gain." It is assumed that the reader will accept that "physicians must play a prominent role in [this] method of execution." Laura-Hill Patton, "A Call For Common Sense: Organ Donation and the Executed Prisoner," 3 *Va. J. Soc. Pol'y & L.* 387, 387–427 (1996).

191. Bayer, *supra* note 110, at A 23.

192. *Breach of Trust, supra* note 73.

193. See *id.* at 17.
194. See *id.* at 45–46.
195. See *id.*
196. *Id.*
197. See *id.*
198. In fact since 1994 two states, New York and Kansas, reinstated the death penalty with lethal injection as the method of execution. See *Kan. Stat. Ann.* § 22–4001 (1999); *N.Y. Correct. Law* § 658 (McKinney 2000).
199. Lethal injection is the sole method of execution in: Colorado; Connecticut; Delaware; Georgia; Illinois; Indiana; Kansas; Louisiana; Maryland; Mississippi; Montana; Nevada; New Jersey; New Mexico; New York; North Carolina; Oklahoma; Oregon; Pennsylvania; South Dakota; Texas; and Wyoming.
    See *Colo. Rev. Stat. Ann.* § 16–11–401 (2000); *Conn. Gen. Stat. Ann.* § 54–100 (West 2000); *Del. Code Ann.* § 11–4209 (1999); *Ga. Code Ann.* § 17–10–38 (2000); 725 *Ill Comp. Stat.* 119–5 (2001); *Ind. Code* § 35–38–6–1 (2000); *Kan. Stat. Ann.* § 22–4001 (1999); *La. Rev. Stat.* § 15:569 (West 2000); *Md. Code Ann.* § 3–905 (2000); *Miss. Code Ann.* § 99–19–51 (2000); *Mont. Code Ann.* § 46–19–103 (2000); *Nev. Rev. Stat. Ann.* 176.355 (Michie 1999); *N.J. Stat. Ann.* § 2C 49–2 (West 2000); *N.M. Stat. Ann.* § 31–14–11 (West 2000); *N.Y. Correct. Law* § 658 (McKinney 2000); *N.C. Gen. Stat.* § 15–187 (2000); *Okla. Stat. tit.* 22, § 1014 (2000); *Or. Rev. Stat.* § 137.473 (1999); *Pa. Stat. Ann.* § 3004 (2000); *S.D. Codified Laws* § 23A–27A–32 (2000); *Tx. Crim. Proc. Code Ann.* § 43.14 (Vernon 2000); *Wyo. Stat. Ann.* § 7–13–904 (Michie 2000).
200. Lethal injection is an option in: Arizona; California; Florida; Idaho; Kentucky; Ohio; Missouri; New Hampshire; South Carolina; Tennessee; Utah; Virginia; and Washington.
    See *Ariz. Rev. Stat. Const. art.* 22 § 22 (2000); *Ca. Penal Code* § 3604 (West 2001); *Fla. Stat. Ann.* § 922.10 (West 2000); *Idaho Code* § 19–2761 (Michie 2000); *Ky. Rev. Stat. Ann* § 22–4001 (Michie 1999); *Ohio Rev. Code Ann.* § 2949.22 (West 2000); *Mo. Rev. Stat.* § 546.720 (2000); *N.H. Rev. Stat. Ann.* § 630.5 (2000); *S.C. Code Ann.* § 24–3–530 (2000); *Tenn. Code Ann.* § 40–23–114 (2000); *Utah Code Ann.* § 77–19–10 (2000); *Va. Code Ann.* § 53.1–234 (Michie 2000); *Wash. Rev. Code.* § 10.95.180 (2000).
201. See *Ark. Code Ann.* § 5–4–617 (Michie 1999). If sentenced to death prior to 4 July 1983 defendant must affirmatively choose lethal injection or he will be electrocuted. *Id.*
202. See S.N. 240, Reg., Sess. (Ala. 2002). Introduced 15 January 2002, the method of execution would be changed to lethal injection unless the prisoner elects electrocution. The bill would also provide that participation in an execution is not the practice of medicine, nursing, or pharmacy. It also presumes that a health care practitioner will dispense the drugs, and mentions medical personnel as a "person authorized by state law to prescribe medication."
203. See H.R. 865, 97th Le.g., 2d Re.g., Sess. (Neb. 2002). Introduced 8 January 2001, this bill would change the method of execution from electrocution to lethal injection. It would also provide that the drugs could be dispensed without a prescription and that participation in an execution is not the practice of medicine, nursing, or pharmacy.
204. Those states are: Colorado, Idaho, Illinois, Maryland, Mississippi (and or the country coroner), New Hampshire, Oklahoma, South Dakota, and Wyoming.
    See *Colo. Rev. Stat. Ann.* § 16–11–401 (West 2000); *Idaho Code* § 19–2761 (Michie 2000); 725 *Ill. Comp. Stat.* 119–5 (2001); *Md. Code Ann.* § 3–905 (2000); *Miss. Code Ann.* § 99–19–51 (2000); *N.H. Rev. Stat. Ann.* § 630.5 (2000); *Ok. Stat. tit.* 22, § 1014 (2000); *S.D. Codified Laws* § 23A–27A (2000); *Wyo. Stat. Ann.* § 7–13–904 (Michie 2000).
205. Virginia and Washington. See *Va. Code Ann.* § 53–1–233 (Michie 2000); *Wash. Rev. Code* § 10.95.180 (2000).
206. Those states are: Alabama (two physicians, including prison physician may be present); California (shall invite the presence of two physicians); Connecticut (a physician may be present); Florida (qualified physician shall be present); Georgia (two physicians shall be present); Indiana (the prison physician and one other physician may be present); Kentucky (physician of the institution may certify death); Nevada (a competent physician and psychiatrist shall be invited); New Jersey (one licensed physician shall be present); New Mexico (physician must be invited to attend); New York (physician(s) may be present); North Carolina (surgeon or prison physician shall be present); Ohio (physician of correctional institute may be present); Oregon (one or more physicians shall be invited); South

Carolina (statute refers to the attending physician); Tennessee (prison physician is entitled to be present); Texas (two physicians may be present).

See *Ala. Code* § 15–18–83 (2001); *Cal. Penal code* § 3605 (West 2001); *Conn. Gen. Stat. Ann.* § 54–100 (West 2001); *Fla. Stat. Ann.* § 922.11 (West 2001); *Ga. Code Ann.* § 17–10–41 (2000); *Ind. Code* § 35–38–6–6 (2000); *Ky. Rev. Stat. Ann.* § 431.250 (Michie 2001); *Nev. Rev. Stat. Ann.* 176.355 (Michie 2001); *N.J. Rev. Stat* § 2C: 49–7 (2000); *N.M. Rev. Stat. Ann.* § 31–14–15 (2001); *N.Y. Correct. Law* § 660 (McKinney 2001); *N.C. Gen. Stat.* § 15–190 (2000); *Ohio Rev. Code Ann.* § 2949.25 (West 2001); *Or. Rev. Stat.* § 137.473 (1999); *S.C. Code Ann.* § 24–3–560 (2001); *Tenn. Code Ann.* § 40–23–116 (2001); *Tex. Crim. Proc. Code Ann.* § 43.20 (Vernon 2000).

207.   *N.J. Stat. Ann.* § 2C: 49–2 (2000).

208.   *Ark. Code Ann.* § 16–90–502 (Michie 1999). See also *Hill v. Lockhart,* 791 F. Supp. 1388 (E.D. Ark. 1992) (death pronounced by someone qualified to determine the absence of vital signs, need not be a medical doctor.) Clearly one who is qualified to detect the absence of vital signs has necessarily had some medical or health care training.

209.   *Utah Code Ann.* § 77–19–10 (2000). See also *Utah Code Ann.* § 77–19–11 (2000).

210.   *La. Rev. Stat. Ann.* § 15:569 (West 2001).

211.   *Breach of Trust, supra* note 73, at 57.

212.   *Id.*

213.   See *Del. Code Ann.* tit. 11, § 4209 (1999); see also *Breach of Trust, supra* note 73 at 52–53.

214.   See *Breach of Trust, supra* note 73, at 58–59.

215.   *Mont. Code Ann.* § 46–19–103 (2001).

216.   *Ariz. Rev. Stat.* § 13–704 (2001).

217.   *Kan. Stat. Ann.* § 22–4001 (2001).

218.   *Pa. Stat. Ann.* tit. 61, § 3004 (West 2000). See also 2001 Bill Text *Pa. H.B.* 330 (SN).

219.   *Neb. Rev. Stat.* § 29–2532 (2000); see also *supra* note 203.

220.   Those states that declare that participation in lethal injection executions are not the practice of medicine are: Delaware; Idaho, Illinois, Maryland, New Hampshire, New Jersey, Oregon, South Dakota, and Wyoming.

See *Del. Code Ann.* tit. 11, § 4209 (1999); *Idaho Code* § 19–2761 (Michie 2000); 725 *Ill. Comp. Stat.* 5/119–5 (2001); *Md. Code Ann., Corr. Serv.* § 3–905(b) (2000); *N.H. Rev. Stat. Ann.* § 630.5 (2000); *N.J. Stat. Ann.* § 2C: 49–3 (West 2000); *Or. Rev. Stat.* § 137.473 (1999); *S.D. Codified Laws* § 23A–27A (Michie 2000); *Wyo. Stat. Ann.* § 7–13–904 (Michie 2000).

The two states that include other health professions are: Georgia (or any other profession related to health); and Mississippi (medicine and nursing). See *Ga. Code Ann.* § 17–10–41 (2000); *Miss. Code Ann.* § 99–15–53 (2000).

221.   See *Ariz. Rev. Stat.* § 13–704 (2001).

222.   See *Miss. Code Ann.* § 99–15–53 (2000).

223.   Those states are: Arizona; Florida; Illinois; Kansas; Montana; and New York. See *Ariz. Rev. Stat.* § 13–704 (2000); *Fla. Stat. Ann.* § 922.10 (2000); 725 *Ill. Comp. Stat.* 5/119–5 (2001); *Kan. Stat. Ann.* § 22–4001 (1999); *Mont. Code Ann.* § 46–19–103 (2000); *N.Y. Correct. Law* § 660 (McKinney 2000).

224.   Those states are: Delaware; Idaho; Illinois; Maryland; Mississippi; New Hampshire; New Jersey; Oregon; Pennsylvania; and South Dakota. See *Del. Code Ann.* tit. 11, § 4209(f) (1999); *Idaho Code* § 19–2716 (Michie 2000); 725 *Ill. Comp. Stat.* 5/119–5 (2001); *Md. Code Ann. Corr. Serv.* § 3–905(b) (2000); *Miss. Code Ann.* § 99–15–53 (2000); *N.H. Rev. Stat. Ann.* § 630.5 (2000); *N.J. Stat. Ann.* § 2C 49–3 (2000); *Or. Rev. Stat.* § 137.473 (1999); *Pa. Stat. Ann.* 61 P.S. § 3004 (West 2000); *S.D. Codified Laws* § 23A–27A (Michie 2000).

225.   Freedman & Halpern, *supra* note 174, at 169, 172–73.

226.   See Michalos, *supra* note 70, at 13.

227.   Truog & Brennan, *supra* note 169, at 1349.

228.   *Id.*

229.   See *id.*

230.   *Thorburn v. Department of Corrections,* 66 Cal. App. 4th 1284 (1998).

231.   Truog & Brennan, *supra* note 169, at 1349.

232.   See *Thorburn,* 66 Cal. App. 4th at 1290 n.6.

233.   *Id.* at 1293.

234. *Id.* at 1292 (citing Stacy A. Ragon, "A Doctor's Dilemma: Resolving the Conflict Between Physician Participation in Executions and the AMA's Code of Medical Ethics," 20 *U. Dayton L. Rev.* 975, 991 (1995)).

235. *Id.* at 1292.

236. *The Death Penalty in America, supra* note 108, at 10.

237. The Supreme Court has already held, in a different context, that "AMA standards can be used as objective evidence of contemporary norms." Kristina Beard, "Five Under the Eight: Methodology Review And Cruel and Unusual Punishments Clause," 51 *U. Miami L. Rev.* 445 (1997).

238. Press Release, *supra* note 12.

239. Royal Commission on Capital Punishment 1949–1950 Report, *supra* note 95, at 258.

240. *Mont. Code Ann.* § 46–19–103 (2000).

241. *Ariz. Rev. Stat.* § 13–704 (2000).

242. See *supra* note 220.

243. See *supra* notes 204 & 205.

244. See *supra* note 206.

245. See Jack Spensley, "Viewpoint Ethics, The Last Execution," 9 *Nursing Standard* 50 (1995).

256. Elsie L. Bandman & Bertram Bandman, Nursing Ethics Through the Life Span (1995).

247. Lynda Davies, "A Very Peculiar Practice," *Nursing Standard,* 17 July 1996, at 24–26.

248. International Council of Nurses, Mission Statement, *available at* <http://www.icn.ch/abouticn.htm> (visited 18 Feb. 2002).

249. INC Position Statements, "Torture, Death Penalty and Participation by Nurses in Executions," ICN/99/57 (adopted 1998*), available at* <http://www.icn.ch/pstorture.htm> (visited 17 Feb. 2002).

250. Neil Farber et al. "Physicians' Attitudes About Involvement in Lethal Injection for Capital Punishment," 160 *Archives of Internal Med.* 2912–16 (23 Oct. 2000).

15

Maternal Mortality
in Herat Province, Afghanistan
The Need to Protect Women's Rights

Physicians for Human Rights

Executive Summary

This study demonstrates that women in Herat Province, Afghanistan have an extraordinarily high risk of dying during pregnancy and childbirth and the highest maternal mortality ratio in the world outside of Africa.[1] It shows that prenatal care, maternal health care facilities and trained health care personnel are virtually non-existent in the region and it provides evidence that violations of human rights contribute to preventable maternal deaths. These factors include access to and quality of health services, adequate food, shelter and clean water, and denial of personal freedoms such as freely entering into marriage, access to birth control methods and possibly control over the number and spacing of children.[2]

In Afghanistan, the combined effects of more than 20 years of war and persistent human rights violations, including Taliban imposed restrictions on women's rights, have had devastating health consequences for women.[3] Just as maternal health depends on the respect of women's rights,[4] maternal mortality can be an important indicator of the health and human rights status of women, their access to health care and the adequacy of the health care system and its ability to respond to their needs.[5] Disparities in maternal mortality rates may also serve as important indicators of health inequality on local, national, and international levels.[6] More than 515,000 women worldwide die annually of complications of pregnancy and childbirth[7] and 50 million women suffer preventable adverse health complications after childbirth annually. Most of these deaths could be prevented by cost-effective health interventions.[8]

In 1997, maternal mortality in Afghanistan was reported to be one of the worst in the world, 820/100,000.[9] This ratio was determined by a statistical modeling method[10] and no additional assessments of maternal mortality have been available since that time. Given recent opportunities to access populations in Afghanistan which were largely not accessible during the Taliban regime and the need to inform the reconstruction efforts underway in the country, PHR conducted a rapid, regional, population-based assessment to inform policies that may ultimately reduce preventable maternal deaths in Afghanistan.

Purpose of the Study

The purpose of this study was to 1) provide a rapid and accurate estimate of maternal mortality in Herat Province, Afghanistan, 2) assess violations of women's human rights that may contribute to maternal mortality,[11] and 3) assess maternal health services in the region.

Study Design

The study included a randomized, population-based survey of 4,486 women from 34 urban and rural villages/towns in seven of thirteen districts in Herat Province (a province with 1,094,377 people in western Afghanistan, near the Iran border).[12] The women surveyed provided maternal mortality information on 14,085 sisters[13] in structured interviews with local Afghan researchers.

In order to gain insight into individual experiences of health care providers and family members, PHR also conducted more detailed qualitative interviews (case testimonies).

In addition, PHR conducted a comprehensive survey of all health facilities in seven of thirteen districts of Herat Province that were sampled.

Summary of Findings

The findings of the study indicate that women have an extraordinarily high risk of dying during pregnancy and childbirth in Herat Province. The study also provides evidence that ensuring the rights of women may prevent such maternal deaths. The primary findings of PHR's maternal mortality survey are as follows:

Maternal Mortality Ratio:

- The maternal mortality ratio for Herat Province is 593 maternal deaths/ 100,000 live births.
- There were 276 maternal deaths reported among 14,085 sisters.[14]
- Ninety-two percent of the 276 maternal deaths were reported from rural areas.

Demographics:

- The mean age of the respondents was 31 years (range 15–49).
- The majority of respondents were poorly educated with a reported average of 0.35 years of formal education.
- Eighty-eight percent of women reported they were married.

Health and Human Rights Considerations:

- Seventy-four percent of women reported their primary problems to be lack of adequate food, shelter and clean water.
- Respondents reported an average age at marriage of 15 years (range 5–39). However, the average age that respondents indicated would be a desirable age for marriage was 18 years (range 15–30).
- Most women (85%) stated that they wanted to marry at the time of their marriage, although 20% reported that they felt pressured by their family.
- Eighty-six percent of women thought they should have the right to choose a husband and enter into marriage.
- Women reported a mean 5.0 (range 0–20) pregnancies and 4.6 (range 0–18) live births. Only 11% reported having prenatal care.[15]
- Eighty-seven percent of women reported having to obtain permission from their husbands or male relatives to seek health care; however, only 1% of respondents related not being permitted to obtain health care.
- Less than 1% (0.83%) of women reported births that were attended by a trained health care worker.
- Ninety-seven percent reported that they had an untrained traditional birth attendant at the birth.
- Birth control methods were reportedly used by 12% of women whereas 23% of women indicated wanting birth control.
- Seventy-four percent of women stated that husband and wife made decisions about the number and spacing of children equally.

Assessment of Health Facilities and Essential Obstetric Care:

- Sixty-three percent of 27 facilities listed by WHO[16] as functional were found to be operating.
- Only one functional comprehensive Essential Obstetric Care (EOC) facility and four basic EOC facilities existed for the province—less than half of the recommended number of EOC facilities—and all were within a 10–30 minute drive from the center of Herat City.
- Only one district had EOC facilities that met WHO guideline standards and it was in an urban area.

- Fifteen of 19 female physicians were working at the Provincial hospital in Herat City, leaving the rest of the province without trained female health care providers.
- Fewer than half of the 17 operating facilities offered prenatal care.

Individual Interviews with Health Practitioners and Family Members Reported:

- Inadequate supplies of medication and equipment are barriers to appropriate care.
- Traditional society requires that women deliver at home and obtain permission from male family members before seeking healthcare.
- Women and their families do not know the warning signs of potentially lethal conditions during pregnancy and childbirth and cannot therefore avert potential complications.
- Women often cannot afford to pay for health care services even when they know they are in danger.
- Lack of transportation from the villages impedes referrals to hospitals.
- Untrained traditional birth attendants in the villages stated they could save lives with better training and lamented their lack of capacity to deal with the most simple of complications such as infection or bleeding.
- Loss of a mother causes considerable physical and emotional hardship for the families they leave behind.

Families suffered tremendously with the loss of the mother. The story told by a 60-year old widower in a village in Zendajan captures the effects of maternal mortality.

> The TBA did not know what to do so she [my wife] died in a pool of blood without holding or feeding her babies. I am trying to remember if I was by her side, but the years have removed many memories. There was no doctor to help. Even if there was one, I had no money to pay a doctor or a clinic. If I had money, I was going to take her [my wife] to a clinic in the city.
>
> The baby twins needed to be cared for so I brought them to a village woman who had milk in her breasts. One died after three months and the other at six months. I think she did not take good care of them.
>
> Only our two year-old did not understand what happened to their mother. The rest cried for one year. After the year, I decided they needed to be distracted so I sent them to the fields to care for other people's cows. With the money that they earned, I was able to marry a second wife and give my children the chance of another mother.

Individual interviews with health practitioners and family members provided considerable insight into the problems identified in the maternal mortality survey. Dr. Mina, an obstetrician in Enjil Center Clinic, summed up the barriers to good health care for pregnant women as follows:

> There is not enough prenatal and postnatal care for women. They are malnourished, cannot even get Tetanus vaccination and do not have family planning. Even if we suggest family planning, they must discuss this with their husbands and must have money to buy the medicines, which they do not.
>
> Hospitals are culturally unacceptable; a woman has to ask permission to be evaluated by a doctor. If we could get village health workers and TBAs trained in the villages, I think women would do better. But the village health worker and TBAs need to also train the male family members, not just the women, about women's health.

Tamar, a midwife in Zendajan Center Clinic, who is 55 km from Herat City (a three hour drive on a dirt road in a four-wheel drive vehicle), sums up the obstacles that rural women face:

> I deliver babies here but most are delivered in the villages, by untrained TBAs. If there is a very sick woman or a complicated pregnancy, we refer them to Herat but I do not know how many can go since it so far from here. We have health education at the clinic including nutrition since most of the women I see are malnourished. But there are other problems. There is no sanitation in the villages, we do not have enough vaccines for women and it is really not possible to refer women to Herat because of the distance. The biggest problem is that women do not know when they should come for help and neither do the husbands, so women die at home or on a donkey on the way to Herat.

Dr. Saida, Head of the Herat Maternity Hospital and a female obstetrician trained at Kabul Medical Faculty, describes the problems she faces as a doctor in a regional hospital that is supposed to care for women from five different provinces.

> We have been promised so many things and rarely do any of the promises come through. I must go across the campus to the main hospital if I want instruments sterilized. I ask my staff to roll up their sleeves to give blood to patients when the mother needs it since we have no other way of getting blood. My staff is now anemic and I cannot transfuse for a few weeks. I was trained in a time when things were so much better, now I practice "field medicine." My surgery this morning was a hysterectomy but the anesthesiologist could only use a bag to help the patient breathe.

Urgent and Long-Term Recommendations

Three "quick start" initiatives that can be implemented immediately are listed here, followed by seven recommendations for long-term improvement of women's health. These three recommendations are not a substitute for a comprehensive public health infrastructure, or for the food, water, and housing that healthy mothers need.

Urgent Priorities

- First, the donor community should quickly provide the basic equipment needed for complicated births to local clinics and regional health centers. Almost none of them have rudimentary supplies such as intravenous medications to control seizures, bleeding or infection; clean water; or vacuum aspirators. Providing the basic package of such materials and equipment to every facility, and training local health workers to address hemorrhage or obstructed delivery at each location, could save tens of thousands of lives every year. On an urgent basis, recruitment and deployment of trained health professionals to every Essential Obstetric Care (EOC) Facility is necessary.
- Second, the donor community and the Afghan government must recognize that even when services are available and reachable, user fees may preclude life-saving care for many women. The donor community and the Afghan government should work together to develop schemes for ensuring that life saving treatment in emergencies, including obstetric emergencies and prenatal care be available at no cost.
- Third, an initiative to train traditional birth attendants (TBAs) in rural areas should be considered by the donor community. As documented in this study, TBAs are overwhelmingly (97%) the only ones to accompany an Afghan mother in labor. However, they lack basic skills such as how to massage the uterus to expel the placenta or prevent hemorrhage—a frequent cause of death that could be prevented. Although studies in other countries have shown that training of TBAs alone does not reduce maternal mortality rates, given the situation in much of Afghanistan, training TBAs may be a useful short-term measure. TBAs and community members should be taught about common warning signs. The training should be accompanied by assessments of any results, including effects on morbidity, and should not be seen as a replacement for upgrading and increasing the number of EOCs and the number of qualified health professionals.

Long-Term Recommendations for Reducing Maternal Mortality in Afghanistan

The three initiatives above address areas where intensive investment immediately could have a dramatic impact on maternal mortality. Much more needs to be done. Physicians for Human Rights recommends that the Afghan government should make the reduction of maternal mortality a national priority and urges the development of a comprehensive plan to address it. The following recommendations for safe birthing and motherhood will take time to administer and require a long-term and sustained commitment by the Afghan government, international donors, and humanitarian aid groups.

The extraordinarily high numbers of deaths of women during pregnancy and childbirth identified in this report are largely preventable. They are a direct consequence of the very young marriage age for women and girls, poor health and nutrition, too-frequent childbearing, and virtually no access to gynecological and obstetrical services. Afghan authorities, in consultation with Afghan women's groups, civil society, health professionals and local leaders, and assisted by the international community, can and must address these barriers to maternal survival that contribute to the unacceptable death rate of Afghan women.

1. **Maternal health must not be considered a second stage priority and must be integrated into a public health plan.** Because of poor governance, near-constant war, and gross poverty, international humanitarian groups have largely provided health care in Afghanistan through a patchwork of projects. Many are excellent and should be maintained and enhanced, but the country requires an integrated public health plan that will comprehensively address Afghanistan's needs. Furthermore, saving the lives of the thousands of women who die during pregnancy or childbirth in Afghanistan every year literally saves the life of the family as well. Infants and young children who lose their mothers in impoverished families languish and often die themselves.

2. **Afghan women's rights must be protected and promoted.** A national plan must protect and promote a wide range of women's rights (civil, political, economic, social and cultural) over a sustained period of time. This includes ratifying the Convention on the Elimination of Discrimination against Women (CEDAW or "Women's Convention") and including provisions of safe motherhood in Afghan law and health policies. The plan should be based on country-wide discussions with local religious and community leaders, Afghan women's organizations, Afghan health care providers, international humanitarian aid providers, and the Afghan government's Women's Ministry to develop a public education campaign aimed at protecting the right to enter freely into marriage, set and enforce a minimum age of marriage, and choose the timing and spacing of children. In addition, the Afghan government should establish a minimum age of consent for marriage in the constitution that is currently being amended [Article 23, ICCPR acceded by Afghanistan in January 1983]. Similarly, humanitarian assistance providers should employ a rights-based framework in their efforts to prevent maternal deaths.

Family planning services must be enhanced. In the Physicians for Human Rights study, 23% of women respondents indicated that they wanted contraception, but only 12% reported access to it. Expanding information and education about and access to birth control for women and men should be a priority of donors, humanitarian groups, the Afghan Ministry of Public Health, and Afghan civil society.

3. **Women's health services must be extended and improved to meet WHO standards.** One of the key underlying factors contributing to maternal mortality in Afghanistan is the near-total absence of accessible hospital services for complicated births. PHR urges that clinics and hospitals throughout the country be brought up to the World Health Organization's minimum criteria as essential obstetric care facilities, and include the supplies, equipment, and trained personnel required to handle complicated births. Such Essential Obstetric Care (EOC) facilities do not need to be sophisticated hospitals. EOC facilities can and should be accessible to the rural population. Establishing and sustaining them, along with trained health workers, in every province in collaboration with local community leaders, should be a national and international priority. The goal of donors, government and NGOs working together should be to provide the minimal number of appropriate facilities per population, as recommended by the World Health Organization. Minimal supplies, equipment and training to address hemorrhage and other complications are not prohibitively expensive. They include intravenous medications to control bleeding, seizure, and infection, and simple sterile equipment such as forceps and a vacuum extractor to aid birth and after-birth.

4. **Security gaps must be addressed and security provided throughout the country.** Continued internal and international conflict and lack of security throughout Afghanistan is a serious impediment to the development of health infrastructure. Physicians for Human Rights recommends that the United States and its coalition partners assist the Afghan government in providing security throughout Afghanistan, with an emphasis on securing those areas where ongoing conflict is hampering the ability of the national government and humanitarian organizations to extend health services to those most in need. PHR urges that multinational forces be deployed to areas where ethnic minorities are vulnerable to physical attacks, and where banditry and harassment by local warlords has impeded the work of local and international humanitarian groups. Northern Afghanistan is a particularly troubled area that requires international protection. The western region of Afghanistan, where Physicians for Human Rights conducted this study, is another such area. Relief agencies have

difficulty working in this area due to military control by several armed militia groups.

5. **Training of women health care workers at all levels must be a priority.** Physicians for Human Rights urges the Afghan government and donor community, in consultation with Afghan women's organizations, to develop a plan for training and deploying large numbers of nurse midwives and trained traditional birth attendants to under-served areas. In addition, training TBAs to recognize signs of birth complications and schooling them appropriately to refer women to clinics or hospitals is essential. Finally, the donor community, in cooperation with Afghan women's groups and medical associations, should expand the number of female medical students receiving training or retraining in women's health and obstetrics and gynecology, and subsidize their service in poor, rural areas of Afghanistan.

6. **Provision of basic needs including water, food and sanitation must be expedited and targeted to least served areas and those with high maternal mortality.** Lack of adequate nutrition, shelter and clean water are important contributing factors to Afghanistan's high maternal mortality ratio. In the PHR study, women identified all three as lacking. Physicians for Human Rights urges that humanitarian organizations, including non-governmental organizations and United Nations agencies integrate their programs and identify ways to upgrade nutrition and access to clean water in Afghanistan's least-served areas, including communities in Western Afghanistan, Faryab, Ghor, Baghdis, and Farah. In consultation with Afghan women, local community leadership, and traditional birth attendants, relief providers should direct supplemental food and clean water resources to areas of particularly high maternal mortality and ensure that women have access to these.

7. **Assistance for women's mental health problems must be provided.** A very large percentage of Afghan women suffer from major depression or other mental health problems related to trauma and/or the suffering of multiple losses in their lives. Though not the subject of this report, PHR has in previous investigations collected extensive data about widespread depression, suicidal ideation, and other serious indications of poor mental health among Afghan women. Physicians for Human Rights urges that health care providers be trained to identify the signs and symptoms of depression and other mental health problems so that those in need can be referred to trained mental health providers for assistance. Moreover, mental health programs should be integrated into humanitarian assistance, including maternal health programs.

Background

Overview

Afghanistan is one of the poorest countries in the world and in 1997 was reported to have one of the highest infant (152/1,000) and child (257/1,000) mortality rates of all countries.[17] Life expectancy of women was reported to be 44 years in 1997.[18] Only 17% of rural residents and 38% of urban residents had access to safe drinking water.[19] It has been estimated that, annually, diarrhea disease causes 42% of all deaths in Afghanistan[20] and that 85,000 are children under age five.[21] Malnutrition has been reported to affect up to 52% of children under age five.[22] In addition, more than 70% of the health care system in Afghanistan is reportedly dependent on external assistance.[23]

Maternal Mortality in Afghanistan

In 1997, the maternal mortality ratio (number of maternal deaths per 100,000 live births per year) in Afghanistan was reported to be one of the worst in the world, 820/100,000, but no update has been available since that time. Furthermore, this ratio is based on a statistical modeling method[24] used by the World Health Organization (WHO) to estimate maternal mortality in a country that lacks vital registration and other record-based means of estimating of maternal mortality. All estimates of maternal mortality in Afghanistan in the last twelve years have been based on regression model analysis, and not on actual data collected in the field.

The 1995 estimated ratio suggests that in Afghanistan, approximately 16,000 women died annually of childbirth related complications and that a woman died of largely preventable causes every 30 minutes. Under the Taliban regime, which ruled most of Afghanistan between 1996 and 2001, Afghan women experienced persistent deprivations and restrictions of basic freedoms. The effects of the recent war and ongoing skirmishes further diminished women's health status and the already poor health care system.

Maternal Mortality and Human Rights

Increasingly, health professionals have recognized the protection and promotion of human rights as essential conditions for health.[25] Violations of human rights including civil and political rights and economic, social and cultural rights may have profound effects on human health. Furthermore, human rights are interdependent.[26] That is, the realization of one right depends on the realization of other rights. The problem of maternal mortality illustrates well the relationship between health and human rights. Women's health requires social and economic rights such as access to health services, adequate food, shelter, and clean water, and individual freedoms such as freely entering into marriage, access to birth control methods and possibly control over the number and spacing of children to limit the possibility of dying during pregnancy. Furthermore, women require representation in government, equality before the law, access to scientific knowledge, freedom of speech and association, among other civil and political rights, to secure essential economic and social rights. Similarly, lack of access to basic health services, food, shelter, clean water and sanitation, and equal opportunities for work and education may jeopardize women's capacity to survive and participate in society.

Although maternal mortality may reflect a range of violations of women's rights, this study focuses on those rights deemed to have the greatest impact on maternal mortality in the region. These include: 1) access to and quality of maternal health services, 2) rights to food, shelter, clean water, sanitation and education, and 3) individual freedoms including freely entering into marriage, access to birth control methods and possibly control over the number and spacing of children.[27]

Access to and Quality of Maternal Health Service

Lack of access to healthcare may result from a lack of facilities, or where facilities exist, unusable roads, insecurity, and lack of transportation (including ambulances). In addition, the lack of necessary equipment and training to deal with complicated deliveries are frequent problems, as is the absence of trained female health care providers.

In 1997, UNICEF, WHO and UNFPA published guidelines that stated for every population of 500,000 there should be at least four basic essential obstetric care (EOC) facilities and one comprehensive EOC facility.[28] Minimal acceptable levels of care also require that 15% of all births in the population take place in the hospital and 100% of women with obstetric complications are treated in EOC facilities.[29] A basic essential obstetric care (EOC) facility is one that can provide parenteral antibiotics, oxytocic drugs, anticonvulsants for pre-eclampsia, manual removal of placenta, removal of retained products via manual vacuum aspiration, and available assisted vaginal delivery.[30] A comprehensive EOC facility must be able to administer all of the basic services and perform surgery (i.e., caesarian section) and blood transfusions.[31]

Healthcare facilities (hospitals and basic health centers) in most of Afghanistan, especially in rural areas outside of the capital, Kabul, are largely non-functional or do not meet WHO criteria for EOCs. Only 30–40% of the population have access to some health service, with most of these being residents of urban areas.[32] More than half of all hospitals in Afghanistan are located in Kabul and therefore serve approximately only one quarter of the entire population.[33] According to the WHO, approximately 2,700 of 3,900 physicians and 600 of 990 midwives work in Kabul, leaving the remainder of the country with few trained health care professionals.[34] In fact, it was recently estimated that a trained health care provider attended fewer than 8% of deliveries countrywide.[35]

Many of the health care facilities listed by the WHO are, in fact, nonfunctional due to lack of supplies or equipment, lack of structural integrity (windows, doors, electricity, or water) and the absence of trained health care professionals. Facilities surveyed by PHR in Herat Province were noted to be in disrepair. Few if any of the basic health centers had windows, medications, basic equipment such as stethoscopes, electricity or running water. Waiting rooms were empty due to the lack of essential drugs to treat even the most common medical problems and health care professionals lamented that they were helpless to treat patients without the essentials. The combined effects of such conditions of the health care facilities have compounded the problem of maternal mortality in Afghanistan.

Rights to Food, Shelter, Clean Water, Sanitation and Education

Basic human rights to adequate food, shelter, clean water, sanitation and education all may have an effect on maternal mortality. Chronic malnutrition in childhood, a fact of life for children in Afghanistan,[36] frequently results in anemia and stunted growth including the development of a smaller than normal pelvic outlet.[37] Small, anemic mothers with undeveloped pelvic bones are at greater risk of obstructed births with devastating consequences for both mother and baby and may not withstand pregnancy or the usual blood loss during delivery.[38]

Lack of adequate shelter and the absence of clean water or sanitation is likely to contribute to infections and diseases, which can complicate or be complicated by pregnancy and delivery.[39] Lack of education and information also may contribute to maternal mortality. Education is one of the best predictors of health status.[40] Information about birth spacing, contraception, health care and immunizations, and safe pregnancy is essential to the health of mother and baby.[41] Women in Afghanistan over the last two decades have been poorly educated with the average years of formal education reported as one or less years of education, currently leaving a gap in the number of women who can obtain higher education.[42] In addition, a lack of trained female health providers is also likely to contribute to maternal mortality in countries such as Afghanistan in which it is generally culturally unacceptable for women to be examined by male health providers.

Individual Freedoms

Women in Afghanistan, as in many parts of the world, have few rights relating to their sexuality and role in the family. Early/forced marriage, an inability to negotiate terms of sex, including the use of contraception and birth spacing, are all likely to contribute to maternal mortality by leading to a high number of pregnancies starting at an early age.[43] Such pregnancies may place the mother and baby at increased risk for serious complications, especially obstructed births, since this complication is increased when the mother is not fully developed. Restrictions on her movement by government or family are likely to result in death due to inability to access essential maternal health care services.[44]

Application of Relevant International Law

The right to health, including safe motherhood, is acknowledged in many national constitutions, as well as regional and international human rights treaties to which Afghanistan is a party.[45] Together, the International Covenant on Economic, Social and Cultural Rights (ICESCR), which emphasizes such substantive rights as education and health care, and the International Covenant on Civil and Political Rights (ICCPR), which emphasizes women's rights to bodily integrity, information, political participation, association and movement, provide the foundation for many of the rights necessary for women to enjoy health and access to health care.[46]

In recognition of economic limitations on certain States, the ICESCR requires each State Party to "take steps individually and through international assistance and cooperation … to the maximum of its available resources"[47] to achieve progressively the full realization of the rights contained in the treaty. It is a clear violation of the terms of the ICESCR, however, to take any action, through legislation or otherwise, that revokes or removes rights previously enjoyed in that state. State Parties to the ICESCR must also "ensure the equal right of men and women to the enjoyment"[48] of the rights in the convention. Thus, any State policy that restricts the rights of women in Afghanistan in the areas of education[49] or employment[50] would constitute unequivocal violations of Afghanistan's obligations under the ICESCR.

Several provisions in the ICESCR form part of the basis for the right to safe motherhood. Article 11 sets out the right to "adequate food, clothing and housing"[51] and "the fundamental right of everyone to be free from hunger."[52] Malnutrition is a common contributing factor to maternal mortality in Afghanistan. Article 12 of the ICESCR sets out "the right of everyone to the highest attainable standard of physical and mental health."[53] The committee responsible for monitoring adherence to the ICESCR (ESC Committee) gave further authoritative guidance regarding the meaning of this right in General Comment 14 promulgated in 2000.[54] The ESC Committee has stated that the provision of maternal health care "including access to family planning, pre- and post-natal care, emergency obstetric services and access to information as well as to resources necessary to act on that information,"[55] constitutes part of a State's essential or minimum core obligations.[56] The General Comment explicitly includes physical and economic accessibility as components of the right to health.[57]

Like the ICESCR, the ICCPR requires that State Parties must "ensure the equal right of men and women to the enjoyment"[58] of the rights in the convention. The Covenant recognizes "the right of men and women of marriageable age to marry and found a family."[59] Although the term "marriageable age" is not defined, international documents relating to age of marriage[60] suggest that child[61] marriage and betrothal before puberty are not acceptable. Further, the Covenant states that "no marriage shall be entered into without the free and full consent of the intending spouses."[62] The ability or capacity of young girls to give full and free consent is doubtful. Additionally, women may feel coerced by lack of options or pressured by family to marry.

The Convention on the Rights of the Child (CRC) offers further protection to girls, defined as under 18 years of age.[63] The CRC recognizes the "right of the child to the enjoyment of the highest attainable standard of health and to facilities for the treatment of illness."[64] The "full implementation of this right"[65] explicitly includes taking "appropriate measures . . . to ensure appropriate pre- and post-natal health care for expectant mothers,"[66] and "to develop . . . family planning education and services."[67] Recognizing that some countries are better positioned to meet these commitments, the CRC makes realization of this article the responsibility of all state parties stating: "States Parties undertake to promote and encourage international cooperation with a view to achieving progressively the full realization of the right . . . particular account shall be taken of the needs of developing nations."[68] The CRC also sets out the right to education[69] and the state's obligation to protect children from exploitation.[70]

Afghanistan is a party to the ICCPR, the ICESCR, and the CRC and is therefore responsible for ensuring adherence to the commitments it has made including those that form the basis for safe motherhood.

Afghanistan has ratified the Convention on the Political Rights of Women, which provides for universal suffrage for women, their eligibility for election to all publicly elected bodies and their right to hold public office.[71] While Afghanistan is a signatory and not a party to the far more extensive 1979 Convention on the Elimination of All Forms of Discrimination against Women (Women's Convention or CEDAW), its signature indicates an agreement not to contravene its provisions, which include "taking all appropriate measures" to eliminate discrimination against women and to "modify social and cultural patterns of conduct, which are based on the idea of the inferiority or the superiority of either of the sexes or on stereotyped roles for men and women."[72]

The Women's Convention requires States Parties to eliminate discrimination in both public and private spheres; in education, health care, employment, economic and legal programs and rules, and all matters involving marriage and the family. Specifically, Article 10(h) of the Women's Convention addresses the right to equality in education: "Access to specific education information to help to ensure the health and well-being of families, including information and advice on family planning." Article 12(a) of the Women's Convention obligates States Parties to "take all appropriate measures to eliminate discrimination against women in the field of health care in order to ensure, on a basis of equality of men and women, access to health care services, including those related to family planning."[73] Article 12(b) of the Women's Convention[74] states that:

> States Parties shall ensure to women appropriate services in connection with pregnancy, confinement and the post-natal period, granting free services where necessary, as well as adequate nutrition during pregnancy and lactation.

Article 16 addresses marriage and the family and provides that States Parties shall ensure men and women have equal rights. Part (e) of Article 16(1) requires States Parties to ensure "[t]he same rights to decide freely and responsibly on the number and spacing of their children and to have access to the information, education and means to enable them to exercise these rights."[75] That article also states that "the betrothal and the marriage of a child shall have no legal effect and all necessary action, including legislation, shall be taken to specify a minimum age for marriage."[76] Article 2 requires States Parties to implement the substantive provisions of the Women's Convention through domestic law.[77]

The reduction of maternal mortality also is explicitly mentioned in both the 1999 CEDAW General Recommendation on "Women and Health" and the 2000 ESC Committee General Comment on "the Right to the Highest Attainable Standard of Health."[78] The committee which monitors adherence to CEDAW calls for emergency obstetric care (EOC) to be provided and made accessible to women—geographically, economically and culturally—in fulfilling a State's obligations. In its General Recommendation "Women and Health," the monitoring body of the Women's Convention notes that "it is the duty of States parties to ensure women's right to safe motherhood and emergency obstetric services and they should allocate to these services the maximum extent of available resources."[79]

The declarations that emerged from the International Convention on Population and Development held in Cairo in 1994 (Cairo Programme) and the Fourth World Conference on Women held in Beijing (Beijing Platform) further elaborated the binding norms in the ICESCR and the Women's Convention, with respect to maternal mortality, mentioned above.[80] Language in the five-year follow-up documents to the Cairo and Beijing Conferences reiterated the critical need to address the extraordinarily high numbers of maternal deaths worldwide.

In addition to these binding treaties, multiple declarations relating to women's health are relevant for their moral authority and interpretive value. Among these are documents arising from recent global conferences including the declaration and program of action from the World Conference on Human Rights (Vienna Declaration),[81] the Programme of Action for the International Conference on Population and Development (Cairo Programme),[82] and the Platform of Action of the Fourth World Conference on Women (Beijing Platform).[83] The government of Afghanistan was represented at all of these international conferences. Taken together, these declarative documents speak to a strong and growing international consensus regarding certain core principles of women's dignity, opportunities and equality with men.

The Vienna Declaration was the first of these documentary guidelines and was issued in 1993. Part I of the Vienna Declaration states:

> The human rights of women and of the girl-child are an inalienable, integral and indivisible part of universal human rights. The full and equal participation of women in political, civil, economic, social and cultural life, at the national, regional and international levels, and the eradication of all forms of discrimination on the grounds of sex are priority objectives of the international community.[84]

Other relevant sections of the Vienna Declaration establish that the equal status of women and the human rights of women should be integrated in the mainstream activity[85] and urge the full and equal enjoyment by women of all human rights;[86] the elimination of violence against women;[87] and the eradication of all forms of discrimination against women.[88]

The Cairo Programme, which emerged from the International Conference on Population and Development held in Cairo, Egypt in 1994, contains an entire chapter on gender equity and the empowerment of women. Chapter IV of that document states:

> The empowerment and autonomy of women and the improvement of their political, social, economic and health status is a highly important end in itself. In addition, improving the status of women also enhances their decision-making capacity at all levels in all spheres of life, especially in the area of sexuality and reproduction.[89]

In turn, the Cairo Programme calls for, among other things, eliminating inequalities between men and women that affect women's health. For example, it declares the need for State action with respect to: equal political participation, education, skill development and employment; eliminating all practices that discriminate against women; assisting women to establish and realize their rights, including those that relate to reproductive and sexual health; improving women's ability to earn income; eliminating discriminatory practices by employers against women; and making it possible, through laws, regulations and other appropriate measures, for women to combine the roles of child-bearing, breast-feeding and child-rearing with participation in the workforce.

The Beijing Platform, which came out of the Fourth World Conference on Women in 1995, recognized "the basic right of all couples and individuals to decide freely and responsibly the number, spacing and timing of their children and have the information and means to do so, and the right to attain the highest standard of sexual and reproductive health."

Other relevant references in the Beijing Declaration refer to equal rights for men and women;[90] measures governments should take to promote women's rights;[91] the inalienability of women's human rights;[92] the equal enjoyment by women of economic, social and cultural rights;[93] the need to eliminate violence against women, including that based on cultural prejudices;[94] the need to eliminate discrimination based on race, language, ethnicity, culture, religion, disability, or socio-economic class;[95] and the value of human rights education.[96]

Section 76, which deals with gender-biased curricula and teaching materials, specifically mentions reproductive health when it states: "The lack of sexual and reproductive health education has a profound impact on women and men." Strategic objectives in the Beijing Platform include the eradication of illiteracy among women; the improvement of women's access to vocational training, science and technology, and continuing education and the development of non-discriminatory education and training.

Notes

1. See World Health Organization. www.who.int/reproductive-health/publications/ RHR_01_9_maternal_mortality_estimates/figures_and_annexes.e n.pdf. Accessed January 4, 2002. Note: This does not exclude the possibility that some regions within a particular non-African country may not exceed that of Herat. However, data is not readily available for such comparisons. The maternal mortality ratio for Herat (593/100,000) also exceeds that of all six countries bordering Afghanistan: Pakistan (200/100,000), Iran (60/100,000), Turkmenistan (65/100,000), China (60/100,000) and Tajikistan (120/100,000). In contrast, the United States has an estimated ratio of 12/100,000.
2. Although the majority of women stated that they had equal or primary control over number and spacing of children, more than half reported that their husbands had the right to beat them and that it was a wife's duty to have sex with her husband even if she did not want to. These stated beliefs appear to be in conflict with their assertions regarding their stated role in controlling the number and spacing of their children.
3. See Amowitz, L.L., Burkhalter, H., Ely-Yamin, A., and Iacopino, V. *Women's Health and Human Rights in Afghanistan: A Population-Based Study*. Boston, MA: Physicians for Human Rights: May, 2001; Amowitz, L.L. and Iacopino, V.: "Women's Health and Human Rights Needs." *The Lancet Perspectives*. 356 (s65), December 2000; Rasekh, Z., Bauer, H., Manos, M., and Iacopino, V. "Women's Health and Human Rights in Afghanistan." *JAMA* 280(5): 499–455, 1998.
4. World Health Organization. *Advancing Safe Motherhood through Human Rights*. www.who.int/reproductive-health/publications/. Accessed January 4, 2002; Yamin, A.E. and Maine, D.P. "Maternal mortality as a human rights issue: measuring compliance with international treaty obligations." *Human Rights Quarterly* 21.3: 563–607, 1999.
5. Id. supra 7.

6. See Amowitz, L.L., Burkhalter, H., Ely-Yamin, A., and Iacopino, V. *Women's Health and Human Rights in Afghanistan: A Population-Based Study.* Boston, MA: Physicians for Human Rights: May, 2001; Amowitz, L.L. and Iacopino, V. "Women's Health and Human Rights Needs." *The Lancet Perspectives.* 356 (s65), December 2000; Rasekh, Z., Bauer, H., Manos, M., and Iacopino, V. "Women's Health and Human Rights in Afghanistan." *JAMA* 280(5): 499–455, 1998.

7. World Health Organization. *Advancing Safe Motherhood through Human Rights.* http://www.who.int/reproductive-health/publications/ (Accessed January 4, 2002).

8. See World Health Organization. *Advancing Safe Motherhood through Human Rights.* Reproductive Health Publications. www.who.int/reproductive-health/publications. Accessed January 4, 2002.

9. World Health Organization. *The sisterhood method for estimating maternal mortality.* Available at: www.who.int/reproductive-health/publications/RHR_01_9_maternal_mortality—estimates/figures_and_annexes.en.pdf. Accessed January 4, 2002.

10. Id. supra 12.

11. Selection of these factors is based on established causes of maternal mortality reported in the literature and PHR's assessment of relevant regional conditions. For more information on human rights related causes of maternal mortality, see Yamin, A.E. and Maine, D.P. "Maternal Mortality as a Human Rights Issue: Measuring Compliance with International Treaty Obligations." *Human Rights Quarterly* 21:3:563–607, 1999.

12. World Health Organization. *Health Resources by District and Village in Afghanistan.* Herat Sub-Office, Afghanistan. (Unpublished) 2002.

13. The Indirect Sisterhood Method is a measurement technique that involves obtaining information by interviewing respondents about the survival of all their adult sisters.

14. Id. supra 17.

15. Prenatal care was defined as care for a pregnant woman in an area health care facility by trained health care personnel.

16. World Health Organization. *Health Resources by District and Village in Afghanistan.* Herat Sub-Office, Afghanistan. (Unpublished) 2002.

17. United Nations Children's Fund. *State of the World's Children Report, 1997.* New York, NY: United Nations Children's Fund, 1997.

18. Report of the Secretary-General on the situation of women and girls in Afghanistan: The implementation of human rights with regard to women. Geneva, Switzerland: United Nations Commissioner for Human Rights. United Nations document E/CN.4/Sub.2/2000/18.

19. See World Health Organization. Drought in Central Asia, 2000: Background data on affected countries, 2000; United Nations Development Program. Human Development Report, 1997, New York, NY: Oxford University Press, 1997; Information Statistics: Afghanistan. United Nations Children's Fund website: www.unicef.org/statis.

20. United Nations Children's Fund website: www.unicef.org/statis; UNICEF/CIET multiple Indicator Cluster Survey. 1997:2–26.

21. United Nations Department of Humanitarian Affairs. *Report of the DHA mission to Afghanistan.* Geneva, Switzerland: UN Department of Humanitarian Affairs, June 15, 1997:1–24.

22. See World Health Organization. *Drought in Central Asia, 2000: Background data on affected countries, 2000;* United Nations Development Program. *Human Development Report, 1997.* New York, NY: Oxford University Press; 1997.

23. World Health Organization. *Hope.* WHO. December, 1996.

24. World Health Organization. *The sisterhood method for estimating maternal mortality.* Available at: www.who.int/reproductive-health/publications/RHR_01_9_ maternal_mortality_ estimates/figures_and_annexes.en.pdf (Accessed January 4, 2002).

25. Mann, J., Gostin, L., Gruskin, S., Brennan, T., Lazzarini, Z., and Fineberg, H.V. "Health and Human Rights." *Health and Human Rights.* 1(1):6–23, 1994; Iacopino, V. "Human Rights: Health Concern for the Twenty-first Century." In: Majumdar, S.K., Rosenfield, L.M., Nash, D.B., and Auder, A.M. (eds.). *Medicine and Health Care into the Twenty-first Century.* Pennsylvania Academy of Science, PA 376–92, 1995; Benatar, S.R. "Global Disparities in Health and Human Rights: A Critical Commentary." *Am J Pub Health* 88: 295–300, 1998; Yamin, A.E. "Transformative combinations: women's health and human rights." *JAMWA* 1997. 52(4):169–173.

26. United Nations General Assembly. United Nations General Assembly Resolution A/RAS/32/130. Geneva, Switzerland: December 16, 1977; Donnelly J. "Interdependence and Indivisibility of Human Rights." *Universal Human Rights in Theory and Practice*. Ithaca, New York: Cornell University Press, 1989:28–45.

27. Selection of these factors is based on established causes of maternal mortality in the literature and PHR's assessment of relevant regional conditions. See also: Yamin, A.E. and Maine, D.P. "Maternal Mortality as a Human Rights Issue: Measuring Compliance with International Treaty Obligations." *Human Rights Quarterly* 21:3:563–607, 1999.

28. United Nations Children's Fund. *Guidelines for Monitoring the Availability and Use of Obstetric Services*, 1997. www.unicef.org. Accessed June 8, 2002.

29. Id. supra 32.

30. Id. supra 32.

31. Id. supra 32.

32. United Nations Development Program. *Needs Assessment Report, V. Social Protection, Health and Education: B. Health*. undp.org. Accessed February 14, 2002.

33. World Health Organization-Afghanistan, December 2001, Country Health Profile (unpublished), sent to Dr. Arnowitz from WHO/Afghanistan in Islamabad, Pakistan January 2002.

34. Id. supra 36.

35. United Nations Development Program. *Needs Assessment Report, V. Social Protection, Health and Education: B. Health*. undp.org. Accessed February 14, 2002.

36. An estimated 52% of children are malnourished and more than 50% of children have stunted growth. See World Health Organization. *Drought in Central Asia, 2000: Background data on affected countries*. 2000; United Nations Development Program. *Human Development Report* 1997. New York, NY: Oxford University Press, 1997.

37. World Health Organization. *Advancing Safe Motherhood Through Human Rights*. www.who.int/reproductive-health/publications/. Accessed January 4, 2002.

38. Id. supra 40.

39. Id. supra 40.

40. Grossman, 1975. "The correlation between health and schooling." In: *Household Production and Consumption*. ed. Nestor E. Terleckyj. NBER Studies in Income and Wealth, no. 40. New York: National Bureau of Economic Research; Columbia University, Auster, Richard, Irving Levenson, Deborah Sarachek, 1969. "The production of health: an explanatory study." *Journal of Human Resources* 4(Fall): 412–436; Reldman, J. Makuc, D., Kleinman, J., Cornoni-Huntly, J., 1989. "National trends in educational differentials in mortality." *American Journal of Epidemiology* 129:919–933.

41. World Health Organization. *Advancing Safe Motherhood Through Human Rights*. www.who.int/reproductive-health/publications/. Accessed January 4, 2002.

42. See Amowitz, L.L., Burkhalter, H., Ely-Yamin, A., and Iacopino, V. *Women's Health and Human Rights in Afghanistan: A Population-Based Study*. Boston, MA: Physicians for Human Rights: May, 2001; Amowitz, L.L. and Iacopino, V. "Women's Health and Human Rights Needs." *The Lancet Perspectives* 356 (s65), December 2000.

43. Yamin, A.E. and Maine, D.P. "Maternal Mortality as a Human Rights Issue: Measuring Compliance with International Treaty Obligations." *Human Rights Quarterly* 21:3:563–607, 1999.

44. Id.

45. World Health Organization. "Reduction of Maternal Mortality." WHO/UNFPA/UNICEF World Bank Statement. WHO Geneva 1999; and General Comment 14 of the Committee on Economic, Social, and Cultural Rights on the right to the highest attainable standard of health. E/C.12/2000/4, CESCR General Comment 14, July 4, 2000.

46. *International Covenant on Civil and Political Rights*, United Nations G.A. Res. 2200a (XXI), U.N. GAOR, 21st Sess., Supp. no 16., UN Doc A/6316 (1967), reprinted in Center for the Study of Human Rights, *Women and Human Rights: The Basic Documents*. New York, NY: Columbia University, 1996. Afghanistan acceded 24 January 1983 [hereinafter ICCPR]. *International Covenant on Economic, Social and Cultural Rights*, 21 G.A. Res. 2200 (XXI), UN GAOR, Supp. (No. 16) 49, UN Doc A (6316) 1966. Afghanistan acceded 24 January 1983 [hereinafter, ICESCR].

47. ICESCR Art 2(1).

48. ICESCR Art 3.

49. ICESCR Art 13.

50. ICESCR Art 7.
51. ICESCR Art 11(1).
52. ICESCR Art 11(2).
53. ICESCR Art 12(1).
54. United Nations Committee on Economic, Social, and Cultural Rights, General Comment 14. The right to the highest attainable standard of health: 11/08/2000. E/C12/2000/4. [hereafter General Comment 14].
55. General Comment 14 (14).
56. General Comment 14, at Paras 14 and 44.
57. General Comment 14 12(2).
58. ICCPR Art 3.
59. ICCPR Art 23 (2).
60. Declaration on the Elimination of Discrimination against Women (1967) G.A. Res 2263, UN GAOR 22d Sess UN Doc A/6716 (1967); Convention on Consent to Marriage, minimum age for marriage and registration of marriages (1962) 521 UNTS 231.
61. The definition of a child according to the UN Convention on the Rights of the Child is anyone under the age of 18.
62. ICCPR Art 23(3).
63. CRC Art 1.
64. CRC Art 24(1).
65. CRC Art 24(2).
66. CRC Art 24 (2(d).
67. CRC Art 24(2) (f).
68. CRC Art 24(4).
69. CRC Arts 28 and 29.
70. CRC Arts 34 and 36.
71. *Convention on the Political Rights of Women*, 193 U.N.T.S 135, (entered into force 7 July 1954), reprinted in Center for the Study of Human Rights, *Women and Human Rights: The Basic Documents*, New York, NY: Columbia University (1996) Signed 14 August 1980. Article 1,2,3.
72. Article 16(a), *Convention on the Elimination of All Forms of Discrimination Against Women*, adopted 18 Dec 1979, GA Res 34/180, UN GAOR Supp (No 46), UN Doc/A/34/36 (1978), reprinted in ILM 33 (1980)(entered into force 3 Sept. 1981)[hereinafter, Women's Convention].
73. Article 12(2) continues: "Notwithstanding the provisions of paragraph I of this article, States parties shall ensure to women appropriate services in connection with pregnancy, confinement and the post-natal period, granting free services where necessary, as well as adequate nutrition during pregnancy and lactation." Id, Article 12(2).
74. Article 12(2), *Convention on the Elimination of All Forms of Discrimination Against Women* (Women's Convention), adopted 18 Dec 1979, GA Res 34/180, UN GAOR Supp (No 46), UN Doc/A/34/36 (1978), reprinted in ILM 33 (1980) (entered into force 3 Sept 1981).
75. Id. Article 16.
76. CEDAW Art 16(2).
77. Id. Article 2.
78. General Comment, Paras. 14 and 21 (2000); and CEDAW General Recommendation No 24, supra note 21, at Para. 26.
79. CEDAW General Recommendation No 24, supra note 21, at Para. 27.
80. Programme of Action of the International Conference on Population and Development: Report of the International Conference on Population and Development, UN GAOR, 29th Sess, UN Doc A/Conf. 171/13 (1994) 8.21; Action for Equality, Development and Peace: Beijing Declaration and Platform for Action, UN GAOR, Fourth World Conf. On Women, UN Doc A/Conf.177/20 (1995).
81. Vienna Declaration and Programme of Action, World Conference on Human Rights, Vienna. UN Doc A/Conf. 157/23 (12 July 1993).
82. Programme of Action of the United Nations International Conference on Population and Development. UN Doc A/Conf. 171/13. (18 October 1994) [hereinafter, Cairo Programme].
83. Beijing Declaration and Platform for Action, Fourth World Conference on Women. UN Doc A/Conf. 177/20 (17 October 1995) [hereinafter, Beijing Declaration].

84. Part II, Section 3 deals with the equal status of and human rights of women and (40) and (41) reference health in the following way:

> The World Conference on Human Rights recognized the importance of the enjoyment by women of the highest standard of physical and mental health throughout their life span and reaffirms, on the basis of equality between women and men, a woman's right to accessible and adequate health care and the widest range of family planning services, as well as equal access to education at all levels.

85. Id. Article 37.
85. Vienna Declaration, Article 36.
87. Id. Article 38.
88. Id. Article 39.
89. Cairo Programme, Article 4.1.
90. Beijing Declaration, Chapter IV, 214.
91. Id. 215.
92. Id. 216.
93. Id. 220.
94. Id. 224.
95. Id. 225.
96. Id. 227.

16
New Challenges
for Humanitarian Protection

Claude Bruderlein and Jennifer Leaning

The fourth Geneva Convention, adopted 50 years ago, on 12 August 1949, describes the actions that warring parties must take to protect civilian populations from the worst excesses of war. Building on the concept developed in the previous three conventions—that certain activities and people, especially civilians, can be seen as hors de combat—the fourth Geneva Convention defines in detail the many ways in which civilians must be dealt with to shield them from the direct and indirect effects of conflict between combatant forces. Among the responsibilities that this convention sets for the warring parties are explicit actions that would grant medical personnel, and all aspects of the medical enterprise, complete protection from interference or harm. This neutral status for medical relief (and, by extension, all humanitarian aid) rests on the reciprocal assumption that those who deliver this relief are practising in accord with their professional ethics and will take specified steps to maintain their neutral posture vis à vis the warring parties.

The moral impetus for this addition to the Geneva Conventions derived from international reaction to the great civilian death toll of the second world war. In virtually all wars of the subsequent 50 years the fourth Geneva Convention has been variously observed and routinely violated—and there has been no calling to account. Moreover, and this is what prompts new attention to the issue of humanitarian protection in war, in recent wars the warring parties have shown an increasing tendency to flout the fourth convention entirely. The problem is no longer a failure to abide by the rules but a failure to acknowledge that the rules even exist.[1]

This failure is particularly relevant for the medical community. Without the guarantees of protection defined in the fourth convention, civilians can be slaughtered with impunity and physicians and other relief workers swept up in the ensuing carnage. Once the notion of civilian protection is abandoned, the terrain of war is changed utterly. At the very moment we celebrate the 50th anniversary of the Geneva Conventions, we find that effective respect for humanitarian protection has reached its nadir.

Traditional Approach to Humanitarian Protection

The traditional legal effort to protect civilians in war has long centred on distinguishing between civilian persons or objects and military targets. This approach was based on two key assumptions: that attacking civilian targets would provide little military advantage; and that, quite apart from their legal or moral obligations, parties to a conflict would thus seek to optimise their resources by targeting military assets. Therefore the most effective approach to protect civilians in international legal treaties on the conduct of war would be to build on this assumed basic military preference and promote the concept of civilian distinctiveness. This approach has inspired the development of international humanitarian law since its inception.

A corollary of this approach is to designate the armed forces of the warring parties as the principal implementing agents of the protection. International humanitarian law states that those who seek to be protected cannot engage in any hostile activities without losing their protected status. If the armies confirm that the civilians are abiding by these constraints then the armies are obliged to ensure that the civilians are indeed protected. An essential element of this legal regime therefore is the commitment of the parties to the conflict to abide by the rules.

Intensified Threats to Protection of Civilians

The traditional approach taken by international humanitarian law thus rests on a particular and rational view of military interests and behaviour. However, military strategies from the second world war onwards have departed significantly from this classic perception of the non-military worth of civilian assets. The bombardments of London, Rotterdam, Dresden, Hamburg, Hiroshima, and Nagasaki in the second world war were only the precursors of military tactics aimed at obtaining significant military advantage from the destruction, terror, flight, and chaos caused by attacks on civilians. In the 54 years since 1945, civilians have constituted the overwhelming majority of war casualties.[2] What has evolved now, with the waning of the cold war, is a pattern of deliberate war against civilians, waged by relatively untrained forces wielding relatively light arms.[3] Civilian populations have come to acquire a strategic importance, including:

- As a cover for the operations of rebel movements
- As a target of reprisals
- As a shield against air or artillery attacks
- As a lever for exerting pressure on the adverse party, by terrorising and displacing populations, or even
- As a principal target of ethnic cleansing operations and genocide.

In internal conflicts civilian populations are caught in the crossfire between insurgents and state forces and bear most of the casualties. In extreme situations (Rwanda 1994; Bosnia-Herzegovina 1992–4; and Kosovo 1998–9) entire segments of the civilian population have been perceived as a primary military target. Civilian deaths in just these three wars amount to over 1 million people—far greater than the estimated military casualties.

Death is not the only outcome of a war strategy that targets civilians. In the past decade armed conflict has turned over 40 million people into refugees or internally displaced people. The consequences of such displacement are severe and include:

- Breakdown of the social fabric and disintegration of communities
- Production of chaotic situations, where the mixture of civilians and combatants puts civilians at risk and endangers medical and humanitarian relief workers
- Disruption of family groupings, exposing women and girls to sexual violence, prostitution, and sex trafficking
- Forced military recruitment of children, sending those as young as 7 years old into battle.

In addition, warring factions have increasingly denied civilian populations access to humanitarian relief. They defend their actions by appealing to the principle of national sovereignty. Within their national boundaries these warring parties block relief convoys, obstruct ambulances, invade hospitals, destroy clinics, and harass and terrorise national and international medical and other humanitarian relief workers.[4-8] In these circumstances the assumption in international humanitarian law that civilians would be protected simply by establishing their distinct non-military character seems outdistanced by recent changes in warfare and thus fundamentally flawed. In the absence of alternative credible and effective enforcement mechanisms, it would seem that the international community can offer little help to civilian populations targeted in today's wars.

Possible New Strategies

The international community has thus been compelled to reconsider its approach towards protecting civilians. When states or parties to conflicts are unable or unwilling to protect civilians during armed conflict, the international community must develop specific mechanisms to ensure that protection. To that end, new strategies are being developed to expand the concept of humanitarian protection and to consider new alliances with other potential enforcement agents, including the United Nations Security Council and regional organisations and their military outfits.

Accordingly, human rights and humanitarian organisations are pursuing three distinct strategies to bolster the protection given to civilians: reasserting the role and validity of international humanitarian law, and developing new judicial implementation mechanisms; expanding the scope of humanitarian protection; and diversifying the implementation strategies of humanitarian protection, involving the use of various diplomatic and coercive measures, including the use of force under chapter VII of the UN Charter.

Reasserting the Role of International Humanitarian Law

The first strategy has been to recall the objectives of international humanitarian law and promote further efforts nationally and internationally for enforcing these rules. International humanitarian law is seen as essential in determining the illegal character of violence perpetrated against civilians in war. It should therefore be at the centre of any strategy to protect them and to restore the integrity of international law. The proponents of this approach, particularly the International Committee of the Red Cross, acknowledge that war has changed and that civilians have increasingly become the objects of attacks. In their view, however, violations of law do not necessarily signify its obsolescence. On the contrary, international humanitarian law remains highly relevant in contemporary conflicts (such as instances of ethnic cleansing and failed states) and serves to mobilise considerable efforts to further its application.

The key focus of these efforts has been to strengthen international judicial institutions. The culture of impunity that shelters individuals responsible for violent assaults against civilians is one of the biggest obstacles to protecting civilians in most conflicts. The unwillingness or inability of states to bring these people to justice undermines the effectiveness of the entire legal framework. An international remedy for such situations has been identified in the establishment of an International Criminal Court and the creation of the two ad hoc tribunals for the former Yugoslavia and for Rwanda by the UN Security Council.

Action from Professional Groups

Professional groups, including lawyers, doctors, and journalists, have also played a part in reinforcing traditional mechanisms of protection by recalling the legal obligations of parties to armed conflicts under humanitarian law. The successes of "sans-frontières" non-governmental organisations, such as Medecins Sans Frontières, International Commission of Jurists, or Reporter Sans Frontières, is a demonstration of this mobilisation of professionals. The medical and public health communities, through international societies, human rights groups, or relief agencies, played a pioneering role here, taking a strong interest in upholding established international principles of human rights in relation to medical ethics and international humanitarian law and in documenting violations. Beginning with the founding of the World Medical Association in 1947, the world's national medical societies have tried to uphold professional norms in the face of potential or actual confrontation with developments in peace and war. An early leader was the British Medical Association, which in the 1980s spurred organised medicine to combat the participation of physicians in torture.[9][10]

Physician-based human rights organisations have sought to provide governments and judicial bodies with evidence of major violations of the Geneva Conventions during conflict or civil war in the West Bank and Gaza in 1988–90,[11] Somalia in 1992,[12] Bosnia-Herzegovina in 1992–5,[13] Rwanda-Eastern Congo in 1994–7,[14] and Kosovo in 1998–9.[15] A major effort is now underway among several such organisations to provide documentary and forensic evidence to the international criminal tribunals of Yugoslavia and Rwanda.

Relief organisations, under increasing public scrutiny and subject to ever more frequent danger in the field, have also realised that they must educate their staff in the principles of human rights and international humanitarian law.[16] Their staff will thus operate within internationally respected norms and know what should be expected from warring parties and the international community in terms of humanitarian protection.

Expanding the Scope of Humanitarian Protection

The need to expand the scope of humanitarian protection arises directly from the changing nature of war. Were civilians not terrorised into fleeing from their homes, issues relating to internally displaced people would be less acute. Were regular forces fighting according to standard rules of weaponry, the proliferation of unmarked antipersonnel landmines would be less of a problem. Were children not being forcibly inducted into irregular armies and then forced to commit unspeakably brutal acts, the minimum age and its enforcement would not attract such attention.

The increasing involvement, over the past decades, of UN agencies and non-governmental organisations in humanitarian operations has increased the number of humanitarian actors in conflict situations.[17] This in turn has affected the perceived scope of humanitarian protection from one that is basically driven by international humanitarian law to one that is driven by the many needs of specific groups of victims in specific circumstances. Children need caring adults;

terrified refugees need to be able to feel safe; people from diverse cultures seek respectful space for religious practice; women in camps should not be forced into prostitution.

The humanitarian community has sought legal confirmation of this needs based expansion by referring to several key human rights documents that it regards as relevant in conflict settings. These include the 1951 Convention Relating to the Status of Refugees, the 1979 Convention on the Elimination of All Forms of Discrimination against Women, the 1984 Convention against Torture, and the 1989 Convention on the Rights of the Child. The insistence that key provisions of these documents do, indeed, apply in a state of conflict[18] has produced a growing recognition that just because people are trapped in war, they do not in any moral sense, and thus should not legally, lose the protection that they could claim if they were living in a country at peace. International humanitarian law remains the primary legal reference in conflicts. Nevertheless, these developments in humanitarian practice and policy, and the new guidelines on internally displaced peoples (which combine elements of human rights law with international humanitarian law) show an encouraging convergence between these two basic ways of defining protections for civilians in war.

The concept of humanitarian protection is also being extended in terms of time frame. International humanitarian law traditionally applies during the actual conduct of hostilities. From a public health and human rights perspective, however, the phases that lead up to a conflict and the extended reconstruction period afterwards are of equal concern. Issues such as the repatriation of refugees[19] or the status of vulnerable groups, such as women and girls in Afghanistan,[20] become central concerns of those engaged in humanitarian and human rights action in war.

This expansion arises out of a decade of work in which these humanitarian concerns were slowly shaped by bitter experience. The humanitarian community has provided the data that has forced the international legal and political community to develop an expanded scope of protection. As early witnesses to and occasional victims of child soldiers, as surgeons in field hospitals overwhelmed by landmine injuries, or as the only source of help in a region suddenly flooded by internally displaced people, medical relief workers had first to act without the benefit of guidelines and were then compelled to become more systematic. Internal critiques and published reviews of this experience[21] have accelerated our understanding of the complexity of the issues facing those who try to provide relief when established norms of protection are violated and when new forms of attacks on civilians take place in the absence of consensus on what the international community should do next.

International Initiatives

To establish this expanded scope of humanitarian protection in the legal and operational sphere is a complex challenge. Three recent initiatives, undertaken at international legal levels and pursued by many humanitarian and human rights organisations, have focused on protecting civilians against the use of anti-personnel landmines, protecting internally displaced persons, and prohibiting the military recruitment of children.

The 1997 Ottawa Landmines Treaty (entered in force in March 1999) bans the use, production, stockpiling, and transfer of antipersonnel landmines. Groups such as the International Campaign to Ban Landmines (comprising many humanitarian and human rights groups) were critical in mobilising states. This grass roots coalition, and others associated with it, has now embarked on monitoring compliance with the treaty and running local landmine awareness campaigns throughout the world.

The forced displacement of people within the borders of their own countries by armed conflicts has become a central feature of the post cold war era. In its classic form international humanitarian law does not protect internally displaced people since they remain primarily under the protection of their own state. Yet some of the worst assaults on civilians in war have taken place against internally displaced people (Srebrenica),[22] and some of the more intractable humanitarian dilemmas relate to supporting those forced to survive away from home but within the borders of their state (Sudan).[23] As a result the United Nations presented "Guiding Principles for the Protection of Internally Displaced Persons" to the Commission on Human Rights in 1998. These combine elements of humanitarian law and human rights law, which recognise, among other rights, a right not to be unlawfully displaced, the right of access to assistance and protection during displacement, and the right to a secure return and reintegration.

Finally, the use of children in armed conflicts has been another dramatic feature of post cold war hostilities. An estimated 300 000 child soldiers are actively involved in armed conflicts around the world.[24] According to both international human rights and humanitarian law, the current minimum age for participation in armed conflict is 15 years. Although the recruitment of children as young as 7 already falls far below this international standard, Unicef and other humanitarian organisations have tried to raise awareness and affect realities on the ground by crafting the Optional Protocol to the Convention of the Rights of the Child. This sets a minimum age of 18 years. This campaign has also highlighted the many difficulties presented by child soldiers: demobilisation, re-entry into society, and education.

Diversifying Implementation Strategies of Humanitarian Protection

The expansion of the concept of humanitarian protection has resulted in a more sophisticated understanding of the rights of civilians in times of war. Such protection still relies primarily, however, on the ability and willingness of implementing agents (states, the UN Security Council, and regional organisations such as NATO) to enforce this protection. When warring parties fail to abide by the rules of international humanitarian law, it falls to the international community to enforce them.

The practical importance of this responsibility remains unclear. Proponents of more assertive regimes of civilian protection believe that new political and security strategies are required, to provide more tactical options along a continuum within the current legal framework of the UN Charter's chapter VI (entry with the permission of the sovereign state) and chapter VII ("nonpermissive" entry). Such protection strategies need to involve political and military actors, such as the UN Security Council, regional organisations, and specialised agencies (such as the UN Department of Peacekeeping Operations) and would constitute the next generation of international security response to humanitarian crises. The current rationale for international political and military intervention is based on threats to international peace and security; in the next generation this would also include threats to civilian protection.

Throughout this decade we have been in the midst of that transition. In the former Yugoslavia and Rwanda, the international security regime failed to act decisively to end wars that caused great civilian suffering. Humanitarian and human rights organisations decried the role that international relief organisations were forced to play, filling a power vacuum, assuaging the conscience of the international community.[25] In northern Iraq, in Somalia, and again in Kosovo, various sets of international political and military actors took more aggressive action, in each case different, and in each case with mixed and disputed results.

Discussion and Force

As we continue through this transition the humanitarian community, including those in medical relief organisations, must participate in the discussion and develop strategies that would maximise the humanitarian resources available under a given set of political and security constraints. In settings where the consent of warring parties can be obtained such options include establishing humanitarian corridors, delivering targeted relief, planning the safe exit of a population from an emergency, and creating protected areas.

If the warring parties do not consent and civilians continue to be at risk, the international community must consider using force to uphold international humanitarian law. The UN Security Council might consider intervening under chapter VII to re-establish the necessary conditions for providing humanitarian assistance and protecting civilians. These conditions might include creating and enforcing security corridors and areas, protecting humanitarian convoys, disarming populations or groups, and deploying forces to protect civilians. These measures might be particularly relevant in situations that have generated, as a consequence of grave violations of international humanitarian law, major displacements of population and widening social chaos, further contributing to regional and international instability. As in Kosovo, the use of force, in association with diplomatic negotiation, could help to restore a minimal political and security environment, thus permitting delivery of humanitarian assistance and restoration of minimum levels of civilian protection.

Whenever any of these strategies have been attempted during this decade, some humanitarian analysts and practitioners have raised concerns about the mixture of humanitarian and political goals.[26][27] The use of force mandated by the Security Council or regional organisations entails political agendas that may jeopardise the neutrality of protective humanitarian arrangements.[28] Furthermore, the use of force against warring parties may put civilians at even more at risk, as their status and safety become central issues in resolving the conflict. Finally, the extent to which UN Security Council members consider internal conflicts of the magnitude of the Kosovo crisis or the Rwanda genocide to be within the competence of the council remains to be ascertained. The question then arises as to which regional organisation, when, and on what grounds, can be permitted to intervene?

A Role for the Humanitarian Community

Yet many humanitarian organisations, including many engaged in medical relief, have already begun to accumulate experience in humanitarian interventions that involve a mixture of players—civilian, security, and military.[29] The future success of these strategies of humanitarian intervention will depend to a large extent on the ability of humanitarian organisations to engage the interest of political and security authorities in the task of developing clear, adequate, and practical options for protecting civilians.[30] It is also possible that, having participated in and witnessed a series of failures and partial small gains, having played a bit part in a drama determined by others, the humanitarian community could in future decide to play a significant role in mobilising political authorities around specific preferred strategic options.[31] It comes back to the aim of creating in times of war a distinct and neutral place for civilians, where medical and relief workers can reach the population and build a system of adequate supports, sustainable for as long as is necessary. The end is the same as that described in the fourth Geneva Convention of 1949, but the means no longer obtain. The world and its wars have changed, so other means to secure that same high purpose have to be developed and deployed.

Notes

1. Russbach, R. and Fink D. Humanitarian action in current armed conflicts: Opportunities and obstacles. *Med Global Survival* 1994;1:188–99.
2. Sivard, R.L. *World military and social expenditures 1996.* Washington, D.C.: World Priorities, 1996.
3. Kaldor, M. and Vashec, B., eds. *Restructuring the global military sector.* Vol 1. *New wars.* London: Pinter, 1997.

4. Leaning, J. When the system doesn't work: Somalia 1992. In: Cahill, K.M., ed. *A framework for survival: health, human rights, and humanitarian assistance in conflicts and disasters.* New York: Basic Books, Council on Foreign Relations, 1993:103–20.

5. Ramsbotham, O. and Woodhouse, T. *Humanitarian intervention in contemporary conflict.* Cambridge: Polity Press, 1996:167–92.

6. Jean, F. The problems of medical relief in the Chechen war zone. *Central Asian Survey* 1996;15:255–8.

7. Hansen, G. Aid in war-ravaged Chechnya: a severe test for humanitarians. *Christian Science Monitor* 1997 Dec 31:19.

8. Physicians for Human Rights. *Medical group documents systematic and pervasive abuses by Serbs against Albanian Kosovar health professionals and Albanian Kosovar patients.* Boston: PHR, 1998. (Preliminary report 23 December.)

9. British Medical Association. *Torture report.* London: BMA, 1986.

10. British Medical Association. *Medicine betrayed.* London: Zed Books, 1992.

11. Geiger, H.J., Leaning, J., Shapiro, L.A., and Simon, B. *The casualties of conflict: medical care and human rights in the West Bank and Gaza Strip.* Boston: Physicians for Human Rights, 1988.

12. De Waal, A. and Leaning, J. *No mercy in Mogadishu: the human cost of the conflict and the struggle for relief.* Boston, New York: Physicians for Human Rights, Africa Watch, 1992.

13. Physicians for Human Rights. *Medicine under siege in the former Mugoslavia 1991–1995.* Boston: PHR, 1996.

14. Africa Rights. *Genocide in Rwanda.* London: Africa Rights, 1994.

15. Physicians for Human Rights. *War crimes in Kosovo 1998–1999.* Boston: PHR, 1999.

16. Porter, K. Human rights medicine. 1. An introduction. *Student BMJ* 1996;4:146–7.

17. US Mission to the UN. *Global humanitarian emergencies, 1998.* New York: United Nations, 1998.

18. O'Donnell, D. Trends in the application of international humanitarian law by United Nations human rights mechanisms. *Int Rev Red Cross* 1998;324:481–503.

19. Boutroue, J. *Missed opportunities: the role of the international community in the return of the Rwandan refugees from eastern Zaire July 1994–December 1996.* Cambridge: Massachusetts Institute of Technology, 1998.

20. Iacopino, V., Rasekh, Z., Yamin, A.E., Freedman, L., Burkhalter, H., Atkinson, H., et al. *The Taliban's war on women: a health and human rights crisis in Afghanistan.* Boston: Physicians for Human Rights, 1998.

21. Joint Evaluation of Emergency Assistance to Rwanda. *The International response to conflict and genocide: Lessons from the Rwanda experience.* Copenhagen: Steering Committee of the Joint Evaluation of Emergency Assistance to Rwanda, 1996.

22. Ignatieff, M. *The warrior's honor: ethnic war and the modern conscience.* New York: Henry Holt, 1997.

23. Hart, M. and van Praet, S. The Sudan: dying a slow death. In: *World in crisis: The politics of survival at the end of the 20th century.* London, New York: Medecins Sans Frontières, 1997:181–203.

24. Brett, R. and McCallin, M. *Children: the invisible soldiers.* Stockholm: Swedish Save the Children, 1998.

25. Martin, J. Hard choices after genocide: human rights and political failures in Rwanda. In: Moore, J.M., ed. *Hard choices: moral dilemmas in humanitarian intervention.* Lanham, MD: Rowman and Littlefield, 1998:157–75.

26. De Waal, A. Humanitarianism unbound? *Current dilemmas facing multimandate relief operations in political emergencies.* London: African Rights, 1994.

27. Perrin, P. The risks of military participation. In: Leaning, J., Briggs, S.M., and Chen, L.C., eds. *Humanitarian crises: the medical and public health response.* Cambridge: Harvard University Press, 1999:309–23.

28. Sandoz, Y. The establishment of safety zones for persons displaced within their country of origin. In: Al-Nauimi, N.N. and Meese, R., eds. *International legal issues arising under the United Nations Decade of International Law.* Dordrecht: Kluwer Law International, 1995:899–927.

29. Mincar, L. and Weiss, T.G. *Humanitarian action in times of war: a handbook for practitioners.* London: Lynne Rienner, 1993.
30. Stremlau, J. *People in per it: human rights, humanitarian action, and preventing deadly conflict.* New York: Carnegic Corporation, 1998.
31. Weiss, T.G. *Military-civilian Interactions: intervening in humanitarian crises.* Lanham, MD: Rowman and Littlefield, 1999.

17
Economic Sanctions as Human Rights Violations
Reconciling Political and Public Health Imperatives

Stephen P. Marks

In this chapter I consider the public health impacts of sanctions regimes in their political and legal context and examine several reform proposals designed to reduce their harmful effects on civilians.[1] My purpose is to raise some of the legal and moral problems of treating the impacts of sanctions as human rights violations and to urge a collaborative effort of public health and human rights professionals with policymakers to influence the way sanctions are applied.

The Legal and Political Framework of Sanctions

Sanctions in international law and politics are measures of coercion to induce a recalcitrant party to conform to a norm of international behavior or to the will of the "sending" authority. Technically, the term applies to both military and nonmilitary measures, although it is more commonly used for measures short of force. In the United States, the term is used for the wide range of laws that deny aid and trade preferences, prohibit the export and import of weapons and goods, freeze assets abroad belonging to targeted countries or their elites, and apply other measures explicitly taken for purposes ranging from surrendering for trial persons accused of participating in acts of terrorism (e.g., Libya) to changing a country's basic political and economic system (e.g., Cuba).

According to an international finance and trade advising firm, as of July 1999 the United States was imposing sanctions on no fewer that 28 countries.[2] From World War I to 1990, the United States is reported to have imposed sanctions 77 times.[3] In the case of Libya, the Security Council suspended sanctions on April 5, 1999, when Libya surrendered for trial in the Hague the 2 suspects in the downing of PanAm Flight 103, renounced terrorism, and promised to compensate victims if the suspects are found guilty.[4] In contrast, sanctions applied to Cuba since 1960 have not achieved their purpose of destabilizing the Castro regime and provoking its overthrow and have been overwhelmingly rejected by the United Nations (UN) General Assembly, which "call[ed] on all States to refrain from promulgating and applying laws and measures" like the economic, commercial, and financial embargo against Cuba imposed by the United States.[5] When the United States acts outside the enforcement mechanisms of the UN to impose sanctions, it may be using its legitimate discretionary powers to grant or withdraw aid or to grant or deny trade privileges. It may also be acting out of superpower arrogance (more euphemistically termed "U.S. exceptionalism") with a dubious legal and political basis (e.g., in the case of the Helms-Burton Act, which provides measures against persons from third countries who do business with Cuba).[6]

The UN has imposed economic sanctions in 13 cases, 9 of which are currently enforced.[7] The legal grounding of these sanctions lies in the Security Council's power to "decide what measures not involving the use of armed force are to be employed to give effect to its decisions." Under this authority, the Council "may call upon the Members of the United Nations to apply such measures. These may include the complete or partial interruption of economic relations and of rail, sea, air, postal, telegraphic, radio, and other means of communications and the severance of diplomatic relations."[8]

From this legal basis, which presupposes a threat to or breach of the peace or act of aggression, four types of sanctions not involving military force are available.

Trade embargoes. Economic sanctions are the most commonly applied form of sanctions and the one that has the most significant public health consequences, normally in the form of trade embargoes and cessation of development assistance. Such sanctions were used against Iraq in August and September 1990 to induce withdrawal from Kuwait and after April 1992 to induce compliance with Security Council Resolution 687, which set the conditions Iraq must meet in the aftermath of Operation Desert Storm. They were also used against Yugoslavia (1991–1996) and Serbia and Montenegro (1992–1996), the social consequences of which were surveyed in 1994.[9] In the case of Haiti, the Organization of American States (OAS) called for sanctions in 1991, but the Security Council did not impose binding sanctions until June 1993.[10]

Arms embargoes. Typically, the first response to military aggression or other threats to international peace and security is to limit the target country's access to weapons by means of an arms embargo and by curtailing military assistance. Iraq's invasion of Kuwait was the only case of a UN-mandated multilateral arms embargo following a transboundary attack.[11] Arms embargoes have also been imposed on Yugoslavia,[12] Somalia,[13] Liberia,[14] and Haiti.[15] The direct public health implications of such sanctions are negligible, except for the general impact on civilian populations of prolonging the conflict, a possible consequence if the embargo prevents one side from achieving a decisive military victory.

Severing of communications. Preventing telephone and telegraph communication, delivery of mail, Internet access, and air, sea, and river travel is a means of focusing sanctions on the ruling elite of a recalcitrant regime. By their nature, such sanctions are more suitable for targeting those responsible for wrongdoing and avoiding harm to innocent civilians than is the prohibition of all forms of trade. Related to these measures are diplomatic isolation—withdrawing diplomatic personnel and refusing visas—and cultural and sports boycotts.

International criminal prosecution. In 1993, the Security Council invented an audacious form of sanction by establishing an international penal court to try individuals responsible for war crimes (serious violations of international humanitarian law) in the former Yugoslavia[16]; its jurisdiction was expanded in 1994 to include genocide and crimes against humanity in Rwanda.[17] Because the Security Council acted under Article 41 of the UN Charter, the tribunal is a form of sanction, although it is not often referred to as such in the literature. Like the severing of communications, penal sanctions against individuals are likely to have a deterrent and retributive effect without endangering the health and well-being of the civilian population.

Effectiveness of Sanctions and Their Alternatives

The principal argument in favor of sanctions is that, in the case of a recalcitrant dictator, the preferable coercive measure is to block access to weapons, resources, and trade advantages rather than resort to armed force. Whether such sanctions are effective is disputed in the literature.[18] The claim in a classic study that economic sanctions have an overall success rate of 34%[19] has been challenged,[20] and a theoretical model (spatial theory of crisis bargaining) was applied to the same data set in a study that found sanctions to have infrequent and modest impact.[21] "In most cases," the latter study concluded, "a state imposing sanctions on its opponent can expect an outcome that is just about the same as would be obtained without sanctions."[22]

The utilitarian assumption underlying the decision to impose sanctions is that the political gain will outweight the human pain. In other words, there is a higher purpose that justifies the regrettable but unavoidable civilian suffering. This assumption often proves ill founded in practice; the greater good is rarely achieved and is morally unsustainable in terms of its costs.[23] If the aim of sanctions is to communicate a message or punish wrongdoing, then sanctions are on weak ethical ground because they create situations in which "human suffering becomes merely a device of communication" and "a wrongdoer remains untouched and an innocent person is gratuitously harmed."[24] It is equally hazardous to assume that bombings and deployment of troops will succeed, short of the overwhelming force used to dislodge the Iraqi military from Kuwait. An alternative to both war and sanctions is the neglected realm of "positive sanctions" in the form of rewards, inducements, and incentives,[25] as is proposed in the case of Iraq.[26] In other words, more carrots and fewer sticks may be required. When sticks are necessary, the sending states must confront the risk of civilian harm.

Collateral Harm and Human Rights Accountability

The issue of harmful impact on civilian populations was brought to public attention in a significant way as early as 1991 by the study of the impact of the Gulf War and trade sanctions on epidemics and child mortality in selected Iraqi hospitals. This study was expanded to a nationwide survey of infant and child mortality, conducted by a team of 11 public health and medical professionals.[27] More than 30 major studies have been identified as dealing with the civilian impact of the war and sanctions against Iraq.[28] In 1996, the Center for Economic and Social Rights (CESR) sent a mission of 24 researchers, over half of whom were from the fields of public health and medicine, to review the impact of UN sanctions on Iraq in order to assess whether the sanctions violated human rights. After considering the ethical and legal questions regarding UN sanctions against Iraq in the light of available data concerning economic conditions, health facilities, and health infrastructure, the CESR concluded that the "case of Iraq illustrates why sanctions are not always a humane alternative to war."[29] The CESR argued that the UN Security Council should "hold itself accountable to its human rights obligations" and recommended that the Council "take less drastic means . . . to constrain the Iraqi regime without imposing the costs on the most vulnerable sectors of society." The CESR study raises the complex issue of the relationship between economic sanctions and human rights accountability.

It is tempting to consider that because (a) the rights to an adequate standard of living, to physical and mental health, to just remuneration, to education, to family life, and to other related rights are universally recognized and (b) serious studies by public health experts substantiate the claim that these rights have been violated as a result of economic sanctions, then (c) the "senders" of sanctions regimes—that is, the governmental and intergovernmental decision makers in Congress, the White House, the UN Security Council and the OAS—are perpetrators of human rights violations. The CESR comes close to succumbing to that temptation when it stresses that "the [Security] Council remains accountable to human rights principles regardless of the conduct of the Iraqi government."[30] Elizabeth Gibbons claims that states that enforced sanctions in Haiti "inadvertently participated in violating the rights of Haitian citizens."[31]

The identification of senders of sanctions with perpetrators of human rights violations is not so simple, for two reasons. First, as a matter of law, responsibility for a violation can only be attributed to a duty-holder, in most cases a state that has ratified a treaty establishing the obligation in question, and neither the Security Council nor the UN in general is a party to the International Covenant on Economic, Social and Cultural Rights (ICESCR), the Convention on the Rights of the Child (CRC), or any other relevant convention. Moreover, treaties impose obligations on states to take measures within their jurisdiction—that is, within the national territory and, for a limited range of matters, for its nationals outside the territory—but not for foreigners in their own countries. Thus, the members of the Security Council have no treaty-based duty to ensure treaty rights for the citizens of Haiti, Iraq, Serbia, or other targeted countries.

One can hold states accountable, however, for actions that defeat the object and purpose of a treaty to which they are a party (or even that they have signed and not yet ratified, as is the case with the United States with respect to the ICESCR), and the aim of protecting the human rights set out in the ICESCR is part of that object and purpose. Such is the intention of the following provision of the Maastricht guidelines, adopted by a group of 30 human rights experts in January 1997:

> The obligations of States to protect economic, social and cultural rights extend also to their participation in international organizations, where they act collectively. It is particularly important for States to use their influence to ensure that violations do not result from the programmes and policies of the organizations of which they are members.[32]

The language is not that of firm obligation, but it is designed to acknowledge the importance of states' using their influence to prevent violations—for example, through decisions of the Security Council or the OAS to impose sanctions. There is, moreover, a duty upon the Security Council to "act in accordance with the purposes and principles of the United Nations,"[33] among which is the purpose of "promoting and encouraging respect for human rights and fundamental freedoms for all."[34] Significantly, the Committee on Economic, Social and Cultural Rights, which monitors the application of the ICESCR, requires the state or entity imposing sanctions to take these rights "fully into account" when designing the sanctions regime, to monitor effectively the situation in the targeted country with respect to these rights, and to take steps "to respond to any disproportionate suffering experienced by vulnerable groups within the targeted country."[35] In the case of Haiti, the UN and the OAS did take human rights into account by creating the Human Rights Civilian Observation Mission (MICIVIH), which was described as "a positive action . . . that was quite different in nature from the negative action of sanctions."[36] However, it was also noted that the MICIVIH's mandate excluded economic, social, and cultural rights, as a result of "pragmatic decisions" that "respect for Haitians' economic and social rights would be sacrificed for the sake of advancing their political and civil rights." This dilemma emerged in the functioning of MICIVIH's Medical Unit, an unprecedented addition to a human rights component of a peace operation, which ran into difficulty in trying to reconcile mission headquarters' efforts to restrict its role to documenting abuse of civil and political rights with the participating medical practitioners' duty to provide care when the situation called for medical assistance.[37]

The second problem with the senders-as-perpetrators argument is both moral and legal: Senders of sanctions cannot be held responsible unless they intentionally seek to violate the rights in question or pursue policies that are so blatantly harmful to those rights that they fail to meet a minimum standard of compliance. The humanitarian exemptions that have been voted with sanctions in almost every case, and the supplemental humanitarian assistance programs funded by the "senders," as well as their public statements of concern for the plight of civilian populations, make it difficult to find willful intent on the senders' part.[38]

Nevertheless, the moral outrage of those who would like to hold senders of sanctions accountable as perpetrators of violations is justified, and passing blame to Saddam Hussein, Lt Gen Cédras, or Slobodan Milosevic is not enough. As a study commissioned by the UN concluded, "the amount of information available today on the devastating economic, social, and humanitarian impact of sanctions no longer permits [policymakers] to entertain the notion of 'unintended effects.'"[39] A member of the Security Council has declared that "it is disingenuous to talk of 'unintended side effects' when everybody knows that the sector most affected by sanctions, as presently applied, are precisely civilian populations. There is nothing surprising or unintended about it."[40] His statement was in reaction to a "non-paper" (an informal document used as a flexible tool for negotiation) by the five permanent members of the Security Council (P-5) that insisted that sanctions regimes should "minimize unintended adverse side-effects of sanctions on the most vulnerable segments of targeted countries."[41]

This tension between the sound conclusions of public health surveys of countries targeted by sanctions and the uncertain attribution of responsibility for human rights violations underscores the need for more reflection on the relationship between health and human rights. There can be no doubt that the civilian populations in targeted countries are victims of human rights violations. The Committee on Economic, Social and Cultural Rights authoritatively declared that "the inhabitants of a given country do not forfeit their basic economic, social and cultural rights by virtue of any determination that their leaders have violated norms relating to international peace and security."[42] While it is necessarily true that violations are committed by perpetrators, the principles of accountability for the human rights violations resulting from sanctions do not clearly identify the perpetrators or the consequences they should bear. Therefore, a more fruitful avenue is reform of sanctions to avoid such violations.

Rethinking Economic Sanctions

The policy community has been grappling with the dilemmas of sanctions, and numerous solutions have been proposed. In a widely quoted study for the Council on Foreign Relations, international lawyer Lori Damrosch proposed criteria for evaluating collective sanctions that address internal conflicts. She posits a "conflict containment criterion," by which sanctions are assessed for their capacity to reduce or end conflict, and a "differentiation criterion" that rates higher those collective responses that "target the perpetrators of violence or other wrongdoing and minimize severe adverse consequences on civilians who are not in a position to bring about cessation of wrongful conduct." She further distinguishes, within the differentiation criterion, the civilian impact, the wrong-doer impact, and the relationship between the two ("To the maximum feasible extent, a program of economic sanctions should be designed and implemented so as to avoid enriching the perpetrators of wrongdoing at the expense of their victims").[43]

More recent studies on sanctions in Iraq by David Cortright and George A. Lopez, in 1998[44] and 1999,[45] concluded that sanctions inflict "unacceptably high humanitarian costs."[46] Applying criteria of legitimacy, effectiveness, and morality, they recommended restructuring sanctions to allow Iraq to purchase civilian goods, food and medicine, spare parts, and manufactured goods, while maintaining the arms embargo. They favor the use of "smart sanctions strategies that focus more on the wrongdoer than on the general population and economy." The Global Policy Forum,[47] Gibson,[48] Gibbons,[49] and others have made additional policy recommendations.

One of the most systematic sets of recommendations was compiled in *Toward More Humane and Effective Sanctions Management: Enhancing the Capacity of the United Nations System*, a joint project of three institutions, which proposes a useful methodology for anticipating and tracking the impact of sanctions in public health, economics, population displacement, governance and civil society, and humanitarian activities.[50] The same three sponsors, along with five others, met with the chairpersons of the various sanctions committees, senior diplomats, and nongovernmental organization and private sector representatives during the Symposium on Security Council Targeted Sanctions in New York in December 1998. Drawing on the work of the Interlaken Seminar convened by the Swiss government in March 1998, the New York symposium distinguished between efforts to break the target's "power to resist" (which can have "devastating humanitarian consequences") and efforts to break its "will to resist" (which require "the use of sanctions as tools of inducement rather than punishment").[51] The symposium recommended impact preassessments, fine tuning of sanctions to reduce unintended consequences, technically competent monitoring, more effective administration of humanitarian exemptions, model legislation, and special measures for targeted financial sanctions, arms embargoes, and travel bans. The symposium concluded that "a strategy for more effective sanctions should target pressure on decision-making elites, while avoiding to the greatest extent possible adverse humanitarian consequences."[52]

Reconciling Political Imperatives with Human Rights and Public Health

This reflection leads to several conclusions concerning the legitimate reasons for the preferred types of sanctions, as well as the valuable role human rights and health professionals might play in their implementation.

Legitimacy of sanctions. Unilateral measures for narrow national interests or ideological fervor are dangerous to world order and are usually unjustifiable on legal and moral grounds. Sanctions decided collectively in accordance with Chapter VII of the UN Charter are based on the valid grounds of a collective effort by the international community to preserve international peace and security.

Types of sanctions. It is true, as Minear contends, that "sanctions are not entirely or inherently hostile to humanitarian interests."[53] Economic sanctions are more likely to be hostile to those interests than the other three types of sanctions enumerated at the beginning of this commentary. Indeed, arms embargoes, severing of communication, and criminal prosecutions merit more systematic use by governments and offer greater chances of influencing the political decision makers in the target state than do economic sanctions. The latter place the human rights and public health of the civilian population at considerable risk and must be reformed along the lines proposed in the various studies cited.

The political climate is increasingly favorable to the restructuring of sanctions in ways that are responsive to human rights and public health concerns. In the 1995 UN "non-paper" quoted earlier, the P-5 had already called for "unimpeded access to humanitarian aid," assessment of "the short- and long-term humanitarian consequences of sanctions," review of sanctions "to give due regard to the humanitarian situation," and expeditious consideration of humanitarian applications by sanctions committees. More recently, the UN Secretary-General said he wanted to render "sanctions a less blunt and more effective instrument" by using "smart sanctions," which seek, in his words, "to pressure regimes rather than peoples and thus reduce humanitarian costs."[54] He favors sanctions that, in addition to the normal exemptions, include specific measures to protect the human rights of vulnerable groups, as recommended by the Committee on Economic, Social and Cultural Rights and the Committee on the Rights of the Child, which monitor the ICESCR and the CRC respectively.[55] He warns, however, that "these humanitarian and human rights policy goals cannot easily be reconciled with those of . . . sanctions"[56] that, as tools of enforcement, are expected to do harm.

The role of health and human rights professionals. Independent teams of investigators from the fields of human rights and health, using their own assumptions, methods, and professional standards, are justified in publicizing the unacceptable suffering that sanctions impose on civilians. In doing so, they are likely to cause more "tornadoes" of controversy, as Gibbons described the reaction to the November 1993 release of the Harvard School of Public Health's report *Sanctions in Haiti: Crisis in Humanitarian Action.*[57]

Such tensions would be obviated if there were effective cooperation among public health, human rights, and peacekeeping professionals in implementing the recommendations of the recent studies. Health and human rights professionals are needed to monitor seriously and systematically the consequences of sanctions applying the carefully considered methodology and indicators that have been proposed.[58] Such individuals are invaluable in drawing attention to such consequences and urging funding of humanitarian assistance under sanctions regimes. They are vital to preassessment missions prior to the imposition of sanctions, as occurred with respect to Sudan in 1997.[59] They can make the case that economic, social, and cultural rights should be given as much importance as civil and political rights in monitoring and policy. In sum, they can provide the empirical and analytic basis for the argument that the "smartest" sanctions are those that do not sacrifice the health and human rights of the population of targeted countries for an uncertain political outcome.

Notes

1. See infra notes 43, 47, and 50.
2. Sanctions. Net, a Web site created by James Orr Associations, International Finance and Trade Advisors, Washington, D.C.. The countries listed by Sanctions. Net as under a sanctions regime as of July 9, 1999, are Afghanistan, Angola, Azerbaijan, Burma, Burundi, Cambodia, China, Congo, Cuba, Gambia, Guatemata, Haiti, India, Indonesia, Iran, Iraq, Liberia, Libya, Mauritania, Nigeria, North Korea, Pakistan, Sudan, Syria, Turkey, Ukraine, Vietnam, and the Federal Republic of Yugoslavia, Serbia and Montenegro. Available at http://www.sanctions.net (accessed July 15, 1999).
3. G.C. Hufbauer, J.J. Schott, and K.A. Elliott, *Economic Sanctions Reconsidered, History and Current Policy*, 2d ed. (Washington, D.C.: Institute for International Economics, 1990), 9.
4. In July, the Council reaffirmed its intention to lift sanctions "as soon as possible." Presidential Statement S/PRST/1999/22 of July 9, 1999.
5. General Assembly Resolution 53/4, adopted on October 14, 1998. The vote was 157 in favor to 2 against (United States and Israel), with 12 abstentions.

6. Cuban Liberty and Democratic Solidarity (LIB-ERTAD) Act of 1996. Pub. I., No. 104–114, 110 Stat. 785 (Mar. 12, 1996), 22 U.S.C. 6021–6091. A. F. Lowenfeld, "Agora: The Cuban Liberty And Democratic Solidarity (Libertad) Act: Congress And Cuba: The Helms-Burton Act," *American Journal of International Law* 90 (1996): 419–434; J.B. Busby, "Jurisdiction to Limit Third-Country Interaction With Sanctioned States: The Iran and Libya Sanctions and Helms-Burton Acts," *Columbia Journal of Transnational Law* 36 (1998): 621–658.

7. Sanctions regimes have existed with respect to Southern Rhodesia, South Africa, Serbia-Montenegro, and Sudan and are currently enforced with respect to Iraq, Federal Republic of Yugoslavia, Somalia, Libya, Liberia, Haiti, Angola, Rwanda, and Sierra Leone.

8. UN Charter, Article 41.

9. *Social Conditions for Health in Serbia and Montenegro* (New York, NY: CIET International, 1994). M. P. Doxey, *United Nations Sanctions: Current Policy Issues* (Halifax, Nova Scotia: Center for Foreign Policy Studies, Dalhousie University, 1997), 17.

10. Security Council Resolution 841 of June 16, 1993.

11. Security Council Resolutions 661 of August 6, 1991, and 687 of April 3, 1992.

12. Security Council Resolutions 713 of September 25, 1991, 724 of December 15, 1991, and 727 of January 8, 1992. When the former Yugoslav republics were recognized as new states on or after January 15, 1992, sanctions were applied to all by Resolution 762 of June 30, 1962, and special economic sanctions were applied to Serbia and Montenegro by Resolution 757 of May 30, 1992.

13. Security Council Resolution 733 of January 23, 1992.

14. Security Council Resolution 788 of November 19, 1992 (with an exemption for ECOWAS, the Economic Community of West African States, which provided the peacekeeping forces).

15. OAS MRE/RES/1/91 and MRE/RES/2/91 of October 3, 1991.

16. Security Council Resolution 827 of May 25, 1993.

17. Security Council Resolution 955 of November 8, 1994.

18. Extensively reviewed in S.S. Gibson, "International Economic Sanctions: The Importance of Government Structures," *Emory International Law Review* 13 (1999): 161–245.

19. Hufbauer, Schott, and Elliott, *Economic Sanctions Reconsidered*, 93.

20. R.A. Pape, "Why Economic Sanctions Do Not Work," *International Security* 22 (1997): 90–136.

21. T.C. Morgan and V.L. Schwebach, "Fools Suffer Gladly: The Use of Economic Sanctions in International Crises," *International Studies Quarterly* 41 (1997): 27–50.

22. Ibid., 46.

23. J.A. Gordon, "A Peaceful, Silent, Deadly Remedy: The Ethics of Economic Sanctions," *Ethics & International Affairs* 13 (1999): 128–133.

24. Ibid., 139–140.

25. E.A. Amley, "Peace by Other Means: Using Rewards in UN Efforts to End Conflicts," *Denver Journal of International Law and Policy* 26 (1998): 235.

26. F.G. Gause III, "Getting It Backward on Iraq," *Foreign Affairs* 78 (1999): 54–65.

27. Harvard Study Team, "The Effect of the Gulf Crisis on the Children of Iraq," *New England Journal of Medicine* 325 (1991): 977–980.

28. A. Ascherio, R. Chase, T. Coté, et al. "Effect of the Gulf War on Infant and Child Mortality in Iraq," *New England Journal of Medicine* 327 (1992): 931–936.

29. Center for Economic and Social Rights, *UN Sanctioned Suffering: A Human Rights Assessment of United Nations Sanctions on Iraq* (New York: Center for Economic and Social Rights, May 1996), 42.

30. Ibid., 36.

31. E.D. Gibbons, *Sanctions in Haiti: Human Rights and Democracy Under Assault* (West Port, Conn, and London, England: Praeger, 1999), 97. See also E. Gibbons and R. Garfield, "The Impact of Economic Sanctions on Health and Human Rights in Haiti, 1991 to 1994," *American Journal of Public Health* 89 (1999): 1499–1504.

32. "The Maastricht Guidelines on Violations of Economic, Social and Cultural Rights," (Paragraph 19) *Human Rights Quarterly* 20 (1998): 698.

33. UN Charter, Article 24, paragraph 2.

34. Ibid., Article 1, paragraph 3.

35. Committee on Economic, Social and Cultural Rights, *General Comment No. 8 (1997), The Relationship Between Economic Sanctions and Respect for Economic, Social and Cultural Rights*, UN document E/C.12/1997/8, paragraphs 11–14.
36. Gibbons, *Sanctions in Haiti*, 98.
37. C. Marotte and H.R. Razafimbahiny, "Haiti 1991–1994: The International Civilian Mission's Medical Unit," in *Health and Human Rights: A Reader*, ed. J.M. Mann, S. Gruskin, M.A. Grodin, and G.J. Annas (New York: Routledge, 1999), 106–112.
38. Gibbons, *Sanctions in Haiti*, 97.
39. C. von Braunmühl and M. Kulessa. *The Impact of U.N. Sanctions on Humanitarian Assistance Activities* (Berlin: Gesellschaft für Communication Management Interkultur Training, 1995), iii; cited by L. Minear, "The Morality of Sanctions," in *Hard Choices: Moral Dilemmas in Humanitarian Intervention*, ed. J. Moore (Lanham, Md: Rowman & Littlefield, 1998), 236.
40. Juan Somavía. Permanent Representative of Chile to the UN, *The Humanitarian Responsibility of the United Nations Security Council*, Gilbert Murray Memorial Lecture, Oxford, June 26, 1996; p. 18 of manuscript.
41. "Humanitarian Impact of Sanctions," annex to letter of April 13, 1995, to the president of the Security Council, UN document S/1995/300.
42. Committee on Economic, Social and Cultural Rights, *General Comment No. 8*, paragraph 16.
43. L.F. Damrosch, "The Civilian Impact of Economic Sanctions," in *Enforcing Restraint: Collective Intervention in Internal Conflicts*, ed. L.F. Damrosch (New York: Council on Foreign Relations Press, 1993), 283.
44. G.A. Lopez and D. Cortright, "Economic Sanctions and Human Rights: Part of the Problem, or Part of the Solution?" *International Journal of Human Rights* 1 (1998): 1–25.
45. G.A. Lopez and D. Cortright, "Are Sanctions Just? The Problematic Case of Iraq." *Journal of International Affairs* 52 (1999), 735–755. A book by the same authors entitled *The Sanctions Decade* is scheduled for publication in late 1999.
46. G.A. Lopez and D. Cortright, "Are Sanctions Just?," 750.
47. J. A. Paul, *Sixteen Policy Recommendations on Sanctions*. Proposed at a forum of German parliamentarians in Bonn, March 31, 1998. Available on-line at http://www.globalpolicy.org/security/sanctions/jpreccs.htm (accessed on July 22, 1999).
48. Gibson, "International Economic Sanctions." 229–235.
49. Gibbons, *Sanctions in Haiti*. 100–110.
50. L. Minear, D. Cortright, J. Wagler, G.A. Lopez, and T.G. Weiss, *Toward More Humane and Effective Sanctions Management: Enhancing the Capacity of the United Nations System*. Occasional Paper no. 31 (Providence. RI: Thomas J. Watson Jr. Institute for International Studies, 1998). The sponsoring institutions are the Humanitarianism and War Project at Brown University, the Joan B. Kroc Institute for International Peace Studies at Notre Dame, and the Fourth Freedom Forum of Goshen, Ind.
51. *Toward Smarter, More Effective United Nations Sanctions* (Goshen, Ind: Fourth Freedom Forum, 1998), 2. The new cosponsors were the Carnegie Commission on Preventing Deadly Conflict, the Carter Center, the Center for the Study of International Organizations at New York University Law School, the Institute for International Economics, and the United Nations Association of the USA.
52. Ibid., 8.
53. Minear, "The Morality of Sanctions," 246.
54. *Annual Report of the Secretary-General on the Work of the Organization*, UN document A/53/1 of August 27, 1998, paragraph 62.
55. Ibid., paragraph 63.
56. Ibid., paragraph 64.
57. Gibbons, *Sanctions in Haiti*, 59–62.
58. Minear et al. *Toward More Humane and Effective Sanctions Management*, 23–54.
59. Ibid., 11–13.

VI
Methods in Health and Human Rights

International and national bodies and organizations are increasingly using measures and indicators that specifically bring together the connections between health and human rights. These methods, while still in their infancy, can be grouped into four major categories that (1) take human rights as an entry point to examine the degree to which governments are respecting, protecting, and fulfilling rights in the context of health; (2) design, monitor, and evaluate health programming in ways that are sensitive to human rights issues and concerns; (3) focus on stigma and discrimination within the context of health; and (4) utilize international commitments, such as the Millennium Development Goals. While these methods coexist, they in fact have been constructed for diverse purposes and measure different things. As Raworth notes in her chapter, indicators generally lack clarity about what is to be assessed as well as how issues will be measured. Joining the approaches of traditional public health and human rights may produce new angles on our understanding of old problems and go a long way toward improving our actions. Each has, for example, considered the political and legal context in which health issues occur, but their ways of doing so have been radically different. The selections presented here illustrate this variety and draw attention to some of the issues still to be resolved for successful measurement and assessment of health and human rights concerns within these various methods.

As Mokhiber points out in the first chapter, the question of indicators arose early in the UN's efforts to integrate human rights into more general health and development work. Yet, clarity about how best to do this still remains elusive. An important contribution of human rights to health activities is the focus it brings to transparency and to the accountability of governments for their actions in relation to health. The recognition of health within a human rights context has brought attention to the legal obligations of governments as they relate to addressing health concerns, both in terms of prevention and in dealing with its effects. These obligations extend to ensuring that the national laws, policies, and practices of governments that ratify human rights treaties comply with those treaties, and that concrete benchmarks and targets be set against which progress can be measured.

Human rights indicators derive from and reflect human rights norms and are designed to monitor whether human rights norms are realized, often with a view to holding a duty-bearer to account. With respect to health, states may be assessed on the extent to which their national and local health policies, strategies, and programs are rights-based, or the extent to which financial, technical, and human resources are allocated in order to support rights-based approaches to health concerns. The Committee on the Rights of the Child, for example, recommends that special attention be given to assess the extent to which HIV-related rights of children are dealt with in laws, policies, and practices, with specific attention to discrimination against children on the basis of their HIV status or that of their family members.[1] The focus of the Committee on Economic, Social and Cultural Rights (CESCR), on the other hand, is on "discrimination in access to health care and underlying determinants of health, as well as to means and entitlements for their procurement on the grounds of race, color, sex . . . [and] health status."[2] The Raworth chapter proposes a conceptual framework that attempts to take this a step further, assessing a state's obligations using a context specific approach; but, as she indicates, actual application of this concept to real life efforts is still insufficient.

Many of the instruments in existence to assess health programs and national responses include, at most, a limited focus on human rights issues. In crude terms, their focus centers primarily around the existence of particular health issues, reduction of risk, or the availability of services. Most do not even measure which specific population subgroups, with the occasional exception of pregnant women, have access to services, nor the availability, accessibility, acceptability, and quality of these services to the relevant population subgroups— key rights-related aspects identified by the CSECR. While still rather crude, the health and human rights framework to evaluate the quality of public health programming described in *Health and Human Rights: A Reader* has increasingly been applied to health policy and programming in a variety of settings. The chapter by Hurtig, Porter, and Ogden is an attempt to apply this method to evaluate Directly Observed Therapy (DOT), the international strategy for controlling tuberculosis. Bringing health and human rights together in the design of interventions is the challenge presented to everyone involved in this work. More work is still needed to present a state-of-the-art cataloguing of programs and interventions of scientifically proven effectiveness.

Public health has increasingly given rhetorical attention to human rights, but genuine integration of rights into public health work, although relevant to every stage of planning and program development, remains in its infancy. The last chapter in this part by Yamin and Maine uses recently developed public health indicators in the area of maternal mortality reduction to show how these can be applied using human rights criteria. While these indicators may be insufficient to fully capture human rights issues in the context of health or even the human rights concerns intended, they do potentially provide useful information, as the authors show.

Over the coming years, we need to consider how we wish to approach analysis of the status and trends of health and human rights. What should be monitored and for what purpose? What framework or paradigms should be used to lay out monitoring options, including indicators? This is the work of the future.

Notes

1. See for example, recommendations in General Comment No. 3 (2003) for *HIV/AIDS and the Rights of the Child* developed by the Committee on the Rights of the Child.
2. CESCR. General Comment No. 14 on The Right to the Highest Attainable Standard of Health (Article 12 of the Covenant on Economic, Social and Cultural Rights (ICESC)). E /C.12/ 2000/4. (Geneva: United Nations Economic and Social Council, 2000).

18

Toward a Measure of Dignity
Indicators for Rights-Based Development

Craig G. Mokhiber

The advancement of economic and social development and the promotion and protection of human rights and freedoms have been principal purposes of the United Nations since its founding in 1945.[1] For most of the past half century, however, they have been largely pursued by the international community as distinct, at times even contradictory goals. For those engaged in the cause of development, human rights approaches were often viewed as "political," controversial, and unhelpful to the constructive endeavours of development.[2] For some, human rights could even be sacrificed in the name of development, in an instrumentalist *quid-pro-quo* that saw human rights as a temporally deferrable luxury of rich countries. In this context, it is hardly surprising that, prior to the 1990's, no major aid agency had significantly integrated human rights into its development policies and programmes.[3] At the same time, many human rights advocates emphasized civil and political rights, while neglecting economic and social rights, and opted for strategies of critical scrutiny to the exclusion of support for institution building and constructive engagement.[4]

Today, by contrast, virtually every development organization, including the bilateral donors comprising the Development Assistance Committee of the OECD, the various UN agencies, and the principal private and non-governmental aid organizations, has publicly embraced the integration of human rights in their work.[5] For their part, many international human rights advocates have given increased attention to economic and social rights, and have embraced development cooperation as an indispensable tool for the advancement of human rights.

At least four factors facilitated this rather dramatic shift. First, the end of the Cold War provided something of a thaw in inter-state discourse on human rights, while also launching a number of processes of national transition. An unprecedented number of States began to reach out to the international community for assistance not only in building and reforming health systems, educational capacities, and infrastructure, but also justice systems, and institutions of democratic governance.

Second, the convening of a series of global summits under UN auspices during the 1990s produced important international political consensus on previously highly contentious issues.[6] The inter-relationship between democracy, development and human rights was universally agreed.[7] The symmetry of the human rights framework was restored by the agreement that "all human rights are universal, indivisible, interdependent and interrelated" and that they must be treated "globally and in a fair and equal manner, on the same footing, and with the same emphasis."[8] The existence of the right to development was globally affirmed "as a universal and inalienable right."[9] Consensus was proclaimed around the notion that "the lack of development may not be invoked to justify the abridgement of internationally recognized human rights."[10]

Third, the establishment and appointment of the UN High Commissioner for Human Rights with a mandate[11] that gives priority to "promoting a balanced and sustainable development" and "ensuring realization of the right to development"[12] helped to focus international attention on the crucial nexus between human rights and development. The fact that this authoritative, highly visible, and essentially non-political[13] voice was brought to the cause did much to balance the right to development debate, and to relink the discourse surrounding it to the normative basis of the international human rights instruments.

Finally, the launch by the Secretary-General in 1997 of a system-wide UN reform package[14] that expressly called for the integration of human rights into the development (and other) work of the Organization[15] marked the beginning of a process of the reintegration of the UN Charter objectives. One element of that reform was the introduction of a system-wide approach to development cooperation, framed in the Common Country Assessment (CCA) and the UN Development Assistance framework (UNDAF).[16] For the UN human rights programme, an important entry point into the work of development had been created.

It was in this context that the Office of the High Commissioner for Human Rights was charged with responsibility for the integration of human rights in the Organization's development work–the so-called "*mainstreaming process*." Thus, in addition to the Office's traditional work on the promotion of the right to development as such, OHCHR became directly engaged in the conceptualisation of human rights-based approaches to development, and in supporting its partners in their efforts to integrate human rights into their development work.

The Indicator Challenge

The question of indicators[17] arose early in the mainstreaming process, most directly in the context of the formulation of the CCA indicator framework. The CCA was to frame the UN's development situation assessment and analysis, to inform advocacy and policy dialogue, and to form the basis for producing the UNDAF for each country. Consistent with the Secretary-General's reform proposals, human rights were to be integrated in the framework. Nevertheless, early drafts and proposals did not significantly reflect a rights-based approach to development, opting instead for more traditional development approaches. Economic and social areas were emphasized to the complete exclusion of civil and political development issues. Human rights were included as a separate category, rather than integrated throughout, implying that they were exclusive of the other categories, and their measurement was to be limited to questions of treaty ratification. Economic and social indicators that were included, while measuring status, did not measure the "rights" elements of, for example, health and education. In this sense, the early versions of the framework were consistent with most of the myriad of indicator initiatives underway at that time, both within and outside the UN system.

While the CCA framework may not yet be perfect from a rights perspective (and will likely be subject to further revision), each of these concerns was addressed by the UN team charged with the development and revision of the framework. As a result, the Organization may now boast the first comprehensive rights-based indicator framework for development. The framework today largely mirrors the human rights framework, and thus covers the full range of civil, cultural, economic, political and social development sectors. Thus, for example, it includes, alongside health, education and other socio-economic sectors, the new additions of "administration of justice," "democracy and participation" and "personal security."[18] It also allows for disaggregation beyond the usual questions of gender and geography to include vital questions of race, language, religion, and other categories important to exposing and redressing discrimination. In other words, the CCA framework accommodates a rights-based approach to development, but does not guarantee it.

A Rights-Based Approach to Development

While it has received unprecedented attention in recent years, the idea of rights-based approaches is not a new concept. Many of its elements have been tried and tested for years. There is a growing catalogue of successful case studies registered by many countries, and many programmes. Over a decade ago, the UN Committee on Economic, Social and Cultural Rights discussed the subject, and offered valuable advice, warning that proposals for the integration of human rights into development activities "can too easily remain at a level of generality." The assistance programme administered by OHCHR has been based on international human rights standards since its creation in 1955. ILO has operated within a rights framework that predates the UN itself. UNICEF has experimented with such approaches for several years now. UNDP has long pioneered people-centred approaches. Development NGOs, like Oxfam, Care, Novib, and others have also embraced rights-based approaches. Each has made an important contribution to the evolution of the concept, and of related practice.

A rights-based approach to development is a conceptual framework for the process of human development that is normatively based on international human rights standards and operationally directed to promoting and protecting human rights. Essentially, a rights-based approach integrates the norms, standards, and principles of the international human rights system into the plans, policies and processes of development. The norms and standards are those contained in the wealth of international treaties and declarations, and in the authoritative interpretations of the bodies established to monitor treaty implementation. The principles include those of participation, accountability, non-discrimination, empowerment and direct (and express) linkage to the international human rights instruments and standards themselves.[19]

Indicators for Rights-Based Development

Approaching development from this perspective creates particular demands for data that are not satisfied by traditionally restrictive socio-economic indicators alone. As demonstrated by the CCA development experience, the existence of a number of important gaps in the availability of appropriate indicators is presenting difficult challenges to those seeking to actually implement rights-based approaches to development.

Base Indicators on International Standards

Determining *what* to measure in particular has rights implications. A rights-perspective requires that indicators be based upon the internationally agreed human rights norms and standards. These standards, as contained in the treaties[20] themselves, as well as the authoritative normative interpretations contained in the general comments[21], decisions and observations[22] of the treaty-bodies established to monitor their implementation, are agreed, precise and accessible. In addition to providing guidance on the substantive content of each right, they also define with considerable specificity the requirements for enforcement and realization of the rights in question.

Use a Comprehensive Human Rights Framework

As noted above, a rights-based approach necessitates a comprehensive development framework with sectors mirroring the human rights framework. As such, alongside traditional socio-economic categories of development, the missing sectors, and corresponding indicators, must be added. There are essentially four areas of development neglected by traditional approaches: (1) justice administration; (2) personal security; (3) political participation/democracy, and (4) cultural aspects of development.[23] Because they have not been included in past approaches, there is a paucity of readily available, internationally agreed and field-tested development indicators for these sectors. Whatever sweeping policy commitments development agencies may make to rights-based approaches, filling these lacunae will be a *sine qua non* for actually implementing them on the ground.

Integrate the "Rights Element" into Existing Indicators

As for the socio-economic indicators currently and broadly employed, these too will require a second look, from a rights perspective. The "right to health" is something quite different from "health." Because rights-based development focuses on accountability and incorporates notions of entitlement and obligation, simply measuring status, or degree of realization, is not sufficient. There is a need to ensure the existence of an express right, and to monitor and measure the effectiveness of institutions and mechanisms of redress and enforcement as well. In this sense, socio-economic indicators must also be supplemented if rights-based development is to be effected. Accountability means beginning with the identification of (1) an explicit standard against which to measure performance, (2) a specific person/institution owing performance (3) a particular right-holder (or claim-holder) to whom performance is owed; (4) a mechanism of redress, delivery and accountability.

Measure the Subjective

Also necessary for rights-based development, and lacking in many development frameworks, are appropriate indicators and methodologies for the measurement of a number of subjective factors. The subjective is an important and constant element of international human rights law. It shows itself in the "well-founded fear of persecution" which is determinative of lawful asylum claims.[24] It is present as well in the culture and gender relative notion of "cruel, inhuman or degrading treatment or punishment," as contained in a number of international instruments.[25] It is a necessary element of determining the freedom and fairness of elections, as guaranteed by the Universal Declaration of Human Rights and the International Covenant on Civil and Political Rights.[26]

In the development context, public opinion polls and other such tools can be invaluable in measuring levels of public confidence in institutions of governance, and levels of public fear, including among vulnerable or marginalised groups. They are important, as well, for testing public perceptions about progress—a question that, from a rights-perspective, cannot be left to experts, foreign advisors, and government officials. The emphasis on "active, free and meaningful participation" of the rights-based approach requires that people determine the fundamental questions of their own development.[27]

Measure Status, Capacity, Official Response, and Accessibility

Other necessary elements for measurement include status and outcome, or, in other words, realization of human rights to health, education, justice, etc. Capacity must also be measured, including the existence and functioning of the institutions, resources, and expertise necessary for the population to pursue and realise their civil cultural, economic, political and social rights. So must official willingness and response, including ratification of international instruments, compliance and cooperation with international procedures, the existence and functioning of national laws, State policies, programmes and action. Levels of accessibility, to information, to participation, and to redress require measurement.

Disaggregate Further

As indicated above, rights-based approaches are also concerned with the principles of equality, equity and non-discrimination. Knowing who benefits from development, who does not, on what grounds, and why, is vital for this concept of development. This means, in the first instance, disaggregating data beyond the usual factors of gender and geography (although these remain crucial) to look also at disparities with regard to race, religion, language and other categories of human rights concern. Rights-based development must concern itself with the particular situation of women and children, but it must also focus on domestically unpopular (and therefore vulnerable or marginal) groups, including minorities, prisoners, migrants, and other, including nationally specific categories. Where "the numbers are good," efforts must be made to determine who is actually benefiting-the traditionally privileged or vulnerable and marginalised groups?

Read Indicators in Context

As is generally applicable to the question of indicators, the broader context in which they are employed is every bit as important as the data that they reflect. In matters of human rights, for example, simple numerical increases are not definitive. In fact, more data on shortcomings and violations can reflect more openness in a society, better monitoring mechanisms or stronger non-governmental organizations. Less may suggest that information is covered up, that complainants are intimidated, or an absence of capacity to monitor and collect data.

Design Indicators to Assist Development

Of course, a rights-based approach to development must also take account of the developmental elements of human rights. In other words, rights are not protected by good will alone. Simply abstaining from active violations of civil, cultural, economic, political or social rights is not adequate to meet a government's human rights obligations. States are also obliged to take necessary positive action to give effect to these rights. Realising all rights-civil, cultural, economic, political and social-therefore has resource and capacity implications.

Development is about supplementing those resources and enhancing those capacities. OHCHR's principal objective in strengthening the indicator framework is thus to assist national processes of development. A comprehensive rights-based indicator framework would, for example, be of significant value to informing participatory processes for benchmarking at the national level, where specific, time-bound targets are appropriately determined. It could, as well, serve as a useful reference point for (vital) international assistance in support of independent national data collection and documentation centres in developing countries. It would facilitate a more rational interface between national development processes, and international treaty reporting processes, making both processes more meaningful, more efficient, and less resource-demanding.

Moving Ahead: Filling the Indicator Gaps

With these principles in mind, OHCHR has sought to encourage its partners in development agencies, statistical institutes and academia to work toward filling the indicator gaps presented by efforts to implement rights-based development. Notably, the Office organized last year, in cooperation with UNDP, an expert workshop on the development of civil and political rights indicators.[28] The workshop was designed to provide a forum for building on existing civil and political rights indicators, and to encourage the development of new ones. The principal output of the workshop was a detailed list of rough indicators, or elements for measurement, based on relevant international norms, and the expert consultations. OHCHR has sought to disseminate this list as a starting point for the development and agreement of a comprehensive list of refined and scientifically rigorous development indicators for civil and political rights.

Advancing to the next stage of rights-based development will necessitate four basic accomplishments. The first is the compilation of an internationally agreed and scientifically adequate list of core development indicators for civil and political rights, based upon international standards. This will include three sub-categories:

1. the administration of justice, including crime prevention, policing, detention and imprisonment, fair trial, and adequate redress for violations or victimisation;
2. political participation, including the effective exercise of the freedoms of expression, association, assembly, and rights to participate in the conduct of public affairs, including to vote and stand for elections;
3. personal security, including the phenomena of torture, disappearances, summary and arbitrary executions, or the failure of the State to protect communities from crime and women from rape and from public and domestic violence.

The second is to develop similarly agreed and effective indicators for the measurement of cultural rights in development. This means, *inter alia*, looking at how, and the extent to which, each society secures the right of its people to take part in cultural life, and to enjoy the benefits of progress. It will require as well the development of indicators to gauge the extent to which indigenous, minority and migrant cultures are protected, and how they benefit, are excluded from, or are hurt by development programmes and policies.

Finally, much work remains to be done in effectively integrating attention to the "rights element" in existing lists of socio-economic indicators. This means measuring not just outcome, but also the availability and effect of mechanisms or redress and accountability. In the end, if rights-based development means anything at all, it means moving development out of the vague and nebulous realm of charity, and into the measurable area of accountability, and progress.

Notes

1. Article 1 (3) of the UN Charter links the two concepts as a common purpose of the Organization.
2. Where donors invoked human rights at all, it was often in the form of counter-productive sanctions and selective conditionalities.
3. This division showed itself as much in the work of the United Nations as elsewhere. To be sure, there were plenty of interagency meetings between the human rights programme and the development agencies, references to development in the work of human rights bodies, and even some references to human rights in the documents of the development agencies. But operationally, on the ground—where programmes addressed the realities of health, and housing and governance – the distinction was almost absolute.
4. One effect of the lack of significant cooperation and professional exchange between these two disciplines was a reinforced perception of a false dichotomy between two sets of rights (civil and political on the one hand, and economic social and cultural on the other). By this way of thinking, the former were subjects of critique and condemnation, and the latter the logical focus of development aid.
5. See International Council on Human Rights Policy, Local Perspectives: Foreign aid to the justice sector, ICHRP Geneva, 2000, at Annex III.

6. Among the relevant global conferences convened during this period were the World Summit for Children (1990); the UN Conference on Environment and Development (1992); the World Conference on Human Rights (1993); the International Conference on Population and Development (1994) and; the World Summit for Social Development (1995).

7. Vienna Declaration and Programme of Action, (adopted on 25 June 1993 by the World Conference on Human Rights) part I, paragraph 8, (hereinafter "VDPA").

8. Id. at part I, paragraph 5.

9. Id. at part I paragraph 10.

10. Id.

11. As contained in UNGA res. 48/141 of 20 December 1993.

12. Id. at para. 3[c] and 4[c].

13. While the High Commissioner may not be immune to policy concerns, she is shielded by the independence of the Secretariat in which she is situated, and is entirely independent in the partisan, or national sense.

14. See the Report of the Secretary-General entitled *Renewing the United Nations: A Programme for Reform* (UN Doc. A/51/950).

15. Human rights was designated as a "cross-cutting issue," which was to be integrated into the work of all of the Organization's development, humanitarian affairs, peacekeeping and other activities.

16. See United Nations, *Common Country Assessment (CCA) and United Nations Development Assistance Framework (UNDAF) Guidelines*, United Nations, April 1999, New York.

17. As a participant in, and contributor to the UNDG Working Group on Common Country Assessment Indicators, OHCHR has adopted the CCA definition of "indicator," identifying an indicator as a variable or measurement, conveying information that may be qualitative or quantitative, but which is consistently measurable. We include both positive and negative indicators. The goal is therefore a list of simple development indicators, designed to measure "what is," on a right-by-right basis. This would not include benchmarks, targets or goals, or answer definitively "what should be" or "by when," as these are appropriately developed in country specific, participatory national processes. Neither does our goal relate to the employment of grading systems, or to "score" country performance, or to index countries by level performance.

18. See United Nations, *Common Country Assessment (CCA) and United Nations Development Assistance Framework (UNDAF) Guidelines*, United Nations, April 1999, New York. An additional indicators category included in the framework is "international legal commitments for human rights" (i.e., ratification).

19. In our training and promotional activities, we refer to this as the "PANEL" analysis, taking the first letter of each of the five components of our rights-based approach: Participation, Accountability, Non-discrimination, Empowerment and Linkage to international instruments.

20. See United Nations, *Human Rights: A Compilation of International Instruments* (ST/HR/1, Vol. 1 Part 1, Part 2, and Vol. II), New York, 1993.

21. See United Nations, *Compilation of General Comments and General Recommendations Adopted by the Human Rights Treaty Bodies*, (HRI/GEN/1/Rev.4), UN Geneva, 7 February 2000.

22. These are available at *www.unhchr.ch*, in the *Treaty Bodies Database*.

23. As regards *cultural rights*, UNESCO published, in 1998, the first *World Culture Report* aimed at opening up a new field in analytical and quantitative thinking on the relationship between culture and development while providing scientific and creative inputs that could inform policy makers. The report noted a crippling lack of basic indicators of culture among UNESCO Member States.

24. See the Convention Relating to the Status of Refugees, Art. 1, (adopted on 28 July 1951, and entered into force 22 April 1954), contained in United Nations, *Human Rights: A Compilation of International Instruments* (ST/HR/1, Vol. I, Part 2, at page 634), New York, 1993.

25. See, e.g., article 5 of the Universal Declaration of Human Rights, article 7 of the International Covenant on Civil and Political Rights, and article 16 of the Convention against Torture and Other Cruel, Inhuman or Degrading Treatment or Punishment, all of which are contained in United Nations, *Human Rights: A Compilation of International Instruments* (ST/HR/1, Vol. I, Part 1), New York, 1993.

26. Article 21 of the UDHR and article 25 of the ICCPR, both of which are contained in United Nations, *Human Rights: A Compilation of International Instruments* (ST/HR/1, Vol. I, Part 1), New York, 1993.

27. See, e.g., article 2 (3) of the United Nations Declaration on the Right to Development (UNGA res. 41/128 of 4 December 1986), as contained in United Nations, *Human Rights: A Compilation of International Instruments* (ST/HR/1, Vol. I, Part 2), New York, 1993.

28. The Workshop was held at the Palais Wilson in Geneva from 27 to 29 September 1999. A detailed report is available from the Office of the High Commissioner for Human Rights. See UN OHCHR, *Report to the workshop on civil and political rights indicators*, Geneva, 27 to 29 September 1999.

19
Measuring Human Rights

Kate Raworth

Claims of unjust treatment and demands for policy reform are increasingly being couched in the language of human rights. In order to define human rights more precisely, various efforts are under way to create measurements, or human rights indicators. Creating these instruments for measuring human rights is not just a technical exercise: indicators have long played important roles in social policy evaluation and are central to turning human rights concepts into useful policy tools. To assess human rights effectively, however, indicators must hold the state accountable for its policies, help to guide and improve policy, and be sensitive to local contexts without sacrificing the commitment to the universality of rights. Can indicators be developed to do this? The answer will largely determine the success of human rights claims in moving beyond rhetoric and changing real social and political conditions.

Current proposals for indicators lack clarity both about what is to be assessed and how it will be measured. I propose that a far richer conceptual framework be set out that focuses on assessing state obligations, is sensitive to context-specific issues, and does not ignore the inherent tensions in the policy-making process. Whether or not such indicators can be put into practice will only become clear through case studies—which currently are sorely lacking.

Why Human Rights Indicators Are Needed

Indicators are variables that convey information—either quantitative or qualitative—and are consistently measurable.[1] Quantitative indicators are created by counting events or objects; for example, the percentage of school-aged children enrolled in school or the amount of government spending per pupil per

393

year. Qualitative indicators are created through assessments made by trained observers of characteristics (such as the standard of teaching in a school) that can be rated on a scale (such as "excellent/good/poor" or "from 1 to 10").

Indicators, particularly quantitative ones, have long played important roles in the analysis of development policy. It often takes a shocking statistic in the news to draw public attention to a neglected issue such as gender discrimination in the workplace or homelessness. Indicators can motivate policy change by revealing the ill effects of current practices; the introduction of school fees in a poor country, for instance, can be countered by data that show a rapid decline in the number of children attending primary school. They can also persuade the unconvinced where opinion alone cannot. For example, many claim that African Americans are treated unjustly by the legal system—a claim that is hard to dismiss when backed up by statistics from Amnesty International showing that murderers of white Americans are eight times more likely to receive the death penalty than murderers of African Americans.

One of the most widely cited indicators of development is the United Nations Development Programme's Human Development Index (HDI).[2] Calculated annually for 174 countries, currently ranked from Canada at the top to Sierra Leone at the bottom, the HDI combines four simple indicators—life expectancy at birth, the adult literacy rate, school enrollment rates, and the average annual income per person—to create a composite index that gives a basic measure of the state of human development in a country on a scale of 0 to 1. In Botswana in 1998, for example, life expectancy at birth was 46 years, 76 percent of adults were literate, 71 percent of school-aged children were enrolled in school, and average annual income per person was $6,103 (measured in international dollars for purchasing power parity). The combination of these four indicators gave Botswana a value of 0.593 on the Human Development Index and ranked the country 122nd out of 174. In contrast, Greece ranked 25th with and HDI value of 0.875 because life expectancy was 78 years, 95 percent of adults were literate, 81 percent of school-aged children were enrolled, and average annual income per person was $13,943.[3]

When the HDI is launched worldwide each year, it gains the attention of policymakers and development advocates alike because it provides the simplest and most widely recognized measure of the economic and social condition of people's lives around the world. Some countries have even disaggregated the index at the national level: instead of comparing country against country, they compare district against district. In Brazil the Human Development Index has been disaggregated for all 4,500 municipalities in the country's twenty-seven states, providing detailed data on education, health, and incomes throughout the country. The results caught the attention of local and national media, igniting debate when neighboring communities had disparate outcomes. The data also helped to shape policy. Nationally, the government used the data as the basis for improving targeted assistance for poverty alleviation throughout the country. At the state level, some local governments used the data as the basis for redistributing government spending toward the municipalities with the worst outcomes.[4]

These valuable uses of indicators for development analysis indicate the potential role they could play in assessing the realization of human rights. Tools of this kind are very much in demand because human rights principles are increasingly being advocated as a framework for public policy dialogue and assessments, especially under international human rights law. Since the 1948 Universal Declaration of Human Rights, the United Nations has been promoting human rights with at least nominal success. Between 1990 and 2000, the proportion of UN member countries that had ratified all of the six major treaties of international human rights law rose from 10 percent to just over 50 percent. This increase in the nominal commitment to international human rights law has led to greater focus on developing indicators that would help monitor the implementation of these commitments. Such instruments could show the status of a particular human rights situation, reveal whether a situation is getting better or worse owing to a policy change, and guide the formation of better policy. If we were to claim, for example, that the right to education in a certain country was not being realized, then we would need to provide evidence to substantiate that claim. Indicators would be essential to the task.

Indicators may be needed for assessing the extent to which human rights have been realized, but is it conceptually, politically, and practically possible to create them? It is not obvious that the rich normative concepts of human rights can be turned into policy evaluation tools that are adequately responsive to the complexities of policy-making situations. The question of whether or not adequate indicators can be created is, however, central to determining whether or not the language and commitments of human rights can ever become a workable framework for making policy assessments.

The Shortcomings of Qualitative Indicators

The attempt to use indicators to assess human rights is not new. Indices have been constructed since the 1950s, but over the past ten years the approach to their construction and the kinds of indicators desired have shifted significantly. Early human rights indicators consisted of qualitative ratings, scoring a particular country as 5 out of 10 for freedom of the press, for instance, or 7 out of 10 for freedom of association.[5] These ratings were made by human rights experts on the basis of all the information to which they had access, such as newspaper reports, on-the-ground sources, U.S. State Department reports, and the *Amnesty International Annual Report*. In the politicized realm of human rights assessments, however, this approach to creating qualitative indicators suffers from what can be termed the "who, why, so what?" problem.

First: *who is the rater?* The identity of the individuals giving the ratings is inevitably open to questioning, both of their subjectivity and of the incompleteness and partiality of the sources of information to which they had access.[6] As a result, even in cases in which the rating does give a somewhat accurate assessment of a country's situation, the judge's subjectivity could be used by the aggrieved government to divert attention from the judgment made and instead to attack the alleged political bias of the assessor. Second: *why the rating?* A score of, say, 7 out of 10 for freedom of the press in a particular country is opaque in that it reveals nothing of the set of criteria used for creating that score and nothing of the particular national circumstances that merited it. This prompts the final question: *so what?* If indicators are intended to be a policy tool, such ratings give no indication of how to improve the situation. Without revealing the underlying criteria and the reasons for the rating, the indicator is of little use for policy planning.

Statistically, there are also difficulties. Qualitative ratings are often presented in numerical form, but they do not possess the essential characteristics of statistical data: reliability (different people will come up with consistent results) and validity (being based on identifiable criteria that measure what they are intended to measure).[7] As a result, such ratings cannot validly be used for many of the operations that are in fact routinely performed on them, such as collating the ratings of more than one individual to create a composite result or using the ratings as variables in regression analysis. Sophisticated techniques are beginning to be applied more commonly to qualitative information to tackle these statistical limitations, but this manipulation is the exception rather than the norm and still will not make qualitative information as politically acceptable as quantitative.

Political sensitivity to the need to provide less subjective and opaque measures has shifted the focus of current efforts toward the creation of quantitative, statistical indicators because the data can be verified and, in the case of a good indicator, consistently measured across time. Of course this approach, too, has its limitations: quantitative data can measure only countable events and objects, yet there are many uncountable dimensions to human rights. This is an important caveat, a reminder that, as Einstein noted, "not everything that counts can be counted, and not everything that can be counted counts." With the increasing involvement of professional statisticians in gathering data on human rights, however, it is fortunately the case that much more can be measured quantitatively than was previously assumed.

The Conceptual Commitments of Human Rights

What are the main elements in human rights concepts that have particular implications for developing indicators? There are many competing and widely divergent conceptions of human rights, yet they share several core features. First, almost all of them endorse the idea that social rules should be evaluated in terms of the extent to which they enhance or diminish the personal freedom and dignity of participants within a social system. Human rights are realized within a social system when people within it enjoy certain freedoms and when there are social arrangements in place that are sufficient to protect them against standard threats to their enjoyment of those freedoms. Establishing what the scope of those freedoms should be calls for specifying the object of each right— specifying what the right is a right to—be it freedom of association, an adequate wage, primary education, or freedom from arbitrary arrest.

A second important feature shared by many conceptions of rights is that rights are correlated with duties in that they entail claims on individuals or institutions (collectivities of individuals) to secure these rights for people. Moreover, even in situations in which these rights cannot immediately be secured for all people—for example, owing to resource constraints—individuals or institutions are still duty bound to shape their conduct so as best to promote the realization of these rights. Human rights can thus be understood as claims on the behavior of individuals and on the design of social arrangements. In this way, rights discourse emphasizes the idea of accountability and responsibility for the negative consequences of social structures and requires identifying the primary duty bearers and articulating what duties they are held under.

Arising from these two features of human rights discourse are two concurrent but very different interests that we may have in assessing rights. We care about the condition of people's lives—whether or not they enjoy the objects of their rights—but we also care about whether persons who are held under duties are meeting them. The former interest can be seen as an enjoyment approach to assessment and the latter as an obligations approach. These two concurrent interests are compatible, but obviously different. It is quite conceivable in a particular social system that, for example, not all people have enough to eat due to natural resource constraints, yet all duty-bound persons have met their obligations to provide the maximum possible amount of food fairly to all. In this case, by the enjoyment approach to assessment the right to food has not been realized, yet by the obligations approach all duties have been met. Given this potential divergence between an assessment of the enjoyment of rights and an assessment of the obligations of rights, it will clearly be important to distinguish between the two approaches when developing indicators.

A third important feature shared by many conceptions of human rights is universality. Although we recognize that peoples of diverse cultures can, to some extent, aim to realize divergent ideals of justice in different social contexts, we also recognize that all individual persons have interests of sufficient importance to constrain the social order that can be imposed upon them regardless of its legitimacy within their culture. Though it may not be possible to agree precisely on what makes up the human good, we may still be able to agree that it will include certain vital elements—for example, basic political freedoms, nutrition, shelter, education, and social interaction—which just social orders should secure for all. This commitment to universality expresses itself through two desires, corresponding to the enjoyment and obligation approaches to rights. First is the desire to specify universally those freedoms in which all human beings have a vital interest, such as a primary education for all children or the freedom of association for all people. Second is the desire to specify universally those obligations of conduct that persons are held under, such as the duty not to prohibit any child from attending school, or the obligation of the education authorities to provide adequate buildings and teaching staff. Again, the distinction between these two ways in which universality is reflected in human rights will be important when developing indicators.

Current Attempts to Develop Human Rights Indicators

Current efforts are aimed at creating statistical indicators that could be used as policy tools to monitor the commitments made under international human right law. The particular conception of human rights under international law shares the central features of rights set out above, but with a narrower emphasis on the conduct of official institutions, that is, the state. Although the framework of international law is only one particular conception of human rights, and its focus on state conduct alone is considered by many to be problematic, the issues that arise in the attempt to develop indicators under this framework are also relevant to alternative conceptions of rights.

There are several important ongoing efforts, including projects within the office of the United Nations High Commissioner for Human Rights, the Organization for Economic Cooperation and Development (OECD), and several national think tanks such as the Danish Center for Human Rights.[8] The various tentative proposals emerging from these efforts, however, often lack clarity as to what specifically should be measured and how core characteristics of human rights should be reflected in the way indicators are constructed and used.

Among economic and social rights, the right to education is a common starting point for developing indicators. One broadly representative example of the approach being taken is a proposed set of indicators for the right to education arising out of a workshop held by the World University Service-International.[9] The workshop participants agreed that the desirable result was to propose "a set of common indicators, agreed upon by all treaty bodies and agreed upon by the specialized UN agencies, in order to have a common language currency in which to discuss the right to education." Articles 13 and 14 of the International Covenant on Economic, Social, and Cultural Rights were taken as the primary source from which to derive indicators. The workshop aimed to produce ten universally applicable indicators that were quantitative, simple (as opposed to composite, like the Human Development Index), comparable across countries and time, and reliable in that different people would expect to get the same results if they collected data. For practical reasons, indicators should also be affordable and draw upon good data already available.

The resulting proposal—intended as a provisional, not conclusive, list—included commonly cited indicators such as the adult literacy rate; the net school enrollment rate; the required level of teacher training, percentage of teachers who have reached it, and composition of teaching staff; the percentage of government expenditure spent on education and expenditure per pupil; and the cost of education for a family, including direct (fees) and indirect costs per pupil. Each of these proposed indicators is potentially interesting as part of a human rights assessment, but what the proposal does not explain is how these indicators are to be used in an assessment. As a result, it is unclear what conclusions or implications about the right to education could be drawn from the data. Yet if indicators are to be used as tools for guiding and evaluating policy, clarity about their use in assessment is critical. Three deeper conceptual issues need to be addressed.

First, what should human rights indicators for policy evaluation be measuring? There is a lack of conceptual clarity as to what indicators should be assessing—is it the extent to which people have the objects of their rights, or the extent to which the conduct of officials meets the obligations they are held under? Both are valuable interests, and indicators could be created for each, but for the purpose of creating tools for guiding and evaluating policy, the obligations approach provides the more relevant focus.

Second, in what way should the principle of the universality of human rights be reflected in indicators? The claim that human rights are universal does indeed require that this principle be reflected in their measurement, but how? Current approaches to developing indicators are embedding the principle at the wrong conceptual level by assuming that indicators should be universally applicable across countries. Universality should, in fact, be reflected in the principles underlying the obligations of state conduct. Instead of being universally applicable, indicators should be context-specific so they can reflect the ways that those universal principles of conduct are manifested in culturally, economically, and politically different contexts.

Third, what further work is needed to move forward? Given the importance of the universal obligations of conduct, there is a lack of clarity about how they should be weighed against each other. Particularly lacking is an appreciation of the repeated conflicts of interest occurring between resource needs, social groups, and competing freedoms that characterize the dilemmas of the public policy decision-making process. This is where additional conceptual work needs to be done.

What Indicators Should Be Measuring

Attempts to develop indicators are understandably pulled in two directions because of the two concurrent but very different interests that people commonly have with respect to human rights. As discussed above, we care about the condition of people's lives and their enjoyment of freedoms, but we also care about establishing whether official agents, either individually or collectively, are doing enough to meet their obligations in securing those freedoms.

Both of these approaches to developing indicators are compatible with the interests of international human rights law, which aims to promote the realization of rights and also to monitor the conduct of governments in that process. Current proposals to develop indicators, however, are neither implicitly nor explicitly clear about which assessment approach they are using. Most proposals appear to be focused on creating indicators for assessing the enjoyment of rights; few are specifically designed to assess obligations.

Which approach is in fact appropriate for which goals? If the aim were simply to know the condition of people's lives in each country, then the enjoyment approach would be ideal. The data from each country could be compared directly to the ideal outcome—for example, comparing a primary-school enrollment rate of 72 percent to the 100 percent ideal that would mean all children had secured their right to a primary education. Such an assessment would in many cases use indicators in a similar way to assessments of human development (such as the Human Development Index), looking at average life expectancy at birth, adult literacy rates, maternal mortality rates, and school enrollment rates. The outcomes of such assessments would inevitably be closely related to the country's physical and human capital resources and its historic economic and political situation; hence wealthy countries would tend to be assessed as doing well and poor countries as doing badly. A politically feasible approach to developing indicators, however, must allow for the possibility that a government in a historically poor and underdeveloped country could introduce a set of legislative, budgetary, and institutional policies and that its conduct would be assessed as a fulfillment of all its obligations under human rights law—whatever the prevailing level of development of the country; whatever the prevailing condition of people's lives.

Assessing human rights for the purpose of guiding and evaluating policy must, therefore, be something other than simply assessing people's enjoyment of the objects of their rights. The assessment needs to reveal the conduct of the government, give an indication of what action is required (avoiding the *why* and *so what* questions discussed above), and be responsive to changes in that conduct. The obligations approach is therefore the more appropriate: while focusing on the extent to which states meet their obligations of conduct, it allows for the very different contexts within which they face these challenges.

Much emphasis inevitably falls on developing a sufficiently rich conception of what those obligations are. Within international human rights law, the most basic elements of the framework of principles underpinning state obligations have been broadly set out. First are the obligations of action for the state to respect, protect, and fulfill rights.[10] Respecting rights requires the state to refrain from interfering directly with people's pursuit of their rights, whether the interference is through committing torture or arbitrary arrest, enacting illegal forced housing evictions, or imposing food blockades. Protecting rights requires the state to prevent violations by third parties, whether by ensuring that private employers comply with basic labor standards, preventing monopolistic ownership of the media, preventing parents from withholding their children from school, or regulating and forcing abatement of harmful pollution from private industry. Fulfilling rights requires the state to take action—be it legislative, budgetary, judicial, or other—to provide the best possible set of policies that pursue the realization of the right.

In addition to these obligations of action are four commonly recognized obligations of process that must be met in official conduct: *nondiscrimination, adequate progress, participation,* and *effective remedy*. The principle of nondiscrimination obliges the state to act toward all individuals with respect to their rights without distinction of any kind such as ethnicity, gender, language, religion, or political opinion. The principle of adequate progress obliges states to take steps toward meeting their obligations within a reasonably short time after entering legal commitments and with steps that are deliberate, concrete, and targeted as clearly as possible. The principle of participation obliges states to encourage popular participation in all spheres of development and in achieving the realization of rights. Finally, the principle of effective remedy obliges states to ensure that all persons within its jurisdiction are provided an effective remedy for conduct that violates their rights. These obligations of action and obligations of process together form the foundation under international law of a framework of principles for assessing state conduct.[11]

What are the implications of these principles for the kinds of indicators that are required? In fact, an obligations approach would use many of the same data as an enjoyment approach; the difference lies in how they would be used. Instead of comparing a country's performance against a specified human rights goal (say 72 percent school enrollment against the goal of 100 percent), the data would be used to assess the adequacy of the state's conduct with respect to its various obligations to ensure the realization of the right.

A simple example illustrates this distinction. Imagine a country in which 87 percent of children are enrolled in secondary school. What does this statistic reveal about the right of a child to education? Certainly, from the perspective of the enjoyment approach, it reveals that the right is not being realized because not all children are attending secondary school. But from the perspective of the obligations approach, what implications can be drawn regarding the conduct and accountability of policymakers and state officials? From this information alone, none. We might assess the state's conduct very differently on the basis of this enrollment rate depending on whether the statistic came from, say, a low-income country in sub-Saharan Africa or from a wealthy industrial country in Europe. To better substantiate this requires more detailed data that reveal the reasons for this enrollment rate, and, by implication, whether or not policymakers and officials are accountable for the shortfall.

If additional data show that only 77 percent of girls are enrolled compared to 97 percent of boys, then much of the problem is likely due to discrimination. Surveys of parental attitudes could further reveal whether or not it is parents who are discounting the importance of girls' education (hence the state would be failing to protect the right of girls from this prejudice), and surveys of school facilities could reveal whether the discrepancy was due to something as simple as a lack of toilet facilities for girls, placing the accountability with the school authorities for failing to provide the facilities needed to fulfill girls' right of access to an education without discrimination.

Perhaps there is no discrimination but rather, schools lack resources and hence the ability to attract and retain students. Then the question is whether the government is giving enough priority to fulfilling the right to education. Analysis of the budgetary allocations to education as against alternative spending priorities would reveal whether it was a lack of priority or a lack of overall resources that resulted in low spending on education. Likewise, the direction of change over time would reveal whether the obligation to make adequate progress was being met. A fallback in enrollments from 95 percent to 87 percent over the previous five years would be assessed very differently from an increase in enrollments from 55 percent to 87 percent over the same period.

This example shows that instead of using the data simply to assess the level achieved—here 87 percent—against the enjoyment approach goal of 100 percent, the focus should be on using more detailed data to reveal whether enrollments are 87 percent because some obligations have not been met or because, despite all obligations having been met, a shortage of resources and capacity make it currently impossible for this right to be realized.

Is this distinction between the two approaches really important? Yes. It makes a tremendous political difference, particularly to developing countries. When a new government comes in to a historically underdeveloped situation and implements an impressive set of policies to improve the human rights outlook, an obligations approach can recognize that achievement. It means that even a government in a country with a secondary-school enrollment rate of 50 percent could possibly be given a positive assessment of its conduct with respect to the right to education. Likewise, a wealthy country with more than 95 percent enrollment could possibly be given a negative assessment if it were shown that the state was clearly failing in its obligations toward the final 5 percent of children. Since the language of human rights is being advocated as a framework for policy dialogue particularly in developing countries, the acceptance of this framework within those countries will be critical in deciding whether or not the framework is politically feasible.

The importance of making assessments that are sensitive to context, as discussed above, prompts a second conceptual exploration of the approach being taken to indicators: a re-evaluation of the assumption that indicators should be universally applicable.

Acknowledging Local Contexts without Sacrificing Universal Principles

It is widely assumed at the international level that human rights indicators will be internationally agreed upon and universally applicable across countries. At the International Association for Official Statistics Annual Conference on Human Rights and Statistics in September 2000, for example, Thomas Hammarberg appealed to the international community's "capacity to agree on relevant human rights indicators" as the necessary will needed to move forward.[12] The intuitive appeal of creating such universally applicable indicators is both conceptually and politically understandable.

Conceptually, it is assumed that the universality of human rights entails the universal applicability of indicators for policy evaluation. This assumption is too quick, however, as will be discussed below.

Politically, there would be several advantages to having universally applicable indicators. First, universally applicable indicators would be a high-profile reinforcement of the claim that those human rights set out in international law are indeed universal, whatever the cultural context—helping to counter claims that cultural relativity prevents universal legal obligations from being imposed on all countries. Second, the reporting system of international human rights treaties requires countries to submit reports documenting the status of rights and the progress they have made in realizing them, and quantitative data play an important role in specifying what information is required. The quality and extent of information given in state party reports is currently highly variable, and as a part of strengthening and standardizing the reporting system, universally applicable indicators would be a desirable way of increasing the quality of information presented in every report.

In addition, setting fixed data categories could pressure recalcitrant governments to provide data that they would not otherwise collect or make available. The more that providing a particular piece of data were seen as an international norm, the more political pressure there would be to conform—and such pressure is extremely useful in ensuring greater provision of and access to information for citizens about the conduct of their own government. Finally, universal indicators would enable cross-country comparisons, which are useful for evaluating the effects of different policy stances in otherwise similar countries.

Given this intuitive appeal of creating universal indicators, the reasons for the bias toward creating indicators for assessing the enjoyment approach to rights—instead of the obligations approach—become more evident. In practical terms, it is easier to specify universally desirable goals—objects of rights—for the human condition that are relevant across country contexts, such as a long life expectancy or compulsory primary education for all children, than it is to specify universally the obligations of official conduct and institutional arrangements that would lead to these outcomes. Furthermore, the enjoyment of many objects of rights can be assigned specific desirable outcomes, such as 100 percent for primary-school enrollments, or zero cases of torture, and for many it is clear that either a higher or lower score is better or worse—such as higher school enrollments and fewer incidences of torture both being better outcomes in all contexts. Statistics showing the extent to which people are enjoying the objects of their rights are simple to grasp (although this focus may be the reason why many cynics dismiss economic and social rights as "aspirations"): it enables international comparisons of the condition of people's lives in different countries and creates easy-to-communicate advocacy messages.

Despite the appeal of creating universally applicable indicators, however, such assumptions are misguided. The claim that human rights are universal does indeed entail that the principle of universality should be reflected in their measurement but, for the purposes of evaluating policy, it should be reflected not in the specific indicators chosen but in the principles underlying state obligations—the universal obligations to respect, protect, and fulfill rights, and to do so with nondiscrimination, adequate progress, participation, and effective remedy.

If these principles form the foundation of the obligations of state conduct then indicators to measure the extent to which they are being met cannot be universal, because it is possible to specify universally neither which indicators should be used nor what the value of any particular indicator should be.

First, realizing rights requires different policy mixes in each country, hence different conduct by states to meet their obligations. The transformation of policy measures such as government spending, institutional arrangements, and legislation into desired human conditions such as low infant mortality rates and high school enrollment rates is not deterministic. Not only does the economic, social, and political environment differ from one country to the next, requiring a different policy mix in each case, but even in a given context in which all these environmental variables are known, there is no universal policy equation that can be applied with the certainty of producing the optimal outcome.

More specifically, the conduct required by the state to meet its obligations will differ across contexts—for example, the state obligation to protect the right to health will demand conduct from the state that is contingent on the kinds of threats presented by third parties. In one country the threat may be from a private industry polluting the water sources of communities surrounding its factories. In another country the threat may be from a systemic social culture of domestic violence toward women. In yet another the threat may be from social norms and interactions that cause a particularly rapid spread of HIV/ AIDS. Different indicators would be needed in each case to identify the source of the threat to health and to assess the adequacy of the state's conduct to protect individuals from that threat.

Second, prespecified indicators may be inappropriate to reflect particular national circumstances, resulting in errors of omission, such as the failure to identify a violation of an obligation where a violation has actually occurred, and errors of commission, such as the false identification of certain conduct to be a violation of an obligation. For example, assessing the obligation to respect the right of freedom of speech might include an assessment of whether or not the state has interfered with people's choice to speak in opposition to the state: one indicator proposed might be the number of political demonstrations held by groups other than the ruling political party. A low number of such demonstrations could, however, be either because free speech is respected but general political satisfaction causes few protest rallies, or because a politically repressive regime makes such protest politically impossible. It is easy to imagine the number of additional indicators that would be required as supplements to this one to ensure that such an error of omission was not being committed—but such detailed data requirements would make such prespecification conceptually impossible.

Third, even for those indicators that are relevant across contexts and for which it appears to hold that more is better, such as government spending on secondary education as a percentage of national income, the assumption does not hold across countries or within countries over time. In a global context in which the average annual national income per person in a country ranges from $500 in the poorest countries to $30,000 in the richest (measured in international dollars for purchasing power parity), the range of possible policy measures is obviously tremendously different across countries. Different social arrangements and levels of national income require different proportions of government spending on education: in relatively wealthy countries where much education is provided through the private sector and can adequately be paid for directly by households, government spending may be appropriately lower than in other countries that are less able to rely on the private provision of secondary education. Despite spending proportionately less public money on secondary education, the former countries could feasibly have a higher secondary-school enrollment rate than the latter. An illustration of this type is given by the Third International Mathematics and Science Study, which conducted standardized tests on secondary-school students in many OECD and other high-income countries. In 1993, although state spending per pupil on secondary education in South Korea was less than one third of that in Germany, Denmark, and the United States, the performance of students from South Korea was ranked second overall, compared to students in the other three countries who ranked twenty-third, twenty-seventh, and twenty-eighth respectively.[13] Of course there are many reasons why students in one country do well and in another badly, but the example illustrates the lack of even the most basic certainty of the transformation of financial policy into educational achievements across countries.

Fourth, there are significant practical limitations to data collection. If a complete set of indicators was prespecified to cover all possible contexts, the data requirements would be logistically and financially impossible to fulfill. Much data would be irrelevant in a particular country, and although every additional piece of data would bring additional information—and more information is seen to be a good thing—this perspective must be placed in the context of the situations in a significant number of countries in which even the most basic data such as school enrollments are missing or unreliable and data collection is a competing area of resource allocation. For practical as well as conceptual reasons, the data collected should be those that are the most relevant to the context and best highlight the success or failure of the state to meet its obligations.

Of course it probably would be the case that across many or even all country situations, some particular indicators were, in every case, relevant to the assessment of official conduct—they were in fact universally applicable. But this conclusion would be reached a posteriori, as a result of examining the relevance of measures in different contexts, not because those indicators were assumed *a priori* to be relevant measures across contexts. Though the result of having a universally applicable indicator would be the same under each approach, the rationale would be significantly different.

Given that most ongoing attempts to develop indicators are based on the assumption that the indicators selected should *a priori* be universally applicable, the alternative approach of deriving context-specific indicators has received relatively little attention. This may also be because most attempts to develop indicators are taking place within international discussions of human rights law. Attempts undertaken within national contexts would not be so wedded to universal applicability and so would be more likely to explore alternative options. One example is a case study of the right to health in Ecuador in the 1990s by the Center for Economic and Social Rights.[14] The CESR assessed this right by setting out the principles of state obligation with respect to the right to health and then presenting indicators that would contribute toward a relevant assessment of each obligation within Ecuador's current economic, political, and social context. Although the lack of data available limited the scope of the case study, the CESR's research clearly demonstrated the rich potential of the obligations approach to human rights assessments.

With respect to the obligation of the state to protect rights, the CESR asked whether people suffered systematic, harmful effects to their health from actions by private actors and whether the state was taking adequate measures to protect them. The physical and sexual abuse of women by partners and family members is one of several private sources of threats to health identified: data showed in 1998 that 88 percent of women in Guayaquil, the largest city, said they had suffered some form of intrafamilial violence. Was the state doing enough to protect women from this threat? Previously, between 1989 and 1992, of 1,920 complaints relating to sex crimes against women and girls in Guayaquil, only 2 percent had resulted in convictions—implying that the state did not adequately protect victims through the judicial system. Later in the 1990s the introduction of the Law against Violence against Women and the Family brought additional legal protection. New data are now needed to show whether the law actually is resulting in better protection for women from this particular threat and whether this protection has had any effect on the number of cases of abuse occurring.

With respect to nondiscrimination, the CESR asked whether the state conducted its policy with equity. Data show that despite high inequality and extreme deprivation of rural, poor, and indigenous populations, the state disproportionately allocated scarce resources to urban and better-off social groups. In 1997, 84 percent of urban dwellers had access to health services, compared with only 10 percent of rural dwellers; 80 percent of health personnel were in urban areas, and the state spent six times as much on social security for urban dwellers as for rural ones. These data call for a prompt reallocation of the health budget and institutional capacity toward providing services to rural populations: more extensive data would reveal whether a similar policy shift was required for low-income and indigenous populations.

As a final example, with respect to making adequate progress, the CESR asked whether the state could be judged to be moving fast enough toward realizing the right to health. Taking just one example, in 1970 the state set targets to provide adequate sanitation facilities for 70 percent of the urban and 50 percent of the rural population. Yet more than a decade later, the situation was moving in reverse of those targets. Between 1982 and 1990 the share of households with access to sanitation facilities fell from 46 percent to 38 percent in urban areas, and from 15 percent to 10 percent in rural ones. Even by its own targets, the state was not making adequate progress.

The Ecuadorian example demonstrates the potential of this approach to creating indicators, but its complexity cannot be ignored. More than this partial picture must be provided. Data disaggregated by gender, ethnicity, income level, and region are needed to enable analyses of discrimination. Data relevant to the duration of a specific government are needed to provide an analysis of the effects of its policies. When interpreting these data, analysts face the inevitable complications of defining which failures are the fault of the government and which are due to external conditions. The example from Ecuador illustrates this well. By 1998 only 3 percent of the national budget was allocated to health, in contrast to 30 percent for debt servicing. The influence of the international environment, and international institutions, on this outcome must be considered as part of assessing whether the government of Ecuador could have done more to meet its obligations. These and other complications raise the final question of what needs to be done to make the obligations approach to indicators a feasible tool in practice.

Moving Forward with Indicators: Challenges Ahead

If it is accepted that, for the purposes of evaluating policy, indicators should be focused on the obligations approach to assessing state conduct, and if it is also accepted that the universality of human rights should be reflected in the principles underlying those obligations of conduct, then the focus of future work should not be on continuing to propose lists of indicators but rather on addressing the remaining conceptual and practical complications.

What conceptual complications need to be tackled to make an operational policy tool? Certainly a better elaboration of the principles of conduct is needed, one that does not implicitly assume that all state obligations for all rights can be met and maintained simultaneously. This assumption implicitly underlies the present structure of principles, yet it has not been proved theoretically and has certainly not been demonstrated empirically by any country. The potential conflict between obligations is often waived in dialogue or is dogmatically rejected because, it is claimed, a policy solution must be found that enables all obligations with respect to all rights to be met simultaneously, since countries have ratified the covenants of international law and thus are accountable for meeting the obligations within them.

This deep and unjustified assumption that such a policy stance is always possible flies in the face of reality. There are of course genuine conflicts of interest—indeed, the overriding characteristic of the policy-making process is one of weighing conflicting interests among potential resource allocations, social groups, and competing freedoms. It is interesting to note that this world of tradeoffs is the familiar domain of economists, and so it should not be surprising that they often have little patience with the language of international human rights law, which largely fails to address the existence of such conflicts.

As an example, an elaboration is needed of the priorities to be allocated among the obligations to respect, protect, and fulfill a right, as such conflicts do arise. Is it ever permissible for a state to fail to respect a right of some people in order to promote or fulfill a right of others, or indeed another right of those same people? Curtailing freedoms from unreasonable search and seizure may contribute to significant decreases in rates of violent crime, thereby better fulfilling the rights to integrity of the person.[15] Carlos Bosambrio has noted that "a growing number of people in Latin America believe that civil and political rights can, if necessary, be sacrificed to guarantee one's right to live in peace and in a secure environment."[16] How should human rights advocates evaluate such cases?

Likewise, the obligations of process need further elaboration. For example, what criteria turn differences in the way two people are treated or affected by official institutions into an instance of discrimination? What rate of progress toward realizing rights is adequate and who is the legitimate judge of that? What extent and type of participation on the part of those affected by policy is required in the formulation of that policy?

Furthermore, current approaches to creating indicators focus on making assessments of one right at a time in isolation from other rights, creating "silo rights" assessments with no explicit or even implicit mechanism for interaction or tradeoffs between them. Yet in reality there are always competing claims to be weighed between rights, such as conflicting claims on resource use or conflicts of interest between and impacts on different social groups.

A policymaker weighing a decision on one right would inevitably be taking into consideration the consequences of this policy stance on the state's ability to meet its obligations on other rights. Such a tension lies at the heart of state choices regarding policy impacts on human rights, yet the current framework of obligations is structured in such a way that it does not reflect this dilemma. The complexity of policy-making situations needs to be reflected in the ways that indicators are used, and this will require substantial work on elaborating those principles that guide choices between competing interests.

If, in addition, the influence of external factors is taken into account, specifying the scope of obligations becomes increasingly difficult. When the health spending per person is sharply reduced because of an externally triggered financial crisis in a country, what is the obligation of the government to act, and to what extent can it be held accountable? I have so far largely avoided discussing the complexities introduced by the influences of the external environment, but they would inevitably enter into a full specification of state obligations.

Although it is clear that further conceptual elaboration of the principles of obligations is needed for all the reasons given above, it is not clear how that elaboration should be accomplished. Should, for example, the prioritization of obligations be universally applicable, such as "in any conflict between obligations to respect and to protect, the obligation to respect should prevail," or should it be specific to each right, to the particular context, or to other moral criteria?

Should the interaction of these principles of obligation be decided *a priori* or should it be contingent upon the particular instance of conflict? And should the decision be made externally to any particular conflict of interest by human rights legal experts through jurisprudence or internally to the particular conflict by, say, the popular choice of those people affected by the decision? For any of these options, could an additional category of indicators be developed to help show whether or not the obligations were being prioritized according to the principles? For example, if popular choice were believed to be the correct way to decide the weighting between particular conflicting obligations, could the results of a referendum or a popular survey be used as one element in the assessment of whether the state is meeting its obligations?

These are evidently complex issues, and perhaps they make the creation of human rights indicators even more daunting. But unless the principles underlying the obligations of conduct are better elaborated, any attempt to use indicators as monitoring and policy tools will clearly be inadequate because they will fail to capture the complex reality of conflicts that decision-makers constantly face. Making assessments of obligations is inevitably complicated—there are rarely simple answers—but perhaps it is appropriate that this is so evident within the obligations approach: the complexity of making assessments reflects the fact that human rights often involve the most basic dilemmas of human society.

What practical complications need to be addressed? Given the contextual specificity of assessing obligations and the detailed data required to do it, the assessments clearly need to be rooted in national contexts. With the rise of national human rights commissions and other nongovernmental organizations focused on promoting human rights over the past fifteen years, such national rootedness is increasingly possible—and a far cry from the externally conducted qualitative ratings of the 1950s. Of course, in some countries national assessments still are not possible because of strictures on freedom of expression, either in policy or in practice, or because of the lack of national expertise, and so the need for international or overseas organizations to undertake assessments will still be there.

This point of arrival may be disappointing in its inconclusiveness and frustrating in its complexity: the desire to revert to assessing human rights by universally applicable indicators of the enjoyment of rights would be understandable—but it would be a mistake. Instead, progress must be made simultaneously on several fronts. Philosophers and human rights lawyers need to elaborate further the interrelations of the principles of obligation. Statisticians should collect more detailed and disaggregated data that can be used to assess various obligations. National human rights commissions and other NGOs then can use these improved tools to undertake more case-study assessments, along the lines of the study undertaken in Ecuador. The results will be the judge of whether the concepts of human rights can be turned into a framework for assessing policy, and whether indicators can be developed to accomplish the task.

Notes

1. United Nations Office of the High Commissioner for Human Rights, *The Dignity Measure: Selected Human Rights Indicators* (Geneva: United Nations, 1999).
2. United Nations Development Programme, *Human Development Report 2000* (London: Oxford University Press, 2000), p. 157.
3. Ibid., pp. 157–59.
4. Ibid., p. 96.
5. Kenneth A. Bollen, "Political Rights and Political Liberties in Nations: An Evaluation of Human Rights Measures, 1950 to 1984," *Human Rights Quarterly 8* (Special Issue 1986), p. 577.
6. Ibid., p. 583.
7. UNDP, *Human Development Report 2000*, p. 90.
8. The Danish Centre for Human Rights, *Human Rights Indicators 2000: Country Data and Methodology* (Copenhagen: The Danish Centre for Human Rights, 2000).
9. World University Service-International, "Report of the Workshop on Indicators to Monitor the Progressive Realisation of the Right to Education" (workshop organized by World University Service-International, Geneva, May 1999).
10. This framework of respect, protect, and fulfill was first set out by Ashbjorn Eide in the context of the right to food, but has become the common basis of state obligations as applied to all rights. Asbjorn Eide, "The Human Right to Adequate Food and Freedom from Hunger," in *The Right to Food: In Theory and Practice* (Rome: Food and Agricultural Organisation, 1998).
11. See UNDP, *Human Development Report 2000*, chap. 5, pp. 89–111.
12. Thomas Hammarberg, "Searching for the Truth: The Need to Monitor Human Rights with Relevant and Reliable Means" (paper presented at the Statistics, Development, and Human Rights Conference of the International Association for Official Statistics, Montreux, Switzerland, September 4–8, 2000).
13. "Who's Top?" *The Economist*, March 29, 1997.
14. Center for Economic and Social Rights, *From Needs to Rights: Realizing the Right to Health in Ecuador* (Quito: Genesis Ediciones, 1999).
15. This example is drawn from Christian Barry, "The Challenges of Conceiving and Measuring Human Rights" (paper presented at UNDP Global Forum, Rio De Janeiro, Brazil, October 10–11, 2000); available at www.undp.org/hdro/rioforum/rioagenda.html.
16. Carlos Bosambrio, "Crime: A Latin American Challenge for Human Rights," *Human Rights Dialogue* (Winter 2000); available at www.carnegiecouncil.org/hrdwinter2000.html.

20

Tuberculosis Control and Directly Observed Therapy from the Public Health/Human Rights Perspective

Anna-Karin Hurtig, John D. H. Porter, and Jessica A. Ogden

The enjoyment of the highest attainable standard of health is one of the fundamental rights of every human being.
— Preamble to the WHO Constitution UN, 1948

The 1980s and 1990s have seen a resurgence of interest in tuberculosis. Increasing cases world-wide led to the World Health Organization (WHO) declaring a global emergency in April 1993.[1,2] Despite the availability of tools for controlling TB, programmes have been unable to sustain high cure rates.[3] As a consequence of this, and the increasing problems of drug resistance, the international community, through the WHO, has developed and launched the directly observed therapy short course (DOTS) strategy.[4,5] This strategy is described as: government commitment to a national TB programme; case detection through 'passive' case finding (sputum smear microscopy for pulmonary tuberculosis suspects presenting at a health facility); short course chemotherapy for all smear-positive pulmonary TB cases [under direct observation for, at least, the initial phase of treatment [DOT]; regular, uninterrupted supply of all essential TB drugs; and a monitoring system for programme supervision and evaluation.[4–6]

The DOTS strategy has achieved excellent results in New York, other parts of the US,[7–10] and in China.[11] However, from other parts of the world voices have been raised asking if DOTS is the most effective way to control tuberculosis,[12,13] if DOTS can and should be perceived as a panacea,[14] and if the DOTS strategy is ethical.[15,16]

The control of infectious diseases like tuberculosis lies within the broad framework of public health. A currently accepted definition of public health is 'providing the conditions in which people can be healthy.'[17] Although public health contains within it many perspectives and disciplines, it is the biomedical perspective, the realm of medicine based on knowledge and practice from the natural sciences, which currently dominates thinking and approaches to health care and control of disease. Increasingly, it is being appreciated that biomedicine can benefit from working with other disciplines and perspectives. This interdisciplinarity encourages change and flexibility in approaches to health care and disease control.

A perspective which can complement and improve current approaches to the control of tuberculosis has been developed in recent years at the Harvard School of Public Health.[18,19] This approach looks at control of disease through the human rights framework, using the Universal Declaration of Human Rights as a basis for analysing public health programmes.[19] This framework enables a broader, more socially contextualised perspective on public health programmes (Figure 20.1). In this chapter the current international strategy for tuberculosis control will be analysed using this health and human rights framework.

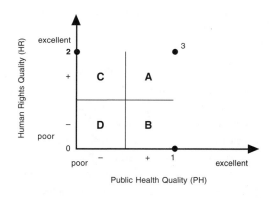

Sector explanation:
A: best case
B: need to improve HR quality
C: need to improve PH quality
D: worst case, need to improve both PH and HR quality

Points explanation:
0: poor quality
1: ideal Ph quality
2: ideal HR quality
3: ideal PH and HR quality

Figure 20.1 A framework for negotiation: human rights and public health. (Reproduced with kind permission from AIDS, Health and Human Rights, the International Federation of Red Cross and Red Crescent Societies, and Francois-Xavier Bagnoud Center for Health & Human Rights, Harvard School of Public Health, Boston, 1995.)

Background

Infectious Disease Control

Current public health control strategies are predominantly framed by the biomedical model and its associated methodologies.[20] Of particular influence is public health's core discipline, epidemiology, which, in investigating infectious diseases, looks primarily at interactions between 'agent', 'host' and 'environment'. Interventions are designed to treat patients, ensure the protection of the population and prevent the occurrence of epidemics. The main strategies for control are to attack the source (e.g., treatment of cases/carriers and the isolation of cases); to interrupt transmission (e.g., environmental and personal hygiene, vector control); and to protect the susceptible population (e.g., immunisation, chemoprophylaxis).[21]

Tuberculosis Control

Current TB control strategies include the following components: case finding and treatment, chemoprophylaxis, vaccination with BCG and the improvement of socio-economic conditions.[22] The biomedical focus for TB control concentrates on reducing the transmission of pulmonary tuberculosis by targeting the most contagious persons (sputum-positive cases), by finding cases of sputum-positive TB and treating them until they become sputum-negative and are eventually cured.

Compliance

Compliance is an important part of TB control and can be defined as the extent to which a person's health-related behaviour coincides with medical advice.[23] It can be a problem for many infectious disease control programmes. The direct observation of treatment (DOT) contained within the DOTS strategy is designed to enhance patient compliance. The strategy requires that the patient take his or her medications in the presence of a health care worker or other 'responsible' third party. In the biomedical/public health terms described above, DOT is part of the strategy for 'attacking the source' of infection and rendering the person non-infectious by treating him/her with the appropriate drugs for an appropriate period of time. DOT is fast becoming the standard approach for control of many infectious diseases, including sexually transmitted diseases, leprosy and tuberculosis.[16] Nevertheless, recent observers have noted that the intervention may be ethically problematic.[16] Embedded within it is the imbalance of power and capacity between the public health profession and the infected person. An uncritical application of DOT may also create problems by placing the onus for cure on the patient, while masking the responsibility of the health care professionals and health care structures to 'provide the conditions in which people can be healthy'.[16] Others have acknowledged the shared obligations of the patient in the need to comply with biomedical treatment, and of society in the need to provide the patient with the necessary treatment facilities.[24,25]

Sumartojo has recently called for the development of an approach to improving compliance which engages with the responsibility of health care structures to provide an appropriate service and which '. . . recognise(s) the needs and dignity of patients'.[26] Similarly, Farmer has noted that '[t]hroughout the world, those least likely to comply are those least able to comply . . . these settings are crying out for measures to improve the quality of care, not the quality of patients'.[27]

Potential Problems with the DOTS Strategy

The increasing use of DOT in infectious disease programmes and the development of the DOTS strategy for TB control have coincided with a reappraisal (in some quarters) of the principles underlying public health interventions.[16,28,29] Also under renewed consideration is the need to understand the interaction and balance between the health needs of the individual and the health needs of the society. The kinds of questions being asked are: Is public health too paternalistic? Is there an imbalance of power and capacity between the public health profession and the infected person? If so, are these imbalances being reinforced by public health control measures? Are there alternative ways of approaching public health interventions that would redress, rather than reinforce, these kinds of imbalances and inequalities?[15,20,24]

Human Rights and Public Health: A Framework for Negotiation

Human Rights

In 1948 the Universal Declaration of Human Rights was accepted and adopted by the participating members of the United Nations.[30,31] Today these principles continue to be relevant, and are being applied to considerations of health. It has recently been suggested, for example, that the extent to which human rights are realised may represent a better and more comprehensive index of well-being than traditional health status indicators.[18] From a public health perspective, while the availability of medical and other health care constitutes one of the essential conditions for health, the availability of these technologies and services does not in itself create 'health'. Indeed only a small fraction of health status variations between populations can be attributed to health care: clearly, then, adequate health care[32] is a necessary, though not sufficient, constituent of health.

The Health and Human Rights Analysis

Public health and human rights can be considered as two complementary, though often conflicting, ways of looking at human well-being. Even when they address similar, or even identical problems their language and underlying assumptions differ. Public health, for example, is built on the principle of seeking the greatest good for the greatest number of people: health is important and public health is considered a valid reason for limiting individual rights under some circumstances. The principles on which the human rights discourse is based, on the other hand, are concerned with promoting the well-being of individuals by ensuring respect for their rights and dignity. Interweaving these perspectives, then, it becomes clear that public health aims and interventions must be the least intrusive and least restrictive measures available to accomplish the public health goal.[19] Any ensuing compromise of an individual's rights must apply equally to all those affected.

In order to explore, negotiate and debate the potential tensions between human rights and public health policies, programmes and practices an approach named here the human rights/public health framework has been developed.[33] The framework can be used to analyse public health programmes in order to provide 'new' ways of intervening which embrace both of these two complementary, but again sometimes conflicting, ways of looking at health issues.

The framework involves: 1) assessing the extent to which the proposed policy or programme represents 'good public health'; 2) discerning whether the proposed policy or programme is respectful and protective of human rights; 3) finding how the best possible combination of public health and human rights quality can be achieved; and finally 4) asking if the proposed policy or programme still appears to be the optimal approach to the public health problem (Figure 20.1).[33] To ensure that the full range of potential burdens on human rights is identified, each of the rights listed in the Universal Declaration of Human Rights (UDHR) should be considered.[33]

Tuberculosis Control from a Human Rights Perspective

To What Extent Does the Proposed Policy or Programme Represent 'Good Public Health'?

As already stated, public health strategies for the control of infections concentrate on disease rather than 'well-being'. From a biomedical perspective, TB control strategies are 'rational' approaches developed from good science. As only people with sputum-positive pulmonary tuberculosis are regarded as being infectious to others, and because control needs to prevent transmission to the wider public, public health interventions are targeted at cases of *infectious* TB only (primarily sputum-positive pulmonary tuberculosis). Forms of TB that are considered non-infectious, such as extra-pulmonary TB or TB in children, are not, therefore, seen to be public health issues. While 'rational' from a positivist, biomedical point of view, the human rights approach would question this perspective. What message does this give to the parents of children with tuberculosis? What message does it give to people with extra-pulmonary disease?

There is an inherent contradiction in the public health approach to the control of infectious diseases like tuberculosis. While the interest of a programme is ultimately the good of the population, the strategy focuses on the individual patient, who is treated without reference to the social conditions that frame his or her life. Take, for example, a TB programme that simply focuses on the act of directly observing patients take their medication, without taking into account the economic and social factors that are associated with the disease. A patient in this situation may be forced to discontinue treatment because a) she cannot travel to the clinic every other day for DOT, either because she lacks resources herself or because her household has refused to support her; b) she may not be able to tell her family that she has TB (and therefore cannot ask for support) because a TB diagnosis may precipitate divorce or obviate her marriage chances; c) she is feeling too unwell to travel the sometimes long distances over difficult roads; and/or d) she simply cannot afford to take the time out of daily life (work, responsibilities for child care, etc.). Such a programme is unlikely to achieve the hoped for results. Barnhoorn and Adriaanse note that before the obstacles to a particular treatment regimen can be cleared away, patients have to understand the system, and the system must be consistent with the underlying health beliefs and social norms of the community.[34] The programme will also need to take account of the practical realities of everyday life which play a role in the ability of people to adhere to any treatment regimen.

Is the Proposed Policy or Programme Respectful and Protective of Human Rights?

In reviewing the UDHR from the perspective of current TB control activities, several broad concepts will be considered: stigma, treatment, adherence to medication, limitations of freedom, education and living conditions. Seeing TB control from a different perspective and addressing these issues with greater sensitivity will lead to better care of TB patients.

Stigma

In many cultures the social stigma of tuberculosis contributes to the abandonment of treatment and lengthy delays in seeking professional care.[35] Article 12 of the UDHR states: "No one shall be subjected to arbitrary interference with his privacy, family, home nor to attacks upon his honour and reputation . . ." DOT affects the TB patient's private life and must therefore be conducted with sensitivity. If treatment takes place at home, the privacy of the patient and his or her family is being jeopardised, whereas if treatment occurs in a public place known for the treatment of TB, there may be stigma or discrimination.[36] A recent study in the West Cape Region of South Africa showed that 6 months of continuous daily attendance at a site of supervision of administering the drugs was considered 'unreasonably long'. Many patients spoke about more pressing issues that they needed to attend to in their daily lives. Participants illustrated how the duration of treatment impacted on their duties to care for children and to provide an income for their families. These feelings appeared to contribute to a temptation to cease treatment once symptoms had abated.[37]

Many TB patients hide knowledge of their illness from employers, friends and family members. Some interpret supervised treatment as the system's distrust of them.[37] These feelings were compounded by the blasé manner in which health professionals informed them of their diagnosis. A lack of empathy exhibited by members of the health team appeared to have an impact on the patient's subsequent relationship with the clinical staff.[38]

Article 16 of the UDHR states: "Men and women of full age, without any limitation due to race, nationality or religion, have the right to marry and to found a family . . ." In Pakistan, divorce and broken engagements occurring as a consequence of tuberculosis are seen more often in female than male patients.[39] In India a diagnosis of TB can be a hindrance to marriage.[40] Parents of girls of marriageable age may be reluctant to send their daughters to the clinic.[34] The belief that pregnancy enhances the risk for relapse also decreases their marriage prospects, and pregnancy is also seen to be a reason for stopping TB treatment.[39]

The voices of two women from Sialkot, Pakistan tell how this right to marry and found a family can be violated by being diagnosed with TB: "*When I go home, people will talk about me. People will say 'She was a TB patient and you should not accept her for your son to marry.' Even if we get well the effect will be the same.*"

We are two sisters and marriage arrangements have been made with men from one family. If my (future) family-in-law knows that I have TB they will be sure to break the engagement. I am not worried for me, but I'm worried for my sister. Her engagement also could break off because of my sickness.[39]

UDHR article 23 states: "Everyone has the right to work, . . . to just and favourable conditions of work and to protection against unemployment . . ." and article 25 continues; "Everyone has the right to . . . medical care and necessary social services, and the right to security in the event of unemployment, sickness, disability. . . ." For people with tuberculosis, it is common to avoid informing employers about the diagnosis, due to fear of the 'consequences' in the workplace and the risk of losing their jobs.[41] In Pakistan TB patients mentioned that they face difficulties in obtaining sick leave, and even in government service they are at risk of losing their jobs. Those who depend on seasonal work for income are particularly affected at certain times of the year like planting and harvesting time.[39] The need to support the family, fear of having to ask for support from employers to buy medicines due to stigmatisation and possible loss of job were factors mentioned by patients in Vietnam.[41]

Treatment

UDHR article 25 states: ". . . motherhood and childhood are entitled to special care and assistance." Two patient categories are excluded from the current international TB control strategy: children and extra-pulmonary TB cases. Between 10% and 20% of new tuberculosis cases occur in children, and approximately 450 000 deaths per year are in children less than 15 years of age.[42] Most children acquire their infection from a smear-positive adult case, but they themselves develop smear-negative disease and are therefore considered to be a relatively unimportant source of infection.[24] In the case of extra-pulmonary TB, it is estimated that there are 1.22 cases of smear-negative and extra-pulmonary tuberculosis for every case of smear-positive tuberculosis in developing countries,[43] and the case fatality rate for untreated smear-negative tuberculosis is between 40 and 50%.[43]

UDHR articles 18 and 19 state: "Everyone has the right to freedom of thought, conscience and religion . . . Everyone has the right to freedom of opinion and expression; this right includes freedom to hold opinions without interference . . ." TB patients need to be treated with dignity and respect. Effective care and a productive health worker-patient relationship require an understanding that different communities may have different perceptions of the disease and its treatment.[34,44] In some societies, for example, attitudes to suffering are profoundly affected by religious beliefs.[45] In addition it is important to recognise that in most societies a range of health care options are now available to people. It cannot be assumed any more that patients will visit the local government health clinic in the first instance. Many patients may choose to visit private practitioners, NGOs (non governmental organisations), or practitioners of alternative kinds of treatment. In countries with a thriving private health care sector, the success of tuberculosis control strategies will depend on the effective involvement of this sector.[12,40,46,47]

Adherence

UDHR article 21 states that "Everyone has the right to equal access to public service in his country . . ." and article 25 adds "Everyone has the right to . . . medical care and necessary social services . . ."

The act of giving DOT is seen as an essential part of control activities within the tuberculosis control structure currently advocated by the WHO. As noted above, however, this process has the effect of placing the primary responsibility for adherence onto the patient, and obscures the role of policy and health care practice. As Chaulet has noted, "adherence is nothing more or less than the outcome of a process involving a long chain of responsibilities, extending from the decision-makers at the Health Ministry to the treating physician."[48]

Others, too, have recognised the need for a 'creative array' of services that go well beyond the observation of drug ingestion.[36,49] The accessibility (social, economic and physical) of a tuberculosis programme is essential for the success of the treatment it offers.[50] In many countries only parts of the population have access to some kind of TB treatment, and even fewer to DOTS. Estimates suggest that fewer than half of patients with tuberculosis in developing countries are in contact with treatment services.[2,51]

Empirical observations of TB patients in Kumasi, Ghana, suggest that non-adherence is largely due to lack of funds for transport to the clinic, non-availability of drugs at the TB clinic, and the refusal of staff in peripheral health posts to inject TB patients with streptomycin supplied at the central TB clinic.[52] In the developing world, self-medication is encouraged through a combination of low quality, unaffordable health services coupled with a lack of effective regulation of the sale of drugs, and aggressive marketing by the pharmaceutical industry.[53] Many patients can only afford to buy a small amount of medication at a time. This inevitably results in the interruption of treatment and often means that patients consume an inadequate or inappropriate combination of drugs.[41] Strengthening of the public sector as well as improving communication with the private sector are therefore crucial elements for improving adherence.

Limitations of Freedom

UDHR article 29 states: "In the exercise of his right and freedom, everyone shall be subjected only to such limitations as are determined by law solely for the purpose of securing due recognition and respect for the rights and freedom of others. . . ."

Within liberal democracies, it is generally accepted that the state may intervene when the exercise of one person's freedom may result in harm to another.[54] This is known as the 'harm principle'. The nineteenth century philosopher John Stuart Mill defined this principle in the following way: "The only purpose for which power can be rightfully exercised over any member of a civilised community, against his will, is to prevent harm to others. His own good, either physical or moral, is not a sufficient warrant." This principle provides the ethical foundation for establishing public health programmes designed to require those with communicable diseases like tuberculosis to behave in ways that are likely to reduce the risk of transmission.

In some industrialised countries, an important question for TB control activities is: When may DOT be imposed by the state? In the United States, universal DOT has been challenged as an unethical intrusion upon autonomy and as a violation of the constitutional requirements that the least restrictive intervention be used.[15]

Education

UDHR article 26 states: "Everyone has the right to education. . . . " Some studies have shown that public health education contributes to the success of tuberculosis control programmes, especially when peers and family members were also exposed to education.[55] The relation between educational background and knowledge of the symptoms and significance to health of tuberculosis, however, varies from region to region, and greater education and knowledge of tuberculosis does not necessarily lead patients to present earlier to the appropriate medical services.[45] Despite the fact that unemployed coloured women in Ravensmead, Cape Town, exhibited a good knowledge of tuberculosis, for example, this knowledge did not necessarily result in biomedically appropriate/ predictable health behaviour. In the event of developing symptoms or disease, individuals either did not seek medical care or failed to complete treatment.[38]

The Indian literature supports these findings. In India it appears that the general public have fairly good 'knowledge' regarding the cause, symptoms and spread of tuberculosis,[40,56–59] although understanding of its diagnosis and treatment does not appear to be present to the same extent.[12,41,56–60] Uplekar and Rangan indicate, however, that even where knowledge regarding the consequences of irregular treatment is good, it does not affect treatment adherence.[40] Narayan and Srikantaramu report that there is no difference in awareness levels between regular and irregular patients.[61] A recent review of this literature notes that education and information regarding tuberculosis must go hand in hand with the provision of a service that 'makes sense' in terms of the realities and priorities of the everyday lives of patients and their families.[50]

Living Conditions

UDHR article 25 states: "Everyone has the right to a standard of living adequate for the health and well-being of himself and his family . . ." Tuberculosis is a disease that is closely associated with poverty.[20] Control of TB can not, and should not, be separated from the development of measures to reduce inequity and poverty.

How Can We Achieve the Best Possible Combination of Public Health and Human Rights Quality?

As already stated, TB control programme structures have been developed from the biomedical perspective. Either as an affect or effect of this, there continues to be a dearth of useful qualitative information on the social and behavioural aspects of TB and other infectious diseases. Available information indicates that there are problematic disjunctions between TB patients and providers, and between the population and the policy makers. The non-medical factors that determine health such as behaviour, the environment, human biology and socio-economic status, remain the most important factors affecting people's health. After the dramatic successes of the sanitary revolution, however, less attention has been paid to these critical, if non-medical, health determinants.[62]

This analysis of TB control from the health and human rights perspectives has highlighted the importance of a wider concept of health and of the need to understand tuberculosis within the context of people's everyday lives. A 'healthy' interaction between patients and providers, another critical element, can only be achieved when health care structures are themselves functioning efficiently and effectively.[44] The best possible approach to TB control will include a consideration of these issues, and will incorporate a complementarity of public health and human rights principles.

Does the Proposed Policy or Programme Still Appear To Be the Optimal Approach To the Public Health Problem?

The positive aspects of the current international TB control strategy are that it has been well constructed from scientific studies and is a rational approach to TB control. It is important to remember that 'DOTS' is more than DOT alone. DOTS as a whole emphasises providing an efficient programme which is able to maintain and sustain high quality laboratory diagnostics, regular drug supplies and a well-trained cadre of health workers who are responsive to patient needs.

The negative aspects of the programme stem largely from its narrowly biomedical orientation. It falls short of embracing the social, economic and cultural dimensions of tuberculosis. Taken in isolation from the rest of the structure, a singular focus on the direct observation component of DOTS has the effect of placing the focus on patient behaviour, highlighting patient 'failures', while effectively masking the failures of the system to enable patients to comply. Managers and others developing TB policy and organising TB control structures need to be more aware of the process of developing appropriate and 'healthy' programmes.

Discussion

The human rights/public health framework encourages a different perspective on the standard biomedical approach to disease control in order to develop improved ways of dealing with diseases like tuberculosis. A concentration on the individual, without an understanding of the wider socio-economic and cultural issues that frame their lives, is likely to create ineffective interventions— interventions which fail to 'provide the conditions in which people can be healthy'. TB patients can only be expected to comply with treatment if they are able to do so. Therefore, in any given setting, the key dimensions of social, economic and physical access to TB services need to be assessed and accounted for in programme design. Shifting the burden of ensuring programme effectiveness from the patient to the programmers will have the added benefit of enabling patients to obtain appropriate treatment whilst retaining their dignity and social and self-respect.

This change in perspective will require more qualitative research and the development of broader outcome indicators than are currently used in TB control programmes. It will entail a shift in focus from DOT alone to DOTS as a process/management structure. Control programmes need to ensure that there is a quality laboratory service and a regular sustained drug supply, but in addition, they need to develop a managerial system that respects the needs of TB patients and takes the importance of the health care worker/patient relationship into account. This can not be achieved with internationally fixed strategies, but rather in locally developed programmes recognising the specific needs and resources of the community.

This analysis also indicates that it is time to view TB control within a wider concept of health. Diseases such as tuberculosis are a reflection of underlying societal conditions of inequity and poverty. They are indicators of wider social, environmental and global conditions, and they need to be seen within the broad context of globalisation and intersectoral collaboration. A health and human rights framework enables us to view public health programmes from a perspective that takes these factors into account. If this perspective leads to changes in practice commensurate with improved human rights, then the framework will have achieved its goal.

Notes

1. World Health Organisation. *TB. A global emergency. WHO Report on the TB Epidemic.* WHO/TB/94.177. Geneva: WHO, 1994.
2. Raviglione. M.C., Dye, C., Schmidt, S., and Kochi, A. Assessment of worldwide tuberculosis control. *Lancet* 1997; 350: 624–629.
3. Porter, J.D.H. and McAdam, K.P.W.J. The re-emergence of tuberculosis. *Ann Rev Public Health* 1994; 15: 303–323.
4. World Health Organization, *WHO Tuberculosis Programme. Framework for effective tuberculosis control.* WHO/TB/94.179, Geneva: WHO, 1994.
5. World Health Organization. *WHO Report on the Tuberculosis Epidemic, 1995. DOTS Stops TB at the Source.* WHO/TB/95.183. Geneva: WHO, 1995.
6. Harries, A.D. and Maher, D. *TB/HIV. A clinical manual.* WHO/TB/96.200. Geneva: WHO, 1996.
7. Morse, D.I. Directly observed therapy for tuberculosis: spend now or pay later. *BMJ* 1996; 312: 719–720.
8. Chaulk, P., Moore-Rice, K., Rizzo, R., and Chaisson, R.E. Eleven years of community-based directly observed therapy for tuberculosis. *JAMA* 1995; 274: 945–951.
9. Frieden, T.R., Fujiwara, P.I., Washko, R.M., and Hamburg, M.A. Tuberculosis in New York City: Turning the tide. *N Engl J Med* 1995; 333: 229–233.
10. McKenna, M.T., McCray, E., Jones, J.L., Onorato, I.M., and Castro, K.G. The fall after the rise: tuberculosis in the United States, 1991 through 1994. *Am J Public Health* 1998; 88: 1059–1063.

11. Zhao, Feng-Zeng, Murray, C., Spinaci, S., Styblo, K., and Broekmans. J. Results of directly observed short-course chemotherapy in 112 842 Chinese patients with smear positive tuberculosis. *Lancet* 1996; 347: 358–362.
12. Juvekar. S.K, Morankar, S.N., Dalal, D.B., et al. Social and operational determinants of patient behaviour in lung tuberculosis. *Indian J Tuberc* 1995; 42: 87–94.
13. Gangadharam, P.R.J. Chemorherapy of tuberculosis under program conditions. [editorial]. *Tubercle Lung Dis* 1994; 75: 241–244.
14. Makubalo, L.E. [editorial]. Epidemiol Comments 1996; 23: 1.
15. Bayer, R. and Dupuis, L. Tuberculosis, public health, and civil liberties. *Ann Rev Public Health* 1995; 16: 307–326.
16. Porter, J.D.H. and Ogden, J .A. Ethics of directly observed therapy for the control of infectious diseases. *Bull Inst Pasteur* 1997; 95: 117–127.
17. Institute of Medicine. *Future of Public Health.* Washington, D.C.: National Academy Press, 1988: pp 1–7.
18. Mann, J.M. Human rights and the new public health. *Health Hum Rights* 1994; 1: 229–233.
19. Mann, J.M., Gostin, L., Gruskin, S., Brennan, T., Lazzarini, Z., and Fineberg, H.V. Health and human rights. *Health Hum Rights* 1994; 1: 7–23.
20. Porter, J.D.H. and Ogden, J.A. Social inequalities in the re-emergence of infectious disease. In: Strickland, S.S., Shetty, P.S., eds. *Human biology and social inequality.* Cambridge, UK: Cambridge University Press, 1998: pp 96–113.
21. Vaughan, J.P. and Morrow, R.H. *Manual of epidemiology for district health management.* Geneva: WHO, 1989.
22. Rodrigues, L.C. and Smith, P.G. Tuberculosis in developing countries and methods for its control. *Trans Roy Soc Trop Med Hyg* 1990; 84: 739–744.
23. Snider, D.E. General view of problems with compliance in programmes for the treatment of tuberculosis. *Bull Int Union Tuberc* 1982; 57(3–4): 55–260.
24. Bayer, R., Neveloff Dubler, N., and Landesman, S. The dual epidemic of tuberculosis and AIDS: ethical and policy issues in screening and treatment. *Am J Public Health* 1993; 83: 649–654.
25. *The tuberculosis revival: individual rights and societal obligations in a time of AIDS.* New York, NY: Publications Program, United Hospital Fund of New York, 1992: 1–75.
26. Sumartojo, E. When tuberculosis treatment fails. A social behavioral account of patient adherence. *Am Rev Respir Dis* 1993; 147: 1311–1320.
27. Farmer, P. Social scientists and the new tuberculosis. *Soc Sci Med* 1997; 44: 347–358.
28. Lupton, D. Risk as moral danger: the social and political functions of risk discourse in public health. *Int J Health Services* 1993; 23: 425–435.
29. Cole, P. The moral bases for public health interventions. *Epidemiology* 1995; 6: 78–83.
30. Bilder, R.B. An overview of International Human Rights Law. In: H. Annum, ed. *Guide to International Human Rights Practice.* Philadelphia, PA: University of Pennsylvania Press, 1994.
31. *Universal Declaration of Human Rights.* Adopted and proclaimed by UN General Assembly Resolution 217 A(III), Dec 10, 1948.
32. McGinnis, J.M. and Foege, W.H. Actual causes of death in the United States. *JAMA.* 1996; 270: 2207–2212.
33. International Federation of Red Cross and Red Crescent Societies and Francois-Xavier Bagnoud Center for Health and Human Rights. *The public health-human rights dialogue in AIDS, health and human rights. An explanatory manual,* Boston, MA: Harvard School of Public Health, 1995.
34. Barnhoorn, F. and Adriaanse, H. In search of factors responsible for non-compliance among tuberculosis patients in Wardha district, India. *Soc Sci Med* 1992; 34: 291–306.
35. Rubel, A.J. and Garro, L.C. Social and cultural factors in the successful control of tuberculosis. *Public Health Rep* 1992; 107: 626–636.
36. Gostin, L.O. Controlling the resurgent tuberculosis epidemic. A 50-state survey of TB statutes and proposals for reform. *JAMA* 1993; 269: 255–261.
37. Dick, J., Schoeman, J.H., Mohammed, A., and Lornbard, C. Tuberculosis in the community: 1. Evaluation of a volunteer health worker programme to enhance adherence to anti-tuberculosis treatment. *Tubercle Lung Dis* 1996; 77: 274–279.

38. Dick, J. and Schoeman, J.H. Tuberculosis in the community: 2. The perceptions of members of a tuberculosis health team towards a voluntary health worker programme. *Tubercle Lung Dis* 1996; 77: 380–388.

39. Liefooghe, R., Michiels, N., Habib, S., Moran, M.B., and De Muynck. A. Perception and social consequences of tuberculosis: a focus group study of tuberculosis patients in Sialkot, Pakistan. *Soc Sci Med* 1995; 41: 1685–1692.

40. Uplekar, M. and Rangan, S. *Tackling TB: the search for solutions.* Bombay: Foundation for Research in Community Health (FRCH), 1996.

41. Johansson, E., Diwan, V.K, Huong, N.D, and Ahlberg, B.M. Staff and patient attitudes to tuberculosis and compliance with treatment: an exploratory study in a district in Vietnam. *Tubercle Lung Dis* 1996; 77: 178–183.

42. Raviglione, M.C., Snider, D.E., and Kochi,A. Global epidemiology of tuberculosis. *JAMA* 1995; 273: 220–226.

43. Murray, C.J.L., Styblo, K., and Rouillon. A. *Tuberculosis. In: Jamison D T, Mosley W H, eds. Disease control priorities in developing countries.* New York: Oxford University Press/World Bank, 1993.

44. Wingerd, J. Communication and credibility: Little Haiti and the public health clinic. 94th Annual Meeting, American Anthropological Association, San Francisco, November 20–24, 1996.

45. Grange, J.M. and Festenstein, F. The human dimension of tuberculosis control. *Tubercle Lung Dis* 1993; 74: 219–222.

46. Brugha, R. and Zwi, A. Improving the quality of private sector delivery of public health services: challenges and strategies. *Health Policy and Planning* 1998; 13: 107–120.

47. Bennett, S., McPake, B., and Mills, A, eds. *Private health providers in developing countries: serving the public interest?* London: Zed Press, 1997.

48. Chaulet, P. Compliance with chemotherapy for tuberculosis: responsibilities of the Health Ministry and of physicians. *Bull Int Union Tuberc* 1990–1991; 66 (Suppl): 33–35.

49. Bloch, A.B, Sumartojo, E., and Castro, K.G. Directly observed therapy for tuberculosis in New York City [letter]. *JAMA* 1994; 272: 435–436.

50. Rangan, S., Uplekar, M., Brugha, R. et al. *Tuberculosis control: a state of the art review.* Delhi, India: UK Department for International Development (DFID), 1997.

51. Anon. The global challenge of tuberculosis. [editorial] *Lancet* 1994; 344: 277–279.

52. Twumasi, P.A. Non compliance with tuberculosis treatment: the Kumasi experience. *Tropical Doctor* 1996; 26: 43–44.

53. Homedes, N. and Ugalde, A. Patients' compliance with medical treatments in the third world: what do we know? *Health Policy Planning* 1993; 8: 291–314.

54. Shindell, S. Legal and ethical aspects of public health. In: J.M. Last, ed. *Maxcy Roseany Public Health and Preventive Medicine.* 11th ed. New York: Appleton-Century-Crofts 1980: pp 1834–1845.

55. Uplekar, M. and Rangan, S. Alternative approaches to improve treatment adherence in tuberculosis control programme. *Indian J Tuberc* 1995; 42: 67–74.

56. Purohit, S.D., Gupta, M.L., Arun Madan, Gupta, P.R., Mathur, B.B., and Sharma, T.N. Awareness about tuberculosis among general population: a pilot study. *Indian J Tuberc* 1988; 35: 183.

57. Geetakrishnan, K., Pappu, K.P., and Roychowdhury, K. A study on knowledge and attitude towards tuberculosis in a rural area of West Bengal. *Indian J Tuberc* 1988; 35: 83.

58. Goyal, S.S., Mathur, G.P., and Pamra, S.P. Tuberculosis trends in an urban community. *Indian J Tuberc* 1978; 25: 77.

59. Ramachandran Rajeswari, Diwakara, A.M, Ganapathy Sudha, Sudarsanam, N.M., Rajaram, K., and Prabhakar, R. Tuberculosis awareness among educated public in two cities in Tamil Nadu. *Lung India* 1995; 13: 108.

60. Nair Dinesh, M., George, A., and Chacko, K.T. Tuberculosis in Bombay: new insights from poor urban patients. *Health Policy and Planning* 1997; 12: 77–85.

61. Narayan Radha, and Srikantaramu, N. Significance of some social factors in the treatment behaviour of tuberculosis patients. *NTI Newsletter* 1987; 23: 76.

62. Lee, P. and Paxman, D. Re-inventing public health, *Ann Rev Public Health* 1997; 18: 1–35.

21

Maternal Mortality as a Human Rights Issue

Measuring Compliance with International Treaty Obligations

Alicia Ely Yamin and Deborah P. Maine

In too many places around the globe, not much has changed since Martin Luther wrote, in the sixteenth century, "And even if women bear themselves weary or they bear themselves out that does not hurt. Let them bear themselves out. This is the purpose for which they exist."[1] Women in developing countries are bleeding to death after giving birth, writhing in the convulsions of eclampsia, and collapsing from days of futile contractions, knowing that they have suffocated their babies to death.[2] The World Health Organization (WHO) and the United Nations Children's Fund (UNICEF) estimate that close to 600,000 women and girls die each year from complications of pregnancy or childbirth, despite the fact that technology that has been available for decades could have been used to avoid these deaths.[3]

Maternal mortality is the leading cause of premature death and disability among women of reproductive age in developing countries.[4] Furthermore, the burden of maternal mortality is not evenly distributed. Ninety-nine percent of pregnancy-related deaths occur in developing countries[5]—and of course, only women are at risk of this fate. Moreover, according to the World Bank, although men and women between the ages of fifteen and forty-four lose approximately the same number of years of healthy life due to disease, there is no single cause of death and disability for men that comes close to the magnitude of maternal death and disability.[6]

The discourse of human rights enables us to place an issue such as maternal mortality on the agenda of public concern and keep it there. Moreover, it provides another crucial reason to be concerned about maternal mortality—beyond even the tragic deaths themselves, women's instrumental role in raising children, and the loss of women's productivity. A rights framework emphasizes that women affected by maternal mortality possess an inherent dignity that makes their preventable deaths a disgraceful social injustice.

As valuable as the rights perspective is, however, it is not sufficient. Without a sound understanding of the epidemiology of maternal mortality (and therefore, the interventions that can prevent it), the concept of a human right to be free from avoidable death during pregnancy and childbirth will remain meaningless. Without a clear understanding of the causal chain leading to maternal mortality (and how to break it), programs intended to reduce maternal deaths are likely to be ineffective.

Indeed, one of the principal problems in implementing economic and social rights (as opposed to civil and political rights, which generally have their basis in national judicial systems and, which often can be measured by counting violations) is that the interpretation and enforcement of economic and social rights requires expertise external to the international legal community.[7] In 1993, the United Nations Centre for Human Rights convened a group of experts to discuss the use of indicators to monitor economic and social rights (the Seminar on Appropriate Indicators), which concluded, in the words of the rapporteur, that although indicators are definitely needed, "the development of [such] indicators requires the conceptualization of the scope of each of the enumerated rights and the related obligations of States Parties. Thus, it is not yet possible to . . . assess progressive realization of these rights."[8]

Rather than beginning with the abstract concept of the right to health and looking for indicators that might infuse substantive meaning into the progressive realization of that right, this chapter begins with the very tangible problem of maternal mortality. From that standpoint, it argues that certain recently developed indicators can be assessed according to human rights criteria and selectively adopted as monitoring tools by national and international institutions in order to evaluate compliance (or noncompliance) with treaty obligations.[9]

Specifically, staff at UNICEF and the Center for Population and Family Health (CPFH) at the Columbia University School of Public Health developed a set of indicators for use in monitoring the availability and use of medical services by women with life-threatening obstetric complications.[10] These indicators, and the guidelines for their use (UN Guidelines), were formally issued in 1997 by WHO, UNICEF, and the United Nations Population Fund (UNPFA).[11] The indicators, more thoroughly described below, go a long way toward providing the human rights community with performance standards regarding a key aspect of women's right to health.

This chapter has two objectives. First, it will give an overview from a public health standpoint of the scope and determinants of maternal morbidity and mortality, together with the issues involved in their detection, treatment, and measurement. Second, it will explain how the UN Guidelines for monitoring national programs can be used as human rights tools to monitor a state's compliance with respect to aspects of the right to health under various international treaties.

This chapter describes the scope of maternal mortality and the public health approaches to addressing it, and then discusses the reasoning behind and implications of using the UN Guidelines. It then describes the legal context for creating a state obligation to reduce maternal mortality as part of guaranteeing the right to health, which is in turn part of states' economic and social rights obligations under specific international treaties. Next, it proposes three ways to use the UN Guidelines in setting enforceable standards with respect to states' obligations to take steps to reduce maternal mortality on a nondiscriminatory basis. The first of these involves the adoption of objectively measurable and verifiable indicators to judge whether states are taking such steps. The second determines whether states are taking the appropriate (i.e., effective) steps. Finally, the third examines whether such steps are being taken on a nondiscriminatory basis.[12]

Understanding and Measuring Maternal Mortality as a Public Health Issue

While maternity-related factors cause a greater proportion of women's deaths and disabilities than any other single cause of death among either men or women,[13] the interventions that could be used to treat pregnancy-related complications and reduce maternal mortality are well-known and readily available. The first step in addressing maternal mortality is a recognition that whatever the benefits of prenatal care for other reasons, the majority of obstetric complications that lead to maternal mortality simply cannot be predicted or prevented through this care. Moreover, unlike the case with many, if not most, other public health problems, history shows that the key to reducing maternal mortality lies not in general social and economic development, but in making effective treatment available and accessible.

Also in contrast to many other health problems, maternal mortality rates and ratios do not provide an effective way of tracking a country's progress with respect to reducing the incidence of maternal deaths over time. Indeed, rates are likely to be the most incomplete and inaccurate in countries where maternal mortality poses the greatest health problem. Therefore, given what is known about the handful of interventions most effective in reducing maternal mortality, the UN Guidelines adopted in 1997 set forth the most straightforward, objectively verifiable indicators available to monitor governments' implementation of those interventions.

Importance of Maternal Mortality and the State of the Field

Of the commonly used health indicators, maternal mortality reveals the greatest disparity between developed and developing countries. As Table 21.1 shows, the maternal mortality ratio (MMR) in North America is eleven deaths per 100,000 live births, while in Africa it is 870—nearly eighty times higher. [14] Moreover, the infant mortality rates in the United States and Nigeria are seven and eighty-four deaths per 1,000 live births, respectively—a twelve-fold difference. [15]

The MMRs cited above express the risk of dying during a single pregnancy. But most women have more than one pregnancy, especially in societies where a woman's value as a person largely depends on the number of children she has. Thus, most women run the risk of maternal death many times. The "lifetime risk" is a statistic that takes into account both the average risk per pregnancy and the average number of pregnancies per woman in a society. [16] This figure gives a more accurate picture of the impact of maternal mortality on women's lives. As Table 21.1 shows, the lifetime risk of maternal death in North America is one woman in 3700–compared to one in sixteen in Africa. [17]

The great variation in the frequency of maternal deaths between more developed and developing countries is in no way attributable to exotic complications of pregnancy and childbirth in developing countries. Indeed, Table 21.2 shows a remarkable similarity between the leading causes of maternal death in the world as a whole and in the United States in particular. Because 99 percent of the maternal deaths in the world occur in developing countries, these WHO estimates are basically a reflection of the causes of maternal deaths in those countries. [18] The proportions of maternal deaths due to hemorrhage, sepsis, and hypertensive disorders (such as eclampsia) [19] are similar in developing countries and the United States: hemorrhage accounts for 25 percent and 29 percent

Table 21.1 Estimated Maternal Mortality Ratios (MMR) and Lifetime Risks for Different Geographic Regions, 1990

Regions	MMR	Lifetime Risk
World Total	430	1 in 60
More Developed	27	1 in 1800
Developing	480	1 in 48
Africa	870	1 in 16
Asia	390	1 in 65
Latin America & Caribbean	190	1 in 130
North America	11	1 in 3700

Source: WHO & UNICEF, 1996

Table 21.2 Obstetric Deaths, By Cause: Global Estimates (1993) and United States (1987–90)

Cause of death	World 1993 Estimates Percentage	United States 1987–90 Percentage
Hemorrhage	25	29
Sepsis	15	13
Hypertensive disorders	12	18
Unsafe abortion	13	*
Obstructed labor	8	*
Embolism	*	20
Cardiomyopathy	*	6
Anesthesia	*	2
Other direct	8	*
Indirect causes	20	*
Unspecified	*	13
Total	100	100
Deaths per 100,000 live births	430	9

* = less than 1 percent
Source: WHO, 1994; Berg et al. 1996, WHO and UNICEF, 1996.

of maternal deaths, respectively; sepsis for 15 percent and 13 percent; and hypertensive disorders for 12 percent and 18 percent.[20] These similarities show that the life-threatening complications faced by pregnant women are much the same around the world. However, a woman's chance of surviving these complications vary greatly, as the MMRs show.

The striking differences that do exist in the proportions of maternal deaths attributable to specific causes result not from different biological risk factors, but from different legal and regulatory contexts and standards of medical care. For example, unsafe abortion and obstructed labor account for 13 percent and 8 percent of maternal deaths, respectively, in developing countries, but each accounts for less than 1 percent of maternal deaths in the United States.[21] Deaths from induced abortion and obstructed labor have been almost eliminated in developed countries due to the availability of safe, legal abortions and the use of cesarean sections.[22]

Thus, given that most maternal deaths are caused by a few familiar complications, the next step from a public health perspective is to find the most efficient ways to reduce the unacceptably high number of deaths from these complications in developing countries. For decades, programs intended to reduce maternal mortality were based on the assumption that life-threatening obstetric complications could usually be predicted or prevented. The result was that in developing countries these programs emphasized prenatal care and the training of traditional birth attendants (TBAs). The programs operated on the belief that enrolling pregnant women in prenatal care would enable clinicians to detect early signs of complications and prevent them from developing further. With emphasis on prenatal care, it became necessary to train TBAs how to conduct deliveries safely so that they could reduce the risk of infection and bleeding caused by traditional practices or ignorance.

Comprehensive reviews of the public health literature, however, have instead shown that most life-threatening obstetric complications can neither be prevented nor predicted, though they can be treated.[23] The reasons that most serious complications cannot be prevented or predicted are both physiological and statistical. Consider hemorrhage, which causes the largest number of deaths.[24] Most deaths from obstetric hemorrhage result from postpartum hemorrhage, in which there is massive bleeding because the blood vessels in the uterus that feed the fetus do not shut down after delivery.[25] This usually happens because there is some material remaining in the uterus (e.g., all or part of the placenta) or because the muscles of the uterus fail to contract. There are no early warning signals for postpartum hemorrhage, but there are some groups of women who have a higher-than-normal risk such as women who have had four or more births, thus stretching and loosening the uterine muscles.[26] However, the vast majority of these "high-risk" women deliver without incident and the majority of hemorrhage cases actually occur among low-risk women.

Most cases of obstructed labor also occur among low-risk women. This seemingly paradoxical result can be illustrated using data from one of the very few studies to evaluate prenatal screening. In the early 1970s in Kasongo, Zaire, more than 3600 women were screened for risk of obstetric complications.[27] When compared to the pregnancy outcomes, the investigators found that their most accurate predictions were those for obstructed labor among women who had given birth before.[28] As Table 21.3 shows, women with poor obstetric histories (e.g., those who had experienced a previous stillbirth) were more than nine times more likely to develop obstructed labor than were women who had better histories (relative risk = 9.2). Looking at the data in another way, about

Table 21.3 Type of Labor, by Obstetric History, Kasongo, Zaire, 1971–1975

| Type of Labor | Obstetric History | | |
	Bad	Good	Total
Obstructed	15	36	51
Not Obstructed	141	3,422	3,563
Total	156	3,458	3,614

Relative Risk: (15/156)/(36/3,458) = 9.2
Sensitivity: 15/51 = 29 percent
Source: Kasongo Project Team, 1984

ten percent of women with poor histories developed obstructed labor (15/156), compared to only about one percent of women with better histories (36/3458). However, *in absolute numbers*, more than twice as many women with better histories as women with poor histories developed obstructed labor (thirty-six compared to fifteen). This is because there are so many low-risk women (those with better histories), that 1 percent of low-risk women is a larger number than 10 percent of high-risk women. For this reason, accurate prediction was not possible even when there was a defined group at very high risk.

Preventative measures might appear to hold the most promise with sepsis and hypertensive diseases of pregnancy, such as eclampsia. After all, the conventional thinking goes, infection can be introduced through unclean delivery practices, and pre-eclampsia can be detected before it becomes life-threatening.[29] But this conventional thinking omits several important facts. In the case of sepsis, there are a number of ways that postpartum infection can develop. It can be introduced by unclean practices on the part of birth attendants (TBAs or physicians) or from premature rupture of the membranes surrounding the amniotic sac or from prolonged labor, in which case no outside source of infection is needed. Moreover, a sizeable proportion of cases of preeclampsia and eclampsia develop suddenly and without warning around the time of delivery.[30]

If the short-term preventative measures discussed above (i.e., prevention of complications among women who are already pregnant) are not effective, policymakers might wonder about the possibilities of long-term prevention. For example, it is often said that good nutrition and education will reduce maternal mortality.[31] But there is evidence to the contrary—evidence from one of history's largest natural experiments: the development of the West. During the last half of the nineteenth century and the early decades of the twentieth century, mortality from many causes declined sharply in Europe and North America. Mortality rates from many of these causes of death, including tuberculosis, fell steeply and steadily, even though there was no effective medical treatment for the diseases.[32] It is generally accepted that improvements in the general standard of living during this period, including better nutrition and sanitation, made people healthier and better able to fight off disease.

The first maternal mortality data available in England and Wales date back to 1850. From 1850 to the mid-1930s, maternal mortality remained relatively constant.[33] In contrast, in the first three decades of this century alone, infant mortality declined by more than half.[34] Thus, maternal mortality was impervious to the changes in standards of living, including improvements in nutrition, that are believed to have transformed public health in now-developed countries.

Moreover, despite the importance of education for women in other arenas of public health, increases in literacy and school attendance in the United Kingdom and the United States were not associated with a reduction in maternal mortality. For example, in 1910, half of all girls aged fourteen to seventeen in the United States attended school.[35] This proportion increased to almost three-quarters by 1930, yet maternal mortality still did not decline.[36] In short, in searching for effective ways to reduce maternal deaths in developing countries, one should not assume that general development measures (such as nutrition and education) will solve the problem of maternal mortality, though they obviously have other important health and social benefits.

However, while it is not possible to prevent or predict most serious complications of pregnancy, delivery, and the postpartum period, the vast majority can be successfully treated. In fact, maternal mortality is one of the few major public health problems for which medical treatment is the key. Again, history shows that after resisting decline for nearly a century, maternal mortality began to fall sharply in the late 1930s. In 1935, the maternal mortality ratio in England and Wales was 394 maternal deaths per 100,000 live births.[37] Within only fifteen years it had fallen by more than three-quarters to eighty-seven deaths.[38] This decline came about with the availability of effective means to treat obstetric complications, including antibiotics for infection, banked blood, and safer surgical techniques for hemorrhage and obstructed labor. As Irvine Loudon, the leading historian in this field, stated, "maternal mortality (but not neonatal or infant mortality, which behave quite differently) is remarkably sensitive to standards of obstetric care but remarkably resistant to the [changes in] levels of socioeconomic deprivation seen in Britain over the last 150 years."[39]

The treatment required to prevent most maternal deaths is not complicated. In the UN Guidelines, two levels of essential obstetric care (EOC) are specified: Basic and Comprehensive.[40] Basic EOC consists of tasks that can be performed by a variety of health workers, including midwives, nurses, and general practice physicians. Comprehensive EOC requires surgical capacity. The "signal functions" of Basic and Comprehensive EOC are shown in Table 21.4.

In general, health centers in developing countries should be able to provide most of the Basic EOC services, and district hospitals should be providing

Table 21.4 Signal Functions Used to Identify Basic and Comprehensive EOC Facilities

Basic EOC Services	Comprehensive EOC Services
(1) Administer parenteral antibiotics*	(1–6) All of those included in Basic EOC
(2) Administer parenteral oxytocic drugs	(7) Perform surgery (caesarean section)
(3) Administer parenteral anticonvulsants for preeclampsia and eclampsia	(8) Perform blood transfusion
(4) Perform manual removal of placenta	
(5) Perform removal of retained products (e.g., manual vacuum aspiration)	
(6) Perform assisted vaginal delivery	

* Parenteral administration of drugs means by injection or intravenous infusion ("drip").

Comprehensive EOC. This, however, is not the case in much of Africa and parts of Asia and Latin America, as data presented in the next section will show.

A New Approach to Monitoring Maternal Mortality

When the Safe Motherhood Initiative began in 1987,[41] it was generally assumed that progress would be measured using maternal mortality rates and ratios. For example, one of the goals of the World Summit for Children in 1990 was to reduce maternal mortality by half by the year 2000.[42] While tracking maternal mortality would seem to be a reasonable way to measure progress, it has several major drawbacks. This section discusses why such tracking is neither technically feasible nor very informative, and then outlines how the UN Guidelines can obviate these drawbacks.

There are two kinds of technical difficulties involved in measuring maternal mortality: gathering the data and interpreting the data.[43] First of all, it is extremely difficult to gather information on maternal deaths because most developing countries do not have adequate vital statistics registration systems. In fact, in many countries, most deaths take place outside health facilities, where reporting is most reliable.[44] Even if a death is reported, the fact that the woman had been pregnant may not be recorded, even in developed countries. For example, a recent study in the United States found that as many as half of all pregnancy-related deaths may be unrecognized.[45] Underreporting is especially likely with deaths that carry a social stigma, such as maternal deaths among unmarried women and deaths from induced abortion.

Because most developing countries do not have functioning vital statistics registration systems, large (and expensive) special studies are necessary to identify maternal deaths. Such studies can be either prospective or retrospective. In a prospective study, the researchers follow a group of pregnant women forward in time. The major drawback of the prospective design is that it is labor-intensive, which limits the number of women who can be followed. On the other hand, in a retrospective study the researchers interview family members and neighbors to identify women who have died during a specified period before the survey (e.g., two years). The major limitation of the retrospective design is that some deaths will not be reported, either intentionally or unintentionally. For example, standard survey questions would not detect the death of the wife/mother in a family where the household subsequently disbands, the husband moves away or remarries, and the children move in with relatives.

In order to lessen the cost of gathering data on maternal deaths, many researchers are now using a new survey method called "the sisterhood method."[46] With this method, rather than asking about the deaths of household members, the interviewer asks adult household members about the deaths of their sisters. Because adults in a household (e.g., husband and wife) often have different sets of siblings, this method greatly expands the number of people on whom information is gathered. Moreover, because the sisterhood method requires only five or six questions per interview, it can be "piggybacked" onto other surveys, thus reducing costs even further.[47]

While the sisterhood method certainly brings advancements in this field, it exemplifies the problems with interpretation of maternal mortality data. First of all, data collected through the sisterhood method, like other methods, is not likely to include deaths that are considered shameful. A study in Matlab, Bangladesh, compared prospective data on maternal deaths to the results of a sisterhood study in the same population.[48] This comparison showed that most of the deaths from induced abortion and deaths of unmarried women were not reported in the sisterhood study.[49] In all, the sisterhood study underreported maternal deaths by one-fifth.[50]

Interpretation of data is also complicated by sample size. Because the number of maternal deaths in a study population over a few years is relatively small, the confidence intervals around the study results are wide.[51] Therefore, if a follow-up study is done some years later, the confidence intervals of the new and old studies may well often overlap, which means that it is not possible to say whether the new study detected a real change or merely a chance variation. Furthermore, analyses of smaller populations (e.g., age groups, ethnic groups, geographic areas) require subdividing the deaths into categories, each of which will have even fewer deaths (and, therefore, wider confidence intervals) than the findings for the population as a whole. To overcome this problem, one must increase the sample size of the study, which again increases cost and difficulty.

Along with these problems, which other survey methods share, the sisterhood method has a special difficulty in that the results usually refer to a period that has its midpoint a decade earlier. Thus, the results do not reflect current levels of maternal mortality. Clearly, such data are not very useful for evaluating the effects of programs.

In addition to these technical issues, a more general limitation applies to all studies of levels of maternal mortality. This limitation arises because maternal mortality studies cannot tell what actions need to be taken to prevent future maternal deaths. If the MMR in a country is 600 or 800 deaths per 100,000 live births, what is the difference in the program implications? The level of maternal mortality does not tell us what needs to be done. In order to design, implement, and monitor programs that will reduce maternal deaths, policymakers and program managers need indicators that clearly show them which activities and areas need more attention. Ideally, these indicators will be sensitive enough to reflect changes quickly, for example, within a year. Fortunately, such indicators do exist.

In 1997, UNICEF, WHO, and UNFPA jointly issued the UN Guidelines, developed by staff at Columbia University and UNICEF.[52] The UN Guidelines provide program managers and policymakers with a set of indicators for assessing and monitoring access to and utilization of services for treatment of serious obstetric complications.[53] Included in the UN Guidelines are forms for gathering and analyzing all the necessary data as well as instructions for their use.[54] These indicators reflect the current understanding of maternal mortality because they focus on women in the general population who develop obstetric complications, rather than on all pregnant women or those obtaining antenatal care. The indicators address the following series of questions for a given geographic area, be it a nation, a province, or a district:

1. Are there enough health facilities providing life-saving care for women with obstetric complications?
2. Are these facilities equitably distributed across the population?
3. Are pregnant women using these facilities?
4. Are pregnant women with obstetric complications using these facilities?
5. Are these facilities providing enough life-saving surgery to meet the needs of the population?
6. Is the quality of these services adequate?

As Table 21.5 shows, the UN Guidelines set minimum and maximum acceptable standards.[55] To understand how the indicators relate to maternal mortality, it is necessary to examine what each factor measures and to what extent its standards are being met.

Table 21.5 Indication of the Availability and Use of Obstetric Services

Indicator	Minimum Acceptable Level
Amount of essential obstetric care (EOC): **Basic** EOC facilities **Comprehensive** EOC facilities	For every 500,000 population, there should be: At least 4 Basic EOC facilities; At least 1 Comprehensive EOC facility.
Geographical distribution of EOC facilities	Minimum level for amount of EOC facilities is met in subnational areas.
Percentage of all births in Basic or Comprehensive EOC facilities	At least 15 percent of all births in the population take place in either Basic or Comprehensive facilities.
Met need for EOC: women treated in EOC facilities as a percentage of those estimated to have obstetric complications	100 percent of women estimated to have obstetric complications are treated in EOC facilities.
Cesarean sections as a percentage of all births	Cesarean sections account for no less than 5 percent nor more than 15 percent of all births in the population.
Case fatality rate: deaths among women with complications in EOC facilities	The case fatality rate among women with obstetric complications in EOC facilities is less than 1 percent.

1. Are There Enough Health Facilities Providing
Life-Saving Care for Women with Obstetric Complications?

The first step in assessing the availability of essential obstetric care (EOC) is to classify health facilities by the level of obstetric care they provide. For purposes of international comparison, two levels of EOC facilities are identified: Basic and Comprehensive.[56] A Basic EOC facility is one that is performing all six of the signal functions shown in Table 21.4.[57] A Comprehensive EOC facility performs the basic functions as well as obstetric surgery and blood transfusion.[58]

According to the UN Guidelines, the minimum acceptable level for availability of EOC facilities is that for every 500,000 persons in the population there should be four Basic EOC facilities and one Comprehensive EOC facility.[59] The rationale is that many life-threatening complications can either be definitively treated at a Basic EOC facility, or else the woman can be given enough treatment so that she will arrive at the Comprehensive facility in better condition than she would have otherwise. For example, while many women with postpartum hemorrhage can be treated at a Basic EOC facility, women with obstructed labor will need to be transferred to a hospital. However, if women with obstructed labor are given antibiotics before their journey to the hospital (which often takes hours) they are less likely to arrive at the hospital with an infection. Similarly, most women with eclampsia will need hospital care, but if they are given drugs to prevent convulsions during the journey, their prognosis is improved.

Early experience with these guidelines showed that many women live in areas that do not meet these standards. For example, in Bangladesh, a study of twenty district hospitals showed that 25 percent of them had not done a single cesarean section in the previous year, even though they all had physicians on staff.[60] A district in Bangladesh contains an average of 1.7 million people, which means that according to the UN Guidelines each district should have three Comprehensive EOC facilities; however six of the twenty districts studied had none.[61]

2. Are These Facilities Equitably Distributed across the Population?

Analyzing information on the number of functioning EOC facilities (indicator one above) by geographic area will reveal regional discrepancies in the availability of life-saving obstetric care. For example, in many countries (e.g., nations in West and North Africa) such an analysis would show that EOC facilities are much more common in major cities on the coastline than they are in the interior.

3. Are Pregnant Women Using these Facilities?

This indicator is included in the series primarily because many countries do not yet have the information available to calculate the much more informative statistic "unmet need for EOC" indicator (indicator four above). Nearly all countries, however, already collect information on the number of deliveries in health facilities. The innovative feature of this indicator (and others that follow) is that the health facility data are used as the numerator of a ratio. The denominator of the ratio is 15 percent of births in the population, which is used as an estimate of the proportion of pregnant women who will need EOC.[62] The interpretation of this indicator is as follows: hospital births include both normal and complicated deliveries. If we accept that at least 15 percent of pregnant women will develop serious complications, then if 15 percent or fewer of pregnant women deliver in EOC facilities, some women with complications are delivering outside the facilities where they could get the care they need.

From a practical point of view, gathering routine information in health facilities is much more feasible than conducting periodic surveys. Estimates of the number of births in a given area and in a given time period are available for most developing countries. Using health facility data in the numerator and a proportion of estimated births in the population as the denominator produces an estimate of unmet need for services in the population as a whole, but without the cost of surveys. Therefore, monitoring can become a continuous (rather than episodic) process.

4. Are Pregnant Women with Obstetric Complications Using These Facilities?

Probably the most promising of the indicators developed for these guidelines is an estimate of "met need" for emergency obstetric care. Again, the denominator is the estimated proportion of pregnant women who develop serious complications (15 percent of live births). In this case, the numerator is the number of women admitted to an EOC facility (Basic or Comprehensive) for treatment of one of the major obstetric complications.[63] While this may be the most eloquent of the indicators, it certainly is not the easiest to measure. Maternity ward registers in many developing countries do not have a column for maternal complications, although there are usually columns for the weight, number, and sex of infants. Thus, information on the number of women with obstetric complications admitted to the hospital (the numerator of unmet need) is often difficult or impossible to collect using existing records. Adding a column on obstetric complications (or reason for admission) to maternity registers seems like a modest and reasonable change to make to improve the survival of women in developing countries.

Information from pretests of the Guidelines, sponsored by UNICEF, show that the level of unmet need is shocking. A study in ten districts in India during 1992 and 1993 showed that only about one-seventh of women experiencing serious obstetric complications received treatment in government facilities.[64] Unmet need ranged from 60 percent in a district in Karnataka to 98 percent in a district in Bihar.[65] A recent study in Egypt also found low levels of met need.

For example, in the Akhmeim District of Upper Egypt, unmet need reached 83 percent.[66]

5. Are These Facilities Providing Enough Life-Saving Surgery to Meet the Needs of the Population?

Because surgical data are more often available than data on treatment of complications, the Guidelines also include an indicator of unmet need for cesarean section.[67] The minimum acceptable level of cesarean section is set at 5 percent of births in the population, which is lower than the level in most developed countries.[68] Because of the danger of overuse of cesarean sections, a maximum acceptable level was also set at 15 percent of births, well under the U.S. level of 22 percent in 1994.[69]

Again, the available data paint a dismal picture. In the study in India mentioned above, five of the ten districts had a cesarean section rate of less than 1 percent of births, two districts had rates of 2 to 4 percent, and only three had rates of 5 to 6 percent, barely meeting the minimum acceptable level set by the UN agencies.[70] Incidentally, these data include cesarean sections performed in private as well as public facilities. In the Bangladesh study, five of the twenty district hospitals had performed no cesarean sections during the previous year.[71] None of the other fifteen hospitals performed enough cesarean sections to equal even 1 percent of births, let alone the minimum of 5 percent.[72] Finally, in East Africa, Erik M. Nordberg found that less than 1 percent of births were done by cesarean section from 1979 to 1981, and the situation may actually have deteriorated since that time.[73]

6. Is the Quality of These Services Adequate?

Assessing the quality of care provided is a complex task. In this series of indicators, designed for use at the national level, only a very crude indicator of quality is used to measure the proportion of women admitted to a facility with obstetric complications who die (called the "case fatality rate"). The maximum acceptable level is set at 1 percent.[74] In other words, if given proper care, at least 99 percent of the women admitted for obstetric complications should survive. This estimate is in line with numerous studies of avoidable factors in maternal deaths.[75] Studies of hospitals in West Africa by the Prevention of Maternal Mortality (PMM) Network found case fatality rates ranging from 1.2 percent to 8 percent between 1983 and 1990.[76] In contrast, obstetric case fatality rates in the United States in 1970 was 0.03 percent.[77]

In sum, the indicators in the UN Guidelines can be extremely helpful to program planners and managers in developing countries as they seek to reduce maternal deaths. Moreover, these indicators have a number of practical advantages over maternal mortality rates and ratios. They are easier and less expensive to measure, they can change quickly (even over the course of one to two years), trends can be measured easily, and they can be used at district as well as national levels.[78] It is hoped that during the next decade, as the UN Guidelines are applied, a substantial body of information will be accumulated, and that this information will help governments in developing countries make their efforts to reduce maternal deaths more effective.

Legal Context for Using the UN Guidelines to Define States' Obligations Under International Human Rights Treaties

In addition to being used by health agencies such as WHO and UNICEF, the UN Guideline indicators can be used to monitor compliance with the existing international human rights obligations to progressively realize this critical aspect of the right to health. Conceptually, the translation of the UN Guidelines from a purely public health tool to a human rights tool requires a shift from a framework of the utility of maternal survival to one of the injustice of maternal mortality. That is, a woman's capacity to bear children is linked to the survival of certain social groups, the division of property, and the productivity of societies as well as to deeply ingrained views of sexuality. Consequently, the definition of women's reproductive roles historically has been fundamental to the ordering of societies, and maternal mortality has often been viewed as an inevitable externality of women's utilitarian, child-bearing role. A human rights perspective, however, rejects the reasoning (so forcefully expressed by Martin Luther) that women possess value as a consequence of fixed, socially-determined roles or purposes.

Indeed, Article 5(a) of the United Nations Convention on the Elimination of All Forms of Discrimination Against Women[79] (the Women's Convention) sets forth an obligation on the part of State parties to "modify the social and cultural practices of men, with a view toward achieving the elimination of prejudices which are based on the idea of the inferiority or superiority of either of the sexes or on stereotyped roles for men and women."[80] From this human rights perspective, maternal mortality is important because human beings must care about women in their own right. Human beings must care that individuals with hopes and promises and self-defined aspirations (all of which may, but need not, include their children, families, and communities) are needlessly condemned to die horrible deaths in the prime of their lives.

As a matter of positive human rights law, the reduction of maternal mortality clearly requires states to respect, ensure, protect, and fulfill a number of different internationally recognized rights, including both civil liberties and economic and social rights, such as the right to health and the right to the benefits of scientific progress.[81] It further requires states to eliminate cultural, religious, and social discrimination that devalues women's health and well-being, establishes barriers to quality health information and services, and promotes inadequate allocation of resources for women's healthcare.[82]

Indeed, when looking at the real-life problems that lead to maternal death, it becomes impossible to separate civil rights involving reproductive choice and freedom of movement, for example, from health rights that are considered to be "economic" rights under international law.[83] For example, lack of access to safe and legal abortions is the single largest contributor to pregnancy-related health problems and mortality in Latin America, resulting in about one-quarter of all maternal deaths in the region.[84] However, while fully acknowledging the indivisibility of civil and economic rights, the focus of this chapter lies in using the UN Guidelines as an example of how certain public health indicators can advance the measurement and enforcement of states' compliance with the right to health as an explicitly economic and social rights obligation under international law.

Applicable Norms

The right to health, including access to healthcare, is set forth as state obligation under a panoply of international human rights instruments.[85] The two international treaties that are most relevant to the reduction of maternal mortality are the International Covenant on Economic, Social and Cultural Rights[86] (ICESCR) and the Women's Convention. However, the International Convention on the Elimination of All Forms of Racial Discrimination[87] (CERD) and the Convention on the Rights of the Child[88] (Children's Convention) are also pertinent. In particular, the Children's Convention is important not just because maternal mortality affects children, but because many women who are dying of pregnancy-related complications are under 18, and are therefore "children" as defined by the convention.[89]

Article 12 of the ICESCR specifies that "States Parties . . . recognize the right of everyone to the enjoyment of the highest attainable standard of physical and mental health,"[90] including "[t]he creation of conditions which would assure to all medical service and medical attention in the event of sickness."[91] Article 12 is supplemented by Article 10(2), which states that "[s]pecial protection should be accorded to mothers during a reasonable period before and after childbirth."[92]

The Women's Convention phrases the right in terms of combating discrimination against women: "States Parties shall take all appropriate measures to eliminate discrimination against women in the field of health care in order to ensure, on a basis of equality of men and women, access to health care services . . ."[93] Article 12(2) of the Women's Convention then goes on to clarify that equality of health services must be judged not from a formalistic standpoint, but in full recognition of the differing health needs of women, including those relating to reproduction, and of the fact that access entails eliminating economic obstacles as well as discriminatory laws and practices. "Notwithstanding the provisions of paragraph 1 of this article, States Parties shall ensure to women appropriate services in connection with pregnancy, confinement and the post-natal period, granting free services where necessary."[94]

Under the ICESCR, State parties are to provide data on indicators defined by WHO with respect to the "proportion of pregnant women having access to trained personnel during pregnancy and proportion attended by such personnel for delivery . . . including maternal mortality rate, both before and after child-birth."[95] On their face, however, neither the ICESCR nor the Women's Convention indicates what would constitute either "conditions that would assure to all medical attention"[96] in the event of obstetric complications or the "appropriate services in connection with pregnancy, confinement and the post-natal period."[97] Nor, more specifically, is there any indication of the necessary minimum proportion of women having access to or receiving the care of the undefined "trained personnel" during pregnancy and delivery, respectively.

Unlike certain classic civil rights violations, such as torture or arbitrary detention, which involve government agents directly committing violations against individuals, the state's compliance with reducing maternal mortality cannot be measured simply by observing and counting up individual instances of maternal deaths. Governments are clearly responsible for the abuse of authority of their agents when committed in their official capacities, but the causal relationship between a government's actions or omissions in establishing conditions or services and the occurrence of maternal deaths is of a different nature. Rather than intentional malfeasance or even the billiard-ball model of cause and effect familiar to many US lawyers,[98] the government's responsibility in terms of maternal mortality lies in establishing a structural framework that excludes certain possibilities (e.g., when pregnant women experiencing eclampsia have no access to a caesarian section) and includes others (e.g., when pregnant women have reasonable access to facilities with the capacity to perform blood transfusions). When those conditions are in place, the state has used its authority to fulfill the right to health even if women later die of maternal causes.

In other words, although any unexplained deaths of prisoners in detention indicate *per se* civil rights violations, the right to be free from avoidable maternal mortality requires an assessment of what is reasonably avoidable. As discussed in Part II *infra*, that assessment in turn requires an understanding of denominators as well as the simple numerators—i.e., the women who die. It is meaningless to compare the number of maternal deaths across countries or times without an estimate of the number of deliveries overall. This is why, as noted above, maternal mortality ratios are generally reported according to deaths per 100,000 live births.

Also unlike the example of deaths in detention, even within a given hospital it is not the number of maternal deaths alone that is *per se* indicative of a problem in the adequacy or quality of care, but as included in indicator six in the UN Guidelines, the case fatality rate—the number of maternal deaths divided by the number of women who are present with obstetric complications in the hospital.[99] For example, if ten prisoners die due to torture or abuse in detention, it is equally a violation of human rights if there are 10,000 prisoners being housed in the facility or 100. By contrast, if 100 women present with complications and ten die, it indicates a very different situation than if 10,000 women present with comparable complications and ten die.

Moreover, unlike in the case of many structural civil and political rights, such as "due process of law" or "free and fair elections," with regard to maternal mortality there are no significant bodies of national jurisprudence and precedent for the international human rights community to draw upon to resolve the questions of what constitutes appropriate conditions or services from a theoretical standpoint. The elements of minimum due process—the right of the accused to know the charges, the right to an effective defense, the right to confront one's accusers, etc.—have been well-established in domestic legal systems. If laws and regulations do not afford such elements, the government involved can be held accountable for not putting the necessary structural conditions in place. However, the analogous elements of the minimal conditions or services required to cope with pregnancy-related complications have generally not been inscribed in legislation or jurisprudence, even where maternal mortality has been effectively eliminated as a public health problem.

Performance Standards

If the normative definition of the right to health–as interpreted with respect to the reduction and prevention of maternal mortality in particular–is vague in comparison with many civil rights, so is the "delineation of performance standards" for states to implement that right, as well as other economic and social rights.[100] In language that is echoed in economic and social rights provisions of other treaties, the ICESCR obligates state parties to "take steps . . . to the maximum of its available resources."[101] Because its enumerated rights are phrased in terms of eliminating discrimination, the Women's Convention uses the somewhat different term "take all appropriate measures" to eliminate discrimination in health care, including special measures for pregnant women.[102] As a matter of law, although the obligations to "take steps . . . toward the full realization" or "take all appropriate measures [toward the elimination of discrimination]" may differ from the presumably immediate and mandatory obligation "to respect and to ensure,"[103] which is set out in the ICCPR, state parties to the ICESCR, the Women's Convention, and other treaties with economic and social rights provisions are by no means free to indefinitely defer taking action with respect to such rights. For instance, the Limburg Principles on the Implementation of the International Covenant on Economic, Social and Cultural Rights (the Limburg Principles) unequivocally state that "[t]he obligation to 'achieve progressively the full realization of the rights' requires States Parties to move as expeditiously as possible towards the realization of the rights . . . [a]ll States Parties have the obligation to begin immediately to take steps to fulfill their obligations under the Covenant."[104]

The Maastricht Guidelines, articulated in 1997, reiterate the requirement of immediate steps:

> The fact that the full realization of most economic, social and cultural rights can only be achieved progressively, which in fact also applies to most civil and political rights, does not alter the nature of the legal obligation of States which requires that certain steps be taken immediately and others as soon as possible.[105]

The Maastricht Guidelines further establish that the burden of proof lies with each state party to the ICESCR to demonstrate that it is making "measurable progress toward the full realization of the rights in question."[106]

Nor, under international law, do states enjoy unframmeled discretion in construing what constitutes the extent of their "maximum available resources."[107] The Economic, Social and Cultural Rights Committee (ESC Committee), the body charged with the monitoring of the implementation of the ICESCR, has forcefully stated that violations of the ICESCR occur when a state fails to satisfy a "minimum core obligation to ensure the satisfaction of, at the very least, *minimum essential levels* of each of the rights."[108] With respect to health, the ESC Committee has stated that there is a minimum core obligation not to deprive "any significant number of individuals 'essential primary health care.'"[109] However, the ESC Committee has not yet elaborated on the positive dimensions of states' obligations with respect to health, or any aspect thereof.[110]

The Maastricht Guidelines reiterated that certain minimum core obligations "apply irrespective of the availability of resources of the country concerned or any other factors and difficulties."[111] The Maastricht Guidelines state, "[a]s established by Limburg Principles 25–28, and confirmed by the developing jurisprudence of the Committee on Economic, Social and Cultural Rights, resource scarcity does not relieve States of certain minimum obligations in respect of the implementation of economic, social and cultural rights."[112] Just as with progressive realization, it is worth noting that civil and political rights also require resource allocation. Resource scarcity does not relieve states of their obligations under the ICCPR or analogous treaties to set up judicial systems that are capable of ensuring fair trials, electoral systems capable of ensuring "genuine and periodic" elections, or correctional systems capable of ensuring decent prison conditions.[113]

In attempting to clarify how a state's "taking of steps" toward progressive realization of economic and social rights would be measured by the ESC Committee, the Maastricht Guidelines further established that states' responsibilities under the ICESCR contain elements of both *obligations of conduct* and *obligations of result*: "The obligation of conduct requires action reasonably calculated to realize the enjoyment of a particular right. . . . The obligation of result requires States to achieve specific targets to satisfy a detailed substantive standard."[114]

This distinction between obligations of conduct and result parallels the traditional distinction in international treaty law between obligations of means and obligations of ends. Rebecca Cook notes that under the Women's Convention, State parties have agreed to pursue obligations of both means and ends.[115] Cook writes that the end is "to embody the principle of equality of men and women in their national Constitutions or other appropriate legislation," while the clause "by all appropriate means" allows state parties to choose the means they will adopt in eliminating discrimination against women.[116]

The Maastricht Guidelines, however, provide far more concrete illustrations of obligations of result/ends and conduct/means than had been previously articulated under international economic and social rights jurisprudence, and interestingly, they single out the issue of reducing maternal mortality as the primary example given.[117] Moreover, in so doing they interpret State parties' obligations in light of the declarations emerging from, respectively, the International Conference on Population and Development held in Cairo in 1994 (Cairo Programme of Action or Cairo Programme)[118] and the Fourth World Conference on Women held in Beijing in 1995 (Beijing Declaration or Beijing Platform).[119] "[T]he obligation of conduct could involve the adoption and implementation of a plan of action to reduce maternal mortality. . . . [T]he obligation of result requires the reduction of maternal mortality to levels agreed at . . . [Cairo and Beijing]."[120] Thus, in the slow iterative process through which international law is created, the Cairo and Beijing documents, while non-binding in themselves, referred to and relied upon the norms in human rights conventions. They, in turn, are referred to by the Maastricht Guidelines as formal interpretations of states' obligations to "take measures . . . towards . . . full realization" under the earlier and vague ICESCR.[121]

Even with the growing jurisprudence of the ESC Committee and the Women's Convention, and the interpretive principles of Limburg and Maastricht, however, there remain problems in defining precisely what essential steps every state should immediately take toward reducing maternal mortality and how such steps should be measured. Without clearly defined elements of what preventing maternal mortality entails, it is impossible to 1) set minimum core levels of the obligation to ensure, *inter alia*, that services are available to all pregnant women who seek them, notwithstanding the level of resources of the country, or 2) set indicators by which to gauge progressive realization.[122] Moreover, unlike the methods used to assess many civil and political rights, the development of appropriate and effective "obligations of conduct" and "obligations of result" to measure states' compliance with the prevention of maternal mortality and economic and social rights generally will ultimately depend upon the use of information and analyses external to the human rights community.

In sum, progress has been and continues to be made in the elaboration and reiteration of economic, social, and cultural norms *qua* rights as well as on consensus-building about the obligatory nature of immediate and concerted state action with respect to achieving those rights. However, for the freedom from avoidable maternal death to be fully realized, the international human rights community must adopt sound epidemiologic guidelines that are in keeping with human rights principles and specify objectively measurable steps for state parties to the ICESCR and the Women's Convention, as well as other regional treaties, to undertake.

The UN Guidelines Provide a Feasible Way of Measuring Compliance with States' Obligations to Reduce Maternal Mortality

If the discourse and philosophy of human rights provides a way of understanding the phenomenon of maternal mortality as an enormous global injustice, the UN Guidelines—and the epidemiology that lies behind those guidelines—provide a way of infusing the norms of human rights instruments with substantive content, thereby demonstrating how to remedy that structural injustice. The UN Guidelines provide for a system-wide analysis of healthcare, which is the responsibility of the government, rather than locating the responsibility for preventing maternal mortality on individual providers and/or women.[123] They thereby allow advocates for economic and social rights in both nongovernmental and intergovernmental organizations to measure State parties' compliance with this key aspect of the right to health by providing concrete meaning to states' obligations under the ICESCR (as well as the analogue in the Women's Convention and other treaties) "to take steps . . . with a view to achieving progressively . . . the rights recognized in the present Covenant by all appropriate means . . . without discrimination of any kind."[124]

While, needless to say, the use of indicators must be supplemented by other human rights monitoring criteria, such as legislative and administrative actions, the UN Guidelines can play a critically important, three-fold role in the enforcement of this aspect of the right to health.[125] First, in contrast to current reliance on governmental statistics of rates and ratios, these process indicators permit a reliable and verifiable indication of states taking steps to reduce and prevent maternal mortality. Second, the UN Guidelines can be used to judge whether the steps or measures states are taking to reduce maternal mortality are in fact the appropriate ones and whether they are aimed at expanding emergency obstetric care coverage. Third, the UN Guidelines go a long way toward permitting an assessment of whether states are taking such steps and measures to reduce maternal mortality on a nondiscriminatory basis, provided that states are required to report on emergency obstetric care coverage and services on the basis of sub-national units and UN Specialized Agencies institute a system to share their data analysis with the treaty monitoring committees.

States' Obligation to Take Steps or Adopt Measures

The first part of the obligation states have is to take steps toward the progressive achievement of the right to be free of avoidable maternal death. The process indicators in the UN Guidelines allow for reporting on state action with respect to reducing maternal mortality to be objectively verified. Indeed, the objective nature of the indicators allows for taking a violations approach to measuring noncompliance of minimum core levels as well as for measuring progressive realization of the right over time.[126] That is, while the accountability of state parties to the ICESCR for providing a minimum essential level of emergency obstetric services is subject to the state's "maximum available resources"[127] for all healthcare—and all social spending at some level–the UN Guidelines establish the core content of standards for emergency obstetric care that can guide priorities in state parties' healthcare expenditures. Any significant deviation from the minimum levels articulated in the UN Guidelines, any discrimination among sub-populations in terms of emergency obstetric coverage, or any back-tracking or active deprivation with respect to the provision of such care should constitute an immediately recognizable violation of this aspect of the right to health. Moreover, combined with information about a country's resources, measured by per capita Gross Domestic Product (GDP), comparisons among state parties of similar resources can be made.[128]

Beyond establishing minimum core standards for emergency obstetric care, the UN Guidelines permit a feasible—and arguably more reliable—method of assessing state performance with respect to the more complex (and hitherto murkier) issue of taking steps or adopting measures toward progressive realization over time. Instead of using the impact indicators referred to in the Maastricht Guidelines and emphasized in the Cairo and Beijing texts, a state party to the ICESCR, the Women's Convention, or another treaty could be judged according to the implementation of readily identifiable interventions that have been found to reduce maternal mortality.

The Cairo Programme, the Beijing Declaration, and the Maastricht Guidelines rely heavily on impact indicators to measure decreases in maternal mortality and states' performance with respect thereto. For example, the Cairo Programme calls for "a reduction in maternal mortality by one half of the 1990 levels by the year 2000 and a further one half by 2015."[129] After setting forth this unequivocal obligation of result, the text goes on to note that "[t]he realization of these goals will have different implications for countries with different 1990 levels of maternal mortality" and further specifies:

Countries with intermediate levels of mortality should aim to achieve by the year 2005 a maternal mortality rate below 100 per 100,000 live births. . . . Countries with the highest levels of mortality should aim to achieve by 2005 a maternal mortality rate below 125 per 100,000 live births and by the year 2015 a maternal mortality rate below 75 per 100,000 live births. However, all countries should reduce maternal morbidity and mortality to levels where they no longer constitute a public health problem.[130]

The language "countries . . . should aim to achieve" indicates that these goals are to be achieved progressively. Certainly the phrase "levels where they no longer constitute a public health problem" suggests some aspirational notion of the full realization of the right to health with respect to freedom from avoidable maternal mortality. However, there is no indication either of what steps state parties must take immediately to meet these impact goals or of what levels of maternal mortality would in fact be acceptable as fulfilling minimum obligations on those deadline dates.

Even if such minimum benchmarks were set, there are two problems with using such obligations of result to enforce states' compliance with core obligations to reduce maternal mortality. First of all, from a purely epidemiologic perspective, these numbers do not provide a feasible way to measure progress in the reduction of maternal mortality for all of the reasons explained in Part II. Second, from a human rights perspective concerned with enforcing states' obligations, the simple fact is that the same countries where maternal mortality poses a significant health problem are unlikely to have the data necessary to generate such figures. As a result, it will be impossible either as a result of the methodology used (i.e., the sisterhood method described in Part II) or simply because of the lack of capacity of the vital registration system to accurately assess or verify whether states are "taking steps" toward implementation.

Therefore, to base compliance with obligations to reduce maternal mortality on impact indicators is, at best, an undertaking which is impossible to carry out accurately from year to year or even every four or five years for the purposes of state parties' reporting requirements under the Women's Convention and the ICESCR, respectively. In all likelihood, to do so is an invitation for government distortion and manipulation of figures because it literally will be impossible to verify. Indeed, in using MMRs to measure compliance, state parties simply have to do a progressively worse job of measuring overall maternal deaths in order to show progress.[131]

For example, in a 1996 publication, Mexican government sources reported its most recently calculated ratio to be forty-eight maternal deaths per 100,000 live births whereas UNICEF estimated that the maternal mortality ratio in

Mexico between 1980 and 1992 was 110 per 100,000 live births. [132] Depending upon the actual number, that would place Mexico among middle-income countries with either relatively low or very high rates of maternal mortality and thereby would affect whether it is in compliance with whatever minimum rates it was supposed to meet. The Mexican government claimed to have reduced maternal mortality by 38 percent between 1980 and 1994, citing as its 1980 figure ninety-four maternal deaths per 100,000 live births,[133] still lower than the UNICEF number. In any case, neither the number nor the progress can be objectively verified. Moreover, the situation in Mexico is in no way aberrational; indeed, it is the norm that in countries where maternal mortality poses a public health problem, accurate or complete data relating to maternal deaths are not available.[134]

Given the total lack of reliability of these numbers and the concern expressed by human rights experts about the use of such invalid data,[135] it seems particularly odd that the Cairo and Beijing documents refer to outcome measures based on reductions from 1990 levels, when at the time of the Cairo and Beijing Conferences, UNICEF, WHO, and other UN agencies were in the process of realizing that their estimates were inaccurate and grossly underestimated the number of maternal deaths occurring in the world. Indeed, the final document emerging from Beijing even lamented, "[r]ecent and reliable data on the mortality and morbidity of women and conditions and diseases particularly affecting women are not available in many countries."[136] The numbers are startling: among the countries reporting vital statistics data to the United Nations for the years 1985 to 1989, more than two-thirds of the countries in Europe reported on maternal deaths specifically, whereas this proportion was only 17 percent in Asia and an unbelievably low 6 percent in Africa.[137]

Appropriateness of Steps or Measures

It seems clear that in order to establish objective steps that states must take or to measure progressive achievement in reducing maternal mortality, the focus should not be on impact indicators or rates, but on what the Maastricht Guidelines refer to as the "obligations of conduct."[138] In specifying obligations of conduct, the programatic means by which states are to achieve the end of reducing maternal mortality, the international legal community must be certain that they are meaningfully associated with the outcome of interest—a population-wide reduction in the number of maternal deaths. According to the best epidemiologic research conducted to date, the measurable and verifiable standards of conduct articulated in the UN Guidelines constitute the most significant interventions aimed at preventing and reducing maternal mortality. Consequently, the UN Guidelines permit an unequivocal judgment of not only whether a state is taking steps to fulfill the right to be free of maternal mortality, but whether a state is taking the *appropriate* steps or measures.

Although the Maastricht Guidelines refer to the Cairo Programme and the Beijing Declaration to establish obligations of conduct, both the documents emerging from the Cairo and Beijing Conferences were heavily negotiated and the products of many different agendas. As a result, by themselves, they do not make it possible to put forth either a set of essential actions that a state needs to undertake to reduce and prevent maternal mortality or the specific way in which states should institute practical improvements and enhancements of strategies and programs to combat maternal mortality. For example, the Cairo Programme states:

> [a]ll countries should design and implement special programmes to address the nutritional needs of women of child-bearing age, especially those who are pregnant or breast-feeding, and should give particular attention to the prevention and management of nutritional anemia and iodine-deficiency disorders. Priority should be accorded to improving the nutritional and health status of young women through education and training as part of maternal health and safe motherhood programmes.[139]

Clearly, it is desirable that the nutritional and educational status of young women be improved, both for the quality of their own lives when they are not pregnant as well as when they are pregnant or breastfeeding, and for the sake of their children. Indeed, these factors speak to women's enjoyment of other human rights and other aspects of the right to health. However, for the sake of clarity, it must be emphasized that the epidemiology behind the UN Guidelines demonstrates that such improvements do not and will not reduce maternal mortality.[140]

Most people would not tolerate the enjoyment of the rights to be free from arbitrary detention or torture being contingent on the restructuring of entire judicial systems in order to create the background conditions necessary for more judicial independence and due process. Similarly, the underlying interdependence of social and economic rights must not be used to justify the deferral of state obligations to take the actions outlined in the UN Guidelines which could immediately reduce the incidence of maternal deaths. On the contrary, it is hoped that the recognition and enforcement of this critical aspect of women's right to health will empower women (and men) to mobilize their communities to demand additional health-related rights, which may indeed involve structural social and economic conditions relating to women's status.

Similarly, if the outcome of interest in setting human rights monitoring standards is the reduction of maternal mortality, behavioristic interventions alone, such as having TBAs educate pregnant women in the importance of maintaining a balanced diet or training them to take their own pulse, will not succeed. These measures avoid the central fact that if women experience pre-eclampsia or begin unexpectedly to hemorrhage in labor, they will require anesthesia, blood transfusions, surgical interventions, etc., in order to survive. To pretend otherwise with women whose lives are at stake is an exercise either in cynicism or in denial.[141]

The Cairo Programme declares that "[i]n order to reduce high-risk pregnancies, maternal health and safe motherhood programs should include counselling and family-planning information."[142] It is unquestionably true that maternal health and safe motherhood programs should include family planning information and counseling about a woman's options as a matter of reproductive choice, but the language of the Cairo document wrongly implies that "high-risk pregnancies" are to be reduced in order to promote safe motherhood and to reduce maternal mortality. However, as discussed in Part II, we know that from a public health standpoint—as opposed to a clinical standpoint—high-risk pregnancies (as usually defined) account for a minority of obstetric complications. Thus, if the overall proportion of the population experiencing complications is the issue of concern in terms of establishing a state's legal obligation, the UN Guidelines clearly tell us that what states should focus on is the distribution of adequate and appropriate emergency obstetric services and not the identification of high-risk pregnancies.[143]

The obligations of conduct set forth in the Beijing Declaration should also be interpreted and narrowed in light of the UN Guidelines. For example, the Beijing Declaration notes, "[w]omen have different and unequal access to and use of basic health resources. . . . In many developing countries, the lack of emergency obstetric services is also of particular concern."[144] In response to this situation, the Beijing Declaration asserts that all states should "ensure that the necessary services are available at each level of the health system and make reproductive healthcare accessible, through the primary healthcare system, to all individuals of appropriate ages as soon as possible and no later than the year 2015."[145] Moreover, although the Beijing Declaration notes that "[i]n many developing countries, the lack of emergency obstetric services is . . . of particular concern," without the specificity provided by the UN Guidelines, it is impossible to assess whether, in accordance with their obligations of conduct, the "necessary services" are being made available at each level of the healthcare system.

Even when the Beijing Declaration calls for governments to "remove all barriers to women's health services and provide a broad range of health-care services, giving particular attention to maternal and emergency obstetric care,"[146] a discussion of the nature of the barriers to such health services remains conspicuously absent. For example, "barriers" could simply be construed as a lack of education, information, or motivation on the part of women to seek care. But information and education are not adequate if, in a developing country context, the appropriate emergency obstetric care is not available at the facilities to which a woman is being directed or if such facilities are inaccessible by available means of transportation.

In contrast, the logic behind the UN Guidelines does not just indicate why simplistic campaigns that promote care-seeking behavior in women when the appropriate care is not genuinely available, accessible, and affordable are misguided. It also substitutes simple indicators to determine whether objective barriers exist. Indicator three (Met Need for EOC), and, when the data are available, Indicator four (Unmet Need for EOC) permit an assessment of whether at least 15 percent of pregnant women (the estimated proportion who experience complications) are delivering in EOC facilities and whether women who actually experience complications are receiving treatment.

The reasons for noncompliance can vary greatly, but with the UN Guidelines the onus is on the government to remove whatever source of barriers exist. For example, in a 1997 mission to Mexico's southern state of Chiapas, Physicians for Human Rights (PHR) found that rural indigenous women often refuse to be taken to government hospitals even in the event of obstetric complications for fear of being sterilized postpartum without consent—a problem that has been documented in various parts of Mexico.[147] In such a situation, ensuring that the standards for met and unmet needs for EOC—and thereby the conditions for reducing maternal mortality–are reached will involve adopting new policies that ensure women's civil rights to reproductive choice and informed consent. However, the obligation of the government is objective and verifiable and cannot be met by governments' facile claims to be educating women about the importance of delivering their babies in hospitals.

Similarly, Mexico is among a number of countries that, in the process of restructuring their healthcare system according to World Bank recommendations, have adopted maternal/child health programs that emphasize the use of community health workers *(promotores)* and health posts, as opposed to the construction and manning of facilities that could provide emergency obstetric care.[148] The Program to Extend Coverage, or PAC by its Spanish acronym, is targeted at eleven of the poorest, most rural, and underdeveloped states in Mexico with the greatest need for health services.[149] In terms of maternal mortality, the PAC theoretically includes among its twelve components a strong emphasis on family planning, and "attention to prenatal, child-birth and post-natal care."[150] In practice however, nongovernmental health-care providers allege that the idea of staffing rural hospitals that have the capacity to store blood with at least one physician who could perform surgery, one nurse, and several community health promoters (*promotores*) has devolved into staffing health posts, which often lack electricity, with only a nurse and *promotores*, and often only the latter. The tangible resources of physicians and blood supplies have been replaced with family planning, nutrition, and other education and behavior modification programs carried out in rural communities.[151]

The UN Guidelines permit an unequivocal judgment that such steps are inadequate with respect to reducing maternal mortality and, therefore, that a state undertaking such measures is not in compliance with international treaty obligations. Furthermore, as states undertake to implement economic and social rights individually and through international assistance and cooperation, it is often aid from international financial institutions that will determine the extent of a state's available resources to fulfill economic and social rights. This example from Mexico illustrates the urgent need for the World Bank to ensure that the health reforms it sponsors is in keeping with sound epidemiologic studies and with the promotion of economic and social rights.[152]

This is not to say, however, that the UN Guidelines dictate the way in which a particular state is to provide for emergency obstetric coverage. That is—as a draft proposal for a General Comment on Article 12 of the ICESCR indicates—provided that the state ensures the accessibility, affordability, availability, and quality of emergency obstetric care, these services "can be satisfied through whatever mix of public and private sector services is appropriate in the national context, given that the full responsibility of implementation rests with the State Party."[153] Thus, state parties to the ICESCR, the Women's Convention, and other regional treaties are not only responsible for the actual provision of services, but for the regulation of both private and public sector services and for the provision of domestic remedies to ensure redress in the absence of quality services.[154]

Moreover the UN Guidelines' focus on monitoring curative care does not obviate the need for mobilization around changing social, economic, and cultural norms and practices that set the stage for the devaluing of healthcare for women. For example, part of taking steps to reduce maternal mortality must include breaking through the attitude that maternal morbidity and mortality are inevitable dangers pregnant women face. As long as this is a prevalent attitude, the ability to mobilize around the creation and utilization of emergency obstetric facilities will be limited. Consequently, in addition to the programatic actions set forth in the UN Guidelines and legislative measures that accompany them, other appropriate means for governments to undertake in the reduction of maternal mortality include not only education in the narrow behavior-modification sense, but raising consciousness around both the epidemiological realities of maternal mortality and the reality of the human right to the conditions needed to prevent maternal death.

In short, while the UN Guidelines do not exhaust all appropriate means by which governments ought to reduce maternal mortality, they do establish highly specific guideposts for progressive improvement that reflect the connections between maternal mortality and the interventions that have in fact proven to be effective in preventing it. Without such concreteness and specificity, the agenda items for safe motherhood programs set forth in Cairo and Beijing, and referred to in the Maastricht Guidelines, remain a laundry list of unconnected social aspirations that states can continue to ignore, circumvent, or implement selectively.

The Immediate Obligation of Nondiscrimination and Other Reporting Issues

Finally, in addition to setting forth concrete and verifiable measures that indicate whether a given state is taking steps to reduce maternal mortality and whether such steps are appropriate, by measuring the distribution of obstetric facilities and allowing for a framework to compare subnational as well as national populations or geographic regions, the UN Guidelines provide one means of measuring nondiscrimination as part of compliance under international treaties. From a human rights perspective, nondiscrimination in access to effective treatment is a fundamental concern. Moreover, it is not only discrimination against women in access to care which is relevant, but discrimination among different groups of women is relevant as well. While the UN Guidelines cannot be used to detect discriminatory practices on the part of individual providers, they can be used to detect, for example, rural-urban disparities in the progressive realization of the right to be free from maternal mortality that may indicate discrimination against certain populations that disproportionately live in underdeveloped regions.[155]

The ICESCR sets out nondiscrimination as a principle that applies to the fulfillment of all of the rights in the Covenant, including the right to conditions that would assure effective medical treatment in the event of sickness.[156] In jurisprudence, nondiscrimination is considered part of the minimum core content of all of the rights in the ICESCR and applies immediately to all state parties. For example, the Maastricht Guidelines unequivocally state that any discrimination on account "of race, colour, sex, language, religion, political or other opinion, national or social origin, property, birth or other status with the purpose or effect of nullifying or impairing the equal enjoyment or exercise of economic, social and cultural rights constitutes a [per se] violation of the Covenant."[157] Thus, if, hypothetically, it could be documented using the UN Guidelines that a country were providing emergency obstetric coverage to areas in which the majority ethnic group lived while not providing the same levels of coverage to minority ethnic areas, that would constitute a per se violation of the ICESCR.

It goes almost without saying that in practice, it is often the case that discrimination—whether intentional or not—on the basis of ethnicity or social group cannot be disconnected from distorted development policies that favor urban areas over rural ones. Many such development policies have a direct impact on access to and quality of emergency obstetric care. For example, a nationwide study in Morocco in 1989 found that the proportion of births that were by cesarean section was 2.3 percent in urban areas—about one-half of the minimum acceptable level in the UN Guidelines.[158] However, in the rural areas cesarean sections accounted for only 0.4 percent of deliveries.[159] Implicitly acknowledging the difficulty of distinguishing the effects of region or ethnicity, the Cairo Programme asserts "[d]isparities in maternal mortality within countries and between geographical regions, socio-economic and ethnic groups should be narrowed."[160] But the UN Guidelines can be interpreted as going much further, indicating that the disparity between rural and urban rates in Morocco reflects discrimination in the realization of the right to be free from avoidable maternal mortality.[161]

The Women's Convention, of course, relates the right to health services to combating discrimination against women in general. But, more particularly, it also focuses on the need to ensure adequate attention to women in underdeveloped and rural areas. Article 14 of the Women's Convention mandates that:

> States Parties shall take all appropriate measures to eliminate discrimination against women in rural areas in order to ensure, on a basis of equality of men and women, that they participate in and benefit from rural development and, in particular, shall ensure to such women the right . . . [t]o have access to adequate health care facilities, including information, counseling and services in family planning.[162]

Again, by using the UN Guidelines to compare subnational units with respect to the adequacy of healthcare facilities—in terms of the number of Basic and Comprehensive facilities, the percentages of caesarian sections, and the crude "case fatality rate" indicator of quality of care—state parties' compliance with the Article 14 requirement of eliminating such discrimination can be objectively measured.

Like the Maastricht Guidelines for the ICESCR, the Women's Convention has specifically stated in a general recommendation that it is discriminatory *effect* as well as *purpose* which triggers a violation of the treaty.[163] Thus, just as Article 3 of the Women's Convention prohibits legislation that is gender-neutral on its face but has a discriminatory impact on women, legislation on health policy or appropriations for health financing that is neutral on its face, but has a discriminatory impact on rural women in terms of emergency obstetric coverage runs afoul of both the ICESCR and the Women's Convention.[164]

Under both the ICESCR and the Women's Convention, State parties ought to report disaggregated data to respond to the issue of misleading national averages that may mask discriminatory policies or effects. Indeed, the ESC Committee has formulated specific reporting requirements with respect to Article 12 that require state parties to provide detailed, disaggregated data on the physical and mental health of the population.[165] Such reporting would in theory apply to the "[p]roportion of pregnant women having access to trained personnel during pregnancy and proportion attended by such personnel for delivery."[166] This reporting is required under the ICESCR and could (and should) be interpreted in terms of the more objective indicators set forth in the UN Guidelines. The reporting guidelines under the ICESCR also attempt to gather health information on groups whose health status is "significantly worse than that of the majority of the population" and the measures the government has adopted to improve their health status.[167] Similarly, the Seminar on Appropriate Indicators called for "new approaches in data collection, analysis, and interpretation," and noted a need for "a particular focus on the status of the poor and disadvantaged groups, best achieved through disaggregated data. . . ."[168]

In practice, states have complied with the requirement calling for provision of disaggregated data to differing degrees, and in general there has been virtually no way for either UN Committees or nongovernmental organizations to monitor the nondiscrimination provisions of the treaties. In Mexico, for example, the Demographic Health Survey of 1987, the most recent to be publicly released, excluded women of municipalities with 90 percent or more non-Spanish speaking populations. This had the effect of excluding many municipalities that were entirely or predominantly indigenous.[169]

As with national units, the UN Guidelines can be used to specify what constitutes a "lack of obstetric services" in any given subnational area. Moreover, comparisons can be made across regions of the number of Basic and Comprehensive obstetric care facilities per 500,000 persons in the population that will effectively achieve the aim of the reporting requirement regarding proportions of women having access to and attended by trained personnel during pregnancy and delivery. If in certain regions, as opposed to others, minimum levels of services are not in place or if an appropriate number of women with obstetric complications are not treated in such facilities, that would indicate a failure to take steps to reduce maternal mortality on a nondiscriminatory basis and could constitute an outright violation of the state's obligations under international economic and social rights treaties.

However, in order to enforce the nondiscrimination provisions of the treaties, the ESC Committee and the Women's Convention require not only objective measures of whether states are taking steps to reduce maternal mortality on a basis of nondiscrimination, such as the indicators in the UN Guidelines. They also require their collection and sharing by WHO and the UN Specialized Agencies. The reality is that effective economic and social rights monitoring requires processing enormous quantities of medical and scientific information that—particularly in light of the exponential increase in that information generated by using disaggregated data to measure realization on a nondiscriminatory basis—presents a daunting practical challenge to the human rights intergovernmental oversight mechanisms. The ESC Committee, for example, meets only once a year for up to three weeks at a time, during which it reviews reports from six states. The members of the Committee are unpaid and have no staff for research or analysis of the country reports.[170]

In light of these realities, the Seminar on Appropriate Indicators called for the "development of an appropriate information management system, including computerization, for evaluating a complex series of data on a disaggregated and time-series basis."[171] The Seminar went on to suggest cross-referencing with information collected by WHO and other UN Specialized Agencies.[172] WHO, together with other Specialized Agencies, is offered an opportunity to set forth observations with respect to each country report under consideration. All of the Specialized Agencies receive copies of the portions of reports relating to their subject matter expertise and may even submit their own reports on issues within their competence.[173] But, in practice, as Audrey Chapman writes, "[c]urrently WHO sends a staff member to attend some of the [ESC] Committee's sessions, but it does not provide staff services or assistance to the [ESC] Committee nor does WHO seek to collect or evaluate health data on a human rights basis."[174]

One commentator compares the role of WHO with that of the International Labor Organization (ILO) with respect to monitoring of worker's rights:

> [u]nlike the ILO, the WHO does not have a tradition of standard-setting through international agreements or of monitoring country progress . . . [The report it has submitted] merely covers those very issues of generic implementation . . . and ignores the kind of country-specific data which Article 18 calls for from specialized agencies and which the ILO has provided.[175]

The virtually unique consensus among three Specialized Agencies (UNICEF, WHO, and UNFPA) around the use of the UN Guidelines provides an unparalleled opportunity for WHO and the other Specialized Agencies to modify their activities in this respect and to develop such a data management and sharing system with respect to this key aspect of women's right to health. That is, if the data required under the UN Guidelines were reported on a province-by-province basis to the same three agencies, including WHO which already requires information regarding these indicators for maternal mortality at the national level, that data could immediately permit such agencies to assess the equality of steps taken in reducing maternal mortality on a regional or subnational basis.

In turn, maternal mortality presents an ideal test case for developing a formal mechanism for sharing this analysis with human rights-treaty-monitoring committee members. The human rights monitoring bodies would then have a basis for objective judgments about whether state parties are indeed complying with the nondiscrimination provisions of the human rights treaties. Moreover, the health agencies, which would receive training in human rights principles and monitoring, would be able to enhance their work significantly through the power and priority that a human rights discourse brings to bear on the issue of maternal mortality. If not WHO, UNICEF, which was involved in the creation of the UN Guidelines and has already developed a task force to monitor compliance with the Children's Convention, is in a particularly good position to take a leading role in monitoring governmental actions to reduce maternal mortality.

Although clearly requiring a multi-institutional political and financial commitment, such a scheme has the advantage of implementing the often invoked interdisciplinary collaboration around a concrete issue of women's health rather than attempting to construct an elaborate bureaucratic procedure for the abstract goal of monitoring economic and social rights. Finally, the nature of the indicators (i.e., the relative ease of both data collection and analysis) used in the UN Guidelines also facilitates use of the indicators by nongovernmental health and human rights advocates at the local level. Such advocates could use the information in national advocacy campaigns in addition to submitting detailed shadow reports relating to this aspect of the right to health,[176] as is routinely done with civil and political rights monitoring.

In sum, if the relevant language in the Beijing and Cairo Programmes of Action were construed using the UN Guidelines, the human rights community would be far closer to imposing meaningful obligations of conduct with respect to reducing maternal mortality under the ICESCR, the Women's Convention, and analogous regional conventions. Indeed, there are three compelling reasons to adopt the UN Guidelines as standards by which to judge states' compliance with the obligation to reduce maternal mortality. First, the UN Guidelines set out objective, verifiable measures of whether states are taking steps toward the realization of women's right to be free of avoidable maternal mortality. Second, they set forth specific obligations of conduct that can be used to assess whether states are taking such steps by the appropriate means. Finally, the UN Guidelines permit an objective assessment, on the basis of population sub-units, of whether states are taking such steps on a nondiscriminatory basis. Moreover, as a matter of process, because of the unique consensus among UNICEF, WHO, and UNPFA, together with the nature of the indicators themselves, maternal mortality provides the ideal test case to begin to develop a data management system that will encourage interdisciplinary collaboration between the health and human rights bodies of the United Nations.

Conclusion

At the close of the twentieth century, the reduction of maternal mortality to levels where it no longer constitutes a major public health problem is an attainable goal for virtually every area of the world. Yet, too many societies and communities continue to consider maternal death in pregnancy or childbirth "normal" or just another danger that women face in the course of their life-times. Rebecca Cook summarizes the implications of this perspective by stating that "premature death during labor or from weakness or exhaustion due to pregnancy . . . [are] explained as destiny and divine will. Maternal mortality and morbidity . . . therefore, [are still] not considered amenable to control through health services, education, and law."[177]

This chapter first illustrated that the epidemiology behind the UN Guidelines definitively demonstrates that maternal mortality is by no means inevitable; while largely unpredictable and unpreventable, complications arising during pregnancy and delivery are highly treatable with long-established health services. Second, the chapter explained how the UN Guidelines can indeed be translated into law, as binding standards by which to judge state parties' compliance with the provisions of international human rights treaties relating to women's access to healthcare.

As a matter of women's fundamental human rights and dignity, the Cairo Programme of Action called for "[t]he underlying causes of maternal morbidity and mortality [to] be identified" and for "attention [to] be given to the development of strategies [for progress to be made] in reducing maternal mortality and morbidity and to enhance the effectiveness of ongoing programmes."[178] Implicit in the Cairo language is some recognition that the human rights community alone cannot determine either the underlying causes of maternal mortality or the strategies necessary to realize the objectives set forth at Cairo and Beijing. In order to elaborate universal standards for reducing maternal mortality, as well as for other aspects of the right to health, human rights lawyers must turn to the field of epidemiology, a discipline dedicated to the analysis of the determinants and distribution of disease among populations. Indeed, the UN Guidelines, based on the most thorough epidemiologic research to date on the subject, not only go a long way toward establishing which are the appropriate "strategies [for progress to be made] in reducing maternal mortality and morbidity,"[179] they can be used to monitor states' progress in combating maternal mortality as a matter of international human rights law.

Notes

1. Deborah Maine et al., "Risks and Rights: The Uses of Reproductive Health Data," *Reproductive Health Matters,* Nov. 1995, at 40, 40 (1995), *quoting* 2 *Martin Luther,* "The Estate of Marriage," in *The Christian in Society* 46 (Walter I. Brandt, ed., 1962).
2. See Peter Adamson, "A Failure of Imagination," in *The Progress of Nations* 3 (1996). For every woman who dies, an estimated thirty more suffer from debilitating infections and painful, often degrading, conditions that can last a lifetime.
3. See *id.* at 3–4. For a discussion of an upward revision of this estimate, see *id.,* at 8–9.
4. See *World Health Organization & UNICEF, Revised 1990 Estimates of Maternal Mortality: A New Approach* 2 (1996) [hereinafter *Revised 1990 Estimates*].
5. See *id.*

6. The World Bank estimates that in 1990 women lost 29.7 million "disability-adjusted life years" (DALYs) due to maternal causes. Men lost an estimated 17.9 million DALYs to their number one cause, HIV. DALYs are a composite indicator that ascribe weights to certain conditions as well as to varying age ranges in order to calculate the global burden of disease as well as to compare conditions and countries. *The World Bank, World Development Report 1993: Investing in Health* 216, 218 (1993).

7. See Audrey R. Chapman, "Monitoring Women's Right to Health Under the International Covenant on Economic, Social and Cultural Rights," 44 *Am. U.L. Rev.* 1157, 1161 (1995); Rebecca J. Cook, "State Responsibility for Violations of Women's Human Rights," 7 *Harv. Hum. Rts. J.* 125, 157 (1994).

8. Chapman, *supra* note 7, at 1164. See also "Report of the Secretariat: Report of the Seminar on Appropriate Indicators to Measure Achievement in the Progressive Realization of Economic, Social and Cultural Rights," U.N. GAOR, World Conf. on Hum. Rts., Prep. Comm., 4th Sess., Agenda Item 6, U.N. Doc. A/CONF.157/PC/73 (1993) [hereinafter *Report of the Seminar on Appropriate Indicators*].

9. Cf., Scott Leckie, "Another Step Towards Indivisibility: Identifying the Key Features of Violations of Economic, Social and Cultural Rights," 20 *Hum. Rts. Q.* 81 (1998). See also "The New International Economic Order and the Promotion of Human Rights: Realization of Economic, Social and Cultural Rights: Progress Report Prepared by Mr. Danilo Türk, Special Rapporteur," U.N. ESCOR, Subcomm'n on the Prevention of Discrimination and Protection of Minorities, 42d Sess., Prov. Agenda Item 7, at 31, U.N. Doc. E/CN.4/Sub.2/1990/19 (1990).

10. See Deborah Maine et al. *Guidelines for Monitoring Progress in the Reduction of Maternal Mortality: A Work in Progress* (1992) [hereinafter *Guidelines for Reduction*] (on file with authors).

11. See Deborah Maine et al. *Guidelines for Monitoring the Availability and Use of Obstetric Services* (2d ed. 1997) [hereinafter *Guidelines for Availability*].

12. See generally "Report of the Seminar on Appropriate Indicators," *supra* note 8, para. 189 (discussing the need for Specialized Agencies to adopt appropriate indicators to measure human rights implementation).

13. See *The World Bank, supra* note 6, at 216, 218.

14. See *Revised 1990 Estimates, supra* note 4, at 3.

15. See *Population Reference Bureau, 1998 World Population Data Sheet (1998).*

16. See Deborah Maine, *Safe Motherhood Programs: Options and Issues* 9 (1991) [hereinafter *Safe Motherhood Programs*].

17. See *Revised 1990 Estimates, supra* note 4, at 3.

18. See *id.* at 2; *World Health Organization, Mother-Baby Package: Implementing Safe Motherhood in Countries* 2 (1994) [hereinafter *Mother-Baby Package*]. See also Cynthia J. Berg et al. "Pregnancy-Related Mortality in the United States, 1987–1990," 88 *Obstetrics & Gynecology* 161 (1996).

19. Eclampsia is the most severe from of hypertensive disease during pregnancy, characterized by convulsions and coma, and usually fatal if not treated. See F.A. Davis, *Taber's Cyclopedic Medical Dictionary* 448–49 (14th ed. 1981).

20. See *Revised 1990 Estimates, supra* note 4, at 2; *Mother-Baby Package, supra* note 18, at 2; Berg et al. *supra* note 18, at 165.

21. See *Revised 1990 Estimates, supra* note 4, at 2; *Mother-Baby Package, supra* note 18, at 2; Berg et al. *supra* note 18, at 165.

22. See Stanley K. Henshaw, "Induced Abortion: A World Review, 1990," 22 *Fam. Plan. Persp.*, Mar./Apr. 1990, at 76.

23. See *Safe Motherhood Programs, supra* note 16, at 18–41.

24. See *Mother-Baby Package, supra* note 18, at 37.

25. See F. Gary Cunningham et al. *Williams Obstetrics* 615–19 (19th ed. 1996).

26. See Dorothy Nortman, *Parental Age as a Factor in Pregnancy Outcomes and Child Development* 14 (Reports on Population/Family Planning No. 16, 1974).

27. See Kasongo Project Team, "Antenatal Screening for Fetopelvic Dystocias: A Cost Effectiveness Approach to the Choice of Simple Indicators for Use by Auxiliary Personnel," 87 *J. Tropical Med. & Hygiene* 173 (1984).

28. See *id.* at 179.

29. Pre-eclampsia is a hypertensive disease of pregnancy characterized by high blood pressure, headaches, abnormal protein in the urine, and swelling of the face, feet, and hands. This condition usually precedes eclampsia, though not always.

30. See Marion H. Hall et al. "Is Routine Antenatal Care Worth While?," *Lancet,* 12 July 1980, at 78, 79.

31. See Kelsey A. Harrison, "Tropical Obstetrics and Gynaecology: 2. Maternal Mortality," 83 *Transactions Royal Soc'y Tropical Med. & Hygiene* 449, 452 (1989).

32. See Thomas McKeown, *The Role of Medicine: Dream, Mirage or Nemesis?* 29–44 (1976).

33. See Irvine Loudon, *Death in Childbirth: An International Study of Maternal Care and Maternal Mortality, 1800–1950,* at 15 fig. 1.3, 16 fig. 1.4 (1992).

34. See *id.* at 489 fig. 28.3.

35. See 1 *Bureau of the Census, U.S. Department of Commerce, Historical Statistics of the United States: Colonial Times to 1970,* at 360–82 (1976).

36. See *id.*

37. See Loudon, *supra* note 33, at 16.

38. *See id.*

39. Irvine Loudon, "Obstetric Care, Social Class, and Maternal Mortality," 293 *Brit. Med. J.* 606, 608 (1986).

40. *Guidelines for Availability, supra* note 11, at 22.

41. See *Mother-Baby Package, supra* note 18, at xiv.

42. See Richard Jolly, "Social Goals and Economic Reality," in *The Progress of Nations* 1 (1995).

43. A maternal death is defined by the WHO as "the death of a woman while pregnant or within 42 days of termination of pregnancy, irrespective of the duration and the site of the pregnancy, from any cause related to or aggravated by the pregnancy or its management but not from accidental causes." 1 *World Health Organization, Manual of the International Statistical Classification of Diseases, Injuries, and Causes of Death* 764 (1977). Thus, a death from complications of induced abortion is a maternal death, since it is considered to be due to the "management" of the pregnancy.

44. See *Guidelines for Reduction, supra* note 10.

45. See Berg et al. *supra* note 18, at 161.

46. See Wendy Graham et al., "Estimating Maternal Mortality in Developing Countries," *Lancet,* 2 Feb. 1988, at 416.

47. See Cynthia Stantion et al., *DHS Maternal Mortality Indicators: An Assessment of Data Quality and Implications for Data Use* 4 (Demographic & Health Surveys Analytical Report No. 4, 1997).

48. See Mohammed Shahidullah, "The Sisterhood Method of Estimating Maternal Mortality: The Matlab Experience," 26 *Stud. Fam. Plan.* 101 (1995).

49. *Id.*

50. *Id.*

51. A confidence interval is "[a] range of values determined by the degree of presumed random variability in the data, within which the value of the parameter (e.g., a mean) is thought to lie with the specified level of confidence." *A Dictionary of Epidemiology* 21 (John M. Last ed., 1983). The most commonly used level of confidence is 95 percent.

52. *Guidelines for Availability, supra* note 11, at iii.

53. *Id.* at 1–2.

54. *Id.* at 54–72.

55. See *id.* at 35.

56. See *Guidelines for Availability, supra* note 11. National or local health officials may wish to add other levels, such as EOC First Aid, in which only some of the Basic EOC functions are performed.

57. *Guidelines for Availability, supra* note 11, at 26 fig. 12.

58. *Id.* at 22, 26 fig. 12.

59. *Id.* at 27.

60. See Yasmin Ali Haque & Golam Mostafa, *A Review of the Emergency Obstetric Care Functions of Selected Facilities in Bangladesh* 4, 5 (1993).

61. *Id.* at 3, 4 & tbl.1.

62. See *Guidelines for Availability, supra* note 11, at 23–24.

63. The major obstetric complications may include any of the following: hemorrhage (ante-or post-partum); prolonged/obstructed labor; postpartum sepsis; complications of abortion; pre-eclampsia/eclampsia; ectopic pregnancy; and ruptured uterus.

64. See S. Nirupam & E. Alexandra Yuster, "Emergency Obstetric Care: Measuring Availability and Monitoring Progress," 50 *Int'l J. Gynecology & Obstetrics* S79, S82 (Supp. 2 1995).

65. See *id.*

66. See Tessa M. Wardlaw, *Preventing Maternal Deaths: Using Process Indicators for Obstetric Services: Previews* (1997).

67. Cesarean section plays an important role in treating a number of life-threatening complications. With prolonged or obstructed labor (due to such causes as the baby being too large to fit through the birth canal, or the mother being too exhausted to push any longer), cesarean section is needed to save the lives of both the mother and the infant. With eclampsia, the most reliable way to stop the convulsions is to deliver the baby immediately through cesarean. Some cases of hemorrhage (such as placenta previa, where the placenta blocks the entrance to the birth canal) require cesarean section as well.

68. See Francis C. Notzon, "International Differences in the Use of Obstetric Interventions," 263 *JAMA* 3286, 3287 (1990).

69. See Sally C. Clarke & Selma M. Taffel, "Rates of Cesarean and VBAC Delivery, United States, 1994," 23(3) *Birth* 166, (1996).

70. See Nirupam & Yuster, *supra* note 64, at S85.

71. See Haque & Mostafa, *supra* note 60, at 4, 5.

72. See *id.* at 5 tbl.2.

73. Erik M. Nordberg, "Incidence and Estimated Need of Caesarean Section, Inguinal Hernia Repair, and Operation for Strangulated Hernia in Rural Africa," 289 *Brit. Med. J.* 92, 93 (1984).

74. See *Guidelines for Availability, supra* note 11, at 38.

75. See *World Health Organization, Studying Maternal Mortality in Developing Countries Rates and Causes: A Guidebook* (1987).

76. See Prevention of Maternal Mortality Network, "Situation Analyses of Emergency Obstetric Care: Examples from Eleven Operations Research Projects in West Africa," 40 *Soc. Sci. & Med.* 657, 662 (1995).

77. See Diana B. Petitti et al. "In-Hospital Maternal Mortality in the United States: Time Trends and Relation to Method of Delivery," 59 *Obstetrics & Gynecology* 7 (1982).

78. See T. McGinn, "Monitoring and Evaluation of PMM Efforts: What Have We Learned?," 59 *Int'l J. Gynecology & Obstetrics* S245 (Supp. 2 1997).

79. "Convention on the Elimination of All Forms of Discrimination Against Women," adopted 18 Dec. 1979, G.A. Res. 34/180, U.N. GAOR 34th Sess., Supp. No. 46, U.N. Doc. A/34/46 (1980), (entered into force 3 Sept. 1981), reprinted in 19 I.L.M. 33 (1980) [hereinafter "Women's Convention"].

80. *Id.* art. 5(a) (emphasis added).

81. See, e.g., International Covenant on Economic, Social and Cultural Rights, adopted 16 Dec. 1966, G.A. Res. 2200 (XXI), U.N. GAOR, 21st Sess., Supp. No. 16, arts. 12, 15, U.N. Doc. A/6316 (1966), 993 U.N.T.S. 3 (entered into force 3 Jan. 1976) [hereinafter ICESCR].

82. See Women's Convention, *supra* note 79, arts. 2, 3, 5, 12.

83. For example, relevant civil liberties include, but are not limited to: the right to life, liberty, and security of person; the right of equality before the law; the right to privacy; and the right to freedom of movement. See, e.g., International Covenant on Civil and Political Rights, adopted 16 Dec. 1966, G.A. Res. 2200 (XXI), U.N. GAOR, 21st Sess., Supp. No. 16, arts. 3 (right for men and women to equally enjoy rights set forth in Covenant), 6 (right to life), 9 (right to security and liberty of person), 12 (right to freedom of movement), 17 (right to privacy), 26 (right to equality before the law), U.N. Doc. A/6316 (1966), 999 U.N.T.S. 171 (entered into force 23 Mar. 1976) [hereinafter ICCPR].

84. See *World Health Organization, Abortion: A Tabulation of Available Data on the Frequency and Mortality of Unsafe Abortion* 8 (2d ed. 1993).

85. Article 25 of the Universal Declaration of Human Rights stated only: "Everyone has the right to a standard of living adequate for the health and well-being of himself and of his family, including . . . medical care." Universal Declaration of Human Rights, adopted 10

Dec. 1948. G.A. Res. 217A (III), U.N. GAOR, 3rd Sess., (Resolutions, part 1), art. 25, U.N. Doc. A/810 (1948), reprinted in 43 *Am. J. Int'l L.* 127 (Supp. 1949). However, the rights to healthcare and healthy living conditions has been further elaborated and specified in other binding treaties and conference documents.

86. ICESCR, *supra* note 81.
87. International Convention on the Elimination of All Forms of Racial Discrimination, adopted 21 Dec. 1965, 660 U.N.T.S. 195 (entered into force 4 Jan. 1969), reprinted in 5 I.L.M. 352 (1966) [hereinafter CERD].
88. "Convention on the Rights of the Child," adopted 20 Nov. 1989, G.A. Res. 44/25, U.N. GAOR, 44th Sess., Supp. No. 49, U.N. Doc. A/44/49 (1989) (entered into force 2 Sept. 1990), reprinted in 28 I.L.M. 1448 (1989) [hereinafter "Children's Convention"].
89. *Id.* art. 1.
90. ICESCR, *supra* note 81, art. 12(1).
91. *Id.* art. 12(2)(d).
92. *Id.* art. 10(2).
93. Women's Convention, *supra* note 79, art. 12(1).
94. *Id.* art. 12(2).
95. Brigit C.A. Toebes, *The Right to Health as a Human Right in International Law,* Annex 1, para. 4(g) (1999).
96. ICESCR, *supra* note 81, art. 12(2)(d). Note that the ICESCR Reporting Guidelines also require "proportions of the population having access to trained personnel for the treatment of common diseases . . . within one hour's walk or travel." However, this requirement appears to refer to primary healthcare and not, in any event, to maternal complications which are addressed separately. *Toebes, supra* note 95, Annex 1, para. 4(f).
97. Women's Convention, *supra* note 79, art. 12(2).
98. For example, note the classic statement of the rule for establishing negligence in a tort case: "Consequences which follow in unbroken sequence, without an intervening efficient cause, from the original negligent act, are natural and proximate; and for such consequences the original wrongdoer is responsible, even though he could not have foreseen the particular results which did follow." *Christianson v. Chicago,* St. Paul, Minneapolis & Omaha Ry. Co., 69 N.W. 640, 641 (Minn. 1896). cf.. *Palsgraf v. Long Island R.R. Co.,* 162 N.E. 99 (N.Y. 1928) (holding that a negligence finding requires a duty of care on the part of the defendant as well as proximate causation).
99. Note that the case fatality rate is not the same as the "hospital maternal mortality rate," which is calculated by dividing maternal deaths by all deliveries or admissions. Calculating and reporting the "hospital maternal mortality rate" implies that women in the hospital are a representative sample of women in the community, which is simply not true. For a discussion of referral bias in hospitals and the effect on calculating maternal mortality indicators, see *Guidelines for Availability, supra* note 11.
100. *See* Chapman, *supra* note 7, at 1158.
101. ICESCR, *supra* note 81, art. 2(1). See also Children's Convention, *supra* note 88, art. 4 (stating that "States Parties shall undertake all appropriate legislative, administrative, and other measures for the implementation of the rights recognized in this Convention."); African Charter on Human and Peoples' Rights, adopted 26 June 1981, O.A.U. Doc. CAB/LEG/67/3 Rev. 5 (entered into force 21 Oct. 1986) reprinted in 21 I.L.M. 58 (1982); Additional Protocol to the American Convention on Human Rights in the Area of Economic, Social and Cultural Rights ("Protocol of San Salvador"), signed 17 Nov. 1988, O.A.S.T.S. No. 69, reprinted in *Organization of American States, Basic Documents Pertaining to Human Rights in the Inter-American System,* O.A.S. Doc. OEA/Ser.L.V/II.82, doc. 6, rev. 1, at 67 (1992).
102. Women's Convention, *supra* note 79, art. 12(1).
103. ICCPR, *supra* note 83, art. 2(1).
104. "The Limburg Principles on the Implementation of the International Covenant on Economic, Social and Cultural Rights," adopted 8 Jan. 1987, U.N. ESCOR, Comm'n on Hum. Rts., 43rd Sess., Agenda Item 8, U.N. Doc. E/CN.4/1987/17/Annex (1987), reprinted in "The Limburg Principles on the Implementation of the International Covenant on Economic, Social and Cultural Rights," 9 *Hum. Rts. Q.* 122 (1987).

In 1986 an important meeting of 29 human rights experts was convened by the International Commission of Jurists, the Faculty of Law of the University of Limburg (Maastricht, the Netherlands) and the Urban Morgan Institute of Human Rights, Univer-sity of Cincinnati (Ohio, USA). That meeting produced the Limburg Principles on the Implementation of the International Covenant on Economic, Social and Cultural Rights (the Limburg Principles). See "Symposium: The Implementation of the International Covenant on Economic, Social and Cultural Rights: Introduction," 9 *Hum. Rts. Q.* 121 (1987). *See also* Philip Alston & Gerard Quinn, "The Nature and Scope of States States Parties' Obligations Under the International Convenant on Economic, Social and Cultural Rights," 9 *Hum. Rts. Q.* 156, 158 (1987) (examining "the nature and scope of the obligations of states parties under Parts I, II, and III of the Covenant.").

105. "The Maastricht Guidelines On Violations of Economic, Social and Cultural Rights," para. 8, 20 *Hum. Rts. Q.* 691, 694 (1998) [hereinafter Maastricht Guidelines]. Ten years after the Limburg Principles were articulated, in January of 1997, another group of human rights experts convened by the same institutions and met in Maastricht to elaborate guidelines to further clarify the Limburg Principles (Maastricht Guidelines), given a dramatically changed world order and the significant work that the Economic, Social and Cultural Rights Committee had managed to accomplish in the intervening decade.

106. *Id.*

107. For a comprehensive discussion of the nature of states' discretion in determining maximum available resources and a proposal to limit such discretion, see Robert E. Robertson, "Measuring State Compliance with the Obligation to Devote the "Maximum Available Resources" to Realizing Economic, Social and Cultural Rights," 16 *Hum. Rts. Q.* 693 (1994).

108. "Compilation of General Comments and General Recommendations Adopted by Human Rights Treaty-bodies: Note by the Secretariat," para. 10, U.N. Doc. HRI/Gen/1 (1992).

109. *Id.*

110. See *Toebes, supra* note 95, Annex 1.

111. Maastricht Guidelines, *supra* note 105, para. 9.

112. *Id.* para. 10.

113. ICCPR, *supra* note 83, arts. 9, 25.

114. Maastricht Guidelines, supra note 105, para. 7. For a discussion of obligations typologies, see Aart Hendriks, "The Right to Health: Promotion and Protection of Women's Right to Sexual and Reproductive Health Under International Law: The Economic Covenant and the Women's Convention," 44 *Am. U.L. Rev.* 1123, 1135–38 (1995).

115. Cook, *supra* note 7, at 163.

116. See *id.* at 163–64; Women's Convention, *supra* note 79, art. 2(a).

117. See Maastricht Guidelines, *supra* note 105, para. 7.

118. "Programme of Action of the International Conference on Population and Development: Report of the International Conference on Population and Development," U.N. GAOR, 29th Sess., U.N. Doc. A/CONF. 171/13 (1994) [hereinafter "Cairo Programme"].

119. "Action for Equality, Development, and Peace: Beijing Declaration and Platform for Action," U.N. GAOR, Fourth World Conf. On Women, U.N. Doc. A/CONF.177/20 (1995), reprinted in *Report of the Fourth World Conference on Women* (1995) (recommended to the UN General Assembly by the Committee on the Status of Women on 7 Oct. 1995) [hereinafter Beijing Declaration].

120. Maastricht Guidelines, *supra* note 105, para. 7.

121. *Id.* While non-binding, to the extent that a large number of states signs onto declarations such as those emerging from the Cairo and Beijing Conferences and adhere to them, they become evidence of trends in developing aspirations and beliefs, as well as of the practice of states in that how states vote and what they declare is a form of state practice. Such declarations, together with non-binding General Assembly Resolutions, fill in some of the substantive content not covered by other secondary sources of international law.

122. See Chapman, *supra* note 7, at 1164.

123. *Guidelines for Availability, supra* note 11, at 1.

124. ICESCR, *supra* note 81, arts. 2 (1)–(2).

125. "Report of the Seminar on Appropriate Indicators," *supra* note 8, para. 126–27.

126. One scholar in particular has suggested that rather than continuing to elaborate unenforceable progressive ideals for rights, the ESC Committee ought to begin amassing a jurisprudence of clearcut violations of minimum levels of rights in order to shame violators into compliance. See Audrey R. Chapman, A "'Violations Approach' for Monitoring the International Covenant on Economic, Social Social and Cultural Rights," 18 *Hum. Rts. Q.* 23 (1996). Thus, if the minimums set out in the UN Guidelines were not met, the state in question would be in violation of the relevant treaty.

127. ICESCR, *supra* note 81, art. 2(1).

128. See Alicia Ely Yamin, "Reflections on Defining, Understanding, and Measuring Poverty In Terms Terms of Violations of Economic and Social Rights Under International Law," 4 *Geo. J. on Fighting Poverty* 273 (1997).

129. Cairo Programme, *supra* note 118, para. 8.21.

130. *Id.* para. 8.20.

131. Some state parties to the ICESCR have included data on maternal deaths but the reliability of such information is unknown. *See, e.g.,* Reports of Ecuador, U.N. Doc. E/1986/3/Add.14; Uruguay, U.N. Doc. E/1990/5/Add.7, para. 206; South Korea, UN Doc. E/1990/5/Add. 19, para. 414. See also *Toebes, supra* note 95, at 111. In fact, Mali was condemned by the ESC Committee in 1994 for having one of the highest maternal mortality rates in the world (1,000 per 100,000 live births). See *Concluding Observations Regarding Mali, Principal Subjects of Concern*, U.N. ESCOR, Comm. on Econ., Soc. & Cult. Rts., para. 13, UN Doc. E/C.12/1994/17 (1994).

132. See UNICEF, *State of the World's Children* 1996, at 93 (1996).

133. See UNICEF, *Mexico and the World Summit for Children: Advances in Maternal Child Health 1980–1994*, at 25 (1995).

134. See *Revised 1990 Estimates, supra* note 4, at 2–4. Cross-national comparisons are equally problematic using rates and ratios. For example, in 1988, the ESC Committee noted that Romania's maternal mortality rate was "eight times the Bulgarian rate, ten times the Polish rate, and fifteen times the Austrian rate." *Toebes, supra* note 95, at 114 (quoting Committee Member Mr. Simma). While the Romanian figures were appalling, such comparisons cannot be made due to methodological differences. See *Mr. Simma With Regard to Romania*, U.N. ESCOR, Comm. on Econ., Soc. & Cult. Rts., para. 16, UN Doc. E/C.12/1988/SR.6 (1988).

135. See "Report of the Seminar on Appropriate Indicators," *supra* note 8, para. 144.

136. Beijing Declaration, *supra* note 119, para. 104.

137. See *United Nations, Demographic Yearbook* 354–57 (3rd ed. 1991).

138. Maastricht Guidelines, *supra* note 105, para. 7.

139. Cairo Progamme, *supra* note 118, para. 8.24.

140. See generally *Safe Motherhood Programs, supra* note 16.

141. The epidemiology behind the UN Guidelines reveals the fallacy of assuming that power over one's well-being is derived from individual control over one's immediate conduct. On the contrary, it is having the structural conditions for the treatment of unexpected complications in place, together with the community's knowledge that they are, that set the scene for an individual pregnant woman to experience any degree of power over her health and life when pregnant and that forms the basis for the state's obligation with respect to reducing maternal mortality. See Alicia Ely Yamin, "Defining Questions: Situating Issues of Power in the Formulation of A Right to Health under International Law," 18 *Hum. Rts. Q.* 398 (1996).

142. Cairo Programme, *supra* note 118, para. 8.26.

143. Contrast the programs currently supported by many governments that focus on reducing high-risk pregnancies. Examples of programs are those that provide women who are over a certain age or have a certain number of children incentives to become sterilized. *Id.*

144. Beijing Platform, *supra* note 119, para. 90.

145. *Id.* para. 196.

146. *Id.* para. 106(c)-(e).

147. See Alicia Ely Yamin et al., *Physicians for Human Rights, Health Care Held Hostage: Violations of Human Rights and Medical Neutrality in Chiapas, Mexico* 29 (1999).

148. See Pan-American Health Organization, *Mexico Undergoing Health Sector Reform* 202 (1996) (on file with authors).

149. See *Mexican Ministry of Health, Evaluación 1996* 85–87 (1997) (on file with authors).

150. *Id.*

151. Interview by Alicia Ely Yamin with Flor Maria Perez and Carlos Burguete, Coordinación de Organizaciones No-gubernmentales por la Paz, San Cristobal de las Casas, Chiapas, Mexico (Aug. 5, 1997).

152. The World Bank avoids involving itself with civil and political rights, but does not apparently construe its Articles of Agreement to limit its involvement in the promotion of economic rights. cf.. Daniel D. Bradlow & Claudio Grossman, "Limited Mandates and Intertwined Problems: A New Challenge for the World Bank and the IMF," 17 Hum. Rts. Q. 411 (1995) (discussing obligations of international financial institutions to incorporate human rights concerns into lending policies).

153. *Toebes, supra* note 95, Annex 1, para. 11.

154. See *id.*

155. Discriminatory practices by providers who are regulated by the state could be monitored under civil rights provisions of various treaties.

156. ICESCR, *supra* note 81, art. 12(2)(d).

157. Maastricht Guidelines, *supra* note 105, para. 11.

158. See Institut National d'Administration Sanitaire (INAS), *Approche de la Mortality et de Morbidite Maternelles au Maroc* (1992).

159. See *id.*

160. Cairo Programme, *supra* note 118, para. 8.21.

161. Note that the ESC Committee has made reference to urban and rural disparities in healthcare generally in Morocco. See "Concluding Observations, Suggestions and Recommendations Regarding Morocco," U.N. ESCOR, Comm. on Econ., Soc. & Cult. Rts., para. 18, U.N. Doc. E/C.12/1994/5 (1994). See also *Toebes, supra* note 95, at 120.

162. Women's Convention, *supra* note 79, art. 14(2), (2)(b).

163. *Toebes, supra* note 95, Annex 1; Maastricht Guidelines, *supra* note 105.

164. Women's Convention, *supra* note 79, art. 3. See also Cook, *supra* note 7, at 165.

165. "The Nature of States Parties Obligations," General Comment No. 3, U.N. ESCOR, Comm. on Econ., Soc. & Cult. Rts., 5th Sess., Supp. No. 3, at 83, U.N. Doc. E/1991/23-E/C.12/1990/8 (1991). See also *Toebes, supra* note 95, Annex 2.

166. *Toebes, supra* note 95, Annex 2, para. 4(f).

167. *Id.* para. 5.

168. "Report of the Seminar on Appropriate Indicators," *supra* note 8, para. 160.

169. See Mexican Ministry of Health, *National Survey on Health and Fertility in Mexico 1987* (1989).

170. See "Provisional Rules of Procedure Adopted by the Committee at Its Third Session (1989)," U.N. ESCOR, Comm. on Econ., Soc. & Cult. Rts., 8th Sess., para. (d), U.N. Doc. E/C.12/1990/4/Rev. 1 (1993). The Women's Convention faces similar obstacles.

171. "Report of Seminar on Appropriate Indicators," *supra* note 8, para. 187.

172. *Id.*

173. See ICESCR, *supra* note 81, arts. 16(2), 18.

174. Chapman, *supra* note 7, at 1168.

175. Minnesota Advocates for Human Rights, *Global Child Survival: A Human Rights Priority* 70 (1998). See also Virginia A. Leary, "Lessons from the Experience of the International Labour Organisation," in *The United Nations and Human Rights: A Critical Appraisal* 580 (Philip Alston ed., 1992).

176. NGO advocates could also use this information to raise questions for the ESC Committee or the Women's Convention to follow up on with the state parties during pre-sessional working groups.

177. Rebecca J. Cook, "International Human Rights and Women's Reproductive Health," 24 *Stud. Fam. Plan.* 73 (1993).

178. Cairo Programme, *supra*, note 118, para. 8.22. Note that "underlying causes" language has historically been used in health literature to refer to nutrition and education.

179. *Id.*

VII

The Human Right to Health

This part focuses on a core substantive issue in health and human rights, the right to health itself. The right to health as understood in international human rights law is defined in article 25 of the Universal Declaration of Human Rights (UDHR) and article 12 of the International Covenant on Economic, Social and Cultural Rights (ICESCR), and is supplemented by the variations and further elaborations of these definitions in numerous other UN and regional human rights treaties. Competent international bodies and domestic courts have interpreted these provisions, expanding our understanding of the content of the right to health. The selections in this part are designed to illustrate both levels of elaboration and interpretation.

First, at the international level, the principal international reference document, article 12 of the ICESCR, was interpreted in 2000 in a General Comment on the Right to Health by the Committee on Economic, Social and Cultural Rights (CESCR), created to monitor the ICESCR. That text, reproduced as the first chapter in this part, analyzes the normative content of the right in terms of accessibility, affordability, appropriateness, and quality of care, and specified the duties of the state to respect, protect, and fulfill this right (paras. 34–37). It also lists the following 14 human rights as "integral components of the right to health": "the rights to food, housing, work, education, human dignity, life, non-discrimination, equality, the prohibition against torture, privacy, access to information, and the freedoms of association, assembly and movement." (para. 3) In other words, these related rights identify, in human rights language, many of the recognized underlying determinants of health. The General Comment is not a binding document; it is rather guidance provided by the independent experts elected to the CESCR by the states parties to the ICESCR to help them fulfill their obligations. In light of its centrality to current efforts to understand the relationship between health and human rights, it is the only official document of an intergovernmental body included in this volume.

The most significant international development since the General Comment was the adoption by the UN Commission on Human Rights on 22 April 2002 of a resolution, proposed by Brazil, on "the right of everyone to the enjoyment of the highest attainable standard of physical and mental health."[1] Through that resolution, the Commission decided to appoint, for a period of three years, a special rapporteur on the right to health, with the following mandate:

(a) To gather, request, receive and exchange information from all relevant sources, including Governments, intergovernmental organizations and non-governmental organizations, on the realization of the right of everyone to the enjoyment of the highest attainable standard of physical and mental health;

(b) To develop a regular dialogue and discuss possible areas of cooperation with all relevant actors, including Governments, relevant United Nations bodies, specialized agencies and programmes, in particular the World Health Organization and the Joint United Nations Programme on HIV/AIDS, as well as non-governmental organizations and international financial institutions;

(c) To report on the status, throughout the world, of the realization of the right of everyone to the enjoyment of the highest attainable standard of physical and mental health, in accordance with the provisions of the instruments listed in paragraph 4 above, and on developments relating to this right, including on laws, policies and good practices most beneficial to its enjoyment and obstacles encountered domestically and internationally to its implementation;

(d) To make recommendations on appropriate measures to promote and protect the realization of the right of everyone to the enjoyment of the highest attainable standard of physical and mental health, with a view to supporting States' efforts to enhance public health.

In his first report, the Special Rapporteur, Paul Hunt, defined the "contours and content" of the right to health, noting that "right to health is an inclusive right, extending not only to timely and appropriate health care, but also to the underlying determinants of health, such as access to safe and potable water and adequate sanitation, healthy occupational and environmental conditions, and access to health-related education and information, including on sexual and reproductive health."[2] He further noted, "the right to health contains both freedoms and entitlements" including "the right to control one's health" and "the right to a system of health protection."[3]

At the national level, much can be learned from the efforts of domestic courts to interpret and apply the provisions on the right to health in national constitutions that are directly influenced by the international definition of the right to health. We provide two examples. The first, by George Annas, considers how the Treatment Action Campaign brought a case in South Africa on behalf of women who were not receiving treatment to prevent mother-to-child transmission of HIV, a case which was finally decided by the Constitutional Court. Mary Ann Torres provides the other example—also relating to access to HIV/AIDS treatment—in a case brought by and organization of people living with HIV/AIDS in Venezuela to receive ARV therapies through the health system. In both cases, the right to health was vindicated judicially as a result of an NGO initiative. Such cases are rare but may stimulate similar national advances in the right to health, notwithstanding initial efforts by the governments concerned to avoid implementing a court's judgment. The longer-term impact of these judgments will largely depend on civil society's strategies to mobilize for the realization of the right to health.

Notes

1. The Right of Everyone to the Enjoyment of the Highest Attainable Standard of Physical and Mental Health, Commission on Human Rights, Resolution 2002/31, April 22, 2002.
2. Preliminary Report of the UN Special Rapporteur on the Right to Health, U.N. doc. E/CN.4/2003/58 of February 13, 2003, para. 23.
3. Ibid., para 24.

22

General Comment No. 14 (2000)

The Right to the Highest Attainable Standard of Health (Article 12 of the International Covenant on Economic, Social, and Cultural Rights)

Committee on Economic, Social, and Cultural Rights

UN doc.E/C.12/2000/4, 4 July 2000

1. Health is a fundamental human right indispensable for the exercise of other human rights. Every human being is entitled to the enjoyment of the highest attainable standard of health conducive to living a life in dignity. The realization of the right to health may be pursued through numerous, complementary approaches, such as the formulation of health policies, or the implementation of health programmes developed by the World Health Organization (WHO), or the adoption of specific legal instruments. Moreover, the right to health includes certain components which are legally enforceable.[1]

2. The human right to health is recognized in numerous international instruments. Article 25.1 of the Universal Declaration of Human Rights affirms: "Everyone has the right to a standard of living adequate for the health of himself and of his family, including food, clothing, housing and medical care and necessary social services." The International Covenant on Economic, Social and Cultural Rights provides the most comprehensive article on the right to health in international human rights law. In accordance with article 12.1 of the Covenant, States parties recognize "the right of everyone to the enjoyment of the highest attainable standard of physical and mental health," while article 12.2 enumerates, by way of illustration, a number of "steps to be taken by the States parties . . . to achieve the full realization of this right." Additionally, the right to

health is recognized, *inter alia*, in article 5 (e) (iv) of the International Convention on the Elimination of All Forms of Racial Discrimination of 1965, in articles 11.1 (f) and 12 of the Convention on the Elimination of All Forms of Discrimination against Women of 1979 and in article 24 of the Convention on the Rights of the Child of 1989. Several regional human rights instruments also recognize the right to health, such as the European Social Charter of 1961 as revised (art. 11), the African Charter on Human and Peoples' Rights of 1981 (art. 16) and the Additional Protocol to the American Convention on Human Rights in the Area of Economic, Social and Cultural Rights of 1988 (art. 10). Similarly, the right to health has been proclaimed by the Commission on Human Rights,[2] as well as in the Vienna Declaration and Programme of Action of 1993 and other international instruments.[3]

3. The right to health is closely related to and dependent upon the realization of other human rights, as contained in the International Bill of Rights, including the rights to food, housing, work, education, human dignity, life, non-discrimination, equality, the prohibition against torture, privacy, access to information, and the freedoms of association, assembly and movement. These and other rights and freedoms address integral components of the right to health.

4. In drafting article 12 of the Covenant, the Third Committee of the United Nations General Assembly did not adopt the definition of health contained in the preamble to the Constitution of WHO, which conceptualizes health as "a state of complete physical, mental and social well-being and not merely the absence of disease or infirmity." However, the reference in article 12.1 of the Covenant to "the highest attainable standard of physical and mental health" is not confined to the right to health care. On the contrary, the drafting history and the express wording of article 12.2 acknowledge that the right to health embraces a wide range of socio-economic factors that promote conditions in which people can lead a healthy life, and extends to the underlying determinants of health, such as food and nutrition, housing, access to safe and potable water and adequate sanitation, safe and healthy working conditions, and a healthy environment.

5. The Committee is aware that, for millions of people throughout the world, the full enjoyment of the right to health still remains a distant goal. Moreover, in many cases, especially for those living in poverty, this goal is becoming increasingly remote. The Committee recognizes the formidable structural and other obstacles resulting from international and other factors beyond the control of States that impede the full realization of article 12 in many States parties.

6. With a view to assisting States parties' implementation of the Covenant and the fulfilment of their reporting obligations, this General Comment focuses on

the normative content of article 12 (Part I), States parties' obligations (Part II), violations (Part III) and implementation at the national level (Part IV), while the obligations of actors other than States parties are addressed in Part V. The General Comment is based on the Committee's experience in examining States parties' reports over many years.

I. Normative Content of Article 12

7. Article 12.1 provides a definition of the right to health, while article 12.2 enumerates illustrative, non-exhaustive examples of States parties' obligations.

8. The right to health is not to be understood as a right to be *healthy*. The right to health contains both freedoms and entitlements. The freedoms include the right to control one's health and body, including sexual and reproductive freedom, and the right to be free from interference, such as the right to be free from torture, non-consensual medical treatment and experimentation. By contrast, the entitlements include the right to a system of health protection which provides equality of opportunity for people to enjoy the highest attainable level of health.

9. The notion of "the highest attainable standard of health" in article 12.1 takes into account both the individual's biological and socio-economic preconditions and a State's available resources. There are a number of aspects which cannot be addressed solely within the relationship between States and individuals; in particular, good health cannot be ensured by a State, nor can States provide protection against every possible cause of human ill health. Thus, genetic factors, individual susceptibility to ill health and the adoption of unhealthy or risky lifestyles may play an important role with respect to an individual's health. Consequently, the right to health must be understood as a right to the enjoyment of a variety of facilities, goods, services and conditions necessary for the realization of the highest attainable standard of health.

10. Since the adoption of the two International Covenants in 1966 the world health situation has changed dramatically and the notion of health has undergone substantial changes and has also widened in scope. More determinants of health are being taken into consideration, such as resource distribution and gender differences. A wider definition of health also takes into account such socially-related concerns as violence and armed conflict.[4] Moreover, formerly unknown diseases, such as Human Immunodeficiency Virus and Acquired Immunodeficiency Syndrome (HIV/AIDS), and others that have become more widespread, such as cancer, as well as the rapid growth of the world population, have created new obstacles for the realization of the right to health which need to be taken into account when interpreting article 12.

11. The Committee interprets the right to health, as defined in article 12.1, as an inclusive right extending not only to timely and appropriate health care but also to the underlying determinants of health, such as access to safe and potable water and adequate sanitation, an adequate supply of safe food, nutrition and housing, healthy occupational and environmental conditions, and access to health-related education and information, including on sexual and reproductive health. A further important aspect is the participation of the population in all health-related decision-making at the community, national and international levels.

12. The right to health in all its forms and at all levels contains the following interrelated and essential elements, the precise application of which will depend on the conditions prevailing in a particular State party:

(a) *Availability*. Functioning public health and health-care facilities, goods and services, as well as programmes, have to be available in sufficient quantity within the State party. The precise nature of the facilities, goods and services will vary depending on numerous factors, including the State party's developmental level. They will include, however, the underlying determinants of health, such as safe and potable drinking water and adequate sanitation facilities, hospitals, clinics and other health-related buildings, trained medical and professional personnel receiving domestically competitive salaries, and essential drugs, as defined by the WHO Action Programme on Essential Drugs.[5]

(b) *Accessibility*. Health facilities, goods and services[6] have to be accessible to everyone without discrimination, within the jurisdiction of the State party. Accessibility has four overlapping dimensions:

Non-discrimination: health facilities, goods and services must be accessible to all, especially the most vulnerable or marginalized sections of the population, in law and in fact, without discrimination on any of the prohibited grounds.[7]

Physical accessibility: health facilities, goods and services must be within safe physical reach for all sections of the population, especially vulnerable or marginalized groups, such as ethnic minorities and indigenous populations, women, children, adolescents, older persons, persons with disabilities and persons with HIV/AIDS. Accessibility also implies that medical services and underlying determinants of health, such as safe and potable water and adequate sanitation facilities, are within safe physical reach, including in rural areas. Accessibility further includes adequate access to buildings for persons with disabilities.

Economic accessibility (affordability): health facilities, goods and services must be affordable for all. Payment for health-care services, as well as services related to the underlying determinants of health, has to be based on the principle of equity, ensuring that these services, whether privately or publicly provided, are affordable for all, including socially disadvantaged groups. Equity demands that poorer households should not be disproportionately burdened with health expenses as compared to richer households.

Information accessibility: accessibility includes the right to seek, receive and impart information and ideas[8] concerning health issues. However, accessibility of information should not impair the right to have personal health data treated with confidentiality.

(c) *Acceptability*. All health facilities, goods and services must be respectful of medical ethics and culturally appropriate, i.e., respectful of the culture of individuals, minorities, peoples and communities, sensitive to gender and life-cycle requirements, as well as being designed to respect confidentiality and improve the health status of those concerned.

(d) *Quality*. As well as being culturally acceptable, health facilities, goods and services must also be scientifically and medically appropriate and of good quality. This requires, *inter alia*, skilled medical personnel, scientifically approved and unexpired drugs and hospital equipment, safe and potable water, and adequate sanitation.

13. The non-exhaustive catalogue of examples in article 12.2 provides guidance in defining the action to be taken by States. It gives specific generic examples of measures arising from the broad definition of the right to health contained in article 12.1, thereby illustrating the content of that right, as exemplified in the following paragraphs.[9]

Article 12.2 (a). The Right to Maternal, Child, and Reproductive Health

14. "The provision for the reduction of the stillbirth rate and of infant mortality and for the healthy development of the child" (art. 12.2 (a))[10] may be understood as requiring measures to improve child and maternal health, sexual and reproductive health services, including access to family planning, pre- and postnatal care,[11] emergency obstetric services and access to information, as well as to resources necessary to act on that information.[12]

Article 12.2 (b). The Right to Healthy Natural and Workplace Environments

15. "The improvement of all aspects of environmental and industrial hygiene" (art. 12.2 (b)) comprises, *inter alia*, preventive measures in respect of occupational accidents and diseases; the requirement to ensure an adequate supply of safe and potable water and basic sanitation; the prevention and reduction of the population's exposure to harmful substances such as radiation and harmful chemicals or other detrimental environmental conditions that directly or indirectly impact upon human health.[13] Furthermore, industrial hygiene refers to

the minimization, so far as is reasonably practicable, of the causes of health hazards inherent in the working environment.[14] Article 12.2 (b) also embraces adequate housing and safe and hygienic working conditions, an adequate supply of food and proper nutrition, and discourages the abuse of alcohol, and the use of tobacco, drugs and other harmful substances.

Article 12.2 (c). The Right to Prevention, Treatment, and Control of Diseases

16. "The prevention, treatment and control of epidemic, endemic, occupational and other diseases" (art. 12.2 (c)) requires the establishment of prevention and education programmes for behaviour-related health concerns such as sexually transmitted diseases, in particular HIV/AIDS, and those adversely affecting sexual and reproductive health, and the promotion of social determinants of good health, such as environmental safety, education, economic development and gender equity. The right to treatment includes the creation of a system of urgent medical care in cases of accidents, epidemics and similar health hazards, and the provision of disaster relief and humanitarian assistance in emergency situations. The control of diseases refers to States' individual and joint efforts to, *inter alia*, make available relevant technologies, using and improving epidemiological surveillance and data collection on a disaggregated basis, the implementation or enhancement of immunization programmes and other strategies of infectious disease control.

Article 12.2 (d). The Right to Health Facilities, Goods, and Services[15]

17. "The creation of conditions which would assure to all medical service and medical attention in the event of sickness" (art. 12.2 (d)), both physical and mental, includes the provision of equal and timely access to basic preventive, curative, rehabilitative health services and health education; regular screening programmes; appropriate treatment of prevalent diseases, illnesses, injuries and disabilities, preferably at community level; the provision of essential drugs; and appropriate mental health treatment and care. A further important aspect is the improvement and furtherance of participation of the population in the provision of preventive and curative health services, such as the organization of the health sector, the insurance system and, in particular, participation in political decisions relating to the right to health taken at both the community and national levels.

Article 12. Special Topics of Broad Application
Non-Discrimination and Equal Treatment

18. By virtue of article 2.2 and article 3, the Covenant proscribes any discrimination in access to health care and underlying determinants of health, as well as to means and entitlements for their procurement, on the grounds of race,

colour, sex, language, religion, political or other opinion, national or social origin, property, birth, physical or mental disability, health status (including HIV/AIDS), sexual orientation and civil, political, social or other status, which has the intention or effect of nullifying or impairing the equal enjoyment or exercise of the right to health. The Committee stresses that many measures, such as most strategies and programmes designed to eliminate health-related discrimination, can be pursued with minimum resource implications through the adoption, modification or abrogation of legislation or the dissemination of information. The Committee recalls General Comment No. 3, paragraph 12, which states that even in times of severe resource constraints, the vulnerable members of society must be protected by the adoption of relatively low-cost targeted programmes.

19. With respect to the right to health, equality of access to health care and health services has to be emphasized. States have a special obligation to provide those who do not have sufficient means with the necessary health insurance and health-care facilities, and to prevent any discrimination on internationally prohibited grounds in the provision of health care and health services, especially with respect to the core obligations of the right to health.[16] Inappropriate health resource allocation can lead to discrimination that may not be overt. For example, investments should not disproportionately favour expensive curative health services which are often accessible only to a small, privileged fraction of the population, rather than primary and preventive health care benefiting a far larger part of the population.

Gender Perspective

20. The Committee recommends that States integrate a gender perspective in their health-related policies, planning, programmes and research in order to promote better health for both women and men. A gender-based approach recognizes that biological and socio-cultural factors play a significant role in influencing the health of men and women. The disaggregation of health and socio-economic data according to sex is essential for identifying and remedying inequalities in health.

Women and the Right to Health

21. To eliminate discrimination against women, there is a need to develop and implement a comprehensive national strategy for promoting women's right to health throughout their life span. Such a strategy should include interventions aimed at the prevention and treatment of diseases affecting women, as well as policies to provide access to a full range of high quality and affordable health care, including sexual and reproductive services. A major goal should be reducing women's health risks, particularly lowering rates of maternal mortality

and protecting women from domestic violence. The realization of women's right to health requires the removal of all barriers interfering with access to health services, education and information, including in the area of sexual and reproductive health. It is also important to undertake preventive, promotive and remedial action to shield women from the impact of harmful traditional cultural practices and norms that deny them their full reproductive rights.

Children and Adolescents

22. Article 12.2 (a) outlines the need to take measures to reduce infant mortality and promote the healthy development of infants and children. Subsequent international human rights instruments recognize that children and adolescents have the right to the enjoyment of the highest standard of health and access to facilities for the treatment of illness.[17]

The Convention on the Rights of the Child directs States to ensure access to essential health services for the child and his or her family, including pre- and post-natal care for mothers. The Convention links these goals with ensuring access to child-friendly information about preventive and health-promoting behaviour and support to families and communities in implementing these practices. Implementation of the principle of non-discrimination requires that girls, as well as boys, have equal access to adequate nutrition, safe environments, and physical as well as mental health services. There is a need to adopt effective and appropriate measures to abolish harmful traditional practices affecting the health of children, particularly girls, including early marriage, female genital mutilation, preferential feeding and care of male children.[18] Children with disabilities should be given the opportunity to enjoy a fulfilling and decent life and to participate within their community.

23. States parties should provide a safe and supportive environment for adolescents, that ensures the opportunity to participate in decisions affecting their health, to build life-skills, to acquire appropriate information, to receive counselling and to negotiate the health-behaviour choices they make. The realization of the right to health of adolescents is dependent on the development of youth-friendly health care, which respects confidentiality and privacy and includes appropriate sexual and reproductive health services.

24. In all policies and programmes aimed at guaranteeing the right to health of children and adolescents their best interests shall be a primary consideration.

Older Persons

25. With regard to the realization of the right to health of older persons, the Committee, in accordance with paragraphs 34 and 35 of General Comment No. 6 (1995), reaffirms the importance of an integrated approach, combining

elements of preventive, curative and rehabilitative health treatment. Such measures should be based on periodical check-ups for both sexes; physical as well as psychological rehabilitative measures aimed at maintaining the functionality and autonomy of older persons; and attention and care for chronically and terminally ill persons, sparing them avoidable pain and enabling them to die with dignity.

Persons with Disabilities

26. The Committee reaffirms paragraph 34 of its General Comment No. 5, which addresses the issue of persons with disabilities in the context of the right to physical and mental health. Moreover, the Committee stresses the need to ensure that not only the public health sector but also private providers of health services and facilities comply with the principle of non-discrimination in relation to persons with disabilities.

Indigenous Peoples

27. In the light of emerging international law and practice and the recent measures taken by States in relation to indigenous peoples,[19] the Committee deems it useful to identify elements that would help to define indigenous peoples' right to health in order better to enable States with indigenous peoples to implement the provisions contained in article 12 of the Covenant. The Committee considers that indigenous peoples have the right to specific measures to improve their access to health services and care. These health services should be culturally appropriate, taking into account traditional preventive care, healing practices and medicines. States should provide resources for indigenous peoples to design, deliver and control such services so that they may enjoy the highest attainable standard of physical and mental health. The vital medicinal plants, animals and minerals necessary to the full enjoyment of health of indigenous peoples should also be protected. The Committee notes that, in indigenous communities, the health of the individual is often linked to the health of the society as a whole and has a collective dimension. In this respect, the Committee considers that development-related activities that lead to the displacement of indigenous peoples against their will from their traditional territories and environment, denying them their sources of nutrition and breaking their symbiotic relationship with their lands, has a deleterious effect on their health.

Limitations

28. Issues of public health are sometimes used by States as grounds for limiting the exercise of other fundamental rights. The Committee wishes to emphasize that the Covenant's limitation clause, article 4, is primarily intended to protect the rights of individuals rather than to permit the imposition of limitations by

States. Consequently a State party which, for example, restricts the movement of, or incarcerates, persons with transmissible diseases such as HIV/AIDS, refuses to allow doctors to treat persons believed to be opposed to a government, or fails to provide immunization against the community's major infectious diseases, on grounds such as national security or the preservation of public order, has the burden of justifying such serious measures in relation to each of the elements identified in article 4. Such restrictions must be in accordance with the law, including international human rights standards, compatible with the nature of the rights protected by the Covenant, in the interest of legitimate aims pursued, and strictly necessary for the promotion of the general welfare in a democratic society.

29. In line with article 5.1, such limitations must be proportional, i.e., the least restrictive alternative must be adopted where several types of limitations are available. Even where such limitations on grounds of protecting public health are basically permitted, they should be of limited duration and subject to review.

II. States Parties' Obligations

General Legal Obligations

30. While the Covenant provides for progressive realization and acknowledges the constraints due to the limits of available resources, it also imposes on States parties various obligations which are of immediate effect. States parties have immediate obligations in relation to the right to health, such as the guarantee that the right will be exercised without discrimination of any kind (art. 2.2) and the obligation to take steps (art. 2.1) towards the full realization of article 12. Such steps must be deliberate, concrete and targeted towards the full realization of the right to health.[20]

31. The progressive realization of the right to health over a period of time should not be interpreted as depriving States parties' obligations of all meaningful content. Rather, progressive realization means that States parties have a specific and continuing obligation to move as expeditiously and effectively as possible towards the full realization of article 12.[21]

32. As with all other rights in the Covenant, there is a strong presumption that retrogressive measures taken in relation to the right to health are not permissible. If any deliberately retrogressive measures are taken, the State party has the burden of proving that they have been introduced after the most careful consideration of all alternatives and that they are duly justified by reference to the totality of the rights provided for in the Covenant in the context of the full use of the State party's maximum available resources.[22]

33. The right to health, like all human rights, imposes three types or levels of obligations on States parties: the obligations to *respect, protect* and *fulfill*. In turn, the obligation to fulfill contains obligations to facilitate, provide and promote.[23] The obligation to *respect* requires States to refrain from interfering directly or indirectly with the enjoyment of the right to health. The obligation to *protect* requires States to take measures that prevent third parties from interfering with article 12 guarantees. Finally, the obligation to *fulfill* requires States to adopt appropriate legislative, administrative, budgetary, judicial, promotional and other measures towards the full realization of the right to health.

Specific Legal Obligations

34. In particular, States are under the obligation to *respect* the right to health by, *inter alia*, refraining from denying or limiting equal access for all persons, including prisoners or detainees, minorities, asylum seekers and illegal immigrants, to preventive, curative and palliative health services; abstaining from enforcing discriminatory practices as a State policy; and abstaining from imposing discriminatory practices relating to women's health status and needs. Furthermore, obligations to respect include a State's obligation to refrain from prohibiting or impeding traditional preventive care, healing practices and medicines, from marketing unsafe drugs and from applying coercive medical treatments, unless on an exceptional basis for the treatment of mental illness or the prevention and control of communicable diseases. Such exceptional cases should be subject to specific and restrictive conditions, respecting best practices and applicable international standards, including the Principles for the Protection of Persons with Mental Illness and the Improvement of Mental Health Care.[24]

In addition, States should refrain from limiting access to contraceptives and other means of maintaining sexual and reproductive health, from censoring, withholding or intentionally misrepresenting health-related information, including sexual education and information, as well as from preventing people's participation in health-related matters. States should also refrain from unlawfully polluting air, water and soil, e.g., through industrial waste from State-owned facilities, from using or testing nuclear, biological or chemical weapons if such testing results in the release of substances harmful to human health, and from limiting access to health services as a punitive measure, e.g., during armed conflicts in violation of international humanitarian law.

35. Obligations to *protect* include, *inter alia*, the duties of States to adopt legislation or to take other measures ensuring equal access to health care and health-related services provided by third parties; to ensure that privatization of the health sector does not constitute a threat to the availability, accessibility, acceptability and quality of health facilities, goods and services; to control the

marketing of medical equipment and medicines by third parties; and to ensure that medical practitioners and other health professionals meet appropriate standards of education, skill and ethical codes of conduct. States are also obliged to ensure that harmful social or traditional practices do not interfere with access to pre- and post-natal care and family-planning; to prevent third parties from coercing women to undergo traditional practices, e.g., female genital mutilation; and to take measures to protect all vulnerable or marginalized groups of society, in particular women, children, adolescents and older persons, in the light of gender-based expressions of violence. States should also ensure that third parties do not limit people's access to health-related information and services.

36. The obligation to *fulfill* requires States parties, *inter alia*, to give sufficient recognition to the right to health in the national political and legal systems, preferably by way of legislative implementation, and to adopt a national health policy with a detailed plan for realizing the right to health. States must ensure provision of health care, including immunization programmes against the major infectious diseases, and ensure equal access for all to the underlying determinants of health, such as nutritiously safe food and potable drinking water, basic sanitation and adequate housing and living conditions. Public health infrastructures should provide for sexual and reproductive health services, including safe motherhood, particularly in rural areas. States have to ensure the appropriate training of doctors and other medical personnel, the provision of a sufficient number of hospitals, clinics and other health-related facilities, and the promotion and support of the establishment of institutions providing counselling and mental health services, with due regard to equitable distribution throughout the country. Further obligations include the provision of a public, private or mixed health insurance system which is affordable for all, the promotion of medical research and health education, as well as information campaigns, in particular with respect to HIV/AIDS, sexual and reproductive health, traditional practices, domestic violence, the abuse of alcohol and the use of cigarettes, drugs and other harmful substances. States are also required to adopt measures against environmental and occupational health hazards and against any other threat as demonstrated by epidemiological data. For this purpose they should formulate and implement national policies aimed at reducing and eliminating pollution of air, water and soil, including pollution by heavy metals such as lead from gasoline. Furthermore, States parties are required to formulate, implement and periodically review a coherent national policy to minimize the risk of occupational accidents and diseases, as well as to provide a coherent national policy on occupational safety and health services.[25]

37. The obligation to *fulfill (facilitate)* requires States *inter alia* to take positive measures that enable and assist individuals and communities to enjoy the right to health. States parties are also obliged to *fulfill (provide)* a specific right

contained in the Covenant when individuals or a group are unable, for reasons beyond their control, to realize that right themselves by the means at their disposal. The obligation to *fulfill (promote)* the right to health requires States to undertake actions that create, maintain and restore the health of the population. Such obligations include: (i) fostering recognition of factors favouring positive health results, e.g., research and provision of information; (ii) ensuring that health services are culturally appropriate and that health care staff are trained to recognize and respond to the specific needs of vulnerable or marginalized groups; (iii) ensuring that the State meets its obligations in the dissemination of appropriate information relating to healthy lifestyles and nutrition, harmful traditional practices and the availability of services; (iv) supporting people in making informed choices about their health.

International Obligations

38. In its General Comment No. 3, the Committee drew attention to the obligation of all States parties to take steps, individually and through international assistance and cooperation, especially economic and technical, towards the full realization of the rights recognized in the Covenant, such as the right to health. In the spirit of article 56 of the Charter of the United Nations, the specific provisions of the Covenant (articles 12, 2.1, 22 and 23) and the Alma-Ata Declaration on primary health care, States parties should recognize the essential role of international cooperation and comply with their commitment to take joint and separate action to achieve the full realization of the right to health. In this regard, States parties are referred to the Alma-Ata Declaration which proclaims that the existing gross inequality in the health status of the people, particularly between developed and developing countries, as well as within countries, is politically, socially and economically unacceptable and is, therefore, of common concern to all countries.[26]

39. To comply with their international obligations in relation to article 12, States parties have to respect the enjoyment of the right to health in other countries, and to prevent third parties from violating the right in other countries, if they are able to influence these third parties by way of legal or political means, in accordance with the Charter of the United Nations and applicable international law. Depending on the availability of resources, States should facilitate access to essential health facilities, goods and services in other countries, wherever possible and provide the necessary aid when required.[27] States parties should ensure that the right to health is given due attention in international agreements and, to that end, should consider the development of further legal instruments. In relation to the conclusion of other international agreements, States parties should take steps to ensure that these instruments do not adversely impact upon the right to health. Similarly, States parties have an obligation to ensure

that their actions as members of international organizations take due account of the right to health. Accordingly, States parties which are members of international financial institutions, notably the International Monetary Fund, the World Bank, and regional development banks, should pay greater attention to the protection of the right to health in influencing the lending policies, credit agreements and international measures of these institutions.

40. States parties have a joint and individual responsibility, in accordance with the Charter of the United Nations and relevant resolutions of the United Nations General Assembly and of the World Health Assembly, to cooperate in providing disaster relief and humanitarian assistance in times of emergency, including assistance to refugees and internally displaced persons. Each State should contribute to this task to the maximum of its capacities. Priority in the provision of international medical aid, distribution and management of resources, such as safe and potable water, food and medical supplies, and financial aid should be given to the most vulnerable or marginalized groups of the population. Moreover, given that some diseases are easily transmissible beyond the frontiers of a State, the international community has a collective responsibility to address this problem. The economically developed States parties have a special responsibility and interest to assist the poorer developing States in this regard.

41. States parties should refrain at all times from imposing embargoes or similar measures restricting the supply of another State with adequate medicines and medical equipment. Restrictions on such goods should never be used as an instrument of political and economic pressure. In this regard, the Committee recalls its position, stated in General Comment No. 8, on the relationship between economic sanctions and respect for economic, social and cultural rights.

42. While only States are parties to the Covenant and thus ultimately accountable for compliance with it, all members of society—individuals, including health professionals, families, local communities, intergovernmental and non-governmental organizations, civil society organizations, as well as the private business sector—have responsibilities regarding the realization of the right to health. State parties should therefore provide an environment which facilitates the discharge of these responsibilities.

Core Obligations

43. In General Comment No. 3, the Committee confirms that States parties have a core obligation to ensure the satisfaction of, at the very least, minimum essential levels of each of the rights enunciated in the Covenant, including essential primary health care. Read in conjunction with more contemporary instruments, such as the Programme of Action of the International Conference on Population and Development,[28] the Alma-Ata Declaration provides

compelling guidance on the core obligations arising from article 12. Accordingly, in the Committee's view, these core obligations include at least the following obligations:

(a) To ensure the right of access to health facilities, goods and services on a non-discriminatory basis, especially for vulnerable or marginalized groups;

(b) To ensure access to the minimum essential food which is nutritionally adequate and safe, to ensure freedom from hunger to everyone;

(c) To ensure access to basic shelter, housing and sanitation, and an adequate supply of safe and potable water;

(d) To provide essential drugs, as from time to time defined under the WHO Action Programme on Essential Drugs;

(e) To ensure equitable distribution of all health facilities, goods and services;

(f) To adopt and implement a national public health strategy and plan of action, on the basis of epidemiological evidence, addressing the health concerns of the whole population; the strategy and plan of action shall be devised, and periodically reviewed, on the basis of a participatory and transparent process; they shall include methods, such as right to health indicators and benchmarks, by which progress can be closely monitored; the process by which the strategy and plan of action are devised, as well as their content, shall give particular attention to all vulnerable or marginalized groups.

44. The Committee also confirms that the following are obligations of comparable priority:

(a) To ensure reproductive, maternal (pre-natal as well as post-natal) and child health care;

(b) To provide immunization against the major infectious diseases occurring in the community;

(c) To take measures to prevent, treat and control epidemic and endemic diseases;

(d) To provide education and access to information concerning the main health problems in the community, including methods of preventing and controlling them;

(e) To provide appropriate training for health personnel, including education on health and human rights.

45. For the avoidance of any doubt, the Committee wishes to emphasize that it is particularly incumbent on States parties and other actors in a position to

assist, to provide "international assistance and cooperation, especially economic and technical"[29] which enable developing countries to fulfil their core and other obligations indicated in paragraphs 43 and 44 above.

III. Violations

46. When the normative content of article 12 (Part I) is applied to the obligations of States parties (Part II), a dynamic process is set in motion which facilitates identification of violations of the right to health. The following paragraphs provide illustrations of violations of article 12.

47. In determining which actions or omissions amount to a violation of the right to health, it is important to distinguish the inability from the unwillingness of a State party to comply with its obligations under article 12. This follows from article 12.1, which speaks of the highest attainable standard of health, as well as from article 2.1 of the Covenant, which obliges each State party to take the necessary steps to the maximum of its available resources. A State which is unwilling to use the maximum of its available resources for the realization of the right to health is in violation of its obligations under article 12. If resource constraints render it impossible for a State to comply fully with its Covenant obligations, it has the burden of justifying that every effort has nevertheless been made to use all available resources at its disposal in order to satisfy, as a matter of priority, the obligations outlined above. It should be stressed, however, that a State party cannot, under any circumstances whatsoever, justify its noncompliance with the core obligations set out in paragraph 43 above, which are non-derogable.

48. Violations of the right to health can occur through the direct action of States or other entities insufficiently regulated by States. The adoption of any retrogressive measures incompatible with the core obligations under the right to health, outlined in paragraph 43 above, constitutes a violation of the right to health. Violations through *acts of commission* include the formal repeal or suspension of legislation necessary for the continued enjoyment of the right to health or the adoption of legislation or policies which are manifestly incompatible with pre-existing domestic or international legal obligations in relation to the right to health.

49. Violations of the right to health can also occur through the omission or failure of States to take necessary measures arising from legal obligations. Violations through *acts of omission* include the failure to take appropriate steps towards the full realization of everyone's right to the enjoyment of the highest attainable standard of physical and mental health, the failure to have a national

policy on occupational safety and health as well as occupational health services, and the failure to enforce relevant laws.

Violations of the Obligation to Respect

50. Violations of the obligation to respect are those State actions, policies or laws that contravene the standards set out in article 12 of the Covenant and are likely to result in bodily harm, unnecessary morbidity and preventable mortality. Examples include the denial of access to health facilities, goods and services to particular individuals or groups as a result of de jure or de facto discrimination; the deliberate withholding or misrepresentation of information vital to health protection or treatment; the suspension of legislation or the adoption of laws or policies that interfere with the enjoyment of any of the components of the right to health; and the failure of the State to take into account its legal obligations regarding the right to health when entering into bilateral or multilateral agreements with other States, international organizations and other entities, such as multinational corporations.

Violations of the Obligation to Protect

51. Violations of the obligation to protect follow from the failure of a State to take all necessary measures to safeguard persons within their jurisdiction from infringements of the right to health by third parties. This category includes such omissions as the failure to regulate the activities of individuals, groups or corporations so as to prevent them from violating the right to health of others; the failure to protect consumers and workers from practices detrimental to health, e.g., by employers and manufacturers of medicines or food; the failure to discourage production, marketing and consumption of tobacco, narcotics and other harmful substances; the failure to protect women against violence or to prosecute perpetrators; the failure to discourage the continued observance of harmful traditional medical or cultural practices; and the failure to enact or enforce laws to prevent the pollution of water, air and soil by extractive and manufacturing industries.

Violations of the Obligation to Fulfill

52. Violations of the obligation to fulfill occur through the failure of States parties to take all necessary steps to ensure the realization of the right to health. Examples include the failure to adopt or implement a national health policy designed to ensure the right to health for everyone; insufficient expenditure or misallocation of public resources which results in the non-enjoyment of the right to health by individuals or groups, particularly the vulnerable or marginalized; the failure to monitor the realization of the right to health at the

national level, for example by identifying right to health indicators and benchmarks; the failure to take measures to reduce the inequitable distribution of health facilities, goods and services; the failure to adopt a gender-sensitive approach to health; and the failure to reduce infant and maternal mortality rates.

IV. Implementation at the National Level

Framework Legislation

53. The most appropriate feasible measures to implement the right to health will vary significantly from one State to another. Every State has a margin of discretion in assessing which measures are most suitable to meet its specific circumstances. The Covenant, however, clearly imposes a duty on each State to take whatever steps are necessary to ensure that everyone has access to health facilities, goods and services so that they can enjoy, as soon as possible, the highest attainable standard of physical and mental health. This requires the adoption of a national strategy to ensure to all the enjoyment of the right to health, based on human rights principles which define the objectives of that strategy, and the formulation of policies and corresponding right to health indicators and benchmarks. The national health strategy should also identify the resources available to attain defined objectives, as well as the most cost-effective way of using those resources.

54. The formulation and implementation of national health strategies and plans of action should respect, *inter alia*, the principles of non-discrimination and people's participation. In particular, the right of individuals and groups to participate in decision-making processes, which may affect their development, must be an integral component of any policy, programme or strategy developed to discharge governmental obligations under article 12. Promoting health must involve effective community action in setting priorities, making decisions, planning, implementing and evaluating strategies to achieve better health. Effective provision of health services can only be assured if people's participation is secured by States.

55. The national health strategy and plan of action should also be based on the principles of accountability, transparency and independence of the judiciary, since good governance is essential to the effective implementation of all human rights, including the realization of the right to health. In order to create a favourable climate for the realization of the right, States parties should take appropriate steps to ensure that the private business sector and civil society are aware of, and consider the importance of, the right to health in pursuing their activities.

56. States should consider adopting a framework law to operationalize their right to health national strategy. The framework law should establish national mechanisms for monitoring the implementation of national health strategies and plans of action. It should include provisions on the targets to be achieved and the time-frame for their achievement; the means by which right to health benchmarks could be achieved; the intended collaboration with civil society, including health experts, the private sector and international organizations; institutional responsibility for the implementation of the right to health national strategy and plan of action; and possible recourse procedures. In monitoring progress towards the realization of the right to health, States parties should identify the factors and difficulties affecting implementation of their obligations.

Right to Health Indicators and Benchmarks

57. National health strategies should identify appropriate right to health indicators and benchmarks. The indicators should be designed to monitor, at the national and international levels, the State party's obligations under article 12. States may obtain guidance on appropriate right to health indicators, which should address different aspects of the right to health, from the ongoing work of WHO and the United Nations Children's Fund (UNICEF) in this field. Right to health indicators require disaggregation on the prohibited grounds of discrimination.

58. Having identified appropriate right to health indicators, States parties are invited to set appropriate national benchmarks in relation to each indicator. During the periodic reporting procedure the Committee will engage in a process of scoping with the State party. Scoping involves the joint consideration by the State party and the Committee of the indicators and national benchmarks which will then provide the targets to be achieved during the next reporting period. In the following five years, the State party will use these national benchmarks to help monitor its implementation of article 12. Thereafter, in the subsequent reporting process, the State party and the Committee will consider whether or not the benchmarks have been achieved, and the reasons for any difficulties that may have been encountered.

Remedies and Accountability

59. Any person or group victim of a violation of the right to health should have access to effective judicial or other appropriate remedies at both national and international levels.[30] All victims of such violations should be entitled to adequate reparation, which may take the form of restitution, compensation, satisfaction or guarantees of non-repetition. National ombudsmen, human rights commissions, consumer forums, patients' rights associations or similar institutions should address violations of the right to health.

60. The incorporation in the domestic legal order of international instruments recognizing the right to health can significantly enhance the scope and effectiveness of remedial measures and should be encouraged in all cases.[31] Incorporation enables courts to adjudicate violations of the right to health, or at least its core obligations, by direct reference to the Covenant.

61. Judges and members of the legal profession should be encouraged by States parties to pay greater attention to violations of the right to health in the exercise of their functions.

62. States parties should respect, protect, facilitate and promote the work of human rights advocates and other members of civil society with a view to assisting vulnerable or marginalized groups in the realization of their right to health.

V. Obligations of Actors Other than States Parties

63. The role of the United Nations agencies and programmes, and in particular the key function assigned to WHO in realizing the right to health at the international, regional and country levels, is of particular importance, as is the function of UNICEF in relation to the right to health of children. When formulating and implementing their right to health national strategies, States parties should avail themselves of technical assistance and cooperation of WHO. Further, when preparing their reports, States parties should utilize the extensive information and advisory services of WHO with regard to data collection, disaggregation, and the development of right to health indicators and benchmarks.

64. Moreover, coordinated efforts for the realization of the right to health should be maintained to enhance the interaction among all the actors concerned, including the various components of civil society. In conformity with articles 22 and 23 of the Covenant, WHO, The International Labour Organization, the United Nations Development Programme, UNICEF, the United Nations Population Fund, the World Bank, regional development banks, the International Monetary Fund, the World Trade Organization and other relevant bodies within the United Nations system, should cooperate effectively with States parties, building on their respective expertise, in relation to the implementation of the right to health at the national level, with due respect to their individual mandates. In particular, the international financial institutions, notably the World Bank and the International Monetary Fund, should pay greater attention to the protection of the right to health in their lending policies, credit agreements and structural adjustment programmes. When examining the reports of States parties and their ability to meet the obligations under article 12, the Committee will consider the effects of the assistance provided by all other actors. The adoption of a human rights-based approach by United

Nations specialized agencies, programmes and bodies will greatly facilitate implementation of the right to health. In the course of its examination of States parties' reports, the Committee will also consider the role of health professional associations and other non-governmental organizations in relation to the States' obligations under article 12.

65. The role of WHO, the Office of the United Nations High Commissioner for Refugees, the International Committee of the Red Cross/Red Crescent and UNICEF, as well as non governmental organizations and national medical associations, is of particular importance in relation to disaster relief and humanitarian assistance in times of emergencies, including assistance to refugees and internally displaced persons. Priority in the provision of international medical aid, distribution and management of resources, such as safe and potable water, food and medical supplies, and financial aid should be given to the most vulnerable or marginalized groups of the population.

Adopted on 11 May 2000.

Notes

1. For example, the principle of non-discrimination in relation to health facilities, goods and services is legally enforceable in numerous national jurisdictions.
2. In its resolution 1989/11.
3. The Principles for the Protection of Persons with Mental Illness and for the Improvement of Mental Health Care adopted by the United Nations General Assembly in 1991 (resolution 46/119) and the Committee's General Comment No. 5 on persons with disabilities apply to persons with mental illness; the Programme of Action of the International Conference on Population and Development held at Cairo in 1994, as well as the Declaration and Programme for Action of the Fourth World Conference on Women held in Beijing in 1995 contain definitions of reproductive health and women's health, respectively.
4. Common article 3 of the Geneva Conventions for the protection of war victims (1949); Additional Protocol I (1977) relating to the Protection of Victims of International Armed Conflicts, art. 75 (2) (a); Additional Protocol II (1977) relating to the Protection of Victims of Non-International Armed Conflicts, art. 4 (a).
5. See WHO Model List of Essential Drugs, revised December 1999, WHO Drug Information, vol. 13, No. 4, 1999.
6. Unless expressly provided otherwise, any reference in this General Comment to health facilities, goods and services includes the underlying determinants of health outlined in paras. 11 and 12 (a) of this General Comment.
7. See paras. 18 and 19 of this General Comment.
8. See article 19.2 of the International Covenant on Civil and Political Rights. This General Comment gives particular emphasis to access to information because of the special importance of this issue in relation to health.
9. In the literature and practice concerning the right to health, three levels of health care are frequently referred to: *primary health care* typically deals with common and relatively minor illnesses and is provided by health professionals and/or generally trained doctors working within the community at relatively low cost; *secondary health care* is provided in centres, usually hospitals, and typically deals with relatively common minor or serious illnesses that cannot be managed at community level, using specialty-trained health professionals and doctors, special equipment and sometimes in-patient care at comparatively higher cost; *tertiary health care* is provided in relatively few centres, typically deals with small numbers of minor or serious illnesses requiring specialty-trained health professionals and doctors

and special equipment, and is often relatively expensive. Since forms of primary, secondary and tertiary health care frequently overlap and often interact, the use of this typology does not always provide sufficient distinguishing criteria to be helpful for assessing which levels of health care States parties must provide, and is therefore of limited assistance in relation to the normative understanding of article 12.

10. According to WHO, the stillbirth rate is no longer commonly used, infant and under-five mortality rates being measured instead.

11. *Prenatal* denotes existing or occurring before birth; *perinatal* refers to the period shortly before and after birth (in medical statistics the period begins with the completion of 28 weeks of gestation and is variously defined as ending one to four weeks after birth); *neonatal*, by contrast, covers the period pertaining to the first four weeks after birth; while *postnatal* denotes occurrence after birth. In this General Comment, the more generic terms preand post-natal are exclusively employed.

12. Reproductive health means that women and men have the freedom to decide if and when to reproduce and the right to be informed and to have access to safe, effective, affordable and acceptable methods of family planning of their choice as well as the right of access to appropriate health-care services that will, for example, enable women to go safely through pregnancy and childbirth.

13. The Committee takes note, in this regard, of Principle 1 of the Stockholm Declaration of 1972 which states: "Man has the fundamental right to freedom, equality and adequate conditions of life, in an environment of a quality that permits a life of dignity and well-being," as well as of recent developments in international law, including General Assembly resolution 45/94 on the need to ensure a healthy environment for the well-being of individuals; Principle 1 of the Rio Declaration; and regional human rights instruments such as article 10 of the San Salvador Protocol to the American Convention on Human Rights.

14. ILO Convention No. 155, art. 4.2.

15. See para. 12 (b) and note 8 above.

16. For the core obligations, see paras. 43 and 44 of the present General Comments.

17. Article 24.1 of the Convention on the Rights of the Child.

18. See World Health Assembly resolution WHA47.10, 1994, entitled "Maternal and child health and family planning: traditional practices harmful to the health of women and children."

19. Recent emerging international norms relevant to indigenous peoples include the ILO Convention No. 169 concerning Indigenous and Tribal Peoples in Independent Countries (1989); articles 29 (c) and (d) and 30 of the Convention on the Rights of the Child (1989); article 8 (j) of the Convention on Biological Diversity (1992), recommending that States respect, preserve and maintain knowledge, innovation and practices of indigenous communities; Agenda 21 of the United Nations Conference on Environment and Development (1992), in particular chapter 26; and Part I, paragraph 20, of the Vienna Declaration and Programme of Action (1993), stating that States should take concerted positive steps to ensure respect for all human rights of indigenous people, on the basis of non-discrimination. See also the preamble and article 3 of the United Nations Framework Convention on Climate Change (1992); and article 10 (2) (e) of the United Nations Convention to Combat Desertification in Countries Experiencing Serious Drought and/or Desertification, Particularly in Africa (1994). During recent years an increasing number of States have changed their constitutions and introduced legislation recognizing specific rights of indigenous peoples.

20. See General Comment No. 13, para. 43.

21. See General Comment No. 3, para. 9; General Comment No. 13, para. 44.

22. See General Comment No. 3, para. 9; General Comment No. 13, para. 45.

23. According to General Comments Nos. 12 and 13, the obligation to fulfil incorporates an obligation to *facilitate* and an obligation to *provide*. In the present General Comment, the obligation to fulfil also incorporates an obligation to *promote* because of the critical importance of health promotion in the work of WHO and elsewhere.

24. General Assembly resolution 46/119 (1991).

25. Elements of such a policy are the identification, determination, authorization and control of dangerous materials, equipment, substances, agents and work processes; the provision of health information to workers and the provision, if needed, of adequate protective clothing and equipment; the enforcement of laws and regulations through adequate inspection; the requirement of notification of occupational accidents and diseases, the conduct of inquiries

into serious accidents and diseases, and the production of annual statistics; the protection of workers and their representatives from disciplinary measures for actions properly taken by them in conformity with such a policy; and the provision of occupational health services with essentially preventive functions. See ILO Occupational Safety and Health Convention, 1981 (No. 155) and Occupational Health Services Convention, 1985 (No. 161).

26. Article II, Alma-Ata Declaration, Report of the International Conference on Primary Health Care, Alma-Ata, 6–12 September 1978, in: World Health Organization, "Health for All" Series, No. 1, WHO, Geneva, 1978.

27. See para. 45 of this General Comment.

28. *Report of the International Conference on Population and Development, Cairo, 5–13 September 1994* (United Nations publication, Sales No. E.95.XIII.18), chap. I, resolution 1, annex, chaps. VII and VIII.

29. Covenant, art. 2.1.

30. Regardless of whether groups as such can seek remedies as distinct holders of rights, States parties are bound by both the collective and individual dimensions of article 12. Collective rights are critical in the field of health; modern public health policy relies heavily on prevention and promotion which are approaches directed primarily to groups.

31. See General Comment No. 2, para. 9.

23
The Right to Health and
the Nevirapine Case in South Africa

George J. Annas

Thanks to activists in South Africa, the right to health as a human right has returned to the international stage, just as it was being displaced by economists who see health through the prism of a globalized economy and by politicians who see it as an issue of national security or charity. The current post-apartheid debate in South Africa is not about race but about health, and in this context, the court victory by AIDS activists in the nevirapine case has been termed not only, as stated in one British newspaper, "the greatest defeat for [President Thabo] Mbeki's government" but also the opening of "legitimate criticism" of the government "over a host of issues from land rights to the pursuit of wealth."[1] Using the nevirapine case as a centerpiece, I will explore the power of the human right to health in improving health generally.

Jonathan Mann rightly observed that "health and human rights are inextricably linked,"[2] and Paul Farmer has argued that "the most important question facing modern medicine involves human rights."[3] Farmer noted that many poor people have no access to modern medicine and concluded, "The more effective the treatment, the greater the injustice meted out to those who do not have access to care."[3] Access to treatment for infection with the human immunodeficiency virus (HIV) and AIDS has been problematic in most countries, but especially in South Africa, where almost five million people are infected with HIV and the government's attitude toward the epidemic has been described as pseudoscientific and dangerous.[4] Political resistance by the South African government to outside funders who want to set the country's health care agenda is, of course, understandable in the context of racism and colonialism.[5] But even understandable politics cannot excuse the government's failure to act more decisively in the face of an unprecedented epidemic.

HIV Infection and the Right to Health

One of the most controversial actions of the South African government was its restriction of the use of nevirapine to prevent the transmission of HIV from mothers to infants. Only two government hospitals per province were allowed to use the drug. The Treatment Action Campaign was formed in 1998 as a coalition of South African AIDS-related organizations to promote affordable treatment for all people with HIV infection or AIDS. This group (and others) scored a victory in 2001, when 39 multinational pharmaceutical companies withdrew their lawsuit against the South African government, which sought to enforce their patents on drugs for the treatment of HIV infection or AIDS, in order to prevent the government from purchasing generic versions of the drugs.[6]

At about the same time, the Treatment Action Campaign brought a suit against the South African government itself, alleging that its restrictions on the availability of nevirapine (limiting it in the public sector to hospitals involved in a pilot study) and its failure to have a reasonable plan to make the drug more widely available violated the right to health of HIV-positive pregnant women and their children guaranteed in the South African constitution. The use of nevirapine remains controversial in Africa, even after a study in Uganda, published in 1999, suggested that administering the drug to a pregnant woman at the onset of labor and to her newborn immediately after birth could result in a 50 percent reduction in the rate of transmission of HIV.[7] This is the basis for the claim that failure to use nevirapine condemns 35,000 newborns a year to HIV infection in South Africa.[1]

The Treatment Action Campaign prevailed in the trial court, which ruled that restricting nevirapine to a limited number of pilot sites in the public sector "is not reasonable and is an unjustifiable barrier to the progressive realization of the right to health care."[8] In July 2002, the Constitutional Court of South Africa, the country's highest court, affirmed the ruling, stating that the government's nevirapine policy violated the health care rights of women and newborns under the South African constitution.[9]

Section 27 of the post-apartheid constitution states,

> (1) Everyone has the right to have access to (a) health care services, including reproductive health care; (b) sufficient food and water; and (c) social security. . . . (2) The state must take reasonable legislative and other measures, within its available resources, to achieve the progressive realization of each of these rights. (3) No one may be refused emergency medical treatment." Section 28 states, "(1) Every child has a right . . . (b)

to family care or parental care, or to appropriate alternative care when removed from the family environment; (c) to basic nutrition, shelter, basic health care services and social services. . . . (2) A child's best interests are of paramount importance in every matter concerning the child.[9]

These rights are part of the bill of rights in the South African constitution, which the constitution itself requires the state to "respect, protect, promote and fulfill." These provisions are modeled on those in the International Covenant on Economic, Social and Cultural Rights (which has been signed, but not yet ratified, by South Africa).[10] Under the covenant, the right to health includes not only appropriate health care, but also the underlying determinants of health, including clean water, adequate sanitation, safe food and housing, and health-related education.[11] South Africa's constitutional health obligations apply to every branch of government. The Constitutional Court considered two questions: what actions the government was constitutionally required to take with regard to nevirapine, and whether the government had an obligation to establish a comprehensive plan for the prevention of HIV transmission from mother to child.

Making Nevirapine Available

As justification for its refusal to make nevirapine generally available in public clinics, the South African government has argued that the drug's safety and efficacy have not been satisfactorily established and that it is of limited benefit in a breast-feeding population (since the number of infants acquiring HIV from breast-feeding would be almost as large as the number infected in the absence of preventive treatment with nevirapine). These views have been articulated by the minister of health, who along with President Mbeki, continues to take positions on HIV infection and its treatment that scientists in the rest of the world find baffling.[4,5]

In January 2001, after a meeting of southern African countries, the World Health Organization recommended the administration of nevirapine to HIV-positive women who are pregnant and to their children at the time of birth. In April 2001, the Medicines Control Council, South Africa's equivalent of the Food and Drug Administration, formally approved nevirapine as safe and effective. Shortly thereafter, in July 2001, the government decided to do the pilot study of nevirapine that was at issue in the lawsuit; this study limited the drug's availability to two sites in each province. The result was that physicians who worked at other facilities in the public sector were unable to prescribe this drug for their patients, even though the manufacturer of the drug, Boehringer Ingelheim, had agreed to make it available at no cost for a five-year period.

The Treatment Action Campaign argued that in the face of the HIV epidemic, which includes the infection of approximately 70,000 infants from their mothers annually, it was irrational and a breach of the bill of rights for the government to prohibit physicians in public clinics from prescribing nevirapine for preventive purposes when medically indicated.[9]

Enforcing the Obligation to Respect Rights

This was the third case in which the Constitutional Court had been asked to enforce a socioeconomic right under the South African constitution. The first, *Soobramoney v. Minister of Health*, was also a right-to-health case.[12] It involved a 41-year-old man with chronic renal failure and a history of stroke, heart disease, and diabetes, who was not eligible for a kidney transplant and therefore required lifelong dialysis to survive. The renal-dialysis unit in the region where he lived, which had 20 dialysis machines—not nearly enough to provide dialysis for everyone who required it—had a policy of accepting only patients with acute renal failure. The health department argued that this policy met the government's duty to provide emergency care under the constitution. Patients with chronic renal failure, like the petitioner, did not automatically qualify.

In considering whether the constitution required the health department to provide a sufficient number of machines to offer dialysis to everyone whose life could be saved by it, the court observed that under the constitution, the state's obligation to provide health care services was qualified by its "available resources." The court noted that offering extremely expensive medical treatments to everyone would make "substantial inroads into the health budget . . . to the prejudice of the other needs which the state has to meet."[12] The Constitutional Court ultimately decided that the administrators of provincial health services, not the courts, should set budgetary priorities and that the courts should not interfere with decisions that are rational and made "in good faith by the political organs and medical authorities whose responsibility it is to deal with such matters."[12]

Likewise, in *South Africa v. Grootboom*, a case involving the right to housing, the Constitutional Court determined that although the state is obligated to act positively to ameliorate the conditions of the homeless, it "is not obligated to go beyond available resources or to realize these rights immediately."[13] The constitutional requirement is that the right to housing be "progressively realized." Nonetheless, the court noted, there is "at the very least, a negative obligation placed upon the state and all other entities and persons to desist from preventing or impairing the right of access to adequate housing."[13,14]

Applying the rulings in these two cases to the nevirapine case, the Constitutional Court reasonably concluded that the right to health care services "does not give rise to a self-standing and independent fulfillment right" that is enforceable irrespective of available resources. Nonetheless, the government's obligation to respect rights, as articulated in the housing case, applies equally to the right to health care services.[9]

Enforcing the Obligation to Protect Rights

The Constitutional Court reframed the two questions it would answer in the light of the South African government's obligation to take "reasonable steps" for the "progressive realization" of the right to health as follows: "Is the policy of confining the supply of nevirapine reasonable in the circumstances; and does the government have a comprehensive policy for the prevention of mother-to-child transmission of HIV?"[9]

The South African government argued that the real cost of delivering nevirapine is not the cost of the drug but the cost of the infrastructure of care: HIV testing, counseling, follow-up, and the provision of formula for parents who cannot currently afford it. The Constitutional Court agreed that the ideal is to make these preventive services universally available but restated the dispute as "whether it was reasonable to exclude the use of nevirapine for the treatment of mother-to-child transmission at those public hospitals and clinics where testing and counseling are available."[9]

The South African government gave four reasons for its restriction of the use of nevirapine: its efficacy would be diminished in settings in which a comprehensive package of services, including breast-milk substitutes, was not available; administration of the drug might produce a drug-resistant form of HIV; the safety of nevirapine has not been adequately demonstrated; and the public health system does not have the capacity to deliver the "full package" of services.[9]

The court addressed each point in turn. With respect to efficacy, the court found that breast-feeding does increase the risk of HIV infection "in some, but not all cases and that nevirapine thus remains to some extent efficacious . . . even if the mother breastfeeds her baby."[9] The court conceded that drug resistance is possible but concluded, "The prospects of the child surviving if infected are so slim and the nature of the suffering [is] so grave that the risk of some resistance manifesting at some time in the future is well worth running."[9] The safety issue was disposed of by reference to the World Health Organization's recommendation of nevirapine and the determination of the Medicines Control Council that the drug is safe. As for capacity, the court concluded that resources are relevant to the universal delivery of the "full package" but are "not relevant to the question of whether nevirapine should be used to reduce mother-to-child transmission of HIV at those public hospitals and clinics outside the research sites where facilities in fact exist for testing and counseling."[9]

The Rights of Children and the Obligation to Fulfill Rights

This case is a right to health case because it concerns the availability of a drug and the circumstances under which the government can reasonably restrict its use. Nonetheless, the case could have been decided solely on the basis of the rights of children. In the words of the Constitutional Court, "This case is concerned with newborn babies whose lives might be saved by the administration of nevirapine to mother and child at the time of birth."[9] The court specifically cites the constitutional rights of children, including their right to "basic health care services." Parents have the primary obligation to provide these services to children but often cannot meet this obligation without help from the state.[15] The court concluded that nevirapine is an "essential" drug for children whose mothers are infected with HIV, that the needs of these children are "most urgent," and that their ability to exercise all other rights is "most in peril."[9] The court did not write about the certainty of the children becoming orphans if their mothers do not also have access to treatment, but treatment of HIV infection and AIDS was beyond the scope of this case, which concerned the prevention of HIV infection.

On the basis of either the right to health or the rights of children, the court's answer to the first question was that the policy of restricting the availability of nevirapine is unreasonable and a violation of the government's obligation to take "reasonable legislative and other measures, within its available resources, to achieve the progressive realization" of the right to "access to health care services, including reproductive health care."[9] In the court's words, "A potentially lifesaving drug was on offer and where testing and counseling facilities were available it could have been administered within the available resources of the state without any known harm to mother and child."[9] The question of whether the cost of nevirapine mattered was not addressed, although the outcome almost certainly would have been different had nevirapine not been available at no or very low cost.

The answer to the second question—whether the government is required to have a reasonable, comprehensive plan to combat mother-to-child transmission of HIV—flowed directly from the answer to the first. The legal question was whether the government's plan of moving slowly from limited research and training programs to more available programs was reasonable. The court decided that because of the "incomprehensible calamity" of the HIV epidemic in South Africa, the government's plan was not reasonable.

The Right to the Progressive Realization of Health

Can the Constitutional Court be accused of taking on the role of the South African government's health department in deciding how money should be spent on health care? The court did not think so, pointing out that all branches of the government have the obligation to "respect, protect, promote and fulfill" the socioeconomic rights spelled out in the constitution. The legislative branch is obligated to pass "reasonable legislative" measures, and the executive branch is obligated to develop and implement "appropriate, well-directed policies and programs."[9] It is, of course, the role of the judiciary to resolve disputes about whether a specific law or policy, or its implementation, is consistent with the terms of the constitution. Since the initiation of the nevirapine lawsuit, three of the country's nine provinces—Western Cape, Gauteng, and KwaZulu-Natal—have publicly announced a plan to realize progressively "the rights of pregnant women and their newborn babies to have access to nevirapine."[9] The court expects the other six provinces to follow suit.

The court was explicit both in defining the rights that were violated and in ordering a remedy. As to the rights, the court declared that "Sections 27(1) and (2) of the Constitution require the government to devise and implement within its available resources a comprehensive and coordinated program to realize progressively the rights of pregnant women and their newborn children to have access to health services to combat mother-to-child transmission of HIV."[9] To implement this right, the court ordered the government to take four specific actions:

> Remove the restrictions that prevent nevirapine from being made available at public hospitals and clinics that are not research and training sites.
>
> Permit and facilitate the use of nevirapine at public hospitals and clinics when this is medically indicated.
>
> Make provision if necessary for counselors based at public hospitals and clinics to be trained for counseling.
>
> Take reasonable measures to extend the testing and counseling facilities at hospitals and clinics throughout the public health sector to facilitate and expedite the use of nevirapine.[9]

Implementing the Right to Health

The decision in the nevirapine case illustrates both the strength and the weakness of relying on courts to determine specific applications of the right to health. The strength is that the right to health is a legal right, and since there can be no legal right without a remedy, courts will provide a remedy for violations of the right to health. In this regard, it is worth noting not only that the right to health and access to health care articulated in the Universal Declaration of Human Rights has been given more specific meaning in the International Covenant on Economic, Social and Cultural Rights[10,11] and other internationally binding documents on human rights, but also that these rights have been written into the constitutions of many countries, including South Africa. The widespread failure of governments to take the right to health seriously, however, means that we are still a long way from the realization of this right. Nonetheless, the recent activism of many new nongovernmental organizations, such as the Treatment Action Campaign, in the area of health rights, provides some ground for optimism that government inaction will not go unchallenged.[16]

The weakness of relying on courts is that the subject matter of the right to health in a courtroom struggle is likely to be narrow, involving interventions such as kidney dialysis or nevirapine therapy. The HIV epidemic demands a comprehensive strategy of treatment, care, and prevention, including education, adequate nutrition, clean water, and non-discrimination.[2,11,17] The government of South Africa has so far been unwilling to designate the HIV epidemic as a national emergency or to take steps to make the prevention and treatment of HIV infection its highest health priority. This stance has apparently changed little since the decision on nevirapine was handed down. The South African government, for example, has asked the Medicines Control Council to review its approval of nevirapine because of continued doubt about its safety and efficacy.[18] Of course, if the council withdraws its approval of the drug, this action will effectively render the Constitutional Court's decision moot, since its orders are based on the finding that nevirapine is safe and effective. On the more positive side, South Africa's cabinet has announced that it is considering universal access to antiretroviral drugs, and Ranbaxy, the largest manufacturer of generic drugs in India, has formed a joint venture with Adcock Ingram to distribute generic antiretroviral agents in South Africa.[19]

Former South African president Nelson Mandela has persuasively argued that an effective strategy for combatting the AIDS epidemic requires the engaged commitment of national leaders to provide not only prevention but also treatment for everyone who needs it, "wherever they may be in the world and regardless of whether they can afford to pay or not."[20] Lack of leadership in addressing the HIV epidemic specifically and the right to health in general is not, of course, confined to South Africa.

Notes

1. McGreal, C. The shame of the new South Africa. *The Guardian* (London), November 1, 2002:2.
2. Mann, J.M. Human rights and AIDS: the future of the pandemic. In: Mann, J.M., Gruskin, S., Grodin, M.A., and Annas, G.J., eds. *Health and human rights: a reader.* New York: Routledge, 1999:216–26.
3. Farmer, P. The major infectious diseases in the world—to treat or not to treat? *N Engl J Med* 2001;345:208–10.
4. Makgoba, M.W. HIV/AIDS: the peril of pseudoscience. *Science* 2000;288:1171.
5. Swarns, R.L. An AIDS skeptic in South Africa feeds simmering doubts. *New York Times.* March 31, 2002(section 1):4.

6. Barnard, D. In the high court of South Africa, case no. 4138/98: the global politics of access to low-cost AIDS drugs in poor countries. *Kennedy Inst Ethics J* 2002;12:159–74.

7. Guay, L.A., Musoke, P., Fleming, T., et al. Intrapartum and neonatal single-dose nevitapine compared with zidovudine for prevention of mother-to-child transmission of HIV-1 in Kampala, Uganda: HIVNET 012 randomised trial. *Lancet* 1999;354:795–802.

8. *Treatment Action Campaign v. Minister of Health, High Court of South Africa, Transvaal Provincial Div., 2002* (4) BCLR 356(T), Dec. 12, 2001.

9. *Minister of Health v. Treatment Action Committee, Constitutional Court of South Africa, 2002* (10) BCLR 1033.

10. Steiner, H.J. and Alston, P., eds. *International human rights in context: law, politics, morals.* 2nd ed. New York: Oxford University Press, 2000:1395–401.

11. United Nations, Economic and Social Council, Committee on Economic, Social and Cultural Rights. *General comment no. 14: the right to the highest attainable standard of health.* New York: United Nations, 2000.

12. *Soobramoney v. Minister of Health (KwaZulu-Natal), Constitutional Court of South Africa,* 1997 (12) BCLR 1696.

13. *South Africa v. Grootboom, Constitutional Court of South Africa, 2000* (11) BCLR 1169.

14. Tarantola, D. and Gruskin, S. Children confronting HIV/AIDS: charting the confluence of rights and health. *Health Hum Rights* 1998;3: 60–86.

15. Ngwena, C. The recognition of access to health care as a human right in South Africa: is it enough? *Health Hum Rights* 2000;5:26–44.

16. Torres, M.A. The human right to health, national courts, and access to HIV/AIDS treatment: a case study from Venezuela. *Chic J Int Law* 2002;3:105–15.

17. De Cock, K.M., Mbori-Ngacha, D., andMarum, E. Shadow on the continent: public health and HIV/AIDS in Africa in the 21st century. *Lancet* 2002;360:67–72.

18. Baleta, A. S Africa soaks up pressure to change HIV/AIDS policy. *Lancet* 2002;360:467.

19. Innocenti, N.G. Ranbaxy in link on AIDS drugs for Africa. *Financial Times* (London). October 18, 2002:29.

20. Mandela, N. Care support and destigmatization. Plenary address presented at the XIV International AIDS Conference, Barcelona, Spain, July 7–12, 2002.

24

The Human Right to Health, National Courts, and Access to HIV/AIDS Treatment

A Case Study from Venezuela

Mary Ann Torres

The human right to health has been part of the discourse on international law and public health since 1946, when the World Health Organization (WHO) proclaimed that the enjoyment of the highest attainable standard of health is a fundamental human right.[1] Numerous treaties and other international instruments subsequently developed the right to health in international law.[2] The right to health has served as inspiration for global public health initiatives, such as WHO's Health for All effort launched in the late 1970s. Controversy has, however, plagued the development of the right to health as an international legal principle, raising the question whether the right to health serves as a guiding light for global public health policy in the twenty-first century.

Recent campaigns to increase access to essential drugs in developing countries, led by local and global non-governmental organizations (NGOs), have brought the human right to health back into the spotlight. Many of these campaigns have focused on increasing access in developing countries to antiretroviral (ARV) therapies to treat HIV/AIDS. ARV therapies, such as Highly Active Anti-Retroviral Therapy (HAART), have helped developed countries treat HIV/AIDS and manage it as a chronic condition. These new therapies provide renewed hope for people living with HIV/AIDS (PLWHAs) because they have proven effective, prolonged survival, reduced mortality, and improved quality of life.

Unfortunately, over one-third of the world's population today does not have access to essential drugs,[3] let alone access to expensive ARV therapies for the treatment of HIV/AIDS.[4]

In addition to activism at the global level, NGOs composed of and working with PLWHAs within individual countries have been mounting efforts to increase access to ARV therapies using arguments informed by the human right to health. These campaigns sometimes involve litigation in national courts in which PLWHAs argue that the government's failure to provide access to ARV therapies violates the right to health enshrined in international and national law. These national cases are important to the international legal discourse on the right to health because they often provide a window on how the right operates at the local level where disease and death ultimately take their toll.

In this chapter, I analyze the 1999 decision of the Venezuelan Supreme Court in the case of *Cruz Bermúdez, et al v Ministerio de Sanidad y Asistencia Social*,[5] in which the Court held the government's failure to provide PLWHAs with access to ARV therapies violated their right to health.

Before analyzing the *Bermúdez* case, I briefly examine the international law concerning the right to health. This analysis focuses on specific problems that have made the right to health a difficult concept to define and implement effectively. These problems become central features of the *Bermúdez* case, as revealed by the status of the right to health in Venezuelan law and the arguments made by the PLWHAs and the government to the Venezuelan Supreme Court. The next part of the analysis considers the Venezuelan Supreme Court's decision and reasoning and its implications for discourse on the right to health in international law. I conclude with general observations about how the *Bermúdez* case helps illuminate not only debates on the right to health in international law, but also on whether the right to health retains importance for global public health in the twenty-first century.

The Right to Health in International Law: A Brief Overview

A number of international legal instruments contain the right to health. One of the best known treaty provisions on the right to health is found in the International Covenant on Economic, Social, and Cultural Rights ("ICESCR"). Under the ICESCR, states parties recognize the human right to enjoy the highest attainable standard of health and undertake to provide for such a standard through measures aimed at: (1) reducing the stillbirth rate and childhood mortality and promoting the development of children; (2) improving environmental and industrial hygiene; (3) preventing, treating, and controlling epidemic, endemic, and other diseases; and (4) creating the conditions for assuring medical services and attention to all.[6] The right to health in the ICESCR is subject to the principle of progressive realization, found in Article 2.1:

Each State Party to the present Covenant undertakes to take steps, individually and through international assistance and co-operation, especially economic and technical, to the maximum of its available resources, with a view to achieving progressively the full realization of the rights recognized in the present Covenant by all appropriate means, including particularly the adoption of legislative measures.

The substantive scope of the right to health and the impact of the principle of progressive realization have been the subject of much debate and analysis that cannot be adequately summarized here. The major themes in this discourse have concerned (1) the scope and nature of the actions governments must take in connection with the right to health, and (2) how much the principle of progressive realization weakens government duties to take action to fulfill the right to health. For example, states parties to the ICESCR accept treaty obligations on a long list of rights, including the rights to an adequate standard of living (Article 11), health (Article 12), education (Articles 13–14), and to share in the benefits of scientific and technological progress (Article 15). For each of these rights, a state party is obliged to take steps to achieve progressively the full realization of the rights to the maximum of its available resources. The open-ended nature of these rights and the flexibility and discretion left to states under the principle of progressive realization create rights that are difficult to define and enforce under international law.

The weak monitoring system established under the ICESCR—self-reporting by states parties—further undermines efforts to clarify the meaning of economic, social, and cultural rights, such as the right to health. Under Article 16 of the ICESCR, states parties must "submit . . . reports on the measures which they have adopted and the progress made in achieving the observance of the rights recognized herein." States parties submit their reports to the Committee on Economic, Social, and Cultural Rights (CESC). But the ICESCR gives the Committee little if any power to criticize or condemn what appears in these reports.

Confronted with the controversies surrounding the right to health, CESC issued a General Comment in 2000 that contributed to the discourse on the meaning of the right within the CESC. The CESC stated:

The right to health, like all human rights, imposes three types of obligations on States parties: the obligations to *respect, protect,* and *fulfill.* In turn, the obligation to fulfil contains obligations to facilitate, provide and promote. The obligation to *respect* requires States to refrain from interfering directly or indirectly with the enjoyment of the right to health. The obligation to *protect* requires States to take measures that prevent third parties from interfering with article 12 guarantees. Finally, the obligation to *fulfill* requires States to adopt appropriate legislative, administrative, budgetary, judicial, promotional and other measures towards the full realization of the right to health.[7]

While this may provide a helpful framework for thinking about the right to health, CESC's interpretation of Article 12 still leaves open the question whether a state party is doing enough to fulfill the right to health in terms of legislative and especially budgetary measures. The principle of progressive realization allows governments to raise scarcity of resources as a legitimate reason for not fulfilling the right to health. Governments must make difficult decisions how to allocate limited public resources, and such budgetary decisions accord with the state's duty to achieve progressively and over time the full realization of many different human rights. Further, the ICESCR leaves to states parties the determination of how public funds are allocated and what constitutes "the maximum of its available resources."[8] Neither CESC nor any other international body has any power under the ICESCR to proclaim a state party is in violation of its obligations under the right to health or to order more money be spent on health or different health policies be pursued. This reality has led some experts to argue that the right to health is not enforceable or justiciable at the international level, raising further questions about the meaning and effectiveness of this human right.

The absence of international case law on the right to health heightens the international legal importance of national cases brought pursuant to the right to health. National court decisions can inform international legal analysis in a number of ways. First, national court decisions involving treaty obligations could be said to constitute subsequent state practice under those treaties for the purpose of treaty interpretation.[9] Second, national court decisions can be considered evidence of state practice and *opinio juris* for purposes of determining rules of customary international law. Third, as Article 38(1)(d) of the Statute of the International Court of Justice provides, national court decisions are subsidiary means for interpreting rules of international law.

The cases being brought by PLWHAs against various governments for failing to provide access to ARV therapies and thus violating the right to health constitute an important set of materials for international legal analysis of the right to health. My attention now turns to the *Bermúdez* case from Venezuela to explore the connections between this national court decision and international law on the right to health.

The Bermúdez Case: Legal Context and Arguments of the Parties

The Right to Health in Venezuelan Law

At the time the *Bermúdez* case came before the Venezuelan Supreme Court in 1999, the right to health found expression in Venezuelan law in two ways. First,

Venezuela is a party to the ICESCR and thus accepted the obligations pursuant to Article 12. Under Venezuelan law, treaty duties such as those found in the ICESCR create obligations for the Venezuelan state that are directly enforceable by citizens against the government; and Venezuelans can invoke such obligations before courts and administrative authorities without the need for implementing legislation.[10] Second, the Venezuelan Constitution contained a constitutional right to health.[11] As a result of both international and constitutional legal sources, the right to health found strong expression in Venezuelan law. Venezuela's legal system thus provided fertile ground for PLWHAs to challenge the government's failure to provide better access to ARV therapies.[12]

Arguments of the Parties

The plaintiffs in this case argued that the Venezuelan government violated their rights to life, health, and access to scientific advances under Venezuelan law by failing to provide them with ARV therapies. The plaintiffs utilized the growing scientific and public health evidence that ARV therapies, if provided, would enable them to live longer and perhaps allow them to benefit from a cure should one arise in the future. The plaintiffs asked the Venezuelan Supreme Court to order the Ministry of Health to remedy these violations of their human rights by (1) providing periodically and regularly all medicines necessary, including ARV therapies and drugs for opportunistic infections, to PLWHAs in Venezuela; (2) covering the expenses of PLWHAs for blood tests needed to monitor the disease and the effect of the medications; and (3) developing and funding policies and programs to provide medical treatment and assistance for PLWHAs in Venezuela.

The Ministry of Health rejected the accusation that the government violated the plaintiffs' rights to life, health, and access to scientific advances protected under Venezuelan law. The Ministry's main defense rested on economics: the government could not pay for ARV therapy and related medicines for all Venezuelan PLWHAs because such expenses would be impossible to sustain. The Ministry pointed to programs on HIV/AIDS prevention it had started (for example, distributing informational booklets and condoms and implementing a "safe sex" initiative) as evidence that it was fulfilling its obligations toward health under Venezuelan law given its financial constraints.

The Ministry of Health's arguments about the financial difficulties of increasing access to ARV therapies dovetail with arguments governments frequently use in connection with questions about their commitment to the right to health under international law. Under the ICESCR, the right to health is to be achieved progressively; and the determination about how resources are allocated in this progressive project is left to the responsible government. The Ministry of Health in the *Bermúdez* case argued that it was progressively achieving improvements in connection with HIV/AIDS under the budget constraints it faced as a health ministry in a developing country.

The Ministry's arguments echo much of what experts have faced in dealing with the HIV/AIDS pandemic since the 1980s. This pandemic highlights the problems that economic, social, and cultural rights confront as elements of contemporary international law. Inadequate financial resources, unequal and uneven economic development, poverty, social injustice, and other problems endemic in the developing world have fueled the HIV/AIDS pandemic and severely constrain what developing-country governments can do to respect, protect, and fulfill the right to health.

The Bermúdez Case: Decision of the Venezuelan Supreme Court

Although the plaintiffs raised claims under the rights to life, health, and access to scientific advances, the Venezuelan Supreme Court focused its opinion on the right to health. Venezuelan law contained strong expressions of the right to health in both constitutional law and international legal obligations accepted by Venezuela. In examining the right to health arguments, the Court noted that

> HIV positive people and people with AIDS, as human beings, are also protected by international law. This Court has taken such international legal principles into account by collecting data about the most current and relevant cases and decisions from the entities that have faced the situation of people with HIV/AIDS before.

Unfortunately, the Court failed to provide any specifics regarding what international legal instruments, international legal principles, cases, or decisions it actually consulted in evaluating the right to health arguments of the parties. Presumably, the Court consulted the ICESCR because Venezuela is a state party, triggering directly enforceable rights for Venezuelans under Article 12's right to health provisions. The Court's decision reads as if constitutional law were the more important source for the right to health analysis, but the Venezuelan Constitution incorporates international legal norms directly into the national legal system, thus producing a seamless legal commitment to the right to health for purposes of the *Bermúdez* case. The Court noted that the right to health was protected by Article 76 of the Venezuelan Constitution *and* international human rights instruments related to this constitutional provision. Its holding in the *Bermúdez* case is, thus, important as an interpretation for both Venezuelan constitutional law and Venezuelan state practice under international law on the right to health, specifically under the ICESCR.

The Court observed that, based on the evidence presented by the parties, the Ministry of Health was not complying with its duty under the right to health, the immediate consequence of which was to place the lives of the plaintiffs at risk. The Court noted, however, that the non-compliance by the Ministry of

Health was not intentional but resulted from its lack of financial resources: "the budgetary capacities of the [Ministry] have been insufficient to fulfill the duty to assist the HIV/AIDS patients." The Court also refers to the Ministry of Health confronting difficult financial situations at a moment Venezuela was facing an economic crisis. As the Court succinctly stated, "everything is reduced to a budgetary problem."

Despite these serious constraints on the Ministry of Health, the Court held that the government violated the plaintiffs' right to health. To reconcile the plaintiffs' need for treatment and the Ministry's budgetary dilemma, the Court argued that the Ministry had available mechanisms under Venezuelan law through which it could seek additional funds for the purpose of dealing with the medical requirements of PLWHAs. The Ministry's failure to utilize these mechanisms contributed to the Court's sense that the Ministry's actions constituted a violation of the right to health.

The Court dramatically expanded the scope of its right to health holding when it reversed prior constitutional jurisprudence on similar constitutional appeals by declaring that its holding applied not only to the plaintiffs before the Court but also to all PLWHAs in Venezuela. This ruling meant that the right to health, as interpreted by the Court, had the broadest possible application in Venezuela, giving every HIV positive person in the country the right to access ARV therapies. While this decision made the right to health in connection with ARV therapies a universal right in Venezuela, the holding also significantly increased the budgetary challenge facing the Ministry of Health.

In the concluding sections of its opinion, the Court ordered the Ministry of Health, among other things, to (1) request immediately from the President the needed funds for HIV/AIDS prevention and control for the remaining fiscal year and an increase in budgetary allocations for future needs and (2) provide ARV therapies and associated medicines to any PLWHAs in Venezuela. "All Venezuelan governmental authorities," the Court concluded, "have to comply immediately with the decision in this constitutional appeal of protection, or they will be in violation of this decision and the constitutional rights it upholds."

Implications of the Bermúdez Case for the Right to Health in International Law

The *Bermúdez* case is important to discourse on the right to health in international law for a number of reasons that relate to both substantive and procedural issues. Substantively, the most striking aspect of the Court's decision is the Court's refusal to accept the Ministry of Health's plea of poverty as a valid justification for the government's failure to provide access to ARV therapies. A perennial difficulty with the substance of the right to health in international law has been the ability of governments to argue that their lack of financial resources means that they are not in violation of the right to health because only progressive realization is required under international law. This dynamic has eroded the duty to fulfill the right to health—to adopt appropriate legislative, administrative, budgetary, judicial, promotional, and other measures towards its full realization—because progressive realization rendered the right to health relative to a country's level of economic development and a government's willingness to spend resources on health. The Court held, however, that the legislative, budgetary, and administrative steps taken by the government in connection with the HIV/AIDS problem in Venezuela were not acceptable under its reading of the right to health.

The ability to challenge countries' decisions on health spending and policy under the right to health in international law is something proponents of the right have desired for a long time. Efforts to blunt the erosion of the principle of progressive realization include arguments that the right to health contains a minimum core that includes the provision of essential drugs not subject to the progressive realization principle.[13] The *Bermúdez* case does not purport to create an irreducible minimum core for the right to health in Venezuela, but it stands as evidence that tolerance for the plea of poverty from governments may be shrinking in countries beset by worsening public health problems that the government refuses to confront adequately. One case from one country certainly does not constitute a seismic shift in state practice for purposes of treaty interpretation or the formation of customary international law; but other countries, notably South Africa, are also experiencing mounting frustrations with government failure to properly address the problems of HIV/AIDS and access to treatment.[14]

Procedurally, the *Bermúdez* case is important for international law because it represents yet another example of the important role NGOs play in contemporary international law. Scholars and policymakers have focused much attention on the growing role NGOs play in creating and monitoring international law at the global level. The *Bermúdez* case illustrates that such NGO activism in connection with human rights norms is also vital at the national and local level. This case may also suggest that, in connection with the human right to health, such national and local activism by the NGO community offers more potential than NGO action on the right to health at the global level. No international institution has ever been in a position to expose Venezuela's inadequate HIV/AIDS policies as the NGOs and PLWHAs that brought the *Bermúdez* case were able to do. The public health cliché that all disease is local also resonates with the notion of transforming the right to health from rhetoric to reality because ultimately the right has to be enjoyed locally.

The *Bermúdez* case is also important for international law because it reaffirms the important role that the right to health can play in the overall public health discourse. Trends in global public health appear to be moving away from a rights-based approach to health concerns (for example, the Health for All campaign) toward a more economics-based, utilitarian paradigm that seeks to improve health because it contributes to more worker productivity and faster rates of economic development (for example, the Commission on Macroeconomics and Health). The framing of the access to treatment issue as a human rights concern in the *Bermúdez* case is perhaps more important today than it was just three years ago.

Connecting access to treatment to human rights concepts also remains critical because of another lesson of the *Bermúdez* case, the enormous distance the human right to health still must travel in many countries around the world. Despite the Venezuelan Supreme Court's holding in the *Bermúdez* case, the Venezuelan government has done little to nothing to improve the access to ARV therapies for PLWHAs. Most of the Venezuelan government is—in the words of the Court—"in violation of this decision and the constitutional right it upholds." The *Bermúdez* case notwithstanding, health as a human right still has not penetrated Venezuelan political and popular culture. The reality that the Venezuelan government ignores the Court's ruling in the *Bermúdez* case with impunity only contributes to the widespread perception that the right to health is symbolic rather than vital to the life of the nation. NGO activism is important; but, as public health experts know, the active and intelligent participation of the government is critical to improving a population's health, especially in the face of disease threats such as HIV/AIDS. The sustained lack of government commitment to health as a human right produces a conspiracy of silence that hides the fatal threat of AIDS and other diseases from innocent and vulnerable people.

Notes

1. See Constitution of the World Health Organization, preamble, 62 Stat 2679, 14 UNTS 185 (1948).
2. See David P. Fidler, *International Law and Public Health: Materials on and Analysis of Global Health Jurisprudence* 303 (Transnational 2000) (listing trearies and other international instruments in which the right to health appears).
3. Médecins Sans Frontières ("MSF"), *What is the MSF Campaign for Access to Essential Medicines?*, available online at <http://www.accessmed.msf.org/campaign/campaign.shem> (visited Mar 24, 2002).
4. Access issues are also discussed by Ellen't Hoen, TRIPS, "Pharmaceutical Patents, and Access to Essential Medicines: A Long Way From Seattle to Doha," 3 *Chi J Intl L* 27 (2002) and Alan O. Sykes, TRIPS, "Pharmaceuticals, Developing Countries, and the Doha 'Solution,'" 3 *Chi J Intl L* 47 (2002).
5. *Cruz Bermúdez et al v Ministerio de Sanidad y Asistencia Social*, Sala Politico Administrativa. Corte Suprema de Justicia, Republica de Venezuela, Expediente Numero: 15.789 (1999), available online at <http://www.csj.gov.ve/sentencias/SPA/spa15071999–15789.html> (visited Mar 24, 2002). All references to the *Bermúdez* case are based on author translation.
6. See International Covenant on Economic, Social, and Cultural Rights (ICESCR), art 12, 993 UNTS 3 (1976).

7. The United Nations Economic and Social Council Committee on Economic, Social and Cultural Rights (CESCR). *The Right to the Highest Attainable Standard of Health* para 33, UN Doc No E/C.12/2000/4. CESCR General Comment 14 (2000) ("General Comment 14").

8. ICESCR at art 2(1) (cited in note 6).

9. Consider Vienna Convention on the Law of Treaties, act 31(3)(b), 1155 UNTS 331 (1969) (noting that "subsequent practice in the application of the treaty which establishes the agreement of the parties regarding its interpretation" is to be taken into account when interpreting a treaty).

10. The Constitution in force at the time of the *Bermúdez* case was the Constitution of 1961, which contained a provision providing that "[t]he enunciation of rights and guarantees contained in this Constitution must not be construed as a denial of others which, being inherent in the human person, are not expressly mentioned herein." Venezuelan Const Art 50 (1961) (Pan Am Union, trans). The Venezuelan Supreme Court held that this provision means that creates protecting human rights have at least the same standing as the Constitution in Venezuelan law. See *Andrés Velázquez*, Corre Suprema de Justicia en Pleno, Sala Politico Administrativa, Republica de Venezuela, Vol I 122 Gacera Forense 166 (1983). The new Venezuelan Constitution, adopted in December 1999 after the *Bermúdez* case was decided, contains the same principle in Article 23:

    Treaties, pacts and covenants related to human rights, which have been subscribed to and ratified by Venezuela have constitutional hierarchy and have prevalence in the internal judicial order to the extent that they contain norms of scope and execution that are more favorable than those contained in the Constitution. These norms are of immediate application by the courts and by all the organs of public administration.

    Venezuelan Const Art 23 (1999).

11. See Venezuelan Const Art 76 (1961) (Pan Am Union, trans):

    Everyone shall have the right to protection of his health. The authorities shall oversee the maintenance of public health and shall provide the means of prevention and attention for those who lack them. Everyone is obliged to submit to health measures established by law, within limits imposed by respect for the human person.

12. The *Bermúdez* case was not the first "right to health" case filed by Venezuelan PLWHAs seeking access to ARV therapies. In *NA, et al v Ministerio de Sanidad y Asistencia Social*, the Venezuelan Supreme Court held in 1998 that the Ministry of Health violated the rights to health and life of twenty-three HIV positive plaintiffs by not providing them with ARV therapy. See *NA, et al v Ministerio de Sanidad y Asistencia Social* (Ministry of Health), Sala Politico Administrativa, Corte Suprema de Justicia, Republica de Venezuela, Expedience numero: 14.625 (1998), available online at <http://www.csj.gov.ve/sentencias/SPA/spa14081998–14625.html> (visited Mar 24, 2002). This decision, however, only benefited the twenty-three plaintiffs and not other HIV positive persons in Venezuela because such constitutional actions (*accion de ampara*) did not affect persons beyond the parties to the dispute. The *Bermúdez* case changes this feature of Venezuelan constitutional law.

13. See, for example, Brigit C.A. Toebes, *The Right to Health as a Human Right in International Law* 283–84 (Intersentia 1999).

14. See, for example, *Treatment Action Campaign et al v Minister of Health et al.* Transvaal Provincial Division of the High Court of South Africa, Case No 21182/2001 (Dec 14, 2001) (holding the South African federal and provincial governments to be in violation of the right to health guaranteed by the South African Constitution for limiting the distribution of, and access to, ARV therapy to prevent mother-to-child transmission of HIV).

VIII
Mobilizing for Health and Human Rights

The final part of this book focuses on ways to use health and human rights frameworks as effective strategies to mobilize for change. The strategies include new methodologies, as well as creative uses of existing techniques, to translate theory into advocacy. Several themes emerge from these chapters: health and human rights education must expand to include all health professionals; NGOs should be creative in their methods even as they keep tightly focused on their goals; progress will require multiple broad approaches to health and human rights; activists must broaden the conceptual scope of traditional human rights while incorporating additional concerns in order to attract the attention of people who might not have been interested otherwise; and there must be a reconceptualizing of theory to promote advocacy, rather than using advocacy simply to carry out theory.

The first chapter, by Easley, Marks, and Morgan, emphasizes the links between public health and human rights, arguing that the protection of human rights is crucial to improving the health status of people everywhere. After reviewing basic health and human rights documents, the authors focus on the international recognition of the right to the highest attainable standard of health. The authors point to increased attention to human rights education as critical to recognizing the potential impact of public health programs and policies on human rights and the need to take into account the effect that improvements in human rights have on health status. Growing acceptance of this approach can be seen in the American Public Health Association's commitment to human rights as fundamental to all its activities.

Some of the most successful and creative strategies for protecting human rights have been developed by advocates for reproductive health and reproductive rights. The second chapter in this part draws on lessons from this movement. Lynn Freedman argues that we must move beyond a narrow conception of the "right to privacy" focused on choice and abortion, and instead more broadly highlight issues of social justice for women, because of the intrinsic value of women as human beings and their vital contributions to society. In order to broaden and reframe the debate in terms of social justice, she examines the false dichotomy of "science vs. politics" and the problems with using legal systems to apportion blame and responsibility for poor health.

The chapter by Sirkin, Iacopino, Grodin, and Danieli addresses the critical role of physicians and other health professionals in promoting and protecting human rights. They argue that the healing professions have a special duty to alleviate suffering and promote health and that there is a need to incorporate a human rights perspective into clinical care. The authors focus on the need for the professions also to address the global victims of human rights abuses and the role of education in bringing about positive change.

Continuing the theme of the importance of education to health and human rights, Iacopino summarizes the current state of teaching human rights in schools of public health, medicine, and nursing. The chapter summarizes existing educational formats, contents, and methods for teaching health and human rights and recommends strategies for increasing the depth and breadth of educational experiences.

In a case study of one of the most successful health and human advocacy rights projects to date—the international campaign to ban the use of land-mines—Kenneth Rutherford describes the vital role of non-governmental human rights organizations in the health and human rights movement. NGOs put banning antipersonnel landmines on the international arms control agenda. Their campaign, which carefully coordinated health and human rights issues, ultimately led to the establishment of an international treaty. These NGOs were awarded the Nobel Peace Prize for their efforts. The case serves as a model for how NGOs can ultimately influence the protection of health and human rights.

25

The Challenge and Place of International Human Rights in Public Health

Cheryl E. Easley, Stephen P. Marks, and Russell E. Morgan Jr.

Human rights workers and practitioners of public health share common concerns for the well-being of people, the alleviation of suffering and want, and the promotion of social justice. The potential for cooperation between these two committed groups has advanced considerably over the past decade or so as scholars, practitioners, administrators, and activists grapple with the differences in disciplinary language and with limited opportunities for contact. It is the intention of the American Public Health Association (APHA) to join others in bridging these differences, so that the combined efforts of these groups can be focused on the shared goal of bettering the human condition around the world.

To advance the dialogue among public health and human rights professionals, there is a growing literature, including several books,[1-3] a peer-reviewed academic journal (*Health and Human Rights: An International Journal*, published by the Harvard-based François Xavier Bagnoud Center for Health and Human Rights), regular features of the *American Journal of Public Health* and of *The Lancet*, and occasional articles in other leading medical journals, such as the *Journal of the American Medical Association* and the *New England Journal of Medicine*. A chapter on the topic is in the fourth edition of *The Oxford Textbook on Public Health*.[4] The movement has been further advanced through several major conferences, such as those organized by the François-Xavier Bagnoud Center for Health and Human Rights in 1994 and 1996, and more recently by the University of Iowa[5] and Temple University,[6] as well as by coalitions and networks such as the Consortium on Health and Human Rights, the International Federation of Health and Human Rights Organizations, and the International Student Association for Health and Human Rights.[7]

As we confront the issues of public health in the 21st century–including the worldwide spread of HIV/AIDS and other infections, the aging of our populations, and the questions raised by burgeoning health-related technology in the face of gross disparities in access to basic health care–human rights and public health professionals are challenged to forge powerful partnerships to help us attain our mutual aims.

Basic Assumptions of Human Rights Documents

Rights are claims or entitlements to something or against someone that are recognized by legal rules or moral principles. In other words, they are legally protected interests of rights-holders, implying obligations on the part of duty-holders to respect and observe them. Human rights constitute a special category of rights. According to natural law theory, a human right is a higher-order kind of right that is morally based and that is universal, in the sense that it belongs equally to all persons simply because they are human beings. Human rights are also grounded in positive law theory, according to which rights are entitlements of individuals and groups that are affirmed and protected by the laws of an organized society, whether national or international.

In the United States, for example, the Declaration of Independence uses natural law doctrine in affirming "that all men [sic] . . . are endowed by their Creator with certain inalienable Rights," whereas the Bill of Rights, amending the Constitution, sets out legal rights in positive law that can be enforced by the courts. The same may be said for practically every country's political and legal development; constitutions with declarations of rights and judicial and other means of enforcement transform the lofty ideals of human rights into practical reality for citizens. In the international system, a similar process occurs. On the one hand, declarations and other texts express the ever evolving consensus on the content of human rights; on the other hand, a web of international treaties and monitoring mechanisms hold the states accountable for meeting their human rights obligations.

Thus, human rights are founded both on moral philosophy, drawing on the meaning and implications of being human, and on legal and political processes by which human societies are governed. Ethics, as a branch of philosophy that deals primarily with defining morally good action, operates in a related but different realm of discourse. As public health professionals, we encounter ethics as descriptions of or prescriptions for moral behavior toward our patients or clients. These ethical mandates are often codified by professional organizations and serve as a guide to decision making in specific practice situations. Human rights also result from moral judgment about good behavior, but in the form of mutually agreed-upon norms articulating the just claims of individuals and groups and the related obligations of the state. The universality of human rights claims derive from the agreement of practically all states to be bound by them, rather than from human nature.

The assertion of international human rights is a historical development that has taken place essentially since the Second World War. Formal codification of human rights, stimulated by abhorrence of the atrocities committed during the war, was launched when the United Nations Charter proclaimed "international co-operation . . . in promoting and encouraging respect for human rights"[8] as one of the purposes of the organization. To advance that purpose, the United Nations General Assembly adopted the Universal Declaration of Human Rights[9] in 1948, followed in 1966 by the International Covenant on Civil and Political Rights[10] and the International Covenant on Economic, Social and Cultural Rights (ICESCR).[11] Collectively, these three documents form what is known as the International Bill of Human Rights.

Other major United Nations treaties address racial discrimination, refugees, discrimination against women, torture, and the rights of the child. These texts, and equivalents adopted by the regional organizations in Europe, the American states, and Africa, contain the bedrock human rights obligations of states, including the right to health.

The Right to Health

The international recognition of the right to health began with the reference to health in the United Nations Charter[12] and took form in the preamble to the 1946 Constitution of the World Health Organization, which affirms, "The enjoyment of the highest attainable standard of health is one of the fundamental rights of every human being without distinction of race, religion, political belief, economic or social condition."[13] The Declaration of Alma-Ata, which was adopted by the International Conference on Primary Health Care in 1978, further proclaimed this right as a "most important world-wide social goal whose realization requires the action of many other social and economic sectors in addition to the health sector."[14] The Universal Declaration of Human Rights affirms everyone's "right to a standard of living adequate for the health and well-being of himself and his family, including food, clothing, housing and medical care and necessary social services, and the right to security in the event of unemployment, sickness, disability, widowhood, old age or other lack of livelihood in circumstances beyond his control."[9]

The right to health is affirmed in the Convention on the Rights of the Child,[15] the Convention on the Elimination of All Forms of Racial Discrimination,[16] the Convention on the Elimination of All Forms of Discrimination Against

Women,[17] and especially in the ICESCR.[11] By ratifying the ICESCR, states recognize "the right of everyone to the enjoyment of the highest attainable standard of physical and mental health" and agree to take steps to achieve the full realization of this right. Both the Convention on the Elimination of All Forms of Discrimination Against Women and the Convention on the Rights of the Child elaborate health-related human rights for their target populations. The Committee on Economic Social and Cultural Rights, which monitors application of the ICESCR, adopted an interpretive document in the form of a "general comment" on the right to health in May 2000, setting out in detail what states are expected to do to fulfill their obligations to realize this right.[18]

Human rights, including the right to health, are often said to be "interdependent." Clearly, the right to the highest attainable standard of health rests on the right to safe and healthy working conditions, clean water, and freedom from environmental toxins, but it depends in equal measure on the recognition of the dignity of the individual and the rights to education, free speech, and participation in the political process. Conversely, the ability to fully exercise other fundamental human rights depends on the right to health. Violation of any human right, including the right to health, contributes to the infringement of other rights.

Limitations on Rights

It is of particular interest to public health practitioners to understand whether human rights are supposed to be absolute or relative to the exigencies of preventing and treating disease and injury and other constraints on government. One scholar noted, regarding the United States, "that public health and individual rights sometimes cannot coexist."[19] International human rights texts acknowledge circumstances under which rights may be suspended in times of national emergency; certain rights, however, are considered nonderogable, such as the right to life; the right to freedom from torture and enslavement; the rights to freedom of thought, conscience, and religion; and the right to recognition as a person before the law.

Other rights may be limited if the restrictions are "prescribed by law and . . . necessary in a democratic society"[10] for certain purposes, such as the need to protect public health. Rights subject to restrictions for such purposes, as specified in the International Covenant on Civil and Political Rights, include the right to freedom of movement and residence, the right to freedom of peaceful assembly, the right to freedom of association, the right to manifest one's religion, and the right to freedom of expression. Thus, some temporary restrictions on certain human rights in the interest of public health may be allowed when the situation leaves no alternative, but this action should always be preceded by a careful and deliberate process of decision making, should be monitored, and should be lifted as soon as possible.

The Role of Education

As public health practitioners understand these general ideas about human rights and recognize the need to be sensitive to the human rights of all people in the communities in which they practice, they are likely to welcome enhanced education about human rights as a component of basic preparation and continued learning for all disciplines of public health work. Their awareness of the potential impact of public health programs and policies on the human rights of the individuals and groups within their country should extend to the realities of public health around the world and the place human rights can have in improving the health status of people everywhere.

Workers in the fields of public health and human rights share concerns for the dignity and well-being of people, and both fields have historically championed the cause of vulnerable groups such as women and children, the aged, the disabled, and the politically disenfranchised. Most members of both professional disciplines recognize health as a human right and are committed to advocacy, policy-making, and other strategies that ensure the achievement of this and other human rights.

The challenge facing public heath professionals wishing to be more engaged in human rights is to go beyond the emotional attachment to social justice and human rights and acquire the knowledge of the field and the skills necessary to put human rights into health practice. Gruskin and Tarantola proposed three levels at which the health and human rights framework can be put into practice.[4] The first level is acquisition of the tools of a systematic human rights analysis to determine best practice for evidence-based health policy and programs. The second is the level of health systems and practice, where a balance is needed between promoting and protecting human rights and promoting and protecting public health as part of national policy. The third level is health and human rights research.

This agenda, or "pathway to health and human rights,"[4] requires a considerable investment in education on these topics for local, state, and national health policymakers, administrators, program developers, students, and health care workers, as well as legislators and the general public. It is, therefore, a legitimate aim of APHA to seek to integrate human rights education into all levels of academic and professional training for health practice.

The Role of APHA

APHA has already demonstrated its commitment to including the human rights framework in public health teaching, research, and practice by sponsoring continuing education institutes and plenary sessions at its annual meetings. APHA's Committee on International Human Rights and the François-Xavier Bagnoud Center for Health and Human Rights are collaborating in the development of a curriculum on health and human rights for students of public health and related fields and for practitioners. The Committee on International Human Rights is also cooperating with an effort to draft an international declaration on health and human rights, spearheaded by Physicians for Human Rights and the François-Xavier Bagnoud Center. Significantly, the *American Journal of Public Health* devoted its October 1999 issue to human rights and has expanded coverage of the topic in subsequent issues. An editorial published in 2000, co-authored by the Executive Director of APHA, concluded, "The time has come to herald human rights as both the foundation of public health practice and the compass of public policy actions."[20]

Consistent with that commitment, the APHA Committee on International Human Rights distributed a statement of principles on public health and human rights at APHA's annual meeting in 2000. The statement reaffirms the basic commitment of public health workers to human rights and the complementarity of health and human rights action. It is a restatement, for the purposes of engaging the community of public health practitioners, of the underlying premises of the Universal Declaration of Human Rights and the implications for the right to health of the interrelatedness of all human rights.

The APHA text, although brief, acknowledges the importance of the cultural context of public health practice. As set out in the Committee on Economic, Social and Cultural Rights' general comment on the right to health, "All health facilities, goods and services must be respectful of medical ethics and culturally appropriate, i.e., respectful of the culture of individuals, minorities, peoples and communities."[18] Of course, the reference in the APHA principles to "culturally acceptable health care" means "culturally appropriate" and excludes practices that are harmful to the health or autonomy of individuals, such as harmful and discriminatory traditional practices.

The APHA principles also acknowledge the need, in limited circumstances defined in international human rights law, to restrict individual freedom to respond to the need to control disease and treat injury. Finally, they seek to encourage APHA and its members to find new and more effective ways to transform the idea of health and human rights into practice benefiting people everywhere.

The pioneering work on the synergy between health and human rights was done in the final decade of the last century. The first decades of this century offer the opportunity for health practitioners to contribute, each in his or her way, to reaching the full potential of this synergy.

Notes

1. Mann, J.M., Gruskin, S., Grodin, M.A., and Annas, G.J., eds. *Health and Human Rights: A Reader.* New York: Routledge, 1999.
2. British Medical Association. *The Medical Profession and Human Rights: Handbook for a Changing Agenda.* London, England: Zed Books, 2001.
3. Health aspects of human rights: a select bibliography (partially annotated). Available at: http://www.edifolini.com/human_rights/human_rights.html.Accessed October 17, 2001.
4. Gruskin, S. and Tarantola, D. Health and human rights. In: Detels, R., McEwen, J., Beaglehole, R., and Tanaka, H., eds. *The Oxford Textbook of Public Health* 4th ed. Oxford, England: Oxford University Press, 2001:311–335.
5. Iowa City appeal on advancing the human right to health. Available at: http://www.hsph.harvard.edu/fxbcenter/Iowa_City_appeal.pdf. Accessed October 17, 2001.
6. Health, Law and Human Rights: Exploring the Connections [conference program]. Available at: http://aslme. org/humanrights2001/. Accessed October 17, 2001.
7. University of Minnesota Human Rights Library. Health and human rights links. Available at: http://www 1.umn. edu/humanrts/links/health.html. Accessed October 17, 2001.
8. Charter of the United Nations, article 1(3). Available at: http://www.un. org/aboutun/charter/index.html. Accessed October 5, 2001.
9. Universal Declaration of Human Rights. Available at http://www.un.org/Overview/rights.html. Accessed October 5, 2001.
10. International Covenant on Civil and Political Rights. Available at http://www.unhchr.ch/html/menu3/b/a_ccpr. htm. Accessed October 5, 2001.
11. International Covenant on Economic, Social and Cultural Rights. Available at: http://www.unhclr.clr/html/menu3/b/a_cescr.htm. Accessed October 5, 2001.
12. Toebes, B.C.A. *The Right to Health as a Human Right in International Law.* Antwerp, Belgium: Intersentia; 1999:15.
13. Constitution of the World Health Organization. July 22, 1946. Available at: http://www.yale.edu/lawweb/avalon/decade/decad051.htm. Accessed October 5, 2001.
14. Declaration of Alma-Ata. Available at: http://www.who.int/hpr/archive/docs/almaata.html. Accessed October 5, 2001.
15. Convention on the Rights of the Child. Article 24. Available at: http://www.unhchr.ch/html/menu3/b/k2crc. htm. Accessed October 8, 2001.
16. Convention on the Elimination of All Forms of Racial Discrimination. UN GA Res 2106A(XX). Article 5. Available at: http://www.unhchr.ch/html/menu3/b/d_icerd.htm. Accessed October 5, 2001.
17. Convention on the Elimination of All Forms of Discrimination Against Women. Articles 11 and 12. Available at: http://www.unhchr.ch/html/menu3/b/e1cedaw.htm. Accessed October 8, 2001.
18. The right to the highest attainable standard of health: 11/08/2000. E/C.12/2000/4, CESCR General comment 14. Available at: http://www.unhchr.ch/tbs/doc.usf. Accessed October 17, 2001.
19. Gostin, L. *Public Health Law: Power, Duty, Restraint.* Berkeley: University of California Press; 2000:109, 113–305.
20. Rodriguez-Garcia, R. and Akhter, M.N. Human rights: the foundation of public health practice. *Am J Public Health*, 2000; 90:693–694.

26
Human Rights and the Politics of Risk and Blame
Lessons from the International Reproductive Health Movement

Lynn P. Freedman

Recent debates about the "politicization" of public health obscure the ways in which epidemiological concepts of risk are routinely used in the legal and political systems to apportion blame and responsibility for poor health. This chapter uses the example of reproductive health and rights to argue that new understandings of the connection between socioeconomic conditions and poor health will only generate change when they are reframed into political claims and pressed by social movements. In this connection, human rights language, principles, and practice hold great potential for the US reproductive rights movement, which has sometimes been constrained by the narrow scope of court rulings.

A small storm is brewing in the hills and valleys of public health. The first gusts began blowing when an op-ed piece entitled "The Politicization of Public Health" appeared in *The Wall Street Journal* last December (*The Wall Street Journal*. December 12, 1996:A12). Scoffing at the official theme of the American Public Health Association's (APHA) 1996 annual conference, "Empowering the Disadvantaged: Social Justice in Public Health," the author, Sally Satel, MD, bemoaned the field's supposed abandonment of science and medicine. As prima facie evidence, she reeled off a selection of conference workshops and symposia that sought to explore the linkages between race- and/or class-based inequality and health and to consider the role of such issues in public health education and practice. Conceding that "the poor do tend to be sicker and to have shorter lives than the better off," and even that limited access to health care was partially responsible for the differential, Dr. Satel went straight to her real concern: "unhealthy habits are more prevalent on the lower rungs of the socioeconomic ladder" and "more than half of all premature deaths are attributable to risky personal behavior." Yet, in Dr. Satel's view, conventional public health strategies designed to change people's behavior were being dismissed by "activist researchers" and abandoned by the APHA in favor of the "glamour" of left-leaning politics. "As the field drifts from its scientific and clinical moorings," she warned, "the health of all Americans stands to suffer. Worse than irrelevant, the politicization of public health is a public menace."

Science versus politics? A perennial straw man; indeed, in this case, a veritable scarecrow. By framing the question as "science vs. politics" (read: truth versus manipulative special interests), Dr. Satel attempts to quash a deeper, more complicated and important debate that is gathering steam in the medical and public health communities. That debate, which far more often takes place without any political consciousness at all, is typically conducted in the language of epidemiology employing the central concept of "risk." Yet, when we talk about risk and the health programs and policies that flow from it, we are always, inevitably, talking about politics—about what kind of society we want to be, about the role of the citizen and his/her entitlements and duties, and about the obligations of the state.

Indeed, our notions about these political questions and relationships actually frame the categories that we use to think about health and to characterize the meaning and consequences of risk. Thus, until we get past the smoke screen thrown up by the false "science vs. politics" dichotomy and come to accept the close and important relationship between science and politics, we will be debating the wrong issues. Far from abandoning science, we think it is time for health professionals to expand the reach of scientific inquiry and simultaneously to develop a deeper, more nuanced and politically savvy understanding of just what is at risk when we talk about risk.

In this chapter, we contend that the debate about the causes and consequences of poor health is in fact outstripping the legal categories that are used in the United States to define political questions. We turn to the field of reproductive health and rights to illustrate our point. Where US political discourse has been stalled in a debate centered on abortion and questions of choice that are largely premised on a narrow conception of a "right to privacy," the international field is employing a much more holistic approach to reproductive health and a far broader conception of human rights. As the public health and medical communities use the tools of science to deepen our understanding of the relationships between an individual, the socioeconomic and cultural conditions in which she lives, and her health, we believe that the field of human rights can have an important role in expanding our understanding of justice, liberating our imagination about the possible, and creating the popular demand and political will needed to craft health policies and programs that can address these issues effectively.

Reconsidering Risk

In medicine, in the media, and in the minds of most Americans, risk is everywhere. It is in the food we eat, the air we breathe, the medicines we take, the places we work, and even the pleasures we choose. One commentator summed it all up this way: "Since life itself is a universally fatal sexually transmitted disease, living it to the full demands a balance between reasonable and unreasonable risk."[1] Indeed, many health professionals have come to see their role from just this perspective, identifying and quantifying the "risk factors" that characterize modern life and then guiding patients and the general public along the best-laid path of avoidance and engagement.

At first glance, this might seem like a straightforward, objective exercise of statistical muscle. Indeed, in the public health and medical literature—where the number of articles using the concept of risk has increased dramatically over the last two decades[2]—risk is usually presented unproblematically as a strictly quantitative question in which the investigator measures the probability that exposure to one or more events or conditions—"risk factors"—will be associated with a particular health-related outcome. These mathematical correlations are then calculated and expressed in different ways, such as "relative risk," "absolute risk," or "lifetime risk," to be used for decision making at different levels of health care; for treatment decisions in the clinical setting, for policy decisions in the government setting, for patient decisions in the course of everyday life.[3]

But risk is not so simple. While a risk measurement can tell us the statistical likelihood that an event will happen, it can never tell us what value to place on that probability. Thus, at one level, the seeming neutrality of risk assessments expressed in mathematical terms often hides the value-laden nature of the decisions they are used to support. For example, a physician who discovers a benign breast lump might tell a patient the statistical probability that she will ultimately develop breast cancer, a seemingly technical, objective statement of risk. But the way the patient herself processes, understands, and acts on that information about her statistical risk can only be understood from within the wider context of her life and her own personal experience and values—a "subjective and highly ambiguous" calculation that Sandra Gifford has aptly called "lived risk."[4] At the same time, outsiders (including physicians) who observe an individual's actions in response to risk calculations often tend to judge such decisions as inherently right or wrong. Thus risk, especially when it concerns such culturally charged matters as human immunodeficiency virus infection, smoking, or drug use, can take on a moral dimension as well.[5]

But the point is not simply that choices made in response to a particular risk calculation will always be value laden. That is true enough. Rather, our bigger point is that risk itself—how it is conceptualized and used in health settings and in public discourse—is a socially constructed category that plays important political functions. Anthropologist Mary Douglas has made the insightful observation that in a secular, globalizing society such as ours, the pervasiveness of "risk" can be explained by its emergence as a key "forensic resource."[6] By this we mean that "risk" has become the key concept used within the legal and political systems (and in popular discourse as well) to assign responsibility for poor health outcomes. For with risk, comes blame. And blame, at bottom, is a social tool for apportioning responsibility and demanding accountability. Thus, risk functions as a forensic resource when it is used to assign responsibility and to distribute the power and resources that interact in complicated ways with such assignments (since sometimes responsibility is assumed by the most powerful and best-resourced while at other times it is foisted on the poor and powerless).

The epidemiologic association between poverty and poor health illustrates the point well. One can structure the relevant risk question by focusing on the proximate factors of individual behavior or lifestyle that are most directly associated with specific causes of ill health. Numerous studies can be marshalled to support the view that people in lower socioeconomic classes engage more often in "risky" behaviors that are associated with leading causes of poor health. If this is the end of the inquiry, the result is likely to be a health care regime that focuses on individual behavior modification and that lodges both fault and responsibility with the individual who fails to make the changes that society demands. Of course, such policy measures are never pristine reflections of neutral epidemiological data; rather correlations between individual behavior and health status yield policies that have been filtered through a variety of sociocultural constructs about gender, race, and class.[7] This plays itself out in very real ways, for example, in the prosecution of pregnant drug abusers and the treatment of pregnant women more generally;[8] and even in welfare and immigration reform, where legislative measures acquire names such as the "Personal Responsibility Act."[9]

Alternatively, one could focus on the epidemiologic fact that the association between low socioeconomic status and higher mortality stubbornly persists, even as the leading causes of death change dramatically, from infectious to chronic disease, for example. That focus leads to a distinctly different set of questions. For instance, one could ask what is the social context of risk, i.e., what puts people at risk of risky behavior, and whether those contextual factors reflect "fundamental social causes" that explain the persistence of the association. Surveying the epidemiological literature with precisely these questions in mind, Bruce Link and Jo Phelan conclude that there are fundamental social causes that involve access to resources that "can be used to avoid risks or to minimize the consequences of disease once it occurs."[10] Such resources include "money, knowledge, power, prestige, and the kinds of interpersonal resources embodied in the concepts of social support and social network." Significantly, the aim here is not just to construct a causal chain that moves from distal social factors to proximate behavioral or lifestyle factors to disease, and then to decide where along that chain to intervene with health measures. Rather, the very point of Link and Phelan's analysis is that these fundamental causes persist and continue to yield inequalities, despite our ability to intervene effectively with respect to particular factors or causes of poor health. Hence, if we care about the inequality, then attention only to proximate causes will not suffice. We will have to look social injustice straight in the eye—and try not to blink.

In sum, the policy implications of a finding that identifies "how general resources like knowledge, money, power, prestige, and social connections are transformed into health-related resources that generate patterns of morbidity and mortality" will be significantly different from those suggested by the assignment of personal responsibility and moral blame to the poor and powerless themselves. The association between poverty and poor health may be uncontested, but the way risk is understood, the way health research questions are structured, and the way policy responses to epidemiological data are formulated, are dramatically different. So how do we choose between the two?

This brings us back to our original point that the attempt to pose the issue as a contest between science and politics is deeply misguided. If risk is indeed a key forensic resource in modern life, then like it or not, health issues are destined to be a basic part of the political landscape. Instead of engaging in the futile exercise of trying (or pretending) to separate science from politics, we should be attempting to understand better the relationship between science and politics so that the public discussion is forced to confront the ways in which the kind of expert knowledge generated by health professionals can be deployed to maintain and reinforce the powerful or, conversely, to subvert the dynamics of power that keep some people both perpetually poor and perpetually sick.

Linking Health to Rights

How, then, do new ways of thinking about health dynamics, new kinds of knowledge get translated into correspondingly effective policies and programs—especially if those policies and programs challenge conventional paradigms or established practices? We suggest that the force of scientific logic, standing alone, will rarely, if ever, effect dramatic change. Rather, there are at least two additional prerequisites: a set of political/legal concepts or vocabulary by which scientific insights can be reframed into political claims, and a social movement that can press such claims.

This is why a human rights perspective is now critical to public health. The debate about the correlation between poverty and poor health, and the different approaches to risk through which that debate is typically conducted, begin to reveal the nature of the problem. An individualist view of risk succeeds forensically because it employs the same categories as the prevailing legal system. In our system, law is seen essentially as a tool to ensure the freedom of each individual to develop to his fullest potential by enabling him to pursue his enlightened self-interest free from interference by the state. Public health measures that focus on self-help and personal empowerment through diet, exercise, stress reduction, and avoiding risky personal behavior, for example, are adopted so readily in public discourse and health practice because they mesh with and even reinforce that vision of law and of "legitimate" expectations as between a citizen and the state.[11] By contrast, a structural view of risk, even when it is scientifically more plausible, generally fails as a forensic tool because the U.S. political/legal system is so deeply resistant to allocating responsibility or demanding accountability and change along these lines.

Yet, in the international arena, where law is notoriously "soft," where there is no adjudication and enforcement system effective against recalcitrant governments, new thinking in health has found much more fertile ground. Recent international developments in the area of women's reproductive and sexual health and rights are a dramatic example. And when these developments are compared to the narrow scope of most domestic reproductive rights discourse, the great potential of human rights thinking and activism for the U.S. women's health movement begins to become clear.

The International Conference on Population and Development (ICPD) held in Cairo in 1994 marked the formal acceptance at the international level of a new paradigm in which health is intimately tied to rights. As defined in the ICPD Programme of Action endorsed by 184 countries (including the United States), reproductive health involves far more than just abortion and contraception:

> Reproductive health is a state of complete physical, mental and social well-being and not merely the absence of disease or infirmity, in all matters related to the reproductive system and to its functions and processes. Reproductive health therefore implies that people are able to have a satisfying and safe sex life and that they have the capability to reproduce and the freedom to decide if, when and how often to do so . . .[12]

Moreover, reproductive rights are explicitly recognized as human rights—but stated far more expansively than simply as the right to choose abortion without government interference (which, significantly, is a right not fully realized in the document). As such, reproductive rights rest on:

the basic right of all couples and individuals to decide freely and responsibly the number, spacing and timing of their children and to have the information and means to do so, and the right to attain the highest standard of sexual and reproductive health. It also includes the right to make decisions concerning reproduction free of discrimination, coercion and violence as expressed in human rights documents . . . [12]

The ICPD declaration is, admittedly, a heavily negotiated, compromised, and imperfect document. But from this document and the political process that led up to it, there has emerged a rich, if still inchoate and evolving, discourse about the connection between health and human rights. Although the "softness" of human rights law clearly makes actual implementation a monumental task, human rights provides the vocabulary and conceptual basis for developing an understanding—and ultimately policies and programs—that link new conceptions of health to the struggle for social justice and respect for the basic dignity of every human being.

Viewed in this way, the ICPD Programme represents a radical departure from previous declarations and policies. Broadly and simply stated, the essence of the change is this: previous governmental and nongovernmental statements, as well as maternal-child health/family planning programs and policies themselves, regularly conceptualized and treated women and their reproductive and sexual capacities *instrumentally*—as the tools through which to implement population control policies, child survival strategies, nationalist or fundamentalist agendas, development schemes, or patriarchal family values and structures. By contrast, the reproductive health and rights approach adopted at ICPD is premised on a view of women as valuable *intrinsically*, as well as for the contribution they make to the broader society. [13] This basic shift in perspective demands a view of both health and rights that begins from and builds on women's lived experience, in its full social, economic, and cultural context.

Thus health is no longer the exclusive domain of the medical expert, trained to consider biological processes as mechanical systems to be fixed according to externally set priorities. Instead, the "reproductive health" approach strives to structure health policies and programs around women as subjects, capable of acting as decision-making agents in their own lives, as well as in their families and communities. While physical well-being is undeniably important, it cannot be understood and treated in isolation from the social, economic, and cultural conditions that influence both its existence and its meaning. Similarly, reproductive rights are not conceived exclusively as an individual right to choose whether or not to bear a child, free from government interference. Certainly that right is basic and profoundly important. But it cannot be the full statement of reproductive rights since a right to choose without regard to the conditions in which choices are made, is a barren right indeed. For example, a theoretical right to use contraception will mean absolutely nothing in the life of a woman who has no access to contraceptives or even to basic quality health care. Context may not be everything, but it is essential to both theory and practice if rights are truly the entitlements of all.

This view of human rights finds expression in international treaties and in the approach championed by the women's human rights movement, which sees civil and political rights, on the one hand, and economic, social, and cultural rights, on the other, as indivisible and interdependent.[14] That view ultimately became a moving force behind the ICPD document and a key organizing principle of the international women's health movement, because it could link increasingly sophisticated understandings of the social causes and consequences of poor health for women, with a language of justice broad enough to address the particular and diverse forces that constrain women's lives around the world. Moreover, it could mobilize a social movement with a constituency broad enough geographically and ideologically to articulate and press its demands for change in an international forum.

Yet this notion of rights is dramatically different from that which prevails in the United States. Here, where reproductive health and rights have been tied so intimately to legislative maneuvers and litigation strategies, our very understanding of what is at stake is heavily influenced by the legal system. Positioned first and foremost as a question of individual choice, reproductive rights have been formulated by the courts primarily on the basis of a constitutional right to privacy. That right has, in turn, been defined essentially as a right to be free of government intrusion into one's personal life, including the relationship between a woman and her private physician. This framing of the issue goes back to the 1965 case of *Griswold v Connecticut*[15] in which the U.S. Supreme Court struck down a Connecticut statute criminalizing the use of contraceptives, including by married couples. The right to privacy first enunciated in Griswold was then applied in 1973 in *Roe v Wade*[16] to uphold a conditional right to abortion.

As multiple commentators, including reproductive rights advocates, have elaborated in the quarter century since *Roe*, the right to privacy, while profoundly important in limiting unwarranted intrusion by the state, is ultimately a flimsy base from which to articulate and defend a woman's reproductive and sexual health and rights.[17,18] First, the right to privacy is simply not broad enough to ensure that all women have access to the health services—much less the social and economic conditions—necessary to exercise even the most narrowly construed right to choose. In 1980, for example, the Supreme Court ruled that no constitutional right was violated if an indigent woman could not obtain a medically necessary abortion because federal legislation prohibited Medicaid from paying for it.[19]

A second problem with reliance on the right to privacy is that it necessarily posits government intrusion in personal decisions as the biggest, most dangerous—indeed, virtually the only—threat to women's reproductive lives. Other major threats to women's well-being—domestic violence, sexual abuse, poverty with all its physical and emotional dimensions, for example—become strictly individual problems conceived as "risk factors" to be treated with education in strategies of avoidance. Thus, as the legal language imposes deeper and deeper constrictions on our expectations of entitlement and our understanding of justice, the corresponding health debate becomes more and more impoverished as well. The strains of that impoverishment have been felt in the US reproductive rights movement, where the health and justice issues of greatest concern to women on the margins of society have become virtually lost to the language of civil rights.

This is not a call to abandon the reproductive rights struggle in the courts or the legislatures. That is basic to every woman's reproductive freedom. But it is a call to expand the struggle outside of the formal legal system, and to use the insights and tools of health research to create the basis for new demands for change. In that struggle, innovative health research and an expanded discourse about social justice reinforce each other by changing the boundaries of what is "culturally credible" as a cause of poor health and as a demand for justice. Such concepts may not yet find validation in the courts; but, as some health activists believe, they provide fertile soil for building a broader, more inclusive movement from the ground up.

Notes

1. Skrabranek, P. and McCormick, J. *Follies and Fallacies in Medicine*. Buffalo, NY: Prometheus Books; 1990.
2. Skolbekken, J. The risk epidemic in medical journals. *Soc Sci Med*. 1995; 40:291–305.
3. Maine, D., Freedman, L., Shaheed, F., Fraurschi, S., and Alkalin, M. Risks and rights: The uses of reproductive health data. *Reproductive Health Matters*, 1995;6:40–51.
4. Gifford, S. The meaning of lumps: A case study of the ambiguities of risk. In: James, C., Stall, R., and Gifford, S., eds. *Anthropology and Epidemiology*. Dordrecht, The Netherlands: D. Reidl; 1986: 213–246.
5. Lupton, D. Risk as moral danger: The social and political functions of risk discourse in public health. *Int J Health Serv*, 1993;23:425–435.
6. Douglas, M. *Risk and Blame: Essays in Cultural Theory*. New York: Routledge; 1992.
7. Chasnoff, I., Landress, H., and Barrett, M. The prevalence of illicit drug or alcohol use during pregnancy and discrepancies in mandatory reporting in Pinellas County, Florida. *N Engl J Med*. 1990; 322:1045–1046.
8. Handwerkerm L. Medical risk: Implicating poor pregnant women. *Soc Sci Med*. 1994; 38:665–675.
9. The Personal Responsibility Act of 1995, HR 4 (104th Congress, 1st session).
10. Link, B. and Phelan, J. Social conditions as fundamental causes of disease. *J Health Soc Behav*. 1995; (Extra Issue):80–94.
11. Petersen, A. and Lupton, D. *The New Public Health: Health and Self in the Age of Risk*. Thousand Oaks, Calif: Sage; 1996.

12. *Report of the International Conference on Population and Development.* New York: United Nations; 1994. Document A/Conf.1771/13.
13. Freedman, L. Reflections on emerging frameworks of health and human rights. *Health and Human Rights*, 1995;1:313–346.
14. Copelon, R. and Petchesky, R. Toward an interdependent approach to reproductive and sexual rights as human rights: Reflections on the ICPD and beyond. In: Schuler, M., ed. *From Basic Needs to Basic Rights: Women's Claim to Human Rights.* Washington, D.C.: Women, Law & Development International; 1995.
15. 381 US 479 (1965).
16. 410 US 113 (1973).
17. Copelon, R. From privacy to autonomy: The conditions for sexual and reproductive freedom. In: Fried M, ed. *From Abortion to Reproductive Freedom.* Boston: South End Press; 1990:27–43.
18. Petchesky, R. *Abortion and Woman's Choice.* Boston: Northeastern University Press; 1990.
19. *Harris v. McRae*, 448 US 297 (1980).

27

The Role of Health Professionals in Protecting and Promoting Human Rights
A Paradigm for Professional Responsibility

Susannah Sirkin, Vincent Iacopino, Michael A. Grodin, and Yael Danieli

In every sector of society, professionals have begun to play critical roles in promoting and protecting human rights: journalists have convened to discuss their responsibilities when they are the first international witnesses of massacres, war crimes, and genocide;[1] business executives have met to develop corporate codes of conduct in relation to labor conditions in general and child and prison labor in particular, as well as trade and aid in countries where gross human rights violations are the norm;[2] international humanitarian workers, agonized over the manipulation by warlords and genocidal killers of their presence and provision of aid, have begun to discuss their responsibilities to develop human rights protocols;[3] clergy of many faiths have used their pulpits, sometimes at great personal risk, to call for an end to injustices and human rights violations; artists, writers, and musicians have organized human rights actions and events for years, and have stood in solidarity with embattled colleagues.

Lawyers have numerous and obvious, specific roles in the struggle for human rights: developing and advocating for international human rights law, trying human rights cases in domestic, regional, and international courts, training human rights lawyers, and supporting the development of judicial systems that protect human rights.

Of all professionals, however, those who take on the ethical oath to protect and promote human life and health, have a unique obligation and contribution ke to human rights. It is a responsibility that has yet to be fully realized.

s chapter, we seek to elaborate on the special connection between health and human rights, the record of health professionals in human rights advocacy, and the betrayal that occurs when members of the health professions engage in or support violations of human rights. We also address the critical role that health professionals must play in attending to and advocating for the healing of the individual, and his or her family, community, society, and nation in the aftermath of traumatic human rights violations.

The Relationship Between Health and Human Rights

Health professionals have a responsibility to protect and promote human rights.[4] This is both because human rights violations have devastating health consequences and because protecting and promoting human rights (civil, political, economic, social, and cultural) can be the most effective means of ensuring the positive conditions for health.[5] A global society must recognize the inherent dignity and equality of all members of the human family.

Throughout history, society has charged healers with the duty of understanding and alleviating causes of suffering. As we enter the twenty-first century, the nature and extent of human suffering have compelled health providers to redefine their understandings of health and the scope of their professional interests and responsibilities. Despite a century of technological progress, poverty, hunger, illiteracy, and disease continue to plague the world community. Today, 1.3 billion people live in deep poverty, and over 85 percent of the world's income is concentrated in the richest 20 percent of the world's people. Seven hundred fifty million people go hungry every day. Nine hundred million adults are illiterate, two-thirds of whom are women. More than one billion people have no access to health care or safe drinking water [1, pp. 30–38]. Each day 40,000 children die from malnutrition and disease, lack of clean water, and inadequate sanitation.[6]

In the past century, the world has witnessed ongoing epidemics of armed conflicts and violations of international human rights, epidemics that have devastated and continue to devastate the health and well-being of people around the world. Armed conflicts have claimed the lives of more than one hundred million people in the twentieth century, and increasingly, civilians have become the victims of war and internal conflicts. Today, 90 percent of war-related deaths are civilians. Twenty-six major civil conflicts raged in 1995. Torture, disappearance, and political killings are systematically practiced in dozens of countries, and tens of millions of landmines threaten the lives and limbs of civilians. In 1995, one in every 200 persons in the world was displaced as a result of war or political repression [1, pp. 5–9].

Health professionals have a great stake in the Universal Declaration of Human Rights, because the document provides the underpinning for the professions' goals of alleviating suffering and promoting the conditions for health and well-being of all people. These goals represent an ideal that cannot be achieved unless the fundamental rights set forth in the UDHR are recognized, respected, protected, and fulfilled. The observance of the 50th Anniversary of the UDHR is an occasion for institutions within the health sector to explore and embrace the critical link between human rights and health.

Historically, human rights have not been among the expressed concerns of health practitioners. Medical training has not yet incorporated human rights into the standard curriculum, and traditional concepts of medical ethics relate primarily to the doctor-patient relationship and the treatment of disease devoid of analysis of societal issues surrounding the patient, his or her community or political, cultural, or economic environment. When conceptualizations of health and human suffering are devoid of human rights concerns, health practitioners can become both willing and unwilling participants in human rights violations. Sometimes, such violations even serve the interests of individual practitioners and may sustain the interests of the state and other actors.

Before reviewing the myriad ways in which health professionals can promote and protect human rights, it is essential to confront the potential within the professions to collaborate in abuses. Health professionals must face the history of a sordid collusion in human rights violations throughout the twentieth century—and sound an alarm at the continued betrayal of their professions on virtually all continents.

The Involvement of Health Professionals in Human Rights Abuses

After World War II, the Allies prosecuted the major surviving Nazi war criminals in an international military tribunal. That trial created new international law and can be properly seen, together with the adoption of the 1948 Universal Declaration of Human Rights, as the birth of the international human rights movement. The trial produced the Nuremberg Principles that recognize that there are crimes against peace, war crimes, and crimes against humanity, and that individuals can be punished for committing these crimes even if such violation is consistent with the laws of their own country, and even if they were "obeying orders" [2].

The 1946–47 trial of Nazi doctors (the Doctors' Trial) documented the most notorious example of physician participation in war crimes and crimes against humanity, specifically murder and torture in the guise of human experimentation [3]. Hitler called upon physicians not only to help justify his racial hatred policies with a "scientific" rationale (racial hygiene), but also to direct his euthanasia programs and ultimately the Nazi death camps. Almost half of all German physicians joined the Nazi Party [4].

Nazi medicine was formed and nurtured by a symbiosis of National Socialist ideology and social Darwinism, mixed with the theory of racial hygiene that viewed some racial and ethnic groups as subhuman and gave physicians an ideological excuse to use their skill to harm people in the name of the state. There is a series of recurrent themes in Nazi medicine: The devaluation and dehumanization of defined segments of the community, the medicalization of social and political problems, the training of physicians to identify with the political goals of the government, fear of the consequences of refusing to cooperate with civil authority, the bureaucratization of the medical role, and the lack of concern for medical ethics and human rights [4]. Nazi physicians failed to see themselves as physicians first, with a calling and an ethic dedicated to healing and caring for the welfare of human beings. Instead, they were seduced by power and ideology to view the state as their "patient" and to see the extermination of an entire people as "treatment" for the state's health.

How could physicians serve as agents of state repression? How could physicians use their skills to torture and murder, rather than to heal and help? Sadly, there is incontrovertible evidence of the continuing involvement of physicians in crimes against humanity [5]. The extent of the involvement of physicians in contemporary human rights violations is horrifyingly broad: the examination of prisoners prior to torture, the monitoring of torture victims, the resuscitation and medical treatment of prisoners after torture, as well as the falsification of medical records, death certificates, and certifications after torture. Physicians also carry out and supervise capital and corporal punishments to which prisoners are sentenced after judicial hearings. Physicians continue to be involved in unethical human experimentation.[7] Physicians and psychologists have also collaborated with brutal regimes to develop and advise on interrogation techniques including sensory deprivation and brainwashing [7]. Physicians have violated medical neutrality during periods of peace and conflict [8]. Finally, they have been silent witnesses to intentional harm and social injustice as well as the neglect of human medical and social needs. For example, in South Africa, government policies under Apartheid were based on indignity and dehumanization. In the past, health professionals, through acts of commission and omission, facilitated and systematically legitimized the debasement of humanity. Under Apartheid, health personnel failed to document forensic evidence of torture and ill-treatment, breached principles of confidentiality, delivered health services on a highly discriminatory basis, and neglected the health consequences of extreme racial disparities in poverty, illiteracy, unemployment, and other social determinants of health. As of this writing, professional organizations, scholars, NGOs, and others within the health sector are examining the role of the health professions under apartheid, developing recommendations for reform and promoting measures to prevent such abuses in the future.[8]

What circumstances and preconditions facilitated these human rights abuses? What were the personal, professional, and political contexts that not only permitted but encouraged these human rights abuses? Why and how did doctors become involved? In examining these profoundly important questions, several recurrent themes have emerged: the devaluation of certain members of society, persistent blaming of the victims of abuse, training physicians to identify with a political cause, fear of refusing to cooperate, bureaucratization of the medical role, and lack of concern for medical ethics [5]. Physicians who resist may be marginalized from their own professional groups. Also, they may themselves be jailed, tortured, and murdered. In recent years, health professionals in Turkey have been prosecuted for treating victims of human rights violations, and health professionals in several countries have disappeared, been arrested, or threatened for treating the sick and wounded in internal armed conflicts or in the course of the violent suppression of public demonstrations.[9]

Additional factors that may facilitate human rights violations within the health sector include: limited conceptualizations of health and human suffering, ineffective leadership of health sector organizations, inadequate accountability among health personnel, lack of independence in the health sector, and lack of human rights and bioethics education. Of course, one cannot exclude the sad fact that some health professionals are witting and willing participants in human rights violations through some major flaw in character and moral standing.

Physicians who use their special skills and knowledge to violate human rights not only violate the rights of their victims, but betray their obligation to their profession. The standing of the entire profession suffers when physicians act as agents of the state to destroy life and health. Physicians themselves should benefit from the articulation of clear international standards that prohibit the use of physicians by the state to violate human rights [9].

Just as it took the world's lawyers and physicians working together to bring the Nazi physicians to justice at Nuremberg, it will take the world's lawyers and physicians working together to prevent wholesale violations of human rights and to support proactively the growth of human rights worldwide. In 1996, Global Lawyers and Physicians (GLP) was established to help accomplish this goal. The world's physicians and lawyers, because of both their moral authority in defending life and justice and their privileged positions in society, have special obligations to humanity and must work together transnationally to identify and publicize physicians, lawyers, and judges involved in human rights abuses. It is our obligation to understand how and why physicians dedicated to health and healing can turn to torture and murder in the service of their country so that repetition of this betrayal of humanity can be avoided. Whenever politics or ideology treat people as objects, we all lose our humanity. Medical ethics devoid of human rights become no more than hollow symbols [9].[10]

The Role of Health Professionals in Protecting and Promoting Human Rights

Although individuals within the health professions have violated their professional oaths, participated in abuses, or acquiesced to human suffering by remaining silent, for the past two decades physicians and other health professionals have also contributed their specialized skills and experience to exposing human rights violations, documenting their serious health consequences, and addressing the needs of victims. Thousands of individual physicians and other health professionals and dozens of national, regional, and international medical and health organizations have adopted human rights principles into their understanding of their professional obligations and incorporated them into codes of ethics.

In Chile, Turkey, and Uruguay for instance, where torture was or has been widespread, medical leaders organized to oppose the practice, condemn medical participation, hold participants in abuses to account, and treat thousands of victims. In the USSR in the late 1970s and early 1980s, courageous Soviet psychiatrists risked long prison sentences to speak out in opposition to the wrongful confinement of dissidents in psychiatric hospitals.

In the 1980s, the anti-apartheid National Medical and Dental Association of South Africa and others documented torture, denial of health care, and other abuses of political detainees. They, too, set up clinics to provide rehabilitative services to survivors of police brutality and prison camps. Amnesty International launched medical groups in many countries to mobilize the profession in its campaigns against torture, the death penalty, and the abysmal health conditions of individual prisoners of conscience. In 1977, the American Association for the Advancement of Science organized a Clearinghouse on Science and Human Rights, initiating medical and scientific delegations to study specific human rights problems and explore the unique contribution of science to the protection of human rights. Together with Argentine doctors, scientists, and students, for instance, they pioneered the use of DNA in the identification of the bodies of the "disappeared" from Argentina's "dirty war" of the 1970s.

In 1986, Physicians for Human Rights (PHR) was established, constituting the first formally-organized group of medical scientists working in the United States to promote human rights worldwide.[11] Since then, similar groups have emerged in Denmark, India, Israel, the Palestinian Authority, South Africa, the United Kingdom, and elsewhere. In the Netherlands, the Johannes Wier Institute has also organized physicians to promote human rights since the mid-1980s.

Physicians, scientists, and other health professionals such as nurses, psychologists, and public health workers fulfill an important need in the worldwide struggle for human rights. Because of their training, they are uniquely qualified to play an important role in human rights investigation, fact-finding, documentation, advocacy, and treatment. Scientists can conduct autopsies, uncover graves, identify remains, and determine cause of death. The evidence doctors and scientists uncover is now routinely used in courts and tribunals to bring perpetrators to justice and hold governments accountable for violations. Health professionals can conduct surveys to quantify in stark figures the morbidity and mortality that result from such violations of human rights as torture, excessive use of force by police and military, and use of chemical weapons and landmines. Medical and psychological examinations and collection of victim histories can provide objective and forceful evidence of abuse by governments and can alert the international community to refugee crises and populations at risk due to hunger, disease, abuse, or neglect [10–12]. Medical and psychological documentation of human rights abuses is more difficult to refute than oral or written testimonies, and is often retrievable even after the witnesses' voices have been silenced.

In addition, when they are well organized, health professionals can put pressure on governments that violate human rights. The grounding of their concerns in professional ethics and their recognized commitment to health render their voices particularly powerful. During the past decades, numerous specialists have made contributions to documentation and advocacy for human rights: internists, pathologists, pediatricians, psychiatrists, psychologists, epidemiologists, gynecologists, nurses, midwives, toxicologists, burn specialists, prison health workers, orthopedic surgeons, social workers, and medical ethicists have conducted investigations, published articles in medical journals, spoken at hearings, presented evidence in national trials, regional courts and the ad-hoc international criminal tribunals for the former Yugoslavia and Rwanda, conducted training sessions, and mobilized their colleagues to promote human rights. Health professionals have also played a central role in documenting the occurrence of rape and child abuse, estimating their incidence, assessing physical and psychological consequences, and helping to develop community-based strategies for helping victim/survivors.

Physicians and their professional associations have mobilized in defense of colleagues who have been imprisoned, tortured, or otherwise abused for performing their duties and adhering to the ethical standards mandating appropriate treatment of the sick and wounded regardless of political affiliation. Major professional societies, such as the British Medical Association, as well as prestigious institutions such as the Institute of Medicine in the United States, have established human rights committees.

Increasingly, health professionals are also engaging in prevention strategies. It is not enough for those whose work is to protect and promote health, to regard their human rights obligations as limited to treating and alleviating the consequences of abuses, reporting on violations, and conducting campaigns after abuses have occurred. The effort to prevent human rights violations extends to monitoring the early signs of outbreaks and to inoculating society against epidemics of abuse through education in tolerance, non-violence, conflict resolution, and basic human standards. Most importantly, health professionals must view addressing the need for truth, justice, and commemoration for victims of human rights abuse as essential to prevention. Failure to meet these needs will open the door to repetition of cycles of violence and revenge, as well as leave a debilitating legacy of trauma for the next generation [13].

The Role of Health Professionals in Addressing Globally the Needs of Victims of Human Rights Abuses

In addressing the needs of victim/survivors, health professionals must see their role in a comprehensive, integrated manner, from the perspective of the totality of the individual's life, as a member of a family, community, society, nation, and the world. To respond effectively to victim/survivor needs, health professionals should be cognizant of their complexity so that they can make informed choices about how to meet them. This will usually be done in collaboration with other relevant professionals such as lawyers, journalists, human rights organizations, community activists and leaders, in addition to cooperative governments and United Nations bodies. In addition to obvious medical treatment, among the important survivor needs and recommended health professional responses are the following.

Acknowledgment by the Caregiver

For decades, survivors of human rights violations have been doubly victimized: first by the abuse itself, and subsequently by a conspiracy of silence that frequently surrounds the victims. Most victims need to tell their story. And they need others to listen to them. Among the first and foremost listeners should be caregivers. In order to listen to and subsequently acknowledge the trauma story, the caregiver must overcome the numbing, denial, avoidance, distancing, and bystander's guilt that frequently accompany the hearing [14]. Whereas society has a moral obligation to share its members' pain, psychotherapists and other health professionals have, in addition, a professional, contractual obligation. When they fail to listen, explore, understand, and help, they participate in the conspiracy of silence and may inflict further trauma on the survivor [14].

Acknowledgment by Society

Recovery from trauma, at least at the cognitive level, involves the ability to develop a realistic perspective of what happened, by whom, to whom, and accepting the reality that it had happened the way it did. Formal and public establishment of the historical record, compilation of eyewitness and survivor accounts, investigation into the roles, motives, and strategies of perpetrators, can validate this perspective for the survivor and the larger society. In the experience of South American psychologists who have worked for years with victims of repression "the victims know that individual therapeutic intervention is not enough. They need to know that their society as a whole acknowledges what has happened to them. . . . Truth means the end of denial and silence. . . . Truth will be achieved only when literally everyone knows and acknowledges what happened during the military regime . . ." [15]. Health professionals have a role to play in supporting and participating in the revelation of these truths, whether through truth commissions, national or international courts and tribunals, or articles, books, archives, and films.

Justice

For victims of serious human rights violations, truth without justice is, in most cases, empty. Impunity for criminals who rape, torture, and kill is an insult to the dead and to survivors and their loved ones. Failure to bring individual perpetrators to justice risks the collectivization of guilt, and can encourage renewed cycles of violence and revenge. Fifty years after Nuremberg, the functioning of two international criminal tribunals to prosecute war crimes, crimes against humanity and genocide in former Yugoslavia and Rwanda, as well as serious prospects of the establishment of an International Criminal Court are cause for hope [16]. Forensic pathologists, archaeologists, anthropologists, radiologists, odontologists, and geneticists, have been and must continue to be central players in the efforts to collect evidence, and promote criminal prosecution of perpetrators of human rights violations. Psychologists and social workers must work with and provide support for witnesses. All health professionals need to view the establishment of justice as a critical part of the healing of individual victims and societies.

Measures of Individual Redress such as Reparation, Restitution, Compensation

Establishing guilt and enforcing punishment for abusers is a real and important form of redress for victims. But victims still need a tangible or symbolic statement from society that they have been grossly wronged. And they should have a right to monetary or other recompense. Reparations for damages, such as restitution of property and possessions or lost income, both real and symbolic compensation for the harm done, and rehabilitation can accomplish the re-establishment of victims' equality of value, power, and self-esteem [17].

Commemoration and Education

There is a deep human need for rituals of mourning and commemoration that transcends all cultures, religions, and society. In the aftermath of gross human rights violations and the devastation caused by war, starvation, and epidemic disease, there is a need for shared context, shared mourning, and shared memory. From the hills of Guatemala, to the villages of Kurdistan; from the parishes of Rwanda to the fields of Srebrenica in Bosnia, forensic scientists who have exhumed graves with Physicians for Human Rights have felt the intense need of the victims for ceremonial reburial, for mourning rituals, and for monuments and memorials. And when all of the bodies cannot be found, recovered, or identified, the anguish of survivors who still wait for the truth and cannot yet grieve fully is incalculable. Recording death and ensuring burial with dignity are essential to demonstrate the value of human life. Mental health professionals in particular, have much to offer in working with individual victims, clergy, and communities to develop and ensure appropriate rituals for reburial, mourning, and commemoration. They can also be instrumental in advocating for special resources to be devoted to memorial and commemoration.

Regarding Human Rights Education

The millions of trained health professionals around the world have yet to embrace fully the notion that human rights are essential for human health. Health professionals should understand that human rights are interdependent and indivisible; that the realization of any one right depends on the realization of other rights. The spectrum of human rights that may affect health includes a broad range of possibilities: civil, political, economic, social, cultural, and others. This understanding will only emerge through human rights education for health professionals.

For health practitioners to promote health and well being, human rights concerns need to be integrated into health education. Throughout the world they have been ill-equipped to address human rights abuses because medicine in the twentieth century has focused almost exclusively on the treatment of disease. But a disease focus marginalizes their roles in society and consequently neglects social conditions that affect health and well being. A prevention orientation offers a more comprehensive perspective that can remove some of these limitations.

Over the past five years, curricular studies in health and human rights have begun to develop in the health sector [18]. Such studies provide students with a basic understanding of human rights issues that are relevant to health professionals and enable students to acquire the knowledge and skills necessary for preventing and alleviating the human suffering caused by human rights abuses. Also, continuing education courses have taught practitioners to document human rights violations and to provide care for survivors of human rights abuses. Hopefully, these pioneering efforts represent the beginning of a global movement for human rights education that will transform effectively the aspirations of the Universal Declaration into action.

The inclusion of human rights in the curriculum of health professionals carries significant implications: it challenges them to redefine health and well-being and focus on causes of human suffering that have been neglected in the past. It requires health professionals to move beyond the traditional physician-patient relationship, and is likely to interfere with the traditional self-protection of the profession and the financial self-interest which is at the core of many health care systems. Furthermore, efforts to integrate human rights into health education are limited by leadership, organization, funding, and policy within the health sector. While no human rights culture can be legislated, many professions have instituted ethical and human rights standards for themselves. The health profession in every country must discipline its own members who violate these standards. But traditional codes of ethics must also extend beyond the doctor-patient relationship to address the relationship between the professional and the larger community. Public health proponents increasingly understand that they must address directly the underlying societal issues that determine, to a large extent, who lives and who dies, when and of what. And human rights activists are ever more aware that limitations to health care based on discrimination exacerbate myriad human rights violations [19].

Notwithstanding these challenges, health and all other professionals, cannot stand by as silent witnesses to the incalculable human suffering caused by human rights violations on a daily basis on a staggering scale worldwide. At stake is not only individual and community well-being and the credibility of all professionals, but the safeguarding of our humanity for centuries to come.

Notes

1. Reporting from the Killing Fields: A Conference on Genocide. Crimes Against Humanity, and War, Berkeley, California, April 5–7, 1997.
2. See Business for Social Responsibility website <www.bsr.org>.
3. J. de Milliano, *The MSF Perspective on the Need for Cooperation between Humanitarian Organisations and Human Rights Organisations*, from Conference on the Cooperation between Humanitarian Organisations and Human Rights Organisations, Final Report of the Conference held in Amsterdam, the Netherlands, pp. 12–16, 1996.
4. See Health and Human Rights Consortium Web Site <www.healthandhumanrights.org>
5. Health is defined as a "state of complete physical, mental and social well-being, and not merely the absence of disease or infirmity." Declaration of Alma Ata. World Health Organization, Primary Health Care. Geneva: World Health Organization, 1978.
6. World Summit on Children, 1990.

7. Final Report of the Advisory Committee on Human Radiation Experiments, U.S. Government Printing Office, October 1995. See also [6].
8. The American Association for the Advancement of Science and Physicians for Human Rights, *Human Rights and Health: The Legacy of Apartheid*, submission at the request of the Truth and Reconciliation Commission, Boston, 1998.
9. Amnesty International, *Prescriptions for Change: Health Professionals and the Exposure of Human Rights Violations*, AI Index: ACT 75/01/96. London, 1996; Physicians for Human Rights, *Torture in Turkey & Its Unwilling Accomplices*, Boston, 1996.
10. See Global Lawyers and Physicians (GLP) Web Site <www.bumc.bu.edu/www/sph/lw/GLPHR.htm>.
11. See PHR Web Site <www.phrusa.org>.

References

1. R. L. Sivard, *World Military and Social Expenditures, 1987–1988*, WMSE Publications, Leesburg, Virginia, 1996.
2. M. Cherif Bassiouni, *Crimes Against Humanity in International Criminal Law*, Martinus Nijhoff Publishers, Dordrecht, The Netherlands, pp. 1–48, 1992.
3. G. Annas and M. Grodin (eds.), *The Nazi Doctors and the Nuremberg Code: Human Rights in Human Experimentation*, Oxford University Press, New York, 1992.
4. M. Grodin and G. Annas, Legacies of Nuremberg: Medical Ethics and Human Rights, *Journal of the American Medical Association,* 276:20, pp. 1682–1683, November 27, 1996.
5. *Medicine Betrayed: The Participation of Doctors in Human Rights Abuses*, Report of a Working Party, British Medical Association, Zed Books, London, United Kingdom and Atlantic Highlands, New Jersey, pp. 1–8, 1992.
6. D. J. Rothman, Ethics and Human Experimentation: Henry Beecher, Revisited, *New England Journal of Medicine*, 317:19, pp. 1195–1199, 1987.
7. R. J. Lifton, *The Nazi Doctors: Medical Killing and the Psychology of Genocide*, Basic Books, New York, pp. 1–18, 1986.
8. B. Levy and V. Sidel, *War and Public Health*, Oxford University Press, New York, 1997.
9. M. Grodin, G. Annas, and L. Glantz, Medicine and Human Rights: A Proposal for International Action, *Hastings Center Report*, 23:4, pp. 8–12, 1995.
10. M. J. Toole and R. J. Waldman, Refugees and Displaced Persons: War, Hunger and Public Health, *Journal of the American Medical Association*, 270:5, pp. 600–605, 1993.
11. H. J. Geiger and R. M. Cook-Deegan, The Role of Physicians in Conficts and Humanitarian Crises: Case Studies from the Field Missions of Physicians for Human Rights, *Journal of the American Medical Association*, 270, pp. 616–620, 1993.
12. R. Desjarlais, L. Eisenberg, B. Good, and A. Kleinman (eds.), *World Mental Health: Problems and Priorities in Low Income Countries*, Oxford University Press, New York, 1995.
13. Y. Danieli (ed.), *International Handbook of Multigenerational Legacies of Trauma*, Plenum Press, New York, 1998.
14. Y. Danieli, Confronting the Unimaginable: Psychotherapists' Reactions to Victims of the Nazi Holocaust, in *Human Adaptation to Extreme Stress*, J. P. Wilson, Z. Harel, and B. Kahana (eds.), Plenum, New York, pp. 219–238, 1988.
15. D. Becker, E. Lira, M. Moses, I. Castillo, E. Gomez, and J. Kovalskys, Therapy with Victims of Political Repression in Chile: The Challenge of Social Reparation, *Journal of Social Issues,* 40:3, pp. 133–149, 1990.
16. E. Stover, In the Shadow of Nuremberg: Pursuing War Criminals in the Former Yugoslavia and Rwanda, *Medicine and Global Survival*, 2:3, pp. 140–147, 1995.
17. Y. Danieli, Preliminary Reflections from a Psychological Perspective, in *The Right to Restitution, Compensation and Rehabilitation for Victims of Gross Violations of Human Rights and Fundamental Freedoms*, T. C. van Boven, C. Flinterman, F. Grunfeld, and I. Westendorp (eds.), Netherlands Institute of Human Rights, Special Issue No. 12, pp. 196–213, 1992.
18. J. Brenner, Human Rights Education in Public Health Graduate Schools, *Health and Human Rights*, 2:1, pp. 129–139, 1996.
19. J. Mann, S. Gruskin, M. Grodin, and G. Annas, Introduction to *Health and Human Rights: A Reader*, Routledge, New York (1999).

28
Teaching Human Rights in Graduate Health Education

Vincent Iacopino

This chapter outlines the state of human rights education in schools of public health, medicine, and nursing and provides a framework for discussions on future development of health and human rights curricula in graduate-level health education. Included here are a review of the need for human rights education in schools for health professionals, the relationship between human rights and bioethics, a profile of current instructors, a summary of content and methodology of present human rights educational initiatives, and considerations for discussions among Health and Human Rights Curriculum Project participants.

Several sources of background information were used in the preparation of this paper: (i) Medline literature searches on health and human rights education topics, (ii) review of relevant human rights course syllabi, (iii) interviews with 9 instructors teaching human rights[1] in schools of public health, medicine and nursing, and (iv) one interview with a representative of the American Nurses Association.

The Need for Human Right Education in Health Professional Schools

The Intrinsic Value of Human Rights in the Health Professions

Health professionals need human rights education because of its intrinsic value in alleviating human suffering and promoting health and well-being. These values operate on both moral and practical levels. The health and human rights discourse not only serves as a unifying framework to understand the role of health practitioners in society, but it also provides practical tools for effective and socially relevant health policy and practice. While the importance of alleviating human suffering and promoting health and well-being may seem self-evident to some, no formal mandate has been set forth in medical ethics to designate human rights concerns as the responsibilities of physicians and other health professionals.[2] In fact, the assertion of a need for human rights education in health professional schools represents a powerful critique of normative health practices and the current state of medical ethics. Since 1978, the World Health Organization (WHO) has defined health as "a state of complete physical, mental and social well-being, and not merely the absence of disease or infirmity."[3] Health concerns in the 20th century have focused almost exclusively on diagnosing, treating, and preventing disease. By focusing on disease as the sole cause of suffering, health practitioners may fail to recognize the critical relationship between health and human rights and consequently marginalize their role in promoting health in society.

Without a formal mandate to protect and promote human rights, social causes of suffering and opportunities for health promotion have been neglected. Perhaps one of the most disturbing examples of such neglect can be found during the practice of "apartheid medicine" in South Africa.[4] Under apartheid, the majority of health practitioners failed to document human rights violations, delivered health services on a highly discriminatory basis, remained silent amid widespread torture of political detainees and forced displacement of more than three million Africans, and neglected the health consequences of extreme racial disparities in poverty, illiteracy, unemployment, and other social determinants of health.

The Significance of Linking Health and Human Rights

In most cases, accepting the linkages between health and human rights requires practitioners to re-examine their definitions of health and the scope of their professional responsibilities. The ways in which health practitioners link matters of health and human rights have significant implications for the ways in which human rights curricula are developed and integrated into graduate health education.

Relationships between health and human rights may be thought of as either "instrumental" or "intrinsic." What most distinguishes these concepts is their implicit definitions of health. An instrumental relationship generally defines health in terms of morbidity and mortality, whereas an intrinsic relationship defines health within the context of an individual's inherent dignity and worth.

Instrumental Linkages

One of the most compelling arguments for educating health practitioners in human rights concerns is that violations of human rights and humanitarian law have extraordinary health consequences. During the last century, the world witnessed epidemics of armed conflict and violations of international human rights—events that have devastated and continue to devastate the health and well-being of humanity.[5] Armed conflicts have claimed the lives of more than 100 million people in the 20th century, and civilians have increasingly been the victims of war and internal conflicts. Recent estimates indicate that civilians make up 90% of war-related deaths.[6] In 1995, 26 major armed conficts occurred. Dozens of countries systematically practice torture, forced disappearance, and politically related killings,[7] and more than 100 million landmines threaten non-combatants.[8] In 1995, one in every 200 persons in the world was displaced as a result of war or political repression.[9]

Despite a century of technological progress, poverty, hunger, illiteracy, and disease continue to plague the health of the world community.[10] According to recent calculations, 1.3 billion people worldwide live in absolute poverty, and more than 85% of the world's income is controlled by the richest 20% of the world's people. Every day, 750 million people go hungry; approximately 900 million adults are illiterate, two-thirds of whom are women. More than one billion people have no access to health care or safe drinking water. Each day, 40,000 children die from malnutrition and preventable diseases, lack of clean water, and inadequate sanitation.[11] That is the equivalent of 100 jumbo jets loaded with children crashing daily with no survivors; it is also equal to the total number of people who died during the bombing of Hiroshima, dying every three days. Within the last five years, there were three times as many people who died as a result of being denied their basic rights as those who died in all the wars, revolutions, and murders in the past 150 years.

Human rights violations, whether civil, political, economic, social, or cultural in nature, have profound effects on morbidity and mortality. Health practitioners have no difficulty understanding the effects that war, torture, famine, forced migration, and the like have on morbidity and mortality. Perhaps the health consequences of other rights violations—such as freedom of speech or the right to marry and found a family—may not be so apparent. Restrictions on freedom of speech, however, have been linked to the large-scale famines that occurred in China between 1958 and 1961 and that claimed the lives of nearly 30 million people.[12] And the right to marry and found a family was developed to prevent such forced sterilization practices as those that preceded Nazi "euthanasia" programs and later genocide.[13]

Social conditions have long been recognized to affect morbidity and mortality. Throughout the 20th century in Europe and in North America, a marked decline in morbidity and mortality was associated with the combined effects of some far-reaching socioeconomic changes. These changes included improving the water supply, sanitary conditions and nutrition, personal hygiene, income from regular employment, social security, education, and preventive measures in public health. More recently, studies on "social determinants of health"[14] have demonstrated that disadvantaged social and economic circumstances increase the risk of serious illness and of premature death. Although the link between social conditions and health status has not been expressed in terms of rights, the health consequences of unrealized economic and social rights are readily apparent.

Another instrumental relationship between health and human rights is that of health policy and human rights. According to Mann, Gostin, Gruskin, et al. "Health policies and programs should be considered discriminatory and burdensome on human rights until proven otherwise."[15] Despite principles of beneficence and nonmaleficence in medicine, health policies have often been developed without considering human rights concerns.[16] Under such circumstances, health policies can be potentially ineffective or even harmful to the populations they are intended to serve.[17] Therefore, new health policies should be evaluated with regard to both positive and negative effects on human rights. Toward that end, human rights impact assessments represent essential and practical tools for attaining the best possible public health outcomes while protecting the human rights of individuals and populations.[18]

Intrinsic Linkages

The need for human rights education in health professional schools can also be argued on the basis of an intrinsic relationship between health and human rights. The intrinsic concept asserts that human rights are essential qualities of health[19] whose justification need not be based solely on morbidity and mortality concerns. Human rights provisions essentially prescribe the conditions for health as defined by WHO. Human rights, as outlined in WHO's definition of health, are intrinsic to the state of well-being and are therefore health outcomes in and of themselves. Education and work opportunities are health ends in and of themselves regardless of their associations with reduced morbidity and mortality. Similarly, freedom of thought, speech, movement, and association are components of health and well-being, independent of their instrumental relationships to death and disease.

The intrinsic perspective focuses on the inherent dignity and the worth of individuals as primary outcomes rather than death and disease. Torture, for example, is a concern of health practitioners because it represents an assault on individuals' dignity and worth and on humanity as a whole—not solely because of its adverse effects on the bodies and the minds of individuals. Consequently, remedial interventions call for protecting and promoting human dignity, not merely improving the morbidity and mortality associated with torture. Respect for human dignity is a concern that all members of the human family can share. Therefore, the intrinsic perspective has the potential of bridging our humanity with professional health practices.

Implications for Health and Human Rights Education:
Principled vs. the Strategic Approach

Whether human rights are thought of in terms of morbidity and mortality or an intrinsic perspective, they represent a significant departure from the normative concept of health as the presence or absence of disease. In the past 10 years, links between health status (morbidity and mortality) and social determinants of health have gained considerable acceptance among health practitioners. Such formulations, however, refer to a limited number of social factors (income or income disparity, education, and race, for instance) and neglect the wide range of human rights considerations that may affect health status.

Instrumental and intrinsic concepts of health and human rights have different implications when integrating human rights in graduate health education. The instrumental perspective has the strategic advantage of relying on traditional concerns of morbidity and mortality. Health practitioners are challenged simply to recognize causes (other than disease, injury, or environmental exposure) of morbidity and mortality. Also, the concept of "social justice" in public health adds credibility and support to instrumental concepts of health and human rights. Although understanding instrumental relationships between health and human rights is relatively easy, practitioners may find that recognizing practical applications of human rights in their everyday work and accepting previously unrecognized interrelations are often difficult. One of the most significant disadvantages of the instrumental perspective is the risk of practitioners' selectively focusing on particular human rights concerns while failing to recognize the interdependence of human rights and their combined effect on health status. For example, social determinants of health, such as poverty, education, and race, may not be effectively addressed when the rights to free speech, association, and representation in government are not ensured. Similarly, efforts to end torture or to institute effective and fair health policies depend on these and other human rights as well.

The intrinsic perspective of health and human rights is a more principled approach that requires health practitioners to recognize rights as conditions for human dignity and essential constituents of health and well-being, independent of morbidity and mortality considerations. It has the advantage of creating a consistent and unified framework for health concerns. Though widely accepted among health and human rights educators, the intrinsic perspective is likely to meet more ideological resistance than the instrumental perspective and, in some cases, may hinder or slow the development of health and human rights curricula in graduate health education. For this reason, project participants should continue to discuss the inherent tension between these strategic and principled approaches.

Objectives of Health and Human Rights Education

The need for human rights education may also be considered in terms of more immediate objectives. The nine health and human rights educators interviewed identified the following objectives.

Awareness and Engagement

Health practitioners, by and large, have not been exposed to human rights concepts. Most students have little or no knowledge of human rights principles or familiarity with international human rights instruments; they have not viewed health within a human rights framework and are unaware of the ways in which the protection and promotion of human rights relate to health promotion. Even in schools that offer health and human rights courses, such courses are typically elective and therefore reach only a small proportion of students. Efforts to improve awareness of and engage students in human rights issues have been facilitated by the following:

1. Interdepartmental collaborations for teaching and other program activities
2. Program activities for student involvement
   - summer research fellowships
   - visiting human rights lecture series
   - facilitating human rights–related internships
   - interactions with local human rights
   - nongovernmental organizations
3. Both required and elective courses
4. Exposure throughout students' graduate education
5. Certificate programs and course concentrations in health and human rights
6. Institutional support from, for example, deans, department chairs, senior faculty, and curriculum boards
7. Financial support
8. Student initiatives
   - health and human rights caucuses
   - local chapters of nongovernmental organizations (NGOs), such as Physicians for Human Rights and Amnesty International
   - film series on human rights topics
9. Human rights issues and research in medical and health journals
10. Exposure to human rights and health policy research, training, and advocacy

Core Knowledge and Skills

An objective of health and human rights education should be to raise awareness of health practitioners and engage them in a human rights discourse that would identify basic knowledge and skills that apply to all health professionals. If human rights concerns are, in fact, essential to health promotion, then health practitioners should be required to develop capacities in the core knowledge and skills of health and human rights.[20] The strategies for including health and human rights courses as part of the required curriculum and mandating health and human rights competency through associations for health professional schools are discussed below.

Development of Practical Applications

Virtually all health and human rights educators interviewed for this study indicated that developing practical applications to address health and human rights concerns is of critical importance. It is not uncommon that students and faculty sometimes view human rights as irrelevant to their daily clinical or health practice. This issue has been addressed by health and human rights instructors in a variety of ways:

- Using group discussion of case examples that relate to local health practices and problems
- Facilitating local field experiences that are human rights related
- Including readings that are relevant to both local and international human rights concerns
- Having students write their required papers on practical human rights concerns
- Providing summer internships and/or research programs for students
- Using human rights impact assessment tools (especially in schools of public health)

Address the Social Context of Health

Health practitioners need to develop knowledge and skills that enable them to address health in a social context. Human rights studies in graduate health education should prepare health practitioners to act in a social and political context in order to protect and promote human rights. It is therefore necessary to integrate human rights concerns into the ethics of health practitioners.

Breakdown Barriers between Human Rights and Health (and other) Discourses

Several health and human rights educators indicated that the language of human rights can sometimes insulate it from other discourses. Finding ways to establish a common language and agenda is therefore important. In recent years, significant progress has been made in overcoming such barriers, for example, rights-based programming in the provision of humanitarian assistance, and interdisciplinary approaches to anthropology and human rights.

Human Rights and Bioethics: The Need for a Common Agenda

The relationship between human rights and bioethics is an important consideration in developing health and human rights curricula in graduate health education for several reasons: First, human rights and bioethics share a common interest of respecting human dignity. Second, although some consider that human rights are essential to health practices, bioethical principles do not formally recognize health practitioners to be responsible for protecting and promoting human rights. Finally, bioethics courses are a primary target for including human rights in graduate health education. Before discussing the possibility of a common agenda for human rights and bioethics, it is important to understand some significant differences between human rights and bioethics.

Although the idea of human rights can be traced to the Magna Carta (1215) and later the English Bill of Rights (1689), France's Declaration of the Rights of Man (1789), and the U.S. Declaration of Independence (1776), the justification of human rights was rhetorical, not philosophical. Such rights were expressions of moral identity in the context of the Holocaust and World War II; they were self-evident and derived from common societal goals of peace and justice and individual goals of human dignity, happiness, and fulfillment. Human rights are social claims or values, which simultaneously impose limits on the power of the state (civil and political rights) and require the state to use its power to promote equity (economic, social, and cultural rights). The realization of such claims or rights is, in effect, a means of achieving the conditions for health and well-being in a global, civil society. The legitimacy of human rights is based on the process of consensus among States.

Bioethical principles—beneficence, nonmaleficence, confidentiality, autonomy, and informed consent—are codes of conduct that regulate clinical encounters with individual patients. These principles do not attempt to define health and well-being, nor do they indicate possible causes of human suffering. In fact, the discipline of bioethics was largely born out of misconduct by physicians and other health practitioners. Historically, the discipline has evolved more in response to increasing ethical dilemmas that have arisen from the practice of clinical medicine from an active agenda for health promotion. Also, while public health practitioners' definition of health includes a wide range of social factors,[21] normative public health practices focus primarily on diagnosis, treatment, and prevention of diseases.[22] In addition, public health does not have a strong tradition of bioethics. During the past year, the APHA released a statement of principles on human rights and is currently in the process of drafting a code of conduct.[23]

Differences between human rights and bioethics underscore the importance of developing an international consensus on the linkages between health and human rights and of formally articulating the responsibilities of health practitioners' in protecting and promoting human rights. In the past year, the François-Xavier Bagnoud Center for Health and Human Rights and Physicians for Human Rights have launched an international effort to develop a Declaration on Human Rights and Health Practice that would formally conceptualize linkages between health and human rights and would articulate ethical responsibilities regarding human rights. Thus far, 75 people from 40 countries have participated in the initial draft of this Declaration.

Despite such efforts to establish a common agenda for human rights and bioethics, human rights educators and bioethicists often disagree on the relative importance of the two discourses (that one discipline subsumes the other). Bioethicists sometimes criticize human rights for lacking a principled approach, and those working in human rights criticize bioethics for lacking an active agenda to address social causes of human suffering and health promotion. Therefore, project participants clearly must continue to discuss an outline for a common human rights and bioethics agenda, and the process by which such an agenda may be attained.

Student's Interest in Human Rights Education

Students' interest in health and human rights may depend on a number of key factors: (i) whether the coursework is required or elective, (ii) students'—especially medical students'—time constraints, (iii) opportunities for human rights experiences outside the classroom, (iv) opportunities for multiple exposures to human rights—at multiple points in time and across various disciplines, (v) the perceived importance of human rights by senior faculty, (vi) the degree to which instructors are perceived as role models, and (vii) the presence of student-led human rights initiatives on campus.

Health and human rights instructors reported that in both subjective assessments and objective course evaluations students have responded to health and human rights courses with great interest and enthusiasm. Increases in class size, growing demand for additional health and human rights courses, and the successful expansion of extracurricular human rights activities all reflect student interest in human rights. Moreover, such interest is greatly enhanced by many of the factors discussed previously, especially opportunities for multiple curricular and extracurricular exposure to human rights.

Since most health and human rights courses are elective, it is not surprising that students choose courses in which they are interested. Also, health and human rights studies in graduate health education have evolved without a formal competency mandate and are taught by instructors who often possess unique firsthand experiences and perspectives and who students regard as role models. These factors have undoubtedly contributed to the success of recent health and human rights initiatives. Currently, human rights material is required in two medical-school programs (for Boston University School of Medicine and for Griffin Hospital, at Yale School of Medicine). The material has been well received by students, and the success of these initiatives is due largely to at least one of the following two factors: the use of case examples that relate to local health practices and problems, and opportunities for extracurricular human rights experiences, such as clinical encounters with refugees.

Exposure to human rights concerns—for example, learning about torture, genocide, and the profound effects of poverty and child labor, and the complicity of health practitioners in human rights violations—can be traumatic for students. In the classroom, students exposed to this information for the first time often exhibit signs of secondary trauma, such as helplessness, hopelessness, anger, avoidance, guilt, and depression. Such reactions may, indeed, interfere with their ability to process information effectively and to respond to human rights challenges constructively. Students who appear to show disinterest in human rights issues may be responding normally to traumatic subject matter. Health and human rights instructors should be aware of these reactions and should help students process the emotions that are inherent to human rights work.

In addition, the development of a human rights perspective among students often involves more than simply acquiring a critical framework for conceptualizing health and health practice; it can be a life-transforming experience. That is, recognizing that respect for human dignity can be a foundation for human interactions often changes individuals' perceptions of themselves and of their place in the world.

Mandatory Requirements versus Elective Courses: Complementary Strategies

Most health and human rights courses are currently offered as electives by a limited number of institutions (see Table 28.1). Twenty-three percent of accredited schools of public health currently offer health and human rights courses compared to 2% of medical schools and less than 1% of nursing schools.

Table 28.1 Health and Human Rights Courses Offered in Schools of Public Health, Medicine, and Nursing

Schools[a]	Health and Human Rights Courses	Institutions Offering Courses	Proportions of Institutions Offering Courses (%)
Public Health (n = 31)[b]	8	7	23
Medicine (n = 125)	4	3	2
Nursing (n = 556)	1	1	0.2

[a] The schools are those listed by the American Association of Schools of Public Health, the American Association of American Medical Colleges (U.S. listings), and the American Association of Colleges of Nursing.
[b] Includes 31 accredited schools of public health.

Table 28.2 Courses on Selected Human Rights Topics Offered in Schools of Public Health

Selected Topics in Health and Human Rights	Number of Institutions Offering Courses
Refugees and Humanitarian Intervention	3
Women, Gender and Sexuality	2
Right to Health Care	1
Health as Social Justice	1
Human Rights and Development	1
Health, Human Rights and the International System	1
Science and Human Rights	1
Rights of Children	1
TOTAL	11

In addition to courses on health and human rights, schools of public health offer at least 11 other courses on selected human rights topics. Only four institutions offer such courses: Harvard School of Public Health, Joseph L. Mailman School of Public Health at Columbia University, Rollins School of Public Health at Emory University, and the School of Public Health at the University of California, at Berkeley. (See Table 28.2 for specific course topics.)

Nearly all of these courses are offered as electives. Consequently, many health and human rights educators describe their teaching efforts as "preaching to the converted." If human rights knowledge and skills are essential to effective health practice, then health practitioners should have some educational exposure to human rights concerns. Most health and human rights educators support a complementary strategy of integrating human rights material into required courses while continuing to offer a range of elective human rights courses, ideally leading to certificates or minor concentrations.

Making human rights studies a requirement can potentially raise awareness and engage many more health practitioners in the human rights discourse. That, in turn, should enable them to incorporate human rights principles in their daily health practice and, over time, to foster a culture of human rights in the health sector. Unfortunately, formidable barriers to such curricular requirements and the potential negative consequences of such requirements must be considered. The health and human rights educators who were interviewed identified the following:

Barriers
- Other demands on students' schedules, especially those of medical students
- Conflicts between concepts of health and the ethical responsibilities of health practitioners

- Skepticism about the relevance human rights has to daily medical and health practices
- Lack of human rights understanding and support among deans, senior faculty and curriculum boards
- Perceptions that health and human rights educators operate on the fringe of mainstream health concerns
- Lack of funding for health and human rights education initiatives

Potential Negative Consequences

- Negative reactions from requirement-weary students
- Decline in the quality assurance for course content and instruction
- The use of human rights resources (i.e., committed individuals) in the classroom rather than in developing substantive human rights work

Perhaps the most critical element to successfully integrating human rights as required components of graduate health education is to firmly ground its content in the very real problems that health practitioners face every day (which is not to discount the importance of international health and human rights concerns). Potential methods for integrating required human rights education, as suggested by the interviewees, included the following:

- Adding modular components in bioethics courses
- Public health courses:
    health policy
    international health
    cross-teaching in required courses, i.e., epidemiology, humanitarian crises, etc.

Medical and nursing school curricula

- introduction to the patient
- community and social medicine or replace current topics
- Identifying health and human rights as a core competency
- Developing continuing health education courses to fulfill licensing requirements, such as those needed to practice medicine
- Web-based courses
- short courses

Profiles of Human Rights Instructors: General Observations in Various Settings

Human rights educators make up a small community of individuals who share a number of common interests and are therefore generally familiar with one another. Besides their common perspectives on health, these educators have developed strong commitments to issues of social justice as a result of their profound life experiences. These may include directly and indirectly witnessing human rights violations, working with disadvantaged individuals and populations, seeing firsthand the suffering that stems from human rights abuses and from unmet human needs, and witnessing gross discrepancies in morbidity and mortality. Such experiences often come from working with NGOs. This work typically gives human rights educators the ability to relate their experiences to their students. Human rights educators also tend to have cross-disciplinary experiences and capabilities including law, health, medicine, science, social sciences, and advocacy, among others, that enrich their perspectives and teaching capabilities.

Human rights educators often believe that the difficulty public health initiatives have in achieving their stated goals has much to do with neglecting human rights concerns. The frustration that may result from such a perspective refers not only to the understanding of human rights as conceptual framework to guide health practice; it refers to the understanding of rights as a rhetorical statement of moral identity, an idea that was evident in the development of the Universal Declaration of Human Rights in the aftermath of World War II.[24] It is not surprising, therefore, that human rights educators and activists generally exhibit extraordinary commitment to their work.

Another observation is that human rights instructors often view their teaching efforts as "upstream" activities that contribute to the development of a culture of human rights as opposed to "downstream" activities, such as documentation of human rights violations or caring for survivors of torture, that are employed only after abuses have occurred.

Implications of the Current Situation for Development of a Curriculum

Human rights educators' unique experiences are critically important in teaching health and human rights in graduate health education. The experiences of human rights educators are the motivating force for teaching human rights and, at the same time, serve as critical examples of practical applications of human rights concerns to students. Such experiences often convey to students the value of human rights perspectives in real and practical terms. The experiences of human rights educators are apparently related to their perceived credibility by both students and faculty and also serve as models for students' career interests and choices.

Instructor profiles indicate that human rights experiences are of critical importance to effective educational initiatives. Human rights include a wide range of human interests—a range that exceeds any one individual educator's experiences. Therefore, gaps in relevant human rights experience or cross-disciplinary expertise underscores the need for collaboration with educators with a wide range of domestic and international experiences and cross-disciplinary expertise.

Content of Health and Human Rights Courses

Using available health and human rights course syllabi, a systematic review of course content and required readings was conducted. Only courses that focused specifically on health and human rights were included in the analysis. A total of 18 course syllabi were available from a total of 21 course listings in schools of public health (n = 8), medicine (n = 2), nursing (n=1), law (n = 3), and in undergraduate programs (n = 4). Twelve different graduate health institutions' offered a total of 14 health and human rights courses, and 6 undergraduate programs included a total of 7 courses. All 18 courses (100%) included a review of two core subjects: human rights law, principles, and/or instruments and conceptual linkages between health and human rights.[25] The courses included a range of 7 to 15 sessions, and each course contained a variety of specific topics. Table 28.3 provides a list of the most common topics.

This analysis provides some insight into the topics that are commonly covered in health and human rights courses. Of course, the small number of courses in each group makes statistical comparisons impossible. In addition, the value

Table 28.3 Content Analysis of Health and Human Rights Courses in Graduate Health Education

Session Subjects	Public Health (n = 8)	Medical & Residency (n = 2)	Nursing (n = 1)	Law (n = 3)	Under- grad (n = 4)	Total (n = 18)
HR Law/Instruments	8	2	1	3	4	18
Health and HR Linkages	8	2	1	3	4	18
Women	8	2	1	2	4	17
Health Policy	7	2	1	2	2	14
War & Refugees	7	2	1	0	3	13
Ethics	4	0	0	3	4	11
Children	4	2	1	2	4	9
Torture	3	1	1	1	3	9
Economic/Social Rights	4	0	0	2	2	8
Universality	4	0	0	2	1	7
Multinational Corporations	3	0	0	2	1	6
Access to Care	1	1	0	1	2	5
Violations/Documentation	2	0	0	0	2	4
Environment	2	0	0	0	2	4
Disabilities	1	0	0	2	1	4
Others*	4	3	0	0	6	13

* Included a total of two courses on each of the topics of race, genocide or sexual identity and one course on each of the following: health practices, human rights violations in the United States, rights of indigenous persons, human rights education, truth and reconciliation, structural violence and terrorism.

Table 28.4 Readings for Health and Human Rights Course

Readings[a]	Public Health (n = 8)	Medical & Residency (n = 2)	Nursing (n = 1)	Law (n = 3)	Under-grad (n = 4)	Total (n = 18)
25 HR Documents[a]	4	1	0	1	2	8
Local Readers	2	4 (n = 5)	1	0	1	8 (n = 21)
Mann et al. Reader[b]	5	0	0	1	1	7
Handouts	1	1	1	2	1	6
Amnesty Ethics Book[c]	2	1	0	0	1	4
Steiner[d]	1	0	0	1	1	3
Others[a]	3	0	1	2	4	10

[a] Center for the Study of Human Rights. Twenty-five Human Rights Documents. New York: Columbia University, 1994.

[b] Mann J, Gruskin S, Grodin M, Annas G. Health and Human Rights: A Reader, New York: Routledge 1999.

[c] Amnesty International, Ethical Codes and Declarations Relevant to the Health Professions, 3rd edition. London: Amnesty International, 1994.

[d] Steiner, HJ and Alston P. International Human Rights in Context: Law, Politics, Morals 2nd Edition, New York: Oxford University Press, 2000.

of this information is limited by three factors: (i) overlap between subject headings, (ii) topics limited to those listed as session subjects and not individual readings within sessions, and (iii) unavailability of several course syllabi at the time of the analysis. Table 28.4 provides a summary of required readings for health and human rights courses.

Ethics Courses with Relevant Human Rights Content

As of January 2002, the status of human rights teaching in ethics courses is unclear. This study did not include a systematic assessment of ethics courses in graduate health education. Human rights relevant content was evident in only two of the medical and/or residency training courses. In 1996, Sonis et al. conducted the only assessment of human rights content in schools of medicine.[26] That study included bioethics course directors and bioethics section directors of 125 U.S. medical schools. The extent of human rights teaching at each school was measured as the percentage of 16 human rights issues. Course directors at 113 (90%) of the 125 U.S. medical schools responded to the survey. Medical schools included about half (45%, 95% confidence interval, 41% to 49%) of 16 human rights issues in their required bioethics curricula. Domestic human rights issues, such as discrimination in the provision of health care to minorities (82% of medical schools), were covered much more frequently than international human rights issues, such as physician participation in torture (17% of schools). The study did not, however, measure the amount of curriculum time devoted to any or all of the human rights issues, nor did it attempt to verify the information reported. The course directors may have over-reported inclusion of human rights issues due to perceived social desirability. Also, the study instrument did not assess whether courses included any reference to human rights law or instruments or conceptual linkages between health and human rights.

Assessing the extent to which human rights relevant content exists in courses on ethics seems to warrant further research, given the importance of outlining a common agenda for human rights and bioethics.

Human Rights–Related Content of Courses on Social Justice, Societal Issues, and Similar Topics

A review of relevant content of courses on social justice, societal issues, and similar topics is beyond the scope of this paper. For the purposes of this paper, it is important to understand that a great number of courses exist on these and other topics in graduate health education. For example, courses on social determinants of health, poverty, gender, violence, environmental justice, hunger, reproductive health policies, HIV/AIDS, the health of vulnerable populations, humanism, and bioethics may be included in the curriculum, but they are not apparently presented within any overarching conceptual framework such as health and human rights.

Teaching Methods

Teaching methods used in graduate-level health and human rights courses often depend on whether the course is offered as an elective or a requirement, the school and department in which it is offered, and, of course, the instructor. In general, health and human rights courses in graduate health education are elective seminars that combine lectures and group discussions.[27] In most cases, lectures are minimized to allow for extensive discussions. Dividing the class into working groups that focus on specific problems or case studies typically enhances the quality of discussion. Discussions may also include student-led reviews of class readings and assignments for debate on specific human rights issues. Regardless of the method of discussion, human rights instructors agree that topics should be grounded in examples that are relevant to students' future health practices.

Many instructors suggest presenting human rights material in a variety of formats. Articles and textbooks are the most common, but students tend to find these readings more interesting when they reflect a range of perspectives, such as scientific, analytical, human rights reports, literary, opinion, and the like. In some cases, articles may be selected to highlights controversies in human rights to help students sort through polarized or oversimplified points of view. Well-chosen audiovisual material is often one of the most compelling formats to present human rights information. For example, an audiotape of a torture survivor's account of her experiences in Guatemala enables instructors to convey such experiences in ways that written material cannot.

Guest speakers are often used in health and human rights classes. They typically provide perspectives on human rights issues that are different from those of the instructors. Such guests are often colleagues in other areas of health study, human rights advocates and experts, clinical patients, survivors of human rights abuses, government representatives, among others. A series of guests may be invited to present in a panel format as well to offer a variety of perspectives on a specific human rights concern. Including guest speakers throughout the course, however, may interrupt the continuity of class discussions.

Formal methods of teaching human rights in graduate health education are most effective when complemented by informal and participatory forms of education. For example:

1. Informal
   - Human rights lecture series
   - Exposure to human rights issues and research in medical and health journals
   - Student film series
2. Participatory
   - Student research fellowships and internships
   - Student caucuses and social meetings
   - Opportunities to interact/volunteer with local NGOs and service organizations
   - Student health and human rights caucuses and informal meetings
   - Human rights symposia on campus

Assessing knowledge is an important teaching method as well. In most graduate-level health and human rights courses, educators generally use participation in discussion and written papers to assess their students' ability to engage in critical thinking and to develop original ideas on human rights.

Conclusions and Future Considerations

For health practitioners to effectively respond to social causes of human suffering in the future, human rights concerns should be integrated into curricular studies of graduate health education. Academic discourse on human rights may be facilitated by undergraduate and graduate courses in schools of medicine, public health, and nursing; in fellowship and graduate-research programs in human rights; and by placing greater emphasis on human rights-related experiences. The degree to which human rights concerns are actively supported by health practitioners will have far-reaching and long-lasting effects on the ways in which students conceptualize health and human suffering, and thus on the impact their professional lives have on society.

The health and human rights discourse that has developed over the past 10 years can provide a comprehensive framework for understanding health and human suffering and for providing practical tools for health promotion. For this reason, the Health and Human Rights Curriculum Project's goal of integrating human rights into graduate health education is important for the realization of health and well-being in the world today.

Notes

1. The institutions represented include Boston University School of Public Health and School of Medicine, Columbia University Joseph L. Mailman School of Public Health, Emory University Rollins School of Public Health, Harvard School of Public Health, Johns Hopkins University School of Hygiene and Public Health, University of California Berkeley School of Public Health, Yale University Department of Epidemiology and Public Health, NYU School of Medicine May Chinn Society for Bioethics and Human Rights, Princeton University Council for Science and Technology, and University of Minnesota Center for Spirituality and Healing.
2. A code of ethics is currently being drafted by the American Public Health Association. For details see www.apha.org/codeofethics/ethics.pdf for the draft code, and www.apha.org/codeofethics/background.pdf for relevant background information.
3. World Health Organization, *Declaration of Alma Ata* (Geneva, Switzerland: Author, 1978), pp. 1–3.
4. A. R. Chapman, L. S. Rubenstein, V. Iacopino, et al. *Human Rights and Health: The Legacy of Apartheid* (Washington, D.C.: American Association for the Advancement of Science, 1998).
5. R. L. Sivard, "World Military and Social Expenditures, 1996," *World Priorities* 1996:1–53.
6. Ibid.
7. Human Rights Watch, *World Report 2001* (New York: Author, 2001); Amnesty International, *World Report 2002* (London: Author, 2002).
8. E. Stover, J. C. Cobey, and J. Fine, "The Public Health Effects of Landmines: Long-Term Consequences for Civilians," In B. S. Levy and V. W. Sidel (Eds.) *War and Public Health* (New York: Oxford University Press, 1997), pp. 137–146.
9. Sivard, 1996.
10. Ibid.
11. United Nations Children's Fund, *World Declaration on the Survival, Protection and Development of Children* (New York: Author, 1990).
12. A. Sen, "Freedoms and Needs," *The New Republic* 1994 (Jan): 31–37.
13. Forced sterilization was practiced extensively in the United States as well. See A. N. Sofair and L. C. Kaldjian, "Eugenic Sterilization and a Qualified Nazi Analogy: The United States and Germany, 1930–1945," *Annals of Internal Medicine* 2000 132(4): 312–319.
14. See A. E. Kunst and J. P. Mackenbach, "The Size of Mortality Differences Associated with Educational Level: A Comparison of Nine Industrialized Countries," *American Journal of Public Health* 1994 84: 932–937; A. J. Fox and H. Aldershot (Eds.), *Health Inequalities in European Countries* (Brookfield, Vermont: Gower Publishing, 1989); and G. Davey Smith, C. Hart, D. Blane, et al. "Lifetime Socioeconomic Position and Mortality: Prospective Observational Study," *British Medical Journal* 1997 314: 547–552.
15. J. Mann, L. O. Gostin, S. Gruskin, et al. "Health and Human Rights," *Health and Human Rights* 1994 1(1):7–23.
16. L. O. Gostin and Z. Lazzarini, *Human Rights and Public Health in the AIDS Pandemic* (New York: Oxford University Press, 1997), pp. 12–32, 49–55.

17. See L. O. Gostin and Z. Lazzarini, *Human Rights and Public Health in the AIDS Pandemic* (New York: Oxford University Press, 1997), pp. 12–32, 49–55; T. A. Ziv and B. Lo, "Denial of Care to Illegal Immigrants: Proposition 187 in California," *New England Journal of Medicine* 1995 332(16): 1095–1098; M. Barry, "The Influence of the U.S. Tobacco Industry on the Health, Economy, and Environment of Developing Countries," *New England Journal of Medicine* 1991 324(13): 917–919; and A. H. Neufeldt and R. Mathieson, "Empirical Dimensions of Discrimination against Disabled People," *Health and Human Rights* 1995 1(2):174–189.

18. L. Gusting and J. Mann, "Towards the Development of a Human Rights Impact Assessment for the Formulation and Evaluation of Public Health Policies," *Human Rights and Health* 1994 1(1):58–80.

19. See J. Mann, L. Gostin, S. Gruskin, et al. "Health and Human Rights," *Health and Human Rights* 1994 1(1): 7–23; and V. Iacopino, "Human Rights: Health Concerns for the Twenty-First Century," In S. K. Majumdar, L. M. Rosenfeld, D. B. Nash, and A. M. Audet (Eds.) *Medicine and Health Care Into the Twenty-First Century* (Philadelphia: Pennsylvania Academy of Science, 1995) pp. 376–392.

20. The development of core knowledge and skills may differ somewhat in schools of public health, medicine, and nursing.

21. See World Health Organization, *Declaration of Alma Ata* (1978) pp. 1–3, and *Ottawa Charter for Health Promotion* (1986) pp. 1–3 (Geneva, Switzerland: Author).

22. World Health Organization, *Health For All in the Twenty-First Century* (Geneva, Switzerland: Author, 1998).

23. For the draft code, go to www.apha.org/codeofethics/ethics.pdf; for relevant background information, go to www.apha.org/codeofethics/background.pdf.

24. L. Henkin, "Introduction: The Human Rights Idea," *The Age of Rights* (New York: Columbia University Press, 1990), pp. 1–10.

25. The most common references included the Universal Declaration of Human Rights, the International Covenant on Civil and Political Rights, and the International Covenant on Economic, Social and Cultural Rights.

26. J. Sonis, D. W. Gorenflo, P. Jha, and C. Williams, "Teaching Human Rights in U.S. Medical Schools," *Journal of the American Medical Association* 1996 276(20): 1676–1678.

27. This tends to be more problematic in medical education where course time is critical and in undergraduate programs because of larger class size.

29

The Evolving Arms Control Agenda
Implications of the Role of NGOs in Banning Antipersonnel Landmines

Kenneth R. Rutherford

No other issue in recent times has mobilized such a broad and diverse coalition of countries, governments and nongovernmental organizations (NGOs). Much of this momentum has been the result of the tremendous efforts made by NGOs to advance the cause to ban AP mines. Their commitment and dedication have contributed to the emergence of a truly global partnership.
— Lloyd Axworthy, Minister of Foreign Affairs, Canada
"AP Mine Ban: Progress Report," February 1997

The twentieth century ended with the entry into force of the Ottawa Treaty to ban antipersonnel landmines.[1] The signing of the treaty was an incredible accomplishment marking, as noted at the time by Canadian Prime Minister Jean Chretien, the "first time, the majority of the nations of the world will agree to ban a weapon which has been in military use by almost every country in the world."[2] However, it also did not have the support of many major powers, which is contrary to most multilateral disarmament agreements.[3] Even as late as 1994, there was a consensus among all states that landmines were legal. In March 1995, Belgium became the first state to pass a domestic law providing for a comprehensive landmine ban.[4] Less than thirty-two months later, on December 2, 1997, Belgium was joined by 122 states in signing the comprehensive ban convention. Currently 138 states have signed the convention, and 101 have ratified it. The convention entered into force on March 1, 1999, becoming the quickest major international agreement ever to enter into force in history.[5] Academics, diplomats, and NGO representatives called the Ottawa Treaty's genesis and negotiations an innovative model for the future development of international law.[6] Even the Nobel committee recognized this unique coalition by awarding the International Campaign to Ban Landmines (ICBL) and its coordinator, Jody Williams, the 1997 Nobel Peace Prize, in part for helping create a fresh form of diplomacy.[7]

Plotting the process through which NGOs set the international political agenda to bring certain issues to the fore has important substantive and theoretical implications. Substantively, this article shows how NGOs can play important roles in getting landmine and various other issue areas, such as the environment and human rights, onto the international political agenda.[8] Furthermore, landmines are a key policy problem, as they cause many injuries and deaths in regional conflicts, hinder postconflict reconstruction, seriously undermine infrastructure, and deny land for civilian use thereby leading to the overuse of existing land.[9]

The chapter has broader significance for the study of comparative foreign policy in that it may help predict the success or failure of current NGO efforts to address other security issues, such as banning child soldiers, ratifying the international criminal court, and restricting the use of small arms and light weapons. If NGOs indeed play a significant role in getting the international community to address the landmine issue, an examination of the conditions under which NGOs controlled and initiated the landmine issue on the international political agenda becomes more relevant. By comparison, several scholars, including Margaret E. Keck and Kathryn Sikkink, address agenda setting through norm diffusion facilitated by NGOs. They show how networks of NGOs persuaded governments to address the value of new norms, such as ensuring human rights in Latin America, protecting the environment, and eliminating violence against women.[10] Reflecting this norm creation process, Richard Price's excellent study of the NGO role in the campaign to ban landmines shows how NGOs were able to delegitimize landmine use by relocating authority away from states.[11] In these analyses, socialization occurs through intensive norm promotion.[12]

In this chapter, I focus specifically on the role of NGOs in setting the agenda for the landmine-banning issue on the international political agenda. It makes two interrelated arguments. First, NGOs initiated the landmine ban by placing the issue on the international political agenda resulting in intense media and public attention. The term 'agenda' is defined in this essay as "objects accorded saliency in the media content or in people's consciousness."[13] Second, NGOs helped articulate and codify the landmines issue into international law by changing how governments perceived the legality of landmines and the effects of landmine use. Addressing both these arguments helps to explain better why the Ottawa Treaty was initiated by NGOs, who in turn helped change state behavior toward landmines. One of the implications is that under certain conditions NGOs contribute to setting the international political agenda, especially legal prohibitions on weapons that cause humanitarian harm, have a dubious military utility, and in turn effect state behavioral changes. In comparison most other major arms control and disarmament treaties, such as the Biological Weapons Convention (BWC), Chemical Weapons Convention (CWC), and Nuclear Weapons Treaty (NPT), are typically negotiated at the behest of major powers, and agenda-setting processes, including the negotiations, do not incorporate NGOs.[14]

These arguments address the agency question concerning the role of NGOs in international politics by showing how NGOs instigated governments to address the landmine issue in a particular way, which eventually culminated in international law. In explaining this proposition, the chapter demonstrates how NGOs affected international legal rules on landmine use by changing the debate from a political to a humanitarian issue, drawing media and public attention to the issue, and ultimately educating states about the limited military utility and dramatic negative humanitarian effects of landmines. This chapter's tentative conclusion suggests that the landmine case illustrates how NGOs can introduce a norm and translate it into a powerful instrument with lasting influence by initiating an issue and then controlling it on the international political agenda.

While this chapter examines the NGO role in the agenda-setting process, it does not seek to evaluate the contents or effectiveness of the Ottawa Treaty.[15] Nevertheless, it does briefly examine alternative explanations to the article's main arguments, examines alternative explanations for landmines agenda setting, and examines alternative theoretical explanations for why the ban was achieved.

Theoretically, the chapter explicitly demonstrates and explains the process of creating and initiating norms and how they are placed and addressed on the international political agenda. Understanding agenda-setting dynamics is central to understanding the achievement of the landmine ban specifically and contemporary international politics more generally. In the landmine agenda-setting process, noticeable attention is transferred in varying degrees to governments, which, in turn, helps to influence policy. Recent agenda-setting studies show that media coverage can shape how the public thinks about American domestic politics.[16] This chapter utilizes recent agenda-setting research to explain how and why the landmine issue arrived on the international agenda and attracted state attention.[17] Specifically, it shows that NGO advocacy and policy work helped generate international attention by frequently and prominently featuring landmine victims. It also highlights how working with high profile individuals, NGOs were able to change state conception of landmine use in a very short time.

The chapter is divided into two sections. The first focuses on level-one agenda setting, labeled "cognitive agenda setting," because NGOs brought the landmine issue to international attention. It investigates how NGOs placed the landmine issue on the governmental and public agenda. The second section addresses level-two agenda setting, labeled "norm agenda setting," because of the NGO role in changing state conception of landmines. It discusses the influence of the particular elements of the landmine issue on the governmental and public agenda. For example, a first-level question might address a statement by governments and the public that landmines are an important issue facing the nation, while a second-level question might look at how governments and the public describe ways of addressing the problem.

Three other important components of agenda setting are also addressed in both sections: framing, schema, and priming. Framing is the selection of elements within a particular issue. These elements are used "to promote a particular problem definition, causal interpretation, moral evaluation, and/or treatment recommendation for the item described."[18] The thesis is that people will think about an issue in a particular way depending on how that issue is presented. This transference of the salience of attributes is the core of second-level agenda setting, while at the same time it holds some implications for level-one agenda setting. Schema is a concept closely linked to framing, but it focuses more on how people organize their thinking.[19] It reduces complicated information into a manageable number of frames in order to handle and process it.[20] Priming is "the process by which the schemas are activated."[21] It assumes that frequency, prominence, or features of a stimulus activates previously learned cognitive structures and influences interpretations of an ambiguous stimulus. Its key factors are frequency and intensity of media exposure.

The chapter also examines neorealist explanations for the ban's achievement, especially focusing on the strategic interests of signatories versus nonsigners and the behavior of landmine-producing states.[22] While neorealism can explain why states either did or did not sign the convention, they cannot explain the placement of the landmine-ban issue on the international agenda. According to this approach, states would not have incorporated NGO actions or a ban on a weapon-retaining military utility into its behavioral calculations. This article takes a constructivist approach because it contends that norms are socially constructed and therefore allow for an NGO role in educating and pressuring other international actors and in establishing the landmine-ban issue on the international political agenda. Furthermore, unlike neorealism, this approach allows nonmaterial relationships, such as discourse about agenda setting, to develop among a variety of international actors, including individuals and NGOs. Thus, this chapter's explanation for the ban is that it resulted from the NGO agenda-setting role in establishing the landmine-ban issue on the international political agenda and in educating and pressuring states to address the issue in a particular way.

Agenda Setting

A thorough evaluation of the NGO role in creating and establishing the Ottawa Convention is critical to the study of international politics because that role is at the heart of constructivist arguments. A clear understanding of the NGO role in initiating the landmine-ban norm through an agenda-setting framework sheds light on the construction of the norm itself (see Table 29.1).

Level One: Cognitive Agenda Setting

Level-one agenda setting addresses the NGO role in getting governments and the public to think about landmines as an important issue. This level deals with transferring landmines from the NGO to the international political agenda and specifically with getting governments to think about landmine use as a major international humanitarian problem. Moreover, one of the chapter's findings is that NGOs helped expedite the enforcement of the convention by condensing negotiations from the usual decades to about fourteen months. The broader argument is that the greater the governmental and public attention created by the NGOs toward a particular issue, the quicker an issue gets on the international political agenda and, most importantly, addressed by states.

Framing: New Issue

As a new issue, landmines attracted tremendous international attention. According to one government diplomat central to the treaty negotiations, the international arms control agenda was bare and therefore arms control negotiators were undistracted by the NGO call for a landmine ban.[23] Even critics of the landmine-ban movement credited NGOs with bringing the landmine issue

TABLE 29.1 NGO Agenda Setting and the Landmine Issue

Agenda-Setting Components	Level One: Cognitive Agenda Setting	Level Two: Norm Agenda Setting
Framing	landmines as a new issue: getting people to think about landmines as a humanitarian issue	horrible effects and disproportionate consequences
Schema	outrageous landmine statistics	leadership games to control the landmine issue
Priming	landmine victim stories	incoherent arguments among anti-ban states

to international attention. One critic writes that "despite its considerable history, little has been recorded about the use of these weapons [landmines]," until they "attracted the attention of the media and humanitarian groups."[24]

Compared with other controversial weapons, such as biological and chemical weapons, poison gas, and nuclear weapons, the legality of landmine use remained an obscure issue for governmental policymakers until the early 1990s. For example, according to Lieutenant Colonel Burris M. Carnahan, there was only one U.S. military manual regarding the use of landmines and international humanitarian law by the early 1980s.[25] Moreover, most of the literature on the legality of landmines was published after the creation of the ICBL in 1992.

Initial NGO interest in the landmine issue began in the 1970s when the International Committee for the Red Cross (ICRC) determined that some weapons should be prohibited both "by customary and treaty-based international humanitarian law because landmines cause superfluous injury and unnecessary suffering (damaging effects disproportionate to the military purpose) and that they are of an indiscriminate nature (no distinction between civilians and combatants)."[26] These legal discussions will be reviewed at greater length in the next section, but here it suffices to say that the ICRC discussions in the 1970s eventually resulted in minimal international legal restrictions being placed on landmine use through the Landmines Protocol of the 1980 Convention on Conventional Weapons (CCW). This particular protocol was strengthened as the Amended Protocol II adopted at the final CCW Review Conference in Geneva on May 6, 1996, when it became apparent that NGOs had the public will to push through a ban.[27] Subsequent to the CCW, landmine use was not a topic of concern for the media, NGOs, or policymakers. There are several proposed reasons why the landmine issue finally attracted international attention in the last decade of the twentieth century; these reasons are discussed below. While reasons are legitimate, this paper argues that the NGO role in getting states to address the landmine problem provides a more comprehensive reason why landmines emerged on the international political agenda.

Introduction to landmines. State militaries traditionally used landmines for defensive purposes, primarily to protect strategic locations or channel enemy forces into specific fire zone areas. Restricted to these particular military uses, landmine casualties were confined primarily to military personnel during combat engagement or related operations. Beginning with the Vietnam War, however, landmines have become more widely used by poorly trained militaries and more offensive in military practice. Many of today's wars are now "long-running, internal, and low intensity, often involving cash starved militaries for whom low-technology, low-cost landmines are a weapon of choice. . . . Consequently, in wars today, mines are frequently placed in areas of high civilian concentration rather than being confined to discrete battlefields of limited size."[28] The result has been an increasing level of destructiveness to civilian

communities. For example, the top three states with landmine-disabled populations are recently emerging from decades of internal conflict that entailed the
use of mines by all parties.[29] According to the US State Department, 59 to 69
million landmines are currently deployed, making them "one of the most toxic
and widespread pollution[s] facing mankind."[30] The State Department finds
further that landmines exacerbate regional conflicts, hinder postconflict reconstruction, seriously undermine infrastructure, and deny land-to-civilian use,
thereby leading to overuse of existing land.[31] Additionally each year landmines
kill more than twenty-four thousand people, most of whom are civilian.[32]

Landmine use among most state professional forces has declined recently.[33]
There are exceptions, however, the most notable being the use of landmines by
Russia in Chechnya, Dagestan, and Georgia, and by Eritrea in its conflict with
Ethiopia.[34] During the 1990s, there were also a few cases of landmines being
deployed by professional troops in which civilians were purposely targeted. In
Bosnia during 1993–94, Bosnian Croatian and Serbian forces used mines to
discourage the return of refugees by other ethnic groups, and Serbian forces
used them in Kosovo in 1999 to harm returning Kosovarian refugees. Nevertheless, many nonstate military forces still rely upon landmines to achieve their
objectives. Recent and current internal wars in Afghanistan, Bosnia, Cambodia,
Rwanda, Somalia, and Uganda show further that landmines are not being used
to conquer the opposing force. Rather the goal is economic and social destabili-
zation or the prevention of the return of refugees. For example, in Afghanistan
"guerrilla forces used mines to force populations off the land and reduce potential support for their opponents," while in Cambodia the Khmer Rouge used
landmines "to destabilize contested areas."[35] Thus these countries host some of
the highest concentrations of landmines in the world. It is estimated, for
example, that Afghanistan currently hosts between 5 and 7 million landmines
while Cambodia hosts between 4 and 6 million.[36]

Explanations for landmines agenda setting. Currently there are three
explanations for landmines agenda setting: terrorism and nonstate actor (NSA)
use, technology, and the end of the cold war. Some claim that the initial legal
interest in restricting landmine use was driven in part by the U.S. military who
wished to limit terrorist access to landmines and other time-delayed weapons,
such as booby traps.[37] Landmines traditionally were used by state militaries for
defensive purposes, primarily to protect strategic locations. In the last few decades, however, landmine use has become more offensive in military practice
and destructive in humanitarian cost. The practice has been compounded by
landmine proliferation to substate militaries, who use them to create social
chaos to bring down states and to target particular groups. While millions of
deployed mines "were randomly laid, with limited tactical rationale, and often
deployed simply to terrorize and demoralize local populations," terrorists did
not deploy them on United States soil or that of its allies.[38] In reality, most

current landmines are not used for terrorist purposes but indiscriminately by inadequately trained soldiers or undisciplined militias. The fact that minefield mapping and marking and mine-awareness education are practically nonexistent increases the landmine threat to civilians in these areas.

These facts, however, do not provide a complete answer for why the landmine issue got onto the international political agenda. The Soviets used landmines irresponsibly in Afghanistan in the 1980s and in greater numbers than all the professional militaries in the 1990s. Yet the landmine issue did not generate international attention. Cambodia, moreover, was also the scene of massive landmine deployment in the 1980s, but no international steps were taken to curtail its use. Finally in the early 1990s, state behavior toward landmine use changed when NGOs raised the landmine-ban issue.

The second purported reason why the landmine issue is now an object of international attention is that technological developments have made the acquisition and deployment of landmines much simpler. By purchasing better technology, more states are now able to produce landmines readily. In addition, aerial dispersal instruments, such as airplanes and artillery, can not deploy a greater number of landmines in a shorter time. Some of the more advanced remote-delivery systems can now deploy thousands of landmines in minutes.[39] Thus, not only has technology increased both the number of landmines being deployed and the speed of deployment, but it has also spurred more indiscriminate deployment of the mines since accurate recording is not possible with aerial-delivery systems.[40] Such use, it is claimed, is increasing because many militaries, especially of the United States, fear casualties among their own forces and therefore put greater emphasis on air power.[41] As one American reporter writes, Americans have "placed extraordinary value on preserving lives of our pilots, sometimes at the possible expense of civilians on the ground."[42] Therefore we can conclude that in the future, aerially delivered mines will increasingly replace manually deployed mines, especially in those states fearing casualties.

Besides reducing casualties, militaries believe that mines deployed by air in large numbers "have the ability to deploy rapidly and to position a considerable obstacle to enemy movement."[43] During the last few decades, the American military expanded this technology by packaging antipersonnel (AP) and anti-tank (AT) mines together because studies showed that by sowing AP mines with AT mines significantly slows down enemy minefield breeching and protects the AT mines from enemy lifting.[44]

While the NGOs complained that such packages blur "the already thin line between antitank and antipersonnel systems," these packages are not the primary cause of landmine casualties or land denial problems.[45] Contrary to the claim that technology is the prime mover of the landmine issue, mines deployed aerially are not a significant percentage of currently deployed mines or a cause of landmine victims.[46] Regardless, the Clinton administration in 1997 still felt public and international pressure regarding U.S. mixed systems, so it attempted to change the definition of the antipersonnel landmines sowed in the mixed systems by reclassifying them as submunitions and antihandling devices for antitank mines.[47] Again, these mixed systems and other aerially deployed mines are not the main reason for the humanitarian disaster caused by mines. Such technology is therefore not the main explanation for the landmine issue getting on the international political agenda.

A realist explanation for the placement of the landmine issue on the international agenda could be the end of the cold war. Its end has enabled state policymakers to focus on less strategic weapons, such as landmines, and allowed many states to pursue unilateral military policies, sometimes in opposition to the major powers. Realists could assert that the end of the cold war has led to irresponsible behavior by non-major states because they no longer feel beholden to major powers and/or have concern for their security. They would argue that these states are acting foolishly and will eventually be punished for weakening their own security by giving up a weapon that retains a military utility on the battlefield. Kenneth Waltz predicts that a post-cold war multipolar system is more unpredictable than a bipolar system because major powers have less flexibility to balance the system and weaker states have greater flexibility to act irresponsibly concerning their security interests.[48] According to this neorealist principle, it would have been difficult to achieve the Ottawa Convention because relative gains would have been more important than they are now. In a multipolar world, for example, weaker states fear war less and "all of them can more freely run the risk of suffering a relative loss."[49] Thus even though Russia, the United States, and other great powers did not sign the Ottawa Convention, most of the NATO and former Warsaw Pact allies have signed.[50]

Moreover, NGO representatives themselves argue, "Governments remained largely unaware of the degree of the landmine epidemic until the end of the Cold War. Yet the devastating, long-term consequences of AP mines were becoming all too apparent to those NGOs who were putting prosthetic limbs on victims, removing the detritus of war from the ground, providing aid and relief to war-torn societies, and documenting violations of human rights and the laws of war."[51] During the cold war, many NGOs did not have access to landmine-infested areas because of instability and politics and accordingly were either unaware of the landmine problem or unable to properly assess the effects of landmine use.

While it is true that the end of the cold war allows governments to focus on less strategic issues, and humanitarian NGOs to operate in previously closed areas, that fact does not provide a complete explanation for the rise of landmines on the international political agenda. It does not explain, for example, why landmines rather than many other worthwhile issues, such as environmental degradation and child soldiers, remain low-priority items for governments.

Emboldened NGOs setting the international agenda. Even though the landmines protocol of the CCW was signed in 1980, it remains relatively unnoticed by the international community as reflected by the fact that after fifteen years only fifty-two states have ratified it.[52] Upset at the lack of universal support for the CCW and the effects of landmines, the ICBL was created in 1991, when the Vietnam Veterans of America Foundation (VVAF), based in Washington, D.C., and MEDICO, the German medical NGO, decided to form a broad-based international campaign to speak with one voice supporting the ban. It was officially launched in October 1992 when six NGOs took "a number of individual and joint steps in the direction of the ban campaign by issuing a 'Joint Call to Ban Antipersonnel' landmines and hosting the first NGO-sponsored international landmine conference in May of 1993."[53]

The ICBL knew that it needed to draw international attention to the landmine issue in order to be successful. They made "this appeal on a moral basis; on a position of political morality,"[54] thus shifting the landmine debate from a political to a humanitarian issue. Issue transformation in other areas that puts "the subject into one category rather than another" helps bring the problem to the attention of those in and around government. The landmine-ban's transformation from a political to a humanitarian issue began when, in January 1991, the Women's Commission for Refugee Women and Children called for a ban in its testimony before the United States Senate about the plight of landmine survivors in the Cambodian border refugee camps.[55] It is interesting to note that this is the first time that landmine use was addressed publicly as a humanitarian concern and not a security issue in the United States.

Schema: Outrageous Statistics

NGOs promoted statistics as systematic indicators in a schema to get states to recognize the landmine problem. These statistics resonated with the media, the public, and policymakers because they were so outrageous that the problem could no longer be ignored. This strategy to garner attention is similar to the assumption that new issues need to encourage action by promoting systematic indicators, such as crises and disasters or by feedback from ongoing programs. Changes in these indicators usually highlight that there is a problem in the system because "a steady state is viewed as less problematic than changing figures." Policymakers use these indicators to decide whether to address an issue, first by assessing the magnitude of the problem and, second, by becoming aware of changes in the problem.[56]

The prime indicator used by NGOs as part of this schema is that landmines kill and maim more than twenty-six thousand people per year of whom an estimated 80 percent are civilian.[57] The claim is also made that this carnage will not end anytime soon because there "may be 200 million landmines scattered in at least sixty-four countries," making them "one of the most toxic and widespread pollution[s] facing mankind."[58]

Moreover, NGOs emphasized that for many civilian communities the nature of war had recently changed from targeting the professional military of the enemy to targeting its civilians. According to UNICEF, for example, more children die from landmines after a war for which those landmines were deployed than do soldiers during the war. Due to the nature of the landmine injury—usually amputation, if not death—those countries infested by landmines have the largest amputee populations in the world. For example, a 1991 study of Cambodia's amputee population found that over thirty thousand of the country's 8.5 million inhabitants were amputees and another five thousand amputees lived in refugee camps along the Thai border.[59] A 1998–99 study found that while Cambodia's population had grown to 10 million people, twenty-four thousand had survived mine injuries and more than fourteen thousand had died.[60]

Furthermore, according to UN demining expert Patrick Blagden, a fifty-fold increase in the world's mine-clearing capability is needed to "stabilize" the current situation. Such an effort would require training 170,000 to 200,000 new mine clearers worldwide costing $1.02 billion to $1.2 billion per year. He warned, however, that accidents happen at a rate of one out of every 1,000 to 2,000 mines destroyed: "a fifty fold increase in manual mines clearance would probably cause a death and injury toll among mine clearers of about 2,000 per year, a rate that in the long term may not be supportable."[61] Kuwait is a case in point. Within the first week after the war, all five Kuwaiti mine-clearing experts were killed attempting to clear landmines. Additionally nearly one hundred international-mine-clearance experts have been killed since the end of the Gulf War.[62]

In another schema that helped policymakers process the landmine issue and encourage the media and the public to get involved, the effects of landmine use were compared with more commonly despised and feared weapon systems: biological, chemical, and nuclear weapons. NGOs currently estimate that more people have been killed and maimed by landmines than by biological, chemical, and nuclear weapons combined.[63]

Many of the statistics generated by NGOs, however, are inflated and, more significantly, regurgitated by the media and policymakers without proper fact-checking and research. Some of the overinflated figures have become so widely used that original sources and methodological data-collection techniques are unknown, and "some land mine figures are repeated so often that they are now regarded as fact."[64] The more common, inflated claims center on the number of currently deployed landmines, such as in Afghanistan where 35 million was the initial estimate, which was later reduced to 10 million "as a conveniently round figure." Even that figure is suspicious because it would have required that the Soviets deploy "3,000 mines per day, every day of the nine-year occupation, which, given the mountainous nature of the terrain and the style of conflict, was unrealistically high."[65] The high estimate of landmines in Angola is also questionable. As one Red Cross deminer stated, "For there to be so many mines in Angola would have required four jumbo jets of mines arriving daily for 20 years."[66] The deployment of mines during the Gulf War provides another example of grossly inflated statistics. It was initially estimated that 9 million landmines were laid by Iraqi forces immediately preceding and during Operation Desert Storm.[67] A few years after the war, however, a survey showed only around 1.7 million mines had been emplaced.[68]

These statistics were promoted via the Internet and through conference mechanisms such as speeches and prepared reports. They were immediately picked up by the media, which, in turn, provided the information to the public and governments. As recently as September 1999, CNN was still quoting NGO estimates that more than forty thousand landmines were being deployed each week,[69] even though the figure had no factual basis and was no longer used by NGOs, especially the ICBL. Since CNN reports are broadcast around the world and are important sources of information for many people, the report is sure to become a major resource for more people learning about landmines. In fact, while Bernard Shaw, the anchor for CNN television's *World News*, attributed the statistic to the ICRC, the less-used CNN website did not refer to the deployment rate. The CNN report used outdated ICRC statistics, which were rough estimates at best. Today's estimates of the weekly rates of deployment are significantly less than the initial estimates of eighty thousand per year, in which more mines were being emplaced than taken out.[70] The CNN report used the unverified statistic as the lead-in to the news story to grab the viewer's attention. This example highlights how information and media technologies were used to get the public to pay attention to the landmine issue by highlighting dramatic statistics, whether or not they were truthful.[71]

These statistics were not seriously questioned until late in the agenda-setting process, primarily in the months leading up to the signing of the Ottawa Treaty in December 1997,[72] when it was too late to distract attention from the landmine issue. By this time, the issue was already on the international political agenda and had attracted tremendous media and public attention. An ICBL critic wrote that the campaign continually used "powerful images of dreadfully wounded civilians." Those images called "attention to the (exaggerated) scale of the problem," which, in turn, "rapidly galvanized public opinion and prompted a number of countries to restrict or prohibit the use of antipersonnel mines unilaterally."[73]

Priming: Landmine Victim Stories

The schema to get people to think about landmines was primed primarily by landmine-victim stories. If policymakers and the public did not completely understand the statistics that were publicized to awaken the memory of a horrible humanitarian disaster, many of them finally did comprehend the magnitude of the situation when they were confronted with the stories of thousands of landmine victims. More often than not, most governmental statements concerning the landmine-ban issue discussed the plight of landmine victims. The ICBL and the ICRC continually featured these stories, which were picked up by the media and pro-ban governments. One of the key points that the campaign emphasized was the dismemberment of people by landmines, which is due to design features that stress maiming, not killing. The resulting injuries are horrifying. The conventional wisdom behind this strategy is that a wounded enemy soldier is less costly to the enemy than a dead one. NGO health workers continually highlighted the effects of landmines on people. For example, landmine victims usually require amputation and long hospitalizations.[74] A study of blood use by ICRC hospitals "found that, overall, for every 100 wounded, 44.9 units of blood were required, while every 100 mine injuries required 103.2 units."[75]

In addition, many media stories and NGO reports discussed the negative social impact that landmines have on many marginalized populations.[76] In addition, the ICBL and ICRC continually featured landmine victims prominently in their educational, fundraising, and promotional literature and sponsored their participation in international conferences.[77] They mounted an effective public-education and media campaign that made it politically difficult for governments to ignore the landmine issue. According to two of the major ICBL leaders, Stephen D. Goose of Human Rights Watch (HRW) and Jody Williams of the ICBL, "most of the early news on AP mines was focused on the victim side of the equation and the tremendous difficulties faced by humanitarian deminers."[78] Another ICBL leader, Rae McGrath of the Mines Advisory Group (MAG), argued that the "deaths and injuries caused to innocent people, and the denial of ground for agricultural and other civilian purposes as a result of the presence of mines, made it inevitable that the aid community must face up to the issue."[79]

The Canadian Government and other core group policymakers—as representatives of the main state sponsors for the landmine ban—also featured landmine victims prominently in their policy speeches in order to attract more states to signing the Ottawa Treaty. Such a priming strategy is perhaps the most significant reason that the movement to ban landmines garnered so much international political action and attention so fast. In essence, the forces who favored a landmine ban used landmine victims as the priming tool with the assumption that the frequency, prominence, or feature of the international community's humanitarian impulse would lead to increased international attention to the issue. Even an anti-ban commentator stated that the strategy worked, saying that "the misery and suffering caused by mines in developing countries caught the imagination of the media and the Western World."[80]

Level Two: Norm Agenda Setting

NGOs successfully placed the landmine issue on the international political agenda, the first level of agenda setting. It was then their task to change how governments viewed landmines, the next agenda-setting level.

Level-two agenda setting addresses the influence of attribute salience of the NGO landmine activities among governmental policy-makers and the public. The level's main theme is the NGO's promotion of the landmine ban and how it changed policymakers' perceptions about landmine use. At this level discussions focus on how NGOs got governmental policymakers to understand landmines in a new way and subsequently why state landmine policies changed. The main thesis is that the more NGOs could convince governments of the horrible effects of landmine use, especially the disproportionate civilian casualties, the greater the possibility of changing state perception and use of landmines.

Framing: Horrible Effects and Disproportionate Consequences

The main framing mechanism to encourage policymakers to view landmines differently was to label them as illegal under *current* international humanitarian law, primarily because their use was causing disproportionate casualities among noncombatants and unnecessary suffering to both the military and civilians. NGOs based their landmine-ban arguments on already established norms and principles. Their key agenda-setting argument in support of the landmine ban concerned proportionality. The 1977 Protocol I to the 1949 Geneva Convention requires belligerents to weigh the expected military utility of a particular weapon against the humanitarian costs.[81] Essentially, the law says that an attack, which may cause more harm to noncombatants than necessary to fulfill the military objective, is illegal. The use of landmines violates this principle in two ways: (1) when the proportionality rule is applied to the whole landmine system, the humanitarian costs out-weigh the military demands; and (2) the time-delay feature of the landmine does not allow the military commander to make the calculations for proportionality.[82]

The NGOs also used the international humanitarian legal argument that landmines are inherently indiscriminate because once deployed they cannot target its victims. Anti-ban forces were able to dispute this argument much more than the proportionality argument. For example, the U.S. position was that landmines could be discriminately used in the right circumstances because landmines were like other "legal" weapons, such as artillery shells, missiles, and air delivered bombs, whose targets may include civilians. Robert Sherman from the U.S. Arms Control and Disarmament Agency (ACDA) responded to the indiscriminate argument in the following manner:

> I frequently hear it said that landmines are indiscriminate; they can't tell the difference between a child or a soldier. That's true, but it's also true of other weapon[s] of war. The shell, bomb, missile that can tell the difference between a child and a soldier has yet to be invented. The military would love it if it were but it doesn't exist and won't in the foreseeable future.[83]

In contrast, even the most ardent critics of the landmine ban admitted that they were causing a humanitarian problem as evidenced by the great *proportion* of civilian casualties among the landmine victims. In his book, *The History of Landmines*, Mike Croll claims that the movement to ban landmines is "unlikely to be beneficial" but that the landmine issue itself came about because of the ICBL's success in attracting international attention to it as a moral issue.[84] Croll and Sherman, ardent ban opponents, defend their positions by admitting to a humanitarian problem caused by landmines. While Sherman compares the humanitarian problem induced by landmines as "not a unique humanitarian problem" when compared with the effects of other weapons, he goes on to say that unlike other weapons, the "time factor" of landmines makes them last a very long time after the war, resulting in "a lot of mines left behind and a lot of civilian casualties."[85] Similarly, Croll says:

> that today it is impossible to cover this subject without reference to the humanitarian perspective and without having one's morals scrutinized. It certainly has not been my objective to glorify what is surely one of the most insidious weapons ever developed nor to condone the suffering of the many innocent people killed and injured by them.[86]

By transforming the landmine-use issue from a strictly political-military problem to a humanitarian question, NGOs provided themselves with the diplomatic space to play important roles in disseminating information about landmines to the media, policymakers, and the public. Even governmental arms-control negotiators considered it a humanitarian issue; as Sheridan stated, "I'm going to make a plea that we treat this not as a political issue but as a humanitarian issue."[87] While the laws of armed conflict will always wrestle with the unclear balances between military demands and humanitarian standards, NGOs argued that a complete prohibition of landmines is the only political and practical way to eliminate the harm caused by landmines to civilian populations and the environment.

Noticeably, the ICBL "never denied the utility of the antipersonnel landmine in certain situations," albeit the United States Campaign to Ban Landmines (USCBL) recently stated that landmines "have no military value."[88] The USCBL misstatement is perhaps due more to ignorance on the part of recent landmine-ban activists of the genesis of the issue and of previous arguments to get states to discuss landmines as a humanitarian issue than to keeping the discussion in the military domain. The indirect consequence, however, is that such statements indeed shift the landmine debate back to the military realm, exactly what the NGOs wanted to avoid.

Contrary to recent USCBL claims that landmines do not have military utility, many of the ICBL leaders, pro-ban state diplomats, and others acknowledge that landmines are used for many reasons, such as to protect strategic locations, channel enemy forces, deny certain positions to the enemy, and slow down enemy movement.[89] In attempting to steer away from landmine-utility arguments, Canadian and other proban state policymakers emulated the NGO strategy of focusing strictly on the humanitarian and legal aspects of the debate rather than of engaging militaries in it. The pro-ban states leading the interstate negotiations also wanted to avoid debating the utility of landmines on the battlefield, which they thought would derail the treaty's development by shifting landmine discussions to the consensus-based negotiating forums of the CCW and Conference on Disarmament (CD).[90] Because landmines are considered a useful military tool, the major powers and many military leaders believed that taking the landmine issue to these alternative forums—the only international forums to address disarmament issues—was more appropriate and conducive to discussing further use restrictions and/or a ban.[91]

The downside to negotiating the ban in the CCW or CD was significant. Both forum processes are lengthy, primarily because they are consensus-based, usually taking decades of negotiations to reach an agreement. In 1997, for example, Mexico blocked the attempt to put the landmine issue on the CD agenda. Since several other states in the CD are also opposed to putting landmines on the agenda or to issuing an immediate landmine ban, the landmine issue currently cannot be discussed within the CD. Similarly, getting a landmine ban on the CCW agenda was impossible because many states, "such as Russia, India, China and the United States, say they still need landmines to protect international borders, and therefore preferred to discuss landmines in the context of restrictions rather than implementing a ban."[92]

While the ICBL did not question the military utility of landmines, they questioned whether their "limited" utility proportionally out-weighed the humanitarian costs. To provide political cover for governmental policymakers, several NGOs sought to collaborate with military leaders and argue that the military utility of landmines was minimal. On April 3, 1996, the Vietnam Veterans of

America Foundation (VVAF) sponsored a full-page letter in the *New York Times* to President Clinton, which was signed by fifteen retired military leaders, including General Norman Schwarzkopf, Commander of Operation Desert Storm, that supported a ban. One month earlier, the ICRC had released "a study of the military use and effectiveness of anti-personnel mines," which was endorsed by more than ten active and retired international leaders from nine countries and concluded that:

> the military utility of AP mines is far outweighed by the appalling humanitarian consequences of their use in actual conflicts. On this basis their prohibition and elimination should be pursued as a matter of utmost urgency by governments and the entire international community.[93]

Furthermore, the ICBL assisted Canada and other pro-ban states in the treaty-negotiating process by developing and delivering public support for the ban and by providing valuable information and analytical reports based on that information. In particular, the ICBL held conferences in Asia, Africa, Europe, and Latin America to help generate public and governmental support for the ban and to draft recommendations for the leading pro-ban states that were drafting the treaty. It also participated as an active member in conferences that took place in 1996 and 1997 in Austria, Belgium, and Sweden. The ICBL was allowed to do so primarily because the conferences "had not been held hostage to rule by consensus," which, in turn, allowed "for the first time, smaller and middle-sized powers" to "come together, to work in close cooperation with NGOs" to achieve, for the first time, "a ban on a weapon in widespread use."[94] Axworthy recognized the importance of the help of NGOs in creating the regime when he stated at the conference in Ottawa in October 1996 that the NGOs "are largely responsible for our being here today. The same effective arguments you used to get us here must now be put to work to get foreign ministers here to sign the treaty."[95]

Human-rights NGOs, such as HRW and Physicians for Human Rights (PHR), have also invoked human-rights treaties, many of which are considered customary law[96] and highlight the proportionality argument. The use of human-rights arguments for banning landmines follows the recent expansion of international NGO human-rights activities from the early 1990s to include economic and social rights.[97] Partially a result of an increased focus on social and economic rights by developing states, it also helped bridge a North-South coalition atypical for arms control and disarmament treaties. Moreover, grafting norms, such as human rights, that previously had been agreed to universally also helped to ensure that the landmine issue would receive sustained attention, unlike more complex international issues.[98]

Schema: Leadership Games

The main schema used in the policy agenda-setting level entailed games concerning who was taking the leadership role in addressing the humanitarian aspects of the landmine issue. The main players were the major powers, especially the United States, and NGOs and their state allies such as Canada and South Africa. NGOs continually argued that major powers were not necessary to achieve the treaty, although they pressured states to join the treaty. While there were other leadership games taking place within the ICBL, between the ICBL and the ICRC and among the pro-ban states to direct the movement, the major game took place between the United States and the pro-ban coalition. Eventually the media joined this particular leadership "game schema" because they had once supported the concept of a landmine ban; they "increasingly recognized the compelling story behind the global humanitarian crisis and the 'David and Goliath' nature of NGOs taking on governments and militaries to ban a weapon used by armies for decades."[99]

The leadership schema presented contrasted the major powers. At the initiation of NGOs, the leadership turning points for each of the states was directly tied to individuals to get their governments to ban landmines. The main point of this section is to highlight the false games played by states initially to oppose a landmine ban and then to support a ban in an effort to gain public-opinion credibility at the initiative of individuals who carry the support of NGOs. Each of these relationships is addressed briefly below.

United States: Senator Leahy and the Vietnam Veterans of America Foundation. The United States came too late to the Ottawa Treaty negotiations, having joined the conference for the final drafting of the treaty in Oslo in September 1997. This conference took place less than three months before the date of the treaty signing scheduled for early December in Ottawa. By coming to the conference with a series of requests that it wanted to incorporate into the treaty, the US delegation attempted to break the treaty package that had already been assembled and presented to the state delegates in Oslo.[100] Its proposal was not well received by states and completely rejected by the ICBL primarily because the Americans wanted a treaty exception for mixed antitank and antipersonnel landmine systems. Subsequent to the rejection, President Clinton explained US opposition to the treaty by saying that the United States "implored the people there [at the Oslo Final Drafting Treaty Conference] to give us the exceptions we needed."[101]

One of this essay's major arguments is that nonsignatory states, such as Russia and the United States, are having difficulty developing a coherent landmine policy because both the transformation of the landmine debate on the international political agenda from a security to a humanitarian issue and the speed of the issue rising to the top of the international political agenda took them by surprise. Opening up the debate to humanitarian issues invites nontraditional decision-making actors in foreign and security policy, such as refugee, religious, and human-rights activists who support a ban, into the public policy-making process. Transforming the debate expands the scope of conflict about landmine policy, thereby helping to increase the visibility of the issue to the American public and, in turn, involving them more actively in policy discourse.[102] The effect is a weakening of the monopoly held by certain government agencies on security and tactical weapon policy. For example, Defense Secretary William Cohen wrote that "the mass media's coverage of the recent talks in Oslo on land mines could easily leave the impression that the United States is largely responsible for this humanitarian tragedy, or at least stands in the way of international efforts to stop the dying and maiming. Such an impression is simply wrong."[103] The debate's transformation to an area where civilians and nonmilitary decision makers have more influence, and therefore are more vulnerable to NGO pressure, has important implications.

The main force behind the US need to address continually the humanitarian aspects of the landmine debate is Patrick Leahy, Democratic senator from Vermont, and the VVAF. Leahy became interested in the humanitarian aspects of the landmine issue in the early 1990s, when he and his wife visited Central America and met several landmine-disabled children. Soon thereafter, he became the first US public official to label landmines as illegal. Since then, he has been the key legislator to introduce measures against landmines. Leahy ultimately moved the United States into a leadership role between 1992 and 1994, when he worked closely with Bobby Mueller, VVAF's executive director, to help push landmine legislation forward. Speaking about Mueller and the VVAF's efforts at the first ever US Senate hearing on landmines, Leahy said, "I think he has done more and had more responsibility for the global campaign against landmines than anybody I know. . . . So, I just want to say publicly that without not only the constant inspiration but the constant push from Bobby Mueller I do not know if we would be even having this hearing today."[104]

In 1992 the VVAF and other NGO allies, such as HRW, encouraged the Senate to pass Leahy's amendment to ban the export of all landmines.[105] The following year the Senate passed (100–0) a three-year extension, which is now permanent. In 1994 President Clinton was the first international leader to address the United Nations about the need for a ban. As part of establishing landmines on the international agenda, Leahy held the "The Global Landmine Crisis"[106] on May 13, 1994, inviting several American landmine victims and representatives of humanitarian NGOs to testify about the effects of landmines. Since then he has introduced new landmine legislation every year working closely with the ICBL to push the United States position closer to a ban and encouraging other states, such as France, to take their own steps toward a ban.[107]

Since these early victories, however, Leahy and his NGO allies have failed to stop the Clinton administration from backtracking in its leadership role to enact international and domestic legislative measures to alleviate landmine use. Subsequent to the Clinton administration's declared opposition to the treaty, Leahy argued that holding states to different standards would defeat the stigmatization force that a comprehensive treaty could deliver. He said during the final treaty negotiations that "an effective international agreement that is based on stigmatizing a weapon cannot have different standards for different nations."[108]

Great Britain: Diana, Princess of Wales, and the British Red Cross, the Mines Advisory Group, and the Landmine Survivors Network. Until mid-1997 Great Britain was among the treaty's strongest opponents, so it came as a surprise to anti-ban supporters that its landmine policy completely reversed in a matter of months. The landmine issue in Great Britain initially gathered attention in January 1997 when Princess Diana visited Angola as a guest of the British Red Cross and Halo Trust, a British NGO working to clear landmines. She called on the British government to ban landmines as the only humanitarian option. At the time of this statement, the British landmine position was similar to that of the U.S. and supported the continued use of landmines. Her remarks "produced a telling conflict with some decision-makers in the government, since her position in favor of a total ban on land mines deviated from official policy." After condemning her remarks, one governmental official called her a "loose cannon."[109] The effects of her Angolan visit with the British NGOs created more publicity about British policy toward landmines than ever before.

Before her trip, British official David Davis stated that supporting a ban would sacrifice "the effectiveness of our armed forces on the altar of political correctness." Several months after Princess Diana's trip to Angola, Davis announced that Great Britain would support a ban. Furthermore, in a complete reversal of policy, the British government started to praise Princess Diana's positive influence on the issue. The newly appointed International Development Secretary, Clare Short, stated that "we need a worldwide ban and the more the Princess can do to bring that about, the better. The Princess has drawn the world's attention to this problem." Responding to past Conservative Party criticism about her involvement into what was then perceived to be a security issue, the Princess said, "I am not a political figure. I'd like to reiterate now, my interests are humanitarian. That is why I felt drawn to this human tragedy. That is why I wanted to play my part in working towards a worldwide ban on these weapons."[110]

Great Britain's opposition to the ban disappeared relatively soon after the rise to power of Tony Blair's Labor Party, which had made banning landmines one of its election-campaign-platform goals. However, it was British NGOs, especially through Princess Diana as patron of the British Red Cross and through her association with British demining NGOs, such as the Halo Trust and MAG, and her visit to Bosnia with the American humanitarian NGO Landmine Survivors Network (LSN), who encouraged the British public to support a ban and Blair to follow through on his campaign pledge. Upon taking office, the Blair government did announce a ban but with significant reservations, including the "the right to use mines in exceptional circumstances."[111] This directly contravened the ICBL's goal to allow no exceptions. It is not surprising therefore, that Blair's government announced a complete ban soon after British NGOs and Princess Diana wanted his government to follow through on its campaign promise. His government rightly feared that once the landmine issue was placed squarely on the political agenda as a humanitarian issue, British policy for continued landmine use would be unsustainable.

In conclusion, Princess Diana's involvement with the NGOs helped encourage a change in British landmine policy, which, in turn, ensured the Ottawa Convention's success two ways. First, it helped bring about Great Britain's support for a ban. This move damaged the position of the U.S., the most vocal of the treaty's opponents, because until then Great Britain and the United States had similar positions. Losing Great Britain as an ally on the ban issue helped isolate the U.S. from landmine discussions, and, more importantly damaged its credibility vis à vis other allies on the issue. More specifically, Great Britain's change in policy resulted in the United State's isolation from its allies and all NATO members, except Turkey, who also did not support the convention.

Second, Princess Diana's support of NGOs and their arguments to ban landmines helped transfer the issue from a political to a humanitarian problem. Moreover, she was able to leverage the media into covering the landmine issue from locations such as Angola and Bosnia and thereby helped to marshal public support for the ban and against the British anti-ban position. Each of her trips to landmine infested states was organized and planned by humanitarian NGOs. Several days after her death on August 31, 1997, the Oslo Conference began to finalize the treaty. In recognition of her influence in the landmine issue, the prime minister of Norway stated at the conference's opening session that the treaty should be titled the Diana, Princess of Wales Treaty, highlighting the fact that she helped the NGO movement to bring attention to the landmine issue, promote assistance to landmine victims, and focus on the landmine ban.

South Africa: Nelson Mandela and the South African Campaign to Ban Landmines. In February 1997, on the eve of the ICBL conference in Maputo, Mozambique, the South African government announced that it would impose an immediate ban on the use, production, export, and transit of landmines, thereby becoming one of the first African states to declare a unilateral ban.[112] This announcement soon led many other African states to support the Ottawa Process.[113] The South African government's decision was brought about through pressure from the South African Campaign to Ban Landmines (SACBL), a coalition of more than 100 South African NGOs.

The SACBL was able to achieve its government's support for a ban by placing the issue on the agenda as a humanitarian problem via several approaches. First, humanitarian NGOs and student associations started campaigning for a ban in 1993. This racially diverse coalition, coupled with the rise to power of Nelson Mandela and the first democratically elected government in 1994, allowed "unprecedented access to senior political and bureaucratic officials" that "greatly facilitated the eventual symbiosis of governmental and nongovernmental activities and policy positions." There were many common bonds and friendships between SACBL members and governmental officials, including Nelson Mandela, because they were "historical partners" in the antiapartheid struggle.[114] Second, even foreign NGOs influenced the South African government's decision to act on the landmine issue. South African Defense Minister Joe Modise said that South Africa's decision was greatly impacted by United States General Norman Schwarzkopf's support of a landmine ban, which was demonstrated publicly in the April 1996 full-page letter in the *New York Times* to President Clinton sponsored by the VVAF.[115]

Canada: Lloyd Axworthy and Mines Action Canada. In 1993, pressured and supported by Canadian NGOs, especially human-rights groups, the newly elected liberal government in Canada transformed its foreign policy decision-making process to include more NGO consultations.[116] This change in policy allowed a coalition of NGOs working under the auspices of Mines Action Canada (MAC) to influence Canada's landmine position directly by placing it on the government's agenda. They also encouraged Canadian Foreign Minister Lloyd Axworthy to take the lead in helping to alleviate its effects as an international social problem. Initial meetings between the NGOs and the government "produced little common ground from which discussions could progress" once it was placed on the agenda.[117] These meetings, however, gave the NGOs an opportunity to educate government officials about the humanitarian problem caused by landmines and thereby gain legitimacy for their arguments and detract from military and strategic arguments for opposing a ban.

Canadian NGOs continued to promote the landmine issue after it was placed on the government's agenda by instituting a toll-free telephone number that people could call for information, recruiting Canadian celebrities, such as singer Bruce Cockburn, to the cause, instituting a letter writing campaign to government officials, and giving landmine victims an opportunity to present personal testimonies. As some members in the government, especially the foreign ministry, became more open to the idea of a ban, they invited MAC representatives to join the Canadian CCW negotiating teams in 1995 and 1996. Subsequently, Axworthy took the lead internationally in banning landmines by initiating and encouraging the Ottawa Process, which precipitated a dramatic transformation of Canada's international role from a faithful NATO arms-control follower during the cold war to a disarmament leader in the post-cold war world. However, Axworthy needed the support of MAC and other Canadian NGOs in order to mobilize public opinion and motivate Canadians to press for this foreign policy change.[118] In particular, MAC and the other Canadian NGOs provided the political cover for Axworthy to put the landmine issue on the agenda and to take the initiative to encourage state action at the international level.

In summary, even though the work of Axworthy, Leahy, Mandela, and the Princess of Wales are excellent examples for highlighting the need for state action, these individuals needed NGOs to help pressure states on a number of fronts. The issue of whether or not landmines were legal touched many constituencies, such as environmental, human-rights, and refugee NGOs. These NGOs provided information, public-opinion support, and resources to these individuals to highlight the landmine issue and pressure states into changing their landmine policies.

Also helping NGOs get the landmine issue transformed from a policy to a normative issue was the cynical view that many people have of governments. It may have contributed to the muting of landmine-ban opposition. Some media scholars imply that rising levels of mistrust and cynicism in the public is correlated with growing consumption of more information from the media, especially television.[119] Unknowingly, NGOs capitalized on those cynical views by using the media to promote landmine-victim stories and point a finger at the "bad guys" to embarrass and isolate governments not supporting the ban. For example, the ICBL developed a "good guy" list as part of a strategy to move the landmine-ban issue forward at the CCW conferences.[120] This list was circulated to the media, which, in turn, pressured governments. Moreover, data from media coverage show "that whereas mine incidents were rarely reported upon before the campaign to ban landmines reached prominence, since that time they have been treated increasingly as newsworthy events deserving of political attention."[121]

In sum, the leadership-game schema influenced how the landmine issue was perceived by many governments and the public. From the NGO perspective, the landmine issue was a humanitarian problem that should be addressed at the international level. In contrast, major powers, such as the United States, argued that landmines were strategically useful tools on the battlefield. For example, the United States argued that retaining their use was essential for maintaining peace in the Korean peninsula and ridding Kuwait of Iraqi occupation. Regardless, the NGOs continually argued that such reasoning was incoherent when examining the landmine issue at the humanitarian level.

NGO support of key individuals, such as Leahy, Princess Diana, Axworthy, and Mandela, through information and political support, guaranteed that the landmine issue would be addressed once it was on the agenda. While Leahy may not have been successful in obtaining a U.S. signature on the treaty, he did move policy closer to a ban and, most importantly, much of his domestic legislation, such as the export moratorium, was modeled by other states and the United Nations. The personal experiences of Leahy, Princess Diana, Axworthy, and Mandela, working with humanitarian NGOs, such as LSN, MAC, MAG, SACBL, and VVAF, attest that individuals can truly make a difference in policy agenda setting. Some international relations theorists argue that transnational entrepreneurs need to be important decision makers themselves or have the ability to influence such decision makers to move an issue into the international arena.[122] These individuals seem to fit the description explained above, but they could not have achieved the landmine-policy results without NGO advice, encouragement, and support.

Priming: Incoherent Arguments

In essence, the forces in favor of a landmine ban used landmine victims as the priming tool, not only to get the landmine issue on the international agenda but also as a moral argument to stigmatize the weapon and anyone that supported its continued use. This strategy proved extremely helpful in countering anti-ban arguments that landmine use was a legitimate military activity under international humanitarian law. By featuring landmine victims frequently and prominently in their promotional literature and reports and in speeches and conferences, the NGO strategy consisted primarily of emotional arguments brought by and on behalf of victims. They were right. There was no real attempt by states opposed to the ban to dispute the humanitarian arguments. Instead, these anti-ban states made strong military and political arguments as to why landmines should not be banned but at the same time expressed humanitarian concern for the landmine victims. These strategies produced incoherent policies that were not compatible with how and why the landmine issue was established on the international agenda.

Governmental policymakers were hesitant to state their opposition to a ban because of media and public opinion condemning landmine use as the main cause of the humanitarian problem. A 1996 poll showed that the international public was increasingly united in their belief that landmines were horrific and indiscriminate killers and should be banned. The response to the question, "would you personally be in favor of or against your country signing the landmine ban treaty?" was overwhelming. Of the twenty-one states surveyed, Japan and the United States scored the lowest in approval at still the relatively high rates of 58 percent and 60 percent respectfully, while Denmark at 92 percent and Spain at 91 percent scored the highest. Even the citizens of other major power states, such as Russia (83 percent) and India (82 percent) favored their country signing landmine-ban treaty.[123]

Alternative Explanation

Neorealism

Neorealists would explain the international norm for banning landmines as epiphenomenal because they believe that such norms do not have an independent effect on state behavior. For example, neorealist scholar John Mearsheimer argues that states do not follow international norms that do not serve their self-interests.[124] Since anarchy remains constant and the units of an anarchic system are functionally undifferentiated, neorealists focus on material capabilities as the most identifiable characteristics of the states rather than on sociological influences, such as norms. Therefore, according to neorealist principles, we can assume that states ban landmines because they perceive some relative gains in prohibiting landmine use. Similarly, states that do not use mines simply agree not to use them. In other words, some states did not sign the ban because continued landmine use is a means to ensure further their own survival, while other states signed because it signals merely an easy way for them to help achieve their goal of survival. The explanation for why states either signed or did not sign the treaty simply reflects the interests of states adhering to the ban.

Another neorealist explanation for why states signed the landmine ban could be that landmines have no military utility to enhance or threaten a state's security interests. Since it asserts that the primary actors in international relations are states, this particular explanation would explain the ban as a process derived from a state-centered perspective. Neorealists could argue that many states banned landmines because these weapons no longer have the utility that they once had; therefore, their prohibition does not affect state interests.[125] According to neorealists, it is easy to achieve an international agreement when no one's interests are threatened or when states do not care deeply about relative gains.[126] They would argue that perhaps the main reason for the ban is the simple fact that landmines do not win wars and are not essential to many states' national security. Many states did not sign the treaty because they still employ landmines for national security purposes, while many signatory states have relatively little security concerns and thus do not require landmines. Table 29.2 highlights regional opposition to the ban. In regions where security tensions are high, a greater percentage of states oppose the treaty. For example, in the Middle East, 71 percent of the states oppose the treaty. In comparison, less than 7 percent of states in the Americas, where security tension is relatively low, oppose the treaty. A neorealist would assert that this divergence most likely reflects more stable governments and recognized borders. Furthermore, neorealists do not have to highlight only the general pattern of regional support for the ban. They can point out that South Korea and the United States are hesitant to join the ban because of landmine use in the DMZ.

TABLE 29.2 Regional Opposition for the Ottawa Treaty[a]

Region	Total Nonsignatory States	Total States in Region	% of States Not Signing
Africa	8	48	17
Americas	2	35	6
Asia-Pacific	21	35	60
Europe/Central Asia	4	43	8
Middle East/North Africa	12	17	71

[a] State support for the treaty as of March 1999. ICRC, *Landmine Monitor Report 1999: Toward a Mine-Free World* (New York: Human Rights Watch, 1999).

Neorealists could also argue that since the major powers did not sign the convention, it is meaningless. While most of the smaller and mid-size states support the ban regime, major powers, such as China, India, Pakistan, Russia, and the United States, did not sign because it is not in their interest to do so.[127] Waltz says that "a general theory of international politics is necessarily based on great powers" and that "so long as major states are major actors, the structure of international politics is defined in terms of them. States set the scene in which, they, along with non-state actors, stage dramas or carry on their humdrum affairs."[128]

Critique of Alternative Explanations

The neorealist ontology skirts a key issue in international relations: when and under what conditions do issues not originating from states get on the international political agenda? Because neorealism's ontology privileges states over other international actors, it cannot explain the NGO role in agenda setting, controlling the landmine issue, and encouraging states to sign. Neorealists believe that NGOs themselves are dependent upon underlying power distributions. This article's main theoretical point is taken from the contructivist approach: state interest and identity formation on the landmine issue are due to the placement of the ban-landmine norm on the international political agenda, and NGOs are able to control and sustain the issue independent of existing state power distributions. Moreover, the reason that states addressed the landmine issue is because NGOs placed it on the international political agenda. In other words, the implication is that if NGOs did not place and control the landmine issue on the international political agenda, states would not even be discussing a ban let alone actually following through with action. Since Waltz posits that the NSA role in international affairs is marginal,[129] he and other neorealists are unable to explain why states were confronted with the landmine issue in the first place.

People, however, may question the ban's effectiveness because the major producers did not sign. While it is true that China and Russia did not sign, most of the other major landmine producers have stopped production, belying criticism that only states that did not produce landmines agreed not to sell them. Specifically, in the past few years the number of states producing landmines has:

> dropped dramatically from 54 to 16. The 38 who have stopped production include a majority of the big producers in the 1970s, 1980s, and early 1990s—those who bear much of the responsibility for the tens of millions of mines now in the ground. Eight of the twelve biggest producers and exporters over the past thirty years have signed the treaty and stopped production: Belgium, Bosnia, Bulgaria, Czech Republic, France, Hungary, Italy, and the United Kingdom. Other significant producers that have signed include Germany, Croatia, Chile and Brazil."[130]

Even though the major states did not sign the treaty, NGO pressure, enforced by public opinion, encouraged them to implement certain landmine-policy changes unilaterally. Despite their opposition to the treaty, they have instituted policy changes that closely reflect the treaty's objectives.[131] Such unilateral policy announcements reflect a nonconventional approach to international law, and, in particular, seem to bode well for the potential effectiveness of the regime to ban landmines. These actions, especially from major powers, such as the United States, Russia, and China, are caused by "the failure of the international legal system, coupled with fundamentally changed circumstances since the time when the relevant texts were agreed."[132] In the case of the landmine ban, the major powers thought they had unique military responsibilities requiring landmine use; after the signing of the treaty, however, they implemented more restrictive landmine policies thus signaling movement toward supporting the treaty's objectives.

Another charge against the convention's effectiveness could be that it does not include extensive verification provisions. While the convention does allow for some minimal compliant procedures in case of state violation, it is a long and torturous process.[133] NGOs supported the exclusion of intensive verification provisions in the convention in order to attract more states to sign the ban.[134] NGOs developed and implemented a strategy that called for bringing as many states as possible into the regime to counter major-power opposition. Eliminating verification provisions was intended to reduce states' fears of meddlesome inspections.

The lack of verification provisions in the ban convention could have disadvantages. In a verification-free convention, states may believe that prohibitions can be easily circumvented by cheating and, therefore, might sign the ban but not worry about compliance. Some scholars believe that the lack of verification provisions is the principal problem in many arms-control and disarmament agreements. Without verification provisions, "legal prohibitions of weapons are mere ploughings of the sand."[135]

Despite this argument, however, the Ottawa Convention holds several important advantages for states that do sign. Most states that sign give up nothing they need to defend themselves. State security does not depend on landmines. The existence of a landmine prohibition, however, gives signatory states a solid moral and political basis for criticizing other states' ownership or use of these weapons. While the ban convention cannot ensure that states will abide by the prohibition, it will increase the economic and political costs of using them. States that do not wish to be internationally isolated may thus be dissuaded from producing and using landmines and from maintaining landmine stockpiles.

The fact that so many states signed the verification-free ban convention also indicates a level of universal agreement on banning landmines. It may also suggest that state attraction to signing the ban is contingent upon the destructiveness of the weapon system. For example, states may not be as vulnerable to the negative effects of defection from bans on lower-level conventional weapons, such as landmines, as they would be to bans on nuclear weapons.

Conclusion

By transforming the landmine-ban debate from a military and security issue to a humanitarian problem, NGOs created an opportunity to negotiate the landmine issue differently from previous arms-control and disarmament treaties. Changing the issue category also helped NGOs to increase state attention and action toward the landmine issue. For example, noted public policy scholar John W. Kingdon says that that by "putting the subject into one category rather than another" helps bring the problem to the attention of those in and around government.[136] Moreover, opening up the debate to humanitarian issues allows significant access to nontraditional foreign and security policy actors, such as humanitarian and religious groups, into the public policy-making process. Lastly, the debate transformation expanded the scope of conflict about landmine policy, thereby helping to increase the visibility of the issue to policymakers and the public and, in turn, involving them more actively in policy discourse.[137]

At the agenda-setting level of norms, opening the debate to nonmilitary experts, such as Axworthy, Leahy, Mandela, and Princess Diana, allows civilians to become more involved in the process and to engage military leaders directly. It is not surprising, therefore, that President Clinton decided to remain outside the Ottawa Convention process for national security reasons, while addressing the humanitarian aspects of the landmine issue with increased funding for landmine-victim assistance and demining programs.

The chapter's broader implication is that under certain conditions NGOs can contribute to creating international law, especially legal prohibitions on weapons that are strategically dubious and humanitarianly suspect, which, in turn, can effect state behavioral changes. Several unique conditions of the Ottawa Convention process are potentially revealing of the role that NGOs can play in this process. First, the role that victims played in NGO strategies to achieve the ban was a significant factor in drawing international attention to the landmine issue that eventually resulted in state action. Landmine victims, whether in their role as part of statistics and NGO stigmatization strategies or through their personal testimonies at international conferences and in media profiles, were a powerful instrument for NGOs to frame the issue. In fact, the first line of the Ottawa Convention's text says that the purpose of the treaty is "to put an end to the suffering and casualties caused by anti-personnel mines, that kill or maim hundreds of people every week, mostly innocent and defenceless civilians and especially children."

Looking at other weapons that were banned or severely restricted by the international community, such as biological, nuclear, and chemical weapons, the role of victims in accomplishing the conventions was not as significant, especially when compared with the NGO role in high-lighting landmine victims to help achieve the Ottawa Treaty.[138] It should be noted here that the 1925 Geneva Protocol on Poisonous Gas also partially resulted from "popular demands for a ban" in light of the more than one million gas victims from World War I, albeit victims were not a major factor in achieving the more recent Chemical Weapons Convention, which was "prompted by the use of herbicides and riot control agents during the Vietnam War."[139]

The lack of victim participation in the great NGO effort to ban nuclear weapons may explain why it has not been as successful as the landmine campaign in attracting international attention.[140] NGO initiatives in the nuclear weapons campaign were composed primarily of experts arguing from specific legal and medical points of view, which resonated less with public and state representatives than did a parade of civilian victims of that particular weapon *and* NGO experts. Another possible explanation for the failure of the movement to ban nuclear weapons is that banning landmines may not be as important to states as banning nuclear weapons. Violations of a landmine ban would not fundamentally threaten national security, while an undetected violation of a nuclear weapons ban could pose a serious threat.

NGOs primarily focused on the humanitarian aspects of the mine issue, addressing the plight of victims rather than focusing on the military and security implications of the ban. This emphasis is reflected in the convention's call for state signatories to "provide assistance for the care and rehabilitation, and social and economic reintegration, of mine victims."[141] Since including victim assistance into an arms control or disarmament convention is not standard practice, strong arguments had to be made to include language that "would require states to accept certain affirmative duties toward individuals injured by mines."[142] For the treaty to accomplish its goal of providing a complete response to the threats presented by landmines, the inclusion of mine-victim assistance was necessary "to prevent mine victims' permanent inability to function, work, or otherwise participate as productive members of society."[143]

The NGO role in setting and controlling the landmine issue on the international political agenda also provides a distinctive form of world politics that this chapter assesses: a collaborative process between moderate states and transnational NGOs—"a new internationalism" that is evident in other settings. This form of world politics provides a process model that could be useful in current and future efforts to promote security, prohibitions, and restrictions. For example, the Coalition to Stop the Use of Child Soldiers is currently attempting to attach to the Convention on the Rights of the Child an optional protocol banning the recruitment and participation of child soldiers. After eight years of negotiations, on January 21, 2000, governments, including the United States, agreed to ban the use of soldiers under the age of eighteen in armed conflicts but not ban the recruitment of soldiers under eighteen.[144] Because the issue is being negotiated in a consensus-negotiating forum, the United States and other states are able to block the adoption of eighteen as the minimum age for voluntary recruitment. United States opposition is based on "concerns over whether setting the minimum recruitment age at 18 would compromise national security or limit sovereignty."[145] Most likely, the NGO coalition and state allies will be forced to mirror the NGO landmine campaign by taking the issue out of a consensus forum and creating a negotiating forum more open to NGO agenda control.

Another effort that evinces this distinctive form of world politics is the Global Campaign on Small Arms and Light Weapons. The campaign is composed of NGOs and seeks to address the problems caused by the proliferation and misuse of small arms and light weapons. The distinctive form of world politics evidenced by the landmine campaign "provided the foundation" for this effort to alleviate the effects of "the widespread availability of light weapons."[146] Again, because of concerns among states, NGOs may also have to take these negotiations out of any state consensus-based forum.

The chapter's findings provide an explanation both for why the landmine-ban issue was absent from the international political agenda before the ICBL's founding in 1991 and for why it drew the rapid attention once it materialized. Its findings are significant for larger concerns in political science. It sheds light on a few conditions under which NGOs can affect state behavior in an area traditionally at the heart of state sovereignty—security and weapons. Importantly, it shows why many states were attracted to the landmine-ban issue. In this article, any arguments that states signed the treaty because of the NGO agenda-setting role are hypothetical. Nevertheless, the chapter shows why states were motivated and pressured by NGOs to address the landmine issue.

Meanwhile, the international legal community should be interested in the chapter's findings because it provides a process model for current and future NGO-state collaborative efforts to alleviate the negative effects of certain weapons, especially those with a dubious military utility. Since the landmine-ban norm originated at the substate level and not with major state powers, the rise of the landmine-ban norm may help explain why particular issues take off. This point leads us to probe further and ask if the emergence of the landmine-ban issue says something more generally about international law and relations.

The chapter also suggests that that NGOs can be productive players in the evolving arms-control agenda by identifying weapons or other security practices that are contrary to humanitarian principles. For example, NGOs can help target weapons currently in development in order to reduce political opposition and lower implementation costs. Perhaps there also should be a clearer obligation for states to review their weapons currently online. NGOs can be integral to this process by identifying these weapons, and placing and controlling the issue on the international political agenda. Finally, the NGO role in placing the landmine issue on the international political agenda and controlling it once it got there suggests ways that international society can address uncontrolled weapons proliferation and use in a timely and unified manner.

Notes

1. Ottawa Convention on the Prohibition of the Use, Stockpiling, Production and Transfer of Anti-Personnel Mines and on Their Destruction, 1997. Unless noted, all references to landmines refer to antipersonnel landmines and not other forms of landmines, such as antitank mines, antivehicle mines, and sea mines.
2. Statement by Canadian Prime Minister Chretien at the signing conference for the Ottawa Convention, December 2, 1997.
3. For further information on the unique features of the Ottawa Convention, see Ken Rutherford, "The Hague and Ottawa Conventions: A Model for Future Weapon Ban Regimes?" *Nonproliferation Review* 6 (Spring–Summer 1999).
4. International Campaign to Ban Landmines, "Report on Activities: Review Conference on the Convention on Conventional Weapons," Vienna, Austria (September 25-October 13, 1995), 6.
5. International Campaign to Ban Landmines, http://www.icbl.org, April 30, 2000.
6. Richard Price, "Reversing the Gun Sights: Transnational Civil Society Targets Land Mines," *International Organization* 52 (Summer 1998); and Maxwell A. Cameron, Robert J. Lawson, and Brian W. Tomlin, "To Walk without Fear," and Jody Williams and Stephen D. Goose, "The International Campaign to Ban Landmines," in Cameron, Lawson, and Tomlin, eds., *To Walk without Fear: The Global Movement to Ban Landmines* (Toronto: Oxford University Press, 1998).
7. The campaign consists of over fourteen hundred arms-control, development, environmental, humanitarian, human rights, medical, and religious NGOs representing some ninety

countries. Liz Bernstein, coordinator, ICBL, letter to *Landmine Monitor 2000* researchers, October 1999.

8. Paul J. Nelson, "Deliberation, Leverage or Coercion? The World Bank, NGOs, and Global Environmental Politics," *Journal of Peace Research* 34, no. 4 (1997); William Korey, *NGOs and the Universal Declaration of Human Rights: A Curious Grapevine* (New York: St. Martin's Press, 1998); Paul Wapner, "Politics beyond the State: Environmental Activism and World Civic Politics," *World Politics* 47 (April 1995).

9. U.S. Department of State, Bureau of Political-Military Affairs, Office of Humanitarian Demining Programs, *1998 Hidden Killers: The Global Landmine Crisis*, September 1998, pp. 8–9, 11.

10. Margaret E. Keck and Kathryn Sikkink, *Activists beyond Borders: Advocacy in International Politics* (Ithaca, NY: Cornell University Press, 1998).

11. Price (fn. 6).

12. Kathryn Sikkink, "Transnational Politics, International Relations Theory, and Human Rights," *Political Science and Politics* 31 (September 1998), 519.

13. Toshio Takeshita, "Exploring the Media's Roles in Defining Reality: From Issue–Agenda Setting to Attribute–Agenda Setting," in Maxwell McCombs, Donald L. Shaw, and David Weaver, eds., *Communication and Democracy: Exploring the Intellectual Frontiers in Agenda-Setting Theory* (London: Lawrence Erlbaum Associates, 1997), 20.

14. Rutherford (fn. 3), 38–39, 45.

15. For an evaluation of the potential effectiveness of the Ottawa Treaty, see Richard Price, "Compliance with International Norms and the Mines Taboo," in Cameron, Lawson, and Tomlin, eds. (fn. 6).

16. Joseph N. Cappella and Kathleen Hall Jamieson, *Spiral of Cynicism: The Press and the Public Good* (New York: Oxford University Press, 1997); Matthew Robert Kerbel, *Remote and Controlled: Media Politics in a Cynical Age* (Boulder, Colo.: Westview Press, 1995); McCombs, Shaw, and Weaver (fn. 13).

17. McCombs, Shaw, and Weaver (fn. 13).

18. R. Entman, *Democracy without Citizens: Media and the Decay of American Politics* (New York: Oxford University Press, 1989), quoted in Salma Ghanem, "Filling in the Tapestry: The Second Level of Agenda Setting," in McCombs, Shaw, and Weaver (fn. 13), 6.

19. Ibid., 8.

20. D. Graber, *Mass Media in American Politics*, 4th ed. (Washington, D.C.: Congressional Quarterly Press), quoted in Ghanem (fn. 18), 8.

21. J. McLeod, S. Sun, H. Chi, and Z. Pan, "Metaphor and the Media: What Shapes Public Understanding of the 'War' against Drugs" (Paper presented at the Association for Education in Journalism and Mass Communication, Minneapolis, Minn., August 1990), quoted in Ghanem (fn. 18), 9.

22. This chapter does not address neoliberalism because the neoliberalists have very little to say about security. Specifically, neoliberal scholars argue that international regimes change state behavior in low political issues, such as economics and the environment. Robert O. Keohane, *After Hegemony: Cooperation and Discord in the World Political Economy* (Princeton: Princeton University Press, 1984), 49–109; Stephen D. Krasner, "Sovereignty, Regimes, and Human Rights," in Volker Rittberger, ed., *Regime Theory and International Relations* (Oxford: Clarendon Press, 1993).

23. Statement made by Mark Gwozdecky, coordinator of the Mine Action Team in the Canadian Department of Foreign Affairs and International Trade, at the Ottawa Process Forum, Ottawa, Canada, on December 5, 1997. Author's notes.

24. Mike Croll, *The History of Landmines* (Barnsley, U.K.: Leo Cooper, 1998), x–xi.

25. U.S. Department of the Air Force, *The Conduct of Armed Conflict and Air Operations*, pamphlet no. 110–31, 1976, quoted in Lieutenant Colonel Burris M. Carnahan, "The Law of Land Mine Warfare: Protocol II to the United Nations Convention on Certain Conventional Weapons," *Military Law Review* 105 (Summer 1984), 73.

26. Ariane Sand-Trigo, ICRC Delegation to the UN, letter to the author, March 3, 1997.

27. The Landmines Protocol is attached to the CCW as Protocol II and is officially known as the Protocol on Prohibitions or Restrictions on the Use of Mines, Booby Traps and Other Devices. The two other Protocols were Non-detectable Fragments (Protocol I) and Prohibitions or Restrictions on the Use of Incendiary Weapons (Protocol III). The CCW Review

held in Vienna in September 1996 adopted Protocol IV, which called for restrictions on the use of laser weapons, while the landmines protocol was amended at the third and final CCW review held in Geneva. The four protocols are regulated by the provisions of the Weapons Convention.

28. Arms Project of Human Rights Watch and Physicians for Human Rights, *Landmines: A Deadly Legacy* (New York: Human Rights Watch and Physicians for Human Rights, 1993), 9.

29. The U.S. State Department has estimated that Afghanistan, Angola, and Cambodia host the largest numbers of landmines in the world. U.S. Department of State, *1994 Hidden Killers: The Global Landmine Crisis*, pub. no. 10225, December 1994, 1.

30. *1998 Hidden Killers* (fn. 9) 9. In *1994 Hidden Killers* the U.S. Department of State estimated that there were 80 to 110 landmines in sixty-four countries; *1994 Hidden Killers* (fn. 29), v. U.S. Department of State, *1993 Hidden Killers: The Global Problem with Uncleared Landmines*, July 1993, 2.

31. *1998 Hidden Killers* (fn. 9), 8–9, 11.

32. International Committee for the Red Cross, *Landmines Must Be Stopped* (Geneva: ICRC, 1998), 16. *1998 Hidden Killers* (fn. 9), 1.

33. International Campaign to Ban Landmines, *Landmine Monitor Report 1999: Toward a Mine-Free World* (New York: Human Rights Watch, 1999), 3.

34. Chechnya: Olivia Ward, "Empire of Ruin: The Corrupt Russian Army Can't Think of Giving Up Its Mines," *New Internationalist* (September 1997), 16–17; and Daniel Williams, "Brutal Retreat from Grozny Led to a Killing Field," *Washington Post*, February 12, 2000, p. A1, A17. Dagestan: "Islamic Extremists in Dagestan Are Also Using Landmines," ICBL press release, Geneva, September 13, 1999; and "Russian Troops Clearing Dagestan Rebel-Planted Mines," FBIS transcribed text, Moscow *Interfax*, no. LD2508105399, August 25, 1999. Georgia: In November 1999, Russian military forces dropped mines in northern Georgia hoping to block potential escape routes of Chechen militants, "Russians Drop Mines in Georgia," *Washington Post*, November 18, 1999, p. A36. Ethiopia: It should be noted that the Ethiopian defense forces claim not to have used anti-personnel landmines in the conflict. According to the ICBL, "there is no evidence to the contrary." *Landmines Monitor Report 1999* (fn. 33), 147, 196–97.

35. United Nations Office for the Coordination of Humanitarian Assistance to Afghanistan (UNOCHA), *Mine Action Programme: Afghanistan* (New York: United Nations, 1999), 10. Robert Eaton, Chris Horwood, and Norah Niland, *Cambodia: The Development of Indigenous Mine Action Capabilities*, report to the United Nations Department of Humanitarian Affairs (New York: United Nations, n.d.), 6.

36. *1998 Hidden Killers* (fn. 9), 58; Eaton, Horwood, and Niland (fn. 35), 38.

37. Carnahan (fn. 25), 74.

38. *Landmine Monitor Report 1999* (fn. 33), 14.

39. One is example is the United Kingdom's "Ranger" that "can fire 1296 mines in one minute." Lt. Col. C. E. E. Sloan, *Mine Warfare on Land*, (Washington, D.C.: Brassey's Defense Publishers, 1986), 38, quoted in Shawn Roberts and Jody Williams, *After the Guns Fall Silent: The Enduring Legacy of Landmines* (Washington, D.C.: Vietnam Veterans of America Foundation 1995), 7. Another example would be the Italian SO-AT system that allows a helicopter to drop 2496 landmines. This is in contrast to minefield laying, which "only a few years ago ... might have required up to eight hours work by a full company of troops." Quoted in Carnahan (fn. 25), 79.

40. Peter J. Ekberg, "Remotely Delivered Land Mines and International Law," *Columbia Journal of Transnational Law* 33, no. 1 (1995), 151; Carnahan (fn. 25), 74.

41. Ekberg (fn. 40), 153.

42. Michael Dobbs, "A War-Torn Reporter Reflects," *Washington Post*, July 11, 1999, B1.

43. Ekberg (fn 40), 156.

44. Statement by Captain Michael Doubleday, U.S. Department of Defense, press regular briefing, August 19, 1997.

45. *Landmines: A Deadly Legacy* (fn. 28). The "mixed mine" systems are one of the major obstacles to the United States signing the Ottawa Convention.

46. The majority of today's deployed landmines were laid by hand and not delivered aerially. Ekberg claims that remotely delivered landmines are significant contributors to "the landmine crisis." Ekberg (fn. 40), 149.

47. United States Campaign to Ban Landmines, "When Is an Antipersonnel Landmine Not a Mine?—When It Is American," press release, September 9, 1997.

48. Kenneth N. Waltz, "The Origins of War in Neorealist Theory," in Richard K. Betts, ed., *Conflict after the Cold War: Arguments on Causes of Peace* (Boston: Allyn and Bacon, 1994), 92–95.

49. Kenneth N. Waltz, *Theory of International Politics* (New York: McGraw-Hill, 1979), 71.

50. Pre-1997 NATO states that signed the Ottawa Treaty were Canada, Belgium, Denmark, France, Germany, Greece, Iceland, Ireland, Italy, Luxembourg, The Netherlands, Norway, Portugal, Spain, United Kingdom; NATO states that did not sign were Turkey and the U.S. Ex-Warsaw Pact states that signed the treaty were Bulgaria, Czechoslovakia (both the Czech and Slovak Republics), Hungary, Poland, Romania; the only Ex-Warsaw Pact state that did not sign was Russia.

51. Willliams and Goose (fn. 6), 21.

52. Christopher S. Wren, "U.N.-Backed Drive to Restrict Land Mines Fails at Talks," *New York Times*, October 13, 1995.

53. The six NGOs were Handicap International (France), Human Rights Watch (United States), Medico International (Germany), Mines Advisory Group (United Kingdon), Physicians for Human Rights (United States), and the Vietnam Veterans of America Foundation (United States) in Williams and Goose (fn. 6), 22.

54. Statement by Kenneth Anderson, director, Arms Project, Human Rights Watch, Global Landmine Crisis Hearing before a Subcommittee of the Committee on Appropriations, United States Senate, May 13, 1994.

55. Williams and Goose (fn. 9), 20–21.

56. John W. Kingdon, *Agendas, Alternatives, and Public Policies* (Glenview, Ill.: Scott, Foresman and Company, 1984), 20–21, 96.

57. Gino Strada, "The Horror of Land Mines," *Scientific American* (May 1996), 42. Most landmine victims are women and children. Donovan Webster, "One Le.g., One Life at a Time," *New York Times Magazine*, January 23, 1994, p. 33.

58. Patrick M. Blagden, UN demining expert, estimates that there may be more than 200 million landmines. Blagden, "Summary of United Nations Demining," *Symposium on Antipersonnel Mines* (Geneva: ICRC, 1993), 117. *1993 Hidden Killers* (fn. 30), 2.

59. Eric Stover and Dan Charles, "The Killing Minefields of Cambodia," *New Scientist*, October 19, 1991, p. 27.

60. *Landmine Monitor Report 1999* (fn. 33), 405.

61. Patrick Blagden, "The Use of Mines and the Impact of Technology," in Kevin M. Cahill, ed., *Clearing the Fields: Solutions to the Global Land Mines Crisis* (New York: Basic Books and Council of Foreign Relations, 1995), 114–15.

62. Webster (fn. 57).

63. America's Defense Monitor, PBS-TV, Spring 1994.

64. Laurie H. Boulden, "A Mine Field, Statistically Speaking: The Dangers of Inflating the Problem," *Washington Post*, February 8, 1998, C2.

65. Croll (fn. 24), 131.

66. Christina Lamb, "Number of Land Mines Challenged: Report Calls U.N. Global Estimate of 110 Million Exaggerated," *Washington Times*, November 30, 1998, A1.

67. ICRC, *Anti-personnel Landmines Friend or Foe? A Study of the Military Use and Effectiveness of Anti-Personnel Mines* (Geneva: ICRC, March 1996), 37.

68. *Landmine Monitor Report 1999* (fn. 33), 15.

69. Bernard Shaw, CNN's *World News Tonight*, September 6, 1999.

70. *Landmine Monitor Report 1999* (fn. 33), 3.

71. See Kenneth R. Rutherford, "Internet Activism: NGOs and the Mine Ban Treaty," *International Journal on Grey Literature* 1, no. 3 (2000).

72. Croll (fn. 24), 151.

73. Ibid., 35.

74. J. Rautio and P. Paavolainen, "Afghan War Wounded: Experience with 200 Cases," *Journal of Trauma* 28 (April 1988); and D. Johnson, J. Crum, and S. Lumjiak, "Medical Consequences of the Various Weapons Systems Used in Combat in Thailand," *Military Medicine* 146 (1981); quoted in Chris Giannou, and J. Jack Geiger, "The Medical Lessons of Land Mine Injuries," in Cahill (fn. 61), 141.

75. B. Eshaya-Chauvin and R. M. Coupland, "Transfusion Requirements for the Management of War Injured: The Experience of the International Committee of the Red Cross," *British Journal of Anesthesia* 68 (1992), quoted in Giannou and Geiger (fn. 74), 140.
76. For example, see Paul Davies, *War of the Mines: Cambodia, Landmines and the Impoverishment of a Nation* (Boulder, Colo.: Pluto Press, 1994); Roberts and Williams (fn. 39); Phillip C. Winslow, *Sowing the Dragon's Teeth: Land Mines and the Global Legacy of War* (Boston: Beacon Press, 1997).
77. For examples, see International Committee for the Red Cross, ICRC *Overview 1998: Landmines Must Be Stopped*; International Campaign to Ban Landmines, *Landmine Monitor Report 1999* (fn. 33); ICBL brochures.
78. Williams and Goose (fn. 6), 23.
79. Rae McGrath, *Landmines: Legacy of Conflict: A Manual for Development Workers* (Oxford: Oxfam, 1994), 2.
80. Croll (fn. 24), 129.
81. 1977 Additional Protocol 1, Geneva Convention, Article 51 (4), 1949.
82. Ekberg (fn. 40), 166.; "The Arms Project," quoted in Roberts and Williams (fn. 39) 490–91.
83. Robert Sherman, "Banning Anti-Personnel Land Mines: The Ottawa Process and Beyond," *Disarmament: The Future of Disarmament*, April 16, 1997, 106.
84. Croll (fn. 24), xi, 151.
85. NGO Committee on Disarmament, UN forums, April 10, September 23, and October 21–23, 1997 (Edited transcripts, 1998).
86. Croll (fn. 24), xi.
87. NGO Committee on Disarmament, (fn. 85).
88. Statement by Jody Williams, Duke University Conference on Land Mines, May 1, 1998. USCBL, "Statement of the United States Campaign to Ban Landmines Condemning Yugoslav Landmine Aggression in Kosovo," April 15, 1999.
89. Williams (fn. 88).
90. The Conference on Disarmament (CD) was created by the United Nations to negotiate arms-control agreements. The CD usually discusses weapons of mass destruction rather than conventional weapons, which is why the UN created the CD outside the auspices of the CCW.
91. Robert J. Lawson, Mark Gwozdecky, Jill Sinclair, and Ralph Lysyshyn, in Cameron, Lawson, and Tomlin, eds. (fn. 6), 165. For an explanation of the negative consequences of consensus-based negotiating for weapon issues, see Stephen D. Goose, "Antipersonnel Landmines and the Conference on Disarmament," http://www.icbl.org, Home>Resources>Documents; Rutherford (fn. 3).
92. Philippe Naughton, "Landmine Pact to Go Ahead after Pakistan Backs Down," *Reuters*, May 3, 1996.
93. ICRC (fn. 67).
94. Williams and Goose (fn. 6), 45.
95. Statement by Lloyd Axworthy, International Strategy Conference, "Towards a Global Ban on Anti-Personnel Mines," Ottawa, Canada, October 5, 1996.
96. Susan Benesch, Glenn McGory, Christina Rodriguez, and Robert Sloane, "International Customary Law and Antipersonnel Landmines: Emergence of a New Customary Norm," *Landmine Monitor Report 1999* (fn. 33), 1032.
97. Korey (fn. 8), 16.
98. Price (fn. 6), 627–31.
99. Williams and Goose (fn. 6), 23.
100. The U.S. demands were presented in a take-it-or-leave-it package and consisted of five interlocking components: exception for landmine use in Korea, deferral of the date when the treaty would enter in force, changes in the definition of an antipersonnel landmine, more intensive verification measures, and a withdrawal clause from the treaty in cases of national emergency.
101. Lineuvid Gollust, "Clinton/Canada/Landmines," *Voice of America*, November 23, 1997.
102. Schattschneider argues that the expansion of conflict signifies a healthy democracy because it allows for increased public participation, usually through "responsible leaders and organizations," in the policy process. Schattschneider, *The Semisovereign People: A Realist's View of Democracy in America* (New York: Holt, Rinehart and Winston, 1976), 142.

103. William S. Cohen, "Necessary and Right," *Washington Post*, September 19, 1997, p. A23.

104. Patrick Leahy, "The Global Landmine Crisis," Subcommittee of the Committee of Appropriations, U.S. Senate, May 13, 1994, 66–67.

105. "The Scourge of Landmines," Vermont's U.S. Senator Patrick Leahy, http://www.senate.gov/~leahy.

106. Leahy (fn. 104). The author provided testimony along with representatives from international NGOs, domestic interest groups, and the Department of State. The DOD declined Leahy's invitation to attend.

107. Senator Patrick Leahy letter to Handicap International encouraging the French government to call for a review of the landmines protocol to the CCW, January 18, 1993. Handicap International, *For the Banning of Massacres of Civilians in Time of Peace: Facts and Chronologies*, 2d ed. (Lyon, France: Impression MEDCOM, June 1997).

108. Patrick Leahy, "Seize the Moment," ICBL *Ban Treaty News*, September 9, 1997, 1, quoted in Robert J. Lawson, Mark Gwozdecky, Jill Sinclair, and Ralph Lysyshyn, "The Ottawa Process," in Cameron, Lawson, and Tomlin, eds. (fn. 6), 178.

109. Fred Barbash, "Royal Spin" *Washington Post*, February 14, 1997, A23.

110. Robert Hardman, "Princess Calls for Greater Efforts to Clear Landmines," *Daily Telegraph*, June 13, 1997, 10.

111. Tim Butcher, "Labour Bans Landmines from 2005," *Electronic Telegraph*, May 22, 1997.

112. Cameron, Lawson, and Tomlin (fn. 6), 172.

113. In addition to encouraging other African states to join the treaty, South Africa's position on banning landmines was significant for two other reasons. First, it was the major producer of arms, including landmines, in Africa, which is the most heavily mined continent in the world. Second, South Africa used mines extensively in neighboring states, helping the southern African region to become the most mined-infested region in the world.

114. Noel Stott, "The South African Campaign," in Cameron, Lawson, and Tomlin, eds. (fn. 6), 68, 72, 74.

115. Joe Modise, interview with the author, Northern Cape Province, South Africa, May 21, 1997.

116. Canadian Government of Foreign Affairs and International Trade, "Canada in the World: Government Statement," 1995, 48–49, quoted in Maxwell A. Cameron, "Democratization of Foreign Policy: The Ottawa Process as a Model," in Cameron, Lawson, and Tomlin, eds. (fn. 6), 433; Valerie Warmington and Celina Tuttle, "The Canadian Campaign," in Cameron, Lawson, and Tomlin, eds. (fn. 6), 49.

117. Warmington and Tuttle (fn. 116), 49.

118. Ibid., 51, 54.

119. Capella and Jamieson (fn. 16); Kerbel (fn. 16).

120. Williams and Goose (fn. 6), 31.

121. Richard Price and Daniel Hope, "Media Coverage of Landmines," in *Landmine Monitor Report 1999* (fn. 33), 1048.

122. Ethan Nadelmann, "Global Prohibition Regimes: The Evolution of Norms in International Society," *International Organization* 44 (Autumn 1990).

123. "Ban of Use Land Mines in Favour or Against," Gallup International Opinion Research, Spring 1996.

124. John Mearsheimer, "The False Promise of Institutions," in Michael E. Brown, Sean M. Lynn Jones, and Steven Miller, eds., *The Perils of Anarchy: Contemporary Realism and International Security* (Cambridge: MIT Press, 1995), 334.

125. Price implies the same. Price (fn. 6), 614.

126. Mearsheimer (fn. 124), 346–51.

127. Five major states did not sign the Ottawa Treaty for the following reasons—China: to prevent foreign military interference, to maintain national unity, and to protect the well-being of its people; India: to maintain security; Pakistan: to maintain security; Russia: to protect nuclear plants and borders; and U.S.: to preserve security in Korea and to maintain mixed landmine systems. The sources for each respective country are: China: "The Issue of Anti-Personnel Landmines," China National Defense White Paper, Information Office of the States Council, Peoples Republic of China, July 27, 1998, quoted in *Landmine Monitor Report 1999* (fn. 33), 455; India: "India Calls for International Consensus on Banning Landmines," *Xinhua English Newswire*, November 15, 1998; Pakistan: BBC Worldwide

Monitoring Source, Radio Pakistan, external source, March 17, 1999; Russia: Timothy Heritage, "Russia Rebuffs Calls to Sign Landmine Treaty, *Reuters*, May 27, 1998, and Michelle Kelemen, "Russia/Landmines," *Voice of America*, May 27, 1998; U.S.: President Bill Clinton, letter to Marissa A. Vitagliano, acting coordinator, U.S. Campaign to Ban Landmines, August 31, 1998.

128. Waltz (fn. 49), 73, 94.

129. Ibid., 94–95.

130. *Landmine Monitor Report 1999* (fn. 33), 5.

131. Five major states changed their landmine policies since the founding of the ICBL in 1991: China instituted a unilateral landmine export moratorium; India supports a ban on all landmine transfers; Pakistan carefully regulates landmine use; Russia instituted a unilateral landmine export moratorium; and the U.S. instituted a unilateral landmine export moratorium, put a cap on landmine stockpiles, and will cease to use landmines in 2006 if alternatives to APLs and mixed munitions are identified and fielded. The sources for each respective country are: China: China National Defense White Paper (fn. 127); India: *Xinhua English Newswire* (fn. 127); Pakistan: Radio Pakistan (fn. 127); Russia: "Yeltsin Affirms Support for Ban on Mines," *Reuters*, October 29, 1997; and U.S.: "Suspension of Transfers of Anti-Personnel Mines," U.S. National Defense Authorization Act for Fiscal Year 1993, U.S. Federal Register, vol. 57 November 25, 1992, p. 228, and Clinton to Vitagliano (fn. 127).

132. Rosalyn Higgins, *Problems and Process: International Law and How We Use It* (Oxford: Oxford University Press, 1995), 252.

133. Article 8 of the Ottawa Convention addresses "facilitation and clarification of compliance," but its verification provisions are minimal. Setting aside the arguments that Article 8 may actually entail verification provisions, this essay takes the ICBL point of view regarding the lack of verification in the convention. Jody Williams, "Talk to America," *Voice of America Radio Service*, December 4, 1998.

134. Ibid.

135. Geoffrey Best, *War and Law since 1945* (Oxford: Clarendon Press, 1994), 308.

136. Kingdon (fn. 56), 21.

137. Schattschneider argues that the expansion of conflict signals a healthy democracy because it allows for increased public participation, usually through "responsible leaders and organizations," into the policy process. Schattschneider (fn. 102), 142.

138. While victims were the main framing issue in the Ottawa Landmine Treaty, for biological, nuclear, and chemical weapons, the central framing issues were repugnance, proliferation, and environmental threat, respectively. Convention on the Prohibition of the Development, Production, and Stockpiling of Bacteriological (Biological) and Toxin Weapons and on Their Destruction, 1972, preamble; Treaty on the Non-Proliferation of Nuclear Weapons, 1968; Organisation for the Prohibition of Chemical Weapons, *Chemical Weapons: Basic Facts* (The Hague: Organisation for the Prohibition of Chemical Weapons), 5; Ottawa Treaty (fn. 1), preamble.

139. Organisation for the Prohibition of Chemical Weapons (fn. 138), 2, 5. The 1925 Geneva Protocol is officially known as the Geneva Protocol for the Prohibition of the Use of Asphyxiating, Poisonous or Other Gases, and Bacteriological Methods of Warfare.

140. There are currently three efforts by NGOs to ban nuclear weapons: (1) Abolition 2000: A Global Network to Eliminate Nuclear Weapons, c/o Waging Peace, www.napf.org/abolition2000; (2) Middle Powers Initiative (MPI)—Fast track to Zero Nuclear Weapons, www.napf.org/mpi; and (3) IALANA—Nuclear Weapons: Dismantling by Law, www.ddh.nl/org/ialana.

141. Ottawa Convention (fn. 1), article 6, para. 3.

142. While the Ottawa Landmine Treaty contained provisions for victim assistance, arms control treaties for biological, nuclear, and chemical weapons did not.

143. Jerry White and Ken Rutherford, "The Role of the Landmine Survivors Network," in Cameron, Lawson, and Tomlin (fn. 6), 113.

144. U.S. Campaign to Stop the Use of Child Soldiers, http://www.us-childsoldiers.org>U.S. Policy.

145. Mike Wessells, "Child Soldiers," *Bulletin of the Atomic Scientists* 53 (November–December 1997), 39.

146. Liz Clegg, "NGOs Take Aim," *Bulletin of the Atomic Scientists* 55 (January–February 1999), 49.

Researching Health and
Human Rights on the Web

The selections in this volume can barely scratch the surface of the vast emerging field of health and human rights. We have structured this volume around eight themes that suggest a broad reach: conceptual underpinnings, development, biotechnology, reproductive and sexual health, violence, methods, the human right to health, and strategies for action. The fact that only three or four chapters appear in each part provides the reader with a highly selective incursion into the literature on health and human rights. Readers wishing to go into greater depth on health and human rights will need to access official documents, institutions, and the literature taking full advantage of the Internet. The purpose of this chapter is to indicate web-based sources for such research. We have created a web site that contains links to documents, institutions and scholarly writing according to the three headings listed below. The site is maintained by Global Lawyers and Physicians at http://www.glphr.org/resources/appendix.

I. International Legal and Political Documents[1]

a. International Bill of Human Rights
b. Other Major United Nations Conventions and Declarations
c. Regional Human Rights Conventions and Declarations
d. Major Instruments of International Humanitarian Law
e. General Comments and Recommendations of Treaty Monitoring Bodies

      i.   Committee on Economic, Social and Cultural Rights
      ii. Committee on the Rights of the Child
      iii. Committee on the Elimination of Discrimination Against Women
   f. Political Documents of International Conferences and Summits[2]
      i.   International conferences and summits
      ii. Special Sessions of the UN General Assembly

II. National and International Institutions Concerned with Health and Human Rights[3]

   a. Academic and research institutions
   b. Intergovernmental agencies
      i.   United Nations system
      ii. Regional and other
   c. National institutions
      i.   National institutions for the promotion and protection of human rights
      ii. National bodies responsible for foreign aid
   d. Non-governmental organizations (NGOs)
      i.   Major international human rights organizations with an interest in health
      ii. Selected national NGOs working on health and human rights

III. Bibliographical References[4]

  1.   Child and Adolescent Health and Development
  2.   Reproductive Health
  3.   Making Pregnancy Safer (Safe Motherhood)
  4.   Women's Health
  5.   HIV/AIDS
  6.   Communicable Diseases
  7.   Non-Communicable Diseases
  8.   Sustainable Development
  9.   Nutrition
 10. Health and Environment
 11. Food Safety
 12. Emergency Preparedness and Response
 13. Health Promotion
 14. Disability
 15. Mental Health
 16. Substance Abuse
 17. Essential Medicines

18. Immunization and Vaccine Development
19. Clinical Technology/Clinical Trials
20. Health Information Management and Dissemination
21. Health Information Medical Record Confidentiality and Privacy
22. Research Policy and Cooperation
23. Organization of Health Services
24. Health Policy

Notes

1. Among the other sources of international documents on health and human rights the reader may wish to consult Stephen P. Marks, *Health and Human Rights: Basic International Documents,* Cambridge, MA: Harvard School of Public Health, distributed by Harvard University Press, 2004; and Gudmunder Alfredsson and Katarina Tomaševski, *A Thematic Guide to Documents on Health and Human Rights: Global and Regional Standards Adopted by Intergovernmental Organizations and Professional Association,* The Hague: Martinus Nijhoff Publishers, 1998. The University of Minnesota Human Rights Library links to the texts at http://www1.umn.edu/humanrts/instree/ainstls1.htm. For UN instruments, one should use primarily the web site of the Office of the UN High Commissioner for Human Rights at http://www.unhchr.ch/. The UN specialized agencies (http://www1.umn.edu/humanrts/unorgs.htm) and the regional organizations (http://www1.umn.edu/humanrts/regional.htm) have the texts of the instruments concerning them on their web sites.
2. Numerous documents adopted by governments, often at the level of heads of state and government, constitute political commitments rather than formal standard-setting instruments. Nevertheless, they guide policy and are particularly important to issues of health and human rights. The main ones are listed by Global Lawyers and Physicians for Human Rights at http://glphr.org/resources/appendix and by the University of Minnesota Human Rights Library at http://www1.umn.edu/humanrts/unorgs.htm. Another valuable source of detailed information on negotiations over a wide range of development and environmental issues of concern to health and human rights is the site of the International Institute for Sustainable Development (IISD) at http://www.iisd.ca/.
3. The web sites of institutions provide an inexhaustible source of information relevant to research on health and human rights. In addition to the web site of resources for further research on health and human rights (http://www.glphr.org/resources/appendix), Human Rights Internet Human Rights Organizations Database holds over 10,000 records and can be searched at http://www.hri.ca/organizations/.
4. The Program on International Health and Human Rights of the François-Xavier Bagnoud Center for Health and Human Rights has prepared a bibliography on health and human rights for the World Health Organization. The bibliography follows the same classification WHO uses for health issues in general, which is reproduced here. The WHO bibliography is also available online at http://www.who.int/hhr/databases/biblio. Additional bibliographical references on human rights, including the topic of health and human rights, are linked in the University of Minnesota web site at http://www1.umn.edu/humanrts/bibliog/biblios.htm.

Permissions

Annas, George J. *Human Rights and Health-The Universal Declaration of Human Rights.* Reprinted from *New England Journal of Medicine,* 339:24 (1998), 1778–1781. Copyright © 1998, George J. Annas. Reprinted with permission.

Annas, George J. Andrews, Lori B. Isasi, Rosario M. *Protecting the Endangered Human: Toward an International Treaty Prohibiting Cloning and Inheritable Alterations.* Reprinted from *American Journal of Law and Medicine,* 28:2&3 (2002), 151–178. Copyright © 2002, George J. Annas. Reprinted with permission.

Annas, George J. *The Right to Health and the Nevirapine Case in South Africa.* Reprinted from *New England Journal of Medicine,* 348:8 (2003), 750–754. Copyright © 2003, George J. Annas. Reprinted with permission.

Bruderlein, Claude. Leaning, Jennifer. *New Challenges for Humanitarian Protection.* Reprinted from *British Medical Journal,* 319:7207 (1999), 430–435. Copyright © 1999, BMJ Publishing Group. Reprinted with permission.

Brundtland, Gro Harlem. *The UDHR: Fifty Years of Synergy Between Health and Human Rights.* Reprinted from *Health and Human Rights,* 3:2 (1998), 21–26, with permission from the François-Xavier Bagnoud Center for Health and Human Rights, Harvard School of Public Health. Copyright © 1998, President and Fellows of Harvard College.

Cullet, Philippe. *Patents and Medicines: The Relationship Between TRIPS and the Human Right to Health.* Reprinted from *International Affairs,* 79:1 (2003), 139–160. Copyright © 2003 by The Royal Institute of International Affairs. Reprinted with permission.

Klugman, Barbara. *Sexual Rights in Southern Africa: A Beijing Discourse or a Strategic Necessity.* Reprinted from *Health and Human Rights*, 4:2 (2000), 144–173, with permission from the François-Xavier Bagnoud Center for Health and Human Rights, Harvard School of Public Health. Copyright © 2000, President and Fellows of Harvard College.

LeGraw, Joan M. Grodin, Michael A. *Health Professionals and Lethal Injection Execution in the United States.* Reprinted from *Human Rights Quarterly*, 24:2 (2002), 382–423. Copyright © 2002, The Johns Hopkins University Press. Reprinted with permission of the Johns Hopkins University Press.

Marks, Stephen P. *Economic Sanctions as Human Rights Violations: Reconciling Political and Public Health Imperatives.* Reprinted from *American Journal of Public Health*, 89:10 (1999), 1509–1513. Copyright © 1999, American Public Health Association. Reprinted with permission.

Marks, Stephen P. *Tying Prometheus Down: The International Law of Genetic Manipulation.* Reprinted from *Chicago Journal of International Law*, 3:1 (2002), 121–135. Copyright © 2002, University of Chicago. Reprinted with permission.

Mokhiber, Craig G. *Towards a Measure of Dignity: Indicators for Rights Based Development.* Session I-PL4 Montreux, 4–8 September 2000. Copyright © 2000, Craig G. Mokhiber. Reprinted with permission.

Physicians for Human Rights. *Maternal Mortality in Herat Province, Afghanistan: The Need to Protect Women's Rights.* Copyright © 2002, Physicians for Human Rights. Reprinted with permission.

Raworth, Kate. *Measuring Human Rights.* Reprinted from *Ethics and International Affairs* 15:1 (2001), 111–131. Copyright © 2001, Carnegie Council on Ethics and International Affairs. Reprinted with permission.

Rutherford, Kenneth R. *The Evolving Arms Control Agenda: Implications of the Role of NGOs in Banning Antipersonnel Landmines.* Reprinted from *World Politics* 53:1 (2000), 74–114. Copyright © 2000, The Johns Hopkins University Press. Reprinted with permission of the Johns Hopkins University Press.

About the Contributors

Lori B. Andrews, JD, is Distinguished Professor of Law and Director of the Institute for Science, Law and Technology, Chicago-Kent College of Law, Chicago, IL, USA.

Claude Bruderlein, LLM, is Jeremiah Smith Lecturer on Law, Harvard University Law School, a Research Scientist and Director of the Harvard Program on Humanitarian Policy and Conflict Research, Harvard School of Public Health, Boston, MA, USA.

Gro Harlem Brundtland, MD, MPH, is former Prime Minister of Norway and former Director-General of the World Health Organization.

Philippe Cullet, LLM, MA, JSM, JSD, is Lecturer in Law, School of Oriental and African Studies, University of London, UK.

Yael Danieli, PhD, is Director and past President of the Group Project for Holocaust Survivors and their Children, and Senior Representative to the United Nations of the Society for Traumatic Stress Studies, New York, NY, USA.

Cheryl E. Easley, PhD, RN, is Dean of College of Health and Social Welfare, University of Alaska Anchorage, AK, USA.

Paul Farmer, MD, PhD, is Professor of Medical Anthropology, Department of Social Medicine, Harvard Medical School and Founding Director of Partners In Health, Boston, MA, USA.

Lynn P. Freedman, JD, MPH, is Director of the Law and Policy Project and Associate Professor of Clinical Population and Family Health, Heilbrunn Department of Population and Family Health, Mailman School of Public Health, Columbia University, New York, NY, USA.

Nicole Gastineau, AB, is a research assistant at Partners In Health and a Master of Science degree candidate in Health Policy and Management, Harvard School of Public Health, Boston, MA, USA.

Claudio González-Parra, PhD, is Full Professor in the Department of Sociology, Universidad de Concepción, Chile.

Anna-Karin Hurtig, MD, DTM&H, DrPH, is Lecturer in Epidemiology and Public Health, Department of Public Health and Clinical Medicine, Umeå University, Umeå, Sweden.

Vincent Iacopino, MD, PhD, is Director of Research for Physicians for Human Rights, Boston, MA, USA, and Health and Human Rights Instructor at the University of California, Berkeley, School of Public Health, Berkeley, CA, USA.

Rosario M. Isasi, JD, MPH, is Postdoctoral Fellow, Genetics and Society Project, Research Center for Public Law, University of Montreal, Canada.

Barbara Klugman, PhD, is Program Officer in Sexuality and Reproductive Health, Ford Foundation, New York, NY, USA and formerly Director of the Women's Health Project, School of Public Health, University of the Witwatersand, South Africa.

Jennifer Leaning, MD, SMH, is Professor of International Health, Department of Population and International Health, and Director of the Humanitarian Crises and Human Rights Program, François-Xavier Bagnoud Center for Health and Human Rights, Harvard School of Public Health, Boston, MA, USA.

Joan M. LeGraw, RN, JD, MPH, is Adjunct Lecturer on Law, New England School of Law, and Medical Ethics Consultant, Cape Cod Research Institute, Boston, MA, USA.

Deborah P. Maine, DrPH, is Director, Averting Maternal Death and Disability Program, and Professor of Clinical Population and Family Health, Heilbrunn Department of Population and Family Health, Mailman School of Public Health, Columbia University, New York, NY, USA.

Craig Mokhiber, JD, is Deputy Director, New York Office of the United Nations High Commissioner for Human Rights, New York, NY, USA.

Russell E. Morgan, Jr., DrPH, is President of the SPRY Foundation and Past Chair, American Public Health Association International Human Rights Committee, Washington, D.C., USA.

Jessica A. Ogden, PhD, is Social Anthropologist and Infectious Disease Specialist, International Center for Research on Women, Washington, D.C., USA.

Physicians for Human Rights is a non-profit organization that promotes health by protecting human rights, Boston, MA, USA.

John D.H. Porter, MD, MPH, is Reader in International Health, London School of Hygiene and Tropical Medicine, University of London, UK.

Kate Raworth, MSc, is a Policy Adviser at Oxfam, Oxford, UK.

Kenneth R. Rutherford, PhD, MBA, is Assistant Professor in the Department of Political Science, Southwest Missouri State University, Springfield, MO, USA, and Co-Founder of the Landmine Survivors Network, Washington, D.C., USA.

Bonnie Shepard, MEd, MPA, is Senior Program Manager for the Program on International Health and Human Rights, François-Xavier Bagnoud Center for Health and Human Rights, Harvard School of Public Health, Boston, MA, USA.

Susannah Sirkin, MEd, is Deputy Director of Physicians for Human Rights, Boston, MA, USA.

Ellen 't Hoen, LLM, is Coordinator of the Access to Essential Medicines Campaign, Doctors Without Borders, Paris, France.

Daniel Tarantola, MD, is Senior Policy Adviser to the Director-General, and Director, Immunization, Vaccines and Biologicals, World Health Organization, Geneva, Switzerland.

Mary Ann Torres, JD, LLM, is Senior Program Officer, International Council of AIDS Service Organizations (ICASO), Toronto, Ontario, Canada.

Alicia Ely Yamin, JD, MPH, is Instructor in the Department of Health Policy and Management, Harvard School of Public Health, Boston, MA, USA.

About the Editors

Sofia Gruskin, JD, MIA, is Director of the Program on International Health and Human Rights at the François-Xavier Bagnoud Center for Health and Human Rights, and Associate Professor of Health and Human Rights in the Department of Population and International Health at the Harvard School of Public Health. She is the editor of the international journal *Health and Human Rights*, an associate editor for the *American Journal of Public Health*, co-editor of *Health and Human Rights: A Reader,* and chair of the UNAIDS Global Reference Group on HIV/AIDS and Human Rights. She is the author of numerous publications in the health and human rights field.

Michael A. Grodin, MD, is Professor of Health Law, Bioethics and Human Rights; Socio-Medical Sciences and Community Medicine; and Psychiatry at the Boston University Schools of Medicine and Public Health. He has edited or co-edited: *The Nazi Doctors and the Nuremberg Code: Human Rights in Human Experimentation; Children as Research Subjects: Science, Ethics and Law; Meta-Medical Ethics: The Philosophical Foundations of Bioethics;* and *Health and Human Rights: A Reader.* He is the co-founder of Global Lawyers and Physicians and co-director of the Boston Center for Refugee Health and Human Rights.

George J. Annas, JD, MPH is Edward R. Utley Professor and Chair, Department of Health Law, Bioethics and Human Rights, Boston University School of Public Health, and Professor, Boston University School of Medicine, and Boston University School of Law. He is the author or editor of more than a dozen books on health law and bioethics, including *American Bioethics: Crossing Human Rights and Health Law Boundaries, The Rights of Patients, Judging Medicine, Standard of Care,* and *Some Choice,* and writes a regular feature on "Legal Issues in Medicine" for the *New England Journal of Medicine.* He is the co-founder of Global Lawyers and Physicians.

Stephen P. Marks, Docteur d'état, Dipl. IHEI., is Director of the François-Xavier Bagnoud Center for Health and Human Rights and François-Xavier Bagnoud Professor of Health and Human Rights in the Department of Population and International Health at the Harvard School of Public Health. He directs the program on Development and Human Rights and the FXB Center and is editor of the Harvard Series on Health and Human Rights, distributed by Harvard University Press. He is the co-editor of *The Future of International Human Rights* (Transnational Publishers) and is the author of numerous articles on human rights, ethics, international institutions, development, biotechnology and other aspects of health and human rights.

Global Lawyers and Physicians (GLP)'s mission is to work collaboratively toward the global implementation of the health-related provisions of the Universal Declaration of Human Rights and the Covenants on Civil and Political Rights and Economic, Social, and Cultural Rights, with a focus on human rights and health. Global Lawyers and Physicians was founded in 1996 at an international symposium held at the United States Holocaust Memorial Museum to commemorate the 50th Anniversary of the Nuremberg Doctors Trial. GLP was formed to reinvigorate the collaboration of the legal and medical/public health professions to protect the human rights and dignity of all persons. Some of our projects include a Universal Declaration of Patients Rights; the Boston Center for Refugee Health and Human Rights; and the Ethics and Law of International Biomedical Research Trials. (www.glphr.org)

The François-Xavier Bagnoud Center for Health and Human Rights was founded in 1993 at the Harvard School of Public Health to promote and catalyze the health and human rights movement; to influence policies and practices in health and human rights; and to expand the knowledge about linkages between health and human rights in specific contexts such as HIV/AIDS, children's rights and health, and women's health and rights. The Center's three programs—International Health and Human Rights, Human Rights in Development, and Humanitarian Crises and Human Rights—seek to influence policies and programs through its collaboration with various UN agencies and in partnership with NGOs, international agencies, and governments worldwide. Current research and thinking in health and human rights is published in the Center's journal, *Health and Human Rights*, and in other publications. The Center develops and conducts a variety of academic and professional training courses focusing on health and human rights. (www.hsph.harvard.edu/fxbcenter)

Index